Promoting and Sustaining
Economic Reform in

ZAMBIA

Promoting and Sustaining Economic Reform in

ZAMBIA

Edited by

Catharine B. Hill and Malcolm F. McPherson

John F. Kennedy School of Government
HARVARD UNIVERSITY

DISTRIBUTED BY HARVARD UNIVERSITY PRESS
CAMBRIDGE, MASSACHUSETTS, AND LONDON, ENGLAND
2004

Published by the John F. Kennedy School of Government

Distributed by Harvard University Press

Copyright © 2004 by the President and Fellows of Harvard College
All Rights Reserved.

Editorial Management: Gillian Charters
Cover Design: Schafer/LaCasse Design
Text Design and Production: Northeastern Graphic, Inc.

CIP data available from the Library of Congress

ISBN: 0-674-01225-9

Printed in the United States of America

Contents

Preface

The essays in this collection have been assembled and edited over several years. Neither of us could set aside periods long enough to finish the volume, so it was wedged among our other activities. The delay, however, has not changed our conclusions about how to move the Zambian economy forward. Those conclusions remain as relevant now as when we began in late 1995. Though it saved the need for a major recasting of our study, this outcome is profoundly distressing for the majority of Zambians. Even with a new democratic government, Zambia's leaders did not break the past pattern of start-stop economic reform. In this respect, the Movement for Multi-Party Democracy (MMD), under President Frederick Chiluba, failed the Zambian people in the same way as its predecessor, the United National Independence Party (UNIP), did under President Kenneth Kaunda.

Since Zambia's economic difficulties began almost three decades ago, no government has promoted reform with the vigor needed to return the economy to a sustainable growth path. There have been too many distractions. Under President Kaunda and UNIP, Zambia was a front-line state in opposing racism in Rhodesia and South Africa. That stance gained diplomatic and financial support from the international community. It was disastrous for the economy, as it enabled the government to postpone fundamental economic reform. Moreover, until the early 1980s Zambia's leaders succeeded in convincing the donor community that the country's difficulties were mainly due to adverse world market conditions or drought rather than distorted policies and economic mismanagement. Foreign aid continued to flow, further delaying the reforms the country so badly needed.

The deteriorating economy ultimately forced President Kaunda's hand. In October 1985, the government adopted a bold program of market liberalization and public retrenchment. That effort was abandoned by mid-1987 and

Zambia's economic slide continued. Once one of Africa's richest countries, it was fast becoming one of the continent's poorest.

The breaking point was the attempted coup in June 1990 by Lieutenant Luchembe. Though government supporters suppressed the rebellion, the spontaneous celebration across Zambia at the prospect that Kaunda and UNIP had been dislodged sealed their fate. Within months, the Constitution was changed, ending the one-party state. The MMD party was formed and began preparing for elections. Those were vigorously contested. UNIP made an unsuccessful last-ditch effort to avoid defeat through a major expansion of government expenditure financed by printing money. The MMD won the elections in October 1991. Frederick Chiluba became president. The transfer of power was peaceful.

Much was expected of the new president and his party. There was wide-spread talk about, and hope for, a new dawn in Zambia. The early months of the new government's tenure were encouraging. Chiluba and the MMD had made many promises in the heat of the election campaign. However, in the afterglow of victory, Zambia's leaders found some of them to be inconvenient. The commitments to govern openly, transparently, and accountably were especially vexing. President Chiluba's book, *The Challenge of Change*, published after the elections, asserted that open and accountable governance was essential for Zambia to progress politically and economically. That basic message was quietly discarded.

A growing number of government actions demonstrated that Zambia's leaders were not prepared to manage the economy in ways that benefited the nation as a whole. Special interests—ZIMCO's principals, members of the Special Branch (Zambia's security wing), ZCCM's managers, the Cabinet's inner circle, and assorted presidential hangers-on—took precedence over those of the nation. The practical challenge for Chiluba and his associates was how to avoid changing the secretive, autocratic, and corrupt processes for administering Zambia that rewarded insiders so handsomely. In retrospect, no one should have been surprised at this outcome. Nation building and the creation of institutions that put the state ahead of sectional and personal interests can take generations. Zambia (like other developing countries) would not short-circuit the process. Expecting Chiluba and the MMD to behave significantly differently from Kaunda and UNIP was, it turns out, naïve.

Yet, many Zambians felt betrayed. When they cast their votes in 1991, the majority of Zambians deeply believed that "the hour had come" (the MMD's election slogan). They were convinced that, as president, Chiluba would govern fairly, respecting due process and the rule of law. The MMD *Manifesto* had declared a new era of open, transparent governance with responsible leadership. Voters generally agreed with the MMD officials that "Zambia is not a poor country, just one that has been poorly managed" and that "the government has no business in business." Zambia's international supporters were equally impressed, especially when the election was peaceful and fair.

The MMD under President Chiluba and, from late December 2001, President Levy Mwanawasa has now held power for more than a decade. Over this period, most Zambians, and the few outsiders who still care to notice, have been disabused of their earlier beliefs. Neither the election in 1991 nor the transition to a new millennium has sparked an economic revival. Under Chiluba and the MMD, Zambia struggled over the threshold of the twenty-first century significantly poorer than it had been a decade earlier. Being poorer, Zambia's development options have narrowed, and most of its economic problems have become less tractable.

From a national perspective, the government's biggest policy mistake was to delay the privatization of the copper company, ZCCM. This, in fact, was a litmus test that Chiluba and the MMD failed. If Zambia's leaders had been fully committed to economic reform to promote growth and reduce poverty, disposing of ZCCM would have been the first item on the agenda not, as it turned out, one of the last. To the country's cost, privatizing ZCCM was delayed. The losses, both direct and indirect, amounted to billions of dollars.

Another fundamental mistake by Chiluba and the MMD was to continue taxing agriculture through an overvalued foreign exchange rate and government interventions that undermined opportunities for agricultural expansion. Rural poverty is now more pervasive than at any time since independence. A third failure by Zambia's leaders was to believe that governance issues could be fudged. President Chiluba made his position perfectly clear at an international forum in Gabon in 1999 when he stated that governance is what elected officials do. Presumably, this attitude helps explain why elected officials suppressed information (among other things) regarding the loss of the national soccer team in Gabon, the torture of those detained following the attempted coup in 1997, the misappropriation of cobalt receipts, and the use of public funds to finance the MMD convention in 2001. It could also explain why President Chiluba believed the Constitution should be changed, giving him a third term. These errors of omission and commission are typical of leaders to whom accountability is a matter of convenience.

These actions were part of a pattern whereby selected individuals and groups gained special advantages under President Chiluba and the MMD. None of them enabled Zambia to progress. In fact, they contributed to a significant worsening of the country's circumstances, a point confirmed by the essays in this volume. Zambia made no substantive economic progress during the 1990s. Average real per capita income fell by roughly 15 percent from 1992 to 2000. This was on top of a decline from 1975 to 1991 of approximately 45 percent. The drop in living standards has been so severe that Zambia has the dubious distinction of being the only country (besides North Korea and Iraq) where infant mortality has risen over the last three decades. This outcome is even more startling, given that over the period 1975 to 2000 Zambia received average annual net inflows of foreign aid in excess of 19 percent of GDP.

What should distress Zambians and their international supporters is that none of this was necessary. The country has always had the potential for rapid economic and social progress. From the end of WWII until the early 1970s, Zambia was among the fastest growing countries in the world. Zambia's economic potential, however, will not be realized while Zambia's leaders fail to promote and sustain reforms that support rapid growth and development. Zambia's large and persistent budget deficits symbolize this failure. Deficits continue even though the country as a whole has been unable to fully service its debt since the late 1970s. The pattern of debt finance (and its concomitant, printing money) has left Zambia with chronically high inflation and an overwhelming dependence on the international community. Billions of dollars of aid have flowed. That aid has not promoted reform or growth.

As we moved nearer to completing these essays, we have continued to hope that a more upbeat story would unfold. Better news has emerged on the political front. Zambians turned back Chiluba's determined efforts to gain a third term. President Mwanawasa has helped expose the corruption of the Chiluba regime. All of Zambia's friends and supporters salute this newfound openness. On the economic front, the situation remains difficult. The world economy sank in 2001, sharply reducing the prices of copper and cobalt. The events of September 11 in the United States accentuated these trends. The government's continued lukewarm approach to economic reform and its willingness to reverse direction for political purposes have compounded the adverse effects of external events. An obvious example was the rigging of the exchange rate beginning in December 2000. That action sharply raised the real exchange rate, further compromising Zambia's international competitiveness.

From our analysis, we have derived a modest set of proposals designed to move the economy forward. A clear lesson from the last three decades is that the government has to sharply scale back its agenda. It should focus only on a small number of critical activities and sustain them. Heretofore, the government has attempted too much and done it poorly. Programs in health, education, infrastructure, and law and order, if properly conceived and executed, would fully occupy every Zambian who is intent on promoting growth and development for the foreseeable future. Once the economy is growing rapidly and generating budget surpluses, the agenda can be expanded.

None of our analysis alters our conviction regarding Zambia's economic potential. It remains huge. Yet, to realize that potential, the government will need to take a more constructive and less intrusive approach to economic management. The following essays provide the outline and many details of such an approach.

Our work has benefited from the encouragement, criticism, and helpful prodding of Professors James Duesenberry and Dwight Perkins of Harvard University. Our colleague, the late Michael Roemer, wished us well when we first raised the subject of compiling a volume on Zambia's economic reforms. The support of Richard Pagett, former executive director of HIID, proved critical in the final stages of the work. Michael Murray offered valuable insights on key issues of governance and management. In Zambia, Jacques Hillinger, Kevin Donovan, James Mtonga, and Simon Zukas, provided timely assistance on a range of issues. At Harvard, Sara Piccicuto helped with data and references. Carrie Main assisted with the formatting and presentation. In addition to her contribution to Chapter 11, Tzvetana Rakovski provided vital data analysis and backup. Gillian Charters's editorial skills greatly improved the volume. We appreciate the talent of Bernie LaCasse, who designed the book cover, and we are especially grateful and proud to feature the artwork of Agnes Buya Yombwe on the cover. To all these people, we express our heartfelt appreciation for their contributions.

Catharine B. Hill, Williams College
Malcolm F. McPherson, Harvard University

The Authors

Bruce R. Bolnick is a fellow in development at the Kennedy School of Government. As a senior associate at the Harvard Institute for International Development (HIID), Dr. Bolnick headed the advisory team at the Ministry of Planning and Finance in Mozambique (1999–2001) and a similar project at the central bank in Malawi (1996–1999). He also served with HIID as resident advisor to the Ministry of Finance in Zambia (1991–1994) and the central bank in Indonesia (1980–82). His academic work has included faculty positions in economics at Northeastern University, Duke University, and the University of Nairobi. Dr. Bolnick has written extensively on economic development issues relating to financial markets, macroeconomic management, and public finance. His current research focuses on growth and poverty reduction, and economic policy management in Africa. He holds a Ph.D. in economics from Yale University.

Fernando R. Fernholz was a development associate with HIID and is now a member of the Duke Center for International Development at Duke University. During his long association with HIID, Dr. Fernholz served as director of the Program on Investment Appraisal and Management and taught workshops on budgeting and financial management in the public sector and on the management of foreign aid. His overseas assignments for HIID included work in Brunei, Indonesia, Malawi, and Zambia. In Zambia, Dr. Fernholz was the debt and investment advisor from 1991 to 1996. His consulting assignments have taken him to Nicaragua, Egypt, Ethiopia, Kenya, Uganda, and Mexico. Dr. Fernholz holds a master's degree in civil engineering from RWTH Aachen in Germany, a master's degree in public administration from the Kennedy School of Government at Harvard University, and a Ph.D. in economics from Boston University.

Clive S. Gray obtained his Ph.D. in economics from Harvard University in 1965. After resident tours with USAID/Nigeria and Kenya's Ministry of Economic Planning, he served for thirty years with HIID and its predecessor, the Harvard Development Advisory Service. During 1969–90 Dr. Gray led resident HIID teams in Colombia, Ethiopia, Indonesia, and Morocco. He has conducted short-term advisory and research assignments in the former Soviet Union, Eastern Europe, Central America, and Africa. During 1995–2001 he headed HIID's consortium on Equity and Growth through Economic Research (EAGER). His publications relate to capital flows, competition policy, agricultural policy, telecommunications, public finance, education, capacity building, debt monitoring, economics of the bureaucracy, and leadership in Africa.

Catharine B. Hill is John J. Gibson Professor of Economics and provost at Williams College, Williamstown, Massachusetts. Hill was formerly chair of the Center for Development Economics at Williams College. She holds an M.A. from Oxford University and a Ph.D. from Yale. Her research includes trade, public finance, and macroeconomic management in sub-Saharan Africa. Most of her fieldwork has been in Southern Africa, primarily Botswana, Malawi, and Zambia. Her publications include studies of macroeconomic management of commodity booms and busts in Botswana and export promotion policies in developing economies and the United States. Professor Hill was senior resident advisor for HIID on METAP in the Ministry of Finance, Zambia (1996–97).

Deborah A. Hoover earned a master's degree from Cambridge University. Attracted to the field of arts administration and education, she rose to the position of executive director of the Council on the Arts at the Massachusetts Institute of Technology. After leaving MIT, she spent several years in The Gambia (1985–89) and Zambia (1992–96) where she worked with local artists, providing them with the capacity to broaden their opportunities for support. The author of *Supporting Yourself as an Artist* (Oxford University Press, 1985, 1989), Ms. Hoover has devoted her energies to dealing with the problems of working and learning in resource-constrained settings. In Zambia, she was the training officer for the macroeconomic technical assistance project (METAP) and was responsible for organizing the training programs that assisted more than 2,400 Zambian officials.

Malcolm F. McPherson gained his Ph.D. in economics from Harvard University. He is a senior fellow in Development at the John F. Kennedy School of Government at Harvard and a member of the Center for Business and Government. His research includes agricultural development, monetary theory and policy, foreign aid, and macroeconomic management. During his eighteen years with HIID, Dr. McPherson consulted with numerous international agencies and served as resident advisor in The Gambia (1985–89) and Zambia (1992–96). With Steven Radelet he coedited a book on economic recovery in The Gambia (Harvard University Press, 1995). Dr. McPherson was senior advisor to the Public Strategies for Growth with Equity component of the EAGER project. Under that project he edited two volumes, *Restarting and Sustaining Growth and Development in Africa* and *Promoting and Sustaining Trade and Exchange Rate Reform.*

Tzvetana S. Rakovski was a research assistant on the EAGER Project at HIID from September 1997 to June 2000. She holds an M.A. degree in economics from Northeastern University, Boston, and a M.Sc. degree in mathematics from Sofia University, Bulgaria. She is currently working on a Ph.D. in Economics at McGill University, Montreal. Her research interests include international development, trade, growth, and applied econometrics. Her prior work experience included a position as a researcher at the Agency for Economic Analysis and Forecasting (AEAF) in Sofia, Bulgaria.

Glossary of Terms

ACBF	African Capacity Building Foundation
ACBI	African Capacity Building Initiative
ACCA	Association of Chartered Certified Accountants
ACMP	Agricultural Credit Management Program
ACR	African Competitiveness Report
ADI	African Development Indicators
AERC	African Economic Research Consortium
AfDB	African Development Bank
ASIP	Agricultural Sector Investment Program
ASYCUDA	Automated System for Customs Data
BBC	British Broadcasting Commission
BIAO	Banque Industriel d'Afrique de l'Ouest
BoZ	Bank of Zambia
BS	Budget Speech
c.i.f.	Cost, insurance, freight
CAMEL	Financial ranking criteria (mnemonic)
CBI	Cross Border Initiative
CDF	Comprehensive Development Framework
CD-ROM	Compact Disk – Read Only Memory
CG	Consultative Group
CGE	Computable General Equilibrium (models)
CDF	Comprehensive Development Framework (World Bank)
CGIAR	Consultative Group on International Agricultural Research
CFD	Caisse Française de Developpement (French aid agency)
CMTAP	Computerization and Modernization of Tax Administration
CODELCO	Chile's national copper company
COMESA	Common Market for East and Southern Africa
CPI	Consumer Price Index

CSO   Central Statistical Office
CUSA   Credit Union and Savings Association

DAC   Development Assistance Committee
DBZ   Development Bank of Zambia
DFID   Department for International Development
DMC   Data Monitoring Committee
DMFAS   Debt Management and Financial Analysis System
DOD   Debt Outstanding and Disbursed
DRS   Debt Reorganization System (World Bank)
DS   Debt Service
DSA   Debt Sustainability Analysis

EAGER   Equity and Growth through Economic Research
EAZ   Economics Association of Zambia
EBZ   Export Bank of Zambia
ECA   Economic Commission for Africa
EDA   Effective Development Assistance
EPZ   Export Processing Zone
ERP   Economic Recovery Program
ESAF   Enhanced Structural Adjustment Facility
ESAIDARM   East and Southern Africa Institute for Debt and Resource and
               Resource Management
EIU   Economist Intelligence Unit
EU   European Union
EMU   European Monetary Union

FAO   Food and Agricultural Organization
FEMAC   Foreign Exchange Management and Allocation Committee
FNDP   First National Development Plan
FRA   Food Reserve Agency
FRBNY   Federal Reserve Bank of New York

G-7   Group of Seven (rich industrial countries)
GATT   General Agreement on Tariffs and Trade
GDCF   Gross Domestic Capital Formation
GDP   Gross Domestic Product
GEAR   Growth Employment and Reconstruction (South Africa)
GEIS   General Export Incentive Scheme (South Africa)
GoZ   Government on Zambia
GRZ   Government of the Republic of Zambia
GTZ   Gesellschaft für Technische Zusammenarbeit (German agency)

HBS   Harvard Business School
HDI   Human Development Index

HDR	Human Development Report
HIID	Harvard Institute for International Development
HIPC	Highly Indebted Poor Countries
HIV/AIDS	Human Immuno-deficiency Virus/Acquired Immune Deficiency Syndrome
HRDC	Human Resources Development Committee
HRDO	Human Resources Development Officer
HS	Harmonized System (of tariffs)
IBRD	International Bank for Reconstruction and Development
IDA	International Development Association
IDF	Import Declaration Fee
IDS	Institute for Development Studies (Sussex)
IFPRI	International Food Policy Research Institute
IFS	International Financial Statistics (of IMF)
ILO	International Labour Office
IMF	International Monetary Fund
I-PRSP	Interim Poverty Reduction Strategy Paper
IRIS	Institute for Research into the Informal Sector
IRP	Interest Rate Parity
ISIC	International Standardized Industry Classification
ISTP	Interim Short Term Program
KfW	Kreditanstalt für Wiederaufbau (German agency)
KDMP	Konkola Deep Mining Project
KR	Keinbaum Report
LuSE	Lusaka Stock Exchange
mts	Metric tons
M2	Broad Money (currency plus time and savings deposits)
MAFF	Ministry of Agriculture, Food and Fisheries
MB	Meridien/BIAO Bank
MCTI	Ministry of Commerce Trade and Industry
MEFMI	Macroeconomic and Financial Management Institute
MEMACO	Metal Marketing Company
METAP	Macroeconomic Technical Assistance Project
MMD	Movement for Multi-Party Democracy
MoF	Ministry of Finance
MoFED	Ministry of Finance and Economic Development
MP	Member of Parliament
MTEF	Medium Term Expenditure Framework
MTFF	Medium Term Financial Framework
MUB	Manufacture-Under-Bond

MV	Management's View
NAMBoard	National Agricultural Marketing Board
NCCM	Nchanga Consolidated Copper Mines
NCDP	National Commission on Development Planning
NEPAD	New Partnership for African Development
NERP	New Economic Recovery Programme
NGO	Non-Governmental Organization
NORAD	Norwegian Development Agency
NPRAP	National Poverty Reduction Action Program
NPV	Net Present Value
NTE	Non-Traditional Export
OAU	Organisation of African Unity
ODA	Overseas Development Administration (U.K.)
ODA	Official Development Assistance
OECD	Organisation for Economic Cooperation and Development
OER	Official Exchange Rate
OGL	Open General License
OLS	Ordinary Least Squares
OXFAM	Oxford Committee for Famine Relief
PAM	Program Against Malnutrition
PAYE	Pay-as-you-earn (tax)
PEs	Personnel Emoluments
PER	Public Expenditure Review
PFP	Policy Framework Paper
Ph.D.	Doctor of Philosophy
PHI	Presidential Housing Initiative
PL-480	United States Public Law 480 (Food Aid)
PPI	Producer Price Index
PPP	Purchasing Power Parity
PRGF	Poverty Reduction and Growth Facility
PRGS	Poverty Reduction and Growth Strategy
PSI	Pre-Shipment Inspection
PRSP	Poverty Reduction Strategy Paper
PSCAP	Public Sector Capacity Building Project
PSRP	Public Sector Reform Program
PTA	Preferential Trade Area
PWAS	Public Welfare Assistance Scheme
RAP	Rights Accumulation Program
RCCM	Roan Consolidated Copper Mines
RDC	Recurrent Department Charges
REER	Real Effective Exchange Rate

RIB	Removal-in-Bond
RIT	Removal-in-Transit
RMSMX	World Bank projection models
ROADSIP	Road Sector Investment Program
RR	Rothschild Report
SAC	Structural Adjustment Credit
SADC	Southern Africa Development Community
SAF	Structural Adjustment Facility
SAP	Structural Adjustment Program
SI	Statutory Instrument
SIDA	Swedish International Development Agency
SIP	Sector Investment Program
SISERA	Secretariat for Institutional Support for Economic Research in Africa
SITEC	Special Investigation Team for Economic Controls
SPA	Special Program for Africa
SOE	State Owned Enterprises
SSA	Sub Saharan Africa
TA	Technical Assistance
TAZAMA	Tanzania Zambia Pipeline Authority
TB	Tuberculosis
T Bill	Treasury Bill
TBTF	Too-Big-To-Fail
TPTF	Tax Policy Task Force
3SLS	Three Stage Least Squares
UDI	Unilateral Declaration of Independence (Rhodesia)
UK	United Kingdom
UN	United Nations
UNAIDS	United Nations AIDS Agency
UNCTAD	United Nations Commission on Trade and Development
UNDP	United Nations Development Programme
UNESCO	United Nations Education, Scientific, and Cultural Organisation
UNICEF	United Nations Children's Fund
UNIP	United National Independence Party
US	United States
USAID	United States Agency for International Development
VAT	Value Added Tax
VATIC	VAT Implementation Committee
WDI	World Development Indicators
WDR	World Development Report

WTO	World Trade Organization
WWII	World War II
XGS	Exports of Goods and Services
ZCCM	Zambia Consolidated Copper Mines
ZESCO	Zambia Electricity Supply Company
ZICAS	Zambia Institute for Charted Accountancy Studies
ZIMCO	Zambia Industrial and Mining Corporation
ZIMS	Zambia Import Monitoring System
ZNCB	Zambia National Commercial Bank (also ZANACO)
ZNOC	Zambia National Oil Company (formerly ZIMOIL)
ZRA	Zambia Revenue Authority

1

Introduction and Overview

CATHARINE B. HILL AND MALCOLM F. MCPHERSON

1. INTRODUCTION

The essays in this volume examine the efforts of the government of the Republic of Zambia (GRZ) to promote economic reform. Our main focus is the period after 1991 when, following almost two decades of one-party rule, Zambia returned to multiparty democracy. That change brought an end to the attempts by President Kaunda and his United National Independence Party (UNIP) to move Zambia towards economic independence using the public sector to guide and manipulate most aspects of the economy and society.[1] That strategy yielded neither economic growth nor social development. Zambia was significantly poorer in 1991 than when Kaunda began his ill-fated experiment.

Zambia's postindependence economic history has been dominated by two features. The first has been the inability of the general public to benefit from the country's large, and still relatively untapped, natural resource endowment. The second has been the loss of income and wealth resulting from poor leadership, inappropriate policies, and economic mismanagement.

With proper management, Zambia's natural resources could generate and sustain high living standards for every resident. Because of the lack of appropriate policies and effective management, little of Zambia's potential bounty has been used in ways that enhance the general welfare of the population. External factors have contributed to this adverse outcome. With few exceptions,

---

1. President Kaunda announced the takeover of the main economic activities in a series of speeches beginning in 1968 and ending in 1975 (Kaunda 1969, 1975). The basic theme was that Zambia's "full" (political and economic) independence could only be guaranteed if the state controlled the nation's major assets and directed most of the country's economic activity.

however, their impact has been accentuated by government policies. Further-more, those same policies often prevented Zambia from benefiting from fa-vorable trends in the world economy, especially the rapid expansion of world trade and exchange from the late 1960s onwards that helped lift large parts of Asia and Latin America out of poverty.

When Zambia gained independence in 1964, it was one of the richest coun-tries in Africa. Now, as it confronts the challenges of the twenty-first century, many Zambians are among the poorest people in Africa.[2] Real per capita in-come has been falling since the mid-1970s and poverty and inequality have in-creased.[3] The end to the one-party state and President Kaunda's destructive form of "personal rule" resulted from widespread, but long overdue, agitation to halt the erosion of the average Zambian's income and wealth.[4] Yet, as events since then have shown, restoring democracy did not guarantee that the quality of national leadership would improve, that policy makers would become ef-fective economic managers, or that public policy would be directed to the tasks of restarting and sustaining economic growth and development.

Reviving a regressing economy and imbuing a demoralized and dispirited population with a renewed sense of collective purpose are not easy tasks. Al-most two decades of economic decline prior to the 1991 elections seriously damaged Zambia's basic institutions.[5] Two obvious casualties were general attitudes towards public service and perceptions of what constitutes good governance.[6]

---

2. Zambia's economic regression can be traced in several ways. One easily accessible mea-sure is the human development index (HDI) produced by the United Nations Development Programme (UNDP) in its annual *Human Development Report*. Data provided on the UNDP website, at www.undp.org/hdro/, show Zambia's progressive decline. For example, in 1992, Zambia was number 136 in the world with an HDI of .425. By 1995, it was at #146 with an HDI of .378. A recent estimate based on the Human Development Report 2000 (Table 1), ranks Zambia at #153 with an HDI of .42.

3. ILO 1977; Iliffe 1987: Ch.13; World Bank 1993; GRZ/UNDP 1995; *World Development Indicators* 1997, Table 2.6, p.56; *African Development Indicators 1998/99* 1999, Tables 13.2, 13.3. Commenting on the publication by the UNDP of its HDI, *The Boston Globe* (30th June 2000) noted that of 101 countries that have been tracked since 1975, Zambia is the only one whose HDI index has actually fallen.

4. As Sandbrook (1986, 1987) and Ayittey (1992) note, this behavior has been widespread in Africa. African leaders have been subject to few constraints. They have administered their countries in arbitrary ways that provided little scope for sustained growth and development.

5. The decline has been widely noted. The World Bank's country economic memorandum (1981, p. 5) referred to Zambia's economic depression following the copper price collapse of 1974. A later World Bank report (1986, p. 3) noted that "(T)he Zambian economy has been in a continuing state of contraction since 1975." More recently, the World Bank in its study *Assessing Aid* (World Bank 1998) argued that if Zambia had used its resources productively from inde-pendence onward, its per capita income would have been orders of magnitude higher than at present. A similar point was also made in McPherson (1980) and McPherson and Zinnes (1992).

6. Despite its commitments in its *Manifesto* (1991 and 1996 versions), the MMD govern-ment has been unable to change perceptions that governance in Zambia is poor. Evidence can

Upon taking office in 1991, the new government led by the Movement for Multi-Party Democracy (MMD) faced many difficulties. Much was expected of President Chiluba and his team, largely because the Kaunda regime had managed the country so poorly. Moreover, members of the MMD party had boosted those expectations by making many promises to Zambian voters during the election campaign. The MMD government's first few months were highly encouraging. The general public and Zambia's international supporters began to hope that, at last, measures would be taken to move the economy onto a higher growth path and keep it there.

It was not long, however, before the after-glow of the MMD's election victory wore off.[7] Many of the commitments made during the election campaign proved to be inconvenient once President Chiluba and his associates began to consolidate their power. Undertakings to improve leadership were shelved and promises to better manage the economy were fudged. Many of the habits common to the Kaunda regime's autocratic and arbitrary approach to governance re-emerged. Indeed, the MMD government, like its predecessor, has been unwilling and unable to promote and sustain economic reform. In the process, the Zambian people have seen the prospects of prosperity that their country could generate submerged by economic mismanagement.[8] The decline in real per capita income, so stark under the Kaunda regime, continued under Chiluba and the MMD. It is more than a decade since the change of government, and the downward trend in income and welfare shows no sign of being reversed.[9]

---

be found in the *African Competitiveness Report 2000/2001* (Schwab *et al.* 2000, pp. 232-237) where Zambia ranks along with Nigeria, Cameroon, and Mozambique as among the most corrupt countries in Africa.

7. The afterglow has persisted for longer periods in different forums. For example, in 1997 President Chiluba was widely praised for his assertions that "Zambia is open for business" in an address to the World Economic Forum (*The Economist*, May 9, 1998, p. 50). As we note throughout this study, what has been stated by Zambia's leaders and what they would allow in practice have diverged. An example is the reinstitution of exchange controls on the February 18, 2001. The announcement may be found on www.boz.zm under the heading "Government measures to stabilize the foreign exchange market." The statement in Section 2 "Measures," namely that "Government reaffirms that these measures are consistent with the current policy of no exchange controls," does not reflect the actions taken by the BoZ.

8. Lest this judgment seem too harsh, one need only recall President Chiluba's apology to the Zambian people at the State opening of Parliament in January 1999. He apologized on behalf of his government for mistakes it had made and the long time it was taking to reform the economy.

9. Two of the most sensitive measures of changing national welfare are life expectancy at birth and infant mortality. In Zambia, both indexes have moved in adverse directions. The World Bank's *World Development Indicators* 2000 (Table 2.18) reports that in 1980 life expectancy at birth was 50 years, up from 46 in 1974. By 1998, it had fallen to 43 years. Infant mortality in 1980 was 106 per thousand live births, down from 127 in 1974 (World Bank 1981, Table 1.03). In 1998, it had risen to 114. Of all the countries reported in the WDI 2000, only Iraq and North Korea had an increase in infant mortality over the period 1980 to 1998.

Historical experience and detailed analyses suggest that the Zambian economy would grow and develop rapidly if government mismanagement could
be ended. What is unknown is when and how that might occur. Our principal
task in this volume has been to explore these questions. Both the UNIP and
the MMD governments devoted considerable effort *promoting* economic reform, mainly through programs supported by the donor community. Beginning in 1978, the UNIP government formally adopted seven adjustment programs.[10] It sustained none of these. The record for the MMD shows little
improvement. After much indulgence on the part of the International Monetary Fund (IMF), the MMD government completed a Rights Accumulation
Program (RAP) and graduated to an Enhanced Structural Adjustment Facility (ESAF). That program was formally approved in the first week of December 1995 and collapsed within three weeks. Following several attempts to
bring it back on track, the government and the IMF designed a second ESAF.
Commenced in 1999, that, too, unraveled within months of its adoption.

Since then, Zambia and the donor community have designed another adjustment program (a poverty reduction and growth strategy) and Zambia,
with special dispensation from the IMF, has passed the decision point for the
Highly Indebted Poor Country (HIPC) initiative.[11] These programs, yet
again, provide the government with the opportunity to move the economy
forward. Many such opportunities have been available over the last two and a
half decades. Thus, the challenge for the government is not whether it can
formulate and adopt yet another program to reform the economy, but
whether it will act in ways that ensure the economic reforms will be sustained
once they have been adopted. The focus of our work has been to identify and
understand what those conditions are, and to suggest strategies for them to
endure.

Section 2, which follows, provides the background to the study. Section 3
seeks to place the material in its broader analytical context as a case study of

---

10. Formal programs were agreed with the IMF in 1978, 1980, 1981, 1983, 1985, 1990, and
1991. While the formal dates of each program provide a specific starting point, Zambia was
under surveillance by the IMF from 1977 onwards. This was interrupted by the break with the
IMF in May 1987. That break was short-lived. The failure of the government's own adjustment
program found Zambia's policy makers quickly seeking a rapprochement with the donor community (SIDA 1989).

11. Gondwe 2000; IMF/IDA 2000. Chapter 14 comments on the irony of Zambia being
granted the special dispensation. It was to overcome a "hump" in debt service payments that
had been fully foreseen in 1995 when Zambia graduated from the RAP to the ESAF. Such dispensation would not have been required if Zambia had met the conditions under the ESAF of
rebuilding and maintaining its foreign reserves. Then, again, if the IMF had not changed the
rules, it would not have been repaid.

economic reform in Africa. Section 4 briefly describes the contents of each chapter. Section 5 offers an overview and concluding comments.

2. OBJECTIVES OF THE STUDY

The essays assembled in this volume cover the main issues that we, and our colleagues from the Harvard Institute for International Development (HIID), dealt with in our work in Zambia from the latter part of 1990 to mid-1998. Our involvement in Zambia began in early 1990 when the director of HIID was contacted by the government of Zambia to provide technical assistance to the Ministry of Finance (MoF). That assistance, funded by a consortium of donors agencies, was provided under two projects, the macroeconomic technical assistance project (METAP) and the computerization and modernization of tax administration project (CMTAP).[12] METAP had two goals: to assist the government with its new economic recovery program (NERP)[13] and to improve the capacity of MoF staff to formulate and implement the policies needed to promote and sustain rapid economic growth and development. The principal goal of CMTAP was to help Zambia's revenue officials strengthen tax administration using modern information technology and improved management techniques.

These goals were straightforward and easy to interpret.[14] What had not been determined in advance, and only took shape as our work unfolded, was the emphasis that HIID staff would give to each activity. As the following chapters show, during the initial stages, Zambia's difficulties were so pressing that METAP staff spent most of their time helping the government stabilize the economy. Senior policy makers understood that without macroeconomic stability, economic reform could not proceed. Over time, the attention of METAP's staff shifted to capacity building. By the end of the project, that was the principal activity. The main activity of CMTAP staff was capacity building.

---

12. METAP was financed by the governments of Germany, the Netherlands, Norway, and Sweden; CMTAP by the governments of the Netherlands and Norway.

13. The program was outlined in a number of places. The "new" economic recovery program described in GRZ (1989) had much in common with the thrust of the study "Restructuring in the Midst of Crisis" (GRZ 1984). It was not the same as the "new" economic recovery program formulated in 1988 entitled "Growth from Own Resources" (Kayizza-Mugerwa 1990). When the MMD party took power in 1991 it adapted the 1989 program to formulate its own "*new* economic recovery program" (GRZ 1992).

14. The terms of reference were contained in the scope of work appended to the contract signed in January 1991 between the government of Zambia and the President and Fellows of Harvard College.

Some of the shift in emphasis was due to the force of events. In 1991 and 1992, the Zambian economy was drought-stricken and faced the prospect of severe food shortages. Inflation was accelerating, foreign exchange reserves were depleted, and Zambia's massive external arrears, roughly equivalent to its gross domestic product (GDP), prevented further external borrowing and hindered the flow of donor assistance.

Eager to begin the process of transforming the economy, the MMD government made a major effort in early 1992 to bring the budget under control, reduce inflation, deal with the impact of the drought, and reengage the donor community. Assisting the government with these tasks kept METAP staff fully occupied with policy analysis and policy advising. There was little time to organize and conduct the type of training programs required to raise the general level of skills throughout the MoF. Towards the end of the project, and particularly as the government's commitment to economic reform waned, the technical assistance staff had almost completely shifted their activities from economic policy issues to training and capacity building.

The composition of project staff reflected the change in activities. From mid-1996 onwards, as members of the macroeconomic advisory team left Zambia, they were not replaced. The government took the opportunity provided by staff departures to phase out the advisory work, leaving only the training and computerization activities.[15] After a detailed review of the project's activities in 1997, officials from the donor agencies who were financing the technical assistance decided that the Zambian government was not serious enough about economic reform to warrant further support.[16] The project was not renewed and HIID's activities in Zambia ended in June 1998.

The following essays describe Zambia's experience with economic reform. They discuss the actions taken and the difficulties encountered. They also attempt to understand why, after such a promising start, the MMD government began to backslide on its commitment to economic reform. An enduring puzzle in Zambia is why this behavior has been so common, particularly when the nation as a whole has suffered from such recidivism. Every time the government has backpedaled on reform, the economic situation has worsened. That point was clearly demonstrated on the several occasions between 1977 and 1991 when President Kaunda and his UNIP government reversed

---

15. The external assistance advisor continued his activities beyond the completion of the project in June 1998. He made numerous suggestions for moving the reform process forward, but with little effect. His assignment ended in March 1999. He has subsequently produced a monograph outlining his views of Zambia's adjustment program (van der Heijden 2000).

16. Although the external review of the project recommended that the advisory work be continued, local donor officials did not see the point of continuing their support, particularly in view of the government's diminished interest in promoting reform.

direction. That history was thoroughly understood by President Chiluba and the rest of the MMD leadership.[17] What prompted the MMD government to follow this well-trodden and economically destructive path? Whose interests were served when the government abandoned economic reform? How can such behavior be discouraged (or prevented) in the future? For Zambia to move forward, these questions need to be answered.

The task of reviewing Zambia's economic performance has been greatly assisted by detailed policy statements by the political parties and the government. Before the 1991 elections (and again in 1996), the MMD party produced a *Manifesto* giving details of the principles it would follow to restructure and revive the economy. More than a decade has passed. The restructuring remains far from complete, and the economic revival has not occurred. One reason for this is clear. Once it started to govern, the MMD party failed to implement what it had promised.

Numerous attempts have been made to understand why such behavior has been so common in Zambia.[18] Some scholars have stressed the growth-inhibiting interplay of interest groups.[19] According to this analysis, a major consequence of interest group pressure has been to prevent both of Zambia's ruling parties—UNIP and MMD—from managing the economy in ways that promote economic growth and development. Other research has highlighted the lack of leadership.[20] The main argument is that President Kaunda had the authority, were he so inclined, to promote growth and development. Other explanations are also possible. One is that external events have been so disruptive they have undermined Zambia's prospects for growth and development. Two other explanations are developed at length in this study. The first is that Zambia's reforms have been preprogrammed to fail because the government has attempted to implement an agenda that is well beyond its administrative and financial capacities. The second is that aid flows to Zambia have been so large and so unfocused that Zambia's leaders have been under no effective pressure to reform. Indeed, since aid flows have continued irrespective of Zambia's performance, its leaders have had few reasons to sustain reform.[21]

---

17. Direct evidence is the MMD *Manifesto* (1991) published during the run-up to the 1991 elections.

18. Pletcher (2000) refers to Zambia as a "rentier" society. This classifies the system. It does not explain why the country became that way or why, in the face of failed reform, it remains that way.

19. Tordoff 1984, pp.115-119; Callaghy 1990; Fardi 1991; West 1992; Bates and Collier 1992

20. Mwaipaya 1980; Gray and McPherson 1999.

21. *The Economist* (May 7, 1994, pp. 19-21) examined the question of foreign aid under the heading "Why aid is an empty promise." It singled out Zambia as an example of a country that

3. ANALYTICAL BACKGROUND

Many scholars, development specialists, and government officials have devoted significant portions of their careers to attempting to resolve the types of
problems that Zambia has experienced. Periodically, some group has been
bold enough to assert that a "consensus" has been reached.[22] Such statements,
however, invariably prove to be premature. Once-promising solutions have
broken down, their relevance less widespread than initially believed, or the
proposed solutions have been significantly more difficult to implement than
anticipated. Examples are easy to find. Two will illustrate the point.

At the beginning of the 1990s, the World Bank promised lavish financial
support to promote the Africa capacity building initiative (ACBI).[23] A more
recent idea, widely and noisily expounded, has been that many of Africa's
problems would recede if only its foreign debts were written off, or otherwise
sharply reduced.[24]

Despite much earnest administrative effort, large amounts of money, and
numerous conferences and workshops, the ACBI has yet to make a serious
impact on African capacity building.[25] More modest efforts, like the Africa
economic research consortium (AERC), the secretariat for institutional support for economic research in Africa (SISERA), and the training efforts supported by bilateral agencies, have had a more far-reaching effect. Moreover,
relative to the administratively top-heavy and expensive structure required to
implement the ACBI, these alternatives are more likely to be sustained.

With respect to debt relief, its proponents have downplayed an important
but inconvenient fact. Based on the *net* flow of resources, the countries of
sub-Saharan Africa (excluding South Africa and Nigeria) have not serviced

---

had started and then abandoned reform on several occasions. It quoted a minister who had
been asked whether he was concerned that the donor agencies had pulled out of Zambia after
Kaunda abandoned reform in May 1987. The minister was reported as replying: "Concerned?
... Oh no. They always come back." Subsequent events demonstrated that he was right.

22. Such a view is expounded in Ndulo and van de Walle (1996). There were others before
them. The World Bank's Berg Report (1981) and its "From Crisis to Sustainable Growth" report (1989) both state that a broad consensus on how to deal with Africa's problems had been
reached. Many commentators spoke of a "Washington consensus" on the how structural adjustment and development could be achieved (Taylor 1997). Such a meeting of minds (if it
ever existed) fell apart during the financial disruption in Asia during 1997 and 1998.

23. World Bank 1991. The money was to establish and finance the Africa capacity building
foundation (ACBF).

24. The meeting of the World Trade Organization (WTO) in Seattle, Wash., in November
1999, was one such forum where this view was forcefully expressed.

25. In Zambia, the ACBF (referred to above) had plans to develop an advisory program in
macroeconomic analysis in the Ministry of Finance in 1993. Activities in this area did not commence until the latter part of 1998.

their external debts themselves since at least 1970.[26] The available data show that *net* flows of foreign aid have been (and remain) positive. That is, as a group, these countries on average have not been required to divert their domestic savings to service external debt. The question arises: how will removing debt that countries have not been servicing (and thereby incurring a direct domestic opportunity cost) provide such a dramatic boost to their growth prospects?[27] One possible answer is that it would reduce the macroeconomic uncertainty facing each country. Counteracting this positive effect, however, is the distinct possibility, widely believed among local and foreign investors alike, that African governments will begin to borrow excessively once their debts have been cleared.[28]

Most African countries have been politically independent for the better part of four decades. Over that period, a number of common features have emerged. First, with few exceptions, most notably Mauritius and Botswana, overall economic performance has been poor. The oil and food shocks of the mid-1970s are typically seen as the beginning of Africa's difficulties. However, several countries, such as Ghana and Guinea (Conakry), were already declining by the late 1960s. Second, most African countries have never fully recovered from these shocks. Indeed, the various attempts to deal with them, including the provision by donors of large amounts of foreign assistance, often blocked economic recovery. Third, the international community has doggedly used a variety of conditions, largely without success, to induce African countries to adopt and maintain economic reform. Fourth, (again) with few

---

26. Data from the *African Development Indicators 1998/99,* (1999, Table 12.9) show that *net* official development assistance (ODA) to all countries in SSA averaged 4.4 percent of GDP over the period 1975 to 1996. Excluding Nigeria and South Africa, which account for almost half the GDP of SSA but have received minimal foreign assistance, the average was 8.9 percent of GDP. The *World Development Indicators* 2000, Table 6.10 reported that *net* ODA to SSA was $17.5 billion in 1993. In 1998, it was $14.2 billion. The former was 5.7 percent of the GDP of all SSA; the latter was 4.1 percent. Thus, for at least the last three decades, countries in SSA have received adequate resources to service their debts without using resources raised domestically.

27. The CID (1999) proposal is for donor agencies to write off the debt *and* continue aid at present levels. This would require net aid to be increased by the current amount of debt service. In effect, the proposal is as much about increasing aid as it is about reducing debt. Aid effectiveness is ignored. Even with unprecedented flows of net aid over the last three decades, African countries have regressed. The CID paper provides no evidence that additional aid will add to growth in Africa. Past experience suggests that additional aid is more likely to reduce growth. This matter is discussed further in Chapter 14.

28. As shown in Chapter 9, despite debt rescheduling and write-offs of close to $5 billion during the 1990s, Zambia ended the decade with as much debt as it started. A significant part of that debt resulted from the additional borrowing and arrears that accompanied the delay in privatizing ZCCM.

exceptions, by failing to grow, African countries have been "marginalized" in world trade and exchange.[29]

All four features have been evident in Zambia. Its economic performance has been poor, with major sustained declines in per capita real income. The economy has not recovered from the shocks of the mid-1970s despite (in part because of—see Chapter 14) massive international support. The donor community has been both persistent and indulgent in its efforts to help the Zambian government promote economic recovery. Finally, Zambia's contribution to world income *and* world trade has fallen markedly.[30] All four changes have sapped the dynamism of the economy, thereby undermining the country's prospects for sustained growth and development.

Other African countries have had similar experiences. Explanations for these changes have been widely sought and regularly provided. The World Bank has produced many volumes of country-specific research. At periodic intervals this material has been assembled to review Sub-Saharan Africa's (SSA) economic prospects as a whole. The Berg Report of 1981 was the first such study. That report stressed the importance of sustained growth in agriculture within the context of macroeconomic stability.[31] A study in 1984 focused on the need to stimulate growth by raising the rate of investment financed by domestic resource mobilization and large increases in foreign aid.[32] A 1986 report stressed how structural adjustment could foster economic growth by mobilizing more resources domestically.[33] Finally, in its 1989 report, *Sub-Saharan Africa: From Crisis to Sustainable Growth*, the World Bank began to emphasize the importance for growth of enhanced capacity, especially of individuals, organizations, and the state.[34]

In these four studies, World Bank staff emphasized prescriptions. Subsequent contributions have been devoted to assessing the progress of reform and the drawing of lessons. Two studies are noteworthy in this regard. The first examined the lessons of the (so-called) Asian Miracle.[35] The second analyzed the impact of structural adjustment on economic growth and development in Africa.[36] These studies showed that relative to Asia, Africa's eco-

---

29. Collier 1994; World Bank 1995; Yeats *et al.* 1996, 1997; Rodrik 1998.

30. Econometric research reported in McPherson and Rakovski (2000) using data for thirty-three countries over the period 1970 to 1998 confirms Rodrik's (1998) observation that African countries have lost their share of trade because they have not grown, rather than because they have not traded.

31. World Bank 1981a.

32. World Bank 1984a.

33. World Bank 1986a.

34. World Bank 1989. This report was supported by research published in the four-volume *The Long-Term Perspective Study of Sub-Saharan Africa* (World Bank 1990).

35. World Bank 1993.

36. World Bank 1994. This analysis was updated by Bouton, Jones, and Kiguel (1995).

nomic reforms lacked direction and, at best, have been only partially implemented. Not surprisingly, their success has been limited.[37]

An important implication of this work has been that the massive amounts of donor support for reform in Africa has done little to cushion the costs of adjustment. Except for brief intervals such as 1994 to 1997, which can be attributed largely to improved weather, real per capita income across Africa has continued to stagnate and even decline. Several studies contrasting the Asian and African experiences with reform have identified reasons for this outcome.[38] These studies confirm what close to three decades of experience has already shown, namely, that half-hearted reform efforts and indifferent attempts to adjust do not remove the economic imbalances that block growth and development.

In their most recent study of Africa's circumstances, *Can Africa Claim the 21st Century?*,[39] World Bank researchers have posed far more questions and offered fewer answers than previously. The title of the study invites two interpretations. The first reflects the deep sense of frustration (and even despair) that characterizes efforts by the international assistance community to deal with Africa's problems. Indeed, for many people who work on Africa, *The Economist* (May 13, 2000) aptly summarized the situation when it branded Africa as "(T)he hopeless continent."

The second interpretation treats the title as a rhetorical question. Other observers, ourselves included, have few doubts that Africa can *and* will "claim" the twenty-first century. We do not doubt the formidable challenges African countries face: economic instability, civil war, border wars, genocide, displaced populations and refugees, HIV/AIDS, extreme aid dependence, corruption, and increasingly severe (local) water shortages. Nonetheless, history now has many examples of countries and regions, once seen and treated as "basket cases," that have rapidly turned around. The basic question becomes a matter of when rather than if.

Although European history provides a far richer set of examples, one need go no further than the United States to appreciate why Goren Hyden concluded that there are "no short-cuts to progress."[40] Four decades after gaining its independence, the United States was recovering from the war of 1812. The many horrors of slavery, including the Civil War, were yet to come. So, too,

---

37. As pointed out in Chapter 14, there is evidence going back to the Marshall Plan in the 1940s, that countries which are willing to promote reform benefit from aid. A 1997 World Bank study by Burnside and Dollar (subsequently published in the *American Economic Review* September, 2000) has been widely cited (World Bank 1998; Collier and Gunning 1999; Lancaster 1999; *The Economist* June 26, 1999) as providing empirical support for that conclusion.

38. WINROCK 1993; Lindauer and Roemer 1994.

39. World Bank 2000.

40. Hyden 1983.

were the economic depressions of the 1870s, 1890s, and 1930s, the financial panic of 1907, two world wars, numerous smaller conflicts, and the assassination of two presidents. America's diplomats proudly and correctly describe to international audiences that the United States remains a "work in progress."[41] African countries should be seen in the same way.

Those uncomfortable with comparisons between developed and developing countries can usefully recall the experience of countries branded as basket cases in the 1960s (South Korea, Singapore). Three decades later, these same countries were at the forefront of the Asian Miracle. For many observers, Africa may presently appear to be a hopeless continent. Evidence from Asia suggests that hopeless situations can often change radically.

The World Bank's analyses of Africa's problems have been useful and timely. These studies have generated considerable disagreement and the conclusions reached have been widely challenged. The United Nations Economic Commission for Africa (ECA), for example, offered a markedly different view of the sources of Africa's problems and how they should be resolved. Together with the Organisation of African Unity (OAU), the ECA took the view that Africa's problems were not primarily the result of what African governments had, or had not, been doing. In their preparation of the *Lagos Plan of Action*, the ECA/OAU offered a vision for the year 2000 of an Africa at peace, self-sufficient in major staple foods, and benefiting from expanding industrial output and exports. Each country was seen as being fully decolonized, free of outside influence, and the recipient of large flows of untied foreign assistance. Furthermore, because of its expected economic success, the continent as a whole would have assumed a more prominent role in world affairs.[42]

Africa's continued economic decline derailed both the *Lagos Plan* and the agenda contained in the Berg Report. As a means of focusing attention on Africa's problems, the United Nations convened an emergency session of the General Assembly.[43] One outcome was the creation by the donor community of the Special Program for Africa (SPA). This program provided finance for studies, regular high-level meetings to assess Africa's economic progress, and longer-term growth-oriented projects.

The prominent role being taken by the World Bank and IMF in promoting adjustment throughout Africa unsettled many observers. The ECA/OAU, in particular, began to argue that some of the problems in African economies

---

41. Ambassador Roland Kuchel, fourth of July celebrations, U.S. ambassador's residence, Lusaka, 1996.

42. OAU 1979, 1980.

43. United Nations 1986.

resulted from the adjustment measures required by the IMF and World Bank in return for their support. This prompted the ECA/OAU staff to formulate an alternative structural adjustment program.[44] Although the alternative program was widely endorsed by African governments, its success critically depended upon two important assumptions. The first was that African governments would actively promote economic reform. The second was that the donor community would provide massive debt relief coupled with large increases in foreign assistance. Neither of these materialized.[45] After almost two decades of manipulating their economies, African governments lacked the capacity to disengage in ways that would promote growth and development. And, in the wake of the budget-cutting and the conservative fiscal and monetary policies of the Thatcher/Reagan/Kohl era, large-scale debt relief and a major increase in foreign aid to Africa were not in the offing.

Relative to the World Bank and the ECA/OAU, the IMF's activities focused on a narrower set of issues. Furthermore, its time horizon was much shorter. The IMF's main concern was the reduction (and preferably the elimination) of the internal and external imbalances that have been the principal source of macroeconomic instability across Africa. Its programs have sought sharp reductions in budget deficits, realignment (meaning devaluation) of local currencies, the removal of subsidies (as a means of reducing government expenditure), and reductions in the inefficiencies of state-owned enterprises. A common problem in most African countries has been excessive absorption. To deal with this, IMF programs have emphasized demand management. This has been often at odds with the World Bank's attempts to induce a "supply response." It has also conflicted with the ECA/OAU position that, in order to "promote development," governments should continue to manipulate the supply of credit, control the foreign exchange rate, and actively influence the sectoral allocation of investment.

Experience supported by a large amount of empirical research has shown that the IMF's emphasis on macroeconomic stability has been fully justified.

---

44. ECA/OAU 1989.

45. The lack of reform by African governments was widely noted and criticized by African leaders themselves. Meeting in Abidjan on December 9, 1990, the assembled heads of the ECA, OAU, and AfDB noted:

We have reviewed the socio-economic and political conditions in Africa and do express our dismay that, despite the major policies adopted by the Assembly of Heads of State and Government of African Countries, the socio-economic condition in Africa has continued to deteriorate. The adoption of. . .[several major initiatives]. . .did not yield the expected results in the decade of the 1980s. This stems largely from the fact that policy decisions have remained mostly unimplemented and common positions not appropriately and forcefully followed." (quoted in *Rural Progress* vol.10, no.1, 1991, p. 1).

Macroeconomic stability will not guarantee rapid growth, but macroeconomic instability makes sustained growth and development impossible.[46]

Though the issues upon which the IMF focused have proven to be vital, many development specialists have criticized its approach as far too narrow and its conditions as too rigid. This prompted a number of changes. In the mid-1980s, the fund began adding to its programs aspects related to the social dimensions of adjustment. It provided additional concessional finance to countries classified as low income and heavily indebted. The IMF also modified its structural adjustment facility (SAF) to create the enhanced structural adjustment facility (ESAF). Following widespread criticism, the fund sponsored an external review of the ESAF program.[47] That review produced two changes (among others). In principle, the IMF agreed to encourage its members to take responsibility for (i.e., to own) their adjustment programs. It also agreed to focus more closely on poverty reduction. Countries that now seek IMF support (of which Zambia is one) are expected to generate their own poverty reduction and growth strategy.[48]

Because of the size of World Bank assistance to African countries and the intrusiveness of IMF programs in economic policy making, the priorities of these organizations often dominate the development agenda. Nevertheless, the Bank/Fund positions have not always held sway. Other views have been important, and persistent. Included among these are Kwame Nkrumah's warnings about "neocolonialism" and the dangers involved if African countries become (as he called it) a "quarry for the developed countries."[49] Another potent and highly destructive idea has been Marxian antipathy for rural activities in general and agricultural production in particular.[50] Many African leaders were convinced by the Prebisch-Singer arguments that primary product producers invariably face a secular deterioration in their external terms of trade. Finally, the center-periphery analysis has also had many adherents in Africa.[51] A more

---

46. Schmidt-Hebbel 1993; Ghura and Hadjimichael 1996; Mackenzie *et al.* 1997; Calamitsis, Basu and Ghura 1999

47. IMF 1998.

48. IMF 2000; IDS 2000. Chapter 15 describes the key elements of Zambia's interim poverty reduction and growth strategy (I-PRGS) produced in mid-2000.

49. Nkrumah 1965. In 1963, Nkrumah argued that in order for African countries to create the conditions for rapid, sustained growth they should form larger political and economic unions. His views were rejected (*New African* no. 381, January, 2000, pp. 18-25). This idea has been revived by Colonel Ghaddafi of Libya. He asserted that there "is no excuse for Africa not to unite" (*BBC News* March 1, 2001. available on www.news.bbc.co.uk/hi/english/world/africa/newsid_11955000/.)

50. Mitrany 1951.

51. Samir Amin (1974, 1977) argued that African countries have been systematically disadvantaged by their relationships with rich nations. Similar arguments had been made with re-

recent dimension of this argument is reflected in discussions of Africa's marginalization (noted earlier) and the widely held view that globalization and the "digital divide" are leaving Africa behind.

To the detriment of growth and development across Africa, these views have been far too influential.[52] Concern over the prospect of "neocolonialist" influences, prompted African leaders like Kaunda, Nyerere, Touré, Nkrumah, Nimieri, Moi, and Mugabe to act in ways that discouraged foreign investment. Although some important changes have been made over the last decade to reverse this bias, many barriers to foreign investment remain. Potential investors still find their efforts hampered by restrictions on land holding, limits on expatriate employment, and the creation of one-stop investment shops that in practice have become additional gatekeepers, hindering rather than facilitating investment. Thus, even though some progress has been made, African leaders remain deeply suspicious that foreign investors are only interested in exploiting their countries. With foreign investment well below its potential, the majority of foreign investors clearly see Africa as a last resort rather than the last frontier.[53]

The agricultural policies pursued by most African governments have been disastrous and represent a fundamental misunderstanding of how economic transformation occurs. In a report for the United Nations in the mid-1960s, René Dumont argued that African governments should sharply increase their investment in agriculture.[54] With no significant exceptions, African govern-

---

spect to different groups within African countries. Writing in the 1930s, Austen Robinson (1967) traced how resources flowed from rural to urban areas with little compensating reverse flow. The same conclusions have emerged from analyses of dualistic development in Southern Africa (Barber 1961; Baldwin 1965). In Zambia, Martin (1972) branded the exploitation of rural areas by the urban-based population as "inner colonialism." Econometric evidence for this proposition is strong. Using data for 33 African countries for the period 1970 to 1998, McPherson and Rakovski (2000a) report that the growth of the nonagricultural sector has generally occurred at the expense of agricultural growth. This shows up as a highly significant negative coefficient on the growth of nonagricultural GDP when this variable is included in an equation describing the growth of agricultural GDP.

52. They have frequently crowded out more constructive suggestions. One of these is the view of "government as saver" (Heller 1954; Kaldor 1963; Meier 1970). Rather than save, most governments have run large deficits. The outcome is that countries have regressed rather than grown.

53. Even upbeat assessments of Africa's prospects such as Camdessus (1996), Madavo and Sarbib (1997), and Wolfehnson (1998) were unable to show that there had been significant investment in Africa other than in some well-defined natural resource projects. Equatorial Guinea is a common example. With so few locals willing to invest in Africa, few foreign investors have felt inclined to risk their resources. The evidence reflects this. Based on data in the *World Development Indicators* 1999, net foreign direct investment over the period 1970 to 1997 in SSA averaged 0.68 percent of GDP.

54. Dumont 1966.

ments have done the opposite. The outcome has been that, even with surplus land and abundant unskilled labor, Africa as a whole has a major and growing food deficit.[55]

Finally, the data show that for Africa as a whole the international terms of trade have fluctuated rather than declined, especially when quality changes are taken into account.[56] Moreover, these fluctuations have not been confined only to African countries. Developing countries in general have had to contend with the same international shocks. The basic lesson has been that countries that have maintained reasonable buffers (food stocks, foreign exchange reserves, and unused borrowing potential) have been able to respond constructively to fluctuations in their terms of trade and other shocks.

Other ideas have taken time to filter through. René Dumont (again) provided a timely (though largely unheeded) warning of the problems created by influence peddling and corruption.[57] Hyden, mentioned earlier, highlighted the growth-inhibiting effects of what he termed the "economy of affection"[58] where merit and performance were displaced by decisions based on nepotism, ethnicity, and personal advantage. During the 1990s, these issues were subsumed under the broad heading of governance.[59]

With regard to the processes whereby policies have been chosen, Robert Bates provided valuable insights. Drawing on the ideas related to rent-seeking and social unraveling, he explained why policy makers emphasize specific rather than general remedies.[60] Though the examples used by Bates were taken from agricultural marketing, his analysis applies more broadly. For in-

---

55. Evidence for this point is widely available (Lele 1981, 1989; ODI 1982, 1983; Eicher 1982, 1992; Brown and Wolf 1985; Lavy 1991; Eicher and Baker 1992; Pinstrup-Andersen and Pandya-Lorch 1995; IFPRI 1995; von Braun, Teklu, and Webb 1998; Donker and Ohiokpehai 1998; Hazell 1999; Binswanger and Townsend 2000). As a whole, Africa's food production has not kept up with population growth as shown by data in the *World Development Indicators* 2000 (Figure 3.3b, p. 125, and Tables 2.1 and 3.3). Using the base 1989-91 = 100, the food production index for Africa in 1979-81 was 78.8. It was 124.3 in 1996-98, a 57.7 percent increase. Total population over the same period increased by 64.8 percent.

56. Julius Nyerere of Tanzania was fond of using the terms of trade between sisal (a Tanzanian export) and vehicles (a Tanzanian import). He used to point out how many tons of sisal were required to pay for an imported vehicle. Over time, that quantity of sisal had risen as its international value fell relative to the cost of vehicles. This was a powerful illustration convincing many Africans policy makers that their primary producers were condemned to declining incomes. Such simpleminded approaches prove little. A counter example is the sisal cost of computers, which has fallen dramatically over the last three decades.

57. Dumont 1967. There is now a large literature on corruption in Africa (Klitgaard 1988, 1990; Parfitt and Riley 1989; Ayittey 1992, 1998; IRIS 1996).

58. Hyden 1983.

59. World Bank 1989; Landell-Mills and Serageldin 1991; Hyden and Bratton 1992.

60. Bates 1981.

stance, his explanation of how farmers defend themselves from the State's predatory policies[61] has many parallels in analyses of tax administration, capital flight, currency substitution, wage bargaining, and state enterprise reform.

Other political scientists have highlighted the problems of leadership, especially when the outcomes are counterproductive. A widely noted issue has been the destructive effect of personal rule.[62] A related matter has been why the consequences of economic decline have been so politically benign in Africa. It took decades for the general populations in Zambia and Zaire to react adversely to the economic destruction wrought by Presidents Kaunda and Mobutu. A similar situation has been unfolding in Zimbabwe.

A number of other contributions have been important. Based on work in Ghana, a group supported by the United Nations Children's Fund (UNICEF) stressed the need to promote "adjustment with a human face."[63] The basic idea of this work was to identify and highlight the costs of adjustment. After years of restrained commentary, an increasing number of non-governmental organizations (NGOs) have been criticizing what they see as the deficiencies and excesses of the World Bank/IMF "orthodoxy." An example was the critique by the Oxford Committee on Famine Relief (OXFAM) released to coincide with the fiftieth anniversary celebrations of the World Bank and the IMF.[64] This pamphlet reminded the bank and fund that over a period of fifteen years, more than thirty African countries had implemented, but not sustained, over 200 structural adjustment programs. The authors asked, rhetorically, what is so compelling about the bank/fund's approach to structural adjustment when failure rates are so high? By taking such a prominent position, the OXFAM critique, in turn, has raised questions about the role that NGOs have played in Africa's economic decline. Indeed, some observers have asked whether NGOs deserve special treatment or whether they have become simply one more group that lobbies donors for funds and African policy makers for their attention on special issues.[65]

A final issue is the HIV/AIDS epidemic. After years of official neglect,

---

61. An example cited by Bates deals with grain deliveries to a monopoly marketing board. In years when harvests are poor, farmers withhold their output, preferring to sell it on the parallel market at prices well above those offered by the board. Failing to reach its targets, the board has to import grain (often at high prices). In years of good harvests (and low prices in parallel markets) farmers deliver their crop to the board. This overwhelms its transport and storage capacities, raising costs and leading to wastage. In both situations, the board loses money.

62. Sandbrook 1986, 1987, 1993.

63. Cornia, Jolly, and Stewart 1988.

64. OXFAM 1995.

65. Edwards and Hulme 1996.

dubbed politely by one source as "official silence,"[66] some African leaders have begun to take a more constructive view of the measures needed to come to grips with a disease that has been debilitating and killing millions of their citizens. Notwithstanding this progress, there is still a long way to go. This point is underscored by the confusion in the views of President Mbeki of South Africa who went to great lengths to deny that HIV and AIDS are linked. While most African leaders, including President Chiluba have watched from the sidelines, the prevalence of HIV/AIDS has reached extreme levels. A UNAIDS report in June 2000 stated that as many as half the fifteen year-olds in some countries are likely to die.[67] Adding to these woes, the subtype of the HIV virus has shifted in ways that increases its virulence.[68]

Although there are now major efforts to deal with HIV/AIDS in Africa, some important issues still need to be addressed. Specific matters identified by HIID's work in Zambia (and described in more detail in Chapter 12) relate to the problems of training, managing, and motivating those who are HIV-positive and who know (or suspect) they will die prematurely.[69] These questions are part of the broader problem of understanding the systemic impact of the epidemic on the capacity of economies to recover and grow on a sustained basis. Recent research is adding new insights. Using a framework derived by running an endogenous growth model in reverse, researchers have shown that the impact of HIV/AIDS on growth and development of HIV/AIDS is highly nonlinear.[70] (Results that demonstrate this for Zambia can be found in Appendix E to Chapter 11.)

The above review suggests that the pipeline of issues related to growth and development in Africa is full. To illustrate, Presidents Mbeki (South Africa), Obasanjo (Nigeria), Bouteflika (Algeria), and Wade (Senegal) have jointly promoted a new millenium initiative for Africa that after several iterations has become the New Partnership for African Development (NEPAD). Based on past experience, this is unlikely to be the last effort to get Africa moving. Many of the issues raised will be important for Zambia in particular and for Southern Africa in general. They include fostering regional trade, improving water utilization and management, dealing with the financial consequences of globalization, promoting regional cooperation to expand and improve the efficient use of infrastructure, and overcoming the adverse effects of acute aid dependence.

---

66. This point was underscored in *The Boston Globe* series "AIDS and the African" (October 12, 1999).

67. UNAIDS 2000.

68. Essex (1999) noted that subtype HIV III-C has rapidly spread across Southern Africa.

69. Hoover and McPherson 2000.

70. Preliminary approaches have been discussed in McPherson, Hoover, and Snodgrass (2000).

This list could be readily extended. Nonetheless, those who seek to help Zambia and other African countries to promote development should recognize that before they suggest new initiatives, the development agenda is already far too cluttered. As currently structured, it significantly exceeds the implementation capacity of the government of Zambia and its associated organizations. Our study concludes that *if* Zambia is to achieve economic growth and development its development agenda has to be drastically scaled back.[71] For Zambia to move forward, it will have to focus on a small number of selected issues, make progress on these, and build from that base.[72] The present scatter-gun approach to development typified by the World Bank's comprehensive development framework, the IMF's poverty reduction and growth strategies, and, unfortunately, NEPAD, guarantees that Zambia will continue to tackle an agenda that is well beyond its financial, technical, and administrative capacities. If this happens, the Zambian economy will continue to be preprogrammed not to grow and not to develop.

4. THE ESSAYS

The essays in this volume are grouped under four themes – historical background, policy reforms, the way forward, and a critical review of our analysis. Chapters 2 and 3 relate to the first theme. They provide the historical context for Zambia's attempts to promote economic reform. The second theme is covered in Chapters 4 to 12. These deal with the key macro policy reforms undertaken, and examine their effects. The third theme, explored in Chapters 13, 14, and 15, highlights some lessons from Zambia's economic performance and our assessment of what is required for the economy to move forward on a sustained basis. The fourth theme is addressed in Chapter 16. An eminent Africanist, who was not part of the HIID team, critically reviews our analysis of Zambia's reform program. A postscript has a brief account of more recent developments.

Historical Context

Chapter 2: "Economic Reform in Zambia: The Historical Background" describes the state of the economy in 1990 and 1991 during the period of

---

71. This conclusion is also consistent with the findings of a multicountry study entitled "Restarting and Sustaining Growth and Development in Africa" (McPherson 2000, 2002).

72. This, of course, is a major lesson for Africa from Asia (Perkins 1992; 1994). Few African governments or donors have taken heed.

heightened agitation for political (and economic) reform. It traces the Kaunda government's early attempts to deal with the economy's problems. The centerpiece of that effort was the Zambian government's two-volume study prepared in 1984 entitled "Restructuring in the Midst of Crisis." That study outlined a comprehensive program intended to mobilize the nation to confront its acute economic imbalances. Although the government soon abandoned the main elements of that program, the exercise provided a framework for subsequent efforts to reform the economy.

Chapter 3: "The MMD and Zambia's New Economic Recovery Programme (NERP)"examines the main elements of the reform program that the MMD government adopted when it took office. The economy was under severe stress —the harvest had failed, inflation was accelerating, foreign arrears were roughly equivalent to GDP, there was no foreign exchange to service external debts, state-owned enterprises were losing money, and private sector confidence had collapsed. The immediate concerns were to stabilize the economy and counteract the effects of the drought. A key challenge for the government was to rationalize Zambia's relationship with the donor community, particularly the International Monetary Fund (IMF). The chapter describes the efforts made to complete and move beyond the IMF's rights accumulation program (RAP).

The Policy Reforms

Chapter 4: "Fiscal Reform and Public Expenditure Control" reviews the main problems with the public expenditure system in Zambia. Difficulties in this area had been a major source of macro-economic instability in Zambia. Over the period 1970 to 1991, the budget deficit in Zambia *averaged* 12.1 percent of GDP. It ranged from a surplus of 3.2 percent of GDP in 1974[73] to a deficit of 21.4 percent in 1986.[74] Initially the deficit was financed using the government's cash reserves. These reserves were quickly depleted and the government began borrowing heavily. With its access to external finance dwindling, the government accumulated arrears and turned to the central bank for financing. The latter was highly inflationary.

The chapter shows that extensive efforts have been made over an extended period to reform the expenditure side of the budget. Despite some notable accomplishments, much more is required for the reforms to become sustainable. A stumbling block has been the wage bill. Unable (and largely unwilling) to reduce the civil service, even following the launch of a high-profile

---

73. This was only one of two surpluses over the entire 1970 to 1991 period. The other was 1.6 percent of GDP in 1970.

74. *International Financial Statistics Yearbook 1996*, pp. 806-809.

public sector reform program (PSRP) in 1993, excessive wage payments and wage awards have continually undermined the integrity of the budget.[75]

Chapter 5: "Fiscal Policy and Tax Reform" examines budget reform from the revenue side. The analysis focuses on changes in the tax system and the attempts made to improve tax administration. The successful introduction of the value-added tax (VAT) is reviewed in detail. Several other reforms improved the structure of taxes in Zambia. These, however, were compromised by continued problems with tax compliance. By establishing the Zambia Revenue Authority (ZRA) the government enhanced its potential for improving compliance. Because of continuing tax fraud, that potential remains largely unrealized.

In Chapter 6: "Monetary Policy, the Exchange Rate, and Financial Reform" we describe the changes in monetary and financial policies that have been made to help foster sustained growth and development. The large budget deficits (referred to above) created serious financial problems. Over the period 1970 to 1991, for example, the money supply (M2) increased by a factor of 134 (i.e., 13,400 percent) and the price level by a factor of 210 (i.e., 21,000 percent). Throughout most of this period, the exchange rate was either fixed or, even if floating, manipulated. It changed by a factor of 91. The real exchange rate became highly overvalued and has generally remained that way. With such a long history of fiscal excess, the tasks of achieving monetary stability and promoting financial reform have not been easy or straightforward. Asset holders have lacked confidence in the soundness and stability of Zambia's financial system. This has been reflected in widespread capital flight and currency substitution. Financial liberalization, introduced as part of the economic reforms, was intended to address these problems.

Chapter 7: "The Sequencing of Financial Market Liberalization, 1993-94" discusses a particular dimension of financial reform. Bruce Bolnick examines the sequencing of interest rate liberalization in 1993 and 1994. He finds that Zambia's approach to freeing up interest rates was significantly different from the conventional prescriptions. The standard approach urges governments to ensure that they have inflation under control, their budgets in reasonable balance, and their financial systems well supervised, so as to lower the risk of financial stress. The Zambian authorities pressed ahead with interest rate liberalization with none of these requirements in place. Once reserve money growth was brought under control several months into 1993, inflation dropped dramatically, real interest rates turned sharply higher, and the exchange rate appreciated. The system had obviously overshot. Within months

---

75. Government wage payments have been difficult to control. Over the period 1975 to 1985 inclusive, government wages averaged 9.9 percent of GDP (World Bank 1986, Tables 5.04 and 2.01).

it began to correct itself. Bolnick provides a lucid account of the lessons from that experience.

Chapter 8: "Trade Policy Reform During the 1990s" examines the options the new government faced as it began the process of broadening Zambia's links with the international system of trade and exchange. After years of government attempts to insulate the domestic economy from external influences by restricting trade and exchange, the process of opening up has been protracted, and subject to considerable local resistance. To counteract the growing shortage of foreign exchange, most individuals and businesses in Zambia had established numerous informal (and extra-legal) external links. These were reflected in widespread smuggling, parallel accounting procedures, false invoicing of imports and exports, the use of offshore bank accounts, and currency substitution. Government policymakers recognized that further restrictions and controls would only make these problems worse. Dealing with them required broad-based liberalization of both trade and exchange. That, however, posed serious adjustment problems for Zambia's highly protected and internationally uncompetitive manufacturing firms. These firms exerted considerable pressure to slow down (and sometimes reverse) the liberalization. Reform, however, had become inevitable since the government lacked the resources to continue its former intervention.

Chapter 9: "Debt Management and Debt Relief" discusses the government's attempts to rationalize the massive overhang of external debt (including arrears) and the interlocking debt between the government and its various agencies. Zambia's debt problems intensified in the late 1970s because of the government's general unwillingness to change its macroeconomic policies. At one time Zambia had an excellent international credit rating. Rather than protect that rating, the government took advantage of its reputation to borrow. External arrears increased, and Zambia's creditworthiness collapsed.[76] The chapter traces the approaches the government has used to reduce its debt burden. This effort, too, has been subject to a number of reversals due to the government's reluctance to sell ZCCM, the copper company. Zambia's debt remains large. Though Zambia has now passed the decision point with respect to the HIPC debt initiative, its debt situation cannot (and will not) be resolved while the government continues to run large budget and balance of payments deficits.[77]

---

76. Zambia's external financing difficulties began early and quickly intensified. Payment arrears in 1975 were K102 million (approximately $150 million). They remained well above K100 million for the rest of the 1970s (World Bank 1981, Table 14, p. 15).

77. Trends are not encouraging. The budget deficit (excluding grants) in 1999 was 11.9 percent of GDP. In 2000, it was programmed to be 13.9 percent of GDP (IMF/IDA 2000, Table 7, p. 26). The projected deficits for 2001 and 2002 are 13.9 and 12.2 percent of GDP respectively.

Chapter 10: "The Role of Agriculture and Mining in Sustaining Growth and Development in Zambia" examines the performance and problems of two sectors that will be instrumental in *any* successful effort by Zambia to achieve sustained growth and development. Since the discovery of copper at the turn of the twentieth century, mining has always been a dominant economic activity. Its impact pervades the whole economy through its interindustry and revenue linkages. As a land- and labor-abundant country with a relatively favorable (tropical) climate, Zambia has always depended heavily on agriculture as a source of employment, if not of income and wealth. From the end of WWII until the early 1970s, the economy grew rapidly due to the expansion in these two sectors. That growth came to an abrupt halt in the mid-1970s, largely through the policy-induced diversion of resources from both sectors. Despite having some of the richest copper reserves in the world, copper production has now fallen to well below half the level reached in the early 1970s. Zambia's food production per capita is now lower than it was at the end of the 1960s.[78] Some agricultural activities have been boosted through privatization and the decontrol of prices. The government has selectively withdrawn from the sector but continues to intervene in agricultural markets in ways that hinder their expansion. In the mining sector, the several years' delay in privatizing ZCCM exacted a high cost in terms of lost output, increased debt, and delayed investment. Economic revival in Zambia remains impossible while these two sectors perform poorly.

Chapter 11: "A Small Econometric Model of the Zambian Economy" reports the results of a small econometric model of Zambia. It has been structured to illustrate some key economic relationships and their dynamics. Based on data for the period 1970 to 1998, the model highlights the main trends characterizing the economy's decline. It also points to the types of changes that will be needed to revive the economy. These include eliminating the budget deficit, removing the biases in the exchange rate, reviving mining and agriculture, and rationalizing Zambia's use of foreign aid. An appendix modifies the model to include investment, and highlights the nonlinear relationship between real income and factors reflecting the spread of HIV/AIDS.

Chapter 12: "Capacity Building in the Ministry of Finance" describes the efforts made to enhance the ability of MoF officials to formulate and implement policies to promote and sustain growth and development. The chapter begins by placing capacity building in its broader context, both within the development literature and relative to efforts made in Zambia. It then examines

---

78. *African Development Indicators* 1998-99 1998, Table 8.5, p. 225. Based on an index of 1989-91=100, food production per capita in Zambia was 94 in 1980, 78 in 1995, and 92 in 1996. Over the period 1974 to 1984, the index had declined at an annual rate of 4.3 percent.

the challenges confronting the MoF. It has always had two institutional draw-backs. As a second-tier cabinet officer, the minister of finance has lacked the authority to spearhead the type of reforms needed to turn the economy around. Furthermore, due to the scope of the reform agenda, the ministry has been grossly overextended. The capacity building program began to address the second of these problems. A broad-based training effort was undertaken, supported by widespread computerization and networking within the ministry. This effort has been seriously compromised by the time diverted and the personnel lost through HIV/AIDS. Major drawbacks in dealing with the problems created by HIV/AIDS have been the lack of attention given to the changes in training and management needed to respond to situations where large (and growing) numbers of workers face the prospect of a premature death.

The Way Forward

Chapter 13: "Improving Governance in Zambia: The Role of Macroeconomic Management" examines a dimension of governance that tends to be overlooked when discussions turn to the "normal" governance agenda—transparency, accountability, and respect for law and order. We argue that prudent economic management is a crucial feature of good governance. Sustained growth and development will not be achieved in Zambia unless the government responsibly manages the nation's resources. The counterfactual is Zambia's own history. Budget deficits, inflationary finance, and exaggerated levels of debt have led to economic regression, not growth and development.

Chapter 14: "Ending Aid Dependency in Zambia" examines the consequences for sustained economic growth and development of Zambia's acute dependence on continued support from the donor community. It highlights the games between the government and the donors that have emerged (and continue) in the distribution and use of aid. These games have deflected vital parts of the reform agenda. In the process, Zambia has become, and remains, highly aid dependent.[79] We argue that for Zambia to grow and develop in

---

79. This point has been well recognized. In its policy framework paper (PFP) in 1991, the World Bank noted that Zambia could not develop by relying on aid. A decade later, with no fundamental reform, the statement applies with equal force as when it was first written. The World Bank stated:

Zambia is, and will remain for some time, heavily dependent on external assistance. An assured flow of such assistance will depend on a firm commitment to, and continued implementation of, economic reforms and on the utmost effort being made to resume normal relations with external creditors. But Zambia cannot rely indefinitely on excep-

ways that can be sustained, the adverse consequences of aid dependence have to be confronted and overcome. One way of doing this is for the government to formulate and implement an "aid exit" strategy. We describe its features and suggest how such a strategy would lower Zambia's dependence on foreign aid, rationalize the country's foreign debt, and reestablish the local conditions needed to support rapid rates of growth and development.

Chapter 15: "Sustaining Economic Reform: The Way Forward" discusses the policies needed for the Zambian economy to grow and develop. With the general decline in the government's commitment to economic reform from early 1995 onwards, and the economic distortions associated with delaying the sale of ZCCM, confidence in Zambia's economic future has been seriously damaged. Rebuilding confidence and trust among investors will require an extended period of solid economic performance. In the meantime, the government has to address the task of cleaning up the financial mess created by the arrears and debt incurred to keep ZCCM operating. "The Way Forward" offers a modest program for eliminating the budget deficit, stabilizing the economy, enhancing investment, and improving productivity so as to boost and sustain economic growth and development.

Critical Review and Postscript

Chapter 16: "Lessons from Zambia for sub-Saharan Africa" is written by Clive Gray, an economist. His task has been to critically review the material in the volume, comment on the soundness of its analysis, and assess how it contributes to the broader understanding of the challenges and opportunities facing African countries that are seeking to promote and sustain economic reform. Dr. Gray brings to his task a deep appreciation of Africa's development problems, having worked and lived in a large number of African countries since the 1960s. The principal reason for including his critique is to provide an independent assessment of the relevance of Zambia's experience for other African countries. Our intention is that other African governments and their advisors will draw upon these lessons in ways that helps them accelerate their own economic reforms.

A postscript updates the volume in a number of areas. Although there has been no dramatic recovery in the Zambian economy, and given some recent developments there is unlikely to be one, an overview of trends helps keep the material presented in context. Zambia held presidential and parliamentary

---

tional levels of foreign aid. Investment and growth can be sustained only if sufficient domestic savings are mobilized, and this will require prompt action to achieve positive real interest rates, reduced fiscal deficits, and a decline in Zambia's import intensity of production and consumption (World Bank 1991a, p. 2).

elections in December 2001. Though reluctant to do so, President Chiluba departed. The MMD presidential candidate, Levy Mwanawasa, gained a plurality with 30 percent of the vote in elections that were widely seen as having been unfree and unfair. This does not auger well for continued political stability in the coming years. The economic situation took a major blow as well when it became apparent that the grain harvest had failed and Anglo American announced that it was pulling out of all mining operations in Zambia. In view of these developments, it is even more critical that the government formulates and adopts a feasible reform program.

5. CONCLUDING COMMENTS

Our choice of topics in this volume has been guided by the overall framework for economic reform adopted by the government of Zambia and the tasks that were assigned to HIID's team of advisors. The tasks covered a broad range including fiscal reform, expenditure control, debt rationalization, financial development, and improving the effectiveness of foreign aid. There are some obvious gaps. For example, we do not *directly* address questions related to political development, democratization, legal reform, or the law and order aspects of governance. There is now a large literature on these topics that supplements what we have done.[80]

Our discussion has typically been confined to areas in which the members of our team worked and in which our activities had some influence. Though this necessarily narrowed the scope of our contribution, we believe the topics considered are broad enough to draw critical insights regarding Zambia's experience with economic reform. Several of the areas that we cover are absolutely essential for the success of *any* reform program.

Given what has been achieved in Zambia since the 1991 elections, one obvious question is whether the MMD government has measured up to its own commitments, the expectations of the international community, the aspirations of the Zambian voters, or, the potential of the economy? At this juncture, the answer to all four questions is no.

---

80. Collier 1991; Bratton 1992; van de Walle 1996; Posner 1998; Collier and Portillo 2000. The international press has been active in reporting on governance problems in Zambia. The BBC News (at www.news.bbc.co.uk) for February 19, 2001 reported a Zambian government study stating that the "coup plotters were tortured." An *Economist* article entitled "Glued to the throne" gave details of President Chiluba's attempts to have the Constitution changed so he could have a third term in office. Commenting on widespread corruption in Zambia, the article noted ". . .the ways people make money in Mr. Chiluba's Zambia are too often crooked" (March 17, 2001, pp. 44-45).

Swept along by the excitement of the election campaign in 1991, it might be argued that the government's promises were extravagant. But, if that were so, the government should have sharply scaled back its activities as the extent of its underachievement became apparent over time. That did not happen.

One factor complicating the government's task has been the frequent modification and reinterpretation of the donor's expectations. For example, the IMF regularly recast the performance criteria of the RAP over the period 1992 to 1995. Since Zambia had huge arrears with the IMF, the latter had little leverage. Zambia's policy makers understood this. They also understood that the RAP was designed primarily to allow the IMF to rationalize its own accounts. It had little immediate benefit for Zambia.[81] The adjustments regularly made to the RAP benchmarks established a pattern of IMF indulgence and Zambian nonperformance that undermined the implementation of the ESAF arrangement that followed the RAP.

By not vigorously promoting reform, the government of Zambia has seriously short-changed the country's population. By their actions, Zambia's leaders have shown that they have had an agenda that attaches a low priority to rapid growth and development. In dispensing with Kaunda and UNIP, Zambia's voters provided Chiluba and the MMD with a mandate to revive the economy. That has not happened. It could not happen with the policies pursued by the government.

The negative answer to the fourth question is unfortunate. As noted in the Introduction, if the economy were properly managed, Zambia could provide a prosperous and expansive future for all its citizens for the foreseeable future. A former minister of finance, the late Ronald Penza, regularly remarked that "Zambia is not a poor country, just one that has been poorly managed." President Chiluba and the MMD party did not reverse that trend.

After a decade of multiparty democracy, does Zambia have the economic foundation that would move the country to a path of sustained growth and development? The analysis presented in this study suggests that the answer is also no. It is likely to remain this way until Zambia's senior policy makers fully grasp the implications of the country's history of the last three decades and craft a reform program that avoids the major mistakes made over this period. This, however, brings us the full circle. Zambia has always had the po-

---

81. Indeed, it is easy to argue that it was against Zambia's short-term interests (especially for its leaders) to graduate from the RAP. Graduation implied that Zambia would shift from a program in which it was not effectively servicing its loans to the IMF, and was subject to flexible benchmarks, to an ESAF program that required adherence to a strict set of performance criteria. That Zambia breached six of ten performance criteria within weeks of moving from the RAP to the ESAF in 1995, suggests that neither the government nor central bank officials were prepared to be bound by the rigors of the ESAF program.

tential for rapid growth and development. Thus far, none of its leaders has been willing to support the actions needed to realize that potential.

Will these circumstances change? We certainly hope so. Indeed, a major reason for this collection of essays is the belief that our analysis provides useful suggestions for moving that process forward.

2

The Historical Context

MALCOLM F. MCPHERSON

1. INTRODUCTION

Upon taking office in late 1991, the newly elected Movement for Multi-Party Democracy (MMD) government confronted many difficulties. Economic activity was declining, the agricultural season proved to be a disaster, and the international donor community, which had suspended most of its support prior to the elections, remained skittish about helping Zambia.[1] Compounding the donors' skepticism was the ambitious nature of the policy reforms contained in the MMD *Manifesto* published during the election campaign. Past experience in Zambia suggested that few of those policies would be fully implemented. At best, their implementation would be delayed. The most likely outcome was that many of the policy changes would be adopted, often with expressions of commitment and good intentions, and then abandoned or modified in ways that undermined their impact.

This chapter examines the historical background to the approach to economic reform taken by the MMD government. Section 2 surveys the economic developments prior to 1991. We focus on the progress of economic reform and the dynamic effects of government intervention. Section 3 discusses the economic situation in 1990 and 1991 and briefly outlines the circumstances that led to the ouster of President Kaunda and the United National Independence Party (UNIP) in the 1991 elections. Section 4 has concluding comments. The appendix compares key economic and social

---

1. Donor displeasure with Zambia is typically reflected through the partial suspension of aid. Zambia's leaders, both before and after the 1991 elections, have never faced the prospect of a complete cutoff of foreign aid. Accordingly, donor threats to suspend aid have lacked credibility.

statistics in Korea and Zambia to cast Zambia's economic performance in a broader context.[2]

2. Economic Developments Prior to the 1991 Elections

At independence in 1964, Zambia's economy was in broad macro balance. Foreign reserves were large, providing close to one years' import coverage. Real per capita income was growing rapidly. Real wages and employment were rising. The budget was in surplus and the expansion of the money supply was consistent with the growth of real income and the progressive deepening of the financial system. The rate of inflation was low and there were minimal levels of external debt.[3] These conditions persisted until the early 1970s, when a series of government decisions set in motion events that soon overwhelmed the country's administrative and financial capacities. Danger signs were evident in 1970 when the budget deficit increased sharply. But, due to high copper prices and favorable agricultural conditions, overall activity remained buoyant.

That came to an abrupt end in 1974. Within the space of several months, Zambia shifted from having budget *and* balance of payments surpluses to massive deficits on both accounts.[4] This was the largest external shock the economy had experienced since the Great Depression.[5] It resulted from the combined effects of rising transport costs, a sharp decline in the price of copper,[6] and a major increase in the cost of petroleum imports. The government's choices were to finance the imbalances or adjust. Expecting the terms-of-trade shock to be temporary, the government chose to finance the imbalances. That quickly proved to be the wrong choice.

Economic Reform in Zambia

Although the economy experienced increasingly severe problems, President Kaunda and the UNIP government were reluctant to promote economic

---

2. Shafer (1990). As the data in the annex show, such a comparison is not as outlandish as it may first appear.

3. A more detailed overview of Zambia's economic history from the earliest days of European settlement to the late 1970s is provided in McPherson (1980, Ch.2).

4. In 1974, the budget *surplus* was 3.4 percent of GDP, and the current account balance of payments *surplus* was 0.5 percent of GDP. Corresponding data for 1975 were *deficits* of 21.5 percent of GDP and 29.4 percent of GDP. (*IFS Yearbook 1994* 1994, pp. 778–781).

5. Baldwin 1965; O'Faircheallaigh 1984, Chs. 4,5; Jourdan 1986; Mikesell 1988; Auty 1993.

6. Based on data in Mikesell (1988) the drop in the real price of copper from 1974 to 1975 was 51 percent. This had been the sharpest year-to-year change since 1900.

reform.[7] During the two decades of one-party rule (1972 to 1991) the government had failed to meet the conditions of no less than seven formal adjustment programs to which it had previously agreed.[8] Notwithstanding the inflow of large amounts of foreign assistance over that period, economic activity experienced a catastrophic, and unprecedented, decline.[9]

International comparisons illustrate the extent of Zambia's collapse. In 1965, Zambia's per capita income in U.S. dollars was more than 175 percent higher than per capita income in South Korea. By 1975, South Korea and Zambia's per capita incomes were at roughly the same level. South Korea's income continued to grow rapidly relative to Zambia's. By 1998, even with the dramatic reduction in income due to the Asian financial crisis, South Korea's per capita income was more than 19 times that of Zambia's.[10] (The appendix has other comparisons between the two countries.) While such Asia/Africa comparisons might appear extreme, Zambia's performance was poor even by African standards. If Zambia's economy had mirrored that of the rest of sub-Saharan Africa over the period 1972 to 1991, its per capita income in 1991 would have been approximately 75 percent higher than it was.

---

7. World Bank 1977; McPherson 1980; GRZ 1984, 1989, 1992; Zuckerman 1986; Kayizza-Mugerwa 1988, 1990; Gulhati 1989; Callaghy 1990; Seshamani 1990; *Economist* 1991; Fardi 1991; West 1992; Bates and Collier 1992; World Bank 1993; and Lewis and McPherson 1994.

8. Based on IMF records, Zambia drew on IMF finance (General Resources Account) in every year between 1971 and 1986 with the exception of 1974 and 1985. It drew on SAF/ESAF and Trust Fund resources in 1979, 1980, 1995, 1997, 1999, and 2000 (Source: "Summary of Disbursement and Repayments, Zambia" at www.imf.org). Apart from the lower tranche drawings in 1971, 1973, and 1976, Zambia entered formal adjustment programs with the IMF in April 1978, April 1981, December 1982, April 1983, July 1984, February 1986, and April 1991. There were ongoing programs under the revived RAP beginning in 1992. Upon the completion of the RAP, Zambia entered an ESAF arrangement (December 1995). This was not completed. A further ESAF was agreed in April 1999 and in December 2000, Zambia reached the decision point for the HIPC. In 2001, preparations began for a poverty reduction and growth facility (PRGF).

9. Much has been written about Zambia's poor performance, but there have been few attempts to critically analyze how the donor community abetted Zambia's economic collapse. An exception is King (1977) whose frank assessment of the problems with the Bank/Fund support for Zambia was never published. It is rare to find discussions of why, for example, the IMF and World Bank (and other donors) continued lending so lavishly to a country that, as early as 1975, could not fully service its external debt. The principal outcome of donor support, which White and Edstrand (1994) noted amounted to $8.5 billion (equivalent to 19 percent of GDP) over the period 1980 to 1993, was to allow Zambia's governments (both UNIP and MMD) to postpone reform.

10. The data are from the World Bank *World Development Indicators*. In 1965, per capita income in Zambia was $294; in South Korea, it was $106. Corresponding data for 1974 were $620 and $545; for 1975, $504 and $600; and for 1997, $416 and $10360.

Zambia's tragedy is that this poor performance could have been avoided. With appropriate economic management, the country could have continued to grow and develop, perhaps even rapidly. But, in the absence of appropriate macroeconomic management, Zambia has had more than two and a half decades of disruption and decline.[11]

The disruption has been dramatic. To put the issue in context, from the end of WWII to 1974, savings and investment in Zambia exceeded 30 percent of GDP. Average per capita income grew at close to 4 percent per annum making Zambia one of the fastest growing economies in the world over that period.[12] From 1975 to 1991, Zambia's savings rate declined sharply, and the rate of investment, though boosted by foreign aid, external borrowing, and the accumulation of external arrears, fell to less than 20 percent of GDP. The result was that Zambia's average per capita income declined by 2.5 percent per annum. This was one of the worst performances during that period among the group of developing countries that avoided disasters such as civil wars and coups.[13]

The data in the following table show the key macroeconomic trends from 1970 to 1998. The first five rows are real GDP in constant U.S. dollars, GDP in current U.S. dollars, real GDP per capita, the growth of real GDP at constant market prices, and the growth of real per capita GDP. Two features stand out. First, there has been virtually no dynamism in the Zambian economy since the mid-1970s. GDP per capita peaked in 1972 and has trended downwards ever since. Second, the per capita growth rates of real income have been highly variable with regular year-to-year changes of six percentage points or more (1973–74, 1974–75, 1988–89, and 1993–94).

Reasons for Zambia's slow and erratic growth are easy to find. Two points evident from the table are the poor performance of agriculture and the slow growth of exports. The latter reflects the decline of mining production. In absolute terms, real agricultural output was no higher towards the end of the 1990s than it had been at the start of the 1970s. This has had major implications for per capita food production, the growth of imports, and Zambia's deepening dependence on foreign assistance. The decline in food production per capita has had an especially adverse impact on food security. During the 1970s, there had been sustained improvements in per capita food production

---

11. These two themes appear in many studies on Zambia for the period up to the end of the 1980s (O'Faircheallaigh 1984, 1986; Kydd 1986; Good 1986; Gulhati 1989; Andersson and Kayizzi-Mugerwa 1989; Geisler 1992; Auty 1993; Mwenda 1993).

12. Growth came from higher copper production, the expansion of associated manufacturing activity, transport, construction, and agriculture (Deane 1953; Baldwin 1965; McPherson 1980).

13. The group is small but it includes Tanzania and Senegal.

primarily due to increases in agricultural production. The drought of 1979 marked the beginning of a downward trend in per capita food production that continued through the 1980s and 1990s and still has not been reversed.

An unusual feature of Zambia's "development" experience, evident in the table, has been the *increased* contribution over time of agriculture to GDP. This trend has been rare even among countries that have undergone serious disruptions. Such a trend runs counter to one of the major empirical regularities that development specialists have identified in their "patterns of growth" studies. Large amounts of empirical research since the 1940s have shown that under normal circumstances the contribution of agriculture to GDP declines as countries make the transition from low income to high income.[14] Zambia's performance is not a "Kuhnian" anomaly that challenges the existing theory. Rather, it reflects the degree to which the economy has collapsed.[15] The changing contribution of agriculture has occurred because the real per capita output of agriculture (and food) has declined more slowly than the decline in real per capita income as a whole. The implication is that over the last three decades Zambia has not developed in the conventional sense. Instead, it has regressed.

One reason for Zambia's rapid growth from the end of WWII until the early 1970s was the high rate of domestic investment. As Table 2–1 shows, the rate of investment remained above 30 percent of GDP through 1976. Until 1974, investment was generally more than matched by the savings rate. From the mid-1970s, Zambia ceased generating large amounts of savings. Public and private consumption became the fastest growing national activities.[16] As savings and investment declined, the growth of income fell.

A further constraint on Zambia's development was the general increase in uncertainty. Several factors contributed. The government's policy of nation-

---

14. Kuznets 1966; Chenery and Syrquin 1975; Syrquin and Chenery 1989.

15. McPherson and Zinnes (1991) modeled the process of economic decline by running an endogenous growth model in reverse. The data in the text are consistent with such a approach. Both savings and investment declined sharply. Recall that in the endogenous growth scenarios, a rising investment rate creates opportunities that are subject to increasing returns. This, in turn, boosts savings and income. In Zambia's case, these processes have been reversed. The declining rate of investment has reduced effective demand, thereby raising unit costs as the advantages of the division of labor and specialization dissipate. For this reason, Zambia's economy is an example of "running Adam Smith in reverse."

16. President Kaunda was quoted in the *Times of Zambia* (May 19, 1986) as having said: "Zambia's cardinal mistake was to subsidize consumption for a long time, thereby delaying diversification." It is curious that, although he recognized the problem, Kaunda did not take steps to shift the balance away from consumption. As the economic situation worsened, Kaunda was again quoted: "We try to spend as little as possible on development to ensure that people do not go hungry" (Source: Andersson and Kayizzi-Mugerwa 1989:4).

Table 2–1 Zambia: Basic Macroeconomic Indicators, 1970–2001

	1970	1971	1972	1973	1974	1975	1976
GDP (bill. USD, 1995 prices)	2.9	2.9	3.2	3.2	3.4	3.3	3.5
GDP (bill. Kwacha, 1994 prices) [3]	1842	1841	2010	1991	2119	2071	2200
GDP growth (annual %)	4.8	−0.1	9.2	−1.0	6.4	−2.3	6.2
GDP per capita growth (annual %)	1.8	−2.7	6.2	−3.8	3.3	−5.3	2.8
Gross domestic investment (% of GDP)	28.2	37.3	35.6	28.9	36.9	40.9	31.5
Gross domestic savings (% of GDP)	45.1	35.2	37.2	44.7	46.5	21.2	36.4
Overall budget balance' (% of GDP) [2]	–	–	−13.0	−16.7	3.4	−21.5	−14.2
Exports of goods and services (% of GDP)	53.6	42.4	43.8	49.1	50.4	36.6	43.3
Imports of goods and services (% of GDP)	36.8	44.5	42.2	33.3	40.9	56.3	38.4
Current account balance" (% of GDP) [2]	–	–	–	–	–	–	–
Treasury bill rate (annual %) [2]	2.40	3.34	4.34	3.94	3.96	4.00	4.15
Official exchange rate (Kwacha/USD, p.a.) [2]	0.71	0.71	0.71	0.65	0.64	0.64	0.70
Real effective exchange rate (1995=100) [2]	–	–	–	–	–	–	–
Parallel Market Ex. Rate (Kwacha/USD, p.a.) [3]	–	–	–	–	–	–	–
Money and quasi money (M2) (% of GDP) [2]	29.2	27.0	25.3	25.8	23.3	31.2	32.9
Money and quasi money growth (annual %) [2]	26.3	−10.4	7.1	20.4	7.3	12.0	26.3
Inflation, consumer prices (annual %) [3]	*−13.2*	*0.0*	*5.4*	*6.2*	*8.1*	*10.1*	*18.8*
Inflation, GDP deflator (annual %)	−11.4	−7.5	3.7	19.9	10.8	−14.2	15.2
Food production index (1989–91 = 100)	54.2	62.6	73.5	65.3	69.6	83.1	95.8
Copper exports (thousand metric tons) [3]	–	–	622.9	627.1	649.8	616.1	712.4
Population growth (annual %)	2.9	2.7	2.8	2.9	3.0	3.1	3.3
Net ODA and official aid (bill. USD)	0.01	0.02	0.02	0.05	0.06	0.09	0.06
External debt, total (DOD, bill. USD)	0.8	0.9	0.9	1.0	1.2	1.7	1.9

Notes:
1—including Grants.
2—excluding Net Official Grants.
Sources:
1) World Development Indicators 2002, World Bank
2) International Financial Statistics, 2002 and February 2003, IMF.
3) African Development Indicators 2002, World Bank.
4) Some series have been completed or updated using observations from "Macroeconomic Indicators," September 2002, Ministry of Finance and National Planning, Lusaka, Zambia. These numbers are given in italics.

1977	1978	1979	1980	1981	1982	1983	1984	1985	1986
3.3	3.4	3.3	3.4	3.6	3.5	3.4	3.4	3.4	3.5
2099	2111	2047	2109	2239	2176	2134	2126	2161	2176
−4.6	0.6	−3.0	3.0	6.2	−2.8	−2.0	−0.3	1.6	0.7
−7.8	−2.9	−6.3	−0.3	2.8	−5.8	−4.9	−3.3	−1.4	−2.2
24.7	23.9	14.1	23.3	19.3	16.8	13.8	14.7	14.9	23.8
22.1	20.5	23.1	19.3	6.8	8.0	15.2	16.5	14.1	22.1
−13.2	−14.4	−9.1	−18.5	−12.9	−18.6	−7.8	−8.4	−15.2	−21.4
39.3	33.6	45.4	41.4	28.6	27.7	32.9	35.1	36.4	42.2
41.9	36.9	36.4	45.4	41.1	36.5	31.5	33.2	37.2	43.9
—	−10.0	2.3	−13.8	−18.0	−14.5	−7.9	−5.4	−17.5	−20.9
4.38	4.38	4.44	4.50	5.75	6.00	7.50	7.67	13.21	24.25
0.79	0.80	0.79	0.79	0.87	0.93	1.26	1.81	3.14	7.79
—	—	—	143.9	147.3	164.1	152.4	131.4	126.5	62.4
—	1.8	1.8	1.3	1.4	1.4	1.6	2.3	4.8	9.8
35.2	28.4	31.3	29.6	28.1	36.4	34.8	34.6	29.7	31.3
12.1	−8.5	30.2	9.0	7.9	33.8	11.1	17.2	23.4	−99.8
19.8	16.3	9.7	11.6	13.0	13.6	19.6	20.0	37.3	51.8
8.3	12.7	21.9	11.8	7.2	6.1	18.6	18.3	41.1	82.0
90.0	82.4	70.4	73.8	74.5	71.3	74.3	72.7	82.0	86.3
647.1	549.9	646.7	617.4	556.0	602.7	570.5	530.1	505.0	466.3
3.4	3.5	3.4	3.3	3.2	3.2	3.1	3.0	3.0	3.0
0.11	0.19	0.28	0.32	0.23	0.32	0.22	0.24	0.32	0.45
2.3	2.6	3.0	3.2	3.6	3.7	3.8	3.8	4.5	5.6

Table 2–1 continued   *Zambia: Basic Macroeconomic Indicators, 1970–2001*

	1987	1988	1989	1990	1991	1992
GDP (bill. USD, 1995 prices)	3.5	3.8	3.7	3.7	3.7	3.6
GDP (bill. Kwacha, 1994 prices)ⁱ	2235	2375	2351	2339	2339	2298
GDP growth (annual %)	2.7	6.3	−1.0	−0.5	0.0	−1.7
GDP per capita growth (annual %)	−0.3	3.2	−4.0	−3.5	−3.0	−4.6
Gross domestic investment (% of GDP)	12.7	11.1	10.8	17.3	11.0	11.9
Gross domestic savings (% of GDP)	16.5	18.2	3.8	16.6	8.4	0.3
Overall budget balance (% of GDP)[2]	−12.6	−11.7	−10.7	−8.3	−7.3	−4.2
Exports of goods and services (% of GDP)	39.5	33.3	26.8	35.9	34.6	36.4
Imports of goods and services (% of GDP)	35.7	26.2	33.8	36.6	37.3	48.0
Current account balance (% of GDP) [2]	−10.8	−7.9	−5.5	−18.1	−9.0	−13.8'
Treasury bill rate (annual %)[2]	16.50	15.17	18.50	25.92	—	—
Official exchange rate (Kwacha/USD, p.a.) [2]	9.52	8.27	13.81	30.29	64.64	172.21
Real effective exchange rate (1995=100) [2]	67.5	101.8	131.0	106.8	99.8	95.7
Parallel Market Ex. Rate (Kwacha/USD, p.a.) [3]	15	30.3	107.8	121.2	133.3	104.2
Money and quasi money (M2) (% of GDP) [2]	31.8	33.7	30.3	21.8	22.4	21.8
Money and quasi money growth (annual %) [2]	53.7	60.3	65.3	47.9	97.6	154.1
Inflation, consumer prices (annual %)	43.0	55.4	127.7	117.4	93.2	169.0
Inflation, GDP deflator (annual %)	62.0	34.5	80.9	106.4	92.7	165.6
Food production index (1989–91 = 100)	86.1	108.1	108.9	93.9	97.2	81.9
Copper exports (thousand metric tons) [3]	499.4	423.8	456.4	460.0	382.0	412.0
Population growth (annual %)	3.0	3.0	3.0	3.1	3.0	2.9
Net ODA and official aid (bill. USD)	0.43	0.48	0.37	0.48	0.88	1.04
External debt, total (DOD, bill. USD)	6.5	6.7	6.6	6.9	7.0	6.7

Notes:
1—including Grants.
2—excluding Net Official Grants.
Sources:
1) World Development Indicators 2002, World Bank
2) International Financial Statistics, 2002 and February 2003, IMF.
3) African Development Indicators 2002, World Bank.
4) Some series have been completed or updated using observations from "Macroeconomic Indicators," September 2002, Ministry of Finance and National Planning, Lusaka, Zambia. These numbers are given in italics.

1993	1994	1995	1996	1997	1998	1999	2000	2001
3.9	3.6	3.5	3.7	3.8	3.8	3.8	4.0	4.2
2454	2241	2185	2329	2406	2360	2413	2500	2629
6.8	−8.7	−2.5	6.6	3.3	−1.9	2.2	3.6	5.2
3.8	−11.2	−5.1	3.9	0.8	−4.1	−0.2	1.3	3.3
15.0	8.2	15.9	12.8	14.6	16.4	17.9	18.3	18.4
8.2	7.4	12.2	5.3	9.4	3.9	−0.9	3.1	—
−9.5	−7.9	−4.3	−3.9	−2.4	−6.9	−5.7	−5.9	−7.9
33.6	36.0	36.1	31.3	30.1	26.7	22.6	30.6	36.8
40.4	36.8	39.8	38.9	35.3	39.2	41.5	45.8	56.6
−8.4'	−7.0'	−7.9'	−7.7'	−9.0	−17.7	−15.2	−18.3	−20.9
124.03	74.21	39.81	52.78	29.48	24.94	36.19	31.37	44.28
452.76	669.37	864.12	1207.90	1314.50	1862.07	2388.02	3110.84	3610.94
108.6	104.5	100.0	104.7	125.4	114.5	111.9	113.3	122.4
531.0	805.4	935.6	1281.8	1583.0	2411.7	—	—	—
14.1	14.8	17.2	17.7	16.9	18.2	18.7	24.1	21.0
68.2	59.2	55.5	35.0	25.1	25.6	27.7	73.8	13.6
188.1	53.6	34.2	46.3	24.8	14.4	36.5	30.1	18.7
143.6	65.6	37.3	23.6	26.0	19.5	20.5	18.1	—
117.4	102.3	94.6	113.7	107.1	93.4	105.9	103.2	—
437.0	361.0	295.0	276.0	304.0	228.0	240.0	234.0	298.0
2.9	2.8	2.7	2.6	2.5	2.3	2.2	2.1	1.9
0.87	0.72	2.03	0.61	0.61	0.35	0.62	0.80	—
6.5	6.8	7.0	7.1	6.8	6.9	6.5	6.3	7.3

alizing productive assets created widespread concern among potential investors about the future role of the private sector. Some entrepreneurs sold out
and transferred their resources abroad, often illegally. Others adapted to the
emerging system by taking advantage of the opportunities to earn "rents"
generated by the burgeoning system of government controls.[17] Macroeconomic instability added to the uncertainty, particularly when the government
began to sharply increase its external borrowing.[18] The country's debts
mounted so rapidly that the government soon had difficulty servicing them.
Gaining access to foreign exchange became increasingly costly and external
arrears rose rapidly. As early as 1975, Zambia had substantial external arrears.[19] By 1978, Zambia's debt was equivalent to 50 percent of GDP.

Rather than deal with the basic source of the problem, namely the
overextension of government activity in a period of declining real resources,
the authorities responded by imposing harsher controls on foreign transactions. This action raised transaction costs throughout the economy, inducing
individuals and firms to search more determinedly for ways to insulate their
activities from the government-induced cost pressures. Some succeeded by
shifting into parallel markets. Those who could not, reduced their output or
went out of business. The government added further to the uncertainty by
periodically indicating that it would reform, only to backpedal once the reforms were underway.

Some of the data in the table illustrate the increase in macroeconomic instability. Foreign debt increased rapidly, especially after 1976. After remaining in the range of 10 to 20 percent per annum until 1984, the rate of inflation
accelerated, reaching triple digits in the late 1980s. The main impetus for rising inflation came from the rapid growth in the money supply.

In this regard, the key datum was the budget deficit. The combined effect
of large budget deficits and declining real per capita output had a devastating
effect on the economy. As Zambia's access to external finance became more
problematic in the late 1970s, the government turned increasingly to its cap-
tive domestic markets. These were "shallow" and provided few resources.
The government began tapping central bank credit, i.e., printing money.
Given that the supply of real resources in the economy was shrinking, this action proved to be highly destructive. Such government behavior has not been
unique to Zambia. It has been a common cause of economic collapse in Central and South America and the economies in transition as well as in Africa.
At one level it reflects a fundamental breakdown in governance, an issue that

---

17. Baylies 1980; Szeftel 1982; Pletcher 2000.

18. World Bank 1981, p. 16.

19. World Bank 1981, Table 14, p. 15. By 1978, Zambia's external arrears were $630 million
(GRZ/UNICEF 1986, Table 25, pp. 36–39).

we explore further in Chapter 13. At another level, it reflects a major confusion among policy makers about the difference between finance capital and real capital, a topic examined in Chapter 6. To the country's detriment, Zambia's leaders have behaved as though the two were the same.

When large deficits continue over such long periods, economic collapse is difficult to avoid, perhaps even inevitable.[20] Zambia's economic performance, therefore, is no surprise. The puzzle is why, with the consequences of its unwillingness to control the budget deficit so visible and so damaging to the economy and the nation for so long, the government continued to reject economic reform.[21]

The Dynamics of Government Intervention

There are many answers to that question. An important factor, however, was the conditions created by the government's decision to take control of most dimensions of economic activity. Having started down this path, it was difficult in principle—and proved impossible in practice—to reverse direction.

Since independence, pressure for the state takeovers had increased with the formal introduction of planning. The First National Development Plan (1966–1970) had been based, in large part, on the "Seers Report."[22] This report had proposed a major increase in government involvement in the economy. The intention was to expand infrastructure, promote agriculture, and direct more resources into regional development.

Government involvement was also seen as a way of dealing with the large gap in incomes between Africans and non-Africans.[23] The newly independent

20. Kindleberger 1989; Friedman 1992. Over the last two decades, many countries—Argentina, Bolivia, Peru, Zaire, Brazil, Turkey, Yugoslavia, Sierra Leone, Ghana, and Uganda—have had similar experiences. Ukraine, Russia, and Serbia are more recent examples.

21. The lack of good economic analysis is *not* an explanation. There were many useful attempts to highlight the key problems facing the economy and to propose constructive ways forward (Goodman 1971; Siedman 1974; IMF 1977; World Bank 1977). Structural adjustment is not an explanation either. As Andersson and Kayizzi-Magerwa (1989:3) noted:

It must, however, be said that though the issues of structural adjustment and diversification, as well as those of the restructuring of the incentive structure and the related pricing and subsidy policies, have been addressed continuously in the 1980s, a suitable formula for their resolution has not been found. This is not surprising. Events have shown that there is a limit to the government's willingness to adopt policies that challenge urban dominance.

22. UN/ECA/FAO "Seers Mission" 1964.

23. Income inequalities in Zambia were large even though racial discrimination had not been pushed to the institutionalized extremes evident in South Africa and Zimbabwe (Gray 1960; Loney 1975).

government was committed to reducing this gap as quickly as possible. Having "surplus" resources, generated by rising mining output and buoyant copper prices, seemed to provide the solution. Conveniently forgotten, however, was the pointed conclusion of the Seers Report that Zambia could have large increases in employment or wages, but not both. Responding to political pressures, Zambia's policymakers pushed both. The government wage bill increased, rapidly absorbing close to 10 percent of GDP.[24]

Independence had swept away restrictions on political activity and other social constraints such as pass laws and residential restrictions. The effects of the "industrial color-bar" that had prevented Africans from holding managerial and senior technical positions were dealt with by the rapid "Zambianization" of employment.[25] A less tractable issue was the concentrated ownership of productive assets. The government decided that the problem should be addressed by broad-based nationalization.[26] Beginning in 1968, the state took over most of the major productive assets in the country (except banking[27] and commercial farming). This process was largely complete by the time President Kaunda delivered his "watershed speech" in 1975.[28]

Yet, at the same time as Zambia was seeking economic independence by taking control of the economy's major assets, the political system had become increasingly authoritarian. Indeed, only eight years after Zambians had cast off one form of political repression under colonialism, another was forced upon them. In 1972, under the guise of promoting participatory democracy, the United National Independence Party (UNIP) declared itself to be the only legal political party.

The stage was set for an economic (and ultimately political) disaster. In retrospect, 1975 *was* the watershed year for Zambia, but not in the way its leaders intended. Due to the collapse of the world copper price in late 1974, Zambia's combined budget and balance of payments deficit shifted by the

---

24. As noted in the Introduction, the government wage bill averaged 9.9 percent of GDP over the period 1975 to 1985 inclusive (World Bank 1986, Table 5.04).

25. Mwanza 1973; McPherson 1980:Ch.2

26. The background to this action has been widely discussed (Martin 1972; Sklar 1975; Cobbe 1979; O'Faircheallaigh 1984).

27. This point is discussed in Chapter 6.

28. This speech was the fourth in a series, dating from 1968, 1970, and 1972, which Zambia's leaders saw as "taking back" the nation's assets. This action was meant to move Zambia ". . . towards complete independence" (Kaunda 1969; Faber and Potter 1971; Harvey 1972; Martin 1972). Yet, as time has shown and Zambians have discovered to their great cost, owning assets is one thing; making them productive, and using them *in the national interest* on a sustainable basis are entirely different matters.

29. Both supply and demand factors were important. The demand for copper was reduced by the development of fiber optics, conservation measures to improve the fuel efficiency of au-

equivalent of 55 percent of GDP in the space of one year.[29] Zambia's attempt to finance the imbalances led to a dramatic and unsustainable increase in the country's external debt.

Reform was postponed due to the general absence of accountability. Much has been written about the politics of economic reform in Zambia, most of it devoted to who did what to whom, when, and with what support.[30] A basic theme of these studies is that economic performance has never been a high priority for Zambia's leaders.[31] Indeed, President Kaunda and UNIP were exceedingly successful convincing most Zambians that their economic problems resulted primarily from external factors.[32]

Since the late 1920s when large-scale mining began, Zambia's prosperity has depended upon the world price of copper. The country has no petroleum resources; it is landlocked, and transport costs are high. Agriculture, particularly in the southern part of the country, is subject to recurrent drought. The price of copper has been highly volatile.

In order to insulate businesses and consumers from sharp changes in the

---

tomobiles by cutting their weight, progressive demobilization of the military as the Vietnam War wound down, the use of hard plastics (rather than copper alloys) in the production of munitions, and improved efficiency in the recycling of copper scrap. The supply of copper was substantially increased by the development of low-cost mines in Chile and Bougainville, among others.

30. Gulhati 1989; Andersson and Kayizzi-Mugerwa 1989; Callaghy 1990; West 1992; Bates and Collier 1992.

31. In his capacity as Chairman of ZIMCO, the parastatal holding company, President Kaunda stated in 1971 that: "...the ZIMCO companies are expected to show a greater consideration for social benefits than would normally apply to privately-owned companies." The implication was that Zambia was prepared to sacrifice efficiency and growth to achieve social goals. The emphasis on nongrowth goals increased to the extent that Kayizzi-Mugerwa (1988) identified a large residual representing factors that detracted from growth even after he had taken account of all external shocks. He concluded that internal responses (including policies and institutional changes) were largely responsible for Zambia's poor performance.

32. President Kaunda regularly attributed Zambia's poor economic performance to such things as fluctuations in copper prices, the oil shock, the closure of the border with Zimbabwe, transport problems, civil wars in neighboring countries, exploitation by transnational corporations, and rising real interest rates in world markets. Official documents produced during the UNIP period focused heavily on external events. These documents, however, did not shy away from suggesting that domestic policies had an impact as well. For example, the Third National Development Plan (1978, Ch.1) and the study *Restructuring in the Midst of Crisis* (GRZ 1984, Ch.1) cited a mix of external and local factors. The first New Economic Recovery Programme (GRZ 1987) ascribed most of Zambia's troubles to external events, particularly the conditions imposed by the IMF. A forthright assessment of Zambia's problems was provided in the Ministry of Finance's annual *Economic Report* (1989, p. 11). It stated:

Zambia remains strongly affected by unfavourable, exogenous developments in the world economy as well as by the rigid monocentric economic structure still extremely dependant (sic!) on only one principal commodity, copper.

relative costs of energy, the government had subsidized petroleum products. This added to the budget deficit and official debt. Zambia's distance from major markets significantly increased the cost of transporting imports and exports. Those costs rose sharply in the early 1970s as a result of the disruptions to conventional transport routes through Angola and Rhodesia/Zimbabwe. Finally, due to the low level of inputs, crop yields and animal productivity have been low by international standards.[33]

While all of these factors were, in some sense, outside the government's control, prudent economic policies could have reduced their burden on the economy. This is not a case, as Harry Johnson used to say, of being "wiser in the blinding light of hindsight." Many other developing countries experienced similar problems without collapsing as Zambia has done. The government's unfortunate policy choices, particularly its unwillingness to sustain broad-based reform, accentuated the economy's weaknesses and seriously compromised its strengths. Copper price fluctuations were of less consequence when foreign exchange reserves were adequate and external debt was small. Transport costs were relatively lower when effective local competition existed and road and rail routes were properly maintained. Rising energy prices would have been more readily accommodated had market-determined pricing obliged both low- and high-priority users to conserve energy. And, the impact of drought was less severe when farm productivity was rising, incentives existed for private sector storage, the public sector had the financial resources needed to import emergency supplies, and farmers were encouraged to raise crops and livestock suited to their agroecological settings.[34]

No one seriously disputes that external factors affected Zambia's economic

---

33. USDA 1990, pp. 545–548; World Bank 1992. The endnotes in the Introduction provide data on food production indexes in Zambia. In per capita terms, these have declined over the last three decades.

34. To pursue their goal of economic independence, Zambia's policy makers explicitly rejected the notion of comparative advantage. This was evident in the strategy of import-substituting industrialization and the quest for food security (World Bank, 1977). In fact, the government's objective was self-sufficiency, especially for staple foods. To achieve this, the government adopted a policy beginning with the 1974/75 season of fixing the price of maize and fertilizer pan-territorially and pan-seasonally. This was reinforced by a ban on maize exports. Farmers in all regions of the country were encouraged to grow maize, thereby ignoring regional competitive advantage based on agronomic conditions, transport differentials, and seasonal storage potential. As Chapter 10 shows, this was costly to the budget, with food and transport subsidies regularly accounting for 3 to 4 percent of GDP. Over the period 1975 to 1985, subsidies averaged 3.7 percent of GDP (World Bank 1986, Table 5.04; World Bank 1993, Table 4.2). That these subsidies failed is evident by the progressive decline in per capita food production (noted earlier) and the disastrous collapse of the food supply in the drought of 1991–92.

performance. Nevertheless, we are reminded that external factors do not provide a permanent excuse for poor economic performance.[35] In fact, external factors became critical only when buffer stocks (food supplies, foreign reserves, and unused borrowing capacity) that had been built up during good times were run down beyond prudent limits. As noted earlier, the Zambian economy was beginning to unravel in the early 1970s. The deteriorating situation could have been arrested then if the government had changed its policies, particularly if it had avoided the extreme overvaluation of the real exchange rate and its huge budget deficits.

While Zambia's leaders were able to gain some political advantage by blaming the country's problems on external factors, it is hard to understand why they should have believed their own rhetoric. External events made economic management difficult. But, none of these events required the government to run such large budget deficits for so long, or to borrow abroad so excessively. Similarly, external factors do not explain why the government allowed vital economic organizations, such as the central bank, the budget office, and the revenue departments—which at one time were among the best in Africa—to become dysfunctional.

The outcome was the steady dissipation of Zambia's capacity to create wealth. Politically, President Kaunda's version of personal rule destroyed the basis for open, accountable governance.[36] Social ideals that were once widely shared, especially during the struggle for independence, were abandoned, along with any effective concern for the poor.[37] Also lost was the ability of Zambia's population to generate income on a sustained basis. To an increasing extent, individuals and firms that had resources were increasingly unwilling to continue their activities in Zambia.

Those able to get their resources out of Zambia did so. Billions of dollars of capital fled Zambia from the mid-1970s onwards.[38] Those who could not shift their resources abroad defended themselves from state action in other ways—tax evasion, the use of parallel markets, currency substitution, smug-

---

35. This point has been made in several contexts (Gulhati, 1989; Mwanakatwe, 1990; King, 1991).

36. A term used by Sandbrook (1987). Examples in Zambia's case can be found in Szeftel (1982), Good (1989), and Crown Agents (1991).

37. The decline in social conditions in Zambia has been widely documented (ILO 1977; GRZ 1984; GRZ/UNICEF 1986, Ch. 11; Iliffe 1987: Ch. 13; Seshamani 1990; Achola 1990; Kelley 1991; ILO 1992; World Bank 1994b). As already noted in Ch. 1, perhaps the most telling datum is that, over the period 1970 to 1992, Zambia's infant mortality did not decline.

38. There are several sources—gaps in the balance of payments, the holdings by Zambian residents of foreign bank accounts and other assets abroad, estimates of the unrecorded gem trade (which World Bank sources suggest have been between $180 and $400 million per annum) and parastatal transfers abroad (World Bank 1992, p. 97).

gling, and by shifting into activities over which the government had little control.[39]

The result was widespread economic disruption. The government agreed with the IMF to adopt a number of structural adjustment programs, in the process gaining access to large amounts of financial support. None of these programs was implemented in ways that could have fundamentally changed the economy.

These failures were costly. The cumulative loss of national income, the rise in external debt, and the deadweight loss of underutilized and poorly utilized capital ran into the billions of dollars.

One positive outcome of the economic failure was that it increased the pressure for political and economic reform. With the economy collapsing, President Kaunda and UNIP were in no position to resist. The general public understood what it *did not* want. This, in turn, helped define what the objectives of economic reform *had* to be.

Another outcome was that Zambia's experience made it clear that further attempts to finance the economic imbalances would be futile. Zambia's international credit-worthiness had been destroyed. By late 1991, economic reform and prudent economic management had become the only options for moving the economy forward.

3. THE ECONOMIC SITUATION IN 1990 AND 1991

Following President Kaunda's termination of the donor-supported adjustment program in May 1987 (at which time the IMF representative was told to leave Zambia), the GRZ formulated and implemented its own adjustment program, "growth from own resources."[40] This program quickly failed, primarily because there were no additional domestic resources to support growth. The government then began to seek ways to repair relations with the donor community. Those attempts eased the government's resistance to economic reform. A useful start was the lifting of most (but not all) controls on agricultural prices. A further signal of the government's intentions was its willingness to begin changing the exchange rate. In December 1989, the kwacha was devalued to K24=$1 and in February 1990 an Open

---

39. Ironically, the June 1989 decontrol of all agricultural prices except those for maize and fertilizer, encouraged commercial farmers to shift from maize production (*EIU Country Report* No. 2 1990, pp. 4–12). This reduced the output of maize in subsequent years, setting the stage for the precipitous drop in supply during the drought of 1991–92.

40. Kayizza-Magerwa 1988; Andersson and Kayizzi-Magerwa 1989; SIDA 1989.

General License (OGL) system of allocation of foreign exchange was introduced.[41]

The economic situation remained precarious. Inflation was high and rising; the budget deficit, though lower than in previous years remained large; and official arrears to foreign creditors continued to increase. In March 1990, the Fifth National Convention of UNIP was held. The prospect of shifting to a multiparty democratic system was debated and rejected. Pressure for political reform continued. As a sign of goodwill, President Kaunda declared a general amnesty for political prisoners on June 25, 1990. The situation, however, was spiraling out of control. Between June 25 and 29 there were food riots, and on June 30 Lieutenant Luchembe attempted a coup. Although the coup attempt failed, the widespread public jubilation at the news that Kaunda and UNIP had been overthrown signaled that the regime's days were numbered.

At the same time as the momentum for political change accelerated, the economic turmoil continued. In October 1990, resident non-Zambians were permitted to hold dollar-denominated accounts locally. This was the first official recognition that currency substitution was a major problem. Inflation for 1990 was 117.4 percent. Real per capita GDP fell by 3.5 percent. Foreign debt and external payment arrears continued to rise.

On December 17, 1990, President Kaunda signed the constitutional (amendment) bill that legalized opposition political parties. Within two months the Movement for Multi-Party Democracy (MMD) was formed. Its constitution was formally adopted on February 28, 1991.

On the economic front, the government and the International Monetary Fund (IMF) agreed in May 1991 to implement the Rights Accumulation Program (RAP). A first for the IMF, this program was designed to allow countries with arrears to the IMF (of which Zambia was one of several) to accumulate in a structured way the "rights" that would enable them to rationalize their arrears. At the completion of the (three-year) program, Zambia could draw on additional IMF funding and convert the arrears to a concessional loan. When it signed this agreement, Zambia's arrears to the IMF were SDR 830 million (approximately $1.2 billion). The agreement triggered the potential for additional foreign assistance. Much of it was not released because, as had happened so often in the past, the government did not honor its commitment to promote reform.

In July 1991, President Kaunda announced that general elections would be

---

41. Under this two-tier system, the official exchange rate of K22=$1 applied to selected importers and imports (ZCCM, Zambia Airways, and oil and fertilizer shipments) and a "second window" initially at K40=$1 but able to "crawl" applied to most of the remaining items (*EIU Country Report* No. 2 Zambia 1990, pp. 4–12; Lewis and McPherson 1996).

held in October. As the election date approached, the government allowed its expenditure to spiral out of control. A hastily organized debt swap, designed to provide financing for UNIP, led to a major increase in reserve money. The rate of inflation, already high, accelerated.

President Kaunda and UNIP were in a bind. The RAP agreement with the IMF obliged them to be economically prudent. But, having committed themselves to the elections, Kaunda and UNIP needed resources to ensure their political success. With no real resources to support its ambitions, the government sought accommodation from the central bank. The rise in domestic credit during the latter part of the year was dramatic. For the year as a whole, domestic credit, driven by government deficit spending, rose by 146.7 percent while broad money (M2) increased by 98.1 percent.[42] As a result, none of the financial benchmarks under the RAP could be met. The IMF program collapsed. The World Bank (reluctantly) suspended its support to Zambia on the September 13, 1991. For Kaunda and UNIP, these developments were largely inconsequential. Their principal concern was political survival.

4. CONCLUDING COMMENTS

The political upheaval from early 1990 until the elections in late 1991 added to Zambia's economic instability. Given the history of economic mismanagement during the Second Republic, it misrepresents the case to argue, as President Kaunda and UNIP officials attempted to do, that the political agitation to end one-party rule had created the economic difficulties. The difficulties were long-standing, and deeply entrenched. They had resulted from the failure of President Kaunda and UNIP to take the steps needed to reform the economy when they had the power and several opportunities to do so. It was the collapse of the economy that gave impetus to the political agitation that eventually undermined the Second Republic.

With the defeat of President Kaunda and UNIP, Zambia had the potential for a fresh start. When given the chance, Zambia's voters had been prepared to jettison the regime whose policies and actions (including inaction, especially with respect to reform) had halved Zambia's real per capita income over a period of fifteen years. In voting for change, Zambians clearly indicated they wanted a government committed to avoiding the mistakes of the Kaunda regime.

A recurring lesson that emerges from any study of Zambia's economic and political history is the general inability of those in control to learn from

---

42. IMF 1992, July 1, Table 2.

events within Zambia and elsewhere. As a result, the same mistakes have been repeated many times. With respect to economic reform, the most obvious lesson is the need to sustain reform. When the government changed in 1991, it was widely hoped that President Chiluba and the MMD party would have learned from their predecessors. The next chapter explores whether that was the case.

APPENDIX: South Korea and Zambia Compared

It was noted in the text that Zambia's leaders had never attached a high priority to economic growth. For South Korea, it was the opposite. Students of South Korea's economic history regularly make the point that rapid economic growth was the main factor legitimizing the regimes of its otherwise unsavory leaders. This divergence in priorities in both countries provides an ideal case study of the merits and demerits of a growth-oriented strategy. Zambia has paid an exceedingly high price for ignoring the critical importance of rapid economic growth in its quest for economic development.

As noted in the text, in 1965 South Korea's per capita income measured in US dollars was roughly one-third of Zambia's. At that time, South Korea was widely seen as one of Asia's "basket cases." By contrast, Zambia was the rising star of Southern Africa. As seen in Table 2–2, the per capita income of South Korea (measured in PPP terms) in 1998 was $12,270 while that of Zambia was $860. (The nonadjusted data show a similar gap.) That is, relative to Zambia's income, the average income in South Korea increased by a factor of around forty over a period of thirty-three years.

Table 2–2 *Zambia and South Korea—Selected Social Indicators*

	Zambia	S. Korea
Expenditure on education (% GDP,1996)	2.2	3.7
Expected years of schooling M/F (1995)	8/7	15/14
Population on less than $2/day (1993)	98%	0%
Urban access to sanitation (1995)	66%	100%
Annual growth of consumption/cap. 1980–97	-2%	7%
Life expectancy at birth (males) 1997	43 years	69 years
Female adult illiteracy (1997)	33%	4%
Maternal mortality/100,000 (1995)	650	30
Food production 1989–91=100 (1995–97)	95.6	119.1
Size of economy 1998 (US $bn.)	3.2	370
GNP per capita 1998 (1993 PPP prices)	860	12,270

Source: *World Development Report 1999/2000* Selected World Development Indicators, Washington, D.C.: The World Bank

Since Zambia's natural resource base is inherently richer than South Korea's, the fundamental difference in economic performance largely reflects the development strategies pursued by each country. South Korea chose to emphasize export-oriented growth.[43] From the late 1960s onwards, Zambia promoted import-substituting industrialization.[44] Further differences were evident in the way that both countries handled economic imbalances. When South Korea encountered major economic difficulties in 1981 and 1998, its policy makers focused on adjusting the economy rather than attempting to finance its internal and external imbalances. Following the major terms-of-trade shock in 1974–75, Zambia's government sought ways of financing its imbalances rather than adjusting.[45]

Due to this choice, Zambia has neither grown nor developed. Moreover, as a result of the accumulation of debt and erosion of its productive capacity, the country has been unable to substantively help the 85 percent of its population who survive on less than $1 per day (in PPP terms) or the 98 percent who survive on less than $2 per day.[46] To the extent that poverty has been reduced in Zambia, it has been primarily through the efforts of the international community.

In Korea, by contrast, the quality of health and education and other social amenities has improved to levels that are consistent with those of a country that is within reach of first-world country status. Having grown rapidly, South Korea has had the resources to take explicit steps to deal with poverty. Not having grown, Zambia has lacked the capacity to prevent poverty from worsening.[47]

Comparing these two countries yields a more general lesson. It provides direct evidence on the merits of emphasizing the *costs of adjustment* versus the *costs of not adjusting*. Zambia's leaders, and the members of the international community that provide assistance, have devoted most of their attention to the former. The outcome has been exceedingly harsh on Zambia's poor. The protracted economic decline has undermined their welfare. It has not spared them from adjusting. If their incomes are to rise, many years of adjustment lie ahead.

43. Gillis *et al.* 1996, p. 85.

44. McPherson 1980, 1995; Lewis and McPherson 1996; McPherson and Rakovski 1999.

45. Lewis and McPherson 1994.

46. World Bank *World Development Indicators* 2000, Table 4, p. 237. The data refer to 1993.

47. It is worth noting that the relative performances of the two economies have not been differentiated by the *fact* of corruption. Both countries have been well known for high-level corruption over extended periods. What has been different, however, is the consequences. In Korea, the amounts misappropriated have been limited and, with few exceptions, the resources corruptly acquired have been reinvested in Korea. In Zambia, corruption has been high as the traffic would bear, or what those involved believed they could get away with. A large part of the misappropriated resources has been moved abroad.

3

The New Economic Recovery Programme: The Second Time Around

MALCOLM F. MCPHERSON

1. INTRODUCTION

Following such a long history of economic mismanagement and disruption, the incoming MMD government faced many challenges. Some of them, such as restoring macroeconomic stability, required immediate action. Others, like economic reconstruction, could only be undertaken over the longer term. None of the tasks would be easy.

An important issue facing the new government was to determine where to start reforming the economy. Those who opposed President Kaunda and UNIP knew what they did not want. They were far less certain about what they wanted, or how fast to proceed. President Chiluba and the MMD party had made many promises during the election campaign, not the least of which was that they would turn the economy around. With the election behind them, MMD policy makers were confronted with the "hard pounding" needed to achieve meaningful reform.

This chapter describes the adjustment program adopted by the MMD government and examines its implementation. Section 2 outlines the main elements of the adjustment program, called (for the second time in four years, but by different governments) the "New Economic Recovery Programme" (NERP). Section 3 reviews the progress made during its early stages while the government was still focused on reform. Section 4 examines the situation from the middle of 1995 forward, when the government's attention shifted away from economic reform. Section 5 discusses the 1998 budget to demonstrate the degree to which the government's policies had lost touch with reality. Section 6 comments on the 1999 and 2000 budgets. The former avoided the hard choices needed to reestablish stability. The latter, formulated by the third minister of finance in less than two years, was an attempt to begin unraveling the financial mess created by the delayed sale of ZCCM. Section 7 has concluding observations. The appendix summarizes four studies undertaken over the period 1993 to 1995 related to Zambia's "prospects" for economic recovery and growth. The studies provide insights regarding what the donors and the government considered had to be done to reform the economy.

2. THE NEW ECONOMIC RECOVERY PROGRAMME: A SECOND TIME

It was not difficult to determine what had to be done to addresss Zambia's economic problems. Major improvements would occur if the MMD government reversed the most destructive elements in its predecessor's policies. Those policies had been based upon the premise that state ownership of productive resources and bureaucratic manipulation of most dimensions of social and economic life would raise the incomes and enhance the welfare of all Zambians. That approach failed so utterly that Zambia, one of the richest countries in Sub-Saharan Africa during the 1960s was well on its way to becoming one of Africa's poorest countries.

The MMD government did not have far to search for a relevant, coherent, economic adjustment program. Numerous studies, produced over the years by consultants, academics, and the staffs of international agencies, were already available. These outlined the basic economic changes needed to stabilize and revive the economy.[1] Government officials had also contributed to the formulation of a number of reform programs.[2] More important, from the mid-1970s onwards, the government had made several attempts to reform the economy. None of those efforts had been sustained. Indeed, just as the economic reforms began to show some signs that they could work, Zambia's leaders found a pretext for abandoning them.[3] Over the period 1976 to 1991, this had happened five times.[4]

Based on their decisive election victory, President Chiluba and the MMD

---

1. ILO 1977; World Bank 1977; 1981; 1984; IMF 1977; SIDA 1989; Good 1989; Gulhati 1989; McPherson 1980; Kagizza-Muzerwa 1988; 1990; Seshamani 1990; Mwanakatwe 1990.

2. The most important of these were "Restructuring in the Midst of Crisis" (GRZ 1984) and the "New Economic Recovery Programme" (GRZ 1989).

3. The politics of economic reform in Zambia have been widely discussed. Most analysts have focused on interest group dynamics (Callaghy 1990; West 1992; Bates and Collier 1992). More recently, Gray and McPherson (1999) have expanded on the theme of leadership that had been raised earlier by Mwaipaya (1980) and Dumont and Mottin (1980).

4. Zambia had formal programs with the IMF in 1976–77, 1978–80, 1980–83, 1984–86, and 1991. All of them broke down (White and Estrand 1994, Table 2.4). In 1988, the government also gave up on its own program "growth from own resources" (Kayizza-Mugerwa 1990).

were widely expected to radically change the government's approach to economic management. That expectation was reinforced by campaign promises (reflected in the MMD *Manifesto*) and the statements by senior government officials upon taking office.[5]

The new government did not waste time devising a new adjustment program. Since Zambia had been a latecomer in promoting economic reform, even by African standards, there was much that could be learned from international experience. Accordingly, the government updated and adopted the New Economic Recovery Programme (NERP). That program had been formulated by the UNIP government in 1988–89 but was not fully implemented.[6]

The NERP provided a useful start. It was comprehensive and timely, and correctly addressed the basic economic imbalances in the economy. The main elements were:[7]

- Privatizing and reforming the state-owned enterprises (SOEs);
- Promoting fiscal discipline and tax reform;
- Implementing appropriate monetary policy and controlling inflation;
- Reducing and rationalizing the external debt;
- Increasing social sector spending, particularly for education and health;
- Reviving agriculture;
- Reforming the mining sector.

Of all these tasks, the most pressing were stabilizing the economy and reengaging the donor community. Due to the dramatic increase in reserve money in the months prior to the 1991 elections, inflation was accelerating and the exchange rate (as measured in the parallel market) was depreciating rapidly. It had become essential to reengage the international community so that Zambia could gain access to balance of payments and additional project support. This would allow the country to begin servicing its external debts (at that time US $7.3 billion, of which more than $3 billion was in arrears) and to reconstruct the economy's infrastructure, most of which was in an advanced state of decay.

The urgency of bringing the donor community "on board" intensified as

---

5. See President Chiluba's statement to the donor community in November 1991 (GRZ 1991) and the government's presentation to the Consultative Group Meeting for Zambia in Paris in December 1991(GRZ 1992).

6. This was the second NERP. The first was the "growth from own resources" program introduced in 1988 following Zambia's break with the IMF in May 1987. The main difference between the two programs was that the first NERP involved the broad-based reintroduction of controls on key economic variables. The second NERP emphasized liberalization and government disengagement.

7. GRZ 1989.

the national food supply dwindled. Within months of the elections the harvest failed, the result of the worst drought in Zambia in more than half a century. Crop production (and the staple food supply) fell to levels that, in per capita terms, had not been recorded in decades.[8] With few food reserves, no foreign exchange available for emergency food imports, and no capacity for further external borrowing, the government and the Zambian population were in a bind.

Based on humanitarian considerations, the donor community was prepared to provide emergency shipments of food as part of its broader effort to relieve the effects of drought in Southern Africa. In Zambia's case, most donors wanted to be sure that their assistance would not be dissipated yet again through the continuation of inappropriate government policies.

At the Consultative Group (CG) meeting for Zambia in December 1991, the new government's economic team, led by minister of finance Emmanuel Kasonde, assured the donor community that fundamental changes would be made. The rhetoric was welcome, but the donors wanted action. That began with the Budget Speech in January 1992. The government announced many changes including:

- Instituting exchange rate reforms including 100 percent retention for nontraditional exporters;
- Devaluing the official exchange rate by 30 percent and promoting an accelerated rate of crawl for the exchange rate (to 8 percent per month);
- Removing subsidies on maize meal (breakfast meal);
- Reducing military expenditure in real terms;
- Planning for privatization of SOEs;
- Eliminating subsidies, loans, and loan guarantees for all parastatals except Zambia Airways and ZCCM;
- Increasing budget allocations for education and health;
- Revoking import preferences, except those in force under the Preferential Trade Agreement (PTA); and
- Establishing a debt management task force.

By adopting these measures, the government was moving much faster than external agents, particularly the IMF, had advised. The initial message from the MMD government was clear. It was committed to economic reform and would act in ways that accelerated the process. This message was enhanced by the accessibility of key members of the economic team and the dynamism imparted to the reform effort by an informal technical committee of economic

---

8. In 1991–92, maize production (Zambia's main staple) was 483.5 thousand metric tons. This was 56 percent less than the harvest of 1.096 million metric tons in 1990/91 (Source: *Macroeconomic Indicators* March 1999:Table 6.1).

ministers. This committee met once a week to oversee the reform effort. The international community was impressed with the government's evident resolve to move forward. Within months, large amounts of balance of payments assistance, commodity aid, and project support began to flow, or were in the pipeline.

The initial reticence of the international community was understandable. Over the years, billions of dollars of aid had been provided to Zambia based on government promises that it would promote reform. Few of the promises had been kept. As noted in Chapter 2, the government had a record of initiating and then abandoning economic reform. What was unclear following the 1991 elections was whether there would be any difference in this respect between Chiluba and MMD and Kaunda and UNIP. The changes made in early 1992—their direction and pace—suggested that there would.

An impressive start does not imply reforms will be sustained. Restoring democracy did not guarantee that economic reform would be pursued more vigorously or diligently than in the past. To understand why, we shall review how the reforms introduced in the NERP were implemented.

3. Zambia 1992 to 1995: Reform Sustained

The elections of 1991 offered the prospect for Zambia to make a major break with the disruption and decline of the past. For slightly more than four years, that prospect was realized. In retrospect, Zambia experienced its longest period of sustained economic reform in the last twenty-five years. That period ended for a number of reasons. The constitution was changed to prevent former president Kaunda from standing for election in 1996. The events that culminated in the closure of Meridien BIAO Bank (described in Chapter 6) placed severe stress on the financial system and undermined confidence in the central bank's ability to supervise effectively the financial system. A change of senior officials in key economic agencies, principally the central bank and the ministry of finance, diminished the transparency of policy making and led to a pattern of economic intervention common to the Second Republic. Perhaps the most important factor, however, was that the government dragged its feet in selling ZCCM.

Although Zambia once more reversed many of its economic reforms after mid-1995, the achievements up to that point had been unprecedented.[9] The impetus for the reforms can be attributed to five factors.

---

9. Although a shift in the approach to economic management had been underway from the first quarter of 1995, it was not evident in the main macroeconomic variables until the end of 1995. The shift, however, was clear to those working within the government (including the au-

First, Zambian voters had overwhelmingly repudiated the economic mismanagement and stagnation that had occurred under Kaunda and UNIP.
Having campaigned as the party that could reform the economy, the MMD
was obliged to begin meeting that promise. Moreover, initially at least, there
were a number of senior MMD officials in key positions who believed that reform was essential and feasible.

Second, the MMD party comprised many people who, for different reasons, had become disenchanted with the unwillingness of the former government to restructure the economy. The MMD *Manifesto*, which featured
prominently in the election campaign, was a blueprint for fundamental economic and social change. In the flush of victory, the MMD government began
to implement some of those changes.

Third, the economy was so close to spiraling out of control that Zambia's
leaders recognized that they had no option but to press forward with economic reform, at least until some degree of stability was restored.

Fourth, after many threats, the international donor community had finally
"pulled the plug" on Kaunda and UNIP. The new government realized that it
could not fully re-engage the donors without practical measures demonstrating that fundamental changes in Zambia's economic and social policies were
underway.

Fifth, just three months after taking office, the failure of the maize harvest
created a national emergency. Zambia had limited food reserves and no foreign exchange. Without donor support, a major humanitarian disaster
loomed.[10]

These considerations produced a fundamentally different approach to
economic management. The Zambian people wanted change, the new government was publicly committed to economic reform, and the resumption of
international support depended upon actions designed to restructure the

---

thor). Debate on economic policy was progressively discouraged, critical assessments of economic options began to be avoided, and an increasing number of economic data (such as
ZCCM's debt, gross foreign reserves, and the government's dollar debt to the central bank)
were systematically withheld. An important (and ultimately destabilizing) change from
mid-1995 was the increasing reluctance of the BoZ to allow the kwacha to depreciate. For example, over the period July 1995 to December 1995, the nominal exchange rate (on a period
average basis) depreciated by only 0.8 percent. For that same period, the real exchange rate relative to the U.S. dollar appreciated by 17.2 percent. (The real appreciation against the South
African rand was even higher.)

10. The donor response was rapid and generous. Approximately 900 thousand metric tons
of food aid was provided. This was equivalent to over half the output of maize in Zambia in the
1991 and 1992 seasons.

economy. The return of multiparty democracy also held the prospect of greater public accountability and improved governance.[11]

During the first few months, particularly when the 1992 budget was brought down, the new government gave every indication that a major shift in policy was underway. One change, important for both practical and symbolic reasons, was the elimination of maize meal subsidies. This was followed by the removal of most import restrictions, the abolition of export licenses, a faster rate of crawl for the official exchange rate, the removal of barriers to entry in the financial and insurance markets, and the lifting of interest rate ceilings. The clearest signal of the government's resolve was the commitment in the 1992 budget to sharply reduce the fiscal deficit.

From a policy perspective, the early part of 1992 was full of promise. The government had set the groundwork for the resumption of international support, and by "balancing" the budget[12] appeared to be taking the steps needed to prevent the fiscal system from further destabilizing the economy.

The promise was not realized. By April 1992, the budget had begun to unravel. The government acceded to the demands of civil servants for wage increases in excess of 100 percent, and it provided operating subsidies to Zambia Airways of approximately $30 million. These extrabudgetary expenditures were in direct contrast with the elimination of maize meal subsidies. That action had been presented to the public as a way of taking pressure off the budget. Questions soon arose about the government's commitment to fairness, equity, and prudent economic management, all of which the MMD had emphasized during the election campaign.

Drought relief added to the problems. A large budget deficit emerged which was financed by money creation (i.e., borrowing from the BoZ). Economic instability intensified. Inflation, which had been 111 percent in 1991, rose to 191 percent in 1992. The exchange rate, which was K64=$1 at the end of 1991, was K184=$1 by the end of 1992. Contrary to the government's expectations and promises, the macroeconomic situation continued to deteriorate.

---

11. These issues had been widely debated during the election campaign. Indeed, the MMD Party sponsored an advertisement stating:

"President Chiluba will answer. . .for all his actions, to YOU! The hour has come for a new President who makes himself answerable, for all his actions, to the people. A man who will also hold himself responsible for the actions of his ministers. That man is President Frederick Chiluba of MMD."

12. As described in Chapter 4, the budget was balanced in the sense that domestic revenues were equal to domestic expenditure. Foreign flows, for debt service, development assistance, and commodity grants, were not included.

The new government had clearly "blown it." It had failed to do the one thing that mattered: it had not distinguished its approach to economic management from that of its predecessor. Asset-holders had seen more than enough. Capital flight and currency substitution, already serious problems, intensified. Consumer and business confidence plummeted, and the general public lost faith in the government's ability to manage the economy. Less than a year after the election, the new government's economic policies were in disarray.[13]

By the third quarter of 1992, senior policy makers began to fully appreciate that the principal source of economic instability was the budget. Doing something about it was difficult. The data needed to conduct a proactive economic policy were not available. Most relevant economic information was months out of date and many data were unreliable. As a result, the government's policy responses were often misdirected, delayed, and ineffective. Worse, two of the key institutions needed to support the reform effort, namely the budget office and the BoZ were ineffective.[14] That situation had to be rectified.

Complicating matters further was the sharp decline in real per capita income and social welfare. Early in 1992, the government had assured the donor community that it would give special emphasis to the social sectors. With inflation so high, and so much of the budget absorbed by wages and subsidies, real social expenditures had declined.[15]

The government's performance was not easy to explain. Apart from some liberalization in the area of trade and finance, one of its few accomplishments during 1992 was the successful distribution of drought relief.[16] Even the steps taken to further liberalize the exchange rate proved to be of little consequence. The 30 percent devaluation and faster rate of crawl of the exchange rate "peg" were totally inadequate in the face of inflation approaching 200 percent per annum.

The main problem was the lack of budget discipline. This was a direct

---

13. Some economists predicted in early 1993 that Zambia was headed for hyperinflation (Adams and Bevan 1993).

14. The operational procedures of both organizations were outdated and better suited to a system of government controls than liberalization. The disarray in the accounts at the BoZ added to the confusion. The accounts were several months out of date. Due to a programming rigidity the computer system arbitrarily truncated large numbers, and the Bank had not produced audited accounts since 1988.

15. Senior government officials were embarrassed by this outcome. They were hoping to request further large amounts of aid from the donors at the CG meeting in Paris in December 1992.

16. Subsequent investigations demonstrated that there had been serious fraud involved in the off-loading of the grain at the ports and in its distribution. No action was taken against the senior government officials (including ministers) involved.

carry-over from past practices. New directions were needed.[17] The first steps were taken in the third quarter of 1992. A concerted attempt was made to meet the end-September benchmarks agreed with the IMF. Though most of them were missed, the effort helped government officials identify the types of measures needed to bring the economy back on track.

During preparations in November 1992, by the Technical Committee of Ministers for the December CG meeting, the issue of "inflation as the cruelest tax on the poor" was raised. President Chiluba picked up on this point. In a speech to the donor community, he stated that such a tax was unacceptable and had to be reduced. He further asserted that the government would take the necessary steps to bring inflation under control.

Within the space of two months (December 1992 and January 1993) a number of initiatives were taken. The exchange rate was unified by allowing ZCCM to sell its earnings at the market rate. The government put itself on a cash budget. A limit was placed on wage increases.[18] A treasury bill (T-bill) tender was introduced to determine interest rates through the market. Import and export licenses were removed, and the government announced steps to eliminate all exchange controls.[19]

To improve the day-to-day management of the reform program, a data monitoring committee (DMC) was established with staff drawn from the MoF and BoZ. This committee met daily until the relevant macroeconomic and financial data were brought up-to-date and a system was established to keep them that way. With those tasks in hand, the meetings were reduced to three per week. The DMC was given overall responsibility for monitoring the day-to-day operations of fiscal and monetary policy. For three years, until the approach unraveled (see Chapter 4), the committee also implemented the cash budget.

The introduction of the cash budget prevented government operations from being a separate source of macroeconomic instability.[20] Monetary excesses continued nonetheless. In the early months of 1993, the government

---

17. Kasonde 1994.

18. The limit was imposed by a fixed allocation in the budget and the threat, subsequently carried out, that taxes would be *raised* to cover wage settlements above the budgeted amount.

19. Exchange controls were not formally removed until January 1994. The government's announcement in January 1993 that it intended lifting them was, in effect, *de facto* removal.

20. In practice, Zambia started by running the "cash budget" with a small surplus. Expenditures were funded (i.e., money was released from BoZ accounts) only when revenue receipts (either in the form of taxes, fees, or direct donor support) would cover the fundings *in advance* on a daily basis. These amounts were released into designated BoZ accounts for use by line ministries and government agencies. It normally took some weeks for these funds to be drawn down. During 1993, the balances in these accounts averaged roughly half the monthly fundings. Thus, the cash budget was tighter than its name suggests.

would not allow the price of petroleum products to rise by "passing through" the price effects of exchange rate depreciation. As a result, ZIMOIL the state-owned oil-marketing corporation could not generate the local currency required to purchase foreign exchange to pay for oil imports. The BoZ provided the foreign exchange on credit. This led to a sharp increase in reserve money.[21]

By late April, BoZ lending to ZIMOIL was stopped and the growth rate of reserve money dropped dramatically. Inflation declined. Prices rose by 15 percent in May, 11.6 percent in June, and 2.7 percent in July. In November 1993, prices declined in Zambia for the first time in more than two decades. Reflecting the moderation of the rate of inflation, nominal interest rates began to fall towards the end of 1993. (Chapter 7 has details of the changes in interest rates.) The exchange rate stabilized.[22]

From mid-1993 until early 1995, there were a few minor bumps to the

---

21. Major confusion surrounded this episode. In mid-February 1993, BoZ management informed the IMF and MoF that it was not lending money to ZIMOIL to cover the foreign exchange cost of oil imports. This was false. But, due to the messy state of BoZ's data, the loan could not be independently verified.

22. The exchange rate appreciated significantly and prices fell in November 1993. This episode has attracted much comment. The IMF, for example, believed that the government squeezed the money supply too severely. Its staff argued, *after the fact*, that the government should have aimed for a gentler reduction in inflation and minimal (or preferably no) appreciation of the kwacha. There were three reasons why this was not feasible. First, MoF officials recognized that the exchange rate and real interest rates would overshoot. (A memo was prepared for the minister on this issue in September 1993.) Second, the IMF did not offer *before the fact* to make the necessary changes in the performance criteria which would have provided the monetary and financial margins to accommodate this scenario. The September and December 1993 targets for reserve money, net international reserves, the debt stock, net claims on government, and reductions in arrears to the IMF remained as had been earlier agreed. (Chapter 7 makes a similar point.) And third, as a practical matter, no one anywhere has demonstrated that the Zambian economy (or any other economy that had been so badly mismanaged for so long) could have been stabilized gradually. The government faced a major credibility problem. No one had any confidence that it would reduce inflation. By standing the economy "on its nose," the government began to build a reputation for economic discipline. Reducing monthly inflation rates from 15.1 percent to *minus* 1.6 percent over a period of five months, while allowing nominal rates of interest on 91-day T-bills to reach 348 percent (in compound annual terms), was a complete break with anything ever done by a government in Zambia. It demonstrated unambiguously that the MMD government was serious about reform. Subsequent analyses will show, I believe, that although the appreciation of the exchange rate was a temporary disruption, it was fully consistent with *reducing* the costs of disinflation (Kahn and Weiner 1990; Posen 1995; Fuhrer 1995). Since economic policy in Zambia lacked credibility prior to the introduction of the cash budget, some purposeful and forceful demonstration of the government's commitment to stability was essential. Anything less would not have created the conditions needed to bring inflation down or offered the prospect of keeping it down.

economy due to donor threats to withdraw support[23] and the run on Meridien BIAO Ltd.[24] Yet overall stability was maintained. Indeed, given the extent of the shocks (in December 1993, December 1994, and February 1995) the economy proved to be remarkably resilient.

One reason was that, in addition to improved monetary management and fiscal control, other reforms were proceeding. Numerous SOEs were privatized. A comprehensive approach to civil service reform (the Public Sector Reform Programme) was announced in November 1993. Thousands of casual daily employees were laid off. With donor support, large amounts of basic infrastructure (roads, bridges, airports, schools, and hospitals) were rehabilitated and reconstructed. And the operational efficiency of government departments and government-supported institutions improved as their recurrent cost problems eased and they gained access to additional materials and supplies.

By the last half of 1994, the economy was stabilizing and there was evidence of a widespread supply response. The investment climate had improved dramatically and a renewed sense of confidence was emerging. The 1995 budget speech, widely acknowledged as advocating a "growth budget," reinforced the message that the government was shifting its efforts from stabilization to growth.

4. Mid-1995 to 1998: Economic Reform Deflected

Macroeconomic data presented in Chapter 2 provide a mixed picture of the economy's performance from 1992 to 1995. During that period, real GDP

---

23. In November 1993, following the lead of the United States, the donor community took a stand on allegations of drug running and corruption by cabinet members. The message was repeated at the December 1993 CG meeting in Paris. Several hundred million dollars of donor pledges to Zambia were put on hold. When the public learned of this, there was a scramble for foreign exchange. The kwacha depreciated sharply. In response, the government reduced the growth rate of reserve money. Treasury bill interest rates, which had been falling during the second half of 1993, rose dramatically. (The average annual T Bill rate was 399 percent in the third week of January 1994.) A similar problem emerged in December 1994 when the government balked on its commitment to liquidate Zambia Airways. Once the government reversed position, the donors reconfirmed their support. The foreign exchange and T-bill markets, which had begun to move, settled down.

24. Meridien BIAO experienced an open run in January and February 1995. The details are described in the annex to Chapter 6. The run on Meridien BIAO Ltd. produced a "flight to quality". Deposits were transferred to the "old" Zambian banks (Standard, Barclays) and the demand for foreign exchange increased. The exchange rate, which had been around K680=$1 for most of 1994 jumped to K820=$1 in February 1995.

remained roughly constant. Gross domestic investment rose marginally, the result of donor support rather of than improved domestic savings. The overall budget deficit fell (though as noted in Chapter 4, arrears increased sharply in 1995). The share of exports in GDP was stable at close to 30 percent, although the share of nontraditional exports increased rapidly. By contrast, the share of imports fluctuated, largely due to changes in flows of foreign assistance following the elections. This is evident in the persistently large current account deficit on the balance of payments (over 10 percent of GDP). The nominal exchange rate depreciated, but much less than the domestic rate of inflation. Consequently, the real exchange rate appreciated sharply after 1993. The food production index, dominated by maize output, was generally flat due to poor seasons. After allowing for population growth, food availability per capita declined.

Output in the mining sector fell, the result of the decapitalization of the mines (due to declining investment and asset stripping) and general inefficiency (resulting from poor management). Gross foreign assistance to Zambia over the period was high, averaging 34.8 percent of GDP.[25] The debt relief component of that aid lowered Zambia's external debt burden. But, as shown below, the improvement was only temporary. Boosted by ZCCM's losses, external debt rose again.[26]

A closer examination of the data reveals some positive trends in the period 1992 to 1995, particularly with respect to inflation, interest rates, the exchange rate, and the growth of the money supply. All of these were moving in the appropriate directions. The momentum, however, was lost early in 1995 when the reform effort encountered serious difficulties. Macroeconomic management began to go awry and the reorganization of key institutions proved to be too slow to support and sustain economic reform. [27]

Problems in Economic Management

Several factors created difficulties for economic management in 1995. The collapse of Meridien BIAO Bank disrupted fiscal and monetary policy. The abrupt end to the rains led to the failure of the maize harvest for the third time in four years. But, perhaps the most important factor that diverted the government's attention from economic reform was the reemergence of former president Kaunda as a political force, following his election as leader of UNIP.

---

25. African Development Indicators 2001, Table 12.9

26. ZCCM's losses in 1996/97 and 1997/98 were $125 million and $220.4 million respectively (IMF Statistical Appendix 1999, Table 15).

27. McPherson 1996.

These events coincided with increasing resistance among Zambia's leaders to the conditions required by the donor community. The attractiveness of some of the government's commitments, made in afterglow of the 1991 elections, had dimmed over time. Donor pressure to restructure ZCCM, close uneconomic SOEs, liquidate ZIMCO, and insist that the GRZ observe principles of good governance and accountability, were increasingly seen as intrusions on Zambia's sovereignty rather than as steps required to reconstruct the economy. Resentment intensified, especially after the donors insisted that the GRZ close Zambia Airways as a condition for moving ahead with the provision of external assistance for 1995.[28]

The collapse of Meridien Bank, one of Zambia's largest commercial banks, resulted from mismanagement at the bank and regulatory indulgence by the BoZ. The government's support for the bank in advance of its collapse put severe pressure on the financial system. With these and other pressures on the economy, there was clear evidence by March 1995 that the economic program was off track.[29] No substantive action was taken. The completion of the RAP with the IMF was postponed until September 1995, and a new set of performance criteria was agreed.[30] Several short-term fixes were adopted to meet the end-September targets. Those fixes did not bring the economy back on a sustainable trajectory. Senior government officials, however, interpreted the completion of the RAP and willingness of the IMF to move forward with an enhanced structural adjustment facility (ESAF) as evidence that government policies were appropriate. That was not the case. Six of ten ESAF performance criteria were missed at the end of December 1995. This was just three weeks after the program had been formally approved.[31]

Macroeconomic management remained problematic during 1996 and 1997. The annual budget targets were met, but only after large, destabilizing first quarter deficits. These were offset by compression of budgeted expendi-

---

28. In the three years before its closure, Zambia Airways had lost around $100 million. Its demise improved the balance of payments and raised Zambia's GDP.

29. In March 1995, advisors within the ministry had briefed senior officials that this was happening. In April 1995, the IMF mission staff independently provided a similar assessment.

30. The IMF and Zambia reached agreement on a RAP in July of 1992 (IMF Press Release No. 92/57). Under the RAP, Zambia could earn rights to clear its arrears with the IMF. The rights entitled Zambia to the first disbursement of a loan from the IMF under a successor arrangement. The RAP was completed on December 4, 1995. On December 6, 1997, the IMF approved loans to Zambia of SDR 883.4 million (about US $1,313 million) under an ESAF arrangement.

31. The ESAF program could not officially start until the RAP was formally complete. The first year of the ESAF was July 1995 to June 1996, with the first performance criteria established for December 31, 1995. With the completion of the RAP delayed until early December 1995, the ESAF benchmarks became effective shortly after the arrangement was officially approved.

tures, *ad hoc* revenue measures, and the accumulation of domestic arrears. Few of the required benchmarks were met. The first formal review of the ESAF was not completed, and the program lapsed in mid-1997. The IMF suggested changes that needed to be made and began a period of "staff monitoring" while awaiting government action.

Institutional Reforms

Following the 1991 elections, a number of important initiatives were taken to promote institutional reform. They included the establishment of the Zambia Revenue Authority (ZRA), the reorganization and recapitalization of the Bank of Zambia, the closure of ZIMCO, the sale of some of ZCCM's assets, and an effort to restructure and reduce the civil service.

The ZRA was set up in 1994 as a means of raising the professional standards of the revenue services and improving tax compliance.[32] The results have been mixed. A value-added tax (VAT) was successfully introduced in mid-1995, replacing a sales tax (see Chapter 5). It eliminated double taxation, improved tax yields, and shifted taxes away from investment to consumption. Tax fraud has remained a problem, largely due to political interference in tax administration. Customs and direct taxes have continued to experience compliance problems. A change in senior management of the ZRA in early 1997 led to more systematic attention to these issues.

With the removal of exchange controls, roughly one-third of the staff of the BoZ became redundant. The bank was down-sized and greater emphasis was given to financial supervision and economic research. Efforts were made to improve the quality of staff and management. There was progress in improving the quality and timeliness of the monetary data. Following overseas practice, the Bank of Zambia Act was revised to provide the BoZ with more independence.[33]

Despite these changes, monetary policy encountered serious problems. At one level, this reflected the fragility of institutional reform where the outcomes of key decisions depend heavily on the personalities involved rather

---

32. At the official launching of the ZRA on April 1, 1994, the chairman of the Zambia Revenue Board stated that it was the ZRA's intention to increase revenue collections by "500 percent." Though some allowance should be made for hyperbole, the ZRA's subsequent performance has shown that, after taking into account changes in tax rates and the tax base, there had been no perceptible increase in the real value of tax collections. This is shown by Kasanga (1996) and in Chapter 5.

33. In practice, "independence" has meant little to the way monetary policy is managed. BoZ officials have shown no more willingness to engage the government in debate than in the past. Nor have they hesitated to finance the government's deficits, keep interest rates "under control" (i.e., low), or hinder the exchange rate from depreciating.

than the procedures being followed. At another level, it was the result of the pressures placed on monetary policy by lack of fiscal discipline. To contain these pressures, the BoZ acted contrary to stated government policies by intervening in the foreign exchange and T-bill markets.[34]

The fundamental problem is that the BoZ's objectives have been inconsistent. As part of the IMF program, the bank adopted targets for the money supply and international reserves. In addition to these quantitative targets, the BoZ management sought to limit movements in exchange rates and interest rates, both of which are politically sensitive. The BoZ has attempted to push interest rates down and prevent the nominal exchange rate from depreciating. By manipulating interest rates, the Bank gave up control over reserve money. And, by resisting exchange rate depreciation, the BoZ has been unable to achieve its goal of accumulating foreign reserves.

A further outcome is that by limiting the increase in the nominal exchange rate, the real exchange rate remained serious overvalued. This trend was particularly damaging because it kept unit labor costs high, thereby undermining Zambia's (already weak) ability to compete internationally.

These actions by the BoZ added to macroeconomic instability. Inflation remained high, foreign exchange reserves fell, and there was significant "redollarization" of economic activity as the business community and international investors reacted adversely to the BoZ's continued interference.

The MMD government came to office committed to reforming both the public service and the SOEs.[35] Both types of reform were considered necessary for improving the effectiveness of the public sector and restoring growth. Though there has been progress in both areas, key reforms were delayed. ZIMCO, the parastatal holding company, and Zambia Airways were liquidated, but the sale of the mines was dragged out. Under donor pressure, the government had made a commitment to privatize the mines by June 1997. The final sale did not occur until early in 2000.

---

34. This issue is dealt with below. The point, however, is that the apparent stability of the exchange rate during 1997 was contrived. Over that period, the kwacha depreciated against the U.S. dollar by less than 9 percent despite major changes in economic fundamentals, both domestically and internationally. This low rate of depreciation can be directly attributed to BoZ manipulation.

35. The MMD *Manifesto* (1991) noted:

"The MMD recognises that the Zambian Public Service has been inefficient mainly due to politicisation and poor incentives. . . ." (p. 3); and "The MMD is committed to privatisation in order to optimise resource utilisation, enhance the productivity and profitability of the public sector and assist in the reduction of the government deficit"(p. 4). As part of adopting "strict financial management and sound budgetary control. . ." the MMD committed itself to ". . .selling off as many state owned enterprises as possible. . . ." (p. 5).

This slippage was exceedingly costly for Zambia and, in policy terms, inexcusable. A major theme of the NERP (itself carried over from the early 1980s) was that immediate action was needed to revive the mining sector. [36] To start that process, the MMD government required ZCCM and ZIMCO to devise a plan to privatize the mines. Nothing substantive emerged. A subsequent report by external consultants in 1993 on how best to sell ZCCM (the *Keinbaum Report*) was shelved. The sale of the mines was further delayed by the government's unwillingness to accept a low sale price even though the price tendered represented a realistic representation of the company's (highly depreciated) value.[37] Further delays accompanied the drop of world copper prices.

Because of its dithering, the government lost all ability to influence the final outcome. The only unknown was the ultimate size of losses, direct and indirect, that would accrue by the time ZCCM was sold. Those losses amounted to billions of dollars.[38]

In the public sector, some reorganization has taken place. But effective action was not taken to reduce the size of the civil service and the public sector wage bill. Plans were developed to lay off large numbers of civil servants during 1998. A schedule of staff reductions was included as part of the draft IMF program. During the first quarter of 1998, the GRZ released K21 billion for retrenchment. That, however, resulted in a smaller decrease in the number of employees than expected because the cost of accumulated leave had not been properly budgeted.[39] With the cost of retrenchment so exorbitant and chronically underestimated, major reductions in the civil service could only occur with donor support.

---

36. There have been many plans for reviving and recapitalizing the mining sector over the last two decades. See, for example, World Bank (1981, pp. ii, 19–20), and GRZ (1984, vol. I, ch. 3). The MMD government adopted an Interim Development Plan for ZCCM in 1993. ZCCM received emergency assistance in the wake of the mission by World Bank mining experts in 1995.

37. The main problem for the government was political. Having publicly stated that it would not dispose of ZCCM for a low price, the government was in a bind when the amounts actually offered for ZCCM's highly depreciated assets were low and would not be raised.

38. The losses were incurred directly by ZCCM itself, and indirectly by the economy in terms of lost output, reduced investment, increased external borrowing to compensate for reduced tax revenue, and lower foreign assistance (when donors withheld aid as the sale of ZCCM dragged out).

39. Given the length of time taken, and the amount of attention devoted to the whole issue of retrenchment, such a "mistake" had to have been contrived. The cost of the retrenchment packages had been the subject of intensive analysis by government officials and consultants for several years.

5. THE 1998 BUDGET

The discussion so far identifies some of the successes and failures of the government's approach to economic reform. What may not be evident, however, is the extent to which the MMD government lost direction as its tenure lengthened. That can be traced by briefly examining the approaches adopted to policy reform in the budgets over the period 1992 to 1998. We conclude with a detailed review of the 1998 budget speech since it illustrates the degree to which the government's policies had unraveled.

In his opening statement of the 1998 budget speech, the minister of finance asserted that the government's goal since it came to power in 1991 had been to ". . .change Zambia forever. . .."[40] A large number of official statements spelling out how that would be done had appeared over the period November 1991 to January 1998. According to the minister, the program in the 1998 speech simply continued with the themes the government had already introduced and was implementing.[41] The specific program in 1998 was based on a "medium-term adjustment programme."[42] This would help Zambia achieve macroeconomic stability, promote economic growth, and reduce poverty.[43] The minister failed to mention that these same goals that had been set several times before in the government's previously announced adjustment programs.[44]

The 1992 budget was the first opportunity for the MMD government to formulate its own economic policy. That budget was designed to move beyond the disorganization and deficits that typified the period of one-party rule. It was intended to stabilize the economy *and* begin the process of economic reform. The principal initiative was to "balance" the budget and thereby reduce inflation. Yet, within months the government had incurred

---

40. Budget speech delivered to the Parliament, January 30, 1998, par. 5. The phrase is taken from the theme of the *MMD Manifesto '96* "changing Zambia for good!"

41. These are contained in the MMD's *Manifestos* (1991 and 1996), documents prepared for the various CG meetings, letters and memoranda of understanding with the IMF, letters of development policy to the World Bank, the president's speeches officially opening Parliament, and the annual budget speech.

42. BS 1998, par. 3.

43. For the three years 1998 to 2000, inclusive, the government intended raising the rate of economic growth to an average of 5.5 percent per annum and lowering the rate of inflation from 18.6 percent in 1997 to 4 percent per annum in 1999 and 2000 (par. 54). These would represent dramatic improvements in economic performance. During the period 1992 to 1997, annual growth of GDP was less than 1 percent, while the annual rate of inflation averaged 98.3 percent.

44. GRZ 1992, 1995, 1997.

major nonbudgeted expenditures. The budget deficit increased and the rate of inflation accelerated.

The 1993 budget was devoted to bringing inflation under control. As explained in Chapter 4, a "cash budget" was adopted, matching expenditure to available revenue. The objective was to prevent government operations from being an independent source of credit expansion. With the cash budget in place, inflation declined sharply. By the end of 1993, the economy was stabilizing. Reflecting this, the 1994 budget was framed with the goal of achieving a high, sustained, rate of economic growth. The central policy initiatives were tax reform supported by such institutional reforms as the creation of the Zambia Revenue Authority. The civil service and ZCCM were also to be restructured. With the cash budget in place, significant improvements in most macroeconomic variables occurred. From all appearances, the economy was headed towards the stability and growth that had been so elusive.

The 1995 budget was intended to reinforce these trends. It specifically focused on growth. Because of the economy's improved performance, the government expected to complete the RAP with the IMF by March 1995, receive generous debt relief from the Paris Club, and adopt a more comprehensive pattern of structural adjustment. Yet, within two months of being delivered, the budget was in tatters. Completion of the RAP slipped, and the Paris Club meeting was canceled. At the insistence of the IMF, special measures to increase revenue were taken in July 1995. These would enable Zambia to complete the RAP by September 1995 making it eligible for an ESAF.[45] The latter was accomplished amid great fanfare and congratulations from the government, donor community, and the IMF. However, at the time the IMF approved the ESAF arrangement (December 6, 1995) the economy was off-track by a wide margin.[46] That became all too evident at the end of December, just three weeks later, when Zambia missed six of the ten ESAF performance criteria.

The 1996 budget could have been used to bring the economy back on track.[47] That was not done. The minister of finance was unwilling to admit

---

45. As explained in both Chapters 4 and 5, the measures to close the financing gap reversed a number of useful elements of the tax reform. They also resulted in large domestic payment arrears.

46. This point was evident from the data being generated by the Data Monitoring Committee and other sources. Senior officials in the MoF (including the minister) were warned that the economy was "off track" as early as October 1995. The minister severely criticized those who gave these warnings (including the author) for being negative.

47. The author wrote two memos to the permanent secretary, MoF, on January 4 and 5, 1996. The first highlighted the difficulties created by breaching so many performance criteria so soon after the ESAF had been approved. The second dealt with the adverse feedback of ris-

publicly that the ESAF was in trouble so soon after it had been approved. Election year politics also played a role. The government, more generally, did not want to open itself to opposition criticism that the reform program had unraveled.[48]

By the time the 1997 budget was formulated, the MMD government had been reelected with an overwhelming majority (due in part to the boycott of the elections by UNIP supporters) and Frederick Chiluba had been elected president for a second term. Negotiations to sell ZCCM appeared to be making progress and there had been a large maize harvest. The 1997 budget was framed on the presumption that, with the elections over, the focus could again shift to economic growth. That presumption was wrong. The donor community was unwilling to overlook the government's manipulation of the constitution. Its members specifically objected to the changes that had barred the principal opposition candidate for president from standing. The government's action was seen as a major breach of democratic principles and evidence that Chiluba and his MMD associates were not committed to improved governance.[49] The sharp fall in the copper price following the financial turmoil in Asia added to ZCCM's already large losses. Furthermore, the continued delay in selling ZCCM scuttled any chance of a broad-based economic recovery. Thus, 1997 ended with the economy in continued decline and the government adopting several stopgap measures to accommodate cuts in donor support.

This was the background against which the goals of the 1998 budget were set. As shown below, those goals were highly ambitious[50] and detached from the experience of earlier years. The government, it appeared, was searching for ways to make a fresh start. The minister of finance presented the budget as the "key instrument of government policy," stating that the budget reflected the ". . .consistent, systematic, and evolving approach to economic policy which the Government has been pursuing for several years" (par. 150). Even when one allows for hyperbole associated with the occasion, this was stretch-

---

ing domestic interest rates on the budget deficit. The memos urged the government to use the forthcoming budget speech to take preemptive measures to bring the economy back on track. When this argument was made to the minister of finance, he angrily rejected it.

48. The IMF did not complete its first annual review of the program until mid-1997 (IMF EBS/97/20, 1997).

49. The shoddy treatment by President Chiluba of the Danish minister for development cooperation shocked many members of the donor community. Reassured by Chiluba's promise that the constitution would not be changed to exclude Kaunda from participating in the election, that minister was criticized harshly in the Danish parliament for having been so gullible.

50. Indeed, the minister insisted that the goals were not ambitious enough (par.156). Both historical evidence and subsequent experience have shown otherwise.

ing the point. How much is evident by a closer study of the budget's scope, consistency, and funding.

Scope of the Budget: The 1998 budget speech made many commitments. New action was promised on housing, roads, electricity (par. 56), and poverty reduction (par. 56, 83). Several existing promises were repeated.[51] Poverty, the Zambian public was told, would be addressed by promoting rapid economic growth (par. 83), and through the formulation of a national poverty reduction action plan.[52]

A specific commitment was made to ". . .reduce the proportion of 70 percent of the population living in poverty to 50 percent by the year 2004" (par. 16).[53] This goal would be achieved if (1) population growth remained below 2 percent per annum (the World Bank projection at that time);[54] (2) real income grew by 5.5 percent per annum until 2004; and (3) Zambia's income distribution did not worsen. The speech did not explain how real per capita income would rise so rapidly. Some explanation should have been given, since real per capita income had been declining since 1992.[55] The relevance of this point emerged as the year progressed and the assumed real growth rate of 5.5 percent with inflation of 9 percent became increasingly untenable.[56]

Consistency of the Message: The budget speech contained a number of mixed messages. Poverty would be reduced but, at the same time, the tax on

51. These include privatization of ZCCM (par. 24), reform of the public service (pars. 51, 56), meeting the conditions agreed with the IMF (par. 55), reducing inflation to single digits (par. 88), controlling monetary growth (par. 57), implementing ASIP (par. 70), liberalizing petroleum marketing and distribution (pars. 77, 78), and refraining from interfering with exchange rates (pars. 58, 98) and agricultural marketing (par. 71).

52. This raised the question of whether the main barrier to reducing poverty is market failure through the lack of economic growth or bureaucratic failure through the collapse of official poverty reduction efforts (Wolf 1988; Squire 1990). Experience in Zambia (and elsewhere in Africa) suggests that government-directed poverty reduction programs have had little sustained positive impact (Stiglitz and Squire 1998). Economic collapse has been the greatest source of poverty. That can only be overcome by a growth strategy. Several such strategies have been promised in Zambia.

53. It is not clear where the figure of 70 percent of Zambians in poverty comes from. The *World Development Indicators* (World Bank 1998: Table 2.3) noted that in 1993, 86.3 percent of Zambians were below the national poverty line. Per capita real income has declined since that date, implying that the percentage of those listed as poor could not have fallen. Thus, the challenge of moving to 50 percent poverty by the year 2004 was far more formidable than the government presumed.

54. World Development Indicators 1998: Part 2.

55. Data from the *Macroeconomic Indicators* show that real per capita income declined by 14 percent over the period 1992 to 1997.

56. Actual data were -1.8 percent for real GDP and +28.7 percent for inflation (*Macroeconomic Indicators* March 1999).

second-hand clothes was being raised to protect domestic textile producers. The government promised to reduce the civil service through a hiring freeze (par. 93) yet announced initiatives, such as the provision of housing, that could only be achieved by adding staff.

Further confusion was evident in statements about the donors and the financing of the budget. In the opening paragraphs, the minister stated that the government was ". . . profoundly grateful to our international cooperating partners. . ." (par. 5). Later, however, he asserted that the donors were ". . .putting in question the basis of our development cooperation partnership. . ." (par. 101) because they were insisting that Zambia abide by its commitment to good governance. The minister concluded by stating that: "(W)e cannot subject the implementation of our economic and social programmes to the changing views of our cooperating partners" (par. 102).

These were tough words from a government that depended on the donors to finance more than one-third of its budget. Given that the donors were annoyed at the antidemocratic actions taken by the government in rigging the constitution, the minister might have been more circumspect.[57]

Funding of the Budget: All budgeting relies on estimates. Unexpected expenditures will always occur. Some anticipated expenditures will not be made. Revenue sources will over- or under-perform. Prudent budgeting requires realism tempered by conservatism. The 1998 budget was a first attempt to present a consolidated budget that included foreign financing. When the budget was framed, a large amount of the financing had not been secured. There were "prior" conditions that the government had agreed to meet, and potentially lengthy negotiations to complete (including a CG meeting at a date that had not been fixed). Thus, the budget could not be fully funded until well into the year.

The government, nonetheless, included the full amounts of donor support in the budget. This can be interpreted in two ways. First, government officials may have been certain that the funds would materialize. Second, it was a strategic move designed to pressure the donors to provide the support needed to ensure consistency in the budget's financing plan.[58] Both positions were

---

57. The minister might also have recalled his exchange with the Swedish ambassador in late 1994. During that meeting (at which all the donors representatives were present) the minister agitatedly asserted that Zambia had a sovereign right to determine its own policies. The ambassador agreed. He reminded the minister, however, that the Zambian government had to understand that donor countries, too, had the sovereign right to withhold their assistance whenever they encountered behavior that breached accepted norms.

58. This is the international equivalent of what Smithies (1955) called a "coercive deficit." It only works, however, when both parties are willing to play the game of bluff involved. Over recent years, most donors have become increasingly reluctant to be drawn into this situation.

risky. Acting prudently, the government should have developed a credible fallback position.

The speech assumed that the donors would willingly finance several activities. These included civil service retrenchment (par. 106), balance of payments support for debt service (par. 99), reform of the rural credit system (par. 72), the revitalization of the Agricultural Sector Investment Program (ASIP, par. 52), and the implementation of other SIPs (par. 56). Most of this support has no effect upon the budget. It enters the budget as revenue that is matched by equivalent expenditure. However, that was *not* the case with the support for civil service retrenchment and debt service (including debt relief).

The announcement of a fall-back strategy would have been a new and constructive departure. The implicit fallback was the conventional practices of compressing recurrent departmental charges (RDCs) and capital expenditure (CAPEX), reducing the "domestic surplus" (K77 billion was included in the 1998 budget), borrowing from the central bank, and/or incurring domestic and external arrears. The budget speech gave no indication that a fallback position would be needed. This was a mistake. Within months of bringing down the budget, the negotiations to sell ZCCM collapsed. This made several of the donors' prior conditions impossible to meet and held up the release of their support. Adding to the difficulties, the minister was fired and replaced by someone who disagreed with many of the policy directions being taken.[59]

Why did the government adopt such an unrealistic budget? Why did it preprogram failure in such an obvious way? There seem to be three explanations, all of which suggest that by 1998 the government had lost interest in promoting reform but remained desperate for donor support to avoid further economic decline. First, the budget was grandstanding by a minister with well-known presidential aspirations, who was intent on being seen as moving ahead even though the economy was declining. Second, the budget was designed to pressure the donor community to look beyond the government's lapses, particularly the rigging of the 1996 election and the torture of detainees of the 1997 coup attempt. Third, the budget reflected the wish list of a government devoid of policy direction and lacking in leadership.

6. THE BUDGETS OF 1999 AND 2000

Though there were no broad differences in the approach to economic policy in either the 1999 or 2000 budgets, there was a distinct softening of the at-

---

59. His replacement was the Hon. Edith Nawakwi, former minister of agriculture, food, and fisheries.

titudes towards the donors. The experience of 1998 seemed to convince some senior policy makers that, although the donors were prickly and sometimes fickle, their support was essential if the economy was to recover.

The 1999 budget speech was fully consistent with its predecessors. Its opening passages set the tone. The new minister paid tribute to her predecessor who, some months after he was fired, had been murdered.[60] She described 1998 as an exceedingly difficult year—international prices had fallen, the sale of ZCCM had been delayed, donors had withheld aid, weather patterns associated with El Niño had wreaked havoc with the agricultural season, foreign exchange reserves were depleted, inflation rose, and real income and employment fell. The minister gave few details, but the value of metal sales had fallen sharply, agricultural output had declined by one-third, and the exchange rate had depreciated by 69 percent. There was also the first hint of major problems with Zambia Commercial Development Bank (ZANACO) that would only become fully evident in 2000.

The minister noted, however, that despite the adversity, the government had remained committed to its economic reform program (par.14). She also announced that the sale of the mines would be finalized by the end of March 1999 and that the World Bank had agreed to the immediate release of a large part of the $140 million in balance of payments support that it would be providing.[61]

There were other positive developments: tourism and manufacturing had risen during 1998 and, for the second time since 1993, the government had cut the civil service by laying off large numbers of casual daily laborers.

For 1999, the minister projected growth of 4 percent, the addition of $120 million to Zambia's international reserves, and a reduction in the rate of inflation to 15 percent for the year. Admitting that there would be little increase in real budgetary resources, the minister stated ". . .this budget has been designed to reverse the economic decline we experienced in 1998, and to restore the economy firmly to the path of growth" (par. 87). Total expenditure was programmed to be K2,227.7 billion, of which 65.5 percent, or K1,460 billion, would come from local resources.

In contrast to her predecessor's combative tone, the minister expressed

---

60. The circumstances have never been fully revealed. Within hours the police had shot and killed a number of suspects. Many suspicions have been aired, ranging from a political assassination to a diamonds-for-guns/war materiel deal with the Angolans that came unstuck.

61. Within weeks the minister had instructed the BoZ to sell a large part of the first tranche of this support to force an appreciation of the exchange rate. During a meeting with the minister in March 1999, I expressed the view that whoever had ordered that action had essentially wasted the foreign exchange. I later learned that it had been the minister's decision. The sale produced a temporary appreciation of the kwacha. The resources, in fact, had been wasted.

gratitude for the donor support, noting that the potential $300 million that had been included in the budget as donor assistance for capital expenditure may actually increase (par. 99). The minister (and the government more broadly) clearly anticipated a significant positive response from the donor community once ZCCM was sold.

The budget contained some tax relief for agriculture and promised to review the statutory exemptions that were costing the government large amounts each year in foregone revenue (par. 126).[62] There was some expenditure for the new presidential housing initiative (PHI) and to support the public welfare assistance scheme (PWAS). The amounts provided K5.1 billion and K2.8 billion, respectively, but paled in comparison to the K75 billion set aside for a civil service wage increase and the K80 billion to lay off 7,000 civil servants.

From the start of the 2000 budget speech, the new minister of finance sought to distance himself from the disruption of the past. Noting that the economy had shown "remarkable resilience" (par. 3) the minister called for a "new beginning" so that the economic reforms could "deliver tangible and lasting improvement in the lives of ordinary Zambians" (par. 5). Stating that the goals of the government were to "accelerate and sustain economic growth and reduce poverty," the minister indicated that the targets for real GDP growth was 4 percent, end-of-year inflation 14 percent, and the accumulation of foreign reserves of $100 million (par. 53). The budget deficit would be kept to 1.3 percent of GDP and the growth rate of the money supply would not exceed 18.6 percent.

Seeking a "new beginning," the minister stated:

> . . .this year's budget will form the bedrock of a prudent and aggressive programme of economic and financial management that will target tangible economic growth and enhance our efforts to combat poverty and improve the delivery of social services (par.56).

To do this, the government would provide the appropriate legal and regulatory setting, press ahead with its several SIPs, foster regional trade agreements, revamp agricultural credit, promote exports, implement the public sector reform program, and ensure that all government activities have a

---

62. The minister noted: "It has come to Government's attention that some 900 companies enjoy various forms of exemptions from trade taxes under Statutory Instruments and Agreements, some of which date back to the 1980s." This was disingenuous for two reasons. The problem of exemptions had been pointedly noted by the IMF beginning in 1995. The statutory exemptions are only provided by the minister. Indeed, so many had been granted by the minister herself that the IMF insisted they be rolled back.

"pro-poor stance" (par. 81). The minister was also optimistic that Zambia would soon qualify for the HIPC initiative (pars. 86, 88).

Sixty-six percent of the funding for the budget of close to K3 trillion (equivalent to US $1.13 billion), was programmed to come from local sources. A major expenditure item was K423 billion (around $159 million and roughly 4 percent of GDP) to pay ZCCM's domestic arrears. In making this payment, the government sought to rejuvenate local businesses (par. 91).

No one doubted the sincerity of the minister's intentions of moving ahead with a pro-growth, pro-poor program. Yet, the budget as a whole was fundamentally flawed. An underlying premise was that the Zambian economy could resume growth *and* provide substantive help to the poor *and* repay (most) of ZCCM's domestic arrears while still running a budget deficit and reducing inflation. That had not happened before. It was unlikely to happen in 2000. Another problem was that the budget implied that the real exchange rate would continue to appreciate. In Zambia (and elsewhere in Africa) such a change has undermined, rather than fostered, growth.[63]

7. Concluding Comments

The NERP was not a new departure for Zambia, but its implementation posed many challenges for the MMD government. From the beginning, the MMD government faced major problems of stabilizing the economy and creating the conditions for sustained growth and development. The new economic team was anxious to move forward. Understanding that Zambia's economic problems had persisted for many years, they adopted the existing NERP rather than "plowing the sand" over what had to be done. The requirements for stabilizing the economy and reviving growth were well known.

Despite a promising start, the reforms unraveled. Inflation accelerated rather than declined. The government responded by introducing a "cash budget." The impact was dramatic. Inflation fell and business confidence rose. Towards the end of 1994, the economy was stabilizing and growth was resuming. Nonetheless, the government's commitment to reform began to wane. Evidence of this was the demise of the cash budget. All too soon the government began adopting financial fudges that resulted in the resumption of deficit financing and money creation.

Policy omissions and missteps occurred for economic and political reasons. On the economic front, the most important of these were the failure to move quickly to sell ZCCM, the slow pace of civil service reform, and manip-

---

63. Calamitsis, Basu, and Ghura 1999.

ulation of interest rates and the exchange rate in an attempt to reduce inflation. On the political front, changing the constitution to enhance President
Chiluba's chance of reelection was a major mistake.

The MMD government had repeated the errors of its predecessor. After
committing itself to fundamental economic reform, it abandoned the effort.
After an impressive start that generated huge amounts of international good
will, the government dissipated its advantages by diverting its attention and
energies from economic reform. The outcome has not been surprising. Delaying and deflecting reform has produced no tangible benefit to the economy. Indeed, a decade of economic stewardship by President Chiluba and the
MMD has left Zambians in general significantly poorer than they were before
the 1991 elections. Those of their successors who seek to repair the damage
face the task with fewer options than previously against a background of partially met promises.

APPENDIX: STUDIES OF ZAMBIA'S PROSPECTS FOR GROWTH AND DEVELOPMENT, 1993–1995

Over the period 1993 to 1995, the World Bank produced three reports on
Zambia's prospects for growth and development. The United Nations Development Programme (UNDP), working with GRZ officials, published a study
on Zambia's prospects for human development. The conclusions of these
studies overlap. All of them were consistent with general directions outlined
by the government in the NERP. The implication is that it was well known
within the government and the donor community what needed to be done to
restart and sustain growth and development in Zambia. This appendix briefly
reviews the main conclusions of each study.

World Bank 1993 "Prospects and Choices"

This study was conducted at a time when the possibility of achieving macroeconomic stability in Zambia appeared to be remote. The study sought to
provide a policy framework for moving the economy in the direction of sustainable growth. Key elements were:

- Provide macroeconomic balance focusing attention on achieving fiscal balance;
- Reform the public sector by concentrating on:
  —parastatal reform
  —public sector management
  —the composition of public spending
  —external policies

- Create social policies that emphasized:
  —a social action program
  —labor-intensive public works
  —public welfare assistance
  —drought relief
- Establish an infrastructure rehabilitation program;
- Plan external policies in areas such as:
  —debt management
  —improved efficiency of project assistance
- Develop the private sector.

The study assumed that copper production would remain around 400,000 metric tons per year. This estimate was thought to be too conservative. In the event, the projection was too optimistic.

A number of long-term policy issues were also included. These were land tenure reform, poverty, population, debt management, environment, health, and education. The study concluded that, with the diligent implementation of the proposed policy package, the economy could enter a period of sustained growth.

World Bank 1995: "Reducing Poverty in Zambia"

This five-volume study highlighted the extent to which Zambia's basic economic conditions and the welfare of its citizens had deteriorated. Concluding that "poverty in Zambia is serious and widespread," the study indicated that it would take years to revitalize the economy. Two recurrent themes were that the "poor have low returns to their labor" and "the poor have inadequate human resources."

The recommendations were designed to foster growth and reduce poverty. The study stressed that economic reform was essential for promoting growth. If poverty reduction were to be *accelerated*, special attention was needed in four areas. These were:

- Design and implement a pro-poor macroeconomic framework;
- Facilitate the participation of the poor in the economy;
- Enhance human resource development;
- Create a social safety net.

Each of these required that numerous additional objectives be met. For instance, a pro-poor macroeconomic stance required sustained stabilization policies, continued efforts to liberalize the economy and promote competition, accelerated parastatal reform and privatization, the direct encourage-

ment of private sector activity, and the promotion of an efficient public service.

The other three elements were equally detailed.

World Bank 1995: "Prospects for Sustainable Growth"

This study concluded that medium- and longer-term growth in Zambia
could be realized with the following seven-item program.[64]

1: Maintain macroeconomic stability and the effective control of inflation.
   This will depend "primarily on eliminating the budget deficit (broadly defined to include debt service, aid flows and parastatal losses)."
2: Create stable and predictable policies based on the continued implementation of the NERP.
3: Actively promote agriculture as a means of raising nonmining exports and
   fostering a supply response.
4: Rationalize tariff and trade policies to help stimulate the expansion of manufacturing activities for which Zambia has a competitive advantage.
5: Design new initiatives for dealing with external debt to produce a less bur-
   densome debt profile. Based on projections provided in the study, that profile was expected to worsen significantly when repayments to the IMF under the ESAF began in 2001.
6: Diversify from mining exports as quickly as possible. However, for this
   transition to take place in a context of economic growth, the health of the
   mining sector must be protected.[65] Such an approach, the study argued, has
   to be Zambia's principal development thrust for the foreseeable future.
7: Improve the operations of key public institutions and provide infrastructure in many areas. Sustained economic growth will only be possible if this
   takes place.[66]

The UNDP/GRZ "Prospects for Sustainable Human Development"

This report argued that in order to promote sustainable human
development[67] the government needed to reinforce its basic growth objectives
with policies that improved equity, eradicated poverty, and raised welfare.

---

64. World Bank (1995: Ch. 7). The bank study was careful to add the following caveats (p.
105): "This is *not* a comprehensive review of all policy issues facing Zambia; it only reviews
those recommendations that are based on the analysis and data that are presented in [the] report" and (p. 106) "Note that this policy agenda does not address specifically the issues of social services, income distribution, AIDS, population growth, or regional political
considerations."
65. World Bank 1995, p. 106.
66. *ibid.*
67. See UNDP/GRZ 1995, Ch. 7, p. 145 and Ch. 8, p. 162.

Achieving these goals would require the following four strategies:

- improve livelihoods by promoting employment and income-earning activities;
- enhance social services, especially those that benefit the poor;
- provide welfare support for the most economically deprived in society; and
- maintain an enabling environment conducive to investment and growth.

Five premises underpinned these strategies. The government would be *selective* in its areas of focus. Radical approaches were required to promote *popular participation* so as to overcome the culture of *dependency*. The whole population would be mobilized to overcome poverty. Initiatives to alleviate poverty would be *people-centered*. And, a social/political/moral consensus would be created to effectively resolve the problems of poverty and deprivation.

Overview

The four studies have complementary analyses and conclusions. The World Bank identified the factors required for economic growth and sustained poverty reduction. The UNDP/GRZ highlighted the elements for achieving rapid improvements in human development.

All of the studies emphasized the need for macroeconomic stability and a predictable, conducive policy setting. All of them underscored the need to strengthen institutions, and all assert that good governance is essential to both growth and development.[68]

Each one of the analyses specified worthy goals. All of the recommended changes are highly desirable. Yet, given Zambia's circumstances, the programs were impractical because they required far more capacity (financial, administrative, and technical) than Zambia could muster. In effect, these initiatives were preprogrammed to fail.

There are two lessons. The GRZ needs to focus on a limited number of policy changes that are critical for growth and development (such as achieve and sustain macroeconomic stability, minimize its interference in the allocation of resources, reduce official corruption) and do them well. Once it registers success in these areas, the policy agenda can be expanded. The donor community needs to ensure that its agenda (however well intentioned) does not outstrip the government's capacities. Attempts to "push" too many goals will undermine, rather than reinforce, economic reform.

---

68. This point is being widely stressed. It was the centerpiece of the Maastricht meeting of the Global Coalition for Africa (GCA 1996).

4

Fiscal Policy and Public Expenditure Control

CATHARINE B. HILL

1. INTRODUCTION

This chapter explores the Zambian government's domestic fiscal stance and the progress that has been made in moving towards a budget surplus since 1991. The focus is on the steps taken to achieve control over public expenditures.

A key aspect of Zambia New Economic Recovery Programme (NERP, see Chapter 3) was a series of policy initiatives designed to change the role of the government in the economy. The intention was to remove the distortions that had emerged through government intervention in the economy during the preceding two decades. This involved a general reversal of the government's perception that the private sector was inadequate for the task of promoting economic development. From the late 1960s, the public sector had come to account for an increasing share of economic activity. In addition to a large number of state-owned enterprises (SOEs), many of which were monopolies, the government regulated and intervened extensively in the activities that had been left to the private sector.

Although the NERP was oriented to reducing the role of government, it was recognized that the government needed to disengage systematically rather than withdraw for its own sake. A number of principles were important. First, the overall fiscal stance is central to macroeconomic stability. Large fiscal deficits lead to increased foreign and domestic debt, money creation, inflation, and ultimately high real interest rates. Second, there are particular goods and services whose provision cannot be left to the private sector, either because they are public goods or because of externalities. National defense, certain components of health and education, and infrastructure are all examples of expenditures normally considered legitimate government undertakings.

These are genuine areas of public responsibility. The goal of expenditure management is to translate the relevant policies into actual expenditures. A properly functioning fiscal system incorporates appropriate levels of total spending relative to revenue and allocates expenditures efficiently and equitably among competing needs within the constraints imposed by the government's capacity to implement and monitor its activities.[1] Zambia has made significant progress in some aspects of expenditure control. Through its brief experiment with a cash budget, the government demonstrated that overall expenditure control was possible. Problems remain, however, in both the allocation of public expenditure and in monitoring of expenditures. Most of these problems arise in the context of severe fiscal compression. They have been common in other African countries struggling with the task of rationalizing the activities of a government and public sector that had become overextended.[2]

Section 2, which follows, discusses the overall domestic fiscal stance. This places in context the problem of expenditure control and provides some idea of the types of issues confronting the MMD government as it sought to impose discipline on the budget. The section also discusses the operations of the cash budget. This was the main policy tool used by the government to control the fiscal situation. Section 3 examines the allocation of public expenditure. Section 4 turns to a variety of public expenditure management issues. Section 5 has concluding comments. The appendix illustrates some of the key problems of expenditure control using the proposed and actual outcome of the 1997 budget.

2. Overall Domestic Fiscal Stance

In 1990 and 1991, Zambia ran domestic deficits of 8.3 percent and 7.3 percent of GDP. As shown in Chapter 2, the average deficit over the period 1970 to 1991 exceeded 10 percent of GDP. Thus, the last two years of the Kaunda regime were not characterized by any major shift in budget behavior. The government continued to run large deficits.

Based on its promises to the voters during the 1991 election campaign, the

---

1. Premchand, 1993.

2. Sahn, 1992. Collier and Gunning (1999) discuss the importance of fiscal management as an explanation of Africa's growth performance.

MMD government came to office committed to stabilizing the economy and sharply curtailing the role of the government in the economy. The latter idea was reflected in a slogan that featured prominently in the campaign—"The government has no business in business." Zambia's senior policy makers understood that reducing the fiscal deficit would contribute to both objectives. Much progress has been made. Table 4–1 reports government expenditures, revenues, and the fiscal balance during the 1990s. The domestic deficit, which excludes grants, foreign financed capital expenditure, and external debt service payments, moved into surplus in 1995, increasing as a share of GDP in 1996, and 1997. In 1998, however, progress was reversed. Having budgeted a domestic surplus of K120 billion, the government ran a smaller surplus of only K25 billion, mainly as a result of payment of arrears of an amount equal to the projected surplus.

Despite the initial fervor of its commitment to economic reform, the government found the task to be difficult politically. An annual budget target has been a component of the agreements reached with the IMF under the Rights Accumulation Programme (RAP) (1992–95) and the two Enhanced Structural Adjustment Facility (ESAF) arrangements initiated (but not completed) since then. All these programs have included domestic deficit targets, reflected in a benchmark on net claims on the government of the banking sector. Reaching agreement with the IMF on a program has been important to the government, because most bilateral balance of payments support, including debt relief, has been contingent upon the existence of a formal agreement with the IMF.[3] It has made sense to reduce the deficit from double digits, but the primacy given the deficit target in the economic program has had some unintended costs. The slow progress on improved tax collections and restructuring government programs, particularly the reform of the civil service, has produced significant expenditure compression. This has been reflected in the sharp rise in arrears, and a breakdown in the relationship between budgeted and actual expenditures.[4]

The Cash Budget

The main policy tool used by the government to reduce the deficit and its contributions to money creation and inflation was a cash budget. It was first introduced in 1993, and quickly brought money creation under control. Its

---

3. World Bank program loans are also technically contingent upon an IMF program being in place, but World Bank lending continued even while the IMF's ESAF was suspended.

4. For a discussion of fiscal reform in other low-income countries with IMF involvement see Abed *et al.* (1993).

Table 4–1   *Zambia Budget, 1990 through 1998 (million current kwacha)*

	1990	1991	1992
Revenue and grants	27,927	71,906	188,113
Revenue	23,001	40,814	107,521
Tax revenue	22,577	39,954	99,819
Company income tax	7,120	9,509	15,651
Personal income tax	1,701	4,825	21,464
Excise taxes	2,166	7,804	15,526
Sales tax/Value–added tax	2,182	4,600	12,765
Trade taxes 1/	8,308	13,216	34,416
Extraction royalty	0	0	0
Nontax revenue	424	860	4,702
Grants	4,926	31,092	83,592
Total expenditures and net lending	37,342	87,828	212,063
Current expenditure	30,283	63,997	155,063
Wages and salaries	5,960	13,372	34,045
Public service retrenchment	0	0	1,703
Recurrent departmental charges	5,157	8,846	20,907
Transfers and pensions	2,909	6,162	13,954
Subsidies	1,606	8,744	4,437
Interest due	8,859	18,445	48,591
Domestic debt	1,584	3,662	15,577
Foreign debt	7,275	14,783	33,014
Other current expenditure	3,337	3,104	14,622
Agricultural expenditure	0	5,324	16,804
Capital expenditure	7,059	23,831	57,000
Financed by the government of Zambia	4,000	6,258	9,670
Foreign financed	3,059	17,573	47,330
Net lending	0	0	0
Overall balance (accrual)	−9,415	−15,922	−23,950
Financing	9,415	15,921	23,950
Domestic	2,224	11,019	726
Non banks	−306	3,577	10,618
Banking system	2,270	10,585	−14,201
Domestic arrears	260	−3,143	4,309
Change in balances and other	0	0	0
Foreign 2/	7,191	4,902	23,244
Memorandum items:			
Domestic balance (cash) 3/ 4/	−3,747	−17,800	−22,889
Overall balance (cash) 4/	−9,155	−19,064	−19,641

Notes: 1/ Includes sales tax/VAT on imports
2/ Includes interest arrears and debt relief
3/ Fiscal balance exluding grants, interest payments on foreign debt, and foreign–financed capital expenditures.
4/ On a cash basis, an adjustment is made for line ministries' payments of arrears and changes in balances at the BoZ.

1993	1994	1995	1996	1997	1998
390,342	676,346	870,808	1,058,415	1,282,895	1,529,054
235,256	449,618	595,911	816,579	1,022,656	1,131,405
227,248	418,879	545,911	751,446	966,923	1,093,819
39,487	43,011	38,355	49,366	60,080	90,000
41,859	86,202	134,153	172,703	236,313	291,000
33,067	70,204	87,616	126,623	168,189	211,000
34,394	76,104	107,678	136,854	183,688	200,000
78,441	138,536	163,155	242,900	387,982	284,819
0	4,821	17,954	23,000	30,671	17,000
8,008	30,739	50,000	65,133	55,733	37,586
155,086	226,728	274,897	241,836	260,239	397,649
530,795	854,435	1,000,169	1,213,888	1,406,848	1,943,165
389,563	624,735	726,913	869,041	1,017,277	1,262,735
70,524	115,051	177,903	221,428	324,226	327,273
4,101	1,980	1,127	0	2,000	76,957
54,425	63,181	100,672	119,637	136,769	161,397
38,498	89,663	106,997	96,165	126,894	149,277
2,500	0	0	0	0	0
182,618	260,493	258,729	322,023	326,237	420,848
71,463	102,538	77,029	121,846	115,228	80,139
111,155	157,955	181,700	200,177	211,009	340,709
1,305	62,444	55,885	79,431	98,037	111,692
35,592	31,923	25,600	30,357	3,114	15,291
141,232	229,700	273,256	344,847	389,571	680,430
18,232	36,700	58,256	40,596	70,026	113,363
123,000	193,001	215,000	304,251	319,545	567,067
0	0	0	0	0	0
−140,453	−178,089	−129,361	−155,473	−123,953	−414,111
140,453	178,089	129,361	155,473	123,953	414,111
−11,374	53,627	7,600	−43,142	−93,028	149,541
5,881	3,024	−4,037	1,494	−14,000	−3,431
−17,122	24,898	−3,861	12,300	10,400	223,803
−133	27,432	1,815	−50,891	−68,900	−116,746
0	−2,727	13,683	−6,045	−20,528	45,915
151,827	125,462	121,761	198,615	216,981	264,570
−61,517	−29,157	7,940	49,180	64,434	25,185
−140,586	−153,384	−113,863	−212,409	−213,381	−484,942

Table 4–1 continued *Zambia Budget, 1990 through 1998 (percent GDP)*

	1990	1991	1992
Nominal GDP (million kwacha)	113,000	218,000	570,000
CPI	4.3	8.6	22.8
Revenue and grants	0.25	0.33	0.33
Revenue	0.20	0.19	0.19
Tax revenue	0.20	0.18	0.18
Company income tax	0.06	0.04	0.03
Personal income tax	0.02	0.02	0.04
Excise taxes	0.02	0.04	0.03
Sales tax/Value–added tax	0.02	0.02	0.02
Trade taxes 1/	0.07	0.06	0.06
Extraction royalty	0.00	0.00	0.00
Nontax revenue	0.00	0.00	0.01
Grants	0.04	0.14	0.15
Total expenditures and net lending	0.33	0.40	0.37
Current expenditure	0.27	0.29	0.27
Wages and salaries	0.05	0.06	0.06
Public service retrenchment	0.00	0.00	0.00
Recurrent departmental charges	0.05	0.04	0.04
Transfers and pensions	0.03	0.03	0.02
Subsidies	0.01	0.04	0.01
Interest due	0.08	0.08	0.09
Domestic debt	0.01	0.02	0.03
Foreign debt	0.06	0.07	0.06
Other current expenditure	0.03	0.01	0.03
Agricultural expenditure	0.00	0.02	0.03
Capital expenditure	0.06	0.11	0.10
Financed by the government of Zambia	0.04	0.03	0.02
Foreign financed	0.03	0.08	0.08
Net lending	0.00	0.00	0.00
Overall balance (accrual)	−0.08	−0.07	−0.04
Financing	0.08	0.07	0.04
Domestic	0.02	0.05	0.00
Non banks	0.00	0.02	0.02
Banking system	0.02	0.05	−0.02
Domestic arrears	0.00	−0.01	0.01
Change in balances and other	0.00	0.00	0.00
Foreign 2/	0.06	0.02	0.04
Memorandum items:			
Domestic balance (cash) 3/ 4/	−0.03	−0.08	−0.04
Overall balance (cash) 4/	−0.08	−0.09	−0.03
Total expenditure, minus foreign debt & foreign financed capital expenditure	0.24	0.25	0.23

1993	1994	1995	1996	1997	1998
1,482,000	2,241,000	2,998,000	3,945,000	5,169,000	6,241,000
64.7	100	134.9	193	240.1	298.9
0.26	0.30	0.29	0.27	0.25	0.25
0.16	0.20	0.20	0.21	0.20	0.18
0.15	0.19	0.18	0.19	0.19	0.18
0.03	0.02	0.01	0.01	0.01	0.01
0.03	0.04	0.04	0.04	0.05	0.05
0.02	0.03	0.03	0.03	0.03	0.03
0.02	0.03	0.04	0.03	0.04	0.03
0.05	0.06	0.05	0.06	0.08	0.05
0.00	0.00	0.01	0.01	0.01	0.00
0.01	0.01	0.02	0.02	0.01	0.01
0.10	0.10	0.09	0.06	0.05	0.06
0.36	0.38	0.33	0.31	0.27	0.31
0.26	0.28	0.24	0.22	0.20	0.20
0.05	0.05	0.06	0.06	0.06	0.05
0.00	0.00	0.00	0.00	0.00	0.01
0.04	0.03	0.03	0.03	0.03	0.03
0.03	0.04	0.04	0.02	0.02	0.02
0.00	0.00	0.00	0.00	0.00	0.00
0.12	0.12	0.09	0.08	0.06	0.07
0.05	0.05	0.03	0.03	0.02	0.01
0.08	0.07	0.06	0.05	0.04	0.05
0.00	0.03	0.02	0.02	0.02	0.02
0.02	0.01	0.01	0.01	0.00	0.00
0.10	0.10	0.09	0.09	0.08	0.11
0.01	0.02	0.02	0.01	0.01	0.02
0.08	0.09	0.07	0.08	0.06	0.09
0.00	0.00	0.00	0.00	0.00	0.00
−0.09	−0.08	−0.04	−0.04	−0.02	−0.07
0.09	0.08	0.04	0.04	0.02	0.07
−0.01	0.02	0.00	−0.01	−0.02	0.02
0.00	0.00	0.00	0.00	0.00	0.00
−0.01	0.01	0.00	0.00	0.00	0.04
0.00	0.01	0.00	−0.01	−0.01	−0.02
0.00	0.00	0.00	0.00	0.00	0.01
0.10	0.06	0.04	0.05	0.04	0.04
−0.04	−0.01	0.00	0.01	0.01	0.00
−0.09	−0.07	−0.04	−0.05	−0.04	−0.08
0.20	0.22	0.20	0.18	0.17	0.17

operation, however, generated other problems that led to its selective abandonment beginning in mid-1995. In the 1992 budget, the government had anticipated a deficit of 1.9 percent of GDP.[5] In fact, the deficit was about 4 percent of GDP, the result of an unbudgeted wage increase, operating subsidies for Zambia Airways, and drought-related expenditures.

The 1993 budget called for overall domestic balance with revenues equal to expenditures, excluding foreign-financed capital expenditures and foreign debt service and grants. Having failed in 1992 to impose budget discipline, the government announced in the 1993 budget speech that it would adopt a cash budget. The government instructed the Bank of Zambia (BoZ) not to finance any expenditure unless there were adequate funds in the relevant government account. In turn, the ministry of finance would only fund expenditure if adequate revenues were already in accounts at the BoZ. A new Treasury bill (T-bill) tender procedure had been instituted earlier, but revenues raised through sales were only to be used to roll over existing debt. The government cited the examples of Bolivia, Israel, and Argentina in support of this policy change. All three countries had experienced dramatic reductions in inflation through the use of cash budgets.

Because of heavy pressure on expenditure, the operation of the cash budget in 1993 applied only to noninterest expenditure. Domestic debt service was capitalized. During 1993, the government ran a primary surplus and, after an initial surge, domestic inflation decelerated dramatically.[6] The credit squeeze, along with the liberalization of financial markets, led to high nominal and then real interest rates. The annualized return on 91-day T-bills reached 380 percent in July 1993. This increased the domestic debt service component in the budget, contributing to the overall domestic budget deficit of K61 billion, or 4.2 percent of GDP.

The 1994 budget called for an overall budget deficit of K11 billion, and a primary surplus of K50 billion. Again, the cash budget was interpreted as applying to noninterest expenditures. In the end, a deficit of K29 billion emerged, in part the result of payment of arrears that had accumulated in 1993. The 1995 budget was the first to call for a balanced budget, with the cash budget applied to both interest and noninterest expenditures. On paper, the target was met by a small margin. Nonetheless, when the full extent of the

---

5. This excludes grants. The 1992 budget speech does not make clear whether the deficit also includes foreign- financed capital expenditure and external debt service.

6. The surge in inflation resulted from extraordinary lending by the BoZ to the Zambia National Oil Company (ZNOC) to import petroleum. The government would not allow the ZNOC to raise prices to levels that would cover its costs. Accordingly, it could not gain access to foreign exchange without central bank accommodation. This led to a surge in reserve money in the first five months of 1993.

arrears carried over from 1995 became known, the target on a commitment basis was, in fact, missed by a significant margin.

At the aggregate level, the cash budget achieved an important objective, namely preventing the types of large fiscal deficits that would lead to high rates of money growth and rapid inflation. The accounts of the monetary authorities demonstrate (see Table 4–2) that in 1995, the growth of net credit to the government declined relative to 1994, contributing to a reduction in reserve money. In 1996, net credit to the government increased slightly, but most of the 60 percent increase in reserve money was explained by central bank lending to the banking system in response to the banking crisis.

Maintaining a cash budget is an extremely simple rule that, when conscientiously applied, had desirable effects in Zambia. Nonetheless, several problems related to government expenditure remain. Some of these have resulted from the operations of the cash budget. Some have simply not been adequately addressed as part of the implementation of the cash budget or other government policies. The control of total public expenditure and its allocation to different types of expenditures remain weak. These latter issues are discussed in the final section of the chapter.

Problems Implementing the Cash Budget

The MoF makes monthly fundings to other ministries based on allocations in the budget approved by Parliament at the beginning of the year. Under the

Table 4–2   *Bank of Zambia Accounts (Twelve-month change as percentage of beginning-period reserve money)*

	1990	1991	1992	1993	1994	1995	1996	1997	1998
Net foreign assets						−56.5	−287.1	34.9	−631.8
Net domestic assets						30.8	347.7	−9.3	667.5
Net domestic credit						37.2	57.6	−10.9	265.5
Net claims on government						−50.0	11.4	5.4	247.5
Claims on non-government						87.2	46.2	−16.3	18.0
OIN						−6.3	290.1	1.7	402
Reserve money (change)	75.5	89.9	66.1	165.1	46.8	−26.0	60.7	25.9	35.7
Reserve money (Kwacha million)	12	22	36	97	142	105	169	212	288

Source: IMF (1997 and 1999), GRZ Macroeconomic Indicators, various issues

cash budget, fundings are not made until there is revenue in the government's account at the BoZ. (In January, a bridge loan has traditionally been arranged with the BoZ, recognizing that the government necessarily faces a cash-flow problem at the beginning of the year. This arises because any remaining balances in the government's accounts are frozen at the end of each year. The need for a bridge loan is mainly, though not entirely, an accounting issue. The bridge loan is then paid back over an agreed time period.) Tying fundings to revenues in the BoZ, has generated several problems. MoF officials argued that releasing funds in this way made it difficult to rationally allocate resources. Senior officials pushed for making fundings at the beginning of each month, based on anticipated revenues. The cash budget was amended accordingly in mid-1996. During the first quarter of 1997, however, relaxing the simple constraint of the cash budget led to a deficit of K31 billion, close to .5 percent of GDP, when the government was committed to a generate a surplus of 1 percent of GDP for the year.

This experience has shown that controlling aggregate expenditure is a major problem. The cash budget had been a relatively simple tool for that purpose. But when relaxed slightly, budget control was lost, confirming that expenditure control had not become engrained in the operations of the government. Until that is the case, the cash budget will be needed.

The cash budget, by definition, enforced a balanced budget. During 1997 and 1998, the government budgeted for a domestic surplus of 1 percent of GDP. It has been difficult for policy makers to adjust. Meeting the benchmarks has typically been left to the last possible moment. This has led to large monthly swings in fiscal stance, with big pushes on both revenues and expenditures concentrated in short periods of time at the end of quarters. Such window-dressing, however, does not achieve the economic effects of a budget surplus. For those to materialize, a more sustained management of the fiscal position is necessary. That will require a variety of outstanding fiscal management problems to be addressed.

Moving Towards a Consolidated Budget

Zambia has taken a number of steps to focus on the consolidated budget deficit, but many of the necessary data to do so are either unavailable or not available in a timely manner. The consolidated deficit has not been a (major) source of money creation. Being able to monitor it enables the government to keep track of changes in international indebtedness. This is critical since Zambia's debt overhang is large.

The operation of the cash budget has been confined to domestic expenditures and revenues. Foreign grants, foreign-financed capital expenditure, and external debt service payments have typically been treated separately. The government has assumed that the first two items will be equal, and therefore will have a neutral impact on the budget. This has justified excluding them from the budget. While the monitoring of external debt service has been strengthened during the 1990s, the monitoring of foreign grants and for-eign-financed capital expenditure has been inadequate. At best, the informa-tion available to the Budget Office about these items is incomplete. Thus, in framing the budget, neither the overall fiscal position nor the allocation of foreign financed items can be carefully measured.

Foreign-financed capital expenditures are a large component of overall public investment. It has been long recognized that these resources, many of which have implications for future recurrent expenditures, should be fully in-tegrated into the budgeting process. Commodity aid also generates counter-part funds that are not consistently incorporated in the budget. Many of these resources are not accounted for, adding to the difficulty of adopting a consol-idated budget.

The MoF monitors project agreements with donors. But the actual dis-bursement of funds by donors and expenditures by ministries are not ade-quately tracked. (This problem is treated in more detail in Chapter 9.) Fur-thermore, incomplete information on donor-funded projects makes it difficult for the MoF to plan necessary counterpart expenditures.

3. EXPENDITURE ALLOCATION ISSUES

With current levels of revenue, the government's commitment to fiscal balance has placed government expenditure under severe pressure. Since 1991, government expenditure has been between 17 and 23 percent of GDP, down from levels approaching 30 percent of GDP during the 1980s.[7] Restric-tions on aggregate expenditure have created problems. First, an increasing share of total expenditure has been devoted to personal emoluments and do-mestic interest payments, with cuts being made in recurrent departmental charges (RDCs) and capital expenditures. Though expedient, these adjust-ments do nothing to promote economic growth.[8] Second, at the ministry level the control of expenditure has been weak and, as discussed below, large domestic arrears now regularly arise.

---

7. The government expenditure data exclude foreign interest payments and foreign-financed capital.

8. The inadequacies of public service delivery is discussed in Isham, Kaufmann, and Pritchett (1995), Pradhan (1996), and Isham and Kaufmann (1999).

Overall Expenditure Allocation Problems

With personal emoluments (PEs) and interest on the domestic debt claim-
ing an increasing share of government expenditure, the balances available for
recurrent and capital expenditures declined sharply. Recurrent expenditures
were below budgeted amounts in 1994, 1995, and 1996 despite total expenditures that exceeded budgeted levels by significant margins. Since inflation
was higher than anticipated, this resulted in deep real cuts in recurrent expenditures. Domestically financed capital expenditures have been similarly
squeezed. In 1996, wages and salaries (personal emoluments plus the wage
adjustment) equaled 30 percent of government expenditure, and interest on
the domestic debt was 17 percent. By contrast, capital expenditure was only 4
percent of government expenditure and RDCs were 16 percent. In 1996,
RDCs were equivalent to 55 percent of wages and salaries. At the start of the
1990s, they had been equal to wages and salaries.

A further problem is that spending on wages and salaries is understated in
the budget tables. A part of RDCs is used to compensate employees, in the
form of travel and subsistence allowances. The budget for travel and subsistence allowances represent 6–7 percent of PEs and 1.2 percent of the total
budget.[9] Thus, wages and salaries, though large, are also understated, while
expenditures on RDCs that truly support the operations of ministries and departments—fuel, spare parts, stationery, and supplies—are overstated.

Personal Emoluments

When it took office, the MMD government acknowledged that public sector reform would be vital to the overall effort to restructure the economy.[10]
The civil service had to be made more efficient. The wage bill needed to be cut
to levels consistent with the fiscal constraints facing the government. At the
same time, real wages of civil servants had declined significantly. Between
1984 and 1991, personal emoluments fell from 30 percent of total expenditure to 18.2 percent. In real terms, the decline was almost 60 percent.[11] During the same period, the size of the civil service had continued to grow, producing an even sharper cut in average real wages.

Trying to rationalize an over-staffed and expensive civil service was not a
new problem in Zambia. For example, in 1979 the government had indicated
the need to reduce by 50 percent the size of the civil service. Little was done
during the 1980s. In 1990, the government engaged a local consulting firm to

---

9. *Public Expenditure Review*, 1994, p. 110 (World Bank Report No. 13854-ZA).

10. MMD *Manifesto* 1991, section 2.g, pp. 3–4.

11. *PER*, 1992, p. 28 (World Bank Report number 11420-ZA).

devise a plan to cut the size of the civil service. Over 10,000 employees who could be dismissed on grounds of "undisciplined and delinquent behavior" were identified. Since there had been an absence of formal documentation on performance it was not legally possible to do anything.

The central government payroll increased from 110,634 in 1989 to 131,712 in 1994.[12] In mid-1997, the comparable number was around 139,000. This expansion occurred during a period when the government was formally committed to sharply cutting the size of its work force. As a result of this reversal, the wage bill rose as a share of total expenditure. In 1990, it was 16.4 percent of total expenditure. In both 1995 and 1996, it exceeded 30 percent. It increased to 39 percent of total expenditure in 1997 and fell to 32 percent in 1998. Personal emoluments account for 35 percent of domestic expenditures in the 2000 budget (excluding foreign-financed interest payments and capital expenditures and the extraordinary amount of K423 billion, approximately 4 percent of GDP, allocated to pay some of ZCCM's domestic debts).

With total expenditure compressed, the ratio of RDCs to wages has fallen, from 1.04 in 1990 to approximately .55 in 1995 and 1996, .43 in 1997, and .5 in 1998. The implication is that civil service employees have fewer resources at their disposal. It is no surprise, therefore, that their efficiency remains low and has not improved.

The decline in the real wages of civil servants has been accompanied by increased wage compression since 1991. The salaries of professionals relative to those with fewer skills declined between 1990 and 1994.[13] Finally, wages in the civil service have remained well below those of equivalent workers in the parastatal and private sectors.

Thus, contrary to the government's stated objective of reforming the civil service, little has been achieved. After years of reform, the civil service remains grossly overstaffed, the wage bill is significantly higher than the country's economic base can sustain, and civil servants continue to be underpaid relative to their parastatal and private sector counterparts. The budget speech of 2000 offered little to indicate that this situation would change substantively in the near term.[14] The government has adopted the rhetoric of reform while adding to the public sector payroll.

---

12. *PER*, 1994, p. 101.

13. *PER*, 1994, p. 108.

14. As noted in Chapter 12, the 2000 budget speech had several indications that the government sought to distance itself from the policy of reducing the size of the civil service. This comes after the government consistently promised since early 1992 to create a "leaner, more efficient" civil service. To illustrate, the minister of finance noted (Budget Speech 2000, par. 75):

... the central objective of the Public Service Reform Programme is to enhance the performance of the public sector in ways that directly benefit the ordinary Zambian. From

Spending on Health and Education

Poverty in Zambia is among the highest in sub-Saharan Africa, and has been increasing during the 1990s.[15] This is primarily the result of the country's inadequate growth performance over the last 30 years. Other social indicators have also deteriorated. Literacy rates and net enrollment rates have declined, infant mortality has risen, and life expectancy has fallen.[16] These trends can be traced in Table 4–3.

The government has an important role to play in reversing the decline in social indicators by promoting growth and emphasizing health and education.[17] The allocation of government expenditures to social sectors has been maintained as a share of total expenditures, in part in response to agreements with the World Bank. Nonetheless, total real expenditures, both aggregate and per capita, have declined.

Real spending on education fell by 35 percent between 1986 and 1990, and then by a further 15 percent from 1990 to 1998 (Table 4–4). In per capita terms, real spending on education fell by 31 percent between 1990 and 1998. Real spending per capita on secondary and tertiary education, and on teacher training have all declined, while real per capita spending on primary education has remained constant. As a share of total domestic education expenditures, primary education has increased slightly, offset by declines in the share going to secondary education.[18] The share for tertiary education has remained approximately constant. Zambia's share of spending on tertiary education is higher, however, than the average for low and middle-income devel-

---

a political perspective, the programme must be seen, not as a numbers game, or an aimless surgical exercise, but as a comprehensive exercise aimed at addressing the expectations of our people from the public service.

This represented a clear shift from earlier government commitments to reduce the size of the civil service.

15. There are several sources. The World Bank's *World Development Indicators*, the World Bank/UNDP *African Development Indicators*, and the UNDP's *Human Development Indicators*. The first-mentioned source shows that poverty in Zambia, measured as the population below $2 ($1) per day in purchasing power parity terms in 1996, was 91.7 (72.6) percent. *(World Development Indicators* 2000, Table 2.7, p. 64).

16. The importance of human capital, including health and education, to economic growth is discussed in Gemmell (1996) and Schultz (1999).

17. The effects on income distribution of spending on health and education are discussed in Chu, Davoodi, and Gupta (2000).

18. For a discussion of the importance of the expenditure allocations within the health and education sectors see Gupta, Verhoeven, and Tiongson (1999).

19. That, however, has not prevented the quality of tertiary education from falling (Achola 1990; Kelley 1991; Saasa *et al.* 1996). The effects of declining quality of education are considered in Chapter 12.

Table 4-3 *Social Indicators, Zambia*

Series Name	1988	1989	1990	1991	1992	1993	1994	1995	1996	1997	1998
Consumer price index (1995 = 100)	1	2	3	6	17	49	75	100	146	183	—
Death rate, crude (per 1,000 people)	—	—	15	—	15	—	—	—	—	19	19
Electricity production (in million kwh)	8,485	6,782	6,330	7,834	7,780	7,785	7,785	7,790	7,796	8,006	—
Fertility rate, total (births per woman)	—	—	6	5	6	—	6	—	—	6	5
Food price index (1995 = 100)	1	1	3	5	17	50	75	100	146	176	219
GDP, PPP x 1 mil (current international $)	5,588	5,715	5,724	5,899	6,120	6,682	6,572	6,584	7,085	7,234	6,954
Illiteracy rate, adult female (% of females aged 15 and above)	44	43	41	40	39	37	36	35	34	32	31
Illiteracy rate, adult male (% of males aged 15 and above)	23	22	22	21	20	19	19	18	17	17	16
Illiteracy rate, adult total (% of people aged 15 and above)	34	33	32	31	30	29	28	27	26	25	24
Immunization, DPT (% of children under 12 months)	63	58	71	91	61	67	86	82	83	70	—
Immunization, measles (% of children under 12 months)	66	59	68	89	60	61	89	85	93	69	—
Life expectancy at birth, female (years)	—	—	50	—	50	—	—	—	—	43	43
Life expectancy at birth, male (years)	—	—	48	—	48	—	—	—	—	43	43
Life expectancy at birth, total (years)	—	—	49	—	49	—	—	—	—	43	43
Low-birthweight babies (% of births)	—	—	—	—	—	—	—	13	—	—	—
Mortality rate, adult, female (per 1,000 female adults)	—	—	377	—	—	—	—	—	—	524	545
Mortality rate, adult, male (per 1,000 male adults)	—	—	434	—	—	—	—	—	—	512	521
Mortality rate, infant (per 1,000 live births)	—	107	107	—	108	—	109	—	—	113	114
Mortality rate, under-5 (per 1,000 live births)	—	191	—	—	194	—	197	—	—	189	192
Population, total (x 1 million)	7.32	7.55	7.78	8.02	8.26	8.50	8.74	8.98	9.21	9.44	9.67
School enrollment, primary (% net)	87	85	84	84	85	79	77	75	74	72	—
School enrollment, secondary (% net)	45	45	45	46	47	45	44	44	43	42	—

oping countries.[19] Most health indicators in Zambia worsened during the 1990s (Table 4–3).[20]

Over the last decade HIV/AIDS has become a major problem, sharply increasing the burden on the healthcare system.[21] HIV/AIDS affects child survival. It also raises the dependency ratio thereby intensifying the effects of poverty and adding to the burden of disease. Medical experts note that tuberculosis (TB) cases are on the rise as a result of the HIV/AIDS epidemic. As the system attempts to respond to these problems, fewer resources will be available to deal with other health issues.

The government has evaluated its spending policies in both sectors.[22] Its proposals represent a reasonable, though modest, public policy response to the challenges facing the country. Two problems remain, however. Implementation has been inadequate. So, too, have been the resources devoted to these sectors even though, as noted above, they have been protected under agreements with the World Bank. This strategy has had a limited impact since the allocation of spending within the health and education sectors remains problematic. Spending on both education and health suffer from the effects of expenditure compression, as have other areas of the budget. The salary share of spending is high, and RDCs and capital expenditures have been squeezed.[23]

Both education and health deserve a larger share of scarce government resources. That could be done if the government reduced expenditures on other less vital areas, for example, official travel. Over the long term, addressing these issues will require increased growth from which additional resources could then be devoted to improving the health and education status of the population.[24]

Overview

Government expenditure poses two serious problems. First, the overall amounts are too large relative to Zambia's revenue base. Second, the alloca-

---

20. *World Development Indicators* 2000, Table 2.17; *Human Development Indicators* 2000, Table 2. Schultz and Tansel (1997) discuss the effects of health on labor productivity.

21. GRZ 1999.

22. For education, a relevant document is *Educating our Future* (GRZ 1996). The health strategy has been outlined in *National Health Policy and Strategy Document* (1992) and *National Strategic Health Plan for 1995–99* (GRZ 1995).

23. Ablo and Reinikka (1998) have a detailed discussion of education and health expenditures in Uganda.

24. This is not a new result. It is fully consistent with the findings of the Chenery *et al.* study *Redistribution with Growth* (1974). Economic growth, it was argued, would provide the resources needed to improve social welfare and therefore the distribution of income and wealth.

tion of expenditure remains distorted despite numerous attempts at reform. In the appendix we have examined the relationship between budgeted and actual revenues and expenditures for 1997. This exercise shows how these problems are manifest in practice and provides an idea of the magnitudes involved.

4. Public Expenditure Management Issues[25]

In broad terms, the cash budget reduced the extent to which budget deficits added to money creation and inflationary pressure. But it was only a start. For the government to bring its expenditure under control numerous changes still need to be made.

Off-budget Spending

The MoF has generally attempted to avoid off-budget expenditures. Yet, debt swaps and the use of T-bills to finance extrabudgetary transactions have jeopardized the effective control and reporting of government expenditures. Part of the problem has been the division of responsibility within the ministry. Issuing T Bills is the responsibility of the loans and investments division. It has not been under the director of budget. Although primarily used as a debt instrument, T-bills have in some instances been issued surreptitiously to cover specific off-budget items of government expenditure. When discovered by the budget office, the amounts involved were included as government expenditure. By that time, however, the damage had been done. Moreover, there have been few controls or reporting procedures instituted to prevent further abuse of this system.[26] Based on BoZ data on the outstanding stock of T-bills, the last several years have witnessed some continued use of this system of circumventing "normal" budget controls. The implication is that the budget deficit, as measured by borrowing, has exceeded the deficit reported by the MoF. Starting in 1997, the discrepancy between the MoF and the BoZ measures of the deficit has been included as "other expenditure." Thus, although the nature of the expenditure goes unrecorded, the expenditure itself is recorded.[27]

---

25. For a general discussion of public expenditure management issues, in contrast to policy issues, see Potter and Diamond (1999).

26. The minister of finance is responsible for approving the issue of T-bills to cover off-budget items.

27. It was difficult to discover what the expenditure was for. In 1996, the minister ordered that approximately K13 billion in T-bills be issued to Finance Bank. The nature of the transactions was never adequately explained.

The government has also incurred arrears to the parastatal utilities, for phone service, electricity, water, and fuel. Since these firms have not faced hard budget constraints, it has been possible for them to allow these arrears to accrue. That, however, simply pushes the problem back one level to the organization (often the state-owned bank) that finances these firms. When the bills are presented to the government, it does not have the capacity to pay, having failed to make adequate provision in the budget for clearing the arrears. Since the parastatals providing the services to government also have outstanding debts to government, the interlocking obligations have been handled by debt swaps. This approach has been convenient but it poses several problems. First, there is no mechanism for maintaining control over the government's use of the services it is being provided. In particular, ministries and departments have no incentive to monitor and control the use of resources when their debts can be so readily canceled. Second, while this system continues, the government has difficulty validating the bills being presented to them by the enterprises supplying the services. Finally, the government revenue and expenditure that these swaps represent are rarely recorded in the budget. This gives a distorted view of the overall impact of the government and the public sector on the economy.

Domestic Arrears

One response to the reduction in fundings for recurrent and capital expenditure, combined with weak expenditure control mechanisms, has been an increase in domestic arrears. The 1994 budget speech mentioned that arrears were a problem in 1993. During 1994, arrears of K17 billion were paid, increasing the deficit from its program level of K11 billion to K27 billion. In 1995, arrears of K22.2 billion were paid; in 1996, K41.8 billion; in 1997, K68.9 billion; and in 1998, the amount paid was K116.7 billion. These were respectively 3.7, 5.9, 8.4, and 11.5 percent of total domestic expenditure in those years. The regular (and growing) carry-over of arrears is evidence that the government does not have in place an adequate monitoring mechanism. This makes it unlikely that arrears from any particular year will be completely cleared, or that a mechanism for their prevention in the future can be implemented. Overall, the outstanding stock of arrears remains uncertain. Preliminary estimates showed that the arrears carried into 1997 were on the order of 5 to 10 percent of budgeted expenditure. Relative to what was paid in 1997, this proved to be correct. Little seemed to have been learned from this experience, as even larger arrears were carried into 1998, 1999, and 2000.

Domestic arrears arise, in part, because ministries are allocated money in the budget that then is never released. Ministries consider the number in the budget, the "yellow book," as their entitlement and make commitments based on this allocation. In the end, a significant portion of those commitments is not funded. This occurs because the government redirects expenditure to nonbudgeted items, or the funds needed to cover the yellow book totals are not made available. Despite having been instructed that commitments should not be made until funding is released, ministries anticipate (incorrectly as it turns out) annual allocations and attempt to smooth out some expenditure, often by necessity, not just abuse.[28]

Arrears also arise because the budget allocations to ministries in the yellow book are unrealistic from the start. In some cases, actual allocations are well below what is known to be required to support government programs. This tactic is used to make the budget numbers add up to the pre-determined deficit or surplus target when the budget is published. In other cases, known expenditures are excluded to achieve the same objective. When these expenditures take place "unexpectedly," some other budgeted expenditure has to be cut.

For the same reason, expected revenue for some items is overestimated to meet the target. When the revenue does not materialize, budgeted expenditures must be cut. (This problem has been less frequent over the last few years, because revenue is projected in nominal terms, using an inflation target rather than a forecast of the rate of inflation. The inflation targets have been highly optimistic. Nominal revenues are then higher than projected because realized inflation is higher.) This tactic has made the achievement of the nominal revenue targets easier. Nonetheless, it leads to a compression of real expenditures and undermines the overall real impact of the budget, further aggravating expenditure pressures in subsequent periods.

To address the domestic arrears problem, several actions are needed. First, the actual outstanding stock of arrears has to be verified. (Despite the habitual carry-over of charges from one year to the next, some confusion remains on the part of ministries as to when arrears have arisen.) This has to be followed by adequate provision in the budget, or the next several budgets, to clear the arrears. Procedures must be instituted to prevent new arrears from arising. A variety of changes are required to accomplish this.

---

28. Rather than address the matter of arrears, the budget speech of 2000 simply noted that controlling officers who overspent would be subject to "disciplinary action" (*Budget Speech 2000*, par. 99). The government's own financial regulations require such action. Thus, the minister's threat added nothing new. Indeed, the minister compounded the problem by noting that he had "reluctantly provided K44 billion for the clearance of arrears in 2000. . .." This amount was still insufficient to clear the arrears.

For a start, budget provisions relating to RDCs should be realistic. If inadequate resources are allocated to expenditure items that are not truly discretionary, then arrears will arise. Ministry expenditures need to be carefully monitored, and budget allocations enforced.

Beginning in 1996, the Ministry of Finance introduced a new budgeting procedure, based on a medium-term financial framework (MTFF). It was designed to move away from incremental budgeting towards program budgeting. The ministry agreed to a three-year plan specifying expenditure objectives. The annual budget, in principle, is then designed to be consistent with and implement the objectives of the medium-term plan. For the 1997 budget, this procedure did not eliminate the problems of unrealistic expenditure. With expenditure constrained and few programs being eliminated, the final budget allocations were not based on the programming budget exercises undertaken by the ministries, nor were they realistic. To make the numbers add up to the pre-determined deficit target, many items including domestic interest payments were understated. Because some of these items (such as interest) are not discretionary, other budget items have to be cut to meet the aggregate budget targets. This exacerbates the arrears problem.

Unexpected, *ad hoc* expenditures also worsen the budget situation. Due to the pressures to formally budget for a specific surplus, the contingency included in the budget is too small. There are two ways to deal with this. First, the budget should include a large contingency, recognizing that unbudgeted expenditures always arise. Second, better provision for expenditures needs to be made in the budget. Many of the unexpected expenditures in 1996 should not have been totally unexpected. (Indeed, most of them were not. The estimates, however, had been understated as part of the annual "game" needed to get the budget past the IMF deficit threshold.) The MoF should undertake a study of contingent liabilities, so that adequate provision can be included in the budget process. For example, in 1996, some court cases were settled, with the government liable for K30 billion (equivalent to $25 million at the time). Although the actual liability was not known in advance, the existence of the cases was known. It was also well understood that the government had potential liabilities.

Numerous public expenditure management issues need to be addressed. Yet, these matters will not be resolved until the budget itself becomes more realistic and the size of government is reduced until it is consistent with the economy's resource base. For these to happen, the surplus target has to be the residual, revenue performance must improve, or deep cuts in expenditures need to be made.

Policy makers already know before the budget is sent to the government printer that its expenditure and revenue programs are unrealistic. This knowledge, however, has not produced a consensus on how to address the problem. The budget deficit number is predetermined under the IMF program. To date, the government has taken few of the hard decisions needed to cut programs, improve revenue compliance, or raise additional revenue so as to meet the target on a sustainable basis. Until this happens, the budget will remain unrealistic and many of the problems highlighted here will continue.[29]

Government Deposits in Commercial Banks

During 1996, government deposits at commercial banks increased significantly.[30] They were K12 billion in 1994, K45 billion in 1995, K58 billion in 1996, K64 billion in 1997, and K88 billion in 1998. Through the reports of the commercial banks to the BoZ, the MoF had information on the total, but not broken down by ministry. The use of these accounts, most of which were established to improve the efficiency of ministry operations, add to the problem of controlling expenditures.

Over the period 1995 to 1997, government deposits in commercial banks averaged 23 percent of the outstanding stock of T-bills. That is, government was paying interest on T-bills, significant amounts of which could have been offset by appropriate cash management. Such an improvement would have reduced the government's interest payments.

Despite efforts that began in 1992 to sort out these accounts, the nature of many of them has remained unclear. Concerns linger that nontax revenue is not being appropriately managed, that counterpart funds have been accruing to ministries and not passing through the budget, and that resources released for capital expenditures are not being spent but instead are accruing in bank accounts. The increase in these accounts during 1995 was K33 billion, or 6.3 percent of government current expenditure that year. Such a large total distorts both revenue and expenditure reporting.

---

29. The 2000 budget showed no improvement in this regard. It projected an unrealistically low rate of inflation, and pensions and domestic interest payments that were well below what would ultimately be incurred. And, as pointed out in the previous note, the provision for arrears was too low.

30. Senior policy makers were concerned about the accounts held by ministries outside the central bank in 1992 and 1993. At that time, the government was attempting to control expenditure so as to reduce inflation. The MoF issued instructions regarding the use of these accounts. Some were ordered closed. As new emergencies arose, the attention of policy makers shifted. The operations of these accounts were never fully understood or rationalized.

Lack of Expenditure Reconciliation

The MoF funds the various ministries which then report to the government through expenditure and commitment returns to the accountant general stating how the funds were actually spent. There is no crosschecking of other ministries' actual spending patterns against funding. The government expenditure data in the budget is based on funding and may bear little relationship to the way resources are actually spent.

Improvements in the allocation of government expenditure will require that expenditure reconciliation and crosschecking become institutionalized. That, in turn, will require a major effort to enhance the quantity and quality of accounting staff in the Ministry of Finance. Such an effort was made under the macroeconomic technical assistance project (METAP) and will be described in Chapter 12.

5. CONCLUDING COMMENTS

Effective control of public expenditures requires both short- and long-term measures. Over the short run, the focus has to be on monitoring and reporting systems and on the types of regular crosschecks to ensure that the financing provided keeps the budget on target and expenditures are properly recorded. Better control procedures can be put in place and steps taken to avoid new arrears and to achieve an efficient allocation of expenditure within a compressed total. The government's contingent liabilities should be identified, a large contingency should be included in the budget, realistic allocations should be made for RDCs, and careful estimates of debt servicing costs should be included in the budget. The new system, introduced in 1998, of making releases to commercial banks offers one way of imposing discipline on the aggregate expenditure that was lacking when political pressure could be brought to bear on the BoZ. Use of the commercial banks, however, does not deal with the arrears problem. Nor does it make any headway with the problem that, in relation to the overall economy, the government is simply too large.

Over the longer term, basic solutions to expenditure control problems hinge on the formulation and implementation of budgets that reflect sustainable patterns of expenditures and revenues. Revenue needs to be increased above current levels to cover necessary expenditures and to contribute to government savings. Expenditures have to be controlled through realistic budgeting. The wage bill has to be capped even if it cannot be reduced significantly. Total expenditures could be sharply reduced by cutting nonessential government programs. Reductions in official travel, representation abroad, and the elimination of redundant ministries and departments would be constructive places to start.

For the government to do all of this and meet a fiscal surplus target, revenues will have to be increased and discretionary expenditures kept under control. But, if expenditures and revenues are unrealistically set to achieve a predetermined budget target, it will be impossible to meet the target without encountering the same types of problems that have arisen in the last several years.

APPENDIX: Problems of Expenditure Control Illustrated: The 1997 Budget

This appendix uses the 1997 budget to illustrate some of the basic problems of expenditure control in Zambia. There is nothing distinctive about the choice of year. Many of the problems and patterns noted have been evident for years and could be illustrated just as well by choosing some other year. For example, there were even larger imbalances in the major revenue and expenditure categories in 1999.

While we focus on the problems of revenue and expenditure imbalances, it is worth noting that they are symptomatic of ineffective governance as discussed in Chapter 13. The budget represents a key instrument of government policy. Choices regarding the levels and allocation of expenditure and the levels and distribution of taxation directly reflect the government's commitments to efficiency and equity. The outcome of the budget, in particular the coherence between the intended and actual amounts spent and taxed is an indication of the government's capacity to formulate and implement policy. Finally, the overall balance between expenditure and revenue in relation to the existing debt burden and ability to sustain additional debt service, reflect the government's general commitment to the future growth and stability of the economy. Thus, while the annual analysis of budget proposals and outcomes offers insights into the narrower fiscal issues of matching expenditures to available resources, the overall structure of the budget provides important information about the quality of governance.

Table 4-4 shows budgeted and actual revenues and expenditures for 1997.

On the revenue side, nominal tax collections were close to the amounts expected in the budget. Nonetheless, since inflation during 1997 was 24.5 percent while the budget was framed on the basis of 15 percent inflation, real revenue collections declined by approximately 5 percent. This had serious implications for real expenditures.

Table 4-4 *Central Government Budget Performance 1997, K billions*

	GRZ Budget	1997 Actual
Domestic Revenue	1000.2	1028.4
Tax Revenue	919.7	968.4
Nontax Revenue	80.5	60.0
Domestic Expenditure and		
Net Lending	938.3	893.4
Recurrent Domestic Exp.	715.8	822.5
Personal Emoluments	249.2	324.2
RDCs	145.6	140.0
Transfers and Pensions	130.1	164.2
Interest on Domestic Debt	91.	115.2
Other Current Expenditure	99.9	57.7
Contingency	100.	21.1
Capital Expenditure (GRZ)	122.5	70.8
Surplus/Deficit (accrual)	62.0	135.0
Payment of Arrears (net)	0.	68.9
Change in balances (net)	0.	14.1
DOMESTIC BALANCE (Cash)	62.	80.2

Source: Economic Report 1997 Table 2.6

Nontax revenue was well below the estimates. This has been a long-standing problem. The government has made numerous commitments to address the issue but without success. There are two issues. One is that some nontax revenue is not being collected. Another is that the revenue is being collected but not reported to the MoF. The former is a problem of compliance (discussed in more detail in Chapter 5). The latter is an example of how revenue issues and expenditure control overlap. Although the amounts of revenue do not appear to be large in 1997, at one point nontax revenue was around 13 percent of government revenue. The IMF referred to the problem in its program documents in 1994, and several public expenditure reviews supported by the World Bank have noted the adverse trend in this revenue component. By 1997, it continued to be a problem. The situation has not been remedied. Indeed, the government appears to have given up. Projected nontax revenue in the 2000 budget was K37 billion, significantly less than the actual nominal amount collected in 1997.

On the expenditure side, total domestic spending and net lending, before the payment of arrears, was less than the budgeted amount. With inflation well above the rate used to frame the budget, total real expenditure fell sharply.

Actual expenditure was markedly different from the planned allocation. For example, wages and salaries were higher than projected and capital expenditure was lower.

The data indicate that the target for the domestic surplus was achieved. Yet, based on evidence for arrears that emerged following the presentation of the budget, the surplus was in fact the result of the government having left many bills unpaid.

Since any budgeting exercise always depends on estimates, it is unreasonable to expect a budget to unfold without some modification. However, for budgeting to be a meaningful exercise, there have to be pressing reasons for altering both the amounts spent and their allocation. Moreover, any changes made should be guided by the principles of efficiency, effectiveness, and equity.

The MMD government has regularly reaffirmed its commitment to budget reform. Thus, at an aggregate level, the degree to which actual expenditure deviates from expected expenditure indicates the progress being made in meeting this commitment. In Zambia's case, two particularly relevant issues are whether the expenditure deviations represent a major departure from past trends and, if so, whether the budget is moving in directions that are sustainable. Based on these criteria, the 1997 budget, like those before it and after it, was fundamentally off-track. More important, there is nothing in the government's program to indicate how (and when) measures would be taken to bring the budget back on track. The budget speech 2000 does not address the issue. Indeed, that budget calls for a deficit of K124 billion (or slightly more than 2 percent of projected GDP).

As noted above, even though revenues were close to those expected at the time the budget was formulated, collections in real terms declined significantly. These revenue problems, however, are minor relative to the distortions evident on the expenditure side.

Based on past budgets, none of these distortions is surprising. Personal emoluments *always* exceed the amounts budgeted and capital expenditures *always* fall short of the budgeted amounts. Accordingly, the 1997 budget (like all budgets during the 1990s) failed to balance recurrent and capital expenditure in ways that could enhance efficiency. Moreover, the overexpenditure on wages was not matched by comparable increases in the allocation for operations and maintenance (RDCs). That perpetuated the recurrent cost problem that has been a feature of government budgeting since the economic crisis began in the mid-1970s.[31]

An interesting feature of actual expenditure in 1997 was the payment of K68.9 billion in arrears. The amount budgeted was zero. That is, when the

---

31. The problems created by the underfunding of recurrent costs was highlighted by the government itself in the reports "Restructuring in the Midst of Crisis" (GRZ 1984) and the "New Economic Recovery Program" (GRZ 1989).

budget was assembled no arrears were expected. At best, this was a fudge. As noted in the text, from the time the cash budget was introduced in 1993, some of the pressure on the budget has been reflected in unpaid bills.[32] A realistic approach in 1997 would have made a relatively large allowance for arrears. Doing that, however, would have required the government either to raise additional revenue or cut expenditure further, two choices it did not wish to make.

It is not clear how such a large overrun from the previous year emerged. The size of the arrears contradicted the government's claim that it had run a surplus in 1996. It also raises questions regarding the nature of the arrears payments. Were the amounts in fact overdue? Or did those payments include some current expenditure that would not have been allowed under the IMF agreement? Since arrears have been so poorly monitored, it has been difficult to tell.

A curious anomaly in the budget is the underestimate of the domestic interest payments relative to the amounts actually paid. The stock of government debt and the expected expense for re-capitalizing the BoZ were known at the start of the year. Moreover, since interest rates fell more rapidly[33] than had been anticipated, the error should have been in the other direction. This is a another area where the 1997 budget was fudged. By understating interest payments, it appeared as though total expenditure would be lower. Doing this ensured that the government would need to take fewer measures up-front to raise revenue or cut expenditure. (The same comment applies to the understatement of wage and salary payments.)[34]

A final point is that, contrary to expectations and the assertion of the minister of finance in his 1998 budget speech,[35] the domestic budget "surplus" was not used to retire domestic debt. Total domestic debt (T-bills and bonds) increased by K38 billion during 1997. When grants and foreign-financed cap-

---

32. Although the Kaunda regime incurred huge external arrears, it avoided domestic arrears through the use of "X-accounts" at the BoZ. At the end of each year, all outstanding bills were swept into these accounts, preventing arrears from spilling over to next year's budget. The effect was to increase the budget deficit which, as noted elsewhere in this study, reverberated throughout the whole economy.

33. As noted in Chapter 6, interest rates were "talked down" in 1997 when BoZ officials threatened to force commercial banks to hold cash if they did not raise their bids for T-bills (and therefore lower the rate of interest).

34. Based on its expenditure history, the government could have easily cut its estimate for capital expenditure, thereby reducing the need for additional revenue efforts or expenditure cuts. This approach, however, would have been politically unacceptable because it would have openly advertised that the government intended to make only a minimal contribution to capital expenditure. In the event, the predictable cuts in capital expenditure occurred.

35. Budget speech January 30, 1998, par. 41.

ital expenditures (which reduce financing requirements) and external debt service (which increase them) are considered, the government ran a budget deficit on an accrual basis of approximately K125 billion, or 2.4 percent of GDP.

None of these manipulations would matter if they were one-off adjustments to accommodate extraordinary pressures on the budget. These adjustments—the undercollection of nontax revenue, the overexpenditure on wages and salaries, the underspending on capital items, the strategic understatement of domestic interest payments, and the excess amounts due to settle arrears—are repeated every year. They fit a pattern of budgeting that spares the government from having to take measures that will genuinely reform the economy. All of the above manipulations involved inflating recurrent wage-based expenditure and deflating capital expenditure. This is not budgeting in a genuine sense but window dressing. It reaffirms that, despite years of attempted reforms, the budget continues to be mismanaged in Zambia and, as such, continues to be a source of macroeconomic instability.

5

Tax Reform in Zambia

CATHARINE B. HILL

1. Introduction

This chapter discusses fiscal policy and tax reform in Zambia. A distinguishing feature of economic management in Zambia since the mid-1970s has been large and persistent budget deficits. Since 1974 when the government ran a small surplus of 1 percent of GDP, the deficits have ranged up to 21.5 percent of GDP in 1986.[1] Over the entire period 1970 to 1991, the fiscal deficit in Zambia exceeded 10 percent of GDP. Deficits of this size for such an extended period dominate all aspects of macroeconomic policy.

There have been many explanations for the deficits. Zambia's leaders frequently pointed to the problems created by external events—wars in neighboring countries, transport disruptions, fluctuations in primary commodity prices, and the like—which imposed extra burdens on the government requiring deficit spending. Other commentators have focused on the domestic pressures to spend. Still others have highlighted the overexpansion of the public sector and declining tax yield because of fraud and evasion. All of these elements have been important since the mid-1970s.

A major issue facing the MMD government in 1991 was how to change fiscal policy so that it promoted growth and development. Particular attention was given to ways of reforming the tax system so as to strengthen the government's revenue base and enhance efficiency. Viewed in broad terms, significant progress has been made in the tax reform area. The government has successfully introduced a value-added tax (VAT), undertaken a comprehensive liberalization and rationalization of the tariff structure, eliminated a variety of nuisance and distorting taxes, and reduced and rationalized tax rates gen-

---

1. Overall surplus, including grants. Source, selected *Macroeconomic Indicators*, Section 4.

erally. At the same time, revenue performance has been weak, in part because of slow progress improving tax compliance and reducing evasion. The implication (noted in Chapters 4 and 6) is that tax performance has not significantly improved the fiscal situation in Zambia thus far.

This chapter examines the tax system as it existed when the government changed in 1991. It discusses the major accomplishments of the reform program since then. To illustrate the important links between tax reform and revenue collection, this chapter reviews work done on estimating the revenue implications of switching to a VAT from a sales tax. It concludes with an overview of remaining fiscal problems that need to be addressed.

The analysis is arranged as follows. Section 2 describes the tax regime in 1991 and then gives a brief overview of the tax reform program during the 1990s. Section 3 discusses a major component of the tax reform program—the implementation of the VAT. Section 4 discusses setbacks to the reform program. Section 5 examines additional issues. Section 6 has concluding comments. Two appendices deal with mining taxation and tax compliance.

2. THE TAX REFORM OF THE 1990S

Taxation is one method through which governments can finance expenditures. Borrowing domestically or from abroad are alternatives.[2] Zambia has been running large fiscal deficits for three decades, financed by both foreign and domestic borrowing. Tax reform has been a central component of the economic adjustment program during the 1990s. The government believed that increased revenues, along with greater control of government expenditure, could reduce the deficit as a means of stabilizing the economy and bringing inflation under control. Policy makers also recognized that the existing tax structure was highly distorted, generating unintended effects on prices and incentives, while at the same time significantly complicating compliance and enforcement.[3]

Zambia commenced a major tax reform program in 1991 to strengthen tax administration, raise revenue, and reform the tax code. During the next seven years, a variety of reforms were implemented and the tax regime in 1998 was characterized by a significantly wider tax base, lower rates, and fewer distortions.[4]

---

2. Auerbach and Feldstein 1985, 1987.

3. Ahmed and Stern 1989.

4. For a broad discussion of tax reform in developing countries see Thirsk (1997). Shome (1999) discusses experience in Latin America. There are many parallels to the debates on tax reform in Zambia.

Tax administration and compliance, however, have remained problematic. First mentioned in the 1992 budget speech as an area of concern, a variety of attempts were made to improve both the statutory structure of the tax regime and enforcement of existing laws. The creation of an independent tax administration, the Zambia Revenue Authority (ZRA) in 1994, has not produced the hoped-for results in terms of compliance. Future improvements in revenue collections must come from improved compliance and renewed economic growth. The general economic decline accompanying the demise of ZCCM reduced real incomes and Zambia's taxable capacity. Significant increases in revenue in the absence of economic growth will not be possible. Furthermore, there should also be some additional reductions in tax rates, many of which remain high by international standards.

The Second Republic

Total recurrent revenue (excluding grants) declined from the first half of the 1970s to the first half of the 1990s, contributing to the deteriorating fiscal performance in Zambia over this period. (Tax revenue as a percent of GDP is reported in Table 5–1.) From 1970 to 1974, revenue averaged almost 30 percent of GDP, with 11 percent from mineral revenues and 5.9 percent from nontax revenues. By the period 1990 to 1994, revenue had fallen to 19 percent of GDP, with only 1.5 percent from mining and 0.9 percent from nontax revenues. The declines in mineral revenues and nontax revenues more than explain the decline in recurrent revenues as a share of GDP.[5]

At the same time, until markets in Zambia were liberalized starting in the early 1990s, many of the taxes on the economy were implicit rather than explicit, and therefore not captured in the revenue data. The overvalued exchange rate taxed the tradable goods sector while subsidizing the consumption of imports. Several alternative measures of the real exchange rate can be calculated to measure the extent of overvaluation. A 1993 World Bank report discusses a variety of these measures.[6] All imply significant exchange rate overvaluation during the 1970s and 1980s, and therefore heavy, persistent taxation of tradable goods.

As tax revenues and foreign financing declined during the 1980s, government expenditures were also increasingly paid for by printing money. This type of tax, the "inflation tax," is highly distortionary, falling on those (mainly the poor) who cannot protect themselves. Inflation is a tax on money

---

5. World Bank, *Public Expenditure Review, Zambia* 1995, p. 157.
6. World Bank, Report no.11570-ZA, 1992, pp. 50–55

Table 5–1 *Tax Revenue as a Share of GDP*

YEAR	PAYE	COMPTX	OINCTX	EXCISE	DSALTX	MCORPTX	IMSALTX	CUSTOMS	IMPLVY	MINREV	TXREV
1968	0.020	0.017	0.005	0.025	0.000	0.040	0.000	0.020	0.000	0.126	0.253
1969	0.019	0.024	0.007	0.023	0.000	0.038	0.000	0.024	0.000	0.141	0.274
1970	0.024	0.026	0.005	0.028	0.000	0.063	0.000	0.026	0.000	0.135	0.306
1971	0.029	0.032	0.006	0.031	0.000	0.073	0.000	0.031	0.000	0.023	0.225
1972	0.031	0.029	0.008	0.041	0.000	0.021	0.000	0.031	0.000	0.021	0.181
1973	0.033	0.028	0.012	0.045	0.002	0.010	0.000	0.021	0.000	0.057	0.209
1974	0.029	0.024	0.018	0.052	0.005	0.032	0.000	0.020	0.000	0.107	0.288
1975	0.037	0.041	0.013	0.073	0.022	0.000	0.000	0.023	0.000	0.038	0.246
1976	0.039	0.033	0.012	0.070	0.026	0.000	0.000	0.015	0.000	0.006	0.201
1977	0.045	0.039	0.017	0.077	0.013	0.000	0.000	0.015	0.001	(0.001)	0.222
1978	0.043	0.037	0.017	0.079	0.014	0.000	0.016	0.012	0.002	0.000	0.214
1979	0.037	0.033	0.014	0.076	0.013	0.000	0.013	0.013	0.004	(0.004)	0.202
1980	0.039	0.037	0.013	0.074	0.015	0.000	0.016	0.016	0.005	0.014	0.228
1981	0.038	0.038	0.013	0.077	0.017	0.000	0.017	0.014	0.004	0.000	0.212
1982	0.033	0.037	0.012	0.087	0.017	0.000	0.016	0.015	0.006	0.000	0.213
1983	0.025	0.053	0.010	0.069	0.018	0.000	0.011	0.009	0.002	0.013	0.227
1984	0.021	0.034	0.013	0.049	0.015	0.000	0.012	0.012	0.004	0.019	0.204
1985	0.021	0.029	0.018	0.032	0.014	0.000	0.022	0.019	0.007	0.018	0.197
1986	0.022	0.028	0.015	0.025	0.015	0.000	0.032	0.031	0.006	0.031	0.212
1987	0.014	0.031	0.012	0.022	0.015	0.000	0.038	0.029	0.009	0.024	0.197
1988	0.012	0.030	0.007	0.022	0.015	0.014	0.026	0.018	0.007	0.004	0.156
1989	0.010	0.025	0.011	0.028	0.018	0.027	0.028	0.021	0.007	0.000	0.169
1990	0.010	0.032	0.005	0.036	0.019	0.031	0.038	0.029	0.004	0.000	0.195
1991	0.017	0.028	0.005	0.027	0.021	0.015	0.028	0.029	0.005	0.000	0.184
1992	0.034	0.023	0.004	0.021	0.022	0.017	0.028	0.025	0.007	0.000	0.188
1993	0.022	0.016	0.004	0.031	0.021	0.009	0.025	0.023	0.001	0.000	0.141
1994	0.031	0.019	0.007	0.028	0.034	0.002	0.032	0.030	0.002	0.000	0.187
1995	0.035	0.013	0.010	0.032	0.036	0.000	0.026	0.020	0.008	0.010	0.182
1996	0.032	0.015	0.010	0.032	0.034	0.000	0.028	0.026	0.008	0.005	0.188
1997	0.035	0.012	0.011	0.033	0.036	0.000	0.021	0.026	0.008	0.006	0.187
1998	—	—	—	—	—	—	—	—	—	—	—

Table 5-2 Tax Revenue by Component (millions of kwacha)

	PAYE	COMPTX	OINCTX	EXCISE	DSALTX	MCORPTX	IMSALTX	CUSTOMS	IMPLVY	MINREV	TXREV	NGDP
1968	21.0	17.6	5.5	26.7	N/A	42.2	N/A	21.2	N/A	134.0	268.2	1,062.0
1969	24.6	31.0	8.7	29.8	N/A	49.5	N/A	31.0	N/A	185.6	360.2	1,313.5
1970	30.6	32.9	6.5	34.9	N/A	79.6	N/A	32.5	N/A	171.5	388.5	1,268.5
1971	34.3	38.5	7.3	36.8	N/A	86.9	N/A	36.7	N/A	27.2	267.7	1,188.6
1972	41.3	39.4	10.5	55.6	N/A	28.0	N/A	41.9	N/A	27.7	244.4	1,348.0
1973	52.6	44.3	19.1	72.2	3.5	16.3	N/A	32.7	N/A	91.3	332.0	1,591.3
1974	55.0	46.2	33.8	98.3	10.0	60.5	N/A	37.8	N/A	203.2	544.8	1,892.6
1975	58.0	64.7	19.9	115.9	34.3	—	N/A	36.8	N/A	59.4	389.0	1,583.4
1976	74.0	61.9	23.2	132.5	49.2	—	N/A	29.0	N/A	11.6	381.4	1,895.8
1977	88.9	77.5	33.4	152.6	25.6	—	31.9	29.6	2.7	(1.2)	441.0	1,986.4
1978	96.7	82.9	38.2	177.1	31.7	—	23.5	27.2	4.4	0.1	481.8	2,250.7
1979	98.4	86.9	38.0	211.4	34.2	—	33.5	34.9	9.9	(9.8)	537.4	2,660.4
1980	119.5	113.1	38.7	232.8	40.5	—	49.0	49.1	14.4	41.7	698.8	3,064.0
1981	131.4	131.9	44.5	258.8	51.9	—	59.3	49.0	12.7	1.0	740.5	3,485.4
1982	120.2	132.7	43.5	277.0	59.9	—	58.7	52.3	20.1	—	764.4	3,595.0
1983	105.4	222.6	41.6	363.6	70.9	—	44.5	38.8	9.4	53.4	950.2	4,181.0
1984	104.0	167.3	66.2	341.7	90.3	—	61.0	61.3	18.1	94.5	1,004.4	4,931.0
1985	148.4	201.8	123.9	348.4	109.5	—	153.8	134.3	46.0	129.5	1,395.6	7,072.0
1986	287.9	363.0	194.0	409.4	184.3	—	414.4	406.6	79.2	405.4	2,744.2	12,963.1
1987	281.3	611.1	242.2	487.4	293.8	—	757.3	577.3	171.7	475.2	3,897.3	19,779.0
1988	350.9	908.9	205.2	667.0	458.0	415.3	795.0	550.1	218.3	113.3	4,682.0	30,021.0
1989	549.4	1,394.0	594.6	1,218.0	977.2	1,492.3	1,546.7	1,174.1	358.7	6.7	9,311.7	55,181.2
1990	1,092.3	3,601.3	595.3	3,163.1	2,182.2	3,500.0	4,288.5	3,288.2	433.3	—	22,144.2	113,340.0
1991	3,792.9	6,175.4	1,042.3	7,805.4	4,599.5	3,325.0	6,129.8	6,228.6	1,009.3	3.5	40,111.7	218,274.8
1992	19,249.1	13,050.9	2,215.1	15,597.6	12,765.2	9,939.6	16,207.4	13,974.0	4,160.9	53.9	107,213.7	569,563.6
1993	35,131.5	25,434.3	6,727.0	33,792.7	34,394.0	14,000.0	40,969.8	36,402.0	1,069.1	52.8	227,973.2	1,613,738.0
1994	69,732.0	42,768.0	16,470.0	70,204.0	76,104.0	5,064.0	72,087.0	66,449.0	0.0	65.0	418,879.0	2,240,700.0
1995	104,716.0	38,264.0	29,437.0	84,616.0	107,678.0	—	77,574.0	60,720.0	5,463.0	29,437.0	545,911.0	2,998,400.0
1996	128,123.0	58,256.0	38,239.0	126,623.0	133,154.0	—	110,224.0	101,338.0	31,341.0	20,451.0	747,675.0	3,970,300.0
1997	180,239.0	60,080.0	56,074.0	168,189.0	183,688.0		110,319.0	136,011.0	41,614.0	30,671.0	968,387.0	5,169,000.0
1998	249,000.0	90,000.0	42,000.0	211,000.0	200,000.0		200,000.0	284,819.0		17,000.0	1,093,819.0	

balances and can be estimated as the decline in real money balances that results from inflation, or:

$$M_t - M_t /(1+p) \text{ or } M_t (p/(1+p))$$

where M_t represents nominal money balances at the start of the period and p represents the period average inflation rate.[7] Chart 1 reports the estimate of the inflation tax as a share of GDP in Zambia over the last 20 years. It increased steadily during the 1980s, accelerating toward the end of the decade.[8] The reform program of the MMD government was committed to reducing the deficit and this form of financing government expenditures. In its place, the government adopted policies to improve tax collections and control expenditures.

From 1991 to the Present

By the end of 1991, the tax system was grossly distorted and ineffective, the cumulative result of deteriorating tax administration and *ad hoc* tax measures over the preceding two decades.[9] Tax reform was considered a major component of the MMD government's overall economic program. Macroeconomic stabilization required that the government deficit be reduced, in part by increasing revenue mobilization. The deficit in 1991 was 6.5 percent of GDP. Both expenditure and revenue measures were needed to close this gap. The structural adjustment program required that distortions created by the tax system be reduced.

A tax policy task force (TPTF) was established in 1992 to advise the government on reforming the tax system for the 1993 budget and beyond. It included representatives from the government as well as from the private sector. Its terms of reference called for implementing a tax system that was fair, more buoyant, simpler to administer, and more economically efficient. The task force report was issued in October 1992 and has guided policy reform since that time.[10]

---

7. Gillis *et al.*, 1992, p. 334.

8. One of the ironies of this inflation tax is that it has cost more real resources for the government than it gained. The partial equilibrium estimate of the inflation tax (given in the text) is a reasonable approximation of the real transfers to government when inflation rates are low. At high rates of inflation such as those experienced by Zambia from the mid 1980s onwards, the depreciation of the exchange rate leads to a major capital loss for the government as the local currency cost of servicing external debt rises. Unlike the one-off gain to the government from the inflation tax, the increased local currency cost of debt service is cumulative. This point is examined in more detail in McPherson (1999).

9. Alm, Bahl, and Murray (1991) give a detailed account of the tax base deterioration in developing countries.

10. GRZ 1992, hereafter TPTF.

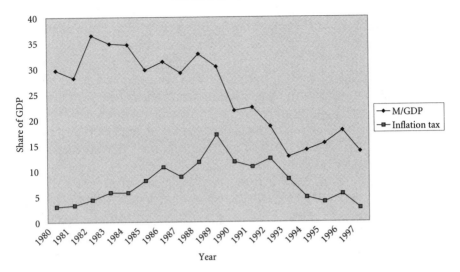

Chart 1.   Inflation Tax

The report stressed the need for major reforms, emphasizing the importance of getting inflation under control by restoring fiscal and monetary balance. It provided many specific recommendations on income taxes, customs
and excise, and the sales tax, having drawn on conclusions reached by working groups in each of these areas. It emphasized the need to shift to a tax system that was broad-based, with moderate and uniform tax rates, and with the
minimum of exemptions and special preferences. It also stressed that the tax
system should be simple and easy to administer. Finally, the report recognized the need to improve significantly the administrative capacity and motivation of the tax authorities.[11]

Initial Reforms: Tax reform began with the MMD government's first
budget. It cited declining compliance over the last decade as a major problem.
"Pay-as-you-earn" (PAYE, an income tax withheld and paid by the employer
on wage income) had declined from over 9 percent of employee compensation to 3 percent in 1990. Similar statistics were cited for company income tax
and the sales tax. The causes cited were excessive tax rates, which led to increasing evasion and inadequate tax enforcement.[12]

The 1992 budget began to address these issues. PAYE income tax brackets
were reduced from seven to three, with the top tax rate declining from 50 per-

---

11. TPTF, p. 3.
12. Budget speech 1992.

cent to 35 percent. At the same time, some previously untaxed allowances were pulled into the tax net.[13] The tax credit was increased to remove many low-income households from the tax rolls, thereby simplifying enforcement and reducing taxes for poorer households. The company income tax rate was reduced from 45 percent to 40 percent. Noncash fringe benefits were made taxable in the hands of the employer, since they were not taxed in the hands of the beneficiary. This was intended to encourage employers to cash out these benefits and offset the loss of revenue from the lower tax rates. Many companies previously exempt from company income tax became liable for the tax. Interest income above a certain level was made subject to a 10 percent tax. The sales tax was harmonized for imports and domestic production and unified at 20 percent. Excise taxes were similarly harmonized. To facilitate enforcement, the government increased penalties and began a program to computerize the tax system.

The PAYE system continued to be adjusted in subsequent budgets. The task force proposed indexing the tax brackets for inflation. The changes incorporated in the 1992 Budget were meant to address previous bracket creep and significantly reduce the tax burden on formal sector employees.[14] Automatic adjustment has not been put in place, however, because of the government's general inability to keep the budget under control. With fiscal targets a key feature of Zambia's agreements with the IMF, significant pressure remained on revenue collections. Instead, with inflation still running in double digits, the tax credit and the bands have been adjusted each year, although seldom adequately to avoid bracket creep.

The company income tax rate was further reduced to 35 percent in the 1993 budget. Preferential rates of 15 percent for farmers and nontraditional exporters were retained. They were recognized to be distortionary but due to political pressure could not be changed. Inflation caused major distortions to the company income tax, but the complexity involved in addressing these issues led them to be postponed. The 1993 budget also streamlined the tax system, eliminating several nuisance taxes, which raised little revenue. These included the selective employment tax, the education levy, and a mineral export tax.

Customs reform under the MMD government started in 1993. The num-

---

13. In the 1996 budget, almost all fringe benefits were finally brought into the tax net. At the same time, the bands were again broadened and the maximum tax rate was reduced to 30 percent.

14. TPTF, pp. 23–24. The exemption was meant to remove all taxpayers from the tax rolls who earned less than 1.65 times GDP per capita. The top marginal tax rate of 35 percent was projected to apply to income above 2.3 times per capita GDP. Because of unexpectedly high inflation, the exemption level was less than per capita income and the 35 percent rate applied to income above 1.25 times per capita GDP.

ber of rates was reduced, while the maximum rate was reduced from 100 percent to 40 percent, and goods previously subject to 15 percent or 20 percent
were taxed at a standard minimum rate of 20 percent. Reforms continued
with each budget, so that Zambia currently has made more progress toward
liberalization than other countries in the region. This is particularly the case
in the area of trade reform, discussed in more detail in Chapter 8. Table 5-3
summarizes the broad changes in the tax system between 1992 and 1998.

3. Major Reform: The Implementation of the VAT

In addition to these changes in tax policy in 1992 and 1993, major reforms
occurred with respect to sales tax, tax administration, customs rates and policy, and the mining sector. We will discuss the first of these here, using as an
example of tax reform the implementation of the VAT. The chapter ends by
describing setbacks to the reform program and the remaining areas where
further reforms are still needed.

Table 5–3   *Changes in the Tax Regime in Zambia—1992 to 1998*

	1992	1998
Income Tax		
CIT	40%	35%
PAYE	15% for farmers and nontraditional exporters	unchanged
	top rate of 35%	top rate of 30%
	benefits excluded in net	benefits included in net
Trade taxes		
Rates	top rate 100%	top rate 25%
Number of rates	six	four
Imports sales tax uplift	20% eliminated	
Exemptions	many (including GRZ, churches, charities, returning residents tightened)	most eliminated
Sales Tax	23%	Replaced by 17.5% VAT with limited list of zero rates and exemptions
Investment Incentives		
Income tax holidays	yes	eliminated
Duty and sales tax		
Exemptions	yes	eliminated
Other taxes		
Education levy	yes	eliminated
Export tax	yes	eliminated

History of the VAT

Zambia introduced a sales tax in 1975. There were numerous problems with the sales tax as it had evolved. There was significant double taxation. The sales tax included a credit mechanism, but only on inputs incorporated into final products. Capital goods, power, and business services were not subject to the credit mechanism.

The sales tax was applied at the border on imports and at the factory gate on domestically produced goods. It therefore excluded from the tax base the value of distribution and retailing activities.[15] In 1991, that value amounted to approximately 7.6 percent of GDP, or 10 percent of private consumption, which is the base of a VAT. Exempting traders from the sales tax also created distortions. Manufacturers were discouraged from undertaking distribution services, even if they could do so efficiently. The tax applied to services provided by manufacturers, while it did not when traders supplied them.

In 1991, administration and compliance of the sales tax were also poor. Administrative responsibility for the sales tax was placed under the customs and excise authorities. Customs and excise officers were not trained in sales tax administration. Moreover, they were rotated in and out of sales tax, undercutting the value of on-the-job training and work experience. The list of companies subject to the sales tax was out of date. Field inspections were cursory at best. Sales tax officers lacked the statutory authority for proper enforcement.

Zambia successfully replaced the sales tax with a VAT in mid-1995. The TPTF had strongly recommended the switch to a VAT and had done the preliminary ground work for the transition. A VAT implementation committee (VATIC) was set up, chaired by the MoF with members from the Ministry of Commerce, Trade and Industry (MCTI), and the ZRA, to oversee the introduction of the tax.

The VAT was intended to broaden the tax base, eliminate the distortions created by the cascading of the sales tax, and improve the competitiveness of Zambia's exports. It shifted the tax burden from investment towards consumption.

To protect the poor, a variety of goods and services were made exempt.[16] These included basic food, health, education, bus fares and house rents. It was understood that zero rating would have been preferable to eliminate the

---

15. TPTF, p. 71.

16. In general, redistribution was a direct objective of tax reform in Zambia. Chu, Davoodi, and Gupta (2000) show that tax (and transfer) policies have had limited impact in developing countries. Tax reform as a component of sound macroeconomic and structural policies can have a positive effect on (i.e., improve) income distribution.

tax from these commodities, because this would have allowed producers to receive a refund for any tax paid on inputs. However, compliance considerations dominated the initial decisions and exemption was chosen rather than zero rating. The possibility of exempting some agricultural inputs was considered as a complement to exempting agricultural output. Exports were zero rated to contribute to international competitiveness. However, exemptions dominated zero rating so that exports were treated as exempt and not zero-rated. This put exporters of exempt goods and small-scale exporters, which were effectively exempt, at a disadvantage because they could not reclaim the VAT paid on inputs. This mostly affected the export of agricultural goods.

After a year of operation, several changes were made. Numerous goods were moved to the zero-rate schedule from the exempt schedule, because of the disadvantage that exemption created for domestic producers whose activities competed with importers. Some goods previously exempt become fully taxable, such as cooking oil, salt, and nondairy products. This eliminated the distortions that exemption created for producers, while the after-tax incomes of poor households were left approximately unchanged. The prices of goods that went from exempt to fully taxable were expected to increase, while those that became zero rated would no longer include the cost of tax on inputs. The share of zero-rated goods in poor consumer households' expenditures in 1994 (37 percent) was three times the share of goods that went from being exempt to fully taxable.[17]

Initially, suppliers with a value of taxable supplies of K30 million (US $34,500 in 1995) and above were required to register for VAT. The government expected that approximately 4,000 firms would register under this threshold. At the time, this was the number that ZRA officials considered manageable. The members of VATIC discussed voluntary registration but decided not to allow it during the first six months of the operation of the VAT. They realized that this would put small firms at a disadvantage. By not allowing registration, small firms effectively became exempt, and any VAT paid on inputs could not be taken as a credit against tax owed. If exporting or selling to other producers, these firms were put at a cost disadvantage relative to firms that could register for the VAT. Effective implementation of the VAT was limited by ZRA's administrative capacity. Accordingly, the government decided to limit registrations. If implementation went smoothly, voluntary registration would be considered during the 1996 budget.

Several goods and services, including phone calls and vehicles, were made

---

17. This percentage was derived from the Consumer Expenditure Survey (1994), published by the Central Statistics Office, Lusaka.

non-deductible under the VAT. In theory, employer-provided benefits are taxable unless otherwise exempted. Given the difficulty of monitoring such benefits, an alternative is not to allow input VAT deductions on a variety of items that are commonly used as employee benefits. At the same time, deductions are allowed where goods are purchased as stock-in-trade or sales inventory to avoid tax cascading. This was an important consideration in the case of vehicles.

The government planned for the VAT to be computerized from the start. In the end, a manual system was introduced. After twelve months, significant parts of the tax were still not computerized. The registration of VAT payers was computerized and a VAT number assigned, but full computerization took several more years.[18]

In designing the VAT, the plan was to set the rate so that the revenue yield would initially equal that of the sales tax. As compliance improved, the intention was to reduce the rate. Initial revenue estimates suggested that a rate of 20 percent would yield adequate revenue to replace the sales tax, even taking into account lost revenue from the transition from the old tax to the VAT. This was important, because the VAT was introduced in mid-1995, while the government was in the midst of completing a Rights Accumulation Program (RAP) with the IMF and negotiating an Enhanced Structural Adjustment Facility (ESAF), both of which included demanding fiscal performance criteria. A significant decline in revenue would have presented problems for the fiscal targets included in these programs. The VAT at a rate of 20 percent was also below the existing sales tax rate of 23 percent. The reduction in the rate helped convince the public that the switch from a sales tax to a VAT was to their advantage.

Revenue Estimates for the VAT[19]

The reform of a country's tax system, especially the substitution of one type of tax for another, causes considerable uncertainty for revenue collection. For example, the shift from a sales tax to a VAT entails a fundamental change in the tax base. Specifically, the credit under the VAT for the tax paid on inputs, while essential for avoiding cascading of the tax, makes the determination of the tax base more complicated than under a sales tax. Further-

---

18. HIID developed a fully operational VAT computer system as part of the Computerization and Tax Administration Project (CMTAP). That system was completed in June 1995. ZRA officials showed no interest in using it. When CMTAP moved to the MoF, key parts of the system were adapted for data recording (especially imports) and for collecting the import declaration fee, IDF.

19. This section draws extensively on Hill and Pellechio (1996).

more, because of the input tax credit, the VAT is the only tax that can pay revenue to taxpayers, in particular, exporters, on a regular basis. Consequently, government officials were understandably concerned about the impact on revenue of such a major change in taxation.

As a result of the concern about revenue implications in countries shifting to a VAT, the estimation of its base and revenue is critical to policymakers. For a particular country, this estimation has generally followed one of two alternative methods.[20] One method starts with GDP, which represents the aggregate value-added from production and distribution activities in the economy, and makes adjustments for imports, exemptions, and zero rating needed to arrive at the value-added included in the base of the VAT.[21] Another method that takes advantage of the fact that the VAT is ultimately paid by consumers. It starts with final consumption and adjusts for exempted and zero-rated goods and services to arrive at the base of the VAT.[22]

The first method follows the production side of the economy by constructing the VAT base from increments to value-added. The second method focuses on the consumption side and concentrates on final sales of goods and services which incorporate total value added from all stages of production and distribution in the economy. In principle, these two methods should arrive at the same result. However, this is not immediately apparent when particular goods and services are exempt from the VAT, as is normally the case, because different adjustments for intermediate sales are required under each method.[23]

In most countries, one or the other of those has been applied to estimate the VAT base and expected revenue. Both methods were used in Zambia to estimate the revenue effects of switching to a VAT. This was done to take advantage of both production and consumption data to cross-check estimates and obtain a better sense of the range of possible outcomes for projected revenue. The remainder of this section demonstrates how these two methods produced different results, explains why, and suggests how these differing estimates were used in the reform program.

Production method: The production method begins with aggregate GDP, which is the total value added from domestic production of goods and services. Because Zambia's VAT is applied to imports, the value of imports must

20. An exception is Gandhi, *et al.*, (1990).

21. An application of this methodology can be found in Aguirre and Shome (1988). Exemptions and zero rating, and their importance in the calculation of the VAT base, are described below.

22. Mackenzie (1992) presents this methodology.

23. Hill and Pellechio (1996) demonstrate the equivalence of these two approaches.

be added to aggregate GDP in the computation of the base. Given the credit for purchases of capital goods, the consumption-based VAT adopted in Zambia requires the subtraction of gross domestic capital formation (GDCF) from the base. However, the residential construction component of GCDF is taxed and, therefore, must be added to the base. Because the exempt sectors will not receive credit for purchases of capital goods, the share of GDCF in exempt sectors also is added to the base. Although all government purchases should be taxed, government expenditure on wages and salaries, which is part of GDP (at market prices), is not taxable and has to be subtracted from the base. Sales tax revenue that is included in GDP and to be replaced by the VAT must be removed from the base. Zambia's VAT has thirteen exempt categories of goods and services and six zero-rated categories, of which the most important is exports. Exempt and zero-rated goods and services have to be subtracted from the base. Exempt imports are also subtracted from the base, while exempt exports must be added back to avoid double counting.

Table 5–4 presents the computation of the VAT base for 1995 based on the production method and shows all additions and subtractions to GDP in column (2). The calculations in column (2) were based on the revised GDP data for 1994 provided by the Central Statistics Office (CSO) in Lusaka. The proportions of exempt and zero-rated supplies in GDP were computed for 1994 and applied to the IMF's projection of GDP in 1995 to compute the VAT base in 1995. The computation also relies on the IMF's projections for imports, exports, GDCF, government wages and salaries, and sales tax revenue in 1995.

It is important to emphasize that categories of exempt and zero-rated supplies specified in a VAT usually do not correspond exactly to sectors reflected in GDP data. This is a common problem in the calculation of the VAT base, not only in Zambia but elsewhere. Often a detailed breakdown of GDP sectors, if available, is needed to calculate the proportions of exempt and zero-rated supplies in GDP. For example, in Zambia, the category of food and livestock supplies which is exempt under the VAT comprises the agriculture sector in the GDP data plus one-half of the food and beverage component of the GDP subsector for food, beverage, and tobacco products. One-half of the food and beverage component is an approximation of the exempt portion. This approximation was necessary because a more detailed breakdown of GDP permitting a closer match with exempt food supplies in the VAT law was not available.

In order to complete the computation of the VAT base, it is necessary to calculate the value of exempt sales to the taxed sector. The information needed for this calculation was obtained from the 1985 input-output table prepared by the CSO. Although it could be argued that the 1985 input-output

Table 5–4   *Zambia: Estimate of VAT Base in 1995—Production Method (billions of kwacha)*

(1)	(2)	(3)
+ Imports	1240.9	
− Exempt imports	110.7	
+ Exempt exports	33.1	
− Gross domestic capital formation	486.1	
+ Residual building	72.9	
+ Capital formation in exempt sectors	78.5	
− Government wages and salaries	130.0	
− Sales tax replaced by VAT	96.8	
+ Output sold to		
Exempt sectors	− **Value added taxed sectors**	
Food and livestock supplies	858.5	159.8
Pesticides and fertilizers	6.5	9.0
Health supplies	16.8	0.3
Educational supplies	55.3	1.7
Books and newspapers	22.9	56.8
Transport services	32.3	63.6
Conveyance of real property	78.2	18.4
Financial and insurance services	45.0	26.1
Gold	0.0	0.0
Funeral services	4.7	10.8
Gaming and betting	0.0	0.0
Privileged supplies	0.0	0.0
Travelers' effects	*0.0*	*0.0*
Total	1,120.3	345.5
Zero-rated sectors		
Exports	974.9	
Services linked to exports	0.0	
Duty free	0.0	
Aircraft stores	0.0	
Aviation kerosene	4.1	
Exported services	*0.0*	
Total	979.0	
Base net of exemptions and zero-rating	1,886.0	
− Loss from turnover threshold	64.5	
− Loss from noncompliance (50 percent)	910.8	
ESTIMATED VAT BASE	910.8	
Share of GDP	0.3	

Memorandum: 1995 GDP estimate K3, 038 billion.
Sources: Central Statistics Office and authors' estimates (Hill and Pellechio, 1996).

table does not closely represent the structure of the Zambian economy in the mid-1990s, it, nonetheless, provided the best available data on the transactions between the exempt and taxed sectors at the time. The value of sales to the taxed sector for each exempt sector was scaled to 1995 levels by the changes in value added of that sector between 1985 and 1995.

As with the GDP data, categories of goods exempt under the VAT often do not match sectors in the input-output table. For example, only 80 percent of the sector for pesticides, fertilizers, and industrial chemicals is estimated to be exempt. Consequently, the entries in the input-output table for this sector were multiplied by .8 on the assumption that 80 percent of the output of this sector used for production in other sectors was exempt. It is important to recognize that the input-output table for transactions between taxed and exempt sectors is not constructed by simply aggregating sectors from a basic input-output table for Zambia. Because sectors in the input-output table did not match the exempt supplies in the VAT law, it was necessary to combine percentages of entries from the input-output table, utilizing informed estimates of exempt portions of certain sectors. In other words, the basic task is to build up each row and column in the matrix from the more detailed input-output table for Zambia. This entails combining percentages of sectors in the input-output table that represent exempt portions of those sectors.

The outcome was a 14x14 input-output matrix for all taxed supplies and the thirteen exempt sectors under the VAT.[24] The thirteen categories of exempt supplies were constructed by aggregating and weighting sectors from the basic input-output table as discussed above. The remaining sectors comprised all taxed supplies and were aggregated into the first sector in the matrix (i.e., taxable goods).

The sales of exempt goods to the taxed sector in the matrix are added to the VAT base (Column 3 of Table 5–4). These sales are added because they are incorporated in the VAT base for the taxed sector.

An adjustment is made for the effect on the base of the threshold for registration as a taxpayer under the VAT in Zambia. This threshold was set at K30 million on an annual basis, meaning that businesses with annual gross sales less than this amount do not have to register and, therefore, do not pay the VAT on their sales. This was assumed to reduce the VAT base by 10 percent from the level already calculated excluding imports. These adjustments result in a potential base of K1,821.5 billion or approximately 60 percent of GDP (not shown in Table 5–4).

The potential base was adjusted for the level of tax compliance in Zambia. Tax compliance has been low in Zambia for a variety of reasons including failure by businesses to register as taxpayers or to file tax returns, underreporting of sales, failure to collect taxes on imports because of smuggling and other forms of evasion. Informed speculation by individuals familiar with Zambia's tax collection system is that only one-third to one-half of potential revenue is collected. The compliance rate was assumed to be 50 per-

---

24. See Hill and Pellechio (1996).

cent so that the loss in potential VAT due to noncompliance is 50 percent. This yields a final estimated VAT base under the production method of K910.8 billion, or 30 percent of GDP, in 1995.

Consumption method: The consumption method for calculating the VAT base for 1995 is presented in Table 5–5. Private consumption is taken from the IMF's GDP projections for 1995. Government expenditure on goods and services is taken from the government's budget for 1995. Purchases of goods and services are a component of recurrent departmental charges (RDCs). Total budgeted government expenditure on goods and services for 1995 is K85 billion. Using the household expenditure survey, approximately 60 percent of private consumption is for exempt goods. The budget breaks down government purchases of goods and services in enough detail to identify exempt purchases. For 1995, approximately K21.4 billion was budgeted for government consumption expenditure on exempt items. According to the budget, a significantly smaller share of government consumption than of private consumption was for exempt goods. This is to be expected because many goods were exempted to eliminate some of the tax on items that are important in the consumption of low-income households. These items account for a smaller share of government consumption expenditure.

The adjustment for VAT paid on residential investment and GDCF in the exempt sectors is identical to that in the production method. The adjustments for sales tax paid and turnover threshold are also the same.

As discussed above, it is necessary to calculate the value of taxable inputs

Table 5–5   *Zambia: Estimate of VAT Base in 1995—Consumption Method (billions of kwacha)*

Final consumer expenditure	
Private consumption expenditure	2,509.7
Government purchases of goods and services	85.0
− Exempted expenditure	
Private consumption expenditure	1,505.8
Government purchases of goods and services	21.4
+ Taxable gross domestic fixed capital formation	
Residential sector	72.9
Capital expenditure in exempt sectors	78.5
+ Taxable inputs into exempted expenditures	170.1
− Sales tax	96.8
− Loss from turnover threshold	64.5
− Loss from noncompliance (50 percent)	613.9
ESTIMATED VAT BASE	613.9
Share of GDP	0.2

Sources: Central Statistics Office and authors' estimates (Hill and Pellechio, 1996)

sold to the exempt sectors. The information for this calculation comes from the same source for computing the sales of exempt goods to the taxed sector under the production method, specifically the 14x14 input-output matrix referred to earlier.

As for the production method, the potential base of K1,227.7 billion (not shown in Table 5–5) was reduced by 50 percent to adjust for noncompliance. The final estimated VAT base equals K613.9 billion in 1995, which is 20 percent of GDP.

Key differences between the production and consumption methods: Both methods rely heavily on the consumption share of GDP in calculating the tax base. The major differences arise in the adjustments to the base that result from exemptions. The adjustment in the production method for the value added of exempt goods is significantly smaller than in the case of household expenditure data. Both sets of data have problems. The GDP data are based on the 1985 input-output table. The production data will be biased to the extent that changes in the structure of the economy are not reflected in that table. This will alter the total value of sales of exempt goods to the taxed sector. For example, an increased share of food and livestock would imply a higher value of sales of exempt goods to the taxed sector, which would increase the VAT base calculated using the production method.

In the household survey, expenditure categories are not detailed enough to assure that the shares assigned to exempt goods are, in fact, exempt. This method may therefore overstate expenditures on exempt items.

A discrepancy between the two methods is also introduced by the way government consumption is handled. In the production method, the base includes total consumption,[25] from which government wages and salaries are subtracted. In the consumption approach, government expenditure on goods and services, obtained directly from the budget, is explicitly included in the base. For 1995, government consumption reported in the GDP accounts does not equal government expenditure on goods and services plus wages and salaries. There is a discrepancy of K32.6 billion, which contributes to the difference in the estimated base obtained using the two methods.

An important difference between the methods remains. For simplicity, the same compliance rate of 50 percent was assumed for both methods, although it is not necessarily the case. Even given this assumption, a change in the compliance rate yields a different magnitude of adjustment of the VAT base under the two methods. For example, if the compliance rate is 10 percentage points

---

25. Computed as consumption equals GDP minus exports plus imports minus gross domestic capital formation.

lower, the estimated VAT base declines by the 6 percentage points of GDP under the production method and 4 percentage points under the consumption method. Uncertainty about compliance introduces considerable variation in the estimate of the VAT base.

Comparison with actual VAT collection in 1995:   As mentioned, Zambia introduced a VAT on July 1, 1995. Given that the VAT rate is 20 percent and the tax was in effect for half of 1995, estimated half-year revenue under either the production or consumption method equals 10 percent of its respective estimated base. Given the estimated VAT bases presented in Tables 5–4 and 5–5, VAT revenue for the second half of 1995 is estimated to range from 2 percent of GDP based on the consumption method to 3 percent based on the production method. This range is wide and somewhat disappointing, given the need for as much precision as possible in projecting government revenue. However, such variation is to be expected, given the deficiencies in data used for both methods, the approximations made to compute categories of exempt and zero-rated goods, and the consequent empirical differences between the two methods discussed above.

In the second half of 1995, that is, the first six months of operation of the VAT, revenue collection totaled K76.3 billion, which is 2.5 percent of GDP. This falls in the middle of the range obtained from the two methods of calculating the VAT base. A benefit of calculating the VAT base using two methods that are supposed to be equivalent is that, even when the two methods in fact produce different estimates for the various reasons discussed here, an estimated range for the outcome is obtained.[26]

Overview

The VAT performed well in its first few years. Revenue collected was close to projections, and significantly above the revenue collected under the sales tax. This assessment needs to be tempered by the fact that the estimates of revenue include an allowance of 50 percent for noncompliance. Thus, while the VAT represents an improvement on the sales tax, considerable room for enhanced performance remains.

Some problems have arisen for firms requesting refunds. The budget has

---

26. Given the variation in the estimated VAT base introduced by uncertainty about compliance, it is important to note that estimates under the production and consumption methods could, depending on the assumed compliance rate, both be above or below the actual outcome. For example, if the compliance rate were 10 percentage points lower, estimated VAT revenue would be 2.4 percent of GDP under the production method and 1.6 percent under the consumption method.

been under severe pressure. While the importance of making refunds under the VAT was emphasized as being vital to its success, repayment problems have dogged the system. Experience under the duty drawback program was used in designing the VAT refund mechanism. Rather than all VAT collections being deposited into the government accounts at the central bank, some are withheld and transferred to an account from which refunds are paid. This is designed to protect revenue for refunds. When facing tight budget conditions, to meet IMF conditionality, the refund account can still be underfunded. In general, however, performance on refunds has continued to improve.

There were expectations that the VAT would considerably improve compliance on other taxes. The VAT provided to the revenue authorities detailed information that could in principle be used to enforce compliance on both the income tax and on customs and excise taxes. These benefits have been slow to materialize. In part, this has been the result of slow computerization of all tax systems. As computerization proceeds, the cross-checking among different taxes may become routine.[27]

4. Setbacks to the Tax Reform Program

As described in Chapter 3, the government was implementing a RAP with the IMF from 1992 to 1995. During the first half of 1995, the program was at risk due to a major budget gap that arose from both the expenditure and revenue sides. Under IMF pressure to complete the RAP and finalize the negotiations for the ESAF, the government adopted an emergency package to bring the budget back on course.

The gap arose for several reasons. The government had underestimated domestic arrears that had arisen during 1994 and were still outstanding at the start of 1995. Only a token amount was budgeted to clear these arrears in 1995, with ministries being informed that they would have to clear any arrears out of their allocations for 1995. These allocations had not been determined taking existing arrears into account, and were highly compressed in any case. The interest expense on the domestic debt was also underestimated. The original estimate was based on an interest rate of 20 to 25 percent, while the rates were close to 50 percent by mid year. Several tax breaks, in particular the reduction on duty on raw materials (discussed in greater detail in Chapter

---

27. It should be noted that the Zambian revenue authorities both pre- and post-ZRA have shown little interest in using data from one part of the tax system to strengthen compliance in other parts.

8) involved greater revenue loss than had been expected. At the same time, expenditure on defense during the first four months of the year exceeded the budget by 75 percent and civil service wage payments also exceeded budgeted amounts.

While some commitment by the government to rescue the economic recovery program was vital, the package of tax measures adopted in mid-1995 was retrogressive. The government had been strongly urged not to let the budget slip earlier in the year. But, given that this was not done, the tax measures were the only feasible option to restore revenue and budget performance.

The measures adopted included making copper production and telephone calls exempt under the VAT, increasing the withholding tax rates from 10 percent to 25 percent, increasing the excise on petroleum from 30 percent to 45 percent, increasing the excise on beer from 75 percent to 100 percent, and introducing a 5 percent fee on imports, the import declaration fee (IDF). Making copper an exempt item under the VAT meant that the copper company, ZCCM, could not reclaim VAT paid on inputs. These indirect taxes would increase ZCCM's costs. This measure was effective at raising revenue, but ran counter to the tax reform program, intended to reduce the indirect taxation of businesses, particularly exporters. All other exports of nonexempt goods were zero-rated, completely eliminating the VAT from their prices. It also placed additional financial stress on ZCCM that, given its inefficiency, increased its losses.

The policy was rationalized on the grounds that efficiency problems at the copper company were primarily the result of factors other than indirect taxation. There was also a feeling that the copper sector was not paying its fair share, with both the royalty and the income tax proving difficult to enforce. It was recognized at the time that the tax would have to be removed, and copper was removed from the exempt schedule on April 1, 1996, in anticipation of privatization.

The increase in withholding tax was widely unpopular. Withholding tax applies to interest income, dividends, rental income, and management and consulting fees.[28] The justification for increasing the rate was that many taxpayers treat the withholding tax as the final tax on income. With income tax rates of 15 percent to 35 percent, withholding of 10 to 15 percent was a regressive tax. Taxation of rental income has been subject to high rates of evasion, so a higher withholding tax on rental income was considered acceptable.

---

28. Contractors and suppliers were subject to withholding on sales. This rate was not increased in 1995, and the tax was eliminated with the 1996 budget.

In any case, the withholding tax was reduced to 15 percent in the following budget.

Policymakers initially proposed doubling the excise tax on petroleum. It is an easy tax to collect, since it is paid by the oil company (ZNOC) and passed on to consumers. Fuel prices in Zambia were low by international standards, so this tax change seemed less regressive and distortionary than alternatives. In the end, the increase in the excise rate was cut in half, and the necessary revenue raised by imposing a 5 percent import surcharge (the IDF). The IDF increased protection at a time when Zambia was trying to reduce tariff distortions. It was declared a temporary measure at the time, to expire by the end of 1996. The IDF was not removed until mid 1998.

The increase in the excise on beer was a political move. There was no evidence that it would actually increase revenue. The government thought it would be difficult to return to Parliament requesting a variety of tax rate increases, having reduced the rate on beer in the budget five months earlier. (The evidence on excise taxes is discussed in greater detail below.)

5. ADDITIONAL MATTERS

Despite significant progress since 1991 in reforming the statutory tax system in Zambia, a variety of areas require further attention. As a result of the TPTF's work and the formation of working groups, an institutional mechanism has been put in place to address these issues. Each year, within the constraints of revenue and administrative capacity, further progress has been made in the tax reform area. Before concluding, several of the remaining issues are briefly discussed.

Property Transfer Tax: Zambia has had a property transfer tax since 1984. It is a flat rate tax on the value realized from the transfer of certain property. Initially, the rate was set at 2.5 percent, but was then increased to 7.5 percent. The property transfer tax is a turnover tax on the sales value of property transactions. The tax applies whether or not profit has been made on the sale, discouraging assets from being traded.

An alternative would be a capital gains tax that would apply the income tax rate to the gain from the sale of property. The TPTF report recognized the distortions created by the property transfer tax, and proposed moving toward a capital gains tax, though not immediately because of the administrative complexity involved. Instead, the TPTF proposed replacing the 7.5 percent rate with a 10 percent tax on the "adjusted value," defined as the gross sale value of an asset less the initial purchase price. To improve compliance, the report proposed that the gross sale value be determined by the taxpayer declaration, but giving the government the right to purchase property at a 20 percent premium over declared value, to minimize underreporting. The report also proposed including payments for land in the property transfer tax. While the act implementing the property transfer tax included land as property, land had no value under the Land Act until it was amended in 1995. [29]

The proposals of the TPTF did not include an adjustment for inflation on the net proceeds from property sales. It was felt that this would introduce excessive complexity and also create distortions since other taxes did not include inflation adjustments. The low tax rate proposed of 10 percent (compared to higher income tax rates) was considered a partial offset to taxing nominal gains.

The 1992 budget speech announced that the property transfer tax would be repealed during the year and replaced with a capital gains tax. This has yet to be done. In the 1994 budget, the property transfer tax rate was reduced from 7.5 percent to 2.5 percent, in an attempt to limit its distortionary effects and improve compliance.

Land Taxation: Zambia does not currently have a property or wealth tax. In an effort to increase the tax to GDP ratio, such a tax has been considered. The change in the Land Act, giving land value, has made it possible to include land in the base of a wealth tax.

The Income Tax Act: Inflation creates distortions in the company income tax. Inflation, for example, results in understatement of wear and tear allowances if based on original cost of assets. Similarly, inventory valuations will be distorted, understating expenses and overstating incomes. The task force considered an inflation adjustment, based on the Chilean model for the company tax, but rejected it for several reasons. It was considered administratively complicated and it involved a large revenue loss that the government did not want to sustain.[30]

There is general dissatisfaction with the Income Tax Act. The TPTF recognized that inflation seriously distorted company tax liabilities, but did not attempt to amend the act. It recommended creating a committee to study possible solutions. Little has been done since.

Excise Taxes: When tariff reform started, the government increased excises on some commodities (wine and spirits) and introduced new excises (on cars and tires). The intention was to sustain revenue and retain taxes on

---

29. TPTF, pp. 33–8.

30. TPTF, Position Paper No. 1, "Company tax reforms for 1993," October 26, 1992, MoF, Lusaka.

goods consumed by higher income groups as tariff rates were reduced. Excise taxes have been changed every year, however, with little consistency on rates and commodities involved.

The excise on clear beer is an example. The rate was initially 125 percent. During October 1994, the rate was reduced to 100 percent, in response to petitions from the beer industry that the high rates were reducing demand significantly and shifting consumption to smuggled beer. Evidence was produced to show that government revenues were in fact declining. Analysis undertaken by the MoF had shown that revenues could increase, or rather not decrease, if rates were lowered. In the 1995 budget, the rate was further reduced to 75 percent. Half way through the year (June 16), however, in response to a fiscal gap, the rate was returned to 100 percent.

Several problems exist with enforcement of the beer excise. The military is entitled to an exemption on the excise on beer, as well as on spirits, soda, and cigarettes (S.I. No. 67 of 1992). Much of this beer makes its way to the private market. The higher the excise rate, the greater the incentive to resell beer. While officials are well aware of the leakage, this exemption has been impossible to eliminate. Similarly, there is much anecdotal evidence of large quantities of beer being smuggled from abroad.

Increasing the excise rate in 1995 did not increase real tax revenues. Using monthly data from 1995 to December 1997, the correlation between real excise revenues from beer and the excise rate is zero. Thus, the rise in beer excise did nothing to raise revenues; it simply complicated tax administration.

The excise on spirits has been equally volatile. Starting at 25 percent in 1992, it was increased to 100 percent in the 1993 budget speech. Then, in response to threatened closure by the domestic bottler, the excise on domestic production was reduced to 35 percent in October of 1994. This effectively increased protection of the domestic bottler by huge proportions. That protection was eliminated with the mid-1995 revenue measures, when the excise was set at 70 percent for both domestic production and imports (June 16, 1995). In 1996 the rate was increased to 125 percent. Again, the domestic bottler effectively lobbied for relief. The excise was applied to imported inputs of ethyl alcohol, rather than the value of output. This reduced the effective excise to below the earlier preferential rate of 35 percent. The real problem for the domestic bottler seems to be that imported spirits enter the country without paying excise. The remedy would be improved enforcement at the border, together with a lower excise rate to reduce the incentive for smuggling.

Similarly, excises on cars and tires were introduced in 1993 to offset the revenue and incidence effects of reductions in customs duties. In the 1996 Budget, custom duties on these goods were further reduced, from 40 percent to 25 percent, while at the same time the excise on vehicles was eliminated.

This reduced the taxes on these commodities by more than 25 percent. The justification was that at the same time, exemptions from taxation on these goods was significantly reduced. Previously, only one in ten vehicles imported paid any taxes. Exemptions existed for charities, new and returning residents, the government, and Zambian foreign service personnel. These were all eliminated with the 1996 budget. Diplomats and technical aid projects continue to enjoy exemptions but to remain exempt from duty they cannot resell vehicles on the domestic market. Charities now pay duty, but can claim refunds on some types of vehicles. New and returning residents pay duty on all vehicle imports.

Excise taxation is an area where further reform is needed. Excise taxes can be used to improve the progressivity of the tax system, but only if the taxes are enforced. Zambia's excise rates are high by regional standards and have generally reached counterproductive levels, thereby reducing government revenue. This in part results from the effects on smuggling, not just as a result of reductions in demand for the commodity. Compliance at the border is low, and higher excises, which are collected on domestic production, makes smuggled imports more attractive. Improved enforcement at the border and adjusted excise rates could improve revenue performance. (Appendix B discusses compliance and ZRA in greater detail.)

6. CONCLUDING COMMENTS

Zambia made impressive progress reforming its tax policy during the MMD's first term in office. It moved from a highly distorted system at the start of the 1990s, to a tax regime characterized by fewer distortions and a broad base, as well as reduced rates. Progress slowed significantly during the second half of the decade, as the government's attention shifted to other, primarily noneconomic, issues. Further progress is needed to reduce tax rates, which are generally high. Given revenue constraints, this must be preceded by improved compliance. Institutional strengthening of the revenue authority, ZRA, is moving this goal forward.

While continued tax reform is important for reducing distortions and contributing to improved fiscal performance, current revenue performance is primarily driven by the shrinking economy. The major focus of the government should be on restoring growth. Government attempts to raise additional revenue may, in fact, be counterproductive. By transferring resources through taxes from the private sector and them using them ineffectively and inefficiently, the government accentuates the economic decline. For tax reform to succeed, it has to complement a growth strategy.

Appendix A. Mining Taxation

The mining sector was heavily taxed during the Second Republic. The decline in world copper prices and reductions in production contributed to deteriorating revenue performance. Production declined from 700,000 tons in the mid-1970s to around 300,000 tons in 1997. The government agreed to privatize ZCCM in an attempt to revitalize the sector. The sale of ZCCM was not completed until early 2000.

One of the policies announced by the MMD government when it took office was to balance the need to produce adequate revenue for government, while not discouraging investment in the mining sector. The slow pace of privatization of ZCCM, however, resulted in continued operational, financial, and management problems. From 1997 onwards, problems at ZCCM were spilling over to the rest of the economy, contributing to poor revenue performance in several areas. A similar problem had arisen in 1993, when the copper price fell to $0.87 per pound. ZCCM incurred arrears on its taxes and payments to its suppliers. These firms then had trouble meeting their tax obligations. Those difficulties demonstrated the importance to the economy of privatizing and revitalizing the mines. Because of the delay, direct tax revenues have fallen, at the same time that the decline in the sector has been a factor in Zambia's slow growth.

From 1989 to 1994, the tax burden on the copper industry had shifted toward indirect taxes (sales tax and import duties) and away from direct taxes (income tax). This reduced the profitability of the mines. Reform of mineral taxation was recognized as important to the ultimate privatization of the mining sector. A committee was formed to consider mining sector tax reform in 1993. The objective was to recommend a tax regime that would attract private sector investment in the mining sector. Tax policy was to be designed to encourage prospecting and exploration and the development of new mines. The existing tax system taxed investors at the start, through import tariffs and sales tax on plant and equipment, discouraging investment. There was also a copper export levy. For these, and other reasons, there had been little exploration in Zambia for 20 years.[31]

The final report of the committee recommended that investors be exempt from duties on imported equipment until the mine started commercial production.[32] To prevent abuse, the exemption was not to apply to a variety of

---

31. Reports of the Committee on Mining Sector Tax Reforms, Ministry of Finance and Ministry of Mines, Lusaka, 10 September, 1993, p. 5 (hereafter Mining Report).

31. Mining Report, p. 6.

32. Mining Report, p. 12.

goods, such as passenger vehicles, computers, and other office equipment. After production started, the mining sector would receive the same treatment as other sectors.

The committee also recommended that a royalty be imposed, a charge for taking minerals which are part of the country's wealth, based on the value of the minerals, not profitability. The committee recommended a flat rate, measured on a net back-to-mine basis.[33]

The report recommended no special treatment be provided with respect to income tax. Capital allowances of 100 percent already applied with unlimited carry forward. Ring fencing was proposed, however, so that capital allowances could not be used to decrease taxable income on mines that were already in production.[34]

In 1994, the Mineral Tax Act of 1989 was revoked, and replaced with a royalty of 3 percent on base metals and industrial minerals and of 5 percent on precious stones and gemstones. Special exemptions to customs duty applicable to other sectors under the Investment Act were extended to the mining sector. (This was implemented through a special statutory instrument (S.I.) for ZCCM, exempting it from import duty on a variety of goods.) A new Minerals and Mines Act was passed in 1995, intended to align Zambia's treatment of the mining sector with international practices. The Rothschild Report (RR) on the privatization of ZCCM observed that the resulting tax environment in Zambia for mining was internationally competitive.[35]

The 1996 budget eliminated most duty exemptions and revoked ZCCM's special S.I. that granted it duty exemptions. However, it left intact the possibility of exemptions for holders of mining rights. Effective April 1, 1996, copper and cobalt were removed from the VAT exempt list, allowing ZCCM to reclaim any VAT paid on inputs. As a result, future tax revenue from the copper industry would come primarily from the mineral royalty and the income tax.

The long delay in privatizing the mines undermined profitability of the sector to such an extent that the government lost the initiative in negotiations with potential buyers. Accordingly, GRZ has conceded more than might have been necessary had the mines been privatized more rapidly. The 1998 budget significantly reduced the taxation of the mining sector, relative to the 1995 Mines and Minerals Act. The 1998 budget included the following concessions:

---

33. Mining Report.

34. International consultants were employed by GRZ to assist with the privatization of the mines. Their tasks included evaluating the tax environment in Zambia and to assist the government in negotiations with possible buyers (Rothschild 1996).

35. TPTF, p. 4.

- the mineral royalty tax rate was reduced from 3 percent to 2 percent;
- the period of carry forward of losses was extended from 5 to 10 years;
- the withholding tax rate on interest and dividends was reduced from 15 percent to 10 percent;
- the restriction on offsetting losses against profits which was limited to 20 percent for those mines with a common owner, but which are noncontiguous geographically, was removed, so that 100 percent of losses could be offset. (This eliminated "ring fencing.")

The government estimated that these measures would cost K18 billion in foregone revenue annually.

The 2000 budget increased these concessions further.

- The mineral royalty rate was reduced from 2 percent to .6 percent of gross value;
- An exemption from the payment of customs duty on consumables was introduced and the mineral royalty up to a cap of U.S. $16 million in the first year and US $15 million per year for the next four years thereafter;
- Copper and cobalt price participation fees were made tax deductible;
- An exemption from excise duty on electricity consumed was introduced;
- The corporate tax rate was reduced from 35 percent to 25 percent and the period for carry forward of losses increased to 20 years;
- An exemption from payment of withholding tax on interest, dividends, royalties, and management fees paid to shareholders and affiliates was introduced;
- The deduction of 100 percent of capital expenditure was extended to additional mines.

The 1998 and 2000 budgets significantly reduced the taxation of the mining sector in Zambia. This was a direct (and unfortunate cost) of delaying privatization of the mines. The contrast is striking between the tax policies included in the 1995 Mines and Minerals Act, considered consistent with international standards by an outside consultant at the time, and the taxation in effect after the 2000 budget. Zambian taxpayers will pay the price of the government's delay for at least several decades.

Appendix B: Improving Tax Compliance and the ZRA

Introduction

The TPTF recognized that weak tax administration and low taxpayer compliance contributed to the low revenue performance. The report recommended, as a high priority, that the government:

- Expedite establishment of the Revenue Board of Zambia, with attractive conditions of service, adequate resources, tight disciplinary procedures, and strong internal audit for tax administration;
- Expedite introduction of a computerized information technology system to modernize tax administration;
- Follow through without delay on the promises to catch tax evaders and prosecute them to the fullest extent of the law;
- Take firm steps to insulate revenue departments from political influence.[36]

The major initiative was the establishment of an independent revenue board, the Zambia Revenue Authority (ZRA). Experience to date has shown that the creation of an independent authority can accomplish little, in the absence of high-level commitment to improve revenue compliance and eliminate political interference with the operation of tax administrators.

Background

When the new government took office, taxes were collected by the Department of Taxes and the Department of Customs and Excise, both in the MoF. There were significant problems with enforcement. Revenues were declining, there were concerns about corruption and political interference with the collection of taxes, and there was little confidence that these problems could be solved within the existing civil service structure. The TPTF strongly recommended that the government move to establish the Revenue Board of Zambia as quickly as possible. It stressed that "strengthening tax administration is an essential precondition for success of the entire tax reform program" (p. 42).[37] Establishing a revenue board and making it independent of the civil service was expected to improve revenue performance through a variety of channels. It was expected to:[38]

- Enable the government to offer better terms and conditions of employment in order to attract and retain qualified employees;
- Allow appointment and promotion based on merit;
- Improve discipline by adhering to a code of conduct and by giving senior management the power to dismiss inefficient or corrupt staff without needing to consult government officials;
- Provide greater flexibility to senior management to determine priorities in enhancing revenue performance and allocating resources accordingly;

36. Faria and Yucelik (1995) highlight the importance of designing a tax structure that the tax authorities can implement.
37. Coopers and Lybrand, 1992, par. 202.
38. Coopers and Lybrand, 1992, par. 701.

- Ensure that resources are available to support the Revenue Authority's operations; and
- Minimize the possibility of direct political involvement in individual tax cases.

Policymakers recognized that few of these tasks could occur given the operation and structure of the civil service. Thus, the recommendation to establish a revenue board. For example, disciplinary procedures in the civil service did not work. In 1995, the secretary to the cabinet noted that more than 40,000 disciplinary cases awaited action. Few disciplinary cases were pursued within the tax departments before they were moved out of the government. In part, this was because pay levels were considered inadequate, resulting in tolerance for staff who derive additional income through extralegal means. Disciplinary actions were also drawn out, with dismissal procedures taking long periods of time and having uncertain results. Independent disciplinary policy and procedures from the civil service were considered vital for the revenue board to function effectively.[39]

The government was persuaded that an independent revenue authority was needed. An implementation committee was appointed to draft the necessary legislation and advise the government on the steps needed to establish the revenue board. A local consulting firm was contracted to develop an organizational structure, propose a budget, and recommend employment policies and a disciplinary code. The minister of finance announced in the 1993 budget that an independent revenue board would be established. The government passed the ZRA Act in March 1993 (No. 28 of 1993). Toward the end of 1993, the British Overseas Development Administration (ODA) agreed to support an interim secretariat and provide consultancy support to assist in the transition to new ZRA management.

The first ZRA board was appointed in September 1993. The nine-member board included the permanent secretary of the MoF (later secretary to the treasury), the permanent secretary of the Ministry of Legal Affairs, the governor of the BoZ, two people appointed by the minister of finance, and four people nominated by private sector institutions. The initial recruitment of the senior management, all expatriate, took longer than expected. The chairman of the ZRA governing board was appointed by the minister of finance to act as the commissioner general from January 1, 1994, until the post was filled nine months later in September.

The ZRA came into being on April 1, 1994, with British government support. About 900 of the 1,540 former employees of the two tax departments were hired by ZRA. The remainder was "retired" from the civil service. Ini-

---

39. Coopers and Lybrand, 1992.

tially expected to start operation on January 1, 1994, the delay proved costly. Revenue performance in the first few months of 1994 was exceedingly poor. Most staff members of the tax department and customs and excise were concentrating on getting jobs in the new ZRA. Tax collections in the first quarter of 1994 were 20 percent lower in real terms than in 1993 and 15 percent lower than in 1995.[40]

The ZRA has faced a variety of problems. Initial recruitment of senior management was slower than expected, and was not in place until September 1994 five months after ZRA commenced operations. The Commissioner of Customs was removed after 10 months, and was not replaced for about a year. Difficulties in filling this position caused disarray in the operations of the customs service. Infrastructure at the border posts remained in disrepair. And, there continued to be reliable reports of corruption and interference in ZRA operations at high levels. This made the post an unattractive one. Computerization proceeded extremely slowly. Coordination with ministry of finance was inadequate and political interference persisted. As a result, real revenue performance did not improve as expected. The following section examines real revenue performance and then discusses reasons why.

Real Revenue Performance

In 1991, tax revenue was 18.4 percent of GDP. It had been 21.2 percent in 1986 and 19.5 percent in 1990. In 1992, it remained below 19 percent. It fell to 14 percent in 1993. Both the tax reform and the establishment of ZRA were directed at improving revenue mobilization.

During the ZRA's first two years, major improvements occurred in its physical and technical capacities. Nonetheless, revenue performance remained weak.[41] As a share of GDP, revenue fell from 18.7 percent in 1994 to 18.2 percent in 1995. In 1996 and 1997, it was 18.8 percent. The change in these shares cannot be fully attributed to the ZRA. Under the tax reform program, there have been significant changes each year in the statutory tax regime. To determine the effects of changes in administration and enforcement

---

40. Calculated using the quarterly CPI index and quarterly revenues deposited at the BoZ, (*Macroeconomic Indicators* various issues Table 4.3).

41. A World Bank sponsored study of ZRA performance (Kasanga 1996) concluded that revenue performance was below expectations. It calculated revenue in U.S. dollars and reported a 5 percent reduction in 1995 over 1994. These numbers, however, do not control for tax policy changes, which have been significant. Indeed, Kasanga was aware of this point and specifically noted that tax policy changes could explain the reduction in trade taxes, but not direct taxes and excises.

on revenues, the effects of changes in tax policy would have to be removed from the revenue data.

There are a number of methods for disentangling the effects of improved administration and changes in tax rates. One is to disaggregate by type of tax. Several taxes have not been significantly changed since the ZRA commenced operation. Changes in real collections, or collections as a share of GDP, therefore are primarily the result of changes in enforcement and compliance. Data in Table 5–6 suggest that company income tax and excises have performed poorly in real terms, with no justification in terms of tax policy changes. Tariff revenues also performed poorly in 1995 compared to 1994, improving in 1996 and 1997(despite rate reductions in 1996.)

Another method (reported in Table 5–7) is to compare actual collections with projections made at budget time. The projections include the proposed tax policy changes, and are based on the projected rate of inflation and real GDP growth that are used in framing the budget. In comparing projected revenues with collections, the projections are stated in real terms using the inflation rate assumed for the projections as the deflator. Actual collections are deflated in the conventional way, using the realized CPI.[42]

In 1994, tax revenue exceeded the projection in real terms by 5.1 percent. All taxes were above their projected levels, with the exception of trade taxes, which were 10 percent below. In 1995, the performance reversed, with projected tax revenue 4.7 percent higher than actual collections in real terms. The main poor performers were company income tax and excise tax, with collections 37 percent and 19 percent below projections. This poor performance in tax revenues in 1995 occurred despite a midyear mini-budget that introduced approximately K40 billion in revenue measures over the remaining half-year. If these measures had not been put in place, performance in real terms relative to the projections would have been significantly worse. As noted in the main text, the revenue measures increased excise, VAT and trade taxes.

In 1996 and 1997, tax revenue was 13.5 percent and 4.5 percent less than projected in real terms, respectively. Customs duties and domestic VAT exceeded projections in real terms, perhaps reflecting improved compliance in these two areas. Direct taxes and excises continued to perform poorly.

Confusing real and nominal benchmarks, the ZRA management repeatedly claimed that it had met and exceeded all revenue benchmarks. In real terms, benchmarks were not met in 1995, 1996, or 1997. Over the period examined, the creation of an independent revenue board did not improve real

---

42. Note that the revenue projections have not assumed any improvement in compliance. This is both conservative and consistent with Zambian experience.

Table 5-6 ZRA Revenue Performance, Zambia 1993-1997

TAX	1993 Actual	1993 %GDP	1994 Actual	1994 % GDP	1995 Actual	1995 %GDP	1996 Actual	1996 % GDP	1997 Actual	1997 % GDP
Total Revenue	232,459.80	14.4	449.616	20.1	595.860	19.9	786.487	19.8	1038352	20.1
Tax Revenue	222,560.70	13.8	418.878	18.7	545.911	18.2	747.754	18.8	968387	18.8
Direct Tax		0.0	128.97	5.8	172.417	5.8	245.069	6.2	327185	6.3
Company Income Tax	25,434.10	1.6	42.768	1.9	38.264	1.3		0.0		0.0
PAYE	35,140.40	2.2	69.732	3.1	104.716	3.5		0.0		0.0
Other Income Tax	6,726.80	0.4	16.47	0.7	29.437	1.0		0.0		0.0
Trade Tax	78,440.60	4.9	138.536	6.2	163.155	5.4	242.908	6.1	287943	5.6
Customs Duties		0.0	66.449	3.0	60.721	2.0	101.388	2.6	136011	2.6
Import VAT		0.0	72.087	3.2	77.572	2.6	110.224	2.8	110319	2.1
IDF		0.0	0	0.0	5.463	0.2	31.341	0.8	41614	0.8
Excise (including fuel levy)	33,792.80	2.1	70.204	3.1	84.616	2.8	126.623	3.2	168189	3.3
Domestic Sales Tax	28,982.30	1.8	76.104	3.4	107.678	3.6	133.154	3.4	185150	3.6
Mineral Revenue	14,052.70	0.9	5.064	0.2	18.045	0.6		0.0	0	0.0
Non Tax Revenue	9,899.10	0.6	30.738	1.4	49.949	1.7	38.733	1.0	59965	1.2
Dividends			6.264	0.3	0.000	0.0		0.0		0.0
Fees and Fines			12.292	0.5	17.255	0.6		0.0	38568	0.7
Privatisation Revenues				0.0	12.468	0.4	38.733	1.0	1500	0.0
Exceptional			12.182	0.5	20.226	0.7	26.009	0.7	18030	0.3
GDP at Market Prices			2240.7		2998.4		3970.3		5157000	

Table 5–7   ZRA Revenue Performance: Real Revenue Collections Relative to Projections

TAX	1993 Actual	1993 %GDP	1994 Actual	1994 % GDP	1995 Actual	1995 %GDP	1996 Actual	1996 % GDP	1997 Actual	1997 % GDP
Total Revenue	232,459.800	0.144	449.616	0.201	595.860	0.199	786.487	0.198	1038352	0.201
Tax Revenue	222,560.700	0.138	418.878	0.187	545.911	0.182	747.754	0.188	968387	0.188
Direct Tax		0.000	128.97	0.058	172.417	0.058	245.069	0.062	327185	0.063
Company Income Tax	25,434.100	0.016	42.768	0.019	38.264	0.013		0.000		0.000
PAYE	35,140.400	0.022	69.732	0.031	104.716	0.035		0.000		0.000
Other Income Tax	6,726.800	0.004	16.47	0.007	29.437	0.010		0.000		0.000
Trade Tax	78,440.600	0.049	138.536	0.062	163.155	0.054	242.908	0.061	287943	0.056
Customs Duties		0.000	66.449	0.030	60.721	0.020	101.388	0.026	136011	0.026
Import VAT		0.000	72.087	0.032	77.572	0.026	110.224	0.028	110319	0.021
IDF		0.000	0	0.000	5.463	0.002	31.341	0.008	41614	0.008
Excise (including fuel levy)	33,792.800	0.021	70.204	0.031	84.616	0.028	126.623	0.032	168189	0.033
Domestic Sales Tax	28,982.300	0.018	76.104	0.034	107.678	0.036	133.154	0.034	185150	0.036
Mineral Revenue	14,052.700	0.009	5.064	0.002	18.045	0.006	0	0.000	0	0.000
Non Tax Revenue	9,899.100	0.006	30.738	0.014	49.949	0.017	38.733	0.010	59965	0.012
Dividends			6.264	0.003	0.000	0.000		0.000		0.000
Fees and Fines			12.292	0.005	17.255	0.006		0.000	38568	0.007
Privatisation Revenues				0.000	12.468	0.004	38.733	0.010	1500	0.000
Exceptional			12.182	0.005	20.226	0.007	26.009	0.007	18030	0.003
GDP at Market Prices			2240.7		2998.4		3970.3		5157000	

revenue performance. Of the several factors that explain this, the most important has been the lack of political commitment to improved revenue collections. The change in management in early 1997, including the removal of the chairman of the ZRA Board, was meant to rectify this situation.

ZRA Operational Issues

Computerization: Computerization within ZRA proceeded slowly. Two years of work supported by the Dutch and Norwegian Governments were abandoned, at high cost to the Government and the computerization program at the ZRA.[43]

The slow computerization was especially costly in the customs area. A data program developed to record customs entries was put in place in two ports of entry in mid-1994. ZRA decided not to extend its use and instead shift to ASYCUDA (Automated System for Customs Data). In the interim, no computerization of records was maintained. ASYCUDA only became fully operational in early 2000. In the meantime, the MoF and BoZ needed data on imports and exports. The data system designed for ZRA was modified and the CSO began to maintain the data, using bills of entry they receive from ZRA. These data could be used for tax enforcement purposes, but ZRA showed no interest in the database until the new commissioner of customs and excise arrived in late 1996.

The cost in terms of revenue foregone has been high. In mid-1995, the data base for the port of Lusaka (one of the two ports computerized) was used to generate a report on outstanding "removals in bond" (RIBs). Many goods enter Zambia from Zimbabwe, via the port of Chirundu, on an RIB that is cleared in Lusaka. This system has been widely abused, since goods allowed entry on an RIB may never be finally cleared. When ZRA fails to clear RIBs, the imports enter duty free.

In mid-1995, the government experienced a revenue shortfall. The program with the IMF required the government to raise additional revenues to meet the agreed budget targets. A report on the port of Lusaka determined that up to K40 billion in duty was owed on goods that had been cleared under RIBs, for which there was no evidence that the RIBs had been acquitted. MoF officials proposed that the collection of duty owed on outstanding RIBs be included as a revenue measure to close the revenue gap. The government and the IMF agreed that about K20 billion in outstanding duty would be collected over the next 12 months. In the end, little was collected and the effort to track

---

43. Large amounts of donor assistance were used to purchase a VAT computer system, after the HIID computer system (referred to earlier) had been cast aside.

RIBs was shelved. This was in part the result of the departure of the commissioner of customs and in part because the revenue shortfall was met through
other taxes, taking pressure off this particular measure. The lack of fol-
low-through on an identified area of major revenue abuse reinforced the
point that improved revenue compliance was not high on the agenda of ZRA
management.

A similar example involves the numbering of bills of entry. Each month at
each port of entry, numbering restarts at 0. This means that the headquarters
cannot be sure of the last bill of entry issued each month at each port. This
creates significant possibilities for abuse. The system of bonded warehouses
has also been identified as a major source of revenue loss, yet efforts to require compliance are minimal or counterproductive. This is another clear
area of political interference. With the arrival of a new commissioner of customs at the end of 1996, a renewed effort at enforcing RIBs (as well as removals in transit, RITs), started in part through expanded efforts to computerize.

Management and Cost Effectiveness: Determining the appropriate role
for the governing board of the ZRA created confusion. Responsibility for the
day-to-day operations of the ZRA rests with the commissioner general. The
governing board should guarantee that the ZRA complies with government
policy and directives. The appointment of the chairman of the governing
board as the acting commissioner general when ZRA was established was a
monumental blunder. It directly undermined accountability leading to lack
of transparency in the operations and oversight of the ZRA.

A further problem has been the misallocation of staff. A detailed report on
ZRA's performance noted that in June 1996, 44 percent of staff were performing administrative support services.[44] Drivers, messengers, and security
guards accounted for 27 percent of the staff. Too few of the total staff were focusing on the main functions of the ZRA, namely tax collections and enforcement.

ZRA receives an allocation from the annual budget. Allocations for 1996 to
1998, plus the commitment for 1997 are reported in Table 5–8.

In addition to GRZ funding, the ZRA has been supported by the British
(ODA). This has included support to the interim secretariat consultancy
(£800,000 plus £700,000, 1994 to 1995). The ODA has also provided funding
for a VAT computer system (£560,000) and salary supplementation for the
commissioner general and the three commissioners (direct taxes, customs,
and VAT) for three years (£800,000). The total was £3.3 million through June
1995. With the ZRA Consolidation Project, overall support amounted to £9

---

44. Kasanga 1996, p. 10.

Table 5–8 ZRA Costs per Kwacha Raised

	GRZ Funding (m Kwacha)	% of Tax Revenue
1996	24,339	3.2
1997	33,146	3.4
1998	48,500	4.4

Source: Macroeconomic Indicators, various issues.

million. This sharply increased the resources used by the ZRA, per kwacha collected.

Coordination between the ZRA and the Ministry of Finance: The relation ship between the ZRA and the MoF has been strained. Rather than being mutually supportive, it became adversarial. One problem has been unclear areas of responsibility. While the ZRA is responsible for collecting revenue, the MoF has ultimate responsibility for revenue policy. Since the establishment of the ZRA, the budget has been under intense pressure. The government has continually pressed the ZRA for improved revenue performance. At the same time, the ministry has made some policy changes that undermine the revenue base. Better coordination would resolve differences before they arise.

The monitoring of revenue performance remains a problem. Targets are based on revenue projections agreed upon by the MoF and the ZRA. However, no mechanism has been established for revising these in response to changes in inflation, real growth, exchange rates, or tax rates.

For the relationship to improve, several changes are needed. A clearer understanding of responsibilities of the ZRA and the MoF must be developed. The MoF needs to monitor the ZRA's performance, and the ZRA must accept that this is the ministry's legitimate role. This will require clarification and enforcement of the ZRA's reporting requirements to the government. Finally, the ministry's tax analysis capacity has to be strengthened, so that the ZRA does not inappropriately begin determining policy on taxation.

Concluding Observations

Despite hopes to the contrary, the creation of the ZRA has had little impact on revenue mobilization in Zambia, largely because there has been no change in the constraints encountered by the former revenue departments in the MoF. Creating the ZRA has not eliminated political interference in revenue collection. Tax fraud by ZRA staff and taxpayers remains highly lucrative attracting, at most, minimal penalties if fraud is detected. Staff caught defrauding the ZRA are fired but restitution has not been required.

An expatriate management team, funded by a donor agency rather than the government, has provided some direction and transparency, but the presence of this team has not prevented real revenues from declining. The poor performance on company income tax, on the collections of RIBs, and on reducing abuse in bonded warehouses can only be attributed to the lack of commitment to improving compliance. Problems in these areas were identified in the early 1990s. Virtually no progress has been made, despite easy technical solutions to these problems.

There has been intense pressure to "Zambianize" the management positions. Based on the ZRA's performance so far, such a change is unlikely to produce any improvement in revenue performance relative to when the departments were part of the civil service.

ZRA compensation is significantly higher than the government's pay scales. This has not eliminated fraud. The rewards of corruption remain large. The probability of being caught is small, and the punishment when caught is mild. Increased computerization will make it significantly easier to detect fraud. But, unless enforcement is strengthened, improved detection will remain a hollow exercise.

Some degree of autonomy for the revenue agency may be necessary to improve tax compliance, but in Zambia's case it has not been sufficient. Many of the problems that lead to low compliance when the civil service collects revenue carried over to the autonomous revenue board. A successful revenue authority has to be founded on the principle that there will be no political interference in its operations. Without that, separating the revenue authority from the civil service can have little impact on revenue performance.

6

Monetary Policy, Exchange Rate Management, and Financial Reform

MALCOLM F. MCPHERSON

1. INTRODUCTION

One of the most persistently destructive features of the Zambian economy over the last three decades has been the rapid growth of the money supply. This has resulted primarily from government budget deficits. With slow income growth, an overvalued nominal exchange rate, and fixed (or controlled) nominal interest rates, rapid monetary expansion led to high rates of inflation, currency substitution, capital flight, and financial disintermediation.

Dealing with rapid money growth requires the reduction (ideally the elimination) of the fiscal deficit. Textbook treatments of monetary and fiscal policy used to emphasize the importance of balancing the budget over the business cycle. Zambia, and most other African countries, e.g., Kenya, South Africa, have had chronic budget deficits for the last three decades. Thus, it is not misplaced to stress the importance of running a budget surplus at least until economic recovery is firmly established. Indeed, the point needs to be underscored: the Zambian economy cannot recover on a sustained basis until the government begins running budget surpluses.

Rationalizing an overvalued exchange rate requires measures that progressively move the exchange rate to levels consistent with Zambia's long-term ability to compete internationally. Addressing the problem of financial disintermediation requires steps that liberalize the financial system in ways that rebuild confidence among the general public in kwacha denominated assets.

This chapter describes the background to the monetary and exchange rate reforms that were included in the New Economic Recovery Program

(NERP). It discusses the main reforms, their impact on the Zambian economy, and lessons from that experience.

Section 2 highlights the trends in monetary, exchange rate, and financial policies prior to the introduction of the NERP. Section 3 examines the types of changes included in the NERP to deal with the problems of inflation, currency substitution, and exchange rate overvaluation. Section 4 assesses the impact of the reforms. It outlines the initial progress made towards stability up to early 1995. Section 5 describes the types of actions required to fully reform the monetary, exchange rate, and financial system in Zambia. A basic requirement is that the government needs to contain its deficit and allow the exchange rate to fully reflect the scarcity of foreign exchange. Section 6 draws lessons from Zambia's experiences in these areas of reform. Section 7 has concluding comments. The appendix provides details on the collapse of Meridien BIAO Bank, one of the factors that derailed Zambia's recovery in the mid-1990s.

2. Historical Background[1]

From a macroeconomic perspective, the government's approach to monetary policy and exchange rate management has created serious problems for the economy over most of the last three decades. The rapid growth of the money supply can be traced to persistent budget deficits and attempts to keep nominal interest rates low both absolutely and relative to inflation. The government also made extraordinary efforts to prevent the exchange rate from depreciating. From mid-1974, Zambia has had a chronically overvalued real exchange rate. A major effort was made to rectify the situation between October 1985 and May 1987 through the introduction of an exchange rate auction, and by floating the kwacha in December 1993. The latter occurred when Zambia Consolidated Copper Mines (ZCCM), Zambia's largest enterprise, was allowed to sell its foreign exchange at the market-determined exchange rate. This was followed by a brief period of official nonintervention. The collapse of a major commercial bank (Meridien BIAO) in early 1995 placed severe stress on the whole financial system. A change in management at the Bank of Zambia (BoZ) led to a shift in policy direction. By mid-1995, the BoZ began to resist depreciation of the exchange rate. With inflation well above the world average, this produced a sharp appreciation of the real exchange

---

1. This section draws freely from McPherson (1993, 1995) and Lewis and McPherson (1994).

rate. Local asset holders once more were induced to shift out of kwacha-denominated assets.

But, this is getting ahead of the story. The following sections describe the basic stance of monetary, financial, and exchange rate policies. It is useful to begin by emphasizing the distinction between real and financial capital. Economists recognize the difference. Senior policy makers in Zambia (and in many other developing countries) have tended to confuse the two. In the process, large amounts of Zambia's national income and wealth have been dissipated.

Finance Capital and Real Capital

A common presumption in developing countries such as Zambia has been that financial capital (i.e. money and credit) will create real capital. This is a major, widespread, and continuing error common to Latin America and Africa and, during the 1990s, many economies in transition. It has fostered the general over-expansion of money and credit leading to rapid inflation, high rates of exchange rate depreciation, capital flight, and financial disintermediation. Indeed, *if* finance had been a source of real capital, Zambia, which has seen extraordinarily high rates of credit expansion over the last three decades, would now be an extremely rich country.[2]

The conditions under which finance can "create" real capital are stringent. They include stable prices, adequate foreign exchange reserves, excess productive capacity, and no adverse affect from credit expansion on the expectations of asset holders and investors.[3] These conditions have rarely been satisfied in Zambia or elsewhere in Africa since the 1960s.[4]

Finance can only increase real capital if it mobilizes (i.e., frees up) real savings, that is, resources which have been set aside from current income flows for purposes other than consumption. This point cannot be overstressed.

Although the existence of a more developed capital market and financial intermediaries will aid in the collection and distribution of investible funds,

---

2. From 1970 to 1994, the kwacha value of domestic credit in Zambia increased by a factor of 1,147 (i.e., approximately 115,000 percent). The outcome was not growth, but stagnation and decline accompanied by capital decumulation.

3. For the economics profession as a whole, the importance of dealing with expectations was sparked by the so-called "rational expectations" revolution. Yet, it was Keynes (1936) who emphasized the importance of feedback from expectations to real activity in a monetary economy when he observed: ". . . a monetary economy . . ., is one in which changing expectations about the future can influence the current rate of employment and not merely its direction. . . ." (*ibid.* p.vii).

4. Botswana and Mauritius are the only exceptions. Both countries have achieved rapid increases in capital formation through policies that encourage high rates of real savings and investment.

they in no way lessen the need for real saving. The rate of investment which is physically possible is limited by saving, and a "shortage of capital"—in the sense of a shortage of real resources available for investment purposes—cannot be solved merely by increasing the supply of finance.[5]

The basic task of any financial system is to transfer resources from those who are willing to lend to those who are willing to borrow. By accepting financial liabilities (i.e., providing credit), individual lenders release their surplus resources (i.e., their savings) to other individuals and firms, who promise to discharge their liabilities from the financial surpluses they expect to generate from their investments.[6]

By aggregating over all borrowers and lenders in the economy (or, more generally, all savers and investors), the familiar national accounting identities emerge[7]:

$$Y = C + S \tag{1}$$

$$Y = C + I + X - M \tag{2}$$

where   Y gross domestic product in current market prices
C aggregate consumption (private and public)
S gross domestic savings
I gross domestic investment (including changes in inventories)
X exports of goods and non-factor services
M imports of goods and non-factor services.

Equating (1) and (2) and rearranging gives:

$$S - I = X - M \tag{3}$$

In an open economy, any difference between domestic investment and domestic saving is balanced by a corresponding difference between imports and exports, and vice-versa.[8]

---

5. Meier 1989, p. 178.

6. Kitchen 1986; Meier 1989, pp. 178–182.

7. Helmers in Appendix B of Dornbusch and Helmers (1988) casts these relationships in terms of gross national income, gross national savings, and the current account of the balance of payments. The difference arises because gross national income (which is equivalent to consumption plus gross national savings) equals gross domestic product minus net factor payments abroad plus net unrequited transfers from abroad. The essential point of these relationships, however, is that any gap between savings and investment is offset (*ex poste*) by corresponding flows to and from the rest of the world.

8. The extended boom in the United States during the 1990s provides an excellent illustration of the linkages among the key components of this identity. Goodley (1999) has shown that

Table 6-1. *Zambia: Selected Indicators, 1970–2001*

	1970	1971	1972	1973	1974	1975	1976	1977	1978	1979	1980	1981	1982	1983	1984	1985	1986
Money plus quasi money growth (annual %)	26.3	-10.4	7.1	20.4	7.3	12.0	26.3	12.1	-8.5	30.2	9.0	7.9	33.8	11.1	17.2	23.4	-99.8
Income velocity of money plus quasi-money[I]	3.8	3.5	4.1	4.2	4.4	3.4	3.4	3.0	3.4	3.6	3.5	3.7	3.1	3.0	3.1	3.7	4.2
Income velocity index (1995=100)[2]	..	..	*58.2*	*59.8*	*57.5*	*51.6*	*49.1*	*40.9*	*47.5*	*52.3*	*50.7*	*53.7*	*46.5*	*44.5*	*46.2*	*56.0*	*65.1*
Inflation, consumer prices (annual %)	*-13.2*	*0.0*	*5.4*	*6.2*	*8.1*	*10.1*	*18.8*	*19.8*	*16.3*	*9.7*	*11.6*	*13.0*	*13.6*	*19.6*	*20.0*	*37.3*	*51.8*
Overall budget balance[II] (% of GDP)	..	..	*-13.0*	*-16.7*	*3.4*	*-21.5*	*-14.2*	*-13.2*	*-14.4*	*-9.1*	*-18.5*	*-12.9*	*-18.6*	*-7.8*	*-8.4*	*-15.2*	*-21.4*
Current account balance[III] (% of GDP)	..	..	..	..	..	..	..	..	*-10.0*	*2.3*	*-13.3*	*-18.0*	*-14.5*	*-7.9*	*-5.4*	*-17.5*	*-20.9*
Official exchange rate (Kwacha/USD, p.a.)[2]	0.71	0.71	0.71	0.65	0.64	0.64	0.70	0.79	0.80	0.79	0.79	0.87	0.93	1.26	1.81	3.14	7.79
Real exchange rate[IV] (Kwacha/USD, p.a.)	24.5	25.3	25.0	24.4	26.3	26.2	25.4	25.3	23.8	24.1	24.8	26.4	25.5	29.1	35.6	44.9	69.2
Treasury bill rate (annual %)[2]	2.43	3.34	4.34	3.94	3.96	4.00	4.15	4.38	4.38	4.44	4.50	5.75	6.00	7.50	7.67	13.21	24.25
Real interest rate[V] (TBR, annual %)[2]	18.0	3.3	-1.0	-2.1	-3.8	-5.6	-12.3	-12.9	-10.3	-4.8	-6.4	-6.4	-6.7	-10.1	-10.3	-17.5	-18.2
Real interest rate differential[VI] (annual %)	..	3.3	-2.1	-2.5	-1.0	-2.7	-11.4	-11.8	-10.0	-3.8	-4.6	-9.8	-11.1	-15.2	-15.2	-21.4	-22.2

Notes:

[I]– Income velocity was calculated as the ratio of GDP to the average broad money for each period using the GDP and monetary series from the International Financial Statistics, IMF; [II]– including Grants; [III]– excluding Net Official Capital Grants; [IV]– Real exchange rate was calculated as the nominal exchange rate times the ratio of the US PPI to Zambian CPI; [V]– Real interest rate was calculated using the Fisher equation; [VI]– Real interest rate differential was calculated as the difference between Zambian and the US real interest rates based on the TBR.

Sources:

1) World Development Indicators 2002, World Bank. 2) International Financial Statistics, 2002 and February 2003, IMF. 3) Some series have been completed or updated using observations from "Macroeconomic Indicators", September 2002, Ministry of Finance and National Planning, Lusaka, Zambia.

These numbers are given in italics.

Table 6-1 continued. *Zambia: Selected Indicators, 1970–2001*

	1987	1988	1989	1990	1991	1992	1993	1994	1995	1996	1997	1998	1999	2000	2001
Money and quasi money growth (annual %)	53.7	60.3	65.3	47.9	97.6	154.1	68.2	59.2	55.5	35.0	25.1	25.6	27.7	73.8	13.6
Income velocity of money plus quasi–money[I]	3.8	3.7	4.1	5.5	5.9	6.6	8.9	8.3	7.1	6.5	6.6	6.1	6.0	5.3	5.1
Income velocity index (1995=100)[2]	57.3	58.3	62.5	83.1	83.6	104.1	123.3	117.1	100.0	89.5	91.8	..	..	..	..
Inflation, consumer prices (annual %)	43.0	55.4	127.7	117.4	93.2	169.0	188.1	53.6	34.2	46.3	24.8	24.4	36.5	30.1	18.7
Overall budget balance[II] (% of GDP)	-12.6	-11.7	-10.7	-8.3	-7.3	-4.2	-9.5	-7.9	-4.3	-3.9	-2.4	-6.9	-5.7	-5.9	-7.9
Current account balance[III] (% of GDP)	-10.8	-7.9	-5.5	-18.1	-9.0	-4.7e	-3.1e	-4.4e	-7.4e	-12.6e	-9.0	-17.7	-15.2	-18.3	-20.9
Official exchange rate (Kwacha/USD, p.a.)[2]	9.52	8.27	13.81	30.29	64.64	172.21	452.76	669.37	864.12	1207.90	1314.50	1862.07	2388.02	3110.84	3610.94
Real exchange rate[IV] (Kwacha/USD, p.a.)	58.9	35.2	27.6	30.3	33.5	33.4	30.9	30.1	30.0	29.4	25.6	28.4	26.9	28.5	28.2
Treasury bill rate (annual %)[2]	16.50	15.17	18.50	25.92	..	..	124.03	74.21	39.81	52.78	29.48	24.94	36.19	31.37	44.28
Real interest rate[V] (TBR, annual %)	-18.5	-25.9	-48.0	-42.1	..	..	-22.2	13.4	4.2	4.4	3.7	0.4	-0.3	0.9	21.6
Real interest rate differential[VI] (annual %)	-20.5	-28.4	-51.0	-44.2	..	..	-22.3	11.8	1.5	2.4	1.1	-2.8	-2.7	-1.4	21.0

Notes:
I – Income velocity was calculated as the ratio of GDP to the average broad money for each period using the GDP and monetary series from the International Financial Statistics, IMF; II – including Grants; III – excluding Net Official Capital Grants; IV – Real exchange rate was calculated as the nominal exchange rate times the ratio of the US PPI to Zambian CPI; V – Real interest rate was calculated using the Fisher equation; VI – Real interest rate differential was calculated as the difference between Zambian and the US real interest rates based on the TBR.

Sources:

1) World Development Indicators 2002, World Bank. 2) International Financial Statistics, 2002 and February 2003, IMF. 3) Some series have been completed or updated using observations from "Macroeconomic Indicators", September 2002, Ministry of Finance and National Planning, Lusaka, Zambia.

These numbers are given in italics.

Identity (3) can be satisfied in a number of ways. Consider, for example, some of the possible adjustments when government expenditure increases without any change in tax rates. The rise in expenditure can result in the following:

- It might crowd out private investment through higher interest rates, or credit rationing;
- If there are idle resources (including ample foreign exchange reserves), the increased demand will increase real output. This will raise the level of imports and tax receipts;
- If there are no idle resources and monetary policy does not limit the growth of demand, prices will rise and government spending will be "financed" by forced saving (through the "inflation tax");
- Alternatively, the increased domestic demand may be matched by higher imports. That may occur through exchange rate depreciation or by capital inflow. The latter could result from foreign aid, government borrowing from foreign banks, or private flows in response to higher interest rates.

In Zambia (and other African countries) there have seldom been adequate idle resources (apart from unskilled labor) to permit a substantial "Keynesian" output response to higher government spending.[9] Increased government spending is often directly linked to increased foreign assistance or deficit financing. Private resources are limited, especially when eroding confidence among investors leads them to shift (or keep) their resources abroad. Exchange rate depreciation has its own costs in terms of inflation and the redistribution of wealth. The "forced saving" solution is costly and counterproductive and ultimately leads to a net loss of resources, especially in highly indebted countries such as Zambia.[10] Finally, changes in interest rates are typically too small relative to other risks to attract capital inflow.[11]

Governments wishing to raise real output on a sustained basis have to mo-

---

the drag on the economy through the fiscal surplus (which has raised S) and the balance of payments deficit (reflected in the fact that X<M) has been offset (in part) by private sector dissaving (which lowers S).

9. This point appears to be contradicted by the general underutilization of industrial capacity and the low productivity of capital and labor throughout Africa. The contradiction disappears when allowance is made for the policy setting (which often acts as a disincentive to higher output) and the limited supply of managerial and organizational skills in the public sector (where much of the surplus capacity exists).

10. McPherson (1999) shows that the real resources captured by the inflation tax (a component of seignorage) are offset by the capital losses (measured in local currency) on external debt due to the depreciation of the exchange rate. He shows that in highly indebted developing countries the gains from seignorage can be more than offset by those capital losses.

11. Collier and Gunning (1999, 1999a) discuss the high risks associated with investing in Africa. A major risk has been that there will be no growth to justify the expansion of capacity.

bilize additional resources.[12] This process requires a stable financial setting in which the individuals and firms who generate surpluses will transfer them to those in the domestic economy who have the capacity to create the additional output. By contrast, the explicit use of financial instruments to extract these surpluses (via inflation, low interest rates, or controls designed to generate rents that can be captured) is counterproductive. It leads to lower saving and investment and slower growth or, as in Zambia, economic decline.

Relying on foreign savings (through external borrowing) does not solve the problem either, especially when those resources are used inefficiently. For Zambia, external borrowing led to the rapid build-up of foreign debt without generating the capacity to service that debt on a sustained basis.[13]

Selected Monetary Indicators

As background to our discussion of the key policy issues in the monetary and exchange rate systems, we have assembled some data in Table 6–1. These data highlight the pressure and challenges facing policy makers. The first row shows the annual growth rate of money and quasi-money (i.e., M2). For most years during the 1970s and early 1980s, the growth rate of M2 was exceedingly high. The second row provides a broad estimate of the income velocity of money. From a level in the range of 3 to 4 up to the mid 1980s, velocity generally doubled in the late 1980s and 1990s. The implication is that asset-holders were less willing to hold monetary assets. The third row reports the annual rate of inflation. Until 1980, inflation was chronic. There was pressure on prices but within the context of the times (oil, food, transport shocks) some price adjustments were to be expected. Not expected were the triple digit rates of inflation over the period 1989 to 1993.

The reason for the rapid inflation and the high growth of the money supply and the selective abandonment of local financial assets can be traced to the fourth row, namely the overall surplus/deficit in the government budget. Beginning in 1971, these deficits have been large and persistent. The next row shows the current account surplus/deficit on the balance of payments. This deficit largely mirrors the public sector dissaving reflected in the budget deficit data.

The next two rows of the table respectively report the official and real exchange rate (measured as kwacha per U.S. dollar). The official exchange rate

---

12. They also need to use their existing resources more efficiently. Typically, low resource mobilization and inefficient resource use occur at the same time, due to macroeconomic instability and price distortions.

13. Fernholz (Chapter 9, this volume) and van der Heijden (2000) explore Zambia's experience with external debt and foreign aid.

showed little upward movement until 1982 by which time the Zambian economy was already in dire straits. From 1983, however, there was rapid depreciation, apart from the period in mid-1987 when the exchange rate was re-fixed. Under pressure from payment arrears and the widening of the premium in the parallel foreign exchange market, the fix proved untenable. Perhaps the most revealing data in the table is the series on the real exchange rate. From an average level of around K25=$1 (from the early 1970s until 1982, with 1990 as the base), the rate depreciated to K69.2=$1 in 1986 (during the unfettered operation of the auction system). It subsequently appreciated to K30=$1 in 1995 and K25.6=$1 in 1997. These data bring out the degree to which the real exchange rate has been manipulated through pressure applied to the official rate in the context of high local inflation.

The last three rows report interest rates. The first is the (three-month) treasury bill rate. The second is the real T-bill rate. The third computes the difference between the T-bill rate in Zambia and the United Kingdom (U.K.) on comparable maturities. These data show the effects of the interest rate controls especially as inflation accelerated in the mid-1970s. The negative real rates of interest explain why Zambia has experienced severe financial disintermediation. Finally, the real interest rate differential implies that Zambian asset holders view U.K. bills (or their equivalent) as yielding a significant premium. This accounts for the large amount of capital flight and currency substitution since the early 1980s.

Monetary Policy and Financial Management

Mismanagement of monetary and financial policies has created serious difficulties for Zambia. Problems began to emerge in 1970 when President Kaunda announced that the government would nationalize the commercial banks.[14] Although the attempt was abandoned within months, it created major uncertainties for all existing and potential investors in the financial system. The response by commercial banks was to further confine their lending to short-term activities such as seasonal credit for agriculture and trade. Longer-term loans were rare. They were available only with a government guarantee, or from the state-owned financial enterprises. But, even those loans were highly selective. That, however, did not make the loans productive.[15]

---

14. As part of the state takeover of key economic sectors, President Kaunda announced (in his speech on November 11, 1970, at Mulungushi Hall, Lusaka "Take up the challenge. . .") that the government would acquire a 51 percent share in both Barclays and Standard Bank. The negotiations broke down (Harvey 1973).

15. ZCCM, the copper company, made a number of loans to government to purchase vehicles for civil servants and to bolster foreign exchange reserves. These activities undermined

President Kaunda's announcement came at around the time the government began drawing down its large cash reserves to cover sharply higher levels of government spending. The Second National Development Plan was also introduced in 1970. The main goal of that plan was to secure Zambia's economic independence by setting in place a system through which the state itself would promote development.[16] That process rapidly became politicized. The government was soon seriously overextended both administratively and financially. These problems were compounded through its pursuit of activities that, in many cases, were often not plan priorities.[17] Real expenditure in the public sector soon outstripped the supply of real domestic resources.

The politicization of economic decisions also coincided with the disappearance of representative government in Zambia. The formal declaration of the one-party state—making the United National Independence Party (UNIP) the only legal party—did not occur until 1972. Yet, for all practical purposes economic policy in Zambia had been subject to the dictates of the party and its government from 1968 onwards. Under the one-party state, formal authority for economic policy shifted from the BoZ and MoF to the Central Committee of UNIP. Never strong organizations at the best of times, the BoZ and MoF were required to implement party policy. Those policies reflected the conviction among Zambia's leaders that economic development would follow if the party directed finance to specific activities, that asset prices should be tightly controlled, and that state-owned enterprises (SOEs) should have a monopoly of financial activities such as insurance, pensions, and small-scale agricultural ("cooperative") credit. This approach undermined financial development. Its destructive effects were compounded by the

---

ZCCM's financial position without enhancing Zambia's growth potential. The loans were ultimately written off under the London and Paris Club agreements or subsumed by government during ZCCM's sale.

16. This approach was stimulated by the goal of the First National Development Plan (FNDP) to foster economic diversification (GRZ 1966, p. 5). It was given greater urgency following Rhodesia's unilateral declaration of independence (UDI) in 1965. This led the Zambian government to invest directly in a number of enterprises such as the oil pipeline from Dar es Salaam and expanded road services (Martin 1972, Ch.3). As explained in Chapter 2, the desire for economic independence led to further investment by the public sector (Kaunda 1969). McPherson (1980, pp. 33–35) has a summary.

17. One priority that did not receive adequate attention was agriculture (McPherson 1980, Ch. 2, Section 5). In the preface to both the first and second plans, President Kaunda had explicitly stated that that agricultural and rural development were essential to the success of the government's plans (GRZ 1966, p.v.; GRZ 1971, p. iii). Yet, in the allocation of resources, agriculture and the rural areas in general were shortchanged even though the amounts the government spent overall were significantly above the allocations in both plans.

selective relaxation of the institutional restraints that had formerly stabilized the financial system.[18] A crucial restraint in this respect was the limit on government borrowing contained in the Bank of Zambia Act. As that limit threatened to deny the government access to credit, it was raised. Eventually, it was ignored entirely.

Initially, the budget deficit was financed using the government's cash reserves. These were soon depleted so the government began to borrow abroad.[19] Following the copper, transport, and oil price "shocks" of the mid-1970s, Zambia's external debt ballooned.[20] Instead of allowing interest rates to rise as a means of attempting to induce the nonbank private sector to supply additional financial resources, the government maintained an elaborate set of interest rate controls. The rationale was that priority sectors could only develop if they were given special access to credit. The government did not have a clearly stipulated set of priorities. All sectors and activities included in the national plans were seen as a priority and in need of special assistance.[21]

The lending behavior of state-owned financial agencies added further pressure to the monetary and financial system. These agencies were established as part of the government's attempt to increase local ownership throughout the economy. The most important were the Zambia National Commercial Bank (ZNCB, founded in 1969)[22] and the Development Bank of Zambia (DBZ, founded in 1972).[23] Attempts were made to strengthen the cooperative move-

---

18. Collier (1991) and Collier and Portillo (2000) argued that an important source of Africa's economic decline has been the weakness of formal "agencies of restraint." Zambia had many such formal restraints in place. The government failed to exercise restraint when it encountered the limits they imposed.

19. Zambia began borrowing abroad fully aware of the consequences. Minister of finance John Mwanakatwe noted in his budget speech for 1973 (January 26) that there was nothing wrong with borrowing abroad provided the proceeds were devoted to development, and not consumption. However, by 1975, when Zambia's export receipts plummeted, the government explicitly decided to borrow abroad. Then minister of finance Alexander Chikwanda announced in his budget speech that Zambia would engage in supplemental borrowing. Markakis and Curry (1976, pp. 412–414) provide details.

20. Zambia had experienced two earlier shocks, one negative and one positive. The cave-in at Mufulira mine in September 1970 killed a large number of miners, cut production, and required costly rehabilitation. The positive shock came in the form of a sharp rise in the price of copper in 1972 that boosted export earnings.

21. McPherson 1980, Ch. 2.

22. The National Commercial Bank was founded under BoZ auspices in 1969. In 1978, it became the Zambia National Commercial Bank and was integrated into the ZIMCO group (World Bank 1991).

23. Legislation establishing the DBZ was passed in 1972. The bank became operational in 1974 (World Bank 1986, par. 1.08).

ment, largely by providing credit to its member organizations. The Grain Marketing Board, a holdover from colonial times, was transformed into the National Agricultural Marking Board (NAMBoard). It, too, was given favored access to finance, largely through direct budget subventions. Finally, the insurance industry was "reformed" by creating a State monopoly.

Although it took a number of years for the activities of these agencies to begin to have important macroeconomic repercussions, some trends were evident. NAMBoard, for example, was required to implement the government's policy, introduced in the 1974/75 season, of pan-territorial and pan-seasonal pricing of maize and fertilizer. Since this policy subverted the principles of comparative advantage and price discovery, it guaranteed that NAMBoard would incur losses.[24]

Many financial difficulties in the operations of these agencies were masked while earnings from copper mining were high and Zambia's international credit-worthiness remained intact. But, the shocks of 1974/75 intensified the pressure on the financial system. That situation was aggravated by the government's response to the shocks. Believing them to be temporary, the government continued spending at rates consistent with the earlier trends in the supply of real resources. This required large amounts of borrowing. With credit becoming tighter abroad (mainly due to credit limits and from 1975 onwards the accumulation by Zambia of external arrears) the government continued borrowing domestically.[25] Debt (both internal and external) grew rapidly, arrears mounted, inflation accelerated, currency substitution intensified, and capital flight became rampant.[26]

These circumstances would have been difficult to manage if the officials involved were honest brokers caught in a tangled web of inconsistent government policies. The financial confusion, however, created opportunities for rent-seeking and corruption at all levels. The examples range from the small-time shakedowns (typically related to exchange control) to larceny on a grand scale.[27] One problem that has been exceedingly costly for Zambia but has passed by virtually unnoted has been the corruption and mismanagement at the BoZ. The accounting system at the bank became dysfunctional in 1988. Crucial records were destroyed. As a result, the bank could not produce for-

---

24. The subsidies mounted rapidly. By 1975 they were K100 million. This was 6.2 percent of GDP and 22.3 percent of the government's recurrent revenue (McPherson 1980, Ch. 2, n.104). See also World Bank (1986, Table A2, p. 122).

25. GRZ/UNICEF 1985, pp. 35–37.

26. Both Kindleberger (1989) and Friedman (1992) provide many examples of governments that have misused their financial systems. Zambia's policy makers repeated the same mistakes.

27. Crown Agents 1991.

mal audited accounts for several years. The situation was only "normalized" in 1994 with the publication of statements of affairs for the bank from 1988 to 1992 and qualified accounts for 1993.[28] Those accounts show qualified assets and liabilities in excess of $1 billion.[29]

This broad-based pattern of monetary and financial mismanagement generated rates of inflation that by 1990 had reached triple digits even in the presence of widespread price controls. Though formally illegal, a parallel market for foreign exchange thrived from the late 1970s.[30] Moreover, despite capital controls, capital flight reached major proportions. As a reflection of increasing financial disintermediation, the demand for kwacha denominated assets declined. The situation was both unstable and unsustainable. Monetary and financial reforms that would produce sharp reductions in the growth of the money supply and the liberalization of financial markets had become long overdue.

Exchange Rate Management[31]

Exchange rate policy has always been contentious in Zambia.[32] In the years immediately following independence, while national income was growing rapidly and the government maintained conservative fiscal and monetary policies,[33] there was little need to consider changes in the exchange rate. Moreover, until 1971, net foreign assets were never below the equivalent of 3.6 month's imports of goods and services,[34] and external public debt was approximately 10 percent of GDP.[35]

---

28. BoZ (1994, 1995). The IMF Statistical Appendix (IMF 1999, Table 17) points to the problem. It contains a note stating "Since January 1995, the balance sheet of the Bank of Zambia has been compiled on the basis of a new chart of accounts. Complete historical data only go back to December 1994."

29. The downside for Zambia was that many of the assets were valueless and most of the liabilities were not.

30. The government had created a special branch of the security forces—Special Investigation Team for Economic Controls (SITEC)—to guard against abuse of exchange controls. A Crown Agents report in 1991 indicated that SITEC was a major part of the problem.

31. This section draws on Lewis and McPherson (1994).

32. SIDA 1989. King (1991) noted that resistance to changes in the exchange rate predates independence. Most policy makers believed that devaluation could not help the economy. Ironically, it was the devaluation of the pound sterling in 1949 and the subsequent mineral boom that provided the basis of Zambia's modern economic growth (Baldwin 1965).

33. From 1965 to 1970, the budget deficit averaged −0.4 percent of GDP. Over this period, the government accumulated cash balances at the central bank. Its domestic borrowing was minimal.

34. Computed from kwacha values in the *IFS Yearbook* (1993, p. 762).

35. At the end of the 1960s, Zambia's external debt was K111 million, of which K56 million had been carried over from colonial days. The former was equivalent to $79 million. GDP for

Policy makers, in particular, were opposed to any modification of the official exchange rate (OER), fixed at the equivalent of K1＝$1.40 since 1949.[36] Their opposition was reinforced by the labor unions, powerful in Zambia due to their dominant position within the copper industry and the civil service. Union members were hostile to any measure (such as exchange rate depreciation) that might reduce their real incomes. So, too, were urban dwellers whose numbers were growing rapidly because of the impoverishment of agriculture (itself the result of inappropriate exchange rate policy).

In the absence of compensating increases in productivity that would have kept Zambia's unit labor costs in line with those of its international competitors, the economic shocks in the early 1970s lowered Zambia's real income. The appropriate policy response would have been to devalue the nominal exchange rate and take steps to contain price increases so that the real exchange rate would depreciate as well. Instead, the government allowed the kwacha to revalue. The negative effects of this action were compounded by the sharp reductions in productivity that accompanied the spread of state intervention.[37] The economy, as a whole, became increasingly uncompetitive. With absorption at elevated levels, the macroeconomic imbalance was financed through a rapid rise in foreign borrowing.

Despite the clear signs of economic crisis and, from 1975, the country's inability to fully service its external debt, the government continued to pursue its strategy of state-directed development and market manipulation. The government was reluctant to change this strategy. When such changes did occur, they came only after major economic damage had been done. The official exchange rate was devalued on a number of occasions, but every adjustment was too little and much too late. Furthermore, that action was not fully supported by the necessary corresponding changes in other policy instruments. The elections of October 1991 created an opening for a new approach to economic management including the adoption of a realistic ex-

---

1969 was $939 million. Thus, the debt/GDP ratio was 8.4 percent. Foreign exchange reserves at the end of 1969 were $354 million, equivalent to 13.5 months' import coverage and three and a half times the country's foreign debt (GRZ/UNICEF 1985, pp. 35–37; *International Financial Statistics* Yearbook 1997, pp.880–883).

36. Zambia's currency, the kwacha, was introduced after independence at a parity of K1 to ten U.K. shillings.

37. The mining production index (1985＝100) reached a post-independence peak of 144.7 in 1976. By 1992, the index was 82.3, a decline of 43 percent. Over the same period, mining sector employment fell by 11.3 percent, implying a decline in labor productivity in mining of almost a third. As noted earlier, productivity declines were evident in other sectors as well. (Sources: *Monthly Digest of Statistics* Jan/March 1984, Table 14c, Feb/March 1991, Tables 11c and 17; IMF Statistical Appendix 1999, Table 5, *African Development Indicators* 2001, Tables 2.3, 2.4).

change rate. Yet, it was not until early 1994 that exchange controls were finally removed.

Over the years, the Zambian authorities adopted several methods for managing the exchange rate. These were: a single fixed rate, dual fixed rates, a crawling peg, an auction, a float with the central bank offering discounts on tied balance of payments support, and, for a period from early 1994 to the latter part of 1995, full liberalization.

Determining when the exchange rate system began to unravel in Zambia is difficult. There were numerous precursors—encroaching state ownership of productive resources, the erosion of accountability under one-party rule, and the revaluation of the kwacha as copper prices fell and oil prices and transport costs rose. However, it was in the early 1970s that the most serious persistent pressures on the exchange rate emerged.

During 1973–75 the Zambian authorities revalued the kwacha against the US dollar by 11.1 percent (in nominal terms).[38] This change was not justified by the economy's capacity to generate and sustain a balance of payments surplus, especially given the dramatic reversal of the fiscal picture in 1974 and 1975. In that period, the budget balance shifted from a surplus of 3.4 percent of GDP to a deficit of 21.5 percent of GDP. The corresponding shift in the balance of payments current account was from a surplus of 0.5 percent of GDP to a deficit of 29.3 percent.

The appropriate response to such imbalances would have been to combine policy adjustment and finance. Expecting copper prices to recover, the government focused on financing the imbalances.[39] Under pressure from the IMF, it devalued the kwacha by 18 percent in 1976 and 10 percent in 1978. However, as data in Table 6–1 show, these changes achieved no significant real devaluation. Furthermore, the changes were inadequate relative to the degree to which Zambia's external accounts had deteriorated. Since little was done to reduce domestic absorption[40] and raise productivity,[41] the nominal devaluation was largely ineffective.

---

38. Due to low inflation in Zambia, the real effective exchange rate appreciated by slightly less, about 9.9 percent (*IFS Yearbook*, 1992, pp. 718, 756).

39. During the period 1974 to 1979, there was no reduction in public expenditure or consumption, or any success in raising additional domestic revenue. Government consumption as a share of GDP was .19 in 1974. It increased to .28 in 1975 and averaged .25 for the next four years (World Bank 1986, Tables A1, A2; *International Finance Statistics* Yearbook 1990, pp. 768–769). In 1975 alone, the government increased its borrowing from the domestic banking system by 16.6 percent of GDP, raised $425 million (17.9 percent of GDP) in extraordinary finance from abroad, and used $108.5 million (4.6 percent of GDP) in reserves and credit with the IMF (*IFS Yearbook*, 1992, pp. 758–759).

40. Absorption declines in response to devaluation because domestic prices rise, reducing real incomes sufficiently to lower the demand for imports.

From 1978 to 1982, the official exchange rate depreciated by only 10 percent in real terms against a background of rapid increases in the dollar value of external debt—43 percent over four years—and mounting payment arrears. Under pressure from the donor community (and as a precondition for continued IMF support) the government devalued the kwacha by 20 percent against the SDR in early 1983. The exchange rate was then allowed to rise gradually against a basket of currencies. This produced a real devaluation of about 35 percent by mid-1985.

Such a gradualist approach was an improvement on previous policies but it did little to help reverse the economy's decline. The budget deficit remained large—15.2 and 21.6 percent of GDP in 1985 and 1986, respectively—and foreign debt (in dollar terms) rose by a further 54 percent between 1982 and 1986. The premium on foreign exchange in the parallel market averaged 223 percent during 1985.

By 1985, the economy was in deeper trouble than usual. Mining production was falling, world prices remained low, and per capita food availability was precarious after a series (1982 to 1984) of poor maize harvests. In October, the government negotiated a stabilization and structural adjustment program with technical and financial support from the IMF, the World Bank, and other donors. Among other measures, the program involved the adoption of a floating exchange rate through a weekly foreign exchange auction. The auction was to be administered by the BoZ and be supported by trade liberalization, deregulation of other economic activities, and tighter controls over fiscal and monetary aggregates.[42]

The performance of the auction from its inception in October 1985 until President Kaunda canceled it in May 1987 has been widely studied.[43] During its initial stages, the auction achieved its primary goal of providing a market-based, nonpolitical mechanism for allocating foreign exchange. The kwacha lost 56 percent of its nominal value at the first auction (dropping from K2.2 to K5/$1). From October 1985 to June 1986, it drifted downward as the real effective exchange rate (REER) remained stable. The premium on the parallel market was almost eliminated.[44]

---

41. The opposite occurred. The fiscal system deterred investment in mining (O'Faircheallaigh, 1986). Management of the mining sector deteriorated, over-staffing was the norm and, as noted earlier, labor productivity declined.

42. The government's presentation to the consultative group in June 1985, provided the elements and the rationale for an action program that, if it had been implemented, would have fundamentally changed the economy's direction (GRZ 1985).

43. Harber, 1987; Kayizzi-Mugerwa, 1988; SIDA, 1989; Aron and Elbadawi, 1992; Lewis and McPherson 1996.

44. SIDA, 1989, pp. 60–66, and Aron and Elbadawi, 1992, p. 111.

The auction's success was short-lived. Because the government did not implement other components of the adjustment package, several donors delayed the disbursement of aid. As noted above, the budget deficit increased to 21.6 percent of GDP in 1986. Monetary growth accelerated, inflation rose, and the kwacha began to depreciate sharply. Influential Zambians began to believe that the auction was *causing* rather than reflecting macroeconomic instability. As a means of offsetting what senior officials called excessive depreciation, the auction procedures were modified in July 1986.[45] These modifications led to an appreciation of the kwacha (see Table 6–1) and raised questions about the sustainability of the auction and the fairness of its procedures. The supply of foreign exchange allocated to the auction was reduced. A pipeline of unfilled obligations emerged and the parallel market reappeared.[46]

The auction's termination in May 1987 was due largely to the government's unwillingness to accept the consequences for relative prices of the shortage of real resources, domestic and foreign. The exchange rate auction did not fail as many government officials contended at the time. It worked far too well! The problem was that it provided evidence unacceptable to the government that the economy was deteriorating at an accelerating rate.[47]

When the government terminated the auction, it set the official exchange rate at K8 to the dollar (compared with an auction rate of K22 in its final week). It also reintroduced foreign exchange controls and import licensing through the foreign exchange management committee (FEMAC).[48] Having rejected price as the basis for allocating foreign exchange, the government once again opted for allowing officials (who were quickly corrupted) and those with special access to dominate the system.

Exchange rate management reverted to its earlier pattern of ad hoc adjustments. In November 1988, the kwacha was devalued from K8 to K10 to the

---

45. The government's attempts to reduce the subsidies on staple foods led to riots in December 1986. Eleven people were killed by police during the riots. President Kaunda restored the subsidies, undercutting the budget (*The Economist* January 10, 1987, pp. 29–30).

46. The auction narrowed the premium on the parallel market but did not eliminate the market.

47. With hindsight, the changes in the auction system were part of a deliberate effort to undermine the reform program and discredit its supporters. At the time the auction was abandoned, the entire pro-stabilization economic management team (including the minister of finance) was sacked. Their replacements were party loyalists opposed to reform (Callaghy, 1990, pp. 294–295; West, 1992; Bates and Collier 1993).

48. There was no objective basis for choosing the figure of K8=$1. It was inconsistent with the economy's productivity, debt-servicing capacity, and future growth prospects (SIDA, 1989, pp. 78–90). Curiously, an Economic Association of Zambia (EAZ) seminar met to consider the choice of exchange rate and despite overwhelming evidence showing that the rate was unsustainable, endorsed the government's actions (Banda *et al.*, 1988).

dollar. It was then officially pegged to the SDR. It depreciated slowly against the dollar until May 1989 when, as part of a new agreement with the IMF, it was devalued from K10.8 to K16 to the dollar and then adjusted regularly (first monthly and then weekly).

The IMF and the World Bank pushed for a faster crawl. The government resisted. As a compromise, in February 1990, by which time the rate was K22=$1, a two-tier system was adopted. There was an "official" rate (primarily for conversion of copper earnings and the importation of oil and fertilizer) set at K22, and a second rate, initially set at K40, applying to other exports and commodity imports through an open general license (OGL) system.

The dual rates were merged in April 1991 as part of an economic recovery program adopted in mid-1989.[49] The unification did not work. A second "retention" market was created, based on the export retention scheme introduced in 1983. Under this arrangement nontraditional exporters were permitted to retain 50 percent of their export proceeds to finance their imports or sell to third parties through an official interbank "retention market." These controls, however, remained a jumble. They lacked coherence and a focus. More to the point, since they did not efficiently value or allocate foreign exchange, they provided no means for moving the economy forward.

3. Policy Reforms under the NERP

The New Economic Recovery Program (NERP) was designed to stabilize and restructure the economy, [50] thereby achieving ". . .positive real per capita growth as quickly as possible while bringing inflation down to an acceptable level. . .."[51] The new government had no doubt that inflation was its most pressing problem (and policy constraint). The NERP stated:

> The most immediate problem of macroeconomic policy is the unfinished business of conquering inflation. The objective is to bring the inflation rate down from about 100 percent in 1991 to 45 percent in 1992, 15 percent in 1993 and 5 percent in 1994. The Government will maintain strict fiscal and monetary disci-

---

49. The NERP calls for the exchange rate to play a ". . . pivotal role in spurring growth in nontraditional exports, reducing reliance on imports, and ensuring that scarce foreign exchange resources are allocated efficiently" (GRZ, 1989, p. 61). There is no explicit recognition that this implied a substantial depreciation of the kwacha.

50. GRZ 1992, p. 1.

51. GRZ 1992, p. 3.

pline to achieve these targets. In doing so, it will demonstrate its determination to reduce inflation.[52]

Given this focus, it is no surprise that the NERP stressed appropriate monetary policies, financial reform, and improved management of the exchange rate.

Monetary Policy

Noting that "(S)tructural reform and durable growth can only proceed once inflation has been brought firmly under control,"[53] the NERP set ambitious goals for reducing inflation. The target for the growth of the money supply in 1993 was 25 percent. This was to be reinforced by increases in nominal interest rates making borrowing rates positive in real terms. The government also intended lowering the costs of financial intermediation. One way to do this in the short term was to alter the mix of required reserves and liquid assets to give banks access to more earning assets. The government, however, was also looking ahead to the broader development of the capital markets. Its objective was to create conditions that would ". . .enable monetary control to be effected indirectly through the purchase and sale of government debt rather than through reliance on reserve and liquid asset requirements."[54]

The desire to move to indirect controls (partly) reflected earlier experience:

> Past attempts to regulate prices—including interest rates and the exchange rate—led to resources being allocated to activities in which Zambia does not necessarily have a comparative advantage. . .[55]

As a means of reinforcing monetary discipline, the NERP noted that the BoZ would strictly limit the volume of debt swaps and restrict the borrowing of the public enterprises from the banking system primarily by allowing them to raise prices to cover their costs. A major goal was to restrict credit to the public sector while providing the opportunity for the private sector to gain access to credit and foreign exchange.[56] It was anticipated that this would stimulate investment and raise the rate of growth.

---

52. GRZ 1992, p. 4.
53. GRZ 1992, p. 9.
54. *ibid.*
55. GRZ 1992, p. 3.
56. GRZ 1992, p. 4.

Financial Reform

Financial reform was included in the NERP as part of the government's efforts to improve competition throughout the economy and re-engage the private sector.[57] During the Second Republic a major premise of economic policy was that key financial sectors could be effectively operated as government-owned monopolies. This was a costly mistake. The NERP indicated that these monopolies would be dismantled.

> The Government will encourage greater competition in the provision of those financial services, such as insurance, pensions, and building society funds, that are presently controlled by state monopolies. This will be accomplished by removing monopoly rights from the state enterprises, and in some cases by privatizing the enterprises themselves.[58]

An element that exacerbated inflation in Zambia was financial disintermediation, especially from the mid-1980s onwards. Disintermediation had been encouraged by high and rising transaction costs due to inflation and the uncertainty associated with economic decline. It was further spurred by the increasing access (through globalization of financial markets) of Zambian asset-holders to low-cost financial services and low-risk assets abroad.

An important dimension of financial reform was to strengthen the operations of the BoZ. By easing foreign exchange controls and shifting to a system of indirect monetary management, the government was requiring the BoZ to change its operating procedures. To do this, the bank's staff had to gain new skills and adopt a more market-oriented (i.e., liberal) approach to monetary and financial management. It would no longer be adequate for the bank to set interest rates and the exchange rate and enforce loan limits for "priority" sectors. BoZ officials would have to understand (and respond to) the role of market forces in determining the cost of credit and its allocation, and the role of market mechanisms in determining the overall demand for and supply of money. This would require a complete overhaul in the way the bank was organized, major improvements in its accounting procedures, and a significant enhancement of its supervisory capacity.

Exchange Rate Reform

The NERP did not directly acknowledge that the kwacha was highly overvalued and the real exchange rate was not mentioned explicitly. Yet, evi-

---

57. The NERP stated:

The economic strategy recognizes the importance of market forces and the conviction that Government should not undertake what the private sector can do at least as well (GRZ 1992, p. 1a).

58. GRZ 1992, p. 12.

dence in the NERP left no doubt that exchange rate overvaluation had been a major problem for Zambia and would have to be addressed. As the data in Table 6–1 show, the real exchange rate depreciated significantly until the mid-1980s. From that point, it has generally appreciated. By 1990 more than half the earlier depreciation had been unwound. Under the NERP, the government indicated that it would maintain "an active exchange rate policy. . .":

> . . .supported by disciplined financial policies and complemented by structural measures—including tariff reform, elimination of barriers to exports, rebuilding infrastructure for trade and tourism, and promoting foreign investment.[59]

The commitment to an "active. . .policy," however, was qualified and limited. Full liberalization of the foreign exchange market was some way off:

> The Government's objective is to complete the process of moving the official exchange rate to a level that would permit the OGL to be shifted to a negative list system as soon as possible, and coverage of the OGL to widen from about 90 percent to at least 95 percent of the base period imports by mid-1992, provided Zambia receives adequate external assistance.[60]

Given the damage that already had been done to Zambia's growth prospects, particularly by exchange rate intervention, these goals were exceedingly modest. Subsequent events demonstrated that they were also grossly inadequate.

Overview

From both the language used and the space devoted to each issue, the officials who framed and approved the NERP were well aware of the urgency of reducing inflation, reforming the financial system, and achieving a realistic value for the foreign exchange rate. The general direction proposed for the reforms was constructive. Nonetheless, some disquieting aspects remained. First, there was a general presumption that the economy could be softlanded. Inflation was to be reduced to single digit levels over three years. Most international experience suggested that after such a long history of monetary and exchange rate mismanagement as Zambia had experienced, economies could not simply be "eased" down to "acceptable" (i.e. low) levels of inflation.[61] The credibility of the relevant authorities (particularly the BoZ)

---

59. GRZ 1992, p. 10.
60. *ibid.*
61. Bruno *et al.* 1991.

and confidence in the value of domestic financial assets had been seriously damaged. Potential investors both local and foreign had no basis for believing that "this time" the government would make the reforms work. It would take concrete results to diminish their skepticism.

Second, the timid approach to exchange rate reform was unwarranted. Exchange rate mismanagement had fundamentally undermined the economy's productive base. The overvaluation of the exchange rate should have been rectified without delay whether or not the donor community provided support. This is a case where the desire of BoZ officials to continue controlling the exchange rate dominated the nation's need to remove the distortions that had been such a barrier to growth.

Third, the commitment to remove the state monopolies in the financial sector was appropriate, but the details were complicated and provided many opportunities for missteps and backsliding. In addition to passing the relevant legislation and amending regulations, many improvements were needed in financial supervision, data reporting and monitoring, and bankruptcy and closure procedures. These would take a long time even under the best circumstances.

Fourth, although not specifically mentioned in the NERP, the government made clear its intention to actively foster financial development. Two areas that have received attention subsequently have been the establishment of the Lusaka Stock Exchange (LuSE) and the revitalization of agricultural credit. So far, the LuSE has played a minor role in Zambia's capital market, largely because the macroeconomic setting has been so unstable. The agricultural credit system has continued to be plagued by bad debts, fraud, and mismanagement.[62]

Notwithstanding these problems, the monetary, financial, and exchange rate reforms proposed in the NERP were a major improvement over what had been attempted by President Kaunda and UNIP. Viewed as a whole, they demonstrated that the new government was aware of the problems facing the economy and understood the types of responses needed to deal with them. The NERP provided an excellent start. But, as Zambia's history has shown, starting reforms has never been a problem. The basic difficulty has been in sustaining them.

4. STABILIZATION AND BEYOND

Despite the government's well-laid plans, the economy spun further out of control. Within months of the 1992 budget speech, the deficit widened.

---

62. MAFF 1996.

Instead of declining, the rate of inflation accelerated. Rallying behind the view that "inflation is the cruelest tax on the poor," the government made the control of inflation its principal economic objective for 1993.[63] A cash budget was introduced. This forced the government to match its expenditure to its revenue. Unfortunately, the government's efforts to curtail its expenditure were not matched by the central bank. During the early part of 1993, the BoZ made large unprogrammed loans to selected parastatals.[64] Reserve money almost doubled in the first five months of the year. Inflation increased sharply leading to rapid depreciation of the exchange rate. In December 1992, the kwacha was 359 to the dollar. By May, it had risen to 545. Interest rates, which had been liberalized with the introduction of the treasury bill tender in January 1993, rose precipitously. From 107 percent in December 1992 the compound annual yield on 91-day bills increased to 348 percent by July 1993.

Once the source of reserve money growth was discovered, [65] the BoZ was instructed to stop lending to parastatals. With both the budget and central bank under control, the growth of reserve money dropped dramatically. Inflation fell abruptly and in July the kwacha began to appreciate. From a June peak of 551 the dollar, it fell to 348 in September. This represented a real appreciation of the kwacha between December 1992 and September 1993 of 52 percent. The government was widely blamed for having engineered the appreciation, when in fact it had not manipulated the rate. The appreciation was an outcome of the government's success, for the first time in more than two decades, controlling the growth of domestic credit and reducing inflation.

The Transition to Stability

Government measures to limit the growth of reserve money began to take effect in late May 1993. But, due to lags, inflation remained high in June (15.8 percent) and July (12.6 percent). By August, the credit squeeze had reduced

---

63. This point was made by an expatriate advisor at one of the weekly meetings of the Technical Committee of Ministers. It was included in a speech that President Chiluba gave at a meeting of the donor community. Ministers attending that meeting picked it up and (for a period at least) the phrase "inflation is the cruelest tax on the poor" became a theme guiding government policy.

64. Most of the central bank credit was provided to ZIMOIL to cover its deficit because of the government's unwillingness to let petroleum prices rise to reflect the cost of imports.

65. BoZ officials had specifically assured MoF staff and the IMF mission in February 1993 that the central bank was not lending to the parastatals. It was not until April that MoF officials discovered otherwise. The BoZ had been providing foreign exchange to ZIMOIL without kwacha cover.

inflation to 2.5 percent. It averaged 0.7 percent over the next three months and was negative in November.

For holders of kwacha-denominated financial assets, there was a marked change in inflationary expectations in July. By this time the market-determined compound annual yield on 91-day T-bills was around 340 percent. The sharp drop in inflation, together with the much slower decline in the T-bill rates caused the real rate of interest to rise dramatically. On 91-day T-bills it reached an annual rate of 181 percent in September. By that time the rise in the demand for T-bills pushed their rates downward to an average rate of 112 percent (92 percent in real terms) in the fourth quarter.

These developments reflected a sharp contraction in the supply of both reserve and broad money. After rising by 92.9 percent from January to May, nominal reserve money went up only 3.4 percent from June to September. In real terms it declined over the whole period. Relative to its December 1992 level, the real value of broad money fell by 8.9 percent to May 1993 and a further 18.9 percent by September 1993. This was the essence of the credit squeeze.

While consumers and some officials welcomed the kwacha's appreciation, the exchange rate had overshot. The main enterprises in the economy, especially ZCCM and commercial farms, were not viable at such an appreciated real exchange rate.[66]

During 1994, the government and the BoZ began to gain more leverage over the exchange rate and the interest rate. With inflation continuing to fall, real interest rates remained highly positive. The T-bill market continued to broaden and deepen. The BoZ established a foreign exchange trading desk. Its operations provided the Bank's senior officials with direct evidence of the importance of consistent policies.[67]

These trends in the exchange rate and interest rates stimulated other changes in the financial system. There was growing evidence of financial re-intermediation. As already noted, while inflation remained high asset-holders had responded by moving out of kwacha-denominated financial

---

66. There has been much second-guessing of why government did not foresee the overshoot and begin to ease off earlier. Given that Zambia had had two decades of high (and often rising) inflation, the MoF and BoZ did not want to ease the credit squeeze prematurely. Their hesitance was reinforced when October's inflation rate, widely expected to be negative, turned out to be 3.7 percent. Moreover, having previously exceeded the IMF's reserve money and net claims on government ceilings, both organizations had made a special effort to meet the September benchmarks. This required the continued withdrawal of liquidity from the system.

67. Some of the panic in the foreign exchange market was triggered when BoZ sales changed sharply. During three weeks in November-December 1993, the BoZ sold $17 million, $6 million, and $11 million, respectively, providing conflicting signals to market participants.

assets. Velocity (i.e., the ratio of GDP to money supply) which had been as low as 3 in the early 1980s, rose to a peak of 9.7 in 1993 due largely to the preceding periods of triple-digit inflation. With the sharp decline of inflation during the latter part of 1993, asset holders were more willing to add kwacha (and kwacha-denominated assets) to their portfolios.

One consequence of the shift out of kwacha as inflation accelerated was that prices became hypersensitive to changes in reserve money. The pass-through from changes in reserve money to inflation was a matter of weeks rather than the more leisurely periods when money creation was more restrained.[68]

In order to reduce inflation, the government had to sharply curtail the growth of reserve money. The basic problem was the budget deficit. As can be seen from Table 6–1, Zambia had large persistent budget deficits beginning in 1970. Indeed, the budget deficit throughout the Second Republic (1972 to 1991) averaged 12.6 percent of GDP. Reserve money issued to cover this deficit averaged 4.6 percent of GDP per annum. Over the whole period (20 years) reserve money increased by approximately 21,600 percent. Since corresponding inflation was roughly 57,750 percent, the government gained virtually nothing from seignorage. Indeed, given that the exchange rate changed by a factor of 91, i.e., 9,100 percent, Zambia probably lost real resources. The latter resulted from the increased domestic cost of external debt service payments not covered by donor flows. In addition to these costs, rapid inflation and the sharp devaluation of the exchange rate caused major damage to the financial system.

The outcomes in Zambia reconfirm, as many governments elsewhere have also discovered, that once the central bank "turns off the monetary spigot," inflation cannot continue. A major problem in Zambia, however, has been that this lesson had an ephemeral impact on senior policy makers. Having broken the back of inflation in the latter part of 1993 and through 1994, they began to presume that inflation was under control. From early 1995, senior policy makers allowed the operation of the cash budget to unravel by adopting two fudges.

The first was an arrangement whereby the central bank made an interest-free loan of an amount that would allow the government to cover a prearranged level of monthly expenditure. The intention of this "bridging finance" was to prevent the irregular monthly flows of government revenue from dis-

---

68. As part his doctoral dissertation, Joseph Kapai estimated inflation equations using monthly data. His results show that during the 1990s, the adjustment of prices in Zambia to shifts in money creation (and ultimately deficit spending) was exceedingly rapid. (Personal communication with Mr. Kapai, October 2000.)

rupting the operations of ministries and departments. In theory, this finance was meant to be temporary and was to be liquidated within each month as government revenue flowed in. This system worked for the first few months until difficulties, created by unprogrammed expenditures, prevented the "bridge" from being repaid.

The second fudge was the payment by the BoZ of official external debt service without government first finding the kwacha counterpart. Also presumed to be temporary, this arrangement was adopted at the urging of the IMF in 1994 as the government and the IMF struggled to meet the original completion date (March 1995) for the RAP. Because the government was reluctant to close Zambia Airways, some donors had withheld balance of payments support. At the time, the IMF staff argued that temporary accommodation from the BoZ would enable Zambia's external debt to be settled without breaching other (domestic) financial targets (particularly net bank claims on government). As is typical in such risky manipulations, extraordinary circumstances intervened and the government, instead of repaying the BoZ, used its available foreign exchange for other purposes. The temporary accommodation became permanent reaching close to $150 million in mid 1997.[69]

As a result of these grants from the BoZ to the government (both of which contravened the Bank of Zambia Act) reserve money grew rapidly. Both fudges should have been avoided—the first by having the government accumulate a small cash "cushion" (i.e., a genuine surplus) so that its monthly payments would face fewer disruptions. That prospect was never considered because the government invariably encountered some activities (both on and off budget) that required "urgent" financing. Moreover, BoZ finance was far more convenient (and more easily hidden from public scrutiny) than having to hold back on government expenditure. The second fudge was a major mistake. It was reserve money creation in its purest form. The BoZ bought foreign exchange in return for kwacha; it then gave the foreign exchange to the government. In monetary formation terms, the first transaction offset the in-

---

69. By late-1995, it was apparent that this temporary accommodation had become permanent. During a meeting of the Data Monitoring Committee, the author suggested that BoZ staff meet with MoF officials to rationalize this financing either by the payment of interest on the outstanding balances or by the issue of T-bills to cover the entire amount. The suggestion was ignored. At the Bournemouth (U.K.) meeting of the Consultative Group meeting in December 1995, I again suggested to Zambian officials that the government's outstanding balance to the BoZ should be included as part of the financing gap. That suggestion was also ignored. It would have pushed the gap to more than $400 million, a figure beyond what the donors were expecting.

crease in net domestic assets with an equivalent amount of net foreign assets. The second transaction simply ran down Zambia's net foreign assets. The full increase in net domestic assets remained.

Despite the government's commitments to macroeconomic stability, repeated assertions that the "cash budget" was operational, and regular statements by senior officials in the government and the BoZ that they were implementing prudent fiscal and monetary policy, the growth of reserve money has remained high. To illustrate, over the years 1995 to 2000 inclusive, reserve money increased by 61.1, 35.4, 48.2, 16.9, 28.4, and 49.8 percent, respectively.[70] For an economy where real income per capita was declining, such high rates of reserve money creation can only produce high rates of inflation. It is no surprise, therefore, that throughout the 1990s Zambia had one of the highest sustained rates of inflation in the world.

Zambia's experience with rapid inflation (above 100 percent per annum) in the early 1990s and chronically high rates ever since, has had an important effect on movements in the exchange rate, particularly the real exchange rate. To put the issue in perspective, it is useful to pick up our earlier narrative.

By the time the MMD government took office, the foreign exchange market consisted of several channels (no funds, retention, OGL, official, market, and parallel) featuring many different rates of exchange. The challenge facing policy makers was to rationalize this system in ways that complemented the broader program of economic reform.

In the budget of January 1992, the government devalued the official exchange rate by 30 percent and raised the retention rate to 100 percent. This effectively moved 50 percent of non-traditional exports from the official market to the retention market. At the same time the BoZ shifted a similar amount of outflows (mostly service payments) to the retention market.[71]

Under pressure from the MoF, the liberalization continued. The exchange rate crawl was accelerated. In October 1992, a *bureau de change* system was introduced. From December 1992, ZCCM was allowed to sell at a market exchange rate derived from the average rate determined in the *bureau de change* market. The budget in January 1993 provided for 100 percent external remittance of profits and announced (without naming a date) that the government intended lifting all exchange controls.

---

70. These data are available in the *Macroeconomic Indicators*. They can also be found in *International Financial Statistics* (April 2001, pp. 886–887).

71. This reaction was typical of the preoccupation by BOZ officials with the gap between the official and retention rates. Focusing on whether this gap was narrowing or widening, bank staff paid less attention to the broader question of whether the overall policy of multiple exchange rates, reinforced by controls, was sustainable.

BoZ officials, however, did not want to relinquish those controls. Preparations dragged out for a further year.[72] The central bank used two arguments for moving slowly. The economy was too unstable, and relaxation of exchange controls would cause capital flight.[73] Bank officials provided no evidence for either proposition. Each was asserted in the expectation that the bank's experience would carry the day.

Under pressure from the MoF, the BoZ agreed to a modest relaxation of the controls in July 1993. The government, however, wanted to move further and faster. A BoZ/MoF subcommittee was formed to develop procedures for removing the controls altogether. In October 1993, the subcommittee recommended removal of all exchange controls except for transitional arrangements in three areas: copper earnings, external debt payments, and large capital items. The January 1994 budget speech announced the elimination of all exchange controls.[74]

For a period, the foreign exchange market functioned well. With improved control over the growth of reserve money, inflation subsided and the nominal exchange rate stabilized.[75] These attempts to achieve stability were occurring against a background of large but variable flows of foreign assistance (see

---

72. The Exchange Control Act of 1965 and accompanying regulations vested power over virtually all foreign transactions in the minister of finance. The minister, in turn, delegated the powers to the BoZ. The bank instructed authorized dealers to operate in a way that would "...facilitate administration of the [Exchange] Control so that it may serve its objective of conserving and increasing the country's foreign exchange resources with the least obstruction to trade and its financing" (BoZ, 1981, p.2). In practice, the BoZ did not follow its own instructions. Most of its regulations had the effect of inhibiting trade.

73. The BoZ (1993: 9–11) argued: "The repeal of the Exchange Control Act would...lead to massive capital flight, at least in the short-run, considering the current instable (sic!) macroeconomic conditions and the rapidly declining value of the kwacha.... The basic requirements for the total abolition of exchange controls are: (a) a reasonable macroeconomic stability, (b) a deep and efficient interbank exchange market, (c) availability of sufficiently large (free) exchange reserves on a sustainable basis to enable the Central Bank to become an active market participant and to intervene in the market effectively, and (d) a well-developed and efficient supervision system for monitoring exchange market operations on an on-going basis." Had the government accepted these "requirements," exchange controls could not have been lifted.

74. As a transitional measure, the minister of finance authorized the BOZ to purchase ZCCM's foreign exchange earnings at market-determined rates and to supervise the foreign exchange operations of financial institutions (powers formerly conferred by the Exchange Control Act).

75. Data from the *Macroeconomic Indicators* (July 1995) show that over the period July to December 1993, the rate of inflation was 8.9 percent whereas during the first six months, January to June, it had been 98.7 percent. The exchange rate was K367.8=$1 in January. It rose to K551=$1 in June, fell to K368=$1 in October, and then rose to K520=$1 in December. (The latter rate was influenced by the donor threat to withhold aid because of allegations of drug

Chapter 9). After some initial hesitancy, the donor community provided large amounts of support to Zambia. During 1992, the net aid flow was $1.04 billion, more than double the amount (of $.48 billion) in 1990. Donor/government relations experienced some difficulties in early 1993. Reacting to what was seen as a threat to political stability, President Chiluba declared a state of emergency in March 1993. Although the emergency was lifted in May 1993, it was widely seen as a serious step backwards for a country that had so recently restored democratic rule.[76] Further trouble was brewing. At the December 1993 Consultative Group meeting in Paris, donors made their support conditional on government action against drug running and corruption among Cabinet members, a move widely applauded in Zambia. President Chiluba reluctantly reshuffled his Cabinet in January 1994.

These events raised uncertainty about the levels of donor support in 1994. The exchange rate depreciated forcing a tightening of credit.[77] These episodes were to be repeated at the end of 1995 when donors began focusing on the performance of ZCCM and continued evidence of high-level corruption. As noted in Chapter 3, the government was becoming increasingly reluctant to respond to donor demands for further reform. Much of the mutual goodwill that had emerged because of Zambia's return to multiparty democracy was being dissipated.[78] In 1996, the ESAF program was off track and President Chiluba, despite promises to the contrary, had the Constitution rigged to exclude his principal rival (and leader of the opposition) from contesting the presidency. Cooperation with the donor community effectively collapsed. Donor assistance, especially for projects, continued but the Chiluba government was unable to regenerate the earlier support it enjoyed among the donors.[79]

---

running by at least two ministers.) Stability in the exchange rate was achieved in 1994. Over the whole year, the exchange rate depreciated by 5.2 percent, from K644.7=$1 in January to K680=$1 in December.

76. Full details about the state of emergency and the "zero option" plan (wherein opposition leaders urged the overthrow of the government) were never made public. A number of prominent opposition politicians were charged with sedition, but all cases were eventually thrown out of court. The most enduring effect of the episode was to undermine donor support for the government.

77. In December 1993, the Statutory Reserve Requirement was raised to 32.5 percent (from 23 percent) and the Liquid Assets Ratio was raised from 35 percent to 50 percent.

78. Without donor support the budget would collapse. Expenditure in 1994 was programmed to be K686.8 billion, including K124.8 billion of foreign-funded capital expenditure and K115 billion in external debt service (interest only). Donor rescheduling of debt amortization and arrears, which was off-budget, accounted for another K565 billion.

79. During a visit to Zambia in January 2000, I met with several senior officials of the donor community to determine if they would support technical assistance along the lines of METAP.

Reintervention by the Bank of Zambia

These developments had a major impact on the operations of the foreign exchange market and overall trends in the nominal and real exchange rates. An added dimension has been the attempt by the BoZ from mid-1995 to manipulate the exchange rate. Unfortunately for the Zambian economy, the BoZ intervention succeeded in stemming the decline in the kwacha. This "success", however, came at the cost of the loss of confidence within the private sector, continued financial disintermediation, and economic decline.

In technical terms the BoZ was the victim of the well-known target/instrument problem. It had too many targets (low inflation, a stable exchange rate, the accumulation of foreign reserves, low interest rates, and overall financial stability) with too few instruments (reserve ratios and the purchase/sale of T-bills). A further handicap is that few Zambians have seen the BoZ as a credible institution. Insiders understood the shakiness of its accounting procedures and the limited capacity of its staff to monitor the financial system. Outsiders have typically seen its policies to reduce inflation and stabilize the exchange rate as being ineffectual. They have also seen BoZ actions as inequitable.

Pressure on the monetary and financial system came from several quarters. First, despite its stated commitment to the policy, the government ceased operating a cash budget in the early months of 1995. Second, the financial system has experienced a number of bank collapses and closures.[80] The support provided to these banks, particularly Meridien/BIAO, whose demise is described in the appendix, led to large increase in reserve money. That experience undermined confidence and left many bad debts. Third, the financial flows from the donor community were seriously disrupted at several points as the government's commitment to reform waxed and waned.

Fourth, the protracted collapse of ZCCM's operations was accompanied by numerous attempts to cut corners and disguise from the public the true state of the company's finances. In the process, some large costs were shifted to ZCCM. For ZCCM, one of the most financially damaging requirements was the use (by the government and BoZ) of its sales of foreign exchange to help stabilize the exchange rate. This largely accounts for the long periods of

---

No donor was enthusiastic. Indeed, representatives of an agency that has been one of Zambia's staunchest supporters stated that the majority of its support was "on hold" and would be reassessed only after the 2001 elections.

80. As noted in the appendix, Meridien/BIAO was closed in May 1995. Two smaller banks were taken over by the BoZ at the end of 1995. Prudence Bank was placed under BoZ management in 1997, Commerce Bank was ordered shut in 1998, and Finance Bank was reorganized. Details may be found on the BoZ website www.boz.zm.

stability of the nominal exchange rate, for example, from May to December 1996 during the run up to the elections and from June to December 1997. In the former period, the exchange rate depreciated by 2.5 percent and during the latter by 6.6 percent. For most observers, these periods of stability were contrived especially in the last half of 1997 when the full force of the Asian financial crisis reverberated through world financial markets. In addition, the government and BoZ adopted measures such as guaranteed loans, forward sales of copper, and tax relief in order to keep the mines operating. None of these measures was adequate and ZCCM's financial position deteriorated. Published accounts from 1995 onwards show rising losses. During 1998 and 1999, the local and international press reported ZCCM's losses on the order of $15-$20 million per month. (Estimates provided in Chapter 10 show that these figures were too low.) ZCCM accumulated large domestic arrears. Clearing these arrears absorbed a significant portion of the 2000 budget. This included an amount of K423 billion (roughly 4.2 percent of GDP) to pay ZCCM's most pressing arrears.[81] The overall direct costs to the government were significantly higher with one source noting that as part of the sale of ZCCM the government assumed debts equivalent to 19 percent of GDP.[82]

Any one of these problems would have tested a well-functioning central bank. Taken together, they overwhelmed the BoZ. The situation began unraveling in 1996 when donors cut their balance of payments support in response to the government's manipulation of the Constitution. To deal with the shortage of foreign exchange, the BoZ accommodated the government. Reserve money grew by 62 percent. Monetary growth was lower, at 28.3 percent, primarily because of a widespread shift out of bank deposits and an increase in the required reserves at the commercial banks. Both changes had a negative effect on financial intermediation. The increase in reserve requirements in 1996 reversed the financial liberalization achieved up to that time.[83] The higher reserve requirements raised the tax on financial intermediation without addressing the underlying cause of the rapid growth in reserve money. During 1996, reserve money increased because of lending by the central bank to a number of commercial banks that experienced liquidity problems. Reserve money also increased because the BoZ was unwilling to force interest rates up so as to sterilize some of the increase in liquidity. The casu-

81. Budget Speech 2000, par. 55.

82. IMF/IDA 2000, p. 6

83. In the 1995 budget, the statutory reserve requirement was reduced from 27 percent to 3 percent. This change dramatically reduced the tax on financial intermediation. To offset the potential monetary impact of releasing such a large amount of liquidity, the government issued statutory reserve bonds to banks. The bonds earned market-based rates of interest. They could be redeemed over a period of five years.

alty was inflation. In 1996, it was 35.2 percent.[84] The 1996 budget speech had projected inflation to be 15 percent for the year.

In 1997, reserve money grew by 26 percent and the money supply by 22 percent. During the first four months of the year, international reserves declined by $40 million. During the last part of 1997, the government ran a large budget surplus. By easing pressure on the growth of reserve money, the BoZ was able to buy foreign exchange without undue pressure on the money supply and interest rates.

The situation reversed in 1998. During January, gross international reserves fell by $37 million from which point they continued to fall.[85] The situation deteriorated with gross reserves declining from $256.4 million at the end of 1997 to $85.3 million at the end of 1998. This precarious situation remained, with gross reserves in 1999 being only $46 million.[86] With the sale of ZCCM and a switch to a less interventionist policy, there has been some recovery. Gross reserves at the end of 2000 were around $146 million.[87]

These policy conflicts raise issues about official "management" of both the exchange rate and interest rates. During 1997 interest rates fell continuously, despite an increase in the treasury bill stock of over 10 percent. A possible explanation might have been a decline in inflation expectations. Evidence suggests that inflation may have moderated, although the monthly data remained highly variable. The widely held expectation that inflation would fall did not materialize. More important, however, was official manipulation of interest rates through BoZ "suggestions" to commercial banks that they should lower their rates or be left holding cash.[88] To the banks, any positive T-bill yield is preferable to holding excess cash. Banks followed these suggestions and made the inevitable choice. But, as interest rates were pushed down, deposit rates at commercial banks became unattractive. With inflation still relatively high, real interest rates became significantly negative.

Similar problems emerged with the exchange rate. Evidence has not supported the government's regularly repeated assertion that the exchange rate was determined by the market.[89] The basic issue is that the government is for-

---

84. *Macroeconomic Indicators* April 2000, Table 1.2. The datum is computed December to December.

85. *Macroeconomic Indicators* January, 1998; *Citibank Treasury Letter* Issue No. 3, March 1998. The latter source put reserves at the end of March at $165.2 million, down from $237.1 million at the end of December 1997. Reserves were $184.7 million in January 1998.

86. Sources: IMF Statistical Appendix 1999, Table 17, IMF/IDA 2000, Table 8.

87. IMF/IDA 2000, Table 8

88. In August 1997, the author met with representatives of several commercial banks in Lusaka who confirmed the BoZ actions.

89. This point is regularly repeated in the government's *Letters of Development Policy*, submissions to the Consultative Groups' meetings in Paris and so on. It was explicitly stated in the 1998 *Budget Speech* (pars 58, 98). Market operators, however, understood that this was not the

mally committed to accumulation of reserves. Its market participation should therefore tend to depreciate the exchange rate. For example, in the first quarter of 1997, foreign reserves declined sharply even though the ESAF agreement with the IMF called for the opposite to happen. Concern about depreciation of the exchange rate dominated the policy response. The result, however, was that the nominal stability of the kwacha achieved by the BoZ led to a marked appreciation of the real exchange rate. That was not in Zambia's interests. Nor was it consistent with economic developments. With donor flows declining, copper export earnings falling, and widespread uncertainty in local and global financial markets, Zambia required a major depreciation of the real exchange rate. The government unwisely resisted this. Its hand, however, was forced through the reemergence of a parallel foreign exchange market.

Promising to reduce the poverty rate to 50 percent of the population by the year 2004, the 1998 budget sought to accelerate economic growth. The budget, however, had been framed on the basis that more than 35 percent of the resources required would be provided by the donor community. That did not occur when one of the main conditions, namely, completion of the sale of ZCCM (to the Kafue Consortium) fell through. Similarly, the 1999 budget assumed that a large share of resources needed to fund the government's programs would be provided by the donor community. The year started out in promising fashion with an ESAF agreement with the IMF. This agreement, however, collapsed within months as the government budget, again, went off track. In the closing months of 1999, the government and Anglo American came closer to a final deal for the sale of ZCCM.

The 2000 budget assumed that the deal would be finalized. It was framed in ways that could allow Zambia to tidy up some of the mess created by ZCCM's financial collapse. As noted earlier, a sizeable share of the budget was devoted to paying off ZCCM's arrears. Because resources were limited and the government would not cut other areas of expenditure, a budget deficit was programmed. This meant that the government was, once more, postponing the time that Zambia could bring inflation down. Again, by mid-2000, the government's inflation targets had been breached. According to the budget speeach, the inflation target was 14 percent. Actual inflation was 22.3 percent.[90]

---

case. The reemergence of the parallel market in foreign exchange is evidence that the exchange rate has not been market-determined. The HIPC "decision point" document repeated the point. (IMF/IDA 2000, par. 14, p. 8). The BoZ, nonetheless, reintroduced exchange controls in December 2000.

90. IMF/IDA 2000, Table 7. The inflation targets for 2001 and 2002 have been set at 16.5 and 11.5 percent respectively. These targets condemn Zambia to two more years of nonrecovery.

MMD has a budget record covering more than a decade. Each budget has promised lower year-end inflation. Only the 1993 budget met that promise and only after a period of inflation in mid-year of 16 percent per month. It is no surprise why the government cannot achieve its inflation target. Large budget deficits continue. While these remain, inflation will be high and economic growth will not revive.

5. Improving Monetary, Exchange Rate, and Financial Management in Zambia

An important aspect of the NERP was the need for the government to improve monetary policy, restructure the financial system, and enhance the overall management of the exchange rate. As noted earlier, the NERP stated that action in all three areas was essential. It was also acknowledged, implicitly at least, that reform in these areas would be complementary. The discussion above gave details of the types of changes the government indicated would be made. What was not known at the time the NERP was formulated (and could not be predicted) was whether the government would follow through with its commitment to reform or, like its predecessor, would abandon or deflect the reforms. The evidence now shows that the government selectively abandoned key elements of its reform program. In view of this experience, what are the options for further monetary, financial, and exchange rate reforms?

Constraints on Reform

A major problem for most of the last three decades in Zambia is that monetary, financial, and exchange rate policies have been implemented against a background of severe constraints. This situation has been especially relevant in the case of exchange rate management. The history of the government adopting and then casting aside different exchange market regimes has made the Zambian public and business community wary of any further changes the government might propose. Several points stand out.

First, the government has lacked clear objectives. It has sought to make the exchange rate serve several purposes—subsidizing imports, keeping the costs of imported machinery and equipment low, reducing inflation, lowering the domestic cost of external debt service, providing evidence of a strong economy, and forestalling pressure for wage increases from the unions. Some of these goals are contradictory. Worse, the government provided no clear indication of its priorities.

Second, since past efforts to manage the exchange rate have been unsuccessful, current and future options are severely limited by the BoZ's lack of credibility. For instance, because the foreign exchange auction was so widely regarded as a failure, memories will have to dim and the idea repackaged before it could be tried again. Similarly, since the economy performed so poorly while the government has attempted to stabilize the exchange rate, there is no basis for arguing that BoZ should (or could) use the exchange rate as a nominal anchor.

Third, because donor support is equivalent to such a high share of GDP, actual and anticipated changes in donor flows can destabilize the exchange rate. More important, Zambia's continued reliance on foreign savings will maintain downward pressure on (i.e., appreciate) the exchange rate. This will continue to undermine Zambia's ability to compete internationally.

Fourth, fluctuations in the exchange rate in Zambia have typically boosted inflation. Prices rise as the kwacha depreciates, but do not fully adjust to any subsequent appreciation.[91] As a result, the real exchange rate has become seriously overvalued. There are a number of ways of computing what the nominal exchange rate would have to be to compensate. Based on developments since the early 1990s, when Zambia began unwinding its external arrears, the exchange rate at the end of December 2000 should have been K5803=$1. It was actually K4157=$1.[92] Due to BoZ manipulation (starting in December 2000, the exchange rate subsequently appreciated sharply averaging K3200=$1 during the first quarter of 2001.)

---

91. This topic relates to the more general fear of a "devaluation-inflation" spiral, to which all governments are sensitive. Recent Zambian experience shows that such a spiral is not inevitable if the budget deficit is kept under control and credit is not allowed to accommodate rising prices. These controls were not in effect when the auction system was in place. The SIDA study noted that: "...with the benefit of hindsight it is clear that by early 1987, the expected one-time inflationary consequences of devaluation had not been contained. They had, instead, been exacerbated by loss of control over the fiscal deficit which, in turn, was being financed by equally uncontrolled growth in money supply. These effects, in a highly liquid yet stagnant ecoomy—constrained mainly by the shortage of foreign exchange—were driving the kwacha down precipitously" (SIDA, 1989: 12).

92. Over the period 1992 to 2000, the kwacha depreciated against the U.S. dollar by 2.1 percent in real terms. Since the United States experienced dramatic expansion (boosted by productivity improvements) and real per capita income continued to fall in Zambia, the real value of the kwacha should be adjusted at least by the productivity differential. In aggregate terms this can be approximated by the change in real per capita GDP. For the U.S., it rose by 26.1 percent between 1992 and 2000. For Zambia, it declined by 13 percent. Thus, to retain the same relative positions in 2000 as in 1992, the real exchange rate should have declined in Zambia by at least 39.6 percent [computed as 1.261*1.13/1.045]. Based on this calculation, the exchange rate at the end of 2000 should have been 4158*1.39.6=K5803. (Source: *International Financial Statistics* February 2001).

The Availability of Data

Monetary and exchange rate reforms have been compromised by lack of data. The impact of policy changes cannot be monitored without up-to-date information. Details of some of the data problems facing policy makers have been described elsewhere (Chapters 3, 4, 9, and 13) and need not be repeated here. A major effort was made to improve a broad range of monetary, fiscal, and other macro data beginning in late 1992. That effort provided the basis for the successful implementation of the cash budget, rationalizing the external debt, managing the T Bill tender, and operating the foreign exchange desk at the BoZ.

What was not anticipated, however, was that senior policy makers would begin withholding key macroeconomic data (such as external indebtedness, gross reserves of the BoZ, ZCCM's outstanding debt) or manipulating the inflation data. Chapter 13 discusses this matter in the context of macroeconomic management and governance. An example cited there was the "talking down" of inflation after a monthly inflation rate (exceeding 5 percent) was recorded in early 1997.[93]

Sustained reform is impossible if such behavior continues. It has created uncertainty and undermined the credibility of the central bank and the government. Senior policy makers have been preoccupied with attempts to disguise adverse movements in key macro variables rather than focusing on the steps needed to remove the economy's imbalances.

The main reason for improving the timeliness and coverage of the basic data is to enable the government and BoZ to take a proactive stance on economic policy. With such an approach, key policy makers are less likely to be surprised ('shocked') by bad news. Furthermore, they will depend less heavily on visiting IMF missions to inform them how the economy is performing and why.

Yet, even with better data, continued improvements are needed in regard to monetary programming and exchange rate projections. Despite intense efforts during most of the 1990s, the BoZ has lacked a credible (and accurate) balance sheet. This problem dates to the accounting irregularities that emerged in 1988 when the bank was unable to produce a coherent set of accounts. For several years, this hindered the BoZ's ability to fully monitor and analyze the monetary formation factors.[94]

Particularly important relationships in Zambia have been the link between

---

93. As pointed out in footnote 54 of Chapter 13, inflation for 1997 derived from the import and GDP deflators should have been at least 31 percent. The official datum was 18.6 percent.

94. Because of rapid inflation, the real value of domestic variables has diminished. This is not the case for external assets and liabilities, whose dollar values do not change.

the budget and changes in money and credit and the effect of exchange rate movements on the fiscal balance. On the revenue side, exchange rate depreciation raises the kwacha equivalent of aid disbursements, import and export taxes, and net government revenues from parastatal exporters (such as ZCCM before it was sold). Similarly, it raises the revenue from import taxes.[95] On the expenditure side, depreciation raises the kwacha cost of government imports and debt service.[96] The net impact of these movements changes the fiscal balance with consequent monetary implications.

These various linkages reinforce the need for the monetary and fiscal agencies to cooperate in identifying and measuring the most important interrelationships and feed-back effects. BoZ management has tended to resist the need for closer cooperation as a way of enhancing its "independence." Such behavior, however, has not been constructive. Moreover, it seriously misconstrues the essential features of having an independent central bank. BoZ managers could usefully be guided by the principle that central banks should be independent within, but not of, the government.[97] The BoZ needs the skilled personnel and resources to make an objective assessment of the economic situation. Nonetheless, if BoZ staff are to contribute effectively to the management of the monetary and financial system, they have to cooperate with other (relevant) agencies of government.

Restoring Confidence

A major purpose of such cooperation is that it eases the task of restoring confidence. Because the economy has been chronically unstable, it will take time (perhaps years) for the government and the BoZ to convince the general public, the business community, and potential foreign investors that they are

---

95. Much of this beneficial effect was offset by widespread tax fraud. An aggregate index of the extent to which fraud is undermining revenue is provided by measures of tax bouyancy. Under normal circumstances taxes on international trade should be buoyant, i.e., have elasticities with respect to income (GDP) greater than unity. Over the period 1992 to 1998, the buoyancy of trade taxes was .76. The buoyancy of government revenue as a whole was .99 (IMF Statistical Appendix 1999, Tables 2, 12.) With the change in ZRA administration in 1997, greater attention was paid to tax fraud.

96. Given Zambia's large debt stock, debt service has been a major concern. With high inflows of aid, the depreciation-debt link has minimal impact on the budget. However, as Zambia rationalizes its debt arrears and re-joins the ranks of creditworthy sovereign borrowers, special efforts will be needed to prevent debt service from undermining fiscal discipline.

97. This idea has been attributed to Robert Roosa, a senior U.S. Treasury official at the time who, when asked about the independence of the Federal Reserve Bank in the United States, replied that the Federal Reserve is "independent within, but not of, the government of the United States." (I thank Professor James Duesenberry of Harvard University for this anecdote.)

determined to take a responsible (and responsive) approach to economic management. Asset-holders have remained highly skeptical. They have only been willing to hold kwacha-denominated assets when the real return has been significantly positive. This has been evident in the difficulties the BoZ has encountered in deepening and lengthening the bill and bond markets.[98]

Of all the steps that the MMD government have taken to restore confidence during the 1990s, the most important were those that sharply reduced inflation during 1993 and the reintegration of the parallel and official foreign exchange markets through the lifting of exchange controls in 1993/94. The positive economic developments that followed these changes demonstrated to the general public that purposeful, constructive government policy could work. That experience contradicts policy makers who believe that controls provide a way out of the economy's difficulties.[99]

With Zambia's exchange rate history in mind, it may seem odd to consider refixing the exchange rate. There is now a widespread view that, as a means of anchoring the financial system, countries that have had a long history of monetary and exchange rate instability should consider fixing the exchange rate. Such an approach, it is believed, helps regenerate confidence and provides a basis for macroeconomic stability and renewed economic growth.[100] We shall briefly explore whether that would be feasible in Zambia.

Refixing the Kwacha?

The essential feature of a high inflation setting is the rapid adjustment of domestic currency variables, notably monetary aggregates, the exchange rate, and the wage rate.[101] The role of a nominal anchor is to break, or at least modify, the dynamics associated with such adjustments. This is accomplished when a government (or central bank) succeeds in fixing one of the domestic currency variables. Alternative anchors include a stable growth of reserve

---

98. Government debt (bonds and bills) has been traded on the Lusaka Stock Exchange (LuSE). The intention has been to create a secondary market for this debt. The 2000 budget speech reported that there have been around two dozen trades in this secondary market for government debt throughout 1999. The market remains exceedingly thin.

99. Intemperate outbursts by senior officials do nothing to lessen the difficulties. When the former minister of finance condemned businesses for pricing in dollars she added to, rather than removed, uncertainty. The headline of the *Zambia Daily Mail* for Saturday, May 14, 1999, read "Nawakwi condemns dollar prices" The paper continued:

Finance Minister Edith Nawakwi, has fired a salvo at businessmen who are pegging their prices in dollars, describing them as greedy people stealing from customers.

100. Welch and McLeod (1993) argued that the key element in establishing a credible commitment to a fixed exchange rate in Latin America has been prudent monetary and fiscal policies. With those policies in place, the choice of an exchange rate regime does not have a marked effect on economic performance (Mills and Wood, 1993; Easterly and Schmidt-Hebbel, 1993).

101. Bruno 1988.

money,[102] the public sector wage bill,[103] nominal interest rates, or a credible commitment to a fixed nominal exchange rate.[104] The use of currency boards (e.g., in Argentina, Bulgaria, Estonia, Lithuania, in addition to well-established arrangements in Hong Kong and Brunei) has been seen as an institutional modification that can help countries stabilize. This institutional fix has been particularly important in countries such as Argentina that have a long history of monetary and exchange rate mismanagement.[105] A currency board fixes the nominal exchange rate. By doing so, it effectively adopts the monetary policy of the country (in Argentina's case, the United States) to which the local currency is linked.

The apparent simplicity of fixing the nominal exchange rate (and calling it an anchor) is also its major drawback. In a system where monetary policy is inappropriate and financial reform has been half-hearted, fixing the exchange rate compounds economic instability. Choosing among alternative anchors is not the same as choosing among alternative strategies for stabilization. The only effective prescription for short- and long-term stability is to eliminate the budget deficit.[106] Indeed, for a heavily indebted country such as Zambia, the only effective foundation for long-term economic stability is to run a budget surplus.

In essence, the choice among anchors is merely a choice among *targets* against which to measure exchange rate performance. The key is choosing a credible target. Without a fundamental overhaul of Zambia's principal economic institutions, namely the BoZ and the MoF, the idea of fixing the exchange rate lacks credibility. Attempting to implement such a policy would undermine, not enhance, confidence.

An Alternative Scenario[107]

If a fixed exchange rate regime is ruled out, what options are viable? Resumption of the auction that President Kaunda canceled in 1987 would be

---

102. For instance, the growth of reserve money might be held close to zero or some low nominal amount. This requires strict control over the public sector deficit, since a major source of reserve money creation is central bank lending to government. In its most drastic form, this type of monetary targeting led countries such as Bolivia (that experienced hyperinflation in the mid-1980s) to require a balanced budget on a daily basis.

103. Where the civil service accounts for much of formal sector employment, a wage freeze provides a nominal anchor. This was a key element in successfully stabilizing the Gambian economy in the mid-1980s (McPherson and Radelet 1995).

104. This was the rationale for the European Union's exchange rate mechanism until it collapsed under the weight of international capital flows (Corden 1994, Ch. 7).

105. Shuler and Hanke 1994.

106. Killick, 1987; Bruno, 1988; and World Bank, 1993.

107. Fischer (2000) discussed the challenges of policy formation in a world of bipolar exchange rate regimes (irrevocably pegged or freely floating). By contrast, Williamson (2000)

preferable to a fixed exchange rate. But, mindful of that history, market participants would lack confidence in the government's willingness to (i) allow the auction to operate without interference, and (ii) maintain an orderly supply of foreign exchange to support the operation of the auction. One consequence of an auction system would be the continuation of a parallel market. Indeed, any scheme that provides a management role for government or the BoZ in the foreign exchange market will be suspect. Capital flight, currency substitution, and evasion of exchange control restrictions have become so ingrained among Zambian businesses that the only regime that can ensure an orderly market is one that minimizes the "tax" (time, paperwork, side payments, fees, and risk of arbitrary disruptions) on foreign exchange operations. This was clearly evident from mid-1995 when, intent on stabilizing the exchange rate, the BoZ would not allow the rate to depreciate until pressures (including a parallel market) emerged that could no longer be contained.

Given these developments at a time when the government and the BoZ insisted they were not interfering, there seems no option except to ensure that the BoZ fully withdraws from any direct responsibility for the exchange rate. This might be achieved by appointing a consortium of commercial banks to act as agents for the BoZ. The BoZ would determine the change in foreign reserves consistent with its other policy objectives and then direct the commercial banks to acquire or dispose of the relevant amounts of foreign exchange. Such an arms length relationship would be constructive because the BoZ does not have the credibility to manage the monetary and exchange rate systems effectively. Its reputation can only be re-built through a sustained period of prudent behavior.

Even if the BoZ is removed from direct participation in the foreign exchange market, the government's operations can have a potentially disruptive effect. Debt service payments and aid flows are large and lumpy. These, however, would be far less consequential if the BoZ would re-build its international reserves and the government would rationalize its own performance so that aid could flow on a more regular basis. Indeed, one advantage of the 'aid exit' strategy (outlined in Chapter 14) is that a regular but declining, and therefore less disruptive, pattern of aid flows can be programmed well in advance.

Overview

Whatever system is adopted for determining the exchange rate, one implication of any attempt to *improve exchange rate management* in Zambia, is that

---

proposed a mechanism for achieving a middle ground between fixed and floating exchange rates.

the authorities will have to promote and sustain a sound monetary policy. This will require the full implementation of the types of monetary, financial, and exchange rate reforms contained in the NERP and subsequent proposals. None of the measures can be fudged. After a decade's experience with these reforms and with many otherwise useful achievements undermined by policy reversals, improvements in exchange rate and monetary management require the government and BoZ to behave prudently.

This will involve:

- Containing the budget deficit and thereby restricting the growth of domestic credit so as to ensure macroeconomic stability. (In the medium term, this will require strict adherence to the cash budget.)
- Continuing development of a market-oriented financial, trade, and foreign exchange system;
- Promoting close MoF/BoZ collaboration to achieve the goals of the economic recovery program.

If appropriately implemented, these actions will produce:

- Interest rates that reflect the supply and demand for credit;
- The effective supervision of banks and financial institutions;
- The rationalization of internal and external public debt;
- The elimination of arrears;
- An end to subsidies and open-ended financial commitments to SOEs;
- Enhanced competition among financial institutions;
- Continued improvements in data monitoring; and
- Further reductions in restrictions on international trade and exchange.

6. Lessons for Monetary, Exchange Rate, and Financial Management

Our review of Zambia's approach to monetary, exchange rate, and financial management raises two questions: how, and why, has such a retrograde system been sustained for so long? In the late 1970s, there was already overwhelming evidence that monetary policies and the exchange rate regime were seriously damaging the economy.[108] Exchange controls were failing to stem capital flight. The budget deficit resulted in the rapid growth in reserve money and high rates of inflation. The increasing premium in the parallel foreign exchange market was evidence of the growing distortions in the offi-

---

108. This point was made in the World Bank country economic memorandum (World Bank 1977). Further evidence of the damage created by the government of Zambia's economic policies was captured in modeling exercises (McPherson 1980, Chs. 3, 5).

cial foreign exchange market. Large balance of payments deficits led to the rapid build-up of foreign debt and mounting external payment arrears.

This information was available to everyone who lived in Zambia and studied its economy. Yet, it had little practical effect on economic policy, including the pace and persistence of efforts to reform the economy. Senior policy makers did not seem to view the exchange rate as a key macroeconomic price that taxes some activities and subsidizes others, or to fully account for the linkages among exchange rate, monetary, fiscal, and trade policies, and debt management. Over the longer term, monetary and exchange rate mismanagement together with the lack of financial reform have compounded rather than ameliorated Zambia's economic problems. The experience yields a number of lessons.

Delaying reform increases its cost: Failure to reform monetary and financial policies and the exchange rate system aggravated Zambia's economic imbalances. Adjustments made over the past two decades illustrate one misstep after another.[109] The exchange rate should not have been allowed to appreciate against the dollar between 1973 to 1975. The devaluations of 1976 and 1978 were too small, given the sharp decline in Zambia's export capacity and international competitiveness. Adjustments in the 1980s were unrelated to the opportunity cost of foreign exchange (as reflected in the parallel market). Instead of abandoning the auction in 1987, the government should have reduced its budget deficit. Unification of the exchange market during 1989–91 *via* an accelerated crawl would have required eliminating exchange controls. That was not done. Finally, when exchange controls were removed in 1994 and the kwacha was floated, the BoZ should have confined its activities to stabilizing the growth of reserve money in ways that avoided exchange rate shocks. Instead, the BoZ began to manipulate the exchange rate by attempting to limit the rate of depreciation.[110]

In the area of monetary policy, delays have been exceedingly costly as well.

---

109. Short-term mismanagement of the exchange rate can be readily explained in political economy terms. Groups enjoying access to foreign exchange at subsidized rates—party stalwarts, unionized workers, import-substituting parastatals and favored traders—gained from the policy. Over the longer term, the economy's decline has been detrimental to all groups. In particular, the distorted exchange rate has been a significant part of the general policies that contributed to a marked rise in poverty in Zambia (Fry, 1974; GRZ/UNICEF 1985; Illiffe, 1988: Ch.13; World Bank 1993).

110. It is easy to criticize the BoZ for its handling of the exchange rate. There has been pressure from the government as well. An example was the sale of foreign exchange in early 1999 in an effort to lower (i.e., appreciate) the exchange rate. This action was taken as a result of pressure from the new minister of finance.

Inflation of 19,260 percent over the period 1972 to 1991[111] and of 5,300 percent over the period 1992 to 2000, are evidence of irresponsible fiscal and monetary management—of governance gone awry. The growth rate of the money supply was far too high relative to changes in the economy's real growth in the late 1970s. That problem was compounded during the 1980s and into the 1990s. The appropriate response was to cut the budget deficit. That did not occur until the cash budget was introduced in 1993. Even that mechanism, though effective, was not sustained.

Resistance to reform is deeply entrenched: The commitment of policy makers to financial and exchange rate reforms will not ensure their success if the main sources of resistance are not neutralized (or brought on board). This requires an understanding of the motivation of key participants. Policy makers responding to national concerns rather than sectional interests would have devalued the exchange rate in 1975, when Zambia's terms of trade deteriorated by 41 percent.[112] The authorities chose not to act, allowing the real exchange rate to become seriously distorted. As the crisis worsened, hesitant and sporadic adjustments were made, and then only under donor pressure.

Over time, the locus of resistance has shifted. During the Second Republic, the party, the unions and the manufacturers supported the status quo. With the change of government, the BoZ became a major obstacle to reform.[113] None of these groups lacked information on the problems created by resisting reform. The problem is rooted in the political economy of controls and rent generation. It also reflects the long-standing problem of ineffective leadership in Zambia.[114]

Slow liberalization cannot cure large imbalances: The MMD government, like its predecessor, greatly underestimated the costs to the economy of continued monetary and financial mismanagement and overvaluation of the exchange rate. Instead of moving quickly to eliminate the budget deficit and remove distortions in the exchange rate system, the government was persuaded (primarily by the BoZ) to remove controls slowly and selectively. Major imbalances remained, and the reform process failed to win public

---

111. *International Financial Statistics Yearbook* 1997, pp. 880–881.

112. World Bank (1992, p. 662) gives terms of trade indices of 215.5 and 126.3 for 1974 and 1975, respectively (1987=100); $126.3/215.5 - 1 = -0.413$.

113. The BoZ governor was widely viewed as the main barrier to exchange rate liberalization. In reality, resistance was institutionalized in the bank. The removal of the governor in June 1992 did not make the organization any more receptive to the idea.

114. Gray and McPherson 1999.

confidence. In effect, the authorities failed to understand that for the economy to move forward, a fundamental (and obvious) break with past policies was needed.

By adjusting slowly, particularly with respect to the elimination of distortions in the exchange rate and reducing the rate of inflation, the authorities retained a highly inequitable *de facto* tax on holding kwacha assets. In ever-increasing numbers, individuals and firms demonstrated they were not prepared to bear that tax. Selective easing of exchange controls in lieu of their abolition encouraged individuals and firms to maintain the arrangements (overseas accounts and the use of foreign currency for local transactions) that they had earlier adopted to evade those controls.

This contrasted with the dramatic response of holders of treasury bills once the real interest rate became positive. While there was some overshooting in the real interest rate as inflation retreated in mid-1993 from annualized rates of close of 500 percent, the T-bill market deepened and broadened significantly during 1994. Unfortunately, subsequent manipulation of the financial system undercut the growth of the T-bill market.

Stabilization is not a precondition for exchange rate reform: In resisting rapid action to remove exchange controls, the BoZ argued that exchange rate liberalization should await stabilization of the economy. The need for stabilization was pressing, but its absence was no reason to delay exchange rate reform.

The fundamental problem facing Zambia in late 1991 was lack of confidence in the economy and in the government's ability to promote and sustain economic reform. Confidence could not be restored as long as the government and its agencies (particularly the BoZ) were perceived as being reluctant to remove the main distortions. Furthermore, with confidence so low, none of the major actors had any reason to believe that reform would occur until the government eliminated the most obvious and counterproductive restrictions.

Improved financial supervision is not a precondition for removing exchange controls: Another BoZ argument for retaining exchange controls was that it needed time to improve financial supervision. In effect, exchange rate reform was held hostage to the central bank's inadequacies.

Numerous specialists have noted[115] and experience during the latter part of the 1990s has shown that financial supervision is a key central bank func-

---

115. Goodhart 1988.

tion whether or not there are exchange controls. After having had sole responsibility for exchange control for more than 25 years, the BoZ should have simultaneously developed its capacity for monitoring and supervision. Otherwise, it is difficult to understand how exchange controls could be properly administered. The BoZ's argument that it needed further time to strengthen supervision (meant as a tactic for delaying the lifting of exchange controls) was, in fact, a convincing case for relieving the bank of that function (and possibly others as well).

Successful exchange rate and financial reform requires complementary policies: Exchange rate and financial reform can succeed only as part of a broad economic adjustment program. Floating the exchange rate ensures that the rate will be determined by the market. It does not guarantee that the rate will be stable. Broadening the offering of financial instruments provides asset-holders with more options. It does not mean that more of these assets will be held. These changes need to be supported by complementary measures—control over the growth of reserve money, enhanced competition among financial enterprises, strengthened financial supervision, and the removal of impediments to trade. Such changes dampen fluctuations in the demand for and supply of foreign exchange, and increase the demand for financial assets.

Of all the complementary measures, the most important are to reduce the public sector deficit to levels that are (at least) covered by the inflows of foreign aid, reforming key financial institutions, and ensuring that the growth of real wages does not exceed changes in labor productivity.

A devaluation-inflation spiral is not inevitable: Policy makers in Zambia have worried that devaluation would induce a devaluation-inflation spiral. As long as some domestic prices are influenced by the official exchange rate and do not fully reflect the opportunity cost of foreign exchange, devaluation will normally lead to a first-round increase in the price level. Yet, Zambia's experience in 1993 demonstrated that a spiral need not follow if the public sector deficit is controlled and credit policy is nonaccommodating. The key is to control credit creation. A spiral reflects accommodating monetary policy. Without that, prices and the exchange rate will stabilize.

Fads do not constitute reform: The government established a stock exchange as a means of deepening the capital market. The central bank has sought to be independent of the government. The former was done before the government had brought its budget under control and the macro economy stabilized. The latter occurred before the central bank could produce a detailed set of audited accounts and a monetary survey on a regular basis. This does not deny that a stock exchange may eventually provide some valuable extensions of the existing assets market or that the central bank should necessarily be dominated by the government. The point is that symbols of modernity have little practical impact if the institutional capacity does not exist to enable them to function effectively. History has shown that the development of stock markets is demand driven. (In Africa one need only look at the stock market in Nigeria. Established in the 1920s, its operations differ little from that of a casino.) As noted earlier, without the capacity to offer independent advice to the government, the legislative proclamation of central bank 'independence' is an empty exercise.

Financial development and economic development take hard work. It is vain for the government in Zambia to believe that it can jump-start the process by a series of quick fixes. Too many corners have been cut already and the Zambian population has paid too high a price for these errors to be repeated.

Capacity and confidence are essential for exchange rate and financial reform: At one level, Zambia's economic history since 1970 has been a case study of how government interventions undermine investor and business confidence. The government intervened too often, in too many areas, and too inconsistently, fostering widespread and systematic abuse by vested interests. To protect the value of their assets, Zambians (both individuals and firms) shifted them abroad, used substitute currencies, and conducted transactions through nonformal and parallel channels.

To change this, the government has to demonstrate its capacity to manage the economy effectively and take explicit steps to regenerate confidence. Given that its technical and analytical capacity is severely limited (see Chapter 12), the most constructive approach is to pursue consistent and transparent policies that leave minimal scope for arbitrary official actions. The cash budget, with its unambiguous criterion of no spending before resources are available, and market liberalization, with its presumption of no official interference, are examples of such policies.

Cycles of self-fulfilling adverse expectations (common to Zambia) can be broken only when asset-holders have an incentive to change their behavior. Tighter foreign exchange controls and financial restrictions do not restore confidence, especially when they are administered by a central bank that the general public and business community do not trust. Continued controls add to the tax on financial intermediation; they do nothing to reduce that tax.

Regenerating confidence will take time: To begin restoring confidence, the actions of the government and the BoZ need to change. The changes should reflect the understanding that: (i) attempts to manipulate the exchange rate typically backfire; and (ii) to influence the exchange rate the BoZ will need to operate indirectly through the market, using its ability to modify the growth of reserve money and foster financial competition.[116] For its part, the government will have to ensure that its budget operations do not create credit.

7. Concluding Comments

Over the past three decades, the formulation and implementation of monetary policy, the pursuit of financial development, and the management of the exchange rate in Zambia, have been characterized by delays, reversals, and outright obstruction. The result has been the systematic undermining of the process of financial intermediation, the excessive expansion of domestic credit, and the persistent overvaluation of the real exchange rate. The reforms adopted by the MMD government in 1992 under the NERP provided a basis for rationalizing the system of monetary and exchange rate management, and stimulating financial deepening.

After a shaky start, due to the failure to bring the budget under control, the government began to stabilize the financial system, and to lay the basis for low inflation and exchange rate stability. During the latter part of 1993, and throughout 1994, there were major improvements in all financial aggregates. These positive developments were short-lived. The government, through the BoZ, began to manipulate the exchange rate (in an effort to reduce inflation) and to use coercion to lower interest rates (in order to reduce the cost of internal debt service). The outcome of this interference was predictable—confidence collapsed, asset-holders (once more) shifted out of kwacha-denominated assets, and inflation and interest rates rose.

Numerous lessons can be derived from this experience. The most important is that the monetary and financial systems and exchange rate cannot be appropriately managed against a background of budget deficits.

After a decade's stewardship by the MMD government, a major monetary lesson from Zambia's past remains unheeded. Zambia cannot reduce its inflation to levels comparable with world rates and stabilize its exchange rate until it brings its budget deficit fully under control and achieves sustained reductions in its debt. Promises to reduce inflation and stabilize the exchange

---

116. Though the principal focus of the chapter has been the domestic market, the globalization of financial markets imposes strict limits on the types of actions that the government and BoZ can sustain (Summers 1995).

rate (common to every budget speech during the 1990s) are hollow unless backed by control over the budget and strict limits on credit creation.

APPENDIX: THE COLLAPSE OF THE MERIDIEN/BIAO BANK[117]

The Origins of the Crisis

In 1994, Meridien/BIAO Bank was the third largest commercial bank in Zambia as measured by deposits and loans and advances, but the second largest when measured by assets. Its principal owner, Andrew Sardanis, was a prominent local businessman who, after modest beginnings as a rural merchant during colonial times, became wealthy as a key official-cum-broker in the early days of the Kaunda regime. His most prominent task was to assist the government of Zambia nationalize the economy's main productive assets over the period 1968 to 1970. The largest of these state takeovers was the country's copper mines. As part of this deal, he became a shareholder in Zambia Consolidated Copper Mines (ZCCM), owning slightly more than six percent of the stock.[118] After leaving government service, Sardanis continued to be closely associated with, and supportive of, the Kaunda regime. As part of his expanding business empire, he established Meridien Bank in the early 1980s. With the change in government following the elections of October 1991, he remained on amicable terms with the Chiluba government. His bank thrived. Among other activities, Meridien provided leasing finance to Zambia Airways, organized loans for other state-owned enterprises, and acted as international broker for ZCCM's metal marketing proceeds.[119]

The rapid growth of Meridien's asset base in Zambia generated resources for expansion. Meridien spread its operations into neighboring countries (Swaziland, Tanzania, and Malawi)[120] as these countries began liberalizing their financial systems. Meridien's principals, however, had bigger plans. They wanted to create a pan-African institution. This could be done in two ways. One was to continue what was already underway, namely to establish

---

117. This appendix is based on a paper prepared for Harvard University's Capacity Building for Economic Decision Making Project, Ministry of Finance and Planning, Maputo, Mozambique. I am grateful to Clive Gray and Bruce Bolnick of Harvard University for helpful comments.

118. Mr. Sardanis's role in the operation has been discussed in several places. Martin (1972) covers the matter well.

119. ZCCM used to consign its output to the Metal Marketing Corporation (MEMACO) a London-based subsidiary.

120. At the time of its collapse, Meridien was in the process of obtaining a banking license in Kenya.

subsidiaries in other countries as financial markets opened up. The other was to buy an established bank. The opportunity for such a purchase arose in 1992 when the Banque Industriel pour Afrique de l'Ouest (BIAO) was offered for sale. Meridien bought the bank, forming Meridien/BIAO (MB hereafter).

By 1994, MB was widely represented in West and Southern Africa. The best-laid plans often go awry. MB's expansion strategy had two weaknesses. The BIAO group had been severely weakened by large loan losses.[121] The rapid expansion of the MB group had overtaxed its managerial capacity. Costly mistakes began to mount. One that was widely known in financial circles in Zambia was one of Sardanis's nephews, based in London, lost millions of dollars speculating in foreign exchange.

Since Zambia was the headquarters of the MB group and because it was so profitable,[122] resources generated in Zambia were used to support the group's international operations.[123] Yet, the profits from MB's Zambia operations were due to a special set of circumstances. One of these was that MB had floated a new high-yield financial instrument (marketed as Meridien investment bonds) that began attracting large deposits. Some of the proceeds were invested in treasury bills that, during late 1993 and throughout most of 1994, earned exceedingly high real returns.[124] To induce people to take up these investment bonds, MB paid above the prevailing bank deposit rate. It could do this because it did not set aside the required (noninterest bearing) statutory reserves.[125] MB's management argued, and Bank of Zambia (BoZ) officials agreed, that the resources raised through the issue of the investment bonds were not deposits as defined under the Banking Act.[126]

---

121. I do not have records giving the details. However, one extenuating circumstance was that the whole francophone zone was under increasingly severe economic pressure during the early 1990s due to the progressive real overvaluation of the CFA franc. This was creating major difficulties for many of BIAO's traditional customers—traders and industrialists. The CFA franc was devalued in 1994.

122. Data from the supervision department of the BoZ reported profits after tax for MB of K3.3billion (equivalent to $7.2 million) for 1993 and K4.1 billion ($6.1 million) for 1994 (BoZ 1995, Appendix 1).

123. It was revealed only in 1995 when the BoZ began to closely scrutinize MB's books that many of its loans had been made within the MB group. A significant number of these were not performing (Records provided in confidence to the author.)

124. To illustrate, the average annualized real return on 28 day T-bills in the first three quarters of 1994 were 86.3, 113, and 58.4 percent, respectively. With the nominal exchange rate moving by only 3.5 percent over that period, these were exceedingly high real dollar returns as well (Source: *Macroeconomic Indicators*, July 1997, Tables 1.3 and 2.6).

125. The statutory reserve was 32.5 percent of deposits until March 1994, at which time it was lowered to 29 percent.

126. Since statutory reserve deposits earned no interest, a large "wedge" existed between deposit and lending rates.

Throughout 1992 and 1993 and into the first part of 1994, MB's operations in Zambia grew rapidly. The bank constructed a large new headquarters in a prime location in downtown Lusaka. Already well-known as an art collector, Sardanis commissioned many new works for these headquarters. He also purchased some of the enterprises that the government had begun to sell as part of its privatization effort. People passing through Lusaka airport could see his private jet parked on the tarmac in between its numerous trips to and from Europe (often with senior government officials aboard).

To all external appearances, everything was going well. Nevertheless, MB's financial standing was badly shaken in September 1994 when *EuroMoney* published an article that questioned the viability of MB's corporate strategy and cast doubt on the bank's solvency.

It was later revealed that when the article appeared, the minister of finance wrote to the governor of the BoZ, seeking assurances that MB's Zambia operations were sound. The governor summoned MB's management and contacted Sardanis, who was living in Paris at the time, and received such assurances. Satisfied, the governor responded to the minister with a favorable report on the bank's financial position and prospects.

It is never easy to identify the precise time that a particular bank encounters trouble. There are, however, at least three stages. The first is typically hidden from all but a few in the bank's inner circle.[127] This is when the fundamentals of the bank become impaired (nonperforming assets rise and liquidity declines) in ways that make it vulnerable to shocks. During this phase, bank supervisors even if they are especially diligent may see little evidence that would cause concern. The problem is that there is little to show that the quality of the bank's portfolio has deteriorated, the loan coverage provided by collateral has become inadequate, or that there are serious maturity mismatches in the structure of assets and liabilities.[128] The second phase is when members of the financial community outside the bank begin to suspect the bank is in difficulty. This information emerges because the bank cannot settle its accounts on time and in full, payments to correspondents are delayed, the interbank market becomes a regular source of extraordinary

---

127. Evidence from the collapse of Barings Bank, the huge losses sustained by Sumitomo Bank on its copper account, and the mega-billions of dollars lost by Long Term Capital Fund shows that the inner circle can remain exceedingly small until the financial institution has suffered major damage.

128. The BoZ supervision report for 1994 showed that MB's nonperforming loans were equivalent to 65.6 percent of its capital and reserves (BoZ 1995, Appendix 9). These were lower than the average for all banks in Zambia. This might appear to excuse bank supervisors from singling out MB, yet had these nonperforming loans been set against MB's capital and reserves, its capital adequacy would have been the lowest of all Zambian banks.

accommodation, or the bank drops out of transactions that have been a normal part of its operations.[129] When these suspicions begin to emerge, interbank accommodation dries up and large depositors begin a "silent run."

This second phase tends to be followed relatively quickly by increased attention from bank supervisors. The effects of the silent run show up in the bank's clearing accounts at the central bank. As its liquid assets drain away, the troubled bank may approach the central bank to rediscount large amounts of bills and other eligible securities. Under more extreme circumstances, the troubled bank may request an emergency loan from the central bank.

By this (third) stage, the bank's troubles are usually widely known and it may experience an overt run. If that happens, the central bank, as lender-of-last-resort, will face the decision whether to support the troubled bank. There is now a long tradition, derived from the history of central banking, setting out the principles involved.[130] The central bank has to decide whether the main problem is illiquidity (lack of readily salable assets to overcome the immediate pressures) or insolvency (lack of sufficient high quality assets to remain in operation). Due to limited information (in many cases aggravated by the inattentiveness of bank supervisors before the difficulties became apparent, or misleading information provided by the troubled bank to the supervisors), the choice is rarely straightforward.

As lender-of-last-resort, the central bank faces the further problem of whether the troubled bank's difficulties are likely to snowball if it fails. This idea of systemic risk has featured prominently in central banking literature, especially in discussions of the notion of "too-big-to-fail" (TBTF).[131] Again, this issue has a long history and much has been written particularly regarding the moral hazard that may arise once a bank's owners or managers perceive their organization as being TBTF. Moral hazard is not confined to financial arrangements; it arises in any circumstance where those who take decisions do not bear their full consequences. [132] This point needs to be emphasized.

---

129. One of the first hints to the local financial community in Zambia of MB's increasing difficulties was that it began rapidly liquidating its T-bill holdings.

130. Economic historians (Sayers 1957; Goodhart 1988) trace the first statement of these principles to Walter Bagehot's book *Lombard Street* published in 1873. Fischer (1999) covers the same principles in his assessment of the need for an international lender of last resort.

131. Relevant references are McDonough (1997), Burnstein *et al.* (1997), and Goodfriend and Lacker (1999).

132. Moral hazard results in a change in risk taking behavior because the risk taker perceives that others cannot afford to (or will not) let them bear the full costs of their actions. The standard example is the insured driver who behaves recklessly because he/she is insured. In financial circles, managers of large banks tend to take on imprudent levels of risk, knowing that the central bank (or the government) cannot afford the knock-on effects of their failure.

For the central bank, the decision about whether to support a particular bank during a financial crisis does not hinge on whether moral hazard created the problem. The TBTF decision hinges entirely upon whether allowing the troubled bank to fail would inflict even greater damage on otherwise sound financial institutions.[133]

Should the central bank decide to deny support to the troubled bank, it has to take over the bank and oversee its orderly closure. In financial systems of developed countries, mechanisms and organizations for undertaking these tasks are well established. In most cases, the troubled bank is placed under new management, restructured, and sold. In developing countries, where financial systems are shallow and fragile, that option is generally not available. Thus, central banks often find themselves having to provide support to banks that, in fact, should be closed.

As subsequent evidence would reveal, MB had been in difficulties for a long time. The principal problem was the nonperformance of intragroup loans. It is likely that MB would have been in serious trouble even without the international attention that followed the *Euromoney* article. By September 1994, MB's capital was totally inadequate and as nominal interest rates in Zambia fell, its earnings were squeezed.[134] Unable to sustain the premium on its investment bond, MB began losing deposits.[135] As already noted, its overseas operations in West Africa and London had experienced losses although, at the time, these particular difficulties were not fully understood by BoZ or MoF officials.

Role of Banking Supervision and Prudential Regulations in Place

Without access to the bank returns submitted by MB to the BoZ, the time at which MB began showing chronic weaknesses cannot be pinpointed. For example, records that became available to the MoF from the BoZ in late December 1994/early January 1995 clearly demonstrated that (when adjusted for nonperforming loans) MB's capital base (equity and reserves) had been equivalent to slightly more than one percent of its assets for the last several

---

133. For public relations purposes, the decision to support a large bank is couched in terms of the damage to the broader economy. For a central bank, the principal concern has to be the soundness and integrity of the financial system. The implications for the rest of the economy can rarely be foreseen, particularly during a financial crisis.

134. In 1994, nominal interest rates on 28 day T-bills fell from an annualized rate of 140.9 percent in the first quarter to 20 percent in the fourth quarter (*Macroeconomic Indicators* July 1997, Table 2.6).

135. Competing banks in Zambia protested to the BoZ that MB should be made to hold statutory reserves against what, in fact, were deposits.

Table 6–2.   *Key Ratios for Meridien/BIAO, December 31, 1994*

Indicator	Meridien/BIAO	All Zambian Banks
Loans and advances	K 13.400bn	K144.900bn
Deposits	K 39.100bn	K290.700bn
Total assets	K103.000bn	K608.300bn
Treasury bills	K 0.130bn	K 81.300bn
Share capital	K 0.463bn	K 5.200bn
Liquidity ratio	22%	34.7%
Capital to deposits	1.2%	4.6%
Capital to total assets	0.45%	2.2%
Nonperforming loans/		
Total loans	29.6%	34.8%

Source: Provided in confidence to the author. For comparison purposes, K1 billion was equivalent to $1.49 million. (The period average exchange rate in 1994 was K670=$1.)
Zambia's GDP at the time was K2.24 trillion, equivalent to $3.35 billion.[138]

months of 1994.[136] As shown in Table 6–2, on December 31, 1994, MB had ratios of capital to deposits of 1.2 percent and capital to total assets of 0.45 percent. By comparison the corresponding averages of the Zambian banking system as a whole were 4.6 and 2.2 percent, respectively. Broader evidence of the pressure to which MB was subject appeared in December 1994 when MB redeemed a large quantity of T-bills to cover its loss of deposits.[137] MB also began borrowing heavily in the inter-bank market. A further indication of its difficulties is that none of Zambia's established banks (Barclays, ZANACO, Stanbic, and Citibank) would provide interbank loans to MB. It was only Zambia's small, local banks that would. For some, their exposure to MB significantly exceeded their capital.

Once these data were made available, it became clear that MB had been in deep trouble for perhaps a year or more. What surprised officials outside the central bank, especially those in the MoF, was why the BoZ had failed to act earlier to ensure that MB maintained appropriate levels of capital (i.e., equity and reserves). Since all banks provide fortnightly returns to the central bank

---

136. It is worth noting that other commercial banks in Zambia had access to this information. In January 1995, I obtained information on the key ratios for all banks from a senior staff member of a major bank in Zambia. These data had been derived from BoZ records.

137. Evidence of the problem can be seen in the shift in BoZ T-bill holdings. After averaging K2.5 billion per month for the period January to September, 1994, BoZ holdings of T-bills were K8, K9.9, and K21.8 billion, respectively, in October, November and December. Corresponding data for T-bill holdings by commercial banks were K107.5, K103.8, and K80 billion (*Macroeconomic Indicators* August 1997, Table 5.1). As noted in Table 1, the holdings of MB in December 1994 had fallen to K130 million. At the end of December exchange rate of K680 = U.S.$1, this amounted to approximately $190,000, effectively zero for such a large bank.

138. *Macroeconomic Indicators* December 1998.

and all the major prudential ratios are tracked, the progressive decline in MB's capital adequacy was well known to BoZ officials. Their failure to insist that MB rebuild its capital and make provisions against nonperforming loans had been indulgence of the grossest kind.[139] Indeed, it was totally inconsistent with the BoZ's long-standing commitment to ensure that Zambia's banks met international capital adequacy standards prescribed by the Basle Accords.[140]

In retrospect, one might wonder how MB would have measured up against commonly accepted performance criteria. One set of criteria widely used by regulators is summarized by the mnemonic CAMEL.[141] It stands for capital adequacy, asset quality, management, earnings, and liquidity. As already noted, MB's capital was inadequate. International standards at the time were that a bank's core capital should exceed 8 percent of its assets.[142] For banks with risky portfolios, the capital requirement was higher. Until late in 1994, a significant portion of MB assets were T-bills. Once these began to be redeemed, the quality of MB's asset base (as measured by risk-weighted returns) deteriorated rapidly. With respect to management, the *Euromoney* article, referred to above, had highlighted the problems. Subsequent noncooperation by MB's management in restructuring the bank reconfirmed the point.

MB's managers reported that earnings during 1992 and 1993, which under Zambian company law were published in the local press, had been impressive. As noted above, they were boosted by high returns on T-bills, MB's lucrative leasing agreements,[143] and the deal with ZCCM's metal marketing

---

139. BoZ officials argued that the Bank of Zambia Act did not provide them with the powers needed to properly monitor and supervise banks and other financial institutions. Some of the explicit gaps were covered in the Banking and Financial Services Act (1994). This, however, does not excuse the BoZ for its indulgence. A 1991 World Bank report on the commercial banking system had explicitly noted that many Zambian banks had weak capital bases, particularly if appropriate provisions for loan losses had been made (World Bank 1991). Thus, BoZ officials had ample warning about the general problem. Moreover, since the BoZ grants banking licenses, it has the authority to withdraw them should any bank fail to follow established banking procedures, one of which is to maintain prescribed amounts of capital.

140. At the time, the standard was 8 percent, with special provisions for additional capital (and/or reserves) when the bank's portfolio included specific risky assets (BIS 1988). These criteria have been revised. Stevens (2000) explains why. As shown by Simons (1996) and Hendricks and Hirtle (1997) financial innovation has broken down many of the standard approaches to risk management.

141. Lopez 1999.

142. As Table 6–2 shows, the banking system in Zambia as a whole did not meet this criterion.

143. During the liquidation of Zambia Airways, it emerged that the MB agreement was well over twice the prevailing international rates for leasing and maintaining aircraft.

proceeds. These leasing agreements ended in December 1994 when Zambia Airways was closed. The deal with ZCCM was lucrative as well. It provided Meridien International with a three-week float (in effect, financed by BoZ reserves). In December 1994, that float amounted to $25 million.[144] Although the return on earning assets was high, MB had a growing number of nonperforming loans. Reported profits would have been far more modest if the bank had made appropriate provisions against bad and doubtful loans. On the last category, liquidity, we have already noted that until the silent run in late 1994, MB had been highly liquid. (From Table 6–2, most banks in Zambia were in that position as well.)

Since the CAMEL criteria have to be seen as an overall assessment of the soundness of a bank, observers would have concluded even before the end of 1994 (i.e., before the concerns about MB's operations became public) that the bank was in trouble. It was undercapitalized, poorly managed, its high earnings were achieved using a number of questionable practices, and if adequate provisions had been made for loan losses, its earnings would have been significantly lower. If the BoZ had been effectively supervising the banking system, MB would have been under regulatory restraint by mid-1994 at least. Whether this would have prevented the bank's subsequent collapse can never be known. It would, however, have reduced the spillover effects associated with allowing MB to remain in business. The basic conclusion is that the BoZ failed to effectively supervise MB. Furthermore, the BoZ governor had had no objective basis for assuring the minister of finance, after the *Euromoney* article appeared, that MB was sound.

Alternative Response Options Considered by Government

The options considered by government (and the BoZ) included:

- Recapitalizing the bank;
- Providing BoZ support;
- Closing the bank

Recapitalizing the Bank: This option was in fact attempted. Andrew Sardanis pledged large amounts of security to the BoZ in return for support. The value of these assets was several billion kwacha. Some of the assets were owned by MB, the most valuable being the just completed MB headquarters. Sardanis indicated that he was prepared to pledge some of his personal prop-

---

144. This datum comes from an IMF report (Aide-Memoire April 1995, page 2) which notes that one of the losses stemming from the collapse of MB was the amount that the central bank had not been able to recover from Meridien International.

erty such as an abattoir, a warehouse, and several parcels of real estate. This latter action, which was totally unnecessary given that MB was a limited liability company, made a deep impression on the minister of finance. It convinced him that Sardanis was determined to rescue the bank.

Though it took a number of weeks, legal title to the pledged property was transferred to the BoZ. Sardanis had hoped to raise additional resources through the sale of shares to close associates. For example, there were discussions with ING Bank about buying the bank. These discussions were inconclusive. In the end, the extra resources were inadequate.[145] They did not cover the overdraft accommodation provided by the BoZ as deposits were withdrawn from MB. Consequently, they did not provide fresh capital that could be used to expand (or even sustain) the bank's asset base.

Providing Bank of Zambia Support: This issue generated the sharpest disagreement between BoZ and MoF officials. In one sense, it was a moot point. Because of its delay in reacting to the silent run, the BoZ had already been providing overdraft accommodation to MB. The decision for the BoZ was whether to cut its losses by denying MB further support. The view at the MoF was that, whatever was decided, further financial disruption should be avoided. After several years of triple-digit inflation, the Zambian economy was reviving. The rate of inflation was falling. Interest rates had declined sharply during 1994. Major progress was being made on economic reform. Business and consumer confidence were rising, and investment (especially in residences and small companies) was increasing rapidly. After several delays, the government's Rights Accumulation Program (RAP) with the International Monetary Fund (IMF) was nearing completion. Following a bruising battle with the donor community over the closure of Zambia Airways in December 1994, much-needed donor support was flowing again.

A major problem was that BoZ and MoF officials were talking past one another. Each viewed the potential problems created by MB from different angles. For BoZ officials, MB was a potential source of large central bank losses. For MoF officials, MB was a potential source of system-wide financial disruption.

Closing the Bank: This was the solution that came to be favored by the BoZ management from around the third week of January 1994. It was prompted by

---

145. In addition to roughly K5 billion of government bonds, MB pledged Meridien Center as collateral. Andrew Sardanis pledged the Chibote Meat Works. The former was valued at K5 billion ($6.5 million); the latter at K6.4 billion ($8.3 million).

several factors including the lack of cooperation of MB's management with central bank supervisors, the realization by senior BoZ managers that they had been 'duped' by earlier assurances the bank was sound, and the sharp increase in financial support that the BoZ had been providing. BoZ management could see little prospect that, even with additional support, MB could ever be viable.

The Course of Action Chosen by the Government

Reaching these divergent positions had not come easily or quickly. With MB under severe pressure, the BoZ sought to examine its records more closely. That was not a straightforward task. During the initial stages, MB's management was uncooperative. They insisted that BoZ supervisors make specific requests in writing rather than examine the books directly. BoZ staff were reluctant to force the issue. They were deterred by the argument, made by MB's management, that if it became widely known that MB was being closely scrutinized the central bank, a run could be provoked leading to MB's ruin. Since Andrew Sardanis had much more political clout than the BoZ governor, this argument was not to be ignored.[146] Lacking information on MB's "true" state of affairs, BoZ officials remained hesitant to push the issue. It was only when the MoF became directly involved in January 1995 that BoZ supervisors gained the access they were seeking. In the meantime, rumors of MB's difficulties began to circulate in Zambia. The bank experienced a further loss of deposits and the small banks that had been providing short-term accommodation to MB became increasingly concerned.

While BoZ officials did not have the type of access to MB records they desired, it was becoming apparent that immediate action was needed to resolve the situation. Other difficulties hindered this. As noted earlier, Sardanis was living in Paris. MB's Lusaka-based management continually deferred to him.

Thus, the first weeks of 1995 were characterized by lack of solid information on MB's overall financial position, together with much confusion and indecision among senior government and BoZ officials on how to proceed. For all those involved, there was a clear sense that, if the situation were mishandled, it could seriously disrupt Zambia's financial system.

By the first week of February, MB's position had deteriorated so sharply that BoZ's senior management concluded that it needed to be closed. Under

---

146. Sardanis was known to be particularly close to the minister of defense who, at that time, was both a trusted advisor to the president and someone with whom few people in Zambia were prepared to tangle.

147. The memorandum announcing the meeting listed as an agenda item consideration to close MB.

the Bank of Zambia Act, such action required the vote of the full bank board. Arrangements were made to do this thereby alerting a broader circle of people in Zambia to MB's fragile state.[147] It took several days to assemble the board because some members were out of town.[148] In the meantime, MoF officials became increasingly concerned that, due to its size, MB's closure would damage the broader economy. One immediate problem for the BoZ (already noted) was the $25 million of its reserves that were held by Meridien International in London. (Earlier instructions by the BoZ to ZCCM to route its sales proceeds through other channels had been ignored.) Furthermore, several local banks remained heavily exposed to MB.

MoF concerns carried the day. Upon being informed of the BoZ board's decision to close the bank, the minister of finance told the governor that this action did not represent government policy. With speculation rising among the public and within the business community that MB would be shut, the minister of finance made a formal statement to the National Assembly outlining government's resolve to take whatever steps were needed to assure the safety and soundness of the entire banking system. At that time, shutting MB was not one of those steps.

The government's action was designed to minimize damage to the economy. What it could not avoid, however, was the sharp increase in reserve money as the BoZ continued to support MB. Despite the government's intentions, serious financial damage was already being done. Interest rates rose sharply and foreign exchange reserves plummeted. The ensuing liquidity squeeze had one salutary effect. It kept inflation under control.

To illustrate: Over the last quarter (Q4) of 1994, reserve money increased at an annualized rate of 24 percent. In Q1 and Q2 of 1995, it rose at annualized rates of 59 and 81 percent, respectively.[149] The interest rate on 28-day T-bills was 20 percent in Q4 of 1994, and 32.3 percent and 42.9 percent, respectively in Q1 and Q2 of 1995.[150] Commercial bank lending rates bottomed out at 39.3 percent in Q4 of 1994 and Q1 of 1995 and rose to 42.9 percent in Q2 of 1995.[151]

The Reaction of the IMF to this Plan

IMF staff members showed little concern about MB's fate. Their main worry was the problems the government would have supporting MB while

---

148. The BoZ board met on February 15 and resolved to place MB in receivership at the end of the following day if specific conditions were not met.

149. *Macroeconomic Indicators* August 1997, Table 2.2.

150. *Ibid.*, Table 2.6.

151. *Ibid.*, Table 2.8.

keeping the economic recovery program on track. The IMF's focus was the government adherence to the timetable for completing the RAP. The IMF was expecting the government to complete the RAP by March 1995, gain access to Paris Club debt relief, and obtain the resources needed to discharge Zambia's arrears to the IMF. The rapid growth of reserve money, together with the loss of foreign exchange reserves (worsened by the block on BoZ funds held in Meridien International in London) breached the end of March benchmarks. An IMF mission indicated that Zambia could not complete the RAP as planned. This was a major blow.

The aide-memoire from the IMF staff's visit of March 28-April 4, 1995 noted:

> Since Fund staff had (sic!) visited Lusaka in February, the economic situation has worsened markedly, and it is apparent that without substantial policy actions, Zambia's economic objectives for 1995 are in jeopardy. . .

The aide-memoire listed three problems: poor revenue performance and higher than anticipated expenditures; "official support for Meridien Bank has increased to about K30 billion"; and a sharp decline in gross official reserves caused in part by the "injections of liquidity to support Meridien. . ."[152]

The IMF made several other observations about support to MB. All of them referred to the operation's high cost and the disruption it caused the government's recovery program. Reporting to the IMF board in June 1995, the IMF staff stated:[153]

> . . . the failure to control expenditure during a period of revenue shortfalls created renewed threats to the fragile economic stability.. . . A sharp acceleration of expenditure on defense contracts, agreement to a civil service pay increase beyond what could be financed from the budget, and hesitation in stemming the losses from Meridien Bank's insolvency were major causes of this.

The statement continued:

> The Meridien Bank difficulties placed severe pressure on the financial system. However, the Government has dealt with the consequences of the financial disruption caused by the liquidation of Meridien Bank by keeping tight control over the budget and by rebuilding foreign exchange reserves.

---

152. "Aide-Memoire International Monetary Fund Mission to Zambia March 28-April 4, 1995" April 1995, p. 1.

153. IMF GRAY/95/196, June 14, 1995. Statement to Executive Board Meeting 95/58, p. 4.

By the time the IMF staff reported on the government's policy actions in September 1995, external agents had been appointed to take over MB on the BoZ's behalf.[154] That report noted:[155]

> The three-month period of the receivership for Meridien Zambia Bank came to an end on August 17. The Zambian office of KPMG Peat Marwick has been appointed to secure maximum recovery for depositors and other creditors through sale or liquidation of the bank, including responsibility for tracing assets with a view to their recovery and pursuit of any criminal activities engaged in by Meridien personnel.

With Zambia's completion of the RAP and IMF approval of the Enhanced Structural Adjustment Facility in December 1995, the MB affair faded from view.[156] The economic effects lingered.

The Outcome of the Crisis

The minister of finance's statement to Parliament on February 16, 1995 firmly committed the government to seek ways of keeping MB operational. Budget pressures limited the government's options. During the two weeks February 13–28, the government provided to MB in excess of K13 billion (roughly $16.9 million). This consisted of shifting deposits of K4.8 billion into MB, providing K3.4 billion in T-bills and K5 billion as a "standby credit." The remaining resources came from the BoZ in the form of overdraft accommodation. The result was a direct injection of reserve money into the system as depositors shifted their funds to other banks. MB's position continued to deteriorate. On May 19, 1995, the BoZ formally closed MB. By this time, it had provided K38.3 billion in support. This was equivalent to $47.9 million or 1.4 percent of GDP. Of this, K15.9 billion was secured by real property and government bonds. The remainder, K22.4 billion, was unsecured.[157]

---

154. A reviewer of an earlier draft of this appendix suggested that the story was contradictory. He arged that, on the one hand, the facts showed that the capacity of the central bank was limited. By contrast, there were several references to the BoZ taking over a bank. In practice, the BoZ appointed highly specialized agents to take the necessary actions to salvage or close the troubled bank. (In MB's case, it was a partner from an international accounting firm.)

155. International Monetary Fund "Zambia—Interim Report on Policy Actions and Economic Developments" EBD/95/122, September 6, 1995, p. 2.

156. The government made a commitment to the Consultative Group meeting in Bournemouth (U.K.) to adopt as a key action the ". . .execution of Meridien receivership according to acceptable norms. . .[d]evelopment of [a] plan for unwinding official support." (GRZ, 1995, Appendix).

157. Records provided in confidence to the author.

The closure of MB received little attention from the government. It had other concerns. Among the most important were the policy changes needed to bring the RAP back on track and making a case to the donor community for emergency food aid (in the wake of the failure of the harvest).[158] The government's attention was also diverted by the reemergence of former president Kaunda as a presidential candidate in the 1996 elections.

Opinions differ on whether the support provided to MB achieved the aim of avoiding systemic damage. At best, it may have minimized it. Towards the end of 1995 two local banks, African Commercial Bank and Commerce Bank, also collapsed. When MoF officials argued for supporting MB in February 1995, five local banks had large outstanding loans to it. By rescuing MB at that time, the BoZ averted the failure of these banks as well. The subsequent failure of these smaller banks can be attributed (in part) to the knock-on effects of MB difficulties. These banks had weak capital bases, highly concentrated portfolios, and a large portfolio of non-performing loans.[159] Some of them should not have been granted banking licenses in the first place.

The support provided to MB by the BoZ further impaired the central bank's capital. Although the BoZ had been grossly undercapitalized for years (a situation compounded by major irregularities in its accounts dating from 1988), dealing with the problem could no longer be postponed.[160] Accordingly, the government agreed to provide the bank with additional capital. In June 1996, the BoZ was issued recapitalization bonds valued at K20 billion (equivalent to $22.3 million).

One casualty of MB's difficulties was the tax reform program to which many officials had devoted a large part of the previous three years. As a means of closing the financing gap and thereby meeting the conditions for the RAP, the government was required to take revenue measures equivalent to 3 percent of GDP.[161] The government implemented them in July 1995. Several of the measures directly reversed key elements of Zambia's comprehensive tax reform.

A further consequence of the MB collapse and the subsequent failure of other banks has been that the BoZ has become a major, though involuntary,

---

158. This was the third crop failure in four years.

159. At December 31, 1994, the nonperforming loans were, respectively, 233 percent and 356 percent of the capital and reserves of Africa Commercial Bank and Commerce Bank (BoZ 1995, Appendix 9).

160. The erosion of central bank capital has been common in developing countries. The issues and remedies are discussed in Sheng (1996), Beckerman (1997), and Stella (1999).

161. Attachment 2 to the aide-memoire of April 1995 describes the fiscal problem (low revenue, expenditure overruns, unreported arrears) and proposes an additional K77 billion (or $96.1 million) in revenue measures.

creditor to the commercial banking system. This appears in the commercial bank accounts under "credit from Bank of Zambia." These accounts show that BoZ credit to the commercial banks was K3 billion in 1994 ($4.5 million), K69 billion ($79.8 million) in 1995, and K87 billion in 1996 ($72.5 million).[162] This credit began to wind down in 1997, and by 1998 had fallen to K21 billion ($11.3 million).[163]

Macroeconomic Impact in the Short and Medium Run

The BoZ's 1995 *Annual Report* summarized the macroeconomic impact of MB's difficulties as follows:

> Government's attempted bail-out of Meridien BIAO Bank, in the early part of the year, caused some serious fiscal slippage in the budget which led to an injection of substantial liquidity into the system. This, along with the overdraft which the Bank of Zambia extended to the bank, led to the depreciation of the exchange rate and a build-up of inflationary pressures in the economy which threatened stability and the smooth conduct of monetary policy. Consequently, monetary policy was tightened further, which resulted in higher interest rates.[164]

On the broader macroeconomic front, the MB affair has had three important effects. The first is that the financial disruption caused Zambia's economic reform program to unravel. The obvious casualty was that the completion of the RAP was delayed from March to September 1995.[165] The second effect has been the general loss of confidence among consumers and the business sector in the soundness and integrity of Zambia's financial system. Despite Zambia's many problems dating from the mid-1970s, the country had maintained a reputation for having solid banks and financial institutions. That reputation was in tatters by the mid-1990s. MB's closure in May 1995 and the collapse of four other banks over the next three years convinced many asset holders that the BoZ (and the government) had fostered "wildcat" banking. Although most of the weak private banks have been closed or reorganized, the state-owned Zambia National Commercial Bank (ZANACO) had also been in trouble for most of the 1990s.[166] The BoZ has been able to

---

162. The respective dollar exchange rates used in these calculations were K670, K864.6, and K1200.5.

163. IMF Statistical Appendix 1999, Table 18.

164. BoZ *Annual Report 1995*, section 2.2, p.6.

165. It is difficult to argue that Zambia lost out by not concluding a Paris Club agreement in early 1995. It was subsequently granted all of the concessions as if there had been no slippage.

166. In December 1994, ZANACO's nonperforming loans were equivalent to 277 percent of its capital and reserves. Its exposure to its top 20 borrowers was 46 percent of its assets (BoZ 1995, Appendix 9).

curtail the operations of the weaker private banks, but it had minimal influence over ZANACO. This does nothing to foster confidence in Zambia among those holding financial assets.

A third effect is that the disruption has undermined the process of financial development. This problem has been compounded by continued macroeconomic mismanagement (as evident in the high persistent rates of inflation). The outcome is that Zambian asset holders have taken full advantage of the opportunities provided by financial globalization to diversify their portfolios internationally. This reduces their financial exposure and minimizes the risks of loss should Zambia's financial system continue to unravel. These adjustments limit the BoZ's ability to manipulate the country's financial system.

Although these three effects can be identified, it would be incorrect to attribute all (or even a significant part) of them to the MB affair. MB's collapse was part of a broader setting in which the BoZ and government have continued to stretch the economy's tolerances. The symptoms have been declining real per capita incomes, chronic inflation, an overvalued real exchange rate, arrested financial development, minimal savings, and low investment. The solution to this general economic malaise is sustained economic reform. Through an ongoing pattern of policy reversals, the government has been unwilling to take the steps needed for that to materialize.

Pertinent Policy Changes Adopted

The principal changes in the wake of the MB affair have been in the area of implementation rather than policy. Most of the relevant policies were in place even before MB experienced difficulties. As a policy matter, the BoZ was meant to supervise banks and other financial institutions effectively. The commercial banks were meant to comply with international standards for capital adequacy, liquidity, asset quality, and managerial competence. Furthermore, the government had committed itself to prudent macroeconomic management.

Based on its experience with MB, the Bank of Zambia has been less willing to indulge any private bank that encounters trouble. Two banks were placed under BoZ management in late 1995. In 1997, Prudence Bank was closed and in 1998, Finance Bank was restructured under BoZ supervision. As already noted, the BoZ has had less success in bringing ZANACO into conformity with prudential requirements. The problems have been a combination of political influence and poor management. ZCCM's demise in the late 1990s added to ZANACO's problems by creating more bad debt.

Viewed overall, however, the BoZ has taken heed of the lessons of the MB crisis and its aftermath. Banking supervision has been strengthened. Reporting systems have been revamped and information flows from financial institutions to the BoZ are now more detailed and regular.

By contrast, it is less clear whether the government learned much from the MB affair. MB's collapse was not due entirely to the problems of the bank alone. These problems were aggravated by the prevailing economic conditions. Since 1995, the government has done little to successfully reform the economy. Economic damage, on an order of magnitude more severe than anything arising from MB's demise, was created by the government's half-hearted attempts to sell ZCCM. The damage inflicted by ZCCM's demise can be measured in billions of dollars. Some of the more obvious costs have been the additional local and foreign debt incurred, the loss of donor support because of delayed reforms, the decline in investment as confidence eroded while the government dithered over ZCCM's sale, and the loss of income as ZCCM collapsed.[167] The costs associated with MB's collapse (direct unsecured support and knock-on disruption) were small by comparison.

One policy change that has been implemented with little positive effect is the granting of independence to the BoZ. This was incorporated in amendments to the Bank of Zambia Act and provisions in the Banking and Financial Services Act of 1994 (and its subsequent amendments). The BoZ has interpreted its independence as freedom from the need to cooperate with the government in setting monetary and fiscal policy. This approach grossly misconstrues the notion of independence and has aggravated the macroeconomic management problems confronting Zambia.

The issue is not whether the BoZ is independent (however that might be defined). The basic problem has been, and remains, one of BoZ capacity. In order to enhance its institutional capacity, the BoZ needs to forge a strong working relationship with the MoF. Direct evidence of the lack of such a relationship has been Zambia's chronic inflation. Despite regular promises by the government and the BoZ to reduce inflation to low single digits, annual inflation rates remained above 20 percent throughout the 1990s. For a country that is manipulating its exchange rate to prevent devaluation, such inflation undermines international competitiveness. Indeed, the inability of the BoZ to meet its inflation objectives (despite its independence) is symbolized by the reintroduction in December 2000 of exchange controls.[168]

---

167. The HIPC decision point document (IMF/IDA 2000, page 6) indicated that the debt assumed by the government on behalf of ZCCM was equivalent to 19 percent of GDP. (In 2000, that represented approximately $625 million.) This was in addition to the 4.3 percent of GDP (K423 billion) provided by the government in the 2000 budget to clear some local arrears incurred by ZCCM.

168. The statement is available on the BoZ web site at www.boz.zm.

Fall-Out from the MB Episode

The MB episode does not show either the BoZ or the MoF in a favorable light. A subtheme of the crisis had been a wrangle between the governor of the BoZ and the minister of finance over an entirely unrelated matter. The minister had been pushing hard at all levels within the government to reach a settlement with Camdex, an offshore enterprise to which had been assigned Zambia's long-overdue debt to the Bank of Kuwait (the amount exceeded $100 million). The governor was resisting this pressure. Adding to the difficulties, there were allegations (of which the governor was aware) that the minister himself had an interest in Camdex. Over the years, the governor had witnessed many schemes into which the GRZ had been bulldozed by one or more pressure groups. He had seen the country lose too often to be rushed at this point.[169]

The dispute over the Camdex payment (the initial claim exceeded $50 million) created a serious rift between the governor and the minister. In a tactical sense, the minister won. As part of the agreement to continue supporting MB rather than closing it, the governor was replaced. His replacement was the former economic advisor to the minister of finance and one of the few Zambians with a Ph.D. in economics. Whether Zambia benefited from this change is arguable. During his tenure at the BoZ, inflation remained high. The exchange rate lost more than three quarters of its value relative to the U.S. dollar. More important, because of continued macroeconomic instability, Zambia failed to grow. Real per capita income declined by approximately 1.6 percent per annum during the second half of the 1990s. While the governor cannot be held responsible for Zambia's persistent decline, he insisted (more than any previous governor) on the BoZ's right to take an independent approach to policy.

It is hard to determine whether the MB affair created any lasting damage for the BoZ or the MoF. Within Zambia's power structure, both organizations have been weak. Both have reputations for facilitating rather than directing government activity. Furthermore, to the general public, both are seen as agents of the IMF and the broader international community. Neither is seen as a source of economic largesse since public announcements of grants

---

169. As noted in Chapter 2, one of these was the redemption by Zambia of the ZIMCO bonds in 1973. These bonds, which had been trading at a heavy discount in the secondary market, were abruptly redeemed by the Zambian government at face value on President Kaunda's instructions. This action depleted Zambia's foreign reserves just as the oil and food crisis and copper price collapse eroded Zambia's international competitiveness. Andrew Sardanis was a party to this transaction. At the time, the governor was a senior official of INDECO (the Industrial Development Corporation). He advised against redeeming the bonds.

and loans from the donor community are typically made by the recipient agencies. From time to time, the public may learn that the BoZ and MoF have met with donors and rescheduled significant parts of Zambia's debt. Since most Zambians cannot relate to the magnitudes involved (often hundreds of millions of dollars) and since few Zambians saw any material benefit from the borrowing, neither organization directly benefits from this publicity.

In sum, the MB affair was yet another of Zambia's many misfortunes. There have been other banking collapses and there have been larger economic losses. There is, however, a bigger issue. Each economic crisis with its disruptions undermines the prospect that economic growth can be revived in Zambia. Moreover, the regularity of such crises (including their predictability) raises doubts about the country's ability to sustain growth even if it were to be revived. The public is informed that the commercial banks are now better supervised than they were. Since this cannot be verified except through the passage of time, the public is justified in remaining skeptical about the BoZ's pronouncements. (A visitor to the BoZ web site receives little assurance. It is several months out of date.)

The MoF (renamed the Ministry of Finance and Economic Development in 1996) continues to struggle. With three ministers in eighteen months during 1998 and 1999, its performance has not inspired confidence. While there is little reason to believe that the MB affair caused the ministry enduring damage, it did not do any good.

Personalities and organizations aside, MB's demise had serious consequences for the economy. It raised doubts about the soundness of the overall banking system. It demonstrated to many Zambians what they had always suspected, namely, that the best-connected businessmen (there are few businesswomen with such connections) receive preferential treatment even when it costs the State billions of kwacha. From a macroeconomic management perspective, the MB affair marked the end of the government's effort to "bring inflation under control." Since taking emergency action in 1993 to pull back from triple digit inflation, the government has tolerated inflation that by all but the most extreme international comparisons (Turkey) is exceedingly high.

The government's willingness to tolerate this level of inflation (and the BoZ's inability to do anything about it) has effectively doomed Zambia to a period of nonrecovery and continued decline in real per capita income. Chronic inflation has eroded confidence and sustained the overvaluation of the real exchange rate. Without confidence so that investment might revive, and without a realistic real exchange rate to reward enterprise and productivity, Zambia's economy cannot recover. This outcome cannot be attributed to MB's demise. The MB affair, however, was part of a larger pattern of missteps and macroeconomic mismanagement that continue to keep Zambia's performance well below its potential.

Lessons from the Crisis

What lessons does the MB affair provide?[170] Can other countries and administrations learn from Zambia's experience?

With the benefit of distance and time, eight points seem relevant.

One: Regulatory indulgence by the central bank is irresponsible. Central banks have primary responsibility for maintaining the integrity and stability of the financial system. Since banks and other financial institutions are the most highly leveraged enterprises in the economy, special efforts are needed to protect them from (silent or overt) runs. Without effective central bank oversight of the financial system, banks that are fundamentally sound can encounter liquidity problems. Heading off that possibility is one of the principal tasks of a properly constituted, staffed, and managed central bank. Fulfilling that task requires the central bank, without fear or favor, to regularly review the operations and portfolios of all banks and take prompt action to remedy any weaknesses (overconcentration of deposits or lending, mismatched maturities, failure to make adequate loan loss provisions). The BoZ's willingness to allow MB to continue operating with grossly inadequate capital was a major, costly, error.

Two: Reviewing and amending central bank legislation to give central banks more autonomy or independence is largely a waste of time if the central bank is incapable of maintaining effective supervision and oversight of the financial system. For many years, the BoZ argued that it did not have the authority to supervise the financial system. The MB affair demonstrated that the central bank failed to use effectively what powers it did have.

Three: When a financial institution encounters difficulties, the central bank should only allow the principals a limited time to recapitalize the institution (i.e., days, not weeks). The mistake made by the BoZ (and the MoF) was failing to place MB under central bank direction while discussions proceeded with the bank's owner about recapitalization. In effect, the commitment by MB's principals to provide additional capital set the process of

---

170. Sheng (1996) has shown that the same lessons emerge from financial crises in a large number of countries. Few governments seem to take heed. Kane and Rice (2000) review bank failures across Africa. Their conclusions reconfirm the lessons that I highlight in the text.

rescuing the bank back by several weeks. When a bank is as badly undercapitalized as MB, the principals should be told to recapitalize it at once or have it placed under central bank management.

Four: Central bank and MoF officials must reach prior agreement on the procedures that they will follow in a financial emergency. Making up rules and responding on-the-fly, as was the case in the MB affair, was both time-consuming and confusing. Agreeing to such a set of procedures before the fact does not mean that when an emergency arises, the central bank and the ministry will have a boiler-plate response. All emergencies have their unique features. However, if preparations have been made in advance for such an eventuality, there will be a better understanding of the types of issues that should be considered and where the relevant responsibilities for crafting a solution lie.

Five: Some observers have been surprised that MB's failure has had no legal ramifications. One of the problems facing those who would bring charges of fraud or misrepresentation is that the demise of MB was the result of a combination of questionable practices (some of which were outside Zambia's legal jurisdiction) and incompetence. The matters were not straightforward. Opinions differed among senior government officials over how the troubles had arisen, the extent of the troubles, and how they should be dealt with. There was bureaucratic turf to protect. There was the political influence of major participants to be weighed. In the final analysis, many observers see MB as a case of shoddy banking practices and poor central bank oversight set against a long history of bad economic management. There may have been criminality involved, but no one in Zambia had the zeal to identify and prosecute the perpetrators.

Six: Systemic risk is a major concern in countries with fragile financial sectors. However, given all the other factors that can disrupt a developing economy undergoing reform (budget deficits, terms of trade shocks, disruptions in donor support, droughts, floods, and civil strife) the prospect of systemic financial risk can be overrated. Since many large asset holders already operate with a foot-in-two-camps, namely, with accounts locally and abroad, the risks of a full financial meltdown are minimal. In retrospect, the prospect of systemic risk in Zambia had MB been shut as the BoZ recommended, was low. More financial damage was done to the economy by the injection of reserve money as the BoZ provided increasing support during February to May 1995.

Seven: While governments have a responsibility to dampen financial crises, it is far more important that they avoid creating the conditions that predispose the financial system (or institutions within that system) to collapse. Many of the pressures faced by the financial system in 1994–95 were created by a long period of macroeconomic mis-management. To its credit the MMD government made an attempt to deal with the external and internal imbalances that had emerged and persisted under the Kaunda regime. From January 1992 to December 1994, there was a genuine effort to reform the economy. To the government's discredit, it allowed the reform effort to unravel in early 1995. Thus, the attempt to rescue MB was set against a background of growing fiscal imbalance and diminished willingness by the government to take the steps needed to move the Zambian economy onto a sustainable growth path.

Eight: Stepping further back from the issue, MB's demise provides the opportunity to better understand the role of financial institutions in a developing country. Banks (and other financial institutions) have one fundamental role in any economy and that is to create value through the process of intermediation. This process is evident in a variety of forms—maturity transformation, risk spreading, mobilizing savings, facilitating investment, and liquidity management. MB failed because it derived its earnings by cutting corners that did nothing substantive to create value through efficient intermediation. Its business with government was not based on the ability to compete by providing quality service at the lowest price. That business depended largely on influence peddling. Furthermore, it boosted its earnings by taking advantage of weak BoZ oversight and a temporary adjustment-driven rise in real returns on government debt. Finally, by taking shortcuts and failing to maintain adequate capital, MB substantially raised the intermediation risks for others, namely its customers and correspondents. Thus, MB's behavior was antithetical to what is required of a value-creating financial intermediary. The obvious lesson is that central banks should remain focused on the proper role of financial institutions in an economy and ensure that all such institutions are managed so as to fulfill that role.

7

The Sequencing of Financial Market Liberalization, 1992–94

BRUCE R. BOLNICK

1. INTRODUCTION

The liberalization of financial markets was a major step in Zambia's stabilization and adjustment program in the early 1990s. It began with the lifting of interest-rate controls for loans and deposits at commercial banks in September 1992, when inflation was at 121 percent (latest three-months, annualized). In January 1993, the Bank of Zambia (BoZ) introduced a tender system to let market forces determine the yield on treasury bills, which in turn determined the central bank rate. By that time inflation had risen to 237 percent due to large fiscal deficits and accommodating money supply growth. In mid-July 1993, real interest rates turned positive for the first time in decades as the compound yield on T-bills increased to over 600 percent. Almost immediately, inflation decelerated, the exchange rate strengthened, and real money balances started to rise. Figures 7–1 to 7–3 show that the ensuing adjustment process was characterized by wild extremes en route to a new plateau of relatively low inflation by the end of 1994.

The decision to abolish interest rate controls at a time of high inflation was a departure from the conventional wisdom on sequencing liberalization policies. According to McKinnon (1991), "premature financial decontrol" was a direct cause of financial crises in Chile, Argentina, and Uruguay in the 1980s.[1] In contrast, successful Asian countries tended to liberalize their financial markets more gradually *after* achieving a reasonable degree of macroeco-

---

1. Also see Diaz-Alejandro, 1985; Corbo and de Melo, 1985.

nomic stability.[2] These case histories were buttressed by theoretical developments establishing that deregulated financial markets do not achieve efficient, market-clearing outcomes in the presence of pervasive information asymmetries.[3] These considerations convinced many scholars and practitioners of the need to reconsider the free-market approach that had been dominating the literature on financial market policies.[4] McKinnon, for example, recommended delaying the liberalization of domestic financial markets until after "the price level is stabilized and fiscal deficits eliminated."[5] Villanueva and Mirakhor likewise concluded that "economic stabilization and improved bank supervision should generally precede complete removal of control on interest rates."[6] Indeed, the two African countries that preceded Zambia in curing triple digit inflation—Ghana and Uganda—both pursued gradualist approaches to liberalizing financial markets.[7]

The aim of this chapter is to explore the motivation behind the sequencing policy adopted in Zambia, and to discuss the consequences. The Zambian experience has broad implications, insofar as it highlights elements of a complicated policy equation that have not been addressed adequately in the literature on sequencing. Three such points bear emphasis:

- Early liberalization can be used as a device to commit political leaders to follow through with a stabilization program, because the market thereafter will transparently penalize policy departures via rising interest rates.
- Risks to the banking system depend on local conditions and need not be as serious as indicated by experience in Latin America.
- During disinflation, donor-supported financial programs should contain contingency mechanisms to sanction adjustments in the monetary targets upon evidence of shifts in money demand behavior, especially at the point when positive real interest rates are established.

The remainder of the chapter is organized as follows. Section 2 outlines the events relating to interest-rate policy in Zambia from 1992 to 1994. Section 3 discusses the consequences of the early liberalization decision. Section

---

2. Tseng and Corker, 1991.

3. Stiglitz and Weiss, 1981; Stiglitz, 1993; Cho, 1986.

4. McKinnon, 1973; Shaw, 1973; Fry, 1988.

5. McKinnon 1991, p.6. McKinnon also favored maintaining controls on international capital flows until late in the adjustment process. In this respect, too, Zambia deviated from the conventional prescription.

6. Villanueva and Mirakhor 1991, p. 509.

7. For Ghana, see Kapur, et al., 1991. For Uganda see Sharer, et al., 1995.

4 appraises the benefits and costs, followed by concluding observations in Section 5.

2. INTEREST-RATE DECONTROL IN ZAMBIA

Conditions prior to decontrol

As explained in Chapter 2, the Zambian economy spiraled downhill during the 1980s. The tailspin was characterized by declines in per capita real GDP and formal sector employment, accompanied by huge fiscal deficits, accelerating inflation, and consistently negative real interest rates. The overvalued exchange rate contributed to a decline in exports, illicit capital flight, and dollarization of domestic transactions. Real money demand stagnated until the late 1980s and then declined rapidly, reflecting a strong vote of no confidence in the government's management of the economy. Overall, Zambia suffered from a classic case of misguided interventionism

In November 1991, the Movement for Multiparty Democracy (MMD) assumed office advocating responsible macroeconomic policies and greater reliance on market forces. Inflation was then around 100 percent and rising due to a preelection surge in deficit spending. The proposed liberalization of repressed prices—including those for food, energy, and foreign exchange—promised to trigger at least a one-off round of further price hikes.

In this environment, the new government took small steps to increase the interest rate on treasury bills in January 1992 and again in April 1992, but these timid measures were insufficient to achieve positive real returns. On the eve of the decision to decontrol commercial bank rates, the maximum bank lending rate was 53 percent (giving a compound yield of 68 percent), the annual rate on saving deposits was 48 percent (53 percent), and the discount rate on 91-day treasury bills was 47 percent (66 percent). The central bank rate was fixed as a simple yield 2 points above the *discount rate* on T-bills. One is struck by the fact that the compound yield on T-bills virtually matched that on risky commercial loans and exceeded the central bank rate. Thus, commercial banks had an incentive simply to hold government paper.[8] Nominal interest rates were far below the rate of inflation. They were also far below the levels required to provide an adequate risk premium for holding kwacha-de-

---

8. In fact, bank holdings of core liquid assets—primarily T-bills—amounted to 45 percent of liabilities to the public, versus a required ratio of 35 percent. Source: Bank of Zambia, *Main Economic Indicators*, August 1993. Combining the statutory reserve requirement of 23.5 percent and the core liquid asset requirement, the total reserve requirement was 58.5 percent.

nominated financial assets, relative to the alternative of holding deposit accounts in foreign currency.[9]

Adverse effects of the interest rate distortions were readily apparent. Among them:

- Households and businesses had a strong incentive to hold commodities as inflation hedges. Bricks for half-built homes and excess business inventory stocks outperformed financial assets as stores of wealth.
- Loans entailed a sizable subsidy to borrowers at the expense of savers; hence, the market for commercial bank loans was beset with arbitrary rationing and serious misallocation of scarce financial resources.
- People had an incentive to engage in illegal capital flight and currency substitution, delay inward remittances, and accelerate outward remittances. Such behavior contributed to disequilibrium in the foreign exchange market and helped to destabilize the exchange rate.
- Efforts by the public to avoid the inflation tax added momentum to inflation by raising the velocity of money.

Zambia's eleven commercial banks were not directly harmed by the negative real interest rates because they maintained a handsome spread between deposit and lending rates.[10] It was the depositors who bore the brunt of negative real returns.

Motives for Early Liberalization

By September 1992, efforts of the new government to implement monetary and fiscal controls were beginning to take effect. Due to new budget controls, the BoZ was no longer monetizing the deficit. This could be seen in BoZ net claims on government, which stabilized after midyear.[11] Also, the

---

9. Anyone holding a saving deposit in kwacha faced the prospect of losing 41.5 percent per annum compared to the alternative of holding a dollar deposit abroad earning the equivalent of LIBOR or better. (This figure assumes adaptive expectations; with perfect foresight, the prospective loss from holding a kwacha account was 55.6 percent per annum.)

10. As a rough gauge, suppose that banks earned a compound yield of 65 percent interest on assets that cover 76.5 percent of deposit liabilities (i.e., 100 percent less 23.5 percent statutory reserve requirement). This gives an average yield of 49 percent. If the average cost of interest-bearing deposits was 46 percent, and zero interest demand deposits represented 43 percent of deposit liabilities, then the average cost of funds was 26 percent. The gross margin is 23 percent.

11. The situation was not as neat as it seemed at the time, due to technical problems with the BoZ accounting system. A major headache faced by the MMD government was that fiscal and monetary control systems had fallen into disarray under the former regime.

three-month growth in reserve money (seasonally adjusted) slowed from an annual rate of 188 percent in June to 26 percent.

At this juncture the BoZ deregulated commercial bank interest rates. While rates remained negative in real terms, the effective rate on bank loans moved significantly above that on treasury bills. This led banks to reduce excess liquid assets by year's-end.[12] Otherwise, the adjustment was sluggish. One reason was that the key anchor for interest rates—the discount rate on treasury bills—was still set administratively at an unchanged level. Four months later, in January 1993, the government introduced a tender system to let the market determine the T-bill yield. By this time, inflation had increased to over 200 percent.

In view of McKinnon's dictum to defer decontrol until "the price level is stabilized," the decision to decontrol interest rates appeared to be premature. Why, then, did Zambia choose to liberalize domestic financial markets at this time? The motivating factors fall under five broad headings:[13]

The political philosophy of liberalization: In view of later events, it is easy to be skeptical of the government's commitment to a reformist, market-oriented strategy of development. Yet the minister of finance was an aggressive proponent of liberalization to reduce government's role in the economy and achieve efficiency gains. He saw little justification for perpetuating controls that subsidized inefficient borrowers at the expense of savers, when the government was in the process of eliminating subsidies for basic foodstuffs. Thus, the minister started from an inclination to decontrol sooner rather than later.[14]

Consequences of not moving quickly: A compelling argument for moving quickly was that real M2 balances fell by 43 percent during the twelve months to December 1992. The erosion of demand for kwacha balances and the corresponding rise in velocity were adding to inflationary pressure, as evident in the fact that inflation nearly doubled from 1991 to 1992, though M2 growth hardly changed. Thus, the government had to weigh the risks of decontrol against the risks of *not taking firm steps to provide incentives for holding kwacha balances.*

---

12. At end-December the core liquid asset ratio was 43.6 percent, versus a requirement of 42.5 percent (effective as of November). Source: the BoZ. Similarly weak responses to decontrol interest rates have been observed in other African countries. See Bolnick (1991) for a discussion of Malawi. Also see Poulson (1993).

13. The following draws heavily on internal government documents and on the author's participation in the policy discussions.

14. Of course, the commitment to reform was not pure and unanimous. Privatization and land reform, especially, bred bitter political disputes within the government.

Expectations of inflation: Reinforcing these considerations was a prevailing view that inflation would quickly come under control *if wealth holders had adequate incentives to rebuild kwacha balances.* This expectation was based on the following observations:

Reserve-money growth during the second half of 1992 was down by half from the same period in 1991 (to an annualized rate of 59 percent). Over the same period, BoZ net claims on government moved very favorably from *positive* K19 billion to *negative* K20 billion.

- Starting in January 1993, the government implemented tough measures to restore fiscal discipline through new "cash budget" procedures.[15] While untested, the cash budget promised to prevent inflationary financing of fiscal deficits, which everyone believed to be the main cause of money growth.
- The economy had absorbed the first round of cost-push effects from floating the exchange rate, based on daily rates at the new bureau de change, which were legalized in October, 1992. By January 1993, the kwacha rate to the dollar had already risen by 95 percent. Given positive real interest rates, the government anticipated that the currency could stabilize or even appreciate slightly, contributing to the prospect of rapid disinflation.

In short, the government's optimism about rapid disinflation rested on the expectation that macroeconomic policy would be managed prudently, and that the market would respond favorably. In this respect, advocates of early decontrol raised a fourth point:

- Early liberalization constituted a commitment to follow through on the fight against inflation. The decontrol of interest rates (and exchange rates) would paint government policy into a corner. Thereafter, any significant departure from prudent macro management would provoke a sharp, highly visible market response via higher interest rates and a weaker kwacha.[16] Any temptation to repress the market response would jeopardize donor support and undermine efforts to establish credibility.

Since inflation, as such, was still extremely high, the *anticipation* of rapid stabilization was a risky basis for action. Again, the decision reflected a balancing of risks, predicated on substantial uncertainty about the impact of the decision to decontrol and the alternative of not doing so.

---

15. Bolnick (1995).

16. Indonesia's example was salient here. Indonesia opened its foreign exchange markets in the early 1970s, contradicting McKinnon's (1991) dictum that the capital account should be liberalized last. Thereafter, spontaneous market movements compelled the policy makers to respond promptly and effectively to macroeconomic problems. See Nasution (1983) and Tseng and Corker (1991).

Technical issues: The case for early liberalization was bolstered by three technicalities. First, the new cash budget process required government to prefund all outlays with banked revenues or banked funds obtained by borrowing from entities other than the BoZ. Domestic interest expenses for 1993 loomed as a major drain on the government's cash flow. The projected cost was more than double the anticipated take-up of treasury bills by financial institutions to satisfy their liquid asset requirements. And as long as the expected real rate of return remained strongly negative, no one else would purchase government securities.

To cover domestic interest expenses the Treasury could: (a) raise taxes and cut noninterest expenses; (b) raise the core liquid asset requirement; or (c) broaden the demand for government securities by paying market-based rates. Since spending was already austere, and the prevailing core liquid asset requirement was already high at 42.5 percent, option (c) looked like the best approach. At the same time, the stock of domestic debt was sufficiently low (under 4 percent of projected GDP) that capitalization of interest expenses was not a daunting prospect, even at high interest rates, as long as the program succeeded in reducing inflation and deepening financial markets. In any case, the budget plan envisioned a large net inflow of foreign assistance, which would limit the need to issue new domestic debt.

A second technicality related to monetary policy. Both the government and the IMF saw the need to deepen financial markets to enable the BoZ to adopt indirect methods of monetary management.[17] The tender system could facilitate the transition to low inflation by providing BoZ with an effective tool to control reserve money growth.

A third technicality was that the 1993 Rights Accumulation Program with the IMF imposed a structural performance criterion requiring the government to ensure that real interest rates on bank loans were positive by the second half of 1993 (using the latest three months of inflation as the gauge for inflation expectations). The IMF evidently believed that moving quickly to establish positive real interest rates was the proper course of action.

A Priori View of the Risks

The IMF team, the government's advisors, and the policy makers themselves (perhaps to a lesser degree) recognized that early decontrol would produce a large initial rise in nominal and real interest rates. Cautionary tales from Latin America about the risk of financial collapse due to high interest rates were well known. But the risk in Zambia was less serious because loans

---

17. See Duesenberry and McPherson (1992).

and advances to nongovernment (including parastatals) represented just 18 percent of total commercial bank assets, compared to 17 percent held in T-bills. Given a high yield on treasury bills, it appeared that most banks could (if necessary) write-off a large fraction of loans and advances without jeopardizing their solvency. Also, nearly half of total commercial bank assets were held by conservatively managed foreign-owned banks, which were subject to close supervision from abroad.[18] A more serious risk was that the real sector could collapse due to high real interest rates. We will return to this in Section 3 below.

Another concern—widely held outside the MoF—was that rising interest rates would add to inflation through cost-push effects. Within the ministry this was not viewed as a significant factor in the equation, since the cost-push effect would be one-off and potentially reversible. (The disinflation process would restore lower interest rates with a lag.) On balance, the impact of establishing positive real interest rates was expected to be favorable.

The Treasury-Bill Tender Mechanism

Prior to 1993, the BoZ offered treasury bills to commercial banks "on tap" at a set interest rate. Redemptions were also available on demand, at a nonpenalty discount rate. Thus, banks were in a position to hold T-bills as a highly liquid substitute for cash. Holdings in excess of the liquid asset requirement were functionally equivalent to reserve money in the hands of the banks.

The "tap" was closed in January 1993 and replaced by a tender system. Each week bids were solicited through a public advertisement stating the amount maturing, the amount sought, and the minimum bid to be allowed. Senior officers from the BoZ and the MoF determined which bids were accepted. The preannounced amount sought was not binding, so the BoZ retained a degree of freedom to influence the average yield by accepting more or fewer bids. Initially, the only instrument on tender was a 91-day bill in the form of a transferable bearer certificate. A 28-day bill was added two months later and quickly became the center of attention. The 91-day bills were also sold over-the-counter in smaller denominations to nonbanks, at the average yield from the previous tender. The BoZ administered all T-bill issues and redemptions.

To inform the public, the government issued statements emphasizing that the sole fiscal purpose of the tender was to roll over maturing bills in a

---

18. For these banks, capital plus reserves significantly exceeded the required 8 percent of deposit liabilities.

non-inflationary manner. Official statements also explained that the tender was designed to provide BoZ with a new tool to control money supply growth in support of the disinflation program.

3. OUTCOMES

The outcomes from early liberalization of domestic financial markets in Zambia fall under five headings: (a) interest rates, inflation, and exchange rates; (b) money and the financial system; (c) the budget; (d) the real economy; and (e) policy credibility.

Interest rates, inflation, and exchange rates

These three variables are treated together because they are tightly linked as determinants of the price of money. For present purposes, the T-bill yield is used as the main indicator of market interest rates.

After the T-bill tender was introduced, nominal interest rates rose rapidly, as anticipated. The magnitude, however, was a great surprise (Figure 7–1). The reason was simple: inflation showed no sign of subsiding. On the contrary, inflation raced along at an average (annualized) rate of nearly 300 percent from January through July 1993. So the yield on T-bills climbed precipitously. From a fixed (compound) rate of 66 percent prior to the eve of the first tender, the yield soared to 333 percent by week nine, and peaked at 687 percent (for 28-day bills) in mid-July.[19] Deposit and loan rates at the commercial banks climbed alongside the rate on T-bills, but less steeply.

Why did inflation remain so high? The problem was a faulty diagnosis of reserve-money growth (Figure 7–2). Attention had focused on fiscal controls to end the excessive expansion of reserve money. After the cash budget came into effect, fiscal transactions became a net source of *reduction* in reserve money during the first half of 1993. It was a therefore great surprise to see that reserve money grew by 70 percent during the first four months of the year. As it became apparent that reserve money was driven by something other than the budget, the problem was traced to BoZ foreign exchange transactions. In particular, the BoZ was paying spot kwacha to purchase foreign exchange from the state copper company (ZCCM) while allowing the

---

19. Few people, even in government, knew how high the rates climbed because most internal documents and all public reports expressed the rates as simple rather than compound yields. When the 28-day yield peaked at 687 percent, newspapers reported the rate as 225.1 percent.

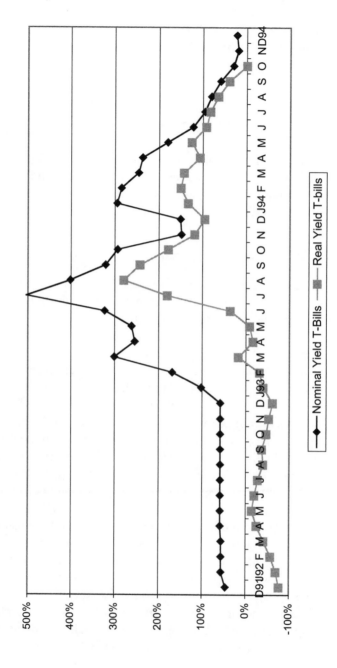

Figure 7-1. Nominal and Real T-Bill Yields December 1991–December 1994

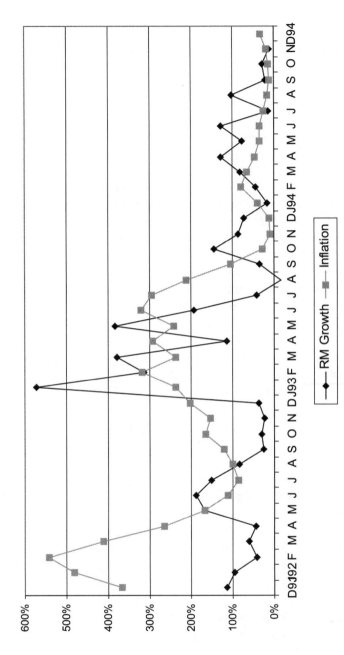

Figure 7-2. Inflation and Reserve Money Growth December 1991–December 1994 (3 month averages)

225

state oil company (ZIMOIL) six months to repay the BoZ for foreign exchange advances to procure petroleum supplies. In effect, the BoZ was extending large quasi-fiscal loans to ZIMOIL, entirely outside the financial program. Until this was fixed in late May, reserve money remained out of control, inflation remained high, the kwacha continued to depreciate, and interest rates soared.

In the end, the BoZ gained a reasonable measure of control over reserve money a half year later than planned. Thereafter, the bank moved aggressively to tighten monetary policy. Between June and August 1993, reserve money shrank by 17 percent, inflation started to fall, and real interest rates turned positive. Extraordinarily so! For nearly a year, the *real* yield on treasury bills exceeded 100 percent (using forward-looking expectations of inflation). The high rates signaled that the public regarded the program with great skepticism, even after inflation was visibly declining.

Another factor supporting the high real interest rates was extreme instability of the exchange rate. In July 1993, the kwacha began to appreciate (Figure 7–3). The BoZ's base rate for buying dollars fell from K560 in late June to K335 in mid-October, before climbing back to K647 by year's-end. A popular explanation for the dramatic appreciation was that the BoZ was dumping donor funds on the market to drive down the price of foreign exchange. This was false. During the appreciation episode, no donor funds were available for the bank to sell. Disbursements of balance of payments support ran far below target, causing serious problems in honoring even top-priority debt-service obligations. Nor were export earnings flooding the market for foreign exchange, because copper prices fell 30 percent between January and November.

Since the appreciation occurred when the supply of foreign exchange to the market was low, the "bubble" can only be explained by insufficient demand. This was entirely unexpected. A few months earlier, no one would willingly hold kwacha if they had access to foreign exchange. The turning point occurred when real interest rates switched from being highly negative to highly positive. When the real cost of funds was negative (and supplies of foreign exchange erratic), every business had an incentive to hold excess inventory. When financing costs became highly positive, the profitable course of action was to economize on stocks (especially since the decontrol of foreign-exchange allocations eliminated the need to hoard imported supplies). With the benefit of hindsight, one can see that the transformation in real interest rates stimulated a widespread, once-off adjustment in inventories. Since most were imported, the adjustment induced a sharp, temporary, decline in the demand for foreign exchange. This analysis cannot be confirmed directly because the government did not compile within-year data on inven-

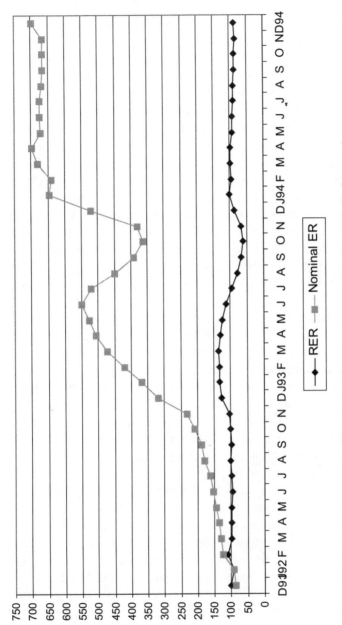

Figure 7-3. Real and Nominal Exchange Rates December 1991–December 1994 (Index numbers, December 1991 = 100)

tories, but it is a plausible explanation of the extremely weak demand for foreign exchange beginning in July 1993.

Rising real interest rates directly affected the demand for foreign exchange by making kwacha balances more attractive. The long-term decline in real money balances bottomed out in July 1993. By October, real balances had risen by 10.4 percent. This is equivalent to an annualized growth of 48.7 percent in real money demand. Unfortunately, the IMF program stipulated virtually zero growth of reserve money between May and September. To meet the program bench mark for the third quarter, the BoZ had to clamp down just when the demand for kwacha balances was starting to rise. The absence of a contingency clause to adjust the reserve money benchmark on evidence of a decline in velocity was a major technical error in the IMF program. The resulting illiquidity meant that many companies could not purchase foreign exchange to buy supplies or stocks even if they wished to do so. This was rectified at the end of September, but not before the exchange rate dropped so low as to threaten the collapse of many domestic producers, including ZCCM.

The strengthening of the kwacha fed high domestic interest rates through the interest rate parity (IRP) condition. At first, with the kwacha appreciating, the IRP relationship worked in Zambia's favor. But by October the kwacha was so overvalued that any thoughtful observer could see that its strength was unsustainable, and a large depreciation was likely. Hence, the return on kwacha-denominated financial assets had to incorporate a large premium to cover exchange rate risks. This explains why the compound yield on 28-day T-bills remained above 140 percent in the fourth quarter of 1993 even though annualized inflation fell to 10.5 percent.[20]

In mid-October, the BoZ relaxed monetary policy to accommodate the rising demand for kwacha balances. The exchange rate reversed course with vigor—much to the dismay of politicians who were boasting about the strong kwacha. The year-end depreciation coincided with a seasonal rise in food prices, generating a new spike of inflation. In the face of renewed inflation fears and exchange-rate uncertainty (in addition to political problems and uncertainty about donor inflows) interest rates remained high in early 1994. Any agent who doubted the government's resolve to stabilize the economy continued to demand a high rate of return on kwacha assets. The lack of *credibility* prevented T-bill yields from declining more quickly.

An element of noncompetitive behavior may also have been sustaining interest rates, since the highly concentrated banking industry dominated the

---

20. Measured inflation understated the underlying inflationary pressures at this time because import prices were unsustainably low due to the appreciation bubble.

tender.[21] In April 1994, when inflation was subsiding, the commercial banks appeared to be taking advantage of the government's need to roll over shorter-term bills. Policy makers were concerned that the treasury and other debtors were bearing unduly high costs due to the uncompetitive market conditions. The evidence was that demand for longer-term bills remained exceedingly thin and their yields remained inexplicably high. This prompted the BoZ at one tender to reject most commercial-bank bids for 28-day bills, and ask the banks to re-bid on 91-day bills. The weighted average yield promptly fell by 14 points, and the term structure of yields became more logical.

All in all, the nominal yield on treasury bills finally came back to earth, reaching 20 percent by November 1994, with inflation below 20 percent (annualized).

4. IMPACT ON THE ECONOMY

This section examines how decontrol affected the monetary system. How were commercial banks affected by the introduction of market-based interest rates? How did the transition to positive real interest rates affect the demand for money balances? Did the T-bill tender process succeed in providing BoZ with an effective tool for monetary management?

The Banking System: During the two years of extreme movements in nominal and real interest rates following liberalization, not one commercial bank failed.[22] Looking carefully at the impact of high interest rates on the banking system, two conditions stand out. First, throughout the period banks held large stocks of treasury bills, the yield on which rose far more than the interest rate on loans or deposits. Second, the banks took advantage of market volatility to widen the spread between the cost of funds and the yield on earning assets. The gross margin, adjusted for zero-interest demand deposits and reserve requirements, widened from an average of 19 percent in 1992 to 97 percent in 1993 (author's calculations).

This is not to say that banks avoided problems. The quality of most commercial loans was seriously impaired when real interest rates rose to extreme levels. Having been habituated to negative real interest rates, most commercial borrowers were highly geared. Many clients were in difficulty due to the

---

21. At the end of June 1994, a year after real interest rates became highly positive, nonbanks still held just 17 percent of the total outstanding stock of T-bills (source: BoZ and MoF data). This includes holdings by non-bank financial institutions.

22. The failure of Meridien Bank came later, for other reasons.

impact of other reforms, as well as the drought conditions in 1991–92 and 1993–94. Consequently, much of the reported rise in loans and advances during the adjustment period represented the capitalization of interest due from illiquid borrowers. Anecdotal evidence suggests that banks did very little voluntary lending at the prevailing high interest rates. To paraphrase one banker: "Anyone who wants to borrow at these interest rates can't be a good credit risk." Both the high premium on treasury bills and the persistence of large spreads suggest that the banks used their market power to avert insolvency from bad debts. Even so, the banks ultimately had to write off or work out a significant portion of their prereform loan portfolio. The portfolio stress underscored the need for careful bank supervision.

Real Money Demand: As noted above, real M2 balances hit bottom in July 1993, when real interest rates turned positive, reversing the long-term flight from kwacha balances. Over the next twelve months, real balances rose by 28 percent and the ratio of M2/M1 rose by 21 percent. In macroeconomic terms, inflation consistently exceeded M2 growth before July 1993, due to rising velocity. Thereafter, financial deepening allowed monetary policy to ease without compromising the target path for disinflation.

Tool for Monetary Management: One rationale for early decontrol was that the tender would provide the BoZ with an effective, market-based tool for monetary management. This did not work out as expected. Problems arose as early as the second tender, which was undersubscribed by half.[23] The BoZ was unable to roll-over maturing notes, causing an unplanned injection of reserve money. Also, commercial banks discovered that they could profit from rising interest rates by purchasing new T-bills and rediscounting old ones, creating a monetary surge through the discount window. The BoZ did not close this arbitrage channel until March, when it increased the penalty rate on rediscounts. Still, undersubscription continued to plague the tenders, particularly after the BoZ tightened up on reserve money. Over the first full year of operation, the tender produced an unintended net injection of K25 billion of reserve money (which started the year at K52 billion). Since few tenders were oversubscribed, the BoZ had little or no discretion to use the system for managing monetary flows.

Yet monetary management would have been even more difficult under the

---

23. Because of thin bidding in the first weeks of the tender, an IMF technical mission concluded that the 91-day bill did not meet the liquidity needs of the commercial banks. The BoZ introduced a 28-day bill in March. Within a few months the 28-day bill dominated trading, creating an enormous administrative burden for the bank.

old "tap" system, with negative real interest rates. By establishing positive real interest rates, the tender prompted banks to hold excess liquid-asset reserves and induced nonbanks to accumulate K26 billion of bills and bonds. These reserve money withdrawals would not have occurred under the tap.

By mid-1994 the tender became more useful as a tool for managing reserve money for two reasons. First, deepening of the market provided more latitude to determine the cut-off for accepting bids. Equally important, the treasury's cash position became less precarious as improvements in tax administration eased the government's borrowing requirement.

The Budget: The shift to market-determined interest rates led to a large rise in the budgetary cost of domestic interest payments. When the policy was adopted, the macroeconomic program provided for interest costs to be capitalized through new domestic borrowing and net foreign assistance. [24] However, the program greatly underestimated the persistence of inflation during the first half of 1993, which caused interest rates to rise higher and stay high longer than expected. Interest expense for 1993 exceeded the program estimate by 74 percent. Adjusting for higher-than-expected inflation, the overrun on interest payments was 18 percent.

Surprisingly, the real stock of treasury bills actually fell by 10 percent in 1993, due to the unintended shortfall of tender sales relative to maturities. The shortfall retarded the growth of real domestic debt, but it caused major problems for the treasury's cash flow, as the gap between maturities (payouts) and tender sales (receipts) crowded out funding for operations and programs under the cash budget rules. To prevent the debt dynamics from following a more explosive time path, the treasury had to impose severe constraints on noninterest expenditures. The cash flow problem was heightened by shortfalls in real tax revenues and nonproject foreign assistance.[25] The critical role of tax collections and foreign assistance in smoothing the adjustment to market-based interest rates can be seen by comparing 1993 to 1994. In 1994, real interest rates were higher on average than in 1993, but aid inflows were above target and tax collections were on target in real terms. This meant that the treasury could cover domestic interest expenses, which were 51 per-

---

24. Source: author's personal records. The financial program took account of domestic interest expenses, but with an estimate that did not adequately allow for rising yields due to liberalization.

25. Adjusting for higher inflation relative to the initial program projection, government revenue and net nonproject foreign assistance fell short by K84 billion (27 percent) and by K30 billion (36 percent), respectively. The latter shortfall was much worse than the figures indicate, because *most* of this assistance arrived at the BoZ at the very end of the year.

cent over budget in real terms, without having to impose such severe cuts in other expenditures.

From the introduction of the tender system to the end of 1994, a period of two years, real domestic debt of the government rose just 28 percent (from a low base, reflecting prior financial repression). By early 1995, the prospects for stabilizing the ratio of debt to GDP at sustainable levels were favorable, given the decline in interest rates to more normal levels, and improvements in revenue performance. Moreover, the increase in the real stock of T-bills was compatible with rising demand for domestic financial assets, virtually matching the increase in real M2.

The Real Economy: The rapid conversion from highly negative to highly positive real interest rates had a serious adverse impact on producers. A full structural model would be needed to isolate the interest-rate effect from other contemporaneous shocks and adjustments, such as the impact of contractionary fiscal and monetary policies, the elimination of foreign-exchange controls (which provided shelter from import competition), and a move towards economic pricing of energy and fuel. The economy was also beset by drought in 1991–92 and 1993–94, and by a 30 percent decline in world copper prices just as real interest rates started to soar.[26] Despite the difficulty isolating the various shock effects, several points can be made about the impact of high real interest rates.

With the shift to positive real interest rates in mid-1993, the extraordinary appreciation of the kwacha (see Section 3 above) placed domestic producers at a large disadvantage compared with competing imports, and undercut export profits. Losses were acute at ZCCM as exchange rate movements exacerbated the adverse impact of declining copper prices and production problems. ZCCM's cash-flow problems were passed on to domestic suppliers in the form of unpaid bills, forcing some to the brink of closure.

Liberalization of interest rates caused special strains on agriculture. When the T-bill tenders were chronically undersubscribed in 1993, the treasury's weak cash position caused delays in the release of funds for marketing the 1992–93 bumper crop of maize, and financing inputs for the next crop season. The problems were compounded by the impact of high interest rates on private-sector participation in the marketing of agricultural inputs and outputs. Food prices had been liberalized in 1992 on the premise that private

---

26. This brings to mind Cooper's (1991) observation that the ease of adjustment "seems to depend in part on *luck*." Note that data on the real economy in Zambia are unreliable.

agents would then handle a substantial share of the agricultural marketing. But private participation fell far short of expectations. Part of the problem can be attributed to mixed signals concerning government policy (see Chapter 10). Yet interest rates undoubtedly played a major role. Consider that the difference between import and export parity prices sets the maximum margin that can be obtained between the procurement price and sale price for grain. Within this range, it was arithmetically impossible for a leveraged trader to profit from holding maize for six months at the interest rates prevailing during the 1993 maize marketing season.[27] Thus, the transition to market-based interest rates impaired both public and private financing of agriculture.

Rising real interest rates further burdened commercial farmers because of unfortunate timing. The 1991–92 drought prevented many farmers from repaying production loans, which were carried forward to 1992–93. Thus, many farmers owed two year's debt at the time when real interest rates rose to triple-digits. They had to cope with liquidity problems and debt workouts for years thereafter.

One must recognize, though, that high real interest rates benefited entrepreneurs in their role as depositors and savers. In addition, entrepreneurs had ways to mitigate the high cost of financing by recapitalizing (e.g., bringing funds home from overseas) or restructuring (e.g., cutting inventory stocks, shutting down inefficient operations).

Politics and Credibility: Virtually from inception, the T-bill tender system was subject to a barrage of criticism from the media, the business community, influential academics, and even commercial bankers. Some critics denounced rising interest rates as a "bonanza for the rich," imposed from Washington. They accused government officials of using the system to earn high yields for their personal accounts at the expense of the treasury and economy at large. Critics blamed high interest rates for causing business failures, draining money balances from circulation, destroying industry, bankrupting farmers, and shutting down capital investment. Critics dominated the public debate and many discussions within government. This uproar

---

27. Simple interest rates above 120 percent produced an unavoidable loss to traders, assuming that maize is procured at the export parity price (as a market floor) and sold at the import parity price (as a market ceiling). This calculation is based on the financial cost of 80 percent leverage. Including the opportunity cost of equity capital would worsen the economic outcome. The calculation assumes an expectation that the exchange rate would rise from K700 per dollar to K750 per dollar over the course of a six-month holding period (actual rate was less favorable), that the world market price per bag would be stable at $12, and that the transportation margin to and from the sea port was 20 percent.

raises vital questions about: (1) the political sustainability of the reforms; (2) the effect of early liberalization on credibility; and (3) the management of information to influence public opinion.

As early as March 1993, mounting criticism compelled the minister of finance to defend his program to a cabinet committee.[28] The most serious challenge to the interest-rate policy arose four months later in conjunction with the maize marketing problem discussed above. When the Ministry of Agriculture requested funds for maize marketing, as budgeted, the treasury did not have enough cash in the bank to cover the expense—in part because T-bill sales had not covered the soaring interest expenses on maturing bills. The Ministry of Agriculture was also hearing bitter complaints from farmers about the adverse effects of high interest rates. Hence, interest-rate policy was singled out as the chief problem facing agriculture.

By this time, both the minister of finance and the budget director had been replaced. The new minister responded to the controversy by considering several options including reintroduction of interest-rate controls, and conversion of treasury bills by fiat into long-term notes. In the end, the politicians judged that reversing the reforms would be more costly than seeing them through. Thus, the decision to decontrol interest rates was sustained, though the controversies continued.

It is worth recalling that one a priori argument in favor of decontrol was the commitment effect: Liberalization would place strong pressure on the government to implement the stabilization program, because departures would be reflected in adverse market developments. In fact, the extraordinary increase in interest rates did compel policy makers to follow through on their commitment to fiscal and monetary discipline. In this respect, the policy was successful. Yet it failed to gain credibility for the government's macroeconomic policy. Even thoughtful observers wrote about the T-bill market as if it were a Ponzi scheme, creating a widespread expectation that the treasury would ultimately default on its domestic debt. The political backlash nearly caused the program to fail.

There is an important lesson here for the political economy of structural adjustment. Effective policy action should be accompanied by a vigorous, sustained and truthful campaign to inform the public about what is happening, why it is being done, how it is working, and what actions are being undertaken to deal with problems that arise in the process. By letting critics dominate the public debate, the government of Zambia contributed to expectations that kept interest rates high for longer than necessary.

---

28. The minister was dismissed shortly thereafter. Commentators viewed the dismissal as being due to the perception that the minister was building an independent political base. Disenchantment about the state of the economy probably played a role.

5. SUMMARY AND CONCLUSION

Zambia's decision to decontrol interest rates early in the adjustment program was the first example of its kind in Africa. Unlike prior experiences in Latin America, early sequencing in Zambia did not provoke a financial crisis for the banking system. This can be explained by differences in the initial conditions. With the exception of one state bank, the large banks were managed conservatively and not controlled by industrial groups. Also, the banks operated with high reserve requirements, which reduced their exposure to potential bad debts. The liquid asset requirement meant, too, that banks held a large portion of their portfolio in treasury bills, which generated extremely high yields during the adjustment process. The large premium on treasury bills helped banks to cover potential losses from loans that were jeopardized by rising interest rates.

The early move to positive real interest rates helped to accelerate disinflation by reversing the adverse trend in velocity, and ending one-way speculation against the kwacha. Equally important, early liberalization raised the government's stake in following through on the stabilization program. Yet early decontrol also caused enormous short-run volatility in interest rates and the exchange rate, generating high costs and risks for the economy.

Two alternative policies might have reduced the economic costs of extreme interest rates, while preserving the stabilization benefits from achieving positive returns. First, the government might have delayed full liberalization until control over the growth of reserve money was firmly established. Specifically, the extraordinary increase in interest rates might have been attenuated if decontrol had been deferred by six to nine months, when the technical problems with monetary management were resolved.

Second, interest rates might have been *managed flexibly* rather than liberalized. As suggested in an IMF paper written shortly after the crises in Latin America,[29] "It may be advisable to gear interest rates. . .to the rate of inflation that is expected to prevail as the new policies take hold." This option was favored by many bankers in Zambia. The advantage, in theory, is that a policy of managed interest rates could produce positive real interest rates without the extremes. Also, nominal interest rates could have fallen more quickly after mid-1993.

Other economies such as Ghana and Uganda successfully pursued disinflation programs without bearing the costs associated with extreme and volatile interest rates. In Zambia, however, it is not so clear that either of the alternatives would have dominated the policy that was actually pursued. Delaying

---

29. IMF, 1983, p. 19.

liberalization might simply have eliminated the pressure to fix the leaks in monetary control. Similarly, attempts to manage interest rates might have bred mismanagement.

In conclusion, several observations can be drawn from Zambia's experience with high interest rates.

- To promote stabilization, the liberalization of interest rates must be accompanied by strong steps to establish fiscal discipline and strict monetary management, consistent with low inflation.
- The extraordinary volatility of the exchange rate could have been avoided by easing the monetary targets once the market revealed that a major shift was occurring in the demand for financial assets, after real interest rates turned positive. The IMF benchmark should have incorporated a contingency clause to this effect.
- Domestic debt of the government remained moderate, despite the extremely high interest rates. Stabilizing the debt ratio depended critically on the government's success in mobilizing revenue to enable the treasury to fund domestic interest expenses.
- Early decontrol of interest rates was ultimately effective, but very costly. Perhaps a less aggressive liberalization path would have produced a better balance of benefits to costs. But perhaps not. What is clear is that the conventional wisdom overstates the case against early decontrol.

8

Trade Policy Reform and Liberalization during the 1990s

CATHARINE B. HILL

1. INTRODUCTION

This chapter examines the progress of trade policy reform in Zambia during the 1990s. Attention is focused on the impact of the tariff reform of 1996 and the fiscal constraints on subsequent efforts to liberalize trade. The discussion also covers other trade related issues such as regional linkages, microeconomic policies to encourage exports, and the importance of the exchange rate.

Trade policy has been a dominant element in determining the pattern of Zambia's modern economic growth. Prior to independence, Zambia had a highly open trading system committed to making the most of its comparative advantage in metal mining. As a member of the Congo Basin Area, Zambia accepted limits on tariff rates, and successive colonial administrations, including the one that was party to the Central African Federation (1953 to 1963), remained committed to free trade. That approach frustrated those who advocated that tariff protection and subsidies should be used to promote industrialization. Images of "trains passing in the night" were invoked as a means of changing government policy about protecting industry.[1]

---

1. This history has been recounted in Baldwin (1965). The image of "trains passing in the night" was taken from a study by W.J.Busschau in 1949 on industrialization in Northern Rhodesia. The image reflects the fact that copper plate was exported from Northern Rhodesia while, at the same time, copper wire was imported from Europe. Zambia's recent efforts to liberalize trade gain some context when it is realized that the Busschau report came down firmly on the side of free trade (McPherson 1980, Ch. 2). The government has been engaged in recreating a system that its illiberal policies destroyed.

There was a major shift in sentiment towards protection when Zambia gained independence. The UN/ECA/FAO "Seers" Mission report of 1964 set the stage for a sharp increase in government activism to promote economic development.[2] Though the Seers report was careful to stress that government intervention should be efficient and cost-effective, the protectionist genie was out of the bottle. In this respect, Zambia was following the path advocated by Kwame Nkrumah, Julius Nyerere, and others who argued that African countries could not be truly independent until they stopped being quarries for European industry and until there was local control over the means of production. Given the historical context and the prevailing orthodoxy that stressed the advantages of planned development, it was no surprise that Zambia became highly protectionist. What perhaps has been unexpected, however, was that a country whose very wealth depended so heavily on trade would take such draconian measures to cut itself off from trade. To Zambia's detriment, the government succeeded only too well. The reforms introduced by President Kaunda between 1968 and 1975, institutionalized a pattern of import-substituting industrialization. As the reforms took hold, the economy lost its dynamism. The situation was aggravated by the shocks of the mid-1970s.

The main shock was the sharp decline in the world price of copper. Because the shock to traditional export earnings was considered temporary, the government made no immediate effort to change its policy so as to reduce the demand for imports. As foreign exchange became increasingly scarce, the government responded by compressing imports through licensing, banning specific imports, and tightening foreign exchange controls. The government allocated foreign exchange by sectors, reinforcing the protective structure of the tariff. Imports were also directed to state-owned enterprises (SOEs), resulting in a highly protected domestic sector that was both capital and import intensive. Consumer goods were restricted more than intermediate and capital goods. According to the World Bank, capital and intermediate goods comprised 66 percent of imports in 1970. By 1985, they accounted for 82 percent. Thus, import-substituting production increasingly took place in the consumer goods sector, behind high barriers.

By the mid-1980s, it was clear that controls and quotas were having a negative effect on the economy. The government study "Restructuring in the Midst of Crisis,"[3] recognized that import substitution was a dead end. To promote growth, trade liberalization and a more outward-oriented strategy were needed. That trend was already well underway in many other develop-

---

2. UN/ECA/FAO "Seers Mission" 1964.
3. GRZ 1984.

ing countries.[4] Though a late-comer, Zambia began shifting to outward-oriented trade policies. That approach produced some favorable results, evident in the rapid growth of non-traditional exports, at least until 1997.[5]

The chapter is organized as follows. Section 2 contains a historical account of the trade reforms in Zambia since the mid-1980s. Sections 3 and 4 examine the major tariff reform adopted in 1996. Section 5 discusses several other issues relating to trade policy reform. Section 6 offers concluding comments.

2. History of Trade Policy Reform in Support of Economic Growth

The government embraced a major program of trade liberalization when it adopted the foreign exchange auction system in October 1985.[6] These reforms were reversed in May 1987 when the auction was halted and quotas and foreign exchange allocation were reintroduced. Some changes were made in 1989, but it was not until 1991 that the liberalization process resumed. The foreign exchange market was liberalized, nontariff barriers were eliminated, and tariff rates were rationalized with many of them being reduced by large amounts. During the 1990s, these policies were generally sustained, although there was some backsliding as the decade wore on.

Exchange Controls[7]

Control over the allocation of foreign exchange was a major means through which the government restricted imports during much of the 1970s and 1980s to reduce absorption. By fixing the official exchange rate and rationing foreign exchange, the government effectively allocated the premium

---

4. Krueger (1997) and Bruton (1998) discuss trade liberalization and growth in developing countries.

5. Empirical evidence on the relationship of trade liberalization and outward orientation is discussed in Dollar (1992), Sachs and Warner (1995, 1997), Easterly and Levine (1998), and Collier and Gunning (1999).

6. In its ʻAction Programme for Economic Structuring" (GRZ 1985, pp. 11–14), the government fully acknowledges the destructive impact of the controls that had been imposed on trade. The basic thrust of the action program was to determine how to unravel the controls that had been adopted. The government noted that the implication of ". . .restoring balance and increasing uniformity in the incentive system, particularly between exports and import-substitutes. . ." was ". . .a major reform in the trade regime with greater reliance on the exchange rate as a mechanism for allocating foreign exchange, rationalisation of the tariff structure, and review of investment incentives.. . ." (p. 13).

7. A detailed review of exchange rate developments in Zambia can be found in Lewis and McPherson (1996). Chapter 6 provides more recent developments.

on foreign exchange to those who gained access to it. This strategy also protected domestic producers, since imports were not readily available at the official exchange rate.

The first major attempt at exchange rate reform was the auction system, in place from October 1985 to May 1987. The auction could not be sustained because it was not supported by complementary macroeconomic stabilization policies. Starting in 1989, reforms were reintroduced. A preexisting export retention scheme (first commenced in 1981) was expanded to allow exporters to receive a market-determined exchange rate. The foreign exchange market was further liberalized, with the introduction of an "Open General License" (OGL) system. The BoZ allocated foreign exchange purchased from the copper company (ZCCM) or provided by donors under the OGL system for imports. The OGL had a negative list, which included luxury goods and precious metals. Bureaux de Change were licensed in October 1992 and in December 1992, the official and market exchange rates were merged. The foreign exchange market was completely liberalized with the suspension of the Exchange Control Act in 1994. As a result, tariffs became the major remaining protective mechanism for traded goods.

Tariffs

Tariffs had been the primary method of limiting imports until 1975. Nominal tariffs varied between 0 and 150 percent, with many exemptions, resulting in both high and variable effective protection. After 1975 nontariff barriers became more important as a method of restricting imports, and the actual tariff rates became less relevant in assessing protection. During the implementation of the exchange rate auction, import licensing was ended and foreign exchange was allocated by the market, making tariffs once again important. With the discontinuation of the auction in May 1987, foreign exchange was again allocated administratively through the foreign exchange management and allocation committee (FEMAC).

Tariff reform began in 1985, the same year the auction was introduced. The maximum rate was reduced to 100 percent, and many zero rates were increased, first to 10 percent and then to 15 percent. Many specific tariffs were changed to *ad valorem* duties. From May 1987 through 1989, further tariff reform was suspended, along with other reforms. Protection was increased in order to reduce import demand. In 1987 the import sales tax was increased, and an "uplift" imposed on imports. A 5 percent import license levy was imposed in 1988 and increased to 10 percent in 1991.

Tariff reform recommenced in 1989 and has continued since that time. In the 1991 budget, tariff rates were set between 0 and 50 percent. In the 1993 budget speech, rates were rationalized at 0, 20, 30, and 40 percent, as recommended by the 1992 tax policy task force (TPTF). The task force highlighted the significant degree of protection provided to domestic firms by the existing tariff structure. To promote economic growth and encourage exports, protection needed to be reduced so that producers faced keener competition. The tariff reform, which decreased the number and dispersion of tariff rates, was also expected to simplify customs administration.

The sales tax uplift of 20 percent was applied to the duty inclusive value of imports. It was a hidden charge on imports that was intended to compensate for the sales tax falling on some domestic production costs that were excluded from the value of competing imports subject to the sales tax. The TPTF recommended elimination of the uplift, but it was only abolished by default with the implementation of the VAT in July of 1995.

The TPTF also recommended abolishing the import license levy. It was considered an extra ad hoc charge on imports and its elimination would have made the tariff system less complex and protectionist. It was eliminated in 1993, but effectively replaced by the Import Declaration Fee (IDF) at the end of 1995 for revenue reasons.

In response to pressures from the manufacturing sector, the 1995 budget reduced the duty rates on five chapters of the Harmonized System (HS): 28, 29, 39, 40, and 72. The rationale was that Zambia's regional commitments to the preferential trade area (PTA, now COMESA) had generated significant negative effective protection for domestic producers. Finished goods from PTA countries were entering Zambia at low rates, while domestic producers had to import raw materials and intermediate goods from non-PTA sources at higher tariff rates. The specific HS chapters were proposed by the private sector as those most relevant to addressing the problem.

There was little empirical evidence that the problem was correctly represented by producers. Poor data on both the pattern of trade and the structure of domestic manufacturing production made it difficult to determine the extent of the problem and therefore the degree to which the duty suspensions would be appropriate. It seemed likely that the manufacturers were blaming the PTA anomaly problem for increased overall competition resulting from liberalization.

The policy was adopted at the last minute in response to intense private sector lobbying. It was understood that there would be costs to this policy. It was known that not all firms would benefit, and there would be pressure to extend the duty suspension to other firms. Domestic firms producing goods on which duty was suspended, or close substitutes for these goods, would face increased competition from duty-free imports. No work had been done to minimize these two problems. This was in part because of inadequate data. It was also clear that effective protection would increase for many firms not facing tariff anomalies.

Within a month of introducing the budget, many of these issues surfaced. The MoF received numerous letters from firms complaining that duty had not been suspended on all of their raw material imports. The duty suspension granted in the 1995 budget only applied to approximately 10 percent of imports subject to the 20 percent duty rate (considered raw materials by importers). There were no clear criteria on which to extend the duty suspension, without extending it to all raw material imports. Doing this, however, had unacceptable implications for revenue and effective rates of protection. During the course of the year, a strategy of resisting new suspensions was adopted. Nonetheless, in response to intense lobbying, some suspensions were granted.

The suspensions also worsened the already problematic compliance on customs duty. In the two months following the duty suspension, goods imported under the HS codes on which duty had been suspended increased as a share of total imports by as much as 400 percent. The most likely explanation was that imported goods were being misclassified to evade duty. Preshipment inspection (PSI) was not performed on goods not subject to duty, so verification of fraud was not possible. This was changed during the course of 1995.

Tax Compliance and Customs Duties

A number of initiatives were taken in the customs area to improve tax compliance. PSI had been used to reduce evasion and fraud, but it was ineffective.[8] To be effective, the PSI required high-level political commitment. That was not forthcoming. At the same time, in response to revenue needs to meet program targets, a flat simple 5 percent import declaration fee (IDF) was introduced, and exemptions from customs duty for investors were eliminated.

Preshipment Inspection for Imports: The 1992 budget made PSI a requirement for import orders valued at more than $5,000. This was designed to improve compliance on customs duties and import sales tax, areas with well-known compliance problems.[9] PSI can be used to improve tax compli-

---

8. In Zambia, PSI was originally used to help enforce foreign exchange control. Rather than cancel the contract with the PSI agency when exchange controls were lifted, the government began using it to combat undervaluation in customs.

9. *Budget Speech,* 1992.

ance in a variety of ways. It reports the valuation of goods and the correct tariff classification, and therefore can be used to minimize undervaluation and misclassification. It also can be used for information on rules of origin, important in countries with preferential tariff rates under regional trading arrangements. The PSI program performs many functions that could be done by Customs Departments, but they can nonetheless be useful, as in Zambia, when institutional capacity is limited or fraud within the customs office is a problem. Ultimately, as capacity is rebuilt and fraud is reduced, the Customs Department should assume full responsibility for the functions performed by the enterprises that supply PSI services.

There is little evidence that PSI has been used effectively by Customs officials to improve revenue collections. Indeed, there was intense hostility to PSI within Customs. It was not effectively used to improve compliance. The $5,000 limit was too high. A review of customs records in 1994 revealed that split shipments designed to evade PSI were common. Goods with exemptions or suspensions were not subject to PSI. This encouraged further abuse. Businesses also argued that PSI frequently held up the delivery of goods.

Hoping to improve the usefulness of PSI, a new tender was opened in mid-1996 to award the next multiyear contract. Little was accomplished. After intense lobbying, the tender was awarded to the original company. PSI has been used effectively to improve customs performance in some countries. It has been ineffective in Zambia largely because of political manipulation and institutional resistance.

The IDF: During 1995, in response to a fiscal gap and underperformance by Customs, a fee was introduced to cover the costs of PSI and to contribute additional revenue. This fee was a 5 percent charge on the cost, insurance, freight (c.i.f.) value of imports. It was implemented, beginning in October 1995, on almost all imports. In response to pressure from the business community, holders of investment licenses with duty exemptions were granted exemption from the IDF. The government, churches, charities and NGOs initially had to pay the fee.

The customs administration within the ZRA has not supported the IDF. They specifically did not want to be responsible for collecting it.[10] Accordingly, the MoF began collecting the fee. Collection was arranged through the commercial banks, to be remitted to the MoF. Proof of payment of the IDF was required to clear goods through Customs. The MoF designed a computer

---

10. Senior officials in the ZRA were exceedingly hostile to the IDF. Prior to its introduction, they made a major effort to derail the effort to the point of circulating a bitter attack on the policy within the government.

program for the commercial banks to record the amount of IDF collected. Once paid, the commercial bank electronically sent the information to the PSI company to initiate inspection, and to the MoF for revenue monitoring purposes.

After the first few months, it became clear that the revenue performance on this tax was extremely strong. It demonstrated the benefits of a low, flat-rate tax with few exemptions. Three to five people administered the program in the MoF, compared to staff numbering in the hundreds at the department of customs and excise at ZRA. During 1996 and 1997, the 5 percent IDF generated revenues equivalent to 30 percent of total customs revenues, with tariff rates of up to 25 percent.

Special Tax Incentives for Investment: The 1991 Investment Act offered investors a variety of special tax incentives, including special income tax holidays and exemptions from customs duty. The Act was passed in 1991, shortly before the elections. The TPTF recommended the elimination of tax holidays. As applied in Zambia, they were unfair, administratively complex, distortionary, and exceedingly costly for the government in terms of foregone revenue.[11]

The 1993 Investment Act took steps to reduce the distortions from the special investment incentives. Exemptions from customs duty and sales tax remained, but special income tax holidays were eliminated. The TPTF report stressed that tax holidays created large distortions. They favored new producers over existing businesses, short-term over long-term investments, and capital-intensive over labor-intensive investments. Furthermore, tax holidays favored import intensive projects over projects that used locally produced capital goods and other inputs and new investment over proper maintenance of existing capital stock. They also required that other taxes be raised to compensate for the foregone revenue.[12]

Inadequate computerization made enforcement of the remaining customs and sales tax exemptions a problem for the tax authorities. The exemptions were granted for a specific list of goods. There is little evidence that goods entering the country under investment licenses were adequately monitored. There has never been any follow-up work to determine whether the investment incentives generated productive investments. Moreover, no convincing cost-benefit analysis of any kind has been undertaken to assess the effects of these subsidies.

The 1996 budget eliminated any new exemptions on customs duty offered

---

11. TPTF, pp. 5, 16.
12. TPTF, p. 51.

to investors, while the introduction of the VAT to replace the sales tax in mid-1995 had effectively eliminated the exemptions from sales tax.[13] The latter was justified on the grounds that investors could claim back the VAT on inputs. Special provisions were made for investors who were not entitled to claim back VAT, such as investors in exempt sectors and mineral exploration companies that were not previously registered for the VAT. The 1996 customs reform significantly lowered customs rates, particularly on capital equipment, reducing the need for special duty exemptions.

Despite the lack of evidence that past preferences have had the desired impact on economic growth or equity, there has been continued pressure to grant investment incentives. Some members of the business community favored their elimination because they gave some firms an unjustified competitive advantage. Revenue concerns in the last few years have helped control the granting of new incentives. The Investment Centre still operates, but has few tax incentives to administer. Its main function is to provide assistance to investors in securing from the government the various approvals needed to establish or operate a business in Zambia.[14]

3. THE 1996 TARIFF REFORM

A tax policy working group was reconstituted in 1995 to propose tax policies for the 1996 budget. In view of the government's commitment to further trade liberalization, tariff reform was a major item on the agenda. The share of imports entering Zambia duty free had increased significantly in 1995 over 1994. (Based on ZRA data, the share was 53 percent in the second half of 1994, and by the first quarter of 1995, it had increased to 65 percent.) This undermined government revenue and the continued liberalization of tariff rates. The large number of exemptions generated anomalies and increased the operational uncertainties facing domestic firms. Pressure for further exemptions continued in response to the perceived inequities in the existing rates. The changes in the 1995 Budget had not dealt with the problem of anomalies arising from COMESA, smuggling, or final goods that had been granted exemptions. The existing duty drawback system was not working effectively. Exporters were at a competitive disadvantage on world markets. Finally, it was clear that weak tax administration, particularly with respect to customs and a complicated tariff structure had stimulated evasion and smuggling. Domestic firms complying with the tax laws were at a disadvantage.

---

13. The exemptions for the mining sector were reinstituted at the last minute.
14. Investment Act 1993, Section 5.

The strategy adopted by the working group was to propose a significant reduction in the number of suspensions and exemptions, while reducing rates across the board. Three alternative policies were discussed. One was a flat duty rate across-the-board, with few exemptions. Another was a 10 percent across-the-board reduction, combined with the elimination of the IDF. The final one, ultimately adopted, was a 15 percent across-the-board reduction, while maintaining the IDF for a further year.

The working group seriously considered the flat rate. The revenue performance of the IDF had been so strong that it highlighted the advantages for compliance of having one rate with few exemptions. The rate, however, would have had to be about 15 percent to generate adequate revenue. It was felt that this rate was too high and some goods would have to be zero-rated. This would reduce the appeal of the flat rate. A flat rate, in the context of COMESA preferences, would still leave some firms with negative effective protection. Finally, domestic manufacturers correctly perceived that this would reduce their effective protection significantly, and lobbied against a single rate.

Though the IDF was unpopular, it was extremely effective at raising revenue. At a flat 5 percent, with few exemptions, it proved to be a buoyant tax. Figure 8–1 shows the value of customs duty collected (at rates from 0 to 40 percent from October 1995 to January 1996; 0 to 25 percent from February 1996) relative to the flat 5 percent IDF for comparable months. Figure 8–2 shows the yield of the IDF and the customs revenue relative to total tax revenue. The tax policy working group recommended reducing tariff rates by 15 percent, while maintaining the IDF. During 1996, it was hoped that compliance on customs would be improved and the IDF could be eliminated in 1997. This would mean a further 5 percent reduction in tariffs across the board, continuing Zambia's trade liberalization program.

Significantly, the 1996 budget speech announced the tariff reform. The major change was to reduce tariff rates while eliminating many suspensions and exemptions. COMESA rates were set at 40 percent of general tariff rates. These changes were designed to contribute to growth by reducing distortions in the tax system, by reducing the antiexport bias in the tariff structure, and by improving compliance on customs duties. Producers faced lower taxes on capital goods, raw materials, and intermediate inputs, thereby increasing their competitiveness and reducing the cost of new investments.

By reducing tariff rates and setting COMESA rates at 40 percent of general tariff rates, almost all existing tariff anomalies were eliminated. Final goods from COMESA entered at 10 percent, while raw materials and intermediate goods from non-COMESA countries entered at 0 to 15 percent. Zambia's commitment to regional trade integration, which remained strong, no longer

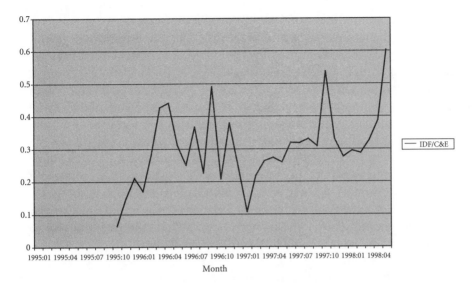

Figure 8-1. Ratio of IDF to Customs and Excise Revenues

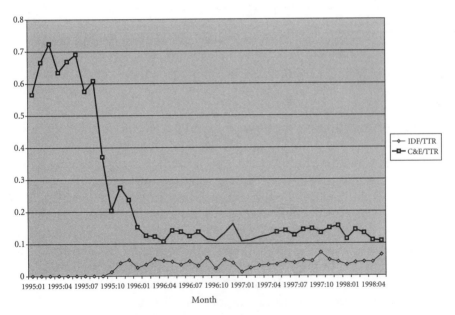

Figure 8-2. IDF and Customs and Excise Revenues relative to Total Tax Revenues

resulted in large numbers of domestic producers facing negative protection. While this change in treatment of COMESA imports was technically in violation of the COMESA treaty, Zambia had proceeded further with tariff reductions on both intra-COMESA and non-COMESA trade than other countries. Its tariffs on intra-COMESA trade were among the lowest in the regional group, and the 1996 budget reduced the trade-weighted tariff on COMESA imports despite increasing some individual duties.

The lower tariff rates were combined with a reduction in exemptions. This improved equity, reduced the variance in effective protection, and maintained revenue. In eliminating exemptions, the government set an example by paying duty on its imports, a policy that had been proposed in the TPTF.[15] The effect on procurement decisions was considered important, since the previous exemption put domestic suppliers at a disadvantage. It was also recognized that the exemption had been a source of tax evasion. Charitable organizations (schools, hospitals, NGOs, churches) also paid duty, but could claim refunds on allowable goods. Exemptions on the importation of motor vehicles were tightened. Based on the ZRA data, only one in ten vehicles imported before the budget reform paid any duty. The existing exemptions had been widely abused. Several imports that previously entered at zero duty rates were subject to 5 percent duty. Specifically, the duty on petroleum feedstock was increased from 0 to 5 percent, to compensate for the revenue loss from reducing duty rates across the board. New customs duty exemptions for investment license holders were also eliminated. Existing exemptions were allowed to run their course, but were not to be renewed.

4. Compliance With the Tariff Reform

Table 8–1 reports the collected duty rates since 1993 and the trade weighted statutory rates. The collected duty rates are below the statutory rates. This is the result of the large number of exemptions and tax fraud. In 1993, 1994, and 1995 the trade-weighted actual duty rates were 9.7, 10.8, and 9.0 percent, respectively. In 1996 and 1997, these rates dropped to 7.3 and 8.2 percent, respectively. As a share of the statutory rate, the trade-weighted actual rate increased from 60 percent and 50 percent in 1994 and 1995 to 69 percent and 72 percent in 1996 and 1997. With the reform in 1996, the difference between collected rates and statutory rates declined significantly. There is also some evidence for improved collections in 1997 over 1996, suggesting improved performance of the revenue authority.

Table 8–2 reports the collected rates, by statutory tariff for four time peri-

---

15. TPTF, p.56.

Table 8–1:   *Average Statutory and Actual Tariff Rates*

	1993	1994	1995	1996	1997	1998
Actual rate	9.70	10.80	9.00	7.30	8.20	8.10
Statutory rate	NA	17.80	18.00	10.70	11.30	10.70
Actual/statutory		0.61	0.50	0.68	0.73	0.75

Notes: * weighted by import values.
February to January used for annual data, because tax policy changes are implemented at beginning of February each year after the annual budget speech at the end of January.

ods. During 1994 and 1995, before the tariff reform of the 1996 budget, the collected rate was a lower share of the statutory rate for the two higher tariff rates of 30 percent and 40 percent, than for the lower rate of 20 percent. The collected rate was less than half the statutory rate for both of these rates in both years. The mean collected rates at the top two statutory rates were less than the collected rate in the lowest statutory tariff band, both in 1994 and 1995. Standard deviations were high and increased with the statutory tariff rate. After the tariff reform of 1996, the ratio of collected rates to statutory rate rose, and the ratio is no longer significantly lower at the higher tariff rates, now 15 percent and 25 percent. In 1996 and 1997, the mean collected rates at the top two rates of the 15 percent and 25 percent were close to the mean rates in 1994 and 1995 for the top rates of 30 percent and 40 percent. Average collections remained unchanged, although rates were reduced by 15 percentage points across-the-board. While the standard deviation still in-

Table 8–2   *Actual Tariff Collections, by Tariff Rate*

	Statutory Rate	Mean Actual Rate	Standard Deviation	Coefficient of Variation	25th Percentile	75th Percentile
1994	20	13.4	9.4	70.1	1.9	20
	30	12.1	14.0	115.7	0	30
	40	15.4	18.0	116.9	0	40
1995	20	10.9	9.9	90.8	0	20
	30	11.4	13.9	121.9	0	30
	40	18.9	18.5	97.9	0	40
1996	5	3.3	3.0	90.9	0	5
	15	10.2	6.8	66.5	0	15
	25	17.4	10.7	61.3	10	25
1997	5	3.7	2.4	64.1	2	5
	15	10.5	6.7	64.3	0	15
	25	18.3	10.3	56.2	10	25
1998	5	4.3	1.8	41.9	5	5
	15	12.9	5.1	39.5	15	15
	25	21.6	8.1	37.5	25	25

Notes: Tariff rates are changed annually on the day of the budget speech, delivered on the fourth Friday of January. The data reported are for the year, starting on the day the tariff rates are changed.

creases as the statutory rates rise, it declines in relation to the mean. This contrasts with the data for 1994 and 1995. There is also an increase in the mean collected rates between 1996 and 1998.

Econometric Results

Following Pritchett and Sethi,[16] it is possible to estimate the following regression for Zambia:

$$\text{Collected rate } (t) = a + b \text{ official rate}(t) + e(t)$$

where a,b are estimated coefficients, e is a random error term, and t indexes time. Pritchett and Sethi estimated this equation for Jamaica, Pakistan, and Kenya for 1991, 1991, and 1987 respectively. They used data on imports and customs revenue aggregated by HS code. In this analysis, the data allow the examination of changes over time as the tariff reform progresses. We do not have data for the period before the reform started or early in the reform process. However, the five or so years for which data are available span significant changes in the tariff structure, as well as several other major changes in tariff and tax policy more generally.

Table 8–3 reports regression results by year. There are four different sets of regressions. The first is the equation above. The second weights each observation by the value of imports in the expectation that a lower proportion of the statutory duty rate is paid on larger import transactions. The third equation excludes observations for which the official rate is zero, since in this case there is no reason for the actual rate to diverge from the statutory rate. And, the fourth equation also weights the observations by import value.

The regressions suggest that the reforms have been working in the expected direction. Actual collections are increasingly related to statutory rates over time. When weighted by import values, with and without items at zero official rates, the improvement shows up more strongly. In 1994 and 1995, collected rates were about 30 to 40 percent of the statutory rates. In 1996 and 1997, this increased to over 70 percent. The coefficients of determination (R^2) also increase, suggesting that the statutory rates play more of a role in explaining collections in the later years. Table 8–3 combines the data for 1995 to 1997, using dummy variables (DV) to test for significant differences across the years. While not large, there are significant increases in 1996 and 1997 over 1995, suggesting that the tariff reform had the desired effect. There is also a small improvement in 1997 over 1996.

---

16. Pritchett and Sethi 1994.

Table 8–3: *Regression Results: Collected Rate as Function of Statutory Rate*

	1994		1995		1996		1997		1995–1997	
	Coefficient	R2	Coefficient	R2	Coefficient	R2	Coefficient	R2	Coefficient	R2
Linear	0.706 (0.003)	0.31	0.749 (0.003)	0.36	0.821 (0.002)	0.46	0.825 (0.002)	0.49	0.788 (0.001)	0.46
Linear weighted by import value	0.326 (0.003)	0.12	0.423 (0.002)	0.19	0.708 (0.002)	0.48	0.724 (0.002)	0.52	0.585 (0.001)	0.37
Linear excluding t=0	0.826 (0.005)	0.24	0.786 (0.004)	0.23	0.822 (0.002)	0.36	0.827 (0.002)	0.39	0.789 (0.002)	0.37
Linear excluding t=0 weighted by import value	0.048 (0.005)	0	0.311 (0.005)	0.036	0.719 (0.002)	0.37	0.727 (0.002)	0.42	0.556 (0.001)	0.28

	1995–1996			1996–1997			1995–1997	1996–1997	
	Coefficient	DV 1996	R2	Coefficient	DV 1997	R2	Coefficient	DV	R2
Linear	0.771 (0.002)	0.033 (0.002)	0.44	0.796 (0.001)	0.018 (0.001)	0.46	0.777 (0.001)	0.036 (0.001)	0.46
Linear weighted by import value	0.785 (0.003)	0.039 (0.002)	0.27	0.765 (0.002)	0.022 (0.001)	0.23	0.786 (0.002)	0.041 (0.001)	0.28

Notes: Standard errors are reported below the coefficient estimates.

Table 8–4 reports regressions that allow the relationship between the statutory rate and the actual rate to vary by statutory rate. The results suggest that the relationship is not constant across rates. In 1996 and 1997, there is evidence that a greater share of the statutory duty rate was collected at higher rates. This contrasts with the evidence for 1995, which suggests that less duty was collected at the middle rate of 30 percent, than at either the 20 or 40 percent rates.

Exemptions

The 1996 budget significantly reduced tariff rates, while eliminating most exemptions as a means of sustaining revenues and reducing distortions. Some of the major changes were the elimination of the blanket exemption for schools and hospitals (interpreted to include nonprofits, churches, and charities more generally) and the government, a significant tightening of the exemption for new and returning residents, and standardization of the tariff preferences given to imports from COMESA countries. As a result of the reform, the share of imports that is subject to a positive tariff rate but enter Zambia duty free fell from 28 percent in 1995 to 23 percent and 20 percent in 1996 and 1997, respectively. The share of imports entering duty free (either because of a zero duty rate or because of an exemption) declined from 51 percent in 1995 to 43 percent and 36 percent in 1996 and 1997 (see Table 8–5).

Until the 1996 tariff reform, goods imported by schools and hospitals and the government entered under HS codes 9901 and 9902 respectively at a zero duty rate. In 1994, the value of imports entering under these codes was 8.9

Table 8–4: *Additional Regression Results (t = 0 dropped, coefficient varies by tariff rate > 0)*

	1995 Coefficient	Standard Errors	1996 Coefficient	Standard Errors	1997 Coefficient	Standard Errors
Not weighted by import value						
Rate	0.841	0.043	0.674	0.079	0.649	0.089
Middle rate*DV1	–0.016	0.015	0.092	0.053	0.113	0.059
High rate*DV2	–0.028	0.021	0.114	0.064	0.138	0.07
R2	0.230		0.360		0.390	
Weighted by import value						
Rate	0.397	0.015	0.606	0.085	0.495	0.066
Middle rate*DV1	–0.117	0.006	0.065	0.057	0.121	0.044
High rate*DV2	0	0.008	0.084	0.068	0.185	0.053
R2	0.050		0.380		0.420	

Actual rate = a + b statutory rate + c statutory rate*DV1 + d statutory rate*DV2 + e
DV1 = 1 if statutory rate = middle rate, DV2 = 1 if statutory rate = high rate

Table 8–5: *Share of Import Value Subject to Tariffs, Exemptions, and Preferences under COMESA*

		Share of Import Value	Share of Import Value t>0, duty=0	Share of Import Value COMESA Preference
1994	0	25.0		
	20	42.1	6.5	
	30	14.2	5.2	
	40	8.4	3	
	Other	10.3	2.6	
	Total	100	17.4	NA
1995	0	23.5		
	20	50.2	17.8	
	30	15.8	7.6	
	40	7.4	2.5	
	Other	3.1		
	Total	100.0	27.9	NA
1996	0	20.5		
	5	30.2	10.8	1
	15	31	8.3	3.2
	25	18.3	3.9	2.5
	Total	100.0	23.0	6.7
1997	0	15.5		
	5	33	7.7	2.2
	15	31.3	8.7	1.4
	25	20.2	3.8	2.7
	Total	100.00	20.2	6.3
1998	0	21.9		
	5	29.5	7.2	3.4
	15	28.4	6.3	0.8
	25	19.8	3.1	2.3
	Total	99.6	16.6	6.5

percent of total imports. By 1996, the value these exemptions was 0.1 of total import value. In eliminating these exemptions in 1996, imports previously entering at a zero tariff rate now are classified by the actual HS code of the import. Some, but not all, of these imports may still be subject to a zero rate (goods such as ambulances, drugs, other medical equipment, and books). The declining share of imports subject to a zero duty rate from 1994 to 1997 has in part resulted from this reform.

Initially, both groups were to pay duty, like all other importers. In the end, it could not be sustained politically. With over 70 percent of Zambians living in poverty, there is a large charitable/NGO sector supplying a variety of services to the poor, including education, health care, family planning, and prevention and treatment of HIV/AIDS. These organizations strongly objected to paying duty on imports. Similarly, members of parliament objected to the government paying duty. More persuasive was the fact that, the MoF had not budgeted on either the expenditure or revenue side assuming that the government would not pay import duty. A compromise solution was reached, which moved to a voucher system. The government would pay the import duty for government and approved churches and charities, either on importation or through a refund. This suggests that the results on improved tariff collections do not translate directly into improved net revenue performance, since some revenue is remitted to both the government and churches and charities.

From the perspective of compliance, however, the voucher system was still a significant improvement. With blanket exemptions, there was no control of items imported by the government or schools/charities/NGOs. With the refund system, the MoF and the ZRA know what is being imported and the amount of duty foregone. There is also a list of approved items for school/churches/NGOs, so that limits can be placed on items that can be re-sold easily on the private market. In addition, a committee of ZRA and the MoF officials must approve each organization. Many organizations, which previously were exempt, now must pay duty. For example, church groups not doing charitable work are no longer eligible for duty-free imports. Because the government system of tracking ministry expenditures is also weak, it is likely that the government exemptions were also abused. An area where there were no controls was the military.

The refund system creates the same distortions as the previous system of exemptions under HS codes 9901 and 9902. Both encourage the government and churches/charities etc. to import items rather than purchase them from domestic producers. The private sector has been lobbying the government for the elimination of this exemption since the tariff reform started. To the extent that the new procedures limit abuse, private domestic producers are marginally better off.

Another exemption that was significantly reduced in the 1996 reforms was for new and returning residents, who were previously allowed to import essentially anything, including vehicles, duty free. With tax on vehicles totaling close to 100 percent (including tariffs, VAT, and an excise tax), this exemption was used to evade the tax. A returning resident was anyone who had been out of the country for two years. With the reform, vehicles were excluded from the exemption, and residents had to be gone for five years to be eligible for the returning resident exemption. In addition, anyone allowed to import a vehicle under an exemption (for example, diplomats and aid agencies) now has to hold the vehicle for five years, rather than two, before being allowed to sell it on the local market (to a nonexempt person) without paying duty.

Table 8–6:   *Imports to Zambia by Region (as percent of total imports)*

	1993	1994	1995	1996	1997	1998
COMESA	na	na	2.1	7.7	6.7	7.0
(US) USA	2.7	2.2	3.8	4.8	3.9	3.1
(GB) UK	10.2	14.0	3.7	10.8	11.2	8.1
(ZA) South Africa	43.2	32.2	36.3	36.9	38.5	40.1
(DE) Germany	na	na	4.9	3.8	1.8	1.6
(JP) Japan	4.4	5.9	6.5	3.2	4.5	4.2
Other	39.5	45.7	36.7	32.8	33.4	35.3

Evidence on the exemption shows that a loophole has been (partially) closed. The data suggest that the average duty collected on motor vehicles has increased from 20 percent and 10 percent in 1994 and 1995, to 75 percent and 85 percent in 1996 and 1997. The high rates in 1996 and 1997 result from vehicles (HS code 8703) being one of only a few goods subject to a minimum specific duty. (The other goods are tires and used clothing.) The data suggest that most vehicle imports are entering under this specific duty and not the *ad valorem* rate of 25 percent. This could be because most imported vehicles subject to duty are previously used and of low value, or it may indicate significant underinvoicing. While casual observation in Zambia suggests that there is significant importation of expensive, new vehicles taking place, many of these enter duty-free through diplomatic or development exemptions, and are ultimately resold on the domestic market.

A remaining loophole is the preferential tariff rates for COMESA imports, currently at 40 percent of the statutory rates. This explains part of the discrepancy between statutory and actual tariff rates. Table 8–6 reports the share of imports entering at preferential COMESA rates for 1996 and 1997. Data from earlier years on this exemption are not available.

In general, the tariff reform achieved substantial reductions in exemptions. This contributed to the improved collections relative to statutory rates.

5. OTHER ISSUES RELATING TO TRADE POLICY REFORM

This section considers a number of issues that help shape the setting in which tariff reform is being undertaken in Zambia. Tariffs cannot be cut too sharply because the government needs revenue. Zambia has entered a number of international agreements placing limits on the extent to which tariffs and other trade restrictions can be applied. South Africa is Zambia's largest trading partner. The sort of reform adopted there and its timing has an important influence on Zambia's growth prospects.

Fiscal Constraints on Trade Liberalization

Zambia relies on customs duties and the IDF (when applied) for a significant share of tax revenue. This share has risen since 1995. Trade liberalization can only proceed and be consistent with macroeconomic stability if alternative revenue sources are found or expenditures are reduced. In 1996, duty rates were lowered while exemptions were reduced significantly to maintain revenue yields. As a share of total tax revenue and in real terms, customs duties rose in 1996 over 1995, and further increased in 1997. This was the result of reductions in exemptions, increased total non-maize imports, and improved compliance.

Improved compliance with existing tariff rates is likely to remain a major source of increased revenue. There is much evidence of smuggling and misclassification of imports. Improved enforcement would allow a reduction in the dispersion of tariffs rates and would reduce the highest rates of effective protection, while leaving the average duty collected unchanged.

Two areas where improvements can be made are in cargo control, namely the clearance of goods at the border under removals in bond (RIB) or removals in transit (RIT), and in the bonded warehouse program. The slow progress made on computerization has made control in these areas problematic. Only in 1997 was a system being put in place to track these transactions.[17]

At the same time, the burden of taxation can be shifted to other taxes. The VAT and improved compliance on the income tax are both possibilities. Increased nontax revenue and improved compliance generally would also generate revenue that could be used to further reduce tariff rates.

Regional integration

Zambia is currently a member of both COMESA and SADC. COMESA replaced the PTA in December 1994. Members of COMESA are committed to eliminating tariff barriers by the end of October 2000 and putting in place a common external tariff by 2004. Zambia applies a 60 percent reduction on the general tariff to imports from COMESA countries. Under COMESA, regional trade liberalization has progressed more rapidly than with the rest of

---

17. A large part of the delay was strategic. Under the Computerization and Modernization of Tax Administration project (CMTAP), one of the first programs developed was for bonded warehouses. Customs officials, both before and after ZRA was established, showed no interest in making this form of control effective. It was, and remains, a major source of customs fraud.

the world. The highest COMESA tariff rate in 1995 was 16 percent, compared to a general tariff rate of 40 percent. In 1996, this rate was reduced to 10 percent, plus the 5 percent IDF. In mid-1998, the IDF was eliminated. As yet, most of Zambia's trade is with non-COMESA countries, so that regional liberalization cannot substitute for liberalized trade with the rest of the world.

Trade liberalization under COMESA has also generated problems for Zambia, including negative effective protection for some domestic producers. This in turn has led to changes in the general tariff structure, which have moved Zambia away from its commitment to trade liberalization. The 1996 budget dealt with these anomalies. In the future, if COMESA rates are reduced faster than the general tariff rates, tariff anomalies will reemerge.

Over the next few years, Zambia will have to decide on a strategy for trade liberalization, including the relative merits of regional versus multilateral liberalization. The best solution would be to proceed with both at the same time. If general duty rates can be reduced while regional integration proceeds, the problems that arise from regional integration can be minimized.

Zambia may also need to decide between COMESA and SADC. If the decision favors SADC (as seems the most logical in view of South Africa's commitments), Zambia should have a strategy for avoiding some of the coordination problems that have arisen within COMESA.

Regional integration involves more than reducing import tariffs. There is potential for increasing efficiency and trade through a variety of other channels. The cross-border initiative (CBI) is a program designed to increase economic growth by improving economic integration in East and Southern Africa. It seeks to facilitate cross-border investment, trade, and payments. Items being addressed include developing a common basis for investment incentives, streamlining customs services, and cooperation in infrastructure development. A major initiative over recent years has been the work on the Southern Africa power pool that seeks to rationalize energy production, distribution, and use across the whole SADC region.[18]

The Importance of South Africa

South Africa is the most important regional market for Zambia's exports, but remains heavily protected. South Africa has imposed high duties on its imports and subsidized its exports through the General Export Incentive Scheme (GEIS). The Government of South Africa is committed to liberalizing its tariff structure and eliminating the GEIS under its agreement with the World Trade Organization (WTO) over the next few years. In the meantime,

---

18. Sparrow, Bowen and Yu 1999.

South Africa's import duties probably cause a reduction in some, but not all, Zambian exports, especially those—such as flowers and vegetables—where seasonal timing and transport costs are important. In cases where transport and other transaction costs are not major concerns, such as textiles, South African trade barriers may reduce Zambian exports only slightly, forcing them to be sold farther abroad at a lower price.

South Africa also subsidizes its exports, especially of manufactured goods, under the GEIS. It is possible, but far from certain, that these export subsidies damage Zambian manufacturers in their home market. In 1994, South Africa's manufactured exports could earn a subsidy of 18 percent on f.o.b. value; by 1995 the maximum rate fell to 14.5 percent. The GEIS is designed to overcome higher costs in South Africa, especially the higher costs associated with the overvaluation of the rand. If it does no more than that, then the only impact on Zambia would be to substitute South African imports for those that would have come in any case from Europe or Asia.

Because export growth and diversification are central to Zambia's structural adjustment program, South African import barriers constitute the greater of these two problems. The main aim of trade policy towards South Africa therefore should be to reduce these trade barriers and to encourage Zambian exports. Any countermeasures should be designed to achieve this goal.

Zambia was entitled under the General Agreement on Tariffs and Trade (GATT, now WTO) to impose countervailing duties against South African exports. But to justify them, Zambia had to document the level of subsidy and the harm to its own producers, requiring a thorough study. The costs of countervailing duties—a confrontational trade policy and more stringent customs enforcement—would likely exceed the benefits, especially as the GEIS is being phased out. Moreover, countervailing duties would apply to a tiny fraction of South Africa's exports and would probably not achieve the main aim of reducing trade barriers in South Africa and encouraging Zambian exports.

A more productive approach might be to work within SADC, in concert with other members, to convince South Africa to lower its duties on imports from SADC members. This approach would be consistent with South Africa's own current preference for dealing with SADC instead of COMESA and would reinforce Zambia's structural adjustment program. Any SADC arrangement should work towards low, but not yet zero, internal tariffs and should either have low common external tariffs or else allow each country to set its own external tariffs. South Africa's preferential trade agreement with the European Union in early 1999 reemphasizes the importance of a concerted effort to liberalize trade flows throughout SADC.

Because a large share of Zambia's imports come from South Africa, fiscal concerns will limit the pace at which Zambia can move toward low regional duties within SADC (see Table 8–6). Zambia needs to proceed slowly towards zero duties within any trade agreement in order to protect its customs revenues. Until the VAT is fully developed or compliance more generally improves and can bear the burden of reductions in customs revenue, Zambia's budget cannot afford the substitution of imports at zero duty from within SADC or COMESA for imports that now bear positive duty rates.

Policies to Encourage Exports

The exchange rate and the tariff structure will be the major policy tools that affect the rate of export growth in Zambia. Other policies can also help encourage exports. These include an improved duty drawback system, manufacturing under bond, EPZs, and assistance for export marketing. While none of these would be effective without the appropriate exchange rate and tariff policies, they should be considered as complementary policies.

During the Second Republic, even when most of Zambia's policies discouraged exports, the government attempted to offset some of the disincentives by special incentives to encourage exports. The Industrial Act of 1977 included provisions along those lines. In 1986, the Industrial Investment Act replaced the Industrial Act. It included new incentives (or reductions in existing disincentives) including an improved duty drawback system and less restrictive export licensing rules. However, within the context of overall economic conditions in Zambia at the time, these had little tangible impact on exports.

Before 1990, export licensing discouraged exports. The export licensing procedures were specifically designed to encourage sales to the domestic market, thereby supporting the import substituting strategy. Since then, the procedures have been liberalized. At present, the only requirement is the single export declaration form that can be filed with a commercial bank. This is largely for data gathering purposes.

With the adoption of the economic reform program, the government has moved toward trade liberalization and reduced the anti-export bias of policies. All export restrictions have been eliminated (with the exception of periodic bans on maize exports), tariffs have been reduced, and the exchange rate liberalized.

Zambia currently has a duty drawback system and allows manufacturing under bond (MUB). The Export Board of Zambia, supported through the Budget, supplies some marketing assistance to exporters. The Ministry of Commerce, Trade and Industry has studied the feasibility of EPZs and is proposing that they be established.

Duty Drawback System: Tariffs on imports are also a tax on exports. To help alleviate this problem, Zambia has a duty drawback system for exporters. In 1994, attempts were made to improve the drawback system. Exporters can claim a refund on customs duty charged on raw materials and intermediate good imports used in producing exports. This system was not working. There were few applications filed for drawback and long delays in obtaining refunds on the few that were filed. The major change to address these problems was to allow those entitled to a duty drawback to claim a credit against future import tax liabilities. As long as firms had additional imports on which they owed duty, this reduced the cash costs of waiting for a drawback.

Few exporters claim and receive refunds. During 1995, credits claimed under the duty drawback system totaled K44.9 million while refunds were K17.1 million. Nontraditional exports in 1995 totaled $201.3 million, equivalent to K174 billion. The credit and refunds on duty paid are insignificant and can have little effect on offsetting the disincentives to exports from duty paid on imported inputs.

The 1997 budget speech called for faster refunds and increased publicity to convince more exporters to use the duty drawback system. This message was repeated in the 1998 budget speech.

Manufacturing Under Bond: Firms that primarily export can manufacture under bond. Enterprises engaged in manufacturing under bond operate under the rules for bonded warehouses, which are licensed on an annual basis. This allows manufacturers to import inputs free of duty and VAT, directly into bonded warehouses. Only direct inputs used in the manufacture of the goods are free of duty. Other items, such as machinery, are subject to duty when they are removed from the warehouse. There is a bond requirement, which increases costs to the manufacturer. There are also problems for firms if they sell some goods locally.

The legislation on bonded warehouses is not specifically designed to benefit exporters. In fact, only three exporters have manufactured under bond (Swarp Spinning, Exel Textiles, and Mukuba Textile Mills).

Export Processing Zones: A study was undertaken in Zambia on the feasibility of establishing export processing zones. Little evidence was presented to show that EPZs would result in positive returns in Zambia. As a first step, it was decided to try to improve the operations of the duty drawback system and manufacturing under bond. If these cannot be made to function, it is not clear that EPZs could be effectively implemented.

Export Marketing: The Export Board of Zambia (EBZ) was established in 1985. Its functions include recommending policies to encourage Zambian exports and to collect and distribute information on trade, particularly relating to potential markets for exports. It also provides technical advice, promotes exports by organizing participation in trade fairs, disseminates information, and coordinates trade visits.

Over the last few years, EBZ has lobbied the government in favor of policies that encourage exports. It has been a useful source of information to government on how policies affect exports. There is little evidence that its other services have much impact on exports.

Overview: There is pressure on the government to give more attention and resources to mechanisms like those above that foster trade. If they are adopted, it will be important for these mechanisms to be operated in ways that benefit the country. In many countries, these changes have not generated net benefits, and Zambia needs to avoid this outcome.

Two points should be kept in mind. The changes listed above should not be considered as substitutes for other adjustments. They cannot substitute for responsible macroeconomic policies, the general reduction in protection, and an appropriately valued real exchange rate. Moreover, they must be set up in ways that minimize the use of government resources, including revenue and administrative capacity, both of which will continue to be severely constrained for the foreseeable future.

Exchange Rate Management

Trade liberalization and policies to promote exports can all be defeated by an overvalued real exchange rate. According to statements of official policy, market forces determine the nominal exchange rate. (A more detailed assessment of the formal and informal pressures that apply to exchange rate determination is given in Chapter 6.) Yet, the government also has an international reserves target. Furthermore, the BoZ has been concerned about inflationary pressures created by rapid growth of reserve money. It has acted in ways that demonstrate that there are limits to acceptable upward movements in the treasury bill interest rate. In practice, the exchange rate is determined by the market within the limits of the manipulations required to deal with these other concerns.

The challenge for the government and the BoZ is to rationalize these manipulations in ways that do not undermine trade reform. With only one policy instrument, the BoZ faces tradeoffs whichever way it turns. The government can assist the process by running a budget surplus. This would reduce the rate of growth of reserve money allowing the bank to accumulate reserves without risking a rise in the rate of inflation.

6. Concluding Comments

During the 1990s, Zambia made significant progress liberalizing its system of trade and international exchange. Many of the positive effects of the changes have been compromised by policy reversals. The government will continue to be pressed for revenue and may find it convenient to "close a financing gap" by raising tariffs. Zambia's history has shown this to be a shortsighted and counterproductive approach to budgeting. Raising tariffs undermines economic growth and adversely affects future prospects for improved revenue performance. A more constructive approach to revenue enhancement remains improved enforcement. Tax fraud in both customs and income tax are serious problems. Reducing the extent of fraud would be far more effective than raising duties.

A further concern is that trade liberalization through tariff reductions and related measures has to be fully supported by an appropriate policy stance with respect to the real exchange rate. Tariff reform provides a useful start in helping to reorient economic activity towards trade. But tariff reform has to be complemented by a real exchange rate that rewards exports rather than taxes them. This brings the problem of trade liberalization full circle to the government's overall stance with respect to macroeconomic policy and management.

9

Debt Management and Debt Relief during the 1990s in Zambia

FERNANDO R. FERNHOLZ

1. INTRODUCTION

External debt in Zambia rose from a level of US$800 million in 1970 to over $7 billion at the start of the 1990s. The latter was equivalent to more than 200 percent of GDP. As a result, Zambia had one of the highest per capita debt ratios in the world.[1] Through a combination of negotiations and international initiatives, the government was able to reverse this trend in the first half of the 1990s, reducing the debt a total of $1.4 billion by 1996. The contracting of new concessional loans during these years partially offset the debt reduction in nominal terms. Furthermore, the momentum to continue reducing debt was not sustained. By the end of the 1990s, the debt had returned to over $7 billion. The financial difficulties of the Zambian Consolidated Cooper Mining Company (ZCCM) during the '90s, resulting from the government's initial reluctance and then inability to sell the company, added to the renewed accumulation of debt.

This chapter discusses successful approaches that the government used to deal with the massive debt problem in the early 1990s and its failure to expand and sustain the strategies. The caution of Easterly and other experts comes to mind. Focusing on debt relief without altering the basic structure of an economy and its policies will only lead to another round of external debt accumulation after the effects of debt relief fade.[2] Zambia's experience specif-

---

1. See various issues of *Global Development Finance*, Washington D.C.: The World Bank, published annually.
2. Easterly 2000.

ically illustrates the relative ineffectiveness of debt relief provided to a country that continues to run public sector deficits and current account deficits on the balance of payments. To reduce dramatically public sector deficits requires appropriate policies and leadership, as the entrenched interests will vigorously defend the allocation of resources that favor them while basic public services have to be maintained to avoid a social explosion.

This chapter is organized as follows. Section 2 discusses the major factors contributing to the build-up of external debt prior to the 1990s. Section 3 examines the debt management strategy set in place during the first years of the MMD government in the context of the overall macroeconomic adjustment program. Section 4 considers Zambia's quest for deeper debt reduction under the Highly Indebted Poor Country initiative (HIPC). Section 5 discusses the institutional and human capacity building aspects of debt monitoring and debt management. Section 6 has concluding comments.

2. ACCUMULATION OF DEBT 1970 TO 1991

The accumulation of external debt in Zambia is a reflection of the high level of deficits in the fiscal and external accounts. Chapter 2 has discussed the historical context of the country's economic decline. Four major shocks, coupled with inappropriate policies, led to a rapid deterioration of economic performance, associated fiscal deficits and consequently to the steep accumulation of debt. Although discussed in Chapter 2, it is important to reiterate here the impact of these shocks on the country's level of external debt.[3] The first shock was political with economic consequences for Zambia. Conflicts in the neighboring countries of Zimbabwe and Angola (Zimbabwe unilater-

---

3. "External Debt Histories of Ten Low-Income Developing Countries—Lessons from Their Experience." IMF, Washington D.C. Working Paper, May 1, 1998. WP/98/72-EAWP/98/72:

The external debt burden of many low-income developing countries has increased significantly since the 1970s. An analysis of developments in a sample of ten countries shows the main factors behind the buildup of debt to be a combination of (1) exogenous shocks, such as adverse terms of trade or bad weather, which particularly affected countries with a concentration of exports in a single or very few products; (2) a lack of sustained macroeconomic adjustment policies and structural reforms, which obstructed a strong policy response to such shocks; (3) lending and refinancing by creditors that was initially predominantly on nonconcessional terms, but since the 1980s has increasingly been shifted toward concessional assistance and grants; (4) a widespread lack of prudent debt management by borrowing countries; and (5) political factors in these countries, such as civil war and social strife that often had devastating economic consequences.

ally declared independence in 1965) led to a disruption in the trade routes, and resulted in spiraling export and import costs for landlocked Zambia. Secondly, a major oil price shock in 1974 dramatically increased oil import costs, a very important cost factor in mining sector production and transportation. Thirdly, a slump in the world price for copper and production difficulties in Zambia in the 1970s affected export earnings and hence the balance of payments. As pointed out in Chapter 2, the combined budget and balance of payments deficit in the country deteriorated by 55 percent of GDP in 1974–75. In addition, the production of copper decreased steadily from about 730,000 tons of copper in 1974 to significantly less than 300,000 tons in 1999. In place of a vigorous program of fiscal adjustment, Zambia turned to external borrowing to finance the growing budget deficits.[4] International financial agencies, flush with bank deposits from oil exporters, were eager to lend. They viewed the Zambian economy as basically sound with export earnings expected to recover. Accordingly, they extended credits for projects and programs such as investments in public sector corporations and public sector holding companies. In addition, the government used credit to import food items, and later to repay debt. Private banks, foreign governments, and commercial enterprises lent to the government, public sector corporations, and the Zambian private sector at variable market rates of interest. The fourth major shock subsequently came when interest rates in the world economy increased substantially at the end of the 1970s and early 1980s. External sector borrowing and grant flows were drastically reduced in 1987 when Zambia defaulted on its external obligations to multilateral institutions.[5]

As the economy began to experience current account deficits and diminishing foreign exchange reserves in the latter part of the 1970s and early 1980s, the state imposed increasingly tighter controls over foreign currency transactions. Many of the outstanding loans were converted into public sector debts when creditors invoked guarantees given by the government. When foreign exchange reserves were practically exhausted in 1987, the public (state-owned corporations) and private sector debtors repaid their obligations to the Bank of Zambia in local currency, while the arrears in foreign exchange mounted. There was a shortfall in the supply of foreign exchange at the fixed exchange rate. A pipeline awaiting foreign exchange allocation built up. Eventually, the government had to make up the shortfall between the official rate and the market clearing rate of exchange. In addition, the unpaid or unsettled balances guaranteed by the creditor and debtor governments or ex-

4. Lewis and McPherson, 1994.
5. World Bank Data, 1993.

port agencies of creditor countries were rescheduled and became public external debt.

Many of the external and internal obligations became unsustainable as the accumulation of debt stocks and arrears from the 1970s grew exponentially. The debt stock of Zambia doubled from US $800 million in 1970 to $1.6 billion in 1975 to $3.3 billion in 1980 and increased to more than US$7.2 billion in 1990. The stock went down during the early 1990s, to climb back to more than $7 billion by the end of 1996. (Figure 9–1).

After 1975, the Zambian government experienced continuing negative trade imbalances. (See Figure 9–2.) World prices for the main export commodity, copper, remained depressed, competition from other copper producers increased, and inefficiencies in the local mining sector resulted in minimal net revenues and even losses from copper production and exports. External debt began to accumulate rapidly, becoming unsustainable as early as 1980. With a debt to GDP ratio exceeding one by 1979, Zambia was in an untenable position well before the world debt crisis erupted in 1982.

Interest arrears also grew at an alarming rate. In 1980, government interest arrears were $6.3 million while principal in arrears was $33 million. Arrears including public and private debt as well as arrears to the IMF, amounted to $500 million in that year. By 1990, the total arrears position of the country was more than $3 billion, about the size of GDP. This is shown in Figure 9–3.

During the period of rapid debt accumulation (1970–91), the Zambian government negotiated its debt payments with Paris Club creditors on four

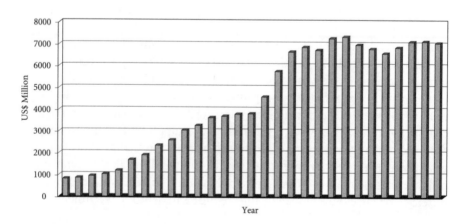

Figure 9–1:   External Debt in US$ Millions DOD: Debt Outstanding and Disbursed World Bank Debt Reorganization System (DRS)

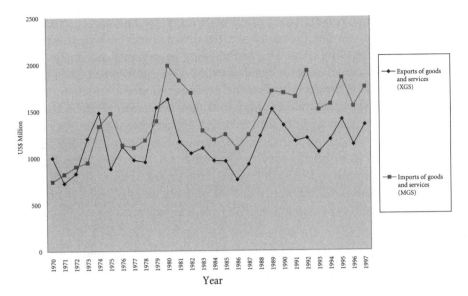

Figure 9–2:   Trade Balances
Source: Global Development Finance. 2000.

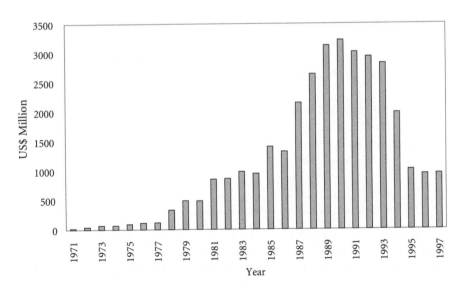

Figure 9–3:   Arrears Position
Source: Global Development Finance 2000, Ministry of Finance and Economic Development, Statistics, Macroeconomic Indicators, various issues, Zambia.

occasions. The first negotiation took place in 1983. January 1, 1983 was agreed as the cut-off date for future negotiations. Another agreement was negotiated and signed in 1984. The rescheduling agreements did not prevent Zambia from accumulating further arrears. In 1986, a third Paris Club agreement was signed as the government partially implemented an IMF supported program. This was abandoned in May 1987, and the arrears buildup accelerated. The government signed a fourth Paris Club agreement in July 1990 under concessional Toronto Terms.[6] The consolidation period for this agreement extended from July 1, 1990 to December 31, 1991. The consolidated amount was more than $927 million, with the largest amount being for arrears of obligations of previously cut off and rescheduled debt (from the 1983, 1984, and 1986 agreements). The Paris Club agreements are discussed further below.

The terms of the 1990 agreement were only partially implemented as Zambia ceased complying with the economic program agreed with the IMF and the schedule of repayments in 1991. This was the first Paris Club agreement for Zambia that included up to 1/3 net present value (NPV) reduction of eligible debt through three options available to creditors: face value reduction; reduction in interest rates; or, extended maturities with a corresponding adjustment of interest rates.[7] Eligible debt is debt that originates from previously cut-off obligations and that is due (or in arrears, depending on the agreement reached) during the consolidation period. Eligible debt represents a fraction of the total Paris Club debt outstanding. Consequently, the 1/3 NPV reduction, under the Paris Club rescheduling agreements, will result only in minor stock reduction in terms of total stock of debt.[8] The advantage of debt rescheduling on concessional terms shows up as lower debt service.

During the debt accumulation period before 1991, it became the norm that a few months after multilateral agreements were signed, the authorities would not implement them. This would lead to further accumulation of arrears, as penalties were then added to contractual interest rates. This has been

---

6. Toronto Terms included up to one-third debt reduction for eligible debt. See IMF (1997).

7. Net present value (NPV) of debt is defined as the sum of all future debt-service obligations (interest and principal) on existing debt, discounted at the market interest rate. The NPV measure takes into account the degree of concessionality. Whenever the interest rate on a loan is lower than the market rate, the resulting NPV of debt is smaller than its face value, with the difference reflecting the grant element (HIPC Documents IMF website 2000).

8. If eligible debt is one-third of Paris Club debt, and Paris Club debt is one-third of total debt, the one-third NPV reduction will be translated to one-twenty-seventh total debt reduction, or about 3.7 percent. And if one-third again of debt is rescheduled under the face value reduction (option A), total debt diminishes by 1.2 percent!

the case with many countries that have repeatedly rescheduled their debts with Paris Club creditors.

A new government took over in November of 1991 on a platform of political and economic reform. As noted earlier, the country by this time had an acute external debt problem. The affairs of state were in disarray. The government lacked a comprehensive record of debt obligations. It did not have a clear debt policy. Furthermore, it lacked a feasible implementation plan to deal with the debt crisis.

3. DEBT MANAGEMENT STRATEGY 1991 TO 1996

Multiparty elections in 1991, which were perceived as peaceful and fair, enabled the government of President Chiluba to start the promised reforms. One major area was that of rationalizing and reducing foreign debt. Creditor countries and international agencies were favorably disposed to help the newly established democracy. Advisory services were welcomed in government offices. Work started almost immediately and collegially to tackle the daunting task of cataloging, managing, and reducing the debt burden.

The government assembled a cabinet team that included officials experienced in economics and finance. The minister of finance, Emmanuel Kasonde (subsequently succeeded by Ronald Penza) and the deputy minister of the national commission on development planning (NCDP) Dean Mung'omba, along with the governor of the Bank of Zambia (BoZ) Dominic Mulaisho (later succeeded by Dr. Jacob Mwanza), gave debt management and debt relief a high priority. A macroeconomic plan was the first step in developing a debt management strategy. It needed the approval of the government and external agencies and donors. Initial attention was given to preparing such a plan. Several government advisors played a substantial role in helping shape this plan and the subsequent system to inform economic policy makers. Further external support came in the form of special grants, project support, and balance of payments support.

Several task forces were established consisting of officials from the ministry of finance, NCDP, and the BoZ. These groups prepared studies and papers, memorandums and briefs on economic management, which were then reviewed at weekly meetings presided over by the minister of finance and the deputy minister of the NCDP.

Once the macroeconomic plan was formulated, the next task was to define the debt situation in the country. This required an examination of all relevant documents within and outside the country to determine the extent of the debt and contractual obligations. At the same time, the task force started reviewing opportunities that were emerging which could result in debt reduction for Zambia.

A debt strategy paper was prepared and approved by the government in early 1992. The paper had clear and detailed targets and timetables for debt reduction by each debt category. The objective was to reduce the external debt service ratio to below 20 percent of exports within five years. The target was to reach a debt service level below $250 million per year. The cabinet paper stated:

"The following could be a tentative scenario if the reduction efforts are successful:

A) Debt stock in US $million

Type:	
Suppliers:	100
Multilaterals:	1400
IMF:	900
Export credits:	100
Bilateral:	500
Total debt:	3000

The debt stock should decrease continually.

B) Debt service:

The target should be a level below US$ 250 million to reach a sustainable level. This scenario assumes continuing donor support and additional resources invested at high rates of return."

Source: Ministry of Finance, Lusaka, January 30, 1992.

The key areas considered to be part of the strategy were:

- Conversion of Zambia's existing obligations to the IMF to a new concessional financial facility through the Rights Accumulation Program (RAP);
- Seeking grants rather than loans; if loans, then only at concessional rates;
- Reducing, and ultimately eliminating, government guarantees for parastatal corporations;
- Negotiating with the Paris Club and with each member country, more favorable terms than normally available;
- Actively seeking debt conversion mechanisms to eliminate eligible bilateral debt;
- Implementing a comprehensive commercial debt buy-back operation with the help of donors and creditors;
- Rationalizing internal debt and implementing cross agency debt reduction to clear in a consistent manner the mutual obligations of public sector agencies;
- Renegotiating on the best possible terms, obligations to non-Paris Club countries. This aspect took into consideration the bilateral net resource flow posi-

tion to Zambia. At this crucial state, debt owed to countries that were transferring positive amounts to Zambia, received priority.

It is worth noting here that while the government was seeking to have others help it reduce the existing debt, there was only partial success (or commitment) to cease running deficits. The failure to follow through with this crucial adjustment was one of the reasons why the debt management strategy subsequently unraveled in the second half of the 1990s.

The First External Agreements on Debt Issues

One of the main priorities of the new government in the early months of 1992 was to renegotiate the implementation of the RAP with the IMF. The intention was to normalize relations with external creditors by resuming debt service payments. With the help of bilateral donors, Zambia also refinanced and cleared World Bank arrears. Hence, conditions were set for the government once again to negotiate with the Paris Club on debt repayment or relief.

Preparation for the Paris Club negotiations started late in 1991 and actual negotiations took place in July 1992 (the 1992 Paris Club agreement). This was followed by bilateral negotiations with each participating creditor. The 1992 Paris Club agreement, under the Enhanced Toronto Terms (or London Terms),[9] called for up to one half of NPV reduction of eligible debt and stretching the maturities of debt obligations up to 25 years. The multiyear agreement rescheduled or wrote off about US $1 billion of obligations.

The consolidation period for the agreement was July 1, 1992 to March 31, 1995. Under Option A, the following countries chose to write off 50 percent of debt at the end of the consolidation period (the accumulated arrears and yearly eligible obligations are gradually converted to a new facility): Canada, France, Germany, Sweden.

Other countries chose Option B: Austria, Belgium, Italy, Japan, U.K., Switzerland with reduced interest rates which resulted in the same NPV reduction as Option A. Option C was selected by Brazil and the U.S.A. combination of extended maturities (23, 25, and 30 years) and reduced interest rates.

For Paris Club agreements, the number of concessions has increased through time, with a higher proportion considered a grant element as compared to commercial terms, but these loans stay on the books at their original

---

9. London Terms refer to the agreement by the Group of Seven industrialized countries (G-7) to reduce the value of the debt in net present value terms (NPV), during the 1991 G-7 meetings in London.

face value. The 1992 Paris Club agreement (Paris V) provided for a stock re-duction possibility at the end of the consolidation period, conditional on Zambia staying on course with the IMF-monitored program.

The officially consolidated amounts under the Paris Club agreement un-derestimates the total amount negotiated in 1992, as some debt was written off. In addition, debt obligations incurred after the first Paris Club agreement of 1983 (post-cut-off debt) were normally not eligible,[10] but part of the post-cut-off arrears were rescheduled. The multilateral agreement separated penalties and arrears from "normal due obligations." The former were re-scheduled under specific provisions. Official development assistance debt, mostly on concessional terms, was also rescheduled under different terms. The NPV reduction is cumulative, debts that had a one-third reduction be-fore, had an additional one-sixth to reach the desired 50 percent reduction.

In addition to the general provisions of the Paris Club agreement, the sub-sequent negotiations with each participating creditor country were prepared carefully and conducted in every possible way favorable to Zambia. For ex-ample, many creditors agreed to waive accumulated penalties, as they recog-nized that the reason for rescheduling was the inability of Zambia to pay on time in the first place. Many also agreed not to apply surcharges in the future for late payments, eliminating charges of up to 2 percent that constituted the penalty. Some creditors also left open the possibility of converting some of the debts owed to them into debt for development. Some countries converted all their outstanding obligations into grants, eliminating some categories of debt outstanding (Sweden in full and Germany in part). Again, in 1993, the opportunity to convert about US $200 million of debt owed to the U.S.A. (PL 480) for food imports into a grant failed as the deadline slipped once Zambia declared the state of emergency. That opportunity was lost, as the U.S. law providing for the debt conversion was amended later that year. It would re-quire now an extra appropriation by the US Treasury of the same amount to eliminate the debt outstanding.[11]

Once the bilateral negotiations were concluded, at least contractually, many millions of dollars of outstanding debt were reduced. For the first time, programs of repayment and annual reconciliation were taking place and Zambia was more or less on track in terms of the implementation of the ex-ternal agreements in 1992 and 1993.

The most dramatic reduction of debt service is normally in the first year of

---

10. So-called "post-cut-off debt." The 1983 first rescheduling agreement establishes the cut-off.

11. Under the new HIPC initiative, supported by the U.S. government, these possibilities are again on the table.

Table 9–1:   *Effects of Rescheduling on Debt Flows. (US$ million)*

	1992	*1993*	*1994*	*1995*
Debt service before Paris Club agreement of 1992				
Total scheduled debt service	697	607	602	534
Debt service after Paris Club agreement of 1992	382	389	432	402
Debt service reduction	315	218	170	132

Source: Paris Club request, Ministry of Finance and World Bank data.

the consolidation period. All obligations eligible for rescheduling are "converted" to the new facility and interest paid on the new balance. During the next period, as balances under the new facility (the new loan) increase on a cumulative basis, so do interest obligations.

As only a few countries chose the stock reduction under option A, the effect was a debt reduction of around $150 million, on an eligible stock of $703 million. In NPV terms, the reduction on eligible debt was close to US $300 million because of lower interest rates and extended maturities. This was less than 7 percent of Zambia's Paris Club debt or less than 4 percent of Zambia's total external debt. What produced the greater reduction of Paris Club debt is the bilateral negotiations and good will shown by some donor countries.

Due to the political uncertainties that culminated in a state of emergency in March 1993, the implementation of the economic program slipped and arrears began to accumulate once more in 1994. Zambia was supposed to seek debt rescheduling at the end of the previous consolidation period but the negotiation took place only in 1996, one year later.

Paris Club Agreement VI of February 28, 1996 (Naples Terms)

Austria, Brazil, Canada, France, Germany, Italy, Japan, the United Kingdom, and the United States participated in the Paris Club Agreement VI. The meeting took place in Paris on February 27 and 28, 1996. The creditor counties agreed to grant debt relief on the maturities of debt service falling due from January 1, 1996, to December 31, 1998 (the consolidation period), conditional upon Zambia meeting the agreed objectives of the enhanced structural adjustment facility (ESAF) program for 1996 onwards.

As a result of the meeting, the creditor countries chose the following options:

Option A: A 67 percent face value reduction of maturities, the rest rescheduled at market interest rates and payable over twenty-three years with six years of grace. The governments of Canada, France, Germany, the United Kingdom, and the United States chose this option.

Option B: Rescheduling at lower interest rates, with a repayment period of thirty-three years, resulting in a reduction of 67 percent in NPV terms. The governments of Austria, Brazil, Italy, and Japan chose this option. ODA loans granted by governments of participating creditor countries will be repaid over a period of forty years inclusive of a sixteen-year grace period. The rates of interest should be at least as favorable as the original concessional rates applicable to these loans.

The cumulative debt service relief including arrears at the end of 1995 amounted to $572 million over the three-year period (see Table 9–2). This was a significant saving and resulted in payments of rescheduled debt to Paris Club creditors of $38 million in 1996, $33 million in 1997 and $32 million in 1998. This level of relief was dependent on Zambia's successful adherence and completion of the ESAF arrangement covering the entire consolidation period from January 1, 1996, to December 31, 1998. Zambia did not meet that condition.

The Naples Terms

Since December 1994, Paris Club member countries have negotiated bilateral agreements with debtor countries under "Naples Terms." A debtor can request relief on either the stock of debt, or on the flow of debt service (maturities), from 50 percent up to a maximum of 67 percent in NPV terms. Relief of 67 percent in NPV, in both stock and flow operations, can be obtained by a face value reduction of 67 percent (Option A), or an equivalent reduction in the present value of debt by extending maturities and reducing the relevant interest rate (Option B).

Table 9–2:   *Debt Relief in US$ Million—Paris Club Debt Only*

	1995	1996	1997	1998
	Arrears			
Debt service before relief	183.87	203.74	147.48	139.65
Post cut-off debt service		29.82	21.92	18.26
Moratorium 1996		8.25	10.82	13.34
Total debt service		38.07	32.74	31.60
Debt relief	183.87	165.66	114.75	108.05
Cumulative	183.87	349.53	464.28	572.34

Stock of Debt Operation: Zambia did not request the stock of debt operation. Existing rules in the Paris Club implied that debt service under this option would have left Zambia with a higher Paris Club debt service (about $100 million a year) than under the flow option. The net stock reduction would have applied to only $300 million, leaving Zambia with a balance of $1.8 billion Paris Club debt. Only "eligible debt" would be reduced and not all creditors could take the face value reduction option (A). A stock of debt operation is also an exit rescheduling, with the implication that a debtor cannot approach the Paris Club for any debt relief on the balance of Paris Club debt in the future. A balance of US $1.8 billion of debt and US $100 million of debt service in addition to all other obligations owed by Zambia, were considered to be unsustainable in the medium run. However, the 1996 Agreement included the option to consider at the end of the consolidation period the debt stock reduction for Zambia, provided that the economic reform program had been sustained.

Flow (Maturities) Restructuring: The 1996 agreement reached with Paris Club creditors confirmed the high level of debt service relief obtained for the next three years. The Agreement covered debt servicing during the consolidation period in respect of loans entered into prior to January 1, 1983, and for previously rescheduled debts under the 1986, 1990, and 1992 agreements (about 90 percent of total Paris Club debt). The relief was cumulative, i.e. where relief in terms of NPV reduction was zero, the full 67 percent applies, if there were previous relief of 33 percent (Toronto Terms, 1990) or 50 percent (Enhanced Toronto Terms, 1992) only the additional top-up relief which would result in 67 percent cumulative reduction would apply.

The eligibility criterion for each category of debt is not automatic. Depending on each debtor's case, the order of inclusion in the agreement starts with pre cut-off debt, previously rescheduled debt without reduction (1986), Toronto Terms agreements (1990) and Enhanced Toronto Terms agreement (1992). Many countries have received only Naples terms on pre cut-off and previously rescheduled debt that had no previous reduction. In Zambia's case that would have resulted in much lower debt relief. Zambia managed to have included in the agreement both the yearly obligations resulting from the 1990 and the 1992 agreements (the rescheduled facility repayments). The Paris Club also agreed to defer the payment of the balances of moratorium interest due under the 1990 agreement, which in turn had been deferred in the 1992 agreement. The outstanding amount would be paid in 10 equal semi-annual installments to commence June 30, 2000, and end December 31, 2004. It was also likely that all these obligations would be subject to further reductions in the future, as they originated is in eligible rescheduled or pre-cut-off debt that was not fully serviced.

Increasing Concessionality from Toronto to Cologne Terms.

Paris Club debt relief has been increasing in terms of real forgiveness: from Toronto Terms with up to 1/3 NPV reduction to London Terms with 1/2 NPV reduction to Naples Terms with 2/3 NPV reduction to Lyons Terms in 1998 with reduction of 80 percent in NPV and to Cologne Terms in 2000 with up to 90 percent in NPV reduction.[12] While nonconcessional rescheduling had ten year maturities and five years of grace, the repayment periods have increased to twenty-five years and fourteen of grace under Toronto Terms, to thirty years and twelve years of grace under Enhanced Toronto or London Terms, to forty years and sixteen of grace under the Naples or Lyons Terms, they now include the possibility of 125 years and sixty-five of grace under Cologne Terms.

Equal burden sharing calls for the equivalent treatment of multilateral and commercial debt. Civic organizations and leaders in recent years have raised the call for complete debt forgiveness for heavily indebted countries, and this will be discussed in the next section. A summary of the Paris Club negotiations is given in the table below.

Non-Paris Club Debt: Debt to non-Paris Club creditors is comparatively small, but the GRZ has made some efforts to negotiate for concessional terms with these bilateral creditors as well (e.g. Russia). At the start of 1990, these debts were estimated at $600 million and by the end of 1999 the amount stood at only $177.2 million. Under the new agreements with the Paris Club, debt to the former Soviet Union, now Russia, has been included as part of the Paris Club Debt, with a discount of 80 percent to post-cut-off debt.[13]

Other Debt Relief Initiatives

In addition to the negotiations taking place at the Paris Club level and on a bilateral level to reduce the debt burden of the country, the debt management task force initiated discussions to explore new initiatives. These included debt buy-back programs, debt conversions, multilateral agency negotiations (fifth

---

12. See HIPC documents, March 1997 onwards. See also *Global Development Finance* 2000, World Bank.

13. See IMF Statistics and *Global Development Finance*, 2000.

Table 9–3:   *Zambia: Summary of Paris Club Agreements*

Paris Club agreement	Date	Amount consolidated [million US$]	Consolidation period [months]	Maturity maximum [in years]	Grace period [years]	NPV reduction
I	05/83	375	12	9.5	5	0
II	07/84	253	12	9.5	5	0
III	03/86	371	12	9.5	5	0
IV	07/90	963	18	25.0	8	1/3
V	07/92	917	33	25.0	16	1/2
VI	02/96	572	36	40.0	16	2/3
VII	04/99	1,060	36	40.0	16	2/3

Note: ODA credits have a longer maturity, some have been gradually written off. ODA credits refer to concessional bilateral credits for emergency food imports and similar purposes.
Source: *Global Development Finance*, various years. World Bank.

dimension, RAP) and more direct negotiations with creditor countries. The Zambian experience in these initiatives is discussed in the following sub sections.

The Commercial Debt Buy-Back Operation: The commercial debt buy-back operation implemented in Zambia, took advantage of the low prices of Zambian commercial paper in the secondary debt market using resources in the form of grants at no direct cost to the economy.

At the time of the operation, a debt-distressed low/middle income (IDA-only) country could take advantage of an IDA debt reduction facility to eliminate its commercial debt that was in arrears and trading at heavy discounts in the secondary market. To be able to access the facility, the country had to meet the following qualifications:

- Have an economic program (such as SAF or ESAF) endorsed by the IMF and be in good standing with IDA and IBRD.
- Have a significant amount of debt which is in arrears and owed to commercial creditors and with high discounts of debt as traded in the secondary market. The high discounts maximize the resources of the facility that includes the contribution of bilateral donors that might participate in a potential operation.
- The buy-back must form part of an overall debt strategy that minimizes the cost of regaining normal financial relations with creditors. It has to contribute significantly to the resolution of the debt problem of a particular country. Additionally, it has to enhance the growth and development prospects of the country.
- Have a current agreement with Paris Club creditors that provide the most favorable treatment for the debtor country.

What is significant in a commercial buy-back operation is that the country stands to benefit twice. Its commercial debt, which is in arrears, is reduced or eliminated, and the country benefits from social programs that can be funded by donated funds from the buy-back operation.

Zambia was eligible for the program after the restoration of payments and resumption of the economic recovery program and the RAP with the IMF in the first half of 1992. As already noted, the government had approved in 1992 a comprehensive debt strategy. The same task force that worked on the debt strategy also prepared a proposal for a debt buy-back and this was presented to the World Bank (IDA) in June 1992. IDA sent a mission, including a representative of the Swiss government in August 1992 to discuss the potential implementation of a commercial buy-back. Since the IDA debt reduction facility was normally limited to about US $10 million per country and it was estimated that the Zambian program would require about $50 million initially, bilateral donors would need to contribute the balance. The task force started the detailed work of reconciling balances with creditors and estimating potential prices for Zambia's commercial debt. Before a formal presentation of the program to the group of donors, the parameters in terms of funding and prices had to be evaluated. In addition, the legal status of a high number of claims (more than 90,000), had to be assessed to be able to judge their inclusion and options for debt reduction in comparable terms.

After the initial approval by IDA, the Swiss government agreed to cofund the first phase of the technical work. For that purpose, financial and legal advisors were contracted, using criteria developed by the Zambian debt buy-back task force and made consistent with IDA guidelines for the selection of technical consultants. Within the general guidelines, it is the implementing country that sets the criteria and procedures for selection, with clear parameters and weights for ranking proposals. The GRZ officially presented the ranking and selection system to the World Bank before the selection committee opened proposals. S.G.Warburg from London was selected as the financial advisor, and Arnold and Porter from Washington D.C. was selected as the legal advisor in December 1992 from six preselected companies in each area. In addition, the Debt for Development Coalition was contracted to help secure the donation of creditor resources out of the buy-back to nongovernmental organizations (NGOs).

More detailed work commenced in January 1993. After several revisions of the data and contacts with different creditors in Zambia and abroad, a clearer picture of the price range of transactions of commercial debt in the secondary market and total amounts and claims began to emerge. This operation was addressing a variety of eligible debt: uninsured commercial banks including refinancing, uninsured trade arrears (pipeline debt at BoZ), and some short-term deposits. As explained earlier, pipeline debt had resulted from the foreign exchange control era. Public sector and private creditors paid BoZ in local currency, BoZ accumulated obligations as there was not enough foreign exchange to cover the repayments. A complete first report of claims was presented and discussed in March 1993. On the basis of a second, fully revised report, a formal request was made to donors in Zambia and later in Switzerland, as lead donor, in July 1993. By that time, the operation had the support of four bilateral donors: Switzerland, Germany, the Netherlands, and Sweden. Confirmation of funding could only occur after the IDA Executive Board had approved the operation.

The price and the amount required for funding had to be finally determined as well as the minimum threshold of participants (normally 67 percent) acceptable to IDA and donors. There was a great level of uncertainty regarding pipeline debt (many creditors, relatively small amounts, long time outstanding), so it was agreed that the threshold for judging success would only apply to fully identified debt (about US $252 million of principal), including part of the pipeline debt. Some data put the situation in perspective.

Principal outstanding at the time of public offer (05/94):[14]

Fully reconciled uninsured commercial debt:	$125 million
Uninsured trade arrears fully reconciled	$ 88 million
Reconciled pipeline debt	$ 39 million
Reconciled principal of commercial debt:	$252 million
Uninsured trade arrears not fully reconciled:	$159 million
Total	$411 million

As a precondition for their participation, creditors waived interest outstanding. That was equivalent to about US $303 million in interest arrears and penalties.

Three options were made available to creditors:

a. Cash for debt at 11 cents on the dollar of principal
b. Bonds equivalent to 11 cents on the dollar, to be used for bids to the privatization process, with a 50 percent premium.
c. Cash to be deposited in an escrow account, to be used by NGOs for funding specific projects approved by GRZ in the social sector as part of the budget

14. Report of the Task Force at the Time of Completion of the buy-back operation, Lusaka, 1994.

process. Disbursements into projects in Zambia would benefit from a 50 percent premium in kwacha from budget resources.

Problems arose regarding donor support as a consequence of the declaration of the state of emergency in 1993. Accordingly, the buy-back was put on hold during the consultative group meeting in Paris in December 1993. Conditions changed in early 1994 and the resumption of donor flows allowed Zambia to be in compliance with debt repayments with multilateral and bilateral creditors. IDA gave its final approval in May 1994, and the operation was made public the same month. On July 24, the date of the first closing, US $181 million was bought back. The second closing, concluded on September 14, 1994, resulted in US $20 million bought back. Thus the result of the operation was considered a full success, with 80 percent acceptance level (200÷250). Some of the remaining debt was under litigation (US $18 million) and the rest had not been tendered for the buy-back. Since the implementation of the operation in 1994, GRZ and BoZ have been able to defend the legal cases in different courts successfully or to settle obligations on comparable terms.

Zambia's commercial debt buy-back operation was completed in September 1994. As a result, US $714 million of commercial debt had been eliminated from the books of the BoZ and the GRZ.[15] For this purpose, US $49 million was pledged by donors and IDA, out of which US $26 million was used to buy back debt and to pay the specialized services of financial and legal advisors to carry out the operation successfully. In addition, more than US $10 million of the payments to creditors out of the buy-back funds, were deposited by former creditors in favor of NGOs with an escrow agent (Bank of New York). An approved debt-for-development program, which commenced in October 1994, ensured that these foreign exchange resources were spent on government-approved projects in the social sector.

Upon disbursement from the escrow account for projects in Zambia, these funds commanded a 50 percent premium from the national budget. First disbursements started in October 1994. By end 1995, all funds were disbursed. Projects financed through the escrow account included: sanitation, schools, training, women's group development, education, health, and small-scale workshops for targeted groups in society.

It should be noted that the option of exchanging debt for bonds for privat-

---

15. "Closing Report. Commercial Debt Reduction Transaction," Republic of Zambia. September 30, 1994.

ization was not taken up by creditors. The possible cause was the slow process of privatization up to the date of closing in 1994.

The commercial debt buy-back operation in Zambia has been considered a success by the different parties involved. Success in this particular program can be attributed to the following factors: a) strong leadership, commitment and support from different levels of government; b) dedication and team work from all parties involved—donors, advisors, and Zambian officials; c) transparent and unbiased selection criteria and procedures which were developed by the implementing country and acceptable to donors; and d) integration of the program as part of an overall debt and macroeconomic strategy. To ensure the support of senior government officials, the debt management committee kept all relevant authorities informed of the objectives, conditions and progress of the operation. It is interesting to note that three of the donors supporting METAP were also financing the buy-back operation for Zambia.

Debt Conversions (Belgium and Switzerland):   Both the governments of Belgium and Switzerland independently agreed to fund debt conversion programs beyond the provisions of the Paris Club. Debts outstanding were converted to project expenditures for projects approved by the GRZ and later by the creditor country or agency. The respective treasuries (in Belgium and Switzerland) would pay their own export credit agencies. As a condition, the expenditures in local currency by the Zambian government needed to be declared as having being financed by the creditor countries. Two Zambian project operations equivalent to more than US $30 million were converted to projects of these countries at zero cost to Zambia from 1994 to 1996.

Rights Accumulation Program: The RAP between Zambia and the IMF aimed at using good economic performance on the part of Zambia as a basis for the 'right' to convert IMF obligations owed by Zambia into a concessional ESAF arrangement. The program formally began in 1991 but soon went off track as election pressures mounted. The MMD government renegotiated the program in 1992. With some slippages, implementation lasted from that date until September 1995. As a result of the program, the equivalent of US $1.2 billion in arrears to the IMF was converted into a facility that carried only an interest charge of 0.5 percent, down from the original rate of 8.5 percent. This operation greatly reduced the yearly debt service level, carried a five-and-a-half-year grace period and five years for repayment of principal.

4. Zambia's Quest for Deeper Debt Reduction: The HIPC Initiative[16]

The Heavily Indebted Poor Countries initiative (HIPC) for debt resolution is intended to address the external debt problem of forty low-income countries.[17] The initiative, established by the IMF and the World Bank in coordination with the Paris Club, presumes that all other creditors will share the same benefits and costs. Established in 1996, HIPC is described by the IMF as being designed "to provide exceptional assistance to eligible countries following sound economic policies to help them reduce their external debt burden to sustainable levels."[18] The initiative was to be implemented in two phases. In the first, the eligible country would receive highly concessional Paris Club rescheduling under Naples Terms and additional donor finance (loans and grants) to support the economic program for three years. At the conclusion of this phase, and after an assessment of the macroeconomic conditions, the country could graduate (exit) from Paris Club rescheduling, or go to the second phase. This is called the decision point.[19] In the second phase, if the country did not graduate, the Paris Club would grant rescheduling terms comparable or equal to Lyons Terms, with a NPV reduction of 80 percent or

---

16. The IMF and the World Bank launched the HIPC initiative in 1996 as the first comprehensive effort to eliminate unsustainable debt in the world's poorest, most heavily indebted countries. In October 1999, the international community agreed to make the initiative broader, deeper, and faster by increasing the number of eligible countries, raising the amount of debt relief each eligible country will receive, and speeding up its delivery. The enhanced initiative aims at reducing the NPV of debt at the decision point to a maximum of 150 percent of exports and 250 percent of government revenue, and will be provided on top of traditional debt relief mechanisms (Paris Club debt rescheduling on Naples terms, involving 67 percent debt reduction in NPV terms and at least comparable action by other bilateral creditors).

17. A group of forty developing countries are classified as being the heavily indebted poor countries. This includes, for analytical purposes, thirty-two countries with a 1993 GNP per capita of US $695 or less and 1993 present value of debt to exports higher than 220 percent or present value of debt to GNP higher than 80 percent. Also included are nine countries that received, or were eligible for, concessional rescheduling from Paris Club creditors. However, any other country meeting the requirements of the initiative could be considered for HIPC assistance. The group comprises: Angola, Benin, Bolivia, Burkina Faso, Burundi, Cameroon, Central African Republic, Chad, Congo, Côte d'Ivoire, Democratic Republic of the Congo, Ethiopia, Ghana, Guinea, Guinea-Bissau, Guyana, Honduras, Kenya, Lao PDR, Liberia, Madagascar, Malawi, Mali, Mauritania, Mozambique, Myanmar, Nicaragua, Niger, Rwanda, São Tomé and Príncipe, Senegal, Sierra Leone, Somalia, Sudan, Tanzania, Togo, Uganda, Vietnam, Yemen, and Zambia.

18. Proposed by the World Bank and the IMF and agreed to by governments around the world in the fall of 1996. HIPC, 1997, 1998. IMF and World Bank.

19. The decision point is the comprehensive assessment of the debt sustainability with and without further debt relief. HIPC Documents, 1999

more of eligible debt due during the consolidation period. This phase was planned to last another three years. At the end of this period, the completion point, all measures necessary to ensure debt sustainability would be adopted by all creditors concerned (all bilateral and multilateral agencies).[20]

Under the enhanced HIPC initiative, approved in September 1999, the thresholds for debt relief have been made more generous, as can be seen from the table below. Lower NPV of debt over exports or revenues, means more debt relief. The argument is that at the completion point the country would exit the debt rescheduling process, grow faster and have made measurable efforts to combat poverty. In addition, there is more flexibility in the duration of the first and second phases. Decision points and completion points can be achieved within months, as has been the case of Uganda in 1999 and 2000. Once debt relief has been granted, it cannot be taken away, and there is retroactive consideration so that even countries that have graduated can receive the most favorable treatment in the coming years, provided they continue to implement successfully their poverty reduction programs.

Zambia is one of the forty countries eligible for debt relief under HIPC with debt to GDP of about 200 percent (well in excess of the 80 percent benchmark) and with low income per capita, about US $300, also well below the US $700 limit. Until the end of 1998, Zambia had an ongoing restructuring agreement with the Paris Club. Hence it could have benefited from HIPC early in 1999. The potential HIPC benefits to Zambia could be substantial.

Initial and Modified Benefits from the HIPC Initiative

	Targets	
Criterion	Original 1996 (percent)	Enhanced 1999 (percent)
NPV debt/exports	200–250	150
"Fiscal window"		
NPV debt/revenue	280	250
Qualifying Thresholds		
Export/GDP	40	30
Revenue/GDP	20	15
Base for assessment of debt relief		
	Completion point	Decision point

Source: IMF, HIPC Documents, 1999

Zambia missed being one of the first countries to benefit from HIPC debt reduction in 1999. The promise of substantial debt relief, however, is still

---

20. The completion point is the time at which all measures are taken to ensure that the country is on a sustainable external debt path, including the reduction of debt stock. HIPC Documents, 1999 (available on www.imf.org).

some important hurdles away, as the implementation of the HIPC initiative requires the concerted effort of the external creditors (multilateral and bilateral) and of the GRZ. To qualify for HIPC eligibility (the decision point), Zambia needed to have an IMF endorsed program. In July 2000, the IMF completed the first review of the country under the Poverty Reduction and Growth Facility (PRGF) supported program and approved a US $13.2 million disbursement. Thus, the framework was set for the next phase of the debt reduction efforts.

> An updated debt sustainability analysis (DSA) for Zambia suggests that, even with strong financial policies, the avoidance of nonconcessional borrowing, and the full use of traditional debt-relief mechanisms, Zambia's external public debt burden would not be reduced to sustainable levels before the middle of the next decade. The baseline scenario indicated that the ratio of the net present value of debt to exports, which was estimated at 510 percent at end-1998, would remain above 250 percent until 2005 and would not fall below 200 percent until 2010. Debt service after rescheduling would not fall below 25 percent of exports of goods and services until 2004, and it would still be equivalent to about 35 percent of government revenue and about 30 percent of expenditure. In addition, the degree of improvement in the debt indicators was shown to be sensitive to assumptions about export prices and growth rates, as well as to the availability of concessional external assistance. In view of this, Zambia will seek exceptional debt relief under the Heavily Indebted Poor Countries (HIPC) Initiative. Subject to satisfactory policy performance under Fund- and World Bank–supported adjustment programs as well as to the confirmation of the excessive weight of the external debt burden on the basis of a detailed DSA prepared jointly by the Fund and the World Bank staffs, Zambia will seek assistance under the Initiative.[21]

Within months, Zambia had been granted this support. Under the heading "HIPC agreement in Support of a Debt Reduction Package for Zambia," the World Bank and IMF noted:

> The International Monetary Fund (IMF) and the World Bank Group's International Development Association (IDA) agreed to support a comprehensive debt reduction package for Zambia under the enhanced Heavily Indebted Poor Countries (HIPC) Initiative. Total debt service relief from all of Zambia's creditors is worth more than US$3.8 billion. This is equivalent to about US$2.5 billion in net present value terms, or approximately 63 percent of the NPV of debt outstanding at end-1999 after the full use of traditional debt relief mechanisms. [22]

It is worth mentioning here that export performance was well below the expectations developed in the middle of the 1990's. It is not surprising then

---

21. IMF (1999) Policy Framework Paper Zambia 1999–2001 (available on www.imf.org).
22. IMF (2000) Press Release December 8, 2000, IMF, HIPC Initiative.

that the ratio of debt service to exports remains so high after rescheduling. The same can be said about the revenue performance.

At the time of writing (early 2001), the next steps are the presentation and approval by the Bretton Woods Institutions of the Poverty Reduction Strategy Paper (PRSP), which is undergoing broad consultation and review within Zambia's civil society, and its implementation. According to the decision point document (November 2000) in July and August of 2000, the IMF and the World Bank reviewed the interim PRSP that formed the basis for their initial support under HIPC. To reach the completion point, essential policies in poverty reduction, social sector reform, and macroeconomic and structural reforms will need to be achieved.[23]

---

23. IMF/IDA (2000)

Zambia's past economic performance has been adversely affected by problems relating to the state-owned copper company ZCCM. Its privatization in early 2000 and the agreement on a program for 2000 under the Poverty Reduction and Growth Facility (PRGF) have substantially improved the prospects for enhanced economic growth and poverty reduction.

In light of the widespread poverty in Zambia, the authorities' firm commitment to poverty reduction, as outlined in their Interim Poverty Reduction Strategy Paper (I-PRSP) is welcome. The authorities' efforts to establish a legal environment that sustains private sector led economic growth, promotes stable macroeconomic conditions conducive to private investment, and targets poverty reduction programs, (clearly prioritized within the available resources), are essential to achieve poverty reduction. The full PRSP, which is scheduled to be completed by the middle of 2001, will develop further the authorities' poverty reduction strategy, expand and broaden the consultative process. The authorities should enhance the effectiveness of policies in the areas of health and education, and give priority to strengthening the poverty database and monitoring mechanisms.

The 2000 program will improve the accountability and transparency of budget management and control. The program's success will depend critically on a sustained strong political commitment to fiscal discipline, especially in the period prior to elections next year. Fiscal policy for 2000 is adversely affected by the large allocation made to settle ZCCM debt, but it is expected that the 2000 budget will provide the basis for a move towards a more sustainable fiscal position in the medium term. Strong revenue efforts, including collections of taxes from the electricity company, ZESCO, and the oil company, ZNOC, and strict adherence to the expenditure targets, including arrears clearance, will be necessary to achieve the program's objectives. The authorities are also committed to abstaining from granting any new tax exemptions, rebates, or any other preferential tax treatment.

The authorities intend to pursue a prudent monetary policy and to limit the credit to public enterprises with a view to reducing inflation. The Bank of Zambia (BoZ) has addressed the weaknesses at the Zambia National Commercial Bank, including through the issuance of a supervisory directive from BOZ to ZNCB. Privatization of the ZNCB in accordance with the timetable envisaged in the program will help to strengthen the financial sector.

In view of the fragility of Zambia's external position, the authorities are seeking to improve external competitiveness in order to diversify the export base. Maintenance of

Poverty Reduction and Growth Facility

The IMF's concessional facility for low-income countries, the Enhanced Structural Adjustment Facility (ESAF), was transformed into a more civil society-oriented arrangement named the Poverty Reduction and Growth Facility (PRGF) in 1999. Instead of pushing unpopular development programs that it could later be blamed for, the IMF decided to encourage the development of country programs formulated using broad-based participatory processes and documented in a poverty reduction strategy paper (PRSP). As with the ESAF, disbursements under the PRGF would provide concessional ten-year loans with a grace period of five-and-a-half years on principal payments and loans with an annual interest rate of 0.5 percent. This is intended to ensure that each PRGF-supported program is consistent with a comprehensive framework for macroeconomic, structural, and social policies that foster growth and reduce poverty.

In July 2000, the IMF approved a US $13.2 million disbursement (for a total of $26.4 million) under a program supported by a Poverty Reduction and Growth Facility (PRGF) credit. As noted by Shigemitsu Sugisaki, Deputy Managing Director and Acting Chairman of the Executive Board of the IMF:

> The government's intention to complete the transition to a private sector-led economy, including through privatization of the remaining public utilities and the operations of the oil sector, is welcome. The authorities are encouraged to take strong actions to improve governance, including through enhancing transparency and eliminating corruption.[24]

Evidence in other chapters of this volume shows that those promises have been only partially fulfilled by the GRZ in the past. A close reading of the different programs since 1991 shows that the same promises had been made several times. There has been a lack of leadership in honoring promises to multilateral and bilateral agencies as well as the Zambian people. If we compare the MMD *Manifesto* (1991) and the different budget proposals with actual delivery, a wide gap emerges. The question still lingers. Will the government be able to implement its plans and objectives during the coming years? Poverty

---

a competitive exchange rate, reducing the cost of utilities through completion of the privatization agenda, and liberalization of the trade system will be essential in this respect. The government's intention to complete the transition to a private sector-led economy, including through privatization of the remaining public utilities and the operations of the oil sector, is welcome. The authorities are encouraged to take strong actions to improve governance, including through enhancing transparency and eliminating corruption.

24. IMF News Brief No. 00/63: July 27, 2000.

continues to increase, deficits have been reduced but not eliminated, and delaying the privatization of ZCCM for all the 1990s undermined the conditions for growth.

Non-Paris Club Creditors: While current debt service due on debt to non-Paris Club bilateral official creditors is small, the government has made a commitment to negotiate concessional rescheduling agreements of arrears and other obligations to these creditors on terms comparable to those granted by Paris Club participants. There is no systematic approach to deal with these debts, but the expectation among debtors is that they will receive similar treatment to those of the Paris Club. Zambia could also try to negotiate buy-back operations based on discounted prices for its commercial debt and possibly financed by donors. An agreement of this nature was signed with the Russian Federation in 1993 but never implemented. Some donors were willing to help finance the operation, but after the declaration of the state of emergency and some arrests of opposition and media personalities, goodwill towards Zambia disappeared. As noted earlier, debts to Russia are now included under the Paris Club.

Debt Service Profile during the 1990s: Debt service to exports ratio (actual payments) fell from a high of 0.45 in 1991 to 0.23 in 1996. Because of the Paris Club agreement of February 1996, the debt service ratio fell below the 0.20 threshold for 1997 onwards. (See Figure 9–4). As noted earlier, because

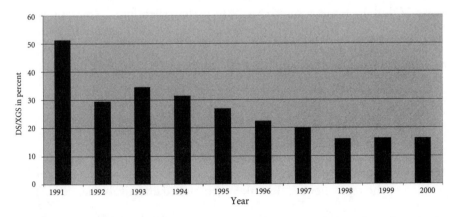

Figure 9–4:   Debt Service Ratio (Actual Debt Service/Exports of Goods and Services)
Source: *Global Development Finance* 2000, MOFED, Zambia, HIPC Working Papers.

of diminishing export levels and obligations due that were not rescheduled, the debt ratios were expected to increase to unsustainable levels without debt relief.

Net external flows to Zambia have been positive during the 1990s. This implies that concessional finance and, in addition, grants exceed the amount of debt service obligations. Nevertheless, the resources available to finance particular projects might not always free up reserves for debt service repayment, imposing some real budget constraints. If these affect the social sector expenditure, the case for prompt debt relief remains valid.

Interlocking Debts Between the Government and Parastatals

Many state-owned corporations had external debts guaranteed by the government and as the process of rescheduling advanced, many of these debts were taken over. In some cases, taxes or dividend payments to the government had not been made and there was a considerable backlog. At the same time, the government owed some of the commercial corporations significant amounts for services and products. To clear these interlocking arrears, a systematic approach was used that resulted in more transparent accounting that cleared the way for a better assessment of the net worth of companies to be privatized. Some of the cases included in the exercise were: Nitrogen Chemicals of Zambia, Zambia Electricity Supply Corporation (ZESCO), Kafue Textiles, ZCCM, and Zambia Airways. Because the privatization of ZCCM was delayed, the company ran progressively larger deficits, thereby increasing both its internal and external debt. At the time of the final settlement for the privatization of ZCCM, the government had to absorb external debt worth US $770 million to complete the transaction.[25] The Zambia National Oil Corporation (ZNOC) was not allowed to raise its prices. Therefore, it could not (and did not) pay taxes. In addition, it received support from the public banking sector during the last part of the 1990s. This placed severe stress on the state-owned bank, ZANACO, and added further to outstanding public debt.

5. Building In-House Capacity for Debt Management

Appropriate macroeconomic policies provide the foundation for effective debt management. With sound fiscal policies, external financing needs can be planned or the repayment of debt already incurred effectively managed. This

---

25. Letter of Intent from Dr. Katele Kalumba, minister of finance and economic development to the IMF, June 30, 2000.

was not the situation in Zambia at the start of the 1990s. Beginning with the state takeovers in 1968, the government of Kenneth Kaunda created a network of largely inefficient state-run agencies. These required significant amounts of government support in the form of direct subsidies or concessional loans. The government believed that copper earnings would continue to increase. This proved to be a mistake. As shown elsewhere in this volume, that mistake was compounded by the lack of concerted efforts to impose fiscal discipline.

The crisis atmosphere in the early 1990s provided the opportunity for the MMD government to bring in the needed economic reforms. Initially, at least, it seized the moment. Hence, at the beginning of the new regime, the government was open to measures that would lead to more effectiveness and efficiency in the delivery of needed services and suggestions from international agencies on programs and advisory services in support of this.

Capacity Building: The effort to strengthen the analytical and managerial capacities of the Zambian agencies dealing with debt issues took several dimensions. One mechanism widely adopted was the use of task forces. Supported with appropriate technical advisory services, they provided a vehicle for the implementation of debt reduction and overall initiatives to improve the economy. Reform-minded policy makers used them to increase interagency cooperation. Some projects and initiatives are worth mentioning.

The macroeconomic technical assistance project (METAP) was a channel for capacity building efforts, with support for domestic and external seminars conducted by METAP personnel or experts from other institutions within and outside Zambia. The World Bank continued its assistance, and numerous capacity building efforts were coordinated through them. In many cases, workshops and in-house discussions took place with the direct participation of World Bank staff, both in Zambia and Washington D.C. In the mid 1990s, a regional program for reserves and debt management was created which also served as a vehicle for capacity building in a systematic way. Initially, the Eastern and Southern Africa Initiative for Debt and Reserves Management (ESAIDARM) provided support for this purpose, and the service was continued by the Macroeconomic and Financial Management Institute (MEFMI).

Systems of debt recording and management introduced in cooperation with the United Nations Commission on Trade and Development (UNCTAD) were supported by METAP in ways that allowed them to become fully functional. An example is the Debt Monitoring and Financial Analysis System (DMFAS) program for debt recording, analysis and monitoring. Other programs used were the Debt Reorganization System (DRS) of the World Bank for evaluation of restructuring terms, and RMSMX model to include debt projections within a consistent recursive macroeconomic framework. Management programs were introduced to track implementation of activities. In a major contribution, METAP computerized and networked the operations of the MoF. Supporting information is an essential element to introduce more transparency in the operations of government, especially in debt management, where critical information about debtors to the government had been lost before 1991.

Human capacity building took place on the job, as METAP and other advisors worked closely with Zambian counterparts on a day-to-day basis at different levels of the administration and with different agencies (the BoZ and sector ministries). As noted in Chapter 12, METAP supported a large amount of training on debt management, negotiation strategies, risk analysis, and debt simulations at different levels, in and out of the country. The training provided a solid foundation for successful negotiations and administration of the economic program. Careful preparation of the analysis and the conduct of negotiations in teams greatly improved the local capacity for further negotiations.

Motivation and Incentives: Initially, there was low motivation in the agencies in charge of debt management, as senior policy makers did not place much importance in trying to resolve the external debt situation. As already noted, this situation changed when the new administration took office, with the ministers and deputy ministers involved in significant efforts to reduce the debt burden. The management meetings provided an opportunity to recognize the quality of the analysis and give credit for the work being done. These opportunities greatly influenced the level of motivation and commitment among the staff.

HIV/AIDS: As noted in more detail in Chapter 12, debt management capacity suffered during the 1990s from the spread of HIV/AIDS. METAP and other organizations supported the executive training as well as long-term academic studies leading to master's degrees for most Zambian officials engaged on debt issues. However, roughly one third of the professional staff in the debt unit died over a period of five years. Numerous others in the unit were debilitated by the disease as well. As a means of helping offset these losses, a broader group of officials was trained in every aspect of debt and economic management.

Key Ratios under Traditional Rescheduling Conditions

After many years of restructuring, most of the existing debt stock is now concessional (UK-DFID, IDA, EU, IMF, Rescheduled Paris Club). This fact is

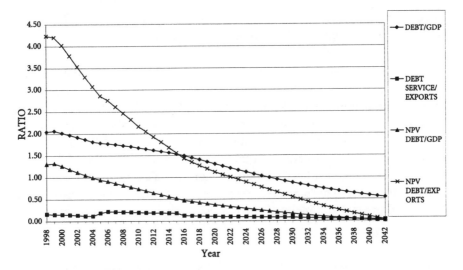

Figure 9–5: *Projection of Key Ratios before HIPC Initiative.*
Source: MOFED data and author's projections.

evident in the downward sloping curves of the NPV of debt to GDP (or debt stock to GDP) and debt service to exports ratios.

In fiscal terms, extracting 10 percent of GDP for debt service, or even 5 percent after soft financing, is not feasible given the public revenue raised in Zambia. With a high level of concessional finance of about US $300 million per year, that goal would still not be practical, as it would necessitate a budget surplus before debt repayment of about 12 percent of GDP. As a reference at the moment, with a small budget surplus of about 1 percent, the ratio of total revenues to GDP is about 16 percent. The size of this burden is one reason the HIPC initiative enabled Zambia to qualify for application of the new terms.

The ratio of debt service to exports would still be higher than 0.20 and decreasing after year 2015; the other criteria for external debt sustainability (namely NPV of debt/exports below 200 percent) would be met under these conditions by 2011.

Key Ratios under HIPC Conditions

In Zambia's case, the target ratio for indebtedness under the HIPC initiative of bringing debt service to exports below 0.20 was reached in the late 1990s. The completion point document notes that the NPV of debt to exports target of 150 percent will be reached in 2004, and the target of 250 percent NPV of debt to revenue will be achieved only in 2007.

Policy Implications: Among the countries eligible for HIPC debt reduction in the first place, Zambia is one of the most urgent cases to be able to accelerate sustainability to the earlier part of the decade. But the effectiveness of debt relief depends on policy performance. Without strong performance by the GRZ, debt relief will be a waste of resources.[26] Now that HIPC has reached the decision point with Zambia, total debt service relief from all of Zambia's creditors is estimated at US $3.8 billion or an equivalent of about US $2.5 billion in NPV terms. This represents 63 percent of the NPV of debt outstanding by the end of 1999 and includes the full use of traditional debt relief mechanisms.

Policy Performance and Exports: If the government succeeds in creating the conditions for vigorous economic growth including the rapid expansion of traditional and nontraditional exports, the present debt relief being offered under HIPC will enable Zambia to achieve debt sustainability within the next decade. A major factor in bringing this about will be the extent to which an appropriate real exchange rate will help Zambia regain its international competitive advantage.[27]

6. Summary and Concluding Observations

Up to the present, Zambia has been one of the four countries that have benefited the most from debt relief efforts. Recent estimates show that the total relief received by Zambia from 1988 to 1997 is US $3.76 billion.[28] Additional debt relief of that magnitude can be expected if Zambia succeeds in implementing the enhanced provisions of the HIPC initiative. The debt stock in nominal terms will remain high, as new finance from multilateral agencies has largely replaced bilateral and commercial debts. Nevertheless, the repayment profile is now more favorable, as the debt has been contracted on highly concessional terms.

While debt management and debt reduction have been high priorities on the policy agenda, another round of unsustainable debt accumulation will only be avoided in Zambia if the structural reforms needed to rebalance the

---

26. Easterly 2000.
27. This point is emphasized in Chapters 6, 10, and 11.
28. Daseking and Powell, IMF. Working Paper. October 1, 1999 WP/99/142-EA.

economy are given the highest priority. Over recent years, the opportunity for achieving exceptional debt relief has gathered the necessary momentum. The challenge for Zambia is to take advantage of the opportunity to reduce its debt burden permanently.

It is noteworthy that the objectives set out in the 1992 debt strategy will be achieved once the full effects of the HIPC initiative take place. The value of debt will be about half its 1991 level while debt service will fall below US $250 million per year, or well below the 20 percent debt service to exports benchmark.

None of the efforts at debt reduction, even complete write-offs, can succeed if the fundamental structure of the economy does not change. If the deficits in the fiscal and balance of payments accounts continue, another round of debt accumulation will be inevitable. All the goodwill and support of the donor community cannot change that. This outcome depends solely upon the decisions of the GRZ and its associated organizations.

10

The Role of Agriculture and Mining in Sustaining Growth and Development in Zambia

MALCOLM F. MCPHERSON

1. INTRODUCTION

This chapter argues that *any* strategy for sustained growth and development in Zambia has to be based on the revitalization of both agriculture and mining. When mining and agriculture were growing rapidly Zambia prospered and per capita incomes rose. When both sectors stagnated, the economy collapsed. Much of the economic decline since the mid-1970s can be traced to the lack of dynamism in these two sectors. Unless they are revitalized in ways that fully exploit their income, employment, and wealth generating linkages, it will be extremely difficult for Zambia to sustain economic and social progress over the foreseeable future.

All official documents beginning with the First National Development Plan (published in 1966) highlight the overwhelming importance to the economy of agriculture and mining.[1] A major problem has been that the formal recognition of the sectors' importance has not been reflected in govern-

---

1. For example, the Third National Development Plan (GRZ 1978) which came at the peak of Zambia's enthusiasm for "socialist planning"(*ibid.*, pp.30–31) stated that agricultural development was essential for achieving "self-sufficiency in staple foods" and for raising "production for exports"(p.35). With respect to mining, the document noted (p.38): "The Plan appreciates that until rural development picks up, copper will continue to play a dominant role in the economy." The development strategy was therefore focused on raising mining output and improving efficiency. The same message appears in the fourth plan (GRZ 1989; Geisler 1992).

ment policies.[2] The opposite has been the case. Both sectors have been heavily taxed as a means of promoting other sectors and to sustain high levels of public consumption. For example, during the first plan (1966–1970), there was significant *underspending* relative to the original plan totals for agriculture and rural development even though there were major overall increases in total government spending.[3] That pattern has continued ever since. Furthermore, even throughout the 1990s, agriculture has been systematically disadvantaged through low producer prices (the result of political interference in agricultural marketing), an overvalued real exchange rate, and the diversion of investment from activities and infrastructure that could have helped raise output.[4] The mining sector has been heavily taxed, directly through the fiscal system and indirectly through an overvalued real exchange rate.[5] Moreover, from the time the mines were nationalized in 1970, the government failed to ensure that they were managed in ways that would sustain their output and productivity. Large amounts of resources generated by mining were diverted to support unrelated and often unproductive activities.

By the time the MMD government took office in late 1991, mining and agriculture had been declining for well over a decade. Based on its promises during the election campaign, the new government was determined to reverse that trend. The MMD *Manifesto* and the NERP (see Chapter 3) stressed the necessity of reviving both agriculture and mining. That did not happen. Indeed, a purely "supply side" interpretation of the failure of the MMD government's strategy since 1991 would underscore its unwillingness and inability to deal decisively with the fundamental problems of low productivity, overtaxation,[6] and declining investment in agriculture and mining. Whether that situation will change now that the mines have been sold is still an open question.[7]

---

2. An International Labour Office (ILO) report noted:
. . . a depressing feature of public policy. . .is the gulf between words and deeds. In contrast with the government's declaration. . ., one is struck by a neglect of agriculture, by the low priority given to rural activities in the allocation of economic resources and skilled manpower. (ILO 1977:78–9; Saasa 1987, Ch.3).

3. McPherson 1980, Ch.2.

4. There are many sources (Good 1986; Kydd 1986; 1988; Geisler 1992; Harvard Business School 1997). This pattern has not been confined to Zambia. Numerous examples are available from other African countries (Eicher and Baker 1992; Pinstrup-Anderson and Pandya-Lorch 1995; Binswanger and Deininger 1997; Binswanger and Townsend 1999; Hazell 1999).

5. O'Faircheallaigh 1986.

6. Chapter 5 shows that the government paid special attention to mining tax reform. Yet, in order to maintain revenue, the tax burden on ZCCM was not lifted until the company had no further capacity to pay.

7. Selling the mines was not the end of government manipulation. As a means of influencing his chances for a third term, the president prevailed upon the 'independent' central bank to

This chapter seeks to identify the changes needed to revive agriculture and mining and, by extension, the whole economy. Section 2 has a brief historical sketch of the factors that have shaped the development of agriculture and mining. A theme common to the postindependence period has been the wealth-destroying effects of persistent government interference. Section 3 examines how the MMD government intended changing the growth paths of both sectors so that they would boost economic recovery. Section 4 discusses the problems and prospects of agriculture. Section 5 has a similar discussion for mining. Section 6 concludes with suggested policy changes for reviving the two sectors.

2. Historical Background

The data contained in Tables 10–1 and 10–2 provide a broad view of the trajectories of both agriculture and mining in Zambia over the period 1970 to 1998. The agricultural data generally portray a sector lacking in dynamism, particularly when related to population growth that over the period 1970 to 1998 increased by 137 percent. Agricultural output measured in constant 1995 prices was K496.8 million in 1970. After peaking at K873.7 million in 1993, it fell to K498.9 million by 1998. The annual growth rate of real output in agriculture (Column 3 of Table 10–1) underwent large swings with outright declines in output in 12 of the 29 years. Agricultural exports (Column 4) generally increased over the whole period with some solid growth from 1988 onwards. Overall, however, agricultural exports have increased at rates well below Zambia's potential. This is illustrated by tobacco. In the mid-1960s, tobacco exports from Zambia were of the same order of magnitude as those from Malawi and Rhodesia/Zimbabwe. Data assembled by the British High Commission in Lusaka show that in 1995/96, Zimbabwe exported 206 million kilograms of tobacco from which it earned US $603.5 million. Malawi exported 130 million kilograms earning $210 million. By contrast, Zambia exported 4.4 million kilograms, earning only $10.5 million. Column 5 of the table reports the share of agriculture in GDP. Over the period under review, the contribution of agriculture to GDP has risen. This is contrary to the "normal" pattern of growth experienced by countries that are genuinely developing. In Zambia's case, the rising share of GDP contributed by agriculture resulted from broad-based economic regression in which the per capita output

---

appreciate the exchange rate, thereby "easing" inflationary pressure. From K4150=$1 in December 2000, the Bank of Zambia pushed the rate to K3100=$1 in April and May 2001.

Table 10-1 *Zambia: Agriculture, Food Production and Aid, Maize Production and Prices, 1970-2001*

Year	Agricultural GDP (mill. 1995 USD)	Agricultural GDP growth (annual %)	Agricultural Exports [3] (mill. USD)	Agriculture (% of GDP)	Food Production per capita [3] (1989-91=100)	Food Aid [3] ('000 metric tons)	Maize Production [4] ('000 metric tons)	Maize Price Index (Chicago) [2] (USD/bushel)
1970	296.3	4.2	6.4	11.6	97.9	..	570.0	48.7
1971	303.5	2.4	9.3	14.2	106.4	0.5	927.9	49.8
1972	317.0	4.5	7.4	14.1	121.8	0.2	1143.3	46.5
1973	313.3	-1.2	14.8	12.4	105.2	0.1	873.6	81.7
1974	327.6	4.6	22.9	11.6	108.8	5.0	1146.4	114.4
1975	342.9	4.7	11.7	14.3	126.0	5.3	1483.1	102.8
1976	366.9	7.0	10.0	15.5	140.3	28.0	1642.0	95.4
1977	370.8	1.1	14.0	18.1	127.1	15.5	1607.9	78.6
1978	373.0	0.6	15.8	18.1	112.2	50.0	1380.9	82.2
1979	352.7	-5.4	5.6	16.4	92.7	166.5	877.8	93.4
1980	346.1	-1.9	13.5	15.1	94.4	84.4	937.3	106.4
1981	374.3	8.2	8.2	17.4	92.8	100.0	1007.3	112.4
1982	330.6	-11.7	5.5	14.9	86.8	83.4	750.2	89.4
1983	358.3	8.4	9.5	16.7	88.7	71.6	935.3	114.7
1984	378.3	5.6	7.8	16.4	84.9	+116.3	871.7	115.8
1985	391.5	3.5	17.4	14.6	93.6	84.6	1122.4	94.4
1986	425.7	8.7	25.0	13.6	95.7	115.6	1230.6	74.7
1987	416.4	-2.2	16.6	12.0	93.1	145.4	1063.4	60.6

1988	496.8	19.3	13.1	17.4	114.3	66.3	1943.2	88.9
1989	483.4	-2.7	20.0	21.2	111.9	3.5	1845.0	93.9
1990	440.4	-8.9	23.8	20.6	93.7	3.7	1092.7	92.5
1991	463.2	5.2	29.5	17.4	95.0	334.6	1095.9	89.0
1992	310.0	-33.1	35.7	23.8	77.0	535.3	483.5	88.0
1993	521.1	68.1	27.2	34.1	109.3	10.8	1597.8	85.2
1994	422.6	-18.9	15.9	13.5	92.0	11.4	1020.7	91.8
1995	563.6	33.4	44.6	18.4	82.0	..	737.8	100.0
1996	559.9	-0.6	52.6	17.2	98.0	..	1409.5	145.3
1997	531.3	-5.1	104.0	15.8	82.0	..	960.2	101.0
1998	537.8	1.2	109.0	16.3	77.0	..	638.1	84.1
1999	592.1	10.1	127.7	17.5	83.0	..	855.9	71.8
2000	601.4	1.6	98.3	17.2	81.0	..	881.6	70.1
2001	586.0	-2.6	..	15.9	..	..	900.0	72.3

Notes: The numbers given in italics are preliminary estimates based on data from "Macroeconomic Indicators", Ministry of Finance and National Planning, Lusaka, Zambia.

Sources: 1) World Development Indicators 2002, World Bank.
2) International Financial Statistics, 2002 and February 2003, IMF.
3) African Development Indicators 2002, World Bank.
4) FAOSTAT 2002, Food and Agriculture Organization.
5) Macroeconomic Indicators, various issues (latest: September 2002), Ministry of Finance and National Planning, Lusaka, Zambia.

of agriculture declined more slowly than the decline in per capita output of non-agricultural activities.

The data in columns 6 and 7, respectively, show that per capita food production has fallen and the volume of food aid has generally increased over the period. These data illustrate the extent to which food insecurity in Zambia has increased. Column 8 traces the production of maize over the three decades. Until 1977, there were sizable increases in output. Agricultural policies had explicitly encouraged maize production even in areas marginal for maize. The growth of output shows that these policies 'worked' for some years at least.[8] Nonetheless, due to fiscal constraints and other impediments, the increases could not be sustained and maize production fell sharply, particularly in drought years (1979, 1981, 1983). With the exception of 1988, in which the growing conditions were excellent, the output of maize has been generally less that half the level reached in 1977. The last column reports the real price per 90 kilogram bag of maize. The trend in prices was generally upward until 1986. Since then, maize prices in constant prices have fallen, undercutting any incentive farmers might have had for expanding maize production.

Table 10–2 has data for the mining (and quarrying) sector. Like agriculture the real income generated in mining has declined over the three decades to 1998 (Column 2 of Table 10–2). Also like agriculture, the year-to-year changes in real output have been large (Column 3). The contribution of mining to GDP has fallen sharply over time. Numerous official documents have asserted that the government's policy has been to diversify the economy away from copper. That has happened through regression rather than growth. A normal pattern of diversification occurs when smaller (and more dynamic) sectors grow faster than the largest sectors. The contribution of mining declined because its real output fell faster than nonmining output declined. The mining and quarrying index (Column 5) shows this decline. Measured relative to a 1990 base, the index was 139.4 in 1970, 125.2 in 1980, and 72.2 in 1998. The dollar earnings from copper production have fallen as well. Measured in 1995 prices, the output of Zambia's mines and quarries declined from levels above $1.5 billion in the 1970s to below $0.5 billion in the 1990s. One reason has been the general decline in copper exports (Column 8) as Zambia's mines became increasingly unproductive and high cost. From levels in the 1970s that at one point exceeded 700 thousand metric tons, copper exports fell to below 300 thousand tons in the 1990s. Another reason for the re-

---

8. We use the term "worked" advisedly. Farmers who expanded maize production, cut their output of other crops, especially drought tolerant crops such as sorghum and millet. These actions undermined food security.

duction in export receipts has been the decline in the world price of copper (Column 9).[9]

Recent data for 1999 and 2000 do not suggest that conditions have changed dramatically. Relative to 1998, the agricultural harvest in 1999 and 2000 were higher. The overall effect was to catch up for output reductions in previous years. In per capita terms, however, food production remained below levels achieved in the mid-1970s. Copper production in 1999 was 286,700 metric tons and in 2000 it was 249,400 mts. Real value added of mining continued to decline. Relative to 1994, it was 57.2 percent lower in 1999, and 59.3 percent lower in 2000. These production figures were reflected in the balance of payments where the contribution of both mining and agriculture to export earnings continued to decline.

The remainder of this section identifies some of the factors that explain the performance of the two sectors.

The Role of Agriculture and Mining

In Zambia, agriculture has provided, directly and indirectly, the bulk of employment whereas mining, directly and indirectly, has generated a major part of the country's income and wealth. This has been a well-established pattern since modern economic growth began in the country.[10] From the time of the major discoveries of copper deposits at the turn of the twentieth century, and their large-scale development in the 1920s,[11] mining has dominated economic activity. This has remained the case over recent years even though the sector has performed poorly. Similarly, with its abundant unskilled labor, large land base, and relatively favorable (though tropical) climate, Zambia has always depended heavily on agriculture as a source of employment, if not income and wealth.[12]

---

9. The declining copper price began soon after independence. Using 1982 as a base, the average price per pound of copper over the period 1950–54 was U.S. $1.09. Below are corresponding prices in U.S.$ per pound for the following periods: 55–59 ($1.19), 60–64 ($1.10), 65–69 ($1.95), 70–74 ($1.54),75–79 ($.83), and 80–84 ($.74) (World Bank 1986, Table 9.04).

10. The first steps in Zambia's development as a world-class mining country began with the decisions by Anglo-American and Roan Selection Trust to begin full-scale expansion of Nchanga and Nkana deposits at the end of the 1920s (Bancroft 1958; Baldwin 1965).

11. To place the scale of the development activity in perspective, copper production was 3,000 tons in 1928, 45,000 tons in 1929, and 120,000 tons in 1930. Thus, within a span of three years, Northern Rhodesia/Zambia had become a major copper producer with some of the lowest production costs in the industry.

12. Recent aggregate studies of economic growth have revived the notions of geographical (particularly tropical) determinism (Gallup, Sachs, and Mellinger 1998; Gallup and Sachs 1998; Bloom and Sachs 1999). The correlations derived by these scholars suggest that tropical countries have low productivity and geographical isolation has been associated with low eco-

Table 10-2. Zambia: Mining and Quarrying, Copper Production and Prices, 1970–2001

Year	Mining and Quarrying (bill. 1994 K.)	Mining and Quarrying (annual growth, %)	Mining and Quarrying (% of GDP)	Mining and Quarrying (1990=100)[3]	Mining and Quarrying (mill. 1995 USD)[3]	Copper Production ('000 metric tons)[3]	Copper Exports (IEC) ('000 metric tons)[3]	Copper Price (London) (USD/pound)[2]
1970	343.0	−12.5	36.0	139.4	1603.9	683.3	..	0.64
1971	309.9	−9.7	23.3	130.4	942.1	633.4		0.49
1972	356.4	15.0	24.3	143.0	1019.9	698.0	622.9	0.49
1973	345.1	−3.2	32.8	140.2	1501.1	633.4	627.1	0.81
1974	353.5	2.4	32.9	146.3	1582.7	663.6	649.8	0.93
1975	318.9	−9.8	13.7	132.7	487.8	619.2	616.1	0.56
1976	375.1	17.6	17.8	144.5	667.3	694.6	712.4	0.64
1977	350.1	−6.7	11.8	135.0	378.0	649.0	647.1	0.59
1978	367.3	4.9	12.7	135.5	407.9	629.0	549.9	0.62
1979	292.3	−20.4	17.6	115.7	588.6	564.4	646.7	0.89
1980	307.4	5.2	16.4	125.2	559.9	607.2	617.4	0.99
1981	321.8	4.7	14.0	114.1	516.0	560.6	556.0	0.79
1982	322.4	0.2	11.0	118.1	405.7	584.5	602.7	0.67
1983	332.1	3.0	15.3	116.0	511.4	575.6	570.5	0.72
1984	299.6	−9.8	13.7	111.8	375.5	522.2	530.1	0.62
1985	278.3	−7.1	15.6	108.6	351.9	479.4	505.0	0.64

1986	264.4	−5.0	18.2	107.1	271.5	459.1	466.3	0.62
1987	275.9	4.4	12.5	104.6	234.7	483.0	499.4	0.81
1988	240.3	−12.9	10.2	100.9	315.1	422.2	423.8	1.18
1989	263.0	9.5	14.0	102.5	472.0	450.4	456.4	1.29
1990	243.7	−7.3	9.0	100.0	243.1	426.6	459.9	1.21
1991	221.7	−9.0	8.4	90.2	236.8	376.9	382.3	1.06
1992	250.0	12.8	5.6	100.9	162.4	441.5	411.9	1.04
1993	227.2	−9.1	8.8	92.1	271.3	403.5	436.5	0.87
1994	373.9	64.5	16.7	76.3	601.6	353.5	360.7	1.05
1995	270.9	−27.6	14.4	68.3	501.0	307.6	291.9	1.33
1996	277.8	2.6	12.1	78.1	379.3	314.7	276.0	1.04
1997	284.4	2.4	9.9	78.8	376.4	321.6	304.0	1.03
1998	213.0	−25.1	6.3	72.2	201.6	298.5	228.0	0.75
1999	160.0	−24.9	3.8	54.2	254.2	286.7	240.0	0.71
2000	160.0	0.0	4.1	54.2	253.7	259.8	234.0	0.82
2001	182.9	14.3	3.9	62.0	289.7	298.7	298.0	0.72

Note: The numbers given in italics are preliminary estimates based on data from "Macroeconomic Indicators", Ministry of Finance and National Planning, Lusaka, Zambia.

Sources: 1) Macroeconomic Indicators, various issues (latest: September 2002), Ministry of Finance and National Planning, Lusaka, Zambia.
2) International Financial Statistics, 2002 and February 2003, IMF.
3) African Development Indicators 2002, World Bank.

Taken together, these two sectors accounted for most of Zambia's rapid economic progress from the end of WWII until the early 1970s. Since the mid-1970s for mining and late 1970s for agriculture, their contributions to economic growth, employment, and national wealth have declined. In 2000, despite a good grain harvest, Zambia's food production per capita was lower than it was at the end of the 1960s,[13] and its mine output was barely 40 percent of levels reached in the early 1970s. For a country that has abundant land and water, and some of the richest copper deposits in the world, these outcomes reflect a degree of economic regression unparalleled by countries other than those wracked by social upheaval or natural calamities.[14]

Fluctuations in mining output and income have been evident from the very beginning of the mining operations.[15] The Depression of the 1930s led to the closure of some mines and delayed the development of others. During WWII, compulsory purchases by the British government provided a stable, remunerative, price. But, the lack of replacement equipment and spare parts decapitalized the mines and related infrastructure, especially for the railroads.[16] This greatly limited the potential for expanding output, especially in the immediate post-war period. Furthermore, the overvaluation of the pound sterling (the so-called dollar shortage) depressed mining returns. Mining profits rose following the devaluation of sterling in 1949 and the commodity boom associated with the Korean War. A major expansion of mine capacity ensued. During the late 1950s, the growth of world demand for copper slowed and prices fell. These trends were reversed in the 1960s as world trade grew rapidly. The Mufulira mine disaster in 1970 cut Zambian production significantly although its effect on mining revenue was largely offset by higher copper prices over the period from 1972 to mid-1974.

The copper price fell sharply during the last half of 1974. Although the

---

nomic growth. (Australia and New Zealand are anomalies that theories of isolation have yet to explain.) Curiously, none of these scholars has described why countries that are isolated and tropical have seen periods of rapid growth when they have been well administered. Zambia and Zimbabwe, now growth and development laggards, were once (1945 to 1970) two of the fastest growing economies in the world despite being landlocked and tropical.

13. The *African Development Indicators* 1998/99 (Table 8.5, p. 225) show that, using an base of 1989–91=100, food production per capita in Zambia in 1980 was 94 while in 1996 it was 92. Longer series from the World Bank *World Development Indicators* database (available on CD-ROM) show that the average food production per capita (with the same base) was 114.3 over the period 1970–1979. From 1990 to 1998, the index averaged 91.6.

14. McPherson and Zinnes (1991, 1992) examined determinants of economic retrogression in a selected number of African countries, including Zambia.

15. This point is illustrated by tracing the fortunes of the Kansanshi mine. The original ore deposit was discovered in 1898. Numerous attempts were made to develop it. All of them, including the present attempt, have been directly affected by sharp swings in copper prices.

16. Baldwin (1965) has an excellent historical account.

proximate cause was the recession in the major industrial countries, the price collapse reflected fundamental shifts in patterns of base metal use, technological innovation in communications, and rapid growth of world copper supply. The shock was so severe and the Zambian government's medium term response so inappropriate that the mining sector has never recovered.[17] The price increases in the early part of the 1990s provided a welcome boost to the revenue of the state-owned copper company, ZCCM. But with production declining as a result of chronic underinvestment and costs rising due to ineffective management, the price rise did little other than slow down the accumulation of ZCCM's debt. Finally, the delay by the MMD government in privatizing ZCCM seriously undercut the productive base of the mining sector. ZCCM's physical capital dissipated as investment declined, senior staff stripped the company's assets, and revenue "disappeared" through fraud (such as the cobalt sales scandal).[18] ZCCM's financial problems were compounded by excessive wage costs (the result of political influence), a chronically overvalued exchange rate (for reasons explained in Chapter 6), continued high indirect taxation (discussed in Chapter 5), and falling productivity (due to aging equipment and inefficient mining techniques).

Like mining, agriculture in Zambia has been through numerous booms and slumps. The expansion of commercial agriculture began in the first decade of the twentieth century when European farmers settled north of the Zambezi River and commenced growing high-valued agricultural crops such as tobacco. The extension of the railway from Livingstone to the mines in the Katanga province of the Belgian Congo over the period 1904 to 1910 attracted more settlers. Agricultural activity remained limited until the rapid development of the Copperbelt in the latter part of the 1920s created large mining townships and raised disposable incomes. The Depression in the 1930s aused extreme hardship for Zambia's farmers, both African and European. Employment and income fell, reducing the demand for farm products.[19] These circumstances began to ease in the late 1930s as the world powers re-armed and the demand for copper increased. This led to a period of re-

17. The government initially treated the decline in copper prices as temporary. That response for the first year or so was (perhaps) appropriate although the government budget quickly became overextended. The government's mistake was to continue believing the price decline was temporary, and reversible.

18. Although the scandal spilled over into the local and international press in 2001, the problems had been noted in earlier IMF documents. The government promised an investigation (IMF/IDA 2000, par.22, p.11).

19. The history of those times and the changing patterns of industrial activity and employment are discussed in Bancroft (1958), Merle Davis (1967), and Baldwin (1965).

newed expansion in the mines and the revival of associated activities, including agriculture.

Following WWII, agricultural activity increased across a broad front. The production of maize, tobacco, and livestock rose rapidly.[20] Major beneficiaries were the European farmers located along the line-of-rail. Steady, modest, progress occurred in African agriculture as well though not at rates rapid enough to reduce the income disparities between African and European farmers.

Following Independence there was intense political pressure to overcome these disparities through special programs to boost African agriculture. President Kaunda responded in 1965 by announcing a "fair price" policy for agriculture.[21] Though originally intended to raise prices received by African producers, the initiative quickly became a "low price" policy designed to reduce the cost of staple food for urban workers. Thus, African farmers moved from one system of discrimination to another. Under the colonial government, there was discrimination in favor of (non-African) commercial farmers, although the effects of high prices (especially for maize) benefited African farmers as well. Under President Kaunda and UNIP, price controls discriminated against all farmers, African and non-African, reducing their incomes and dampening their incentive to invest in agriculture.

The government's price controls were administered through a series of marketing boards. These boards had been established in colonial times largely to influence agricultural supply in ways that benefited European farmers. The largest board was the National Agricultural Marketing Board (NAMBoard).[22] One of its principal functions was to operate the government's policy of pan-territorial and pan-seasonal pricing of maize introduced during the 1974/75 season. This policy was an agronomic and financial disaster. It encouraged maize production in areas that lacked any competitive advantage for the crop. It also discouraged farm-based and private off-farm storage and private investment in transport. The policy was maintained only

---

20. Data from 1954 onwards are presented in *Monthly Digest of Statistics* Issue No.1, April 1964: Tables 23 to 29. They show that over the period 1954 to 1963, the gross value of European agriculture almost doubled, sales of tobacco and maize more than doubled, and sales of milk increased by over 250 percent. The data on African agriculture indicate that the output and sales of a wide range of crops increased rapidly as well.

21. Kaunda quoted in Legum (1966, p.79). Bates (1974, p.40) pointed out that the "government's pricing policy was running in the completely opposite direction." Farmers were being exhorted to expand production but the prices of the main products were being artificially depressed. This issue is examined in more detail in McPherson (1980, Ch.2).

22. This entity had grown out of the former Grain Marketing Board. Its history and functions are discussed in World Bank (1977).

through subsidies that absorbed a significant share of the government budget.[23]

By the time the government changed in 1991, agriculture and mining were in deep decline.[24] Despite a number of donor-supported attempts to address the problems in these sectors,[25] productivity in both sectors had been falling throughout the 1980s.[26] Copper production in 1991 was 376,900 metric tons. Per capita food production in 1990 and 1991, were well below the level achieved in 1970. Indeed, when the harvest failed in 1991/92, Zambia faced a major catastrophe. With no food reserves and no foreign exchange to pay for food imports, the newly elected MMD government solicited the international community for emergency relief. Fundamental changes were needed if both sectors were to revive. During the election campaign, the MMD Party promised that if it became the government, those changes would be made.

---

23. For example, in 1980 these subsidies were K206.4 million, equivalent to 6.7 percent of GDP (World Bank 1986, Tables 5.02, 2.01). By 1991, they still amounted to 11.5 percent of government expenditure, or the equivalent of 3.2 percent of GDP (World Bank 1992, Table 2).

24. All sectors did not suffer. For many years, Zambia has been a major source of semiprecious gemstones. Official data always show their contribution to national income and foreign exchange earnings to be modest. Unofficial reports suggest otherwise. For example, the Public Expenditure Review of 1992 (World Bank 1992, p.97) estimated that the value of smuggled gemstones was between $180 and $400 million per year.

25. With World Bank support, the government made a number of efforts to reverse the decline in mining. Support provided in February 1984 sought to rehabilitate equipment, train critical staff, and rationalize ZCCM's operations. The cost was $300 million (GRZ 1985, pp.32–33). A second rehabilitation program covered the period 1986–90. It was designed to rationalize mining operations, reduce costs, close unprofitable mines, concentrate on profitable (mining) activities, and accelerate mine development. Its investment costs were $375 million per year, a large sum for a country that was already seriously overburdened with debt (World Bank Report no.6355-ZA, 1986, p.viii). This program, however, ran into difficulties when the government abandoned the IMF program in 1987. Some indication of the difficulties is provided by the 1988 *Annual report of the Mines Department* which noted (p.1) "Shortages of operation equipment caused ZCCM to reduce its mine development in order to maintain current production levels, which contributed in subsequent periods to further decrease in production because of inefficiencies in mining operations." At the same time, agriculture was to be liberalized. As part of its 1985 reforms, "The government has completed decontrolling of marketing of all farm products and inputs, and the marketing parastatals and Provincial Cooperative Unions function as the buyers of last resort for all major crops" (*ibid.*, par.12, p.ix).

26. This was a continuation of an already adverse trend. Relative to a base of 1965=100, by 1977, the cost of labor per unit of value added had risen to 462.1 in mining, 342.4 in transport and communication, 155.7 in services and 153.4 in manufacturing (World Bank report no.3007-ZA, 1981, Table 5.05). By this stage, formal sector employment stagnated and the predictions of the UN/ECA/FAO "Seers" Mission report had been validated. That report stated that Zambia could have rapid increases in wages or employment, but not both. Several studies have reconfirmed this point (ILO 1977, 1992).

Overview

Agriculture and mining have always been subject to wide fluctuations of income and output. Though these fluctuations were inconvenient, long-term economic damage was minimized while the government maintained adequate safety margins in the form of physical food stocks and financial reserves. However, as the government's expansionary policies progressively depleted Zambia's cash and foreign exchange reserves, overborrowing destroyed Zambia's international credit rating, and physical reserves were used up, the economy lost the capacity to absorb price and quantity shocks.

While Zambia's experience has been unfortunate, it has differed in degree rather than kind from that of other African countries. They, too, have undergone extensive periods of agricultural stagnation and decline for many of the same reasons—overvalued real exchange rates, urban bias in the allocation of development resources, high rates of implicit and explicit taxation, 'credit' programs that made grants to selected groups, and so on. These issues have been widely analyzed in numerous forums. Bates (1981) described the counterproductive activities of agricultural marketing. The Berg Report (World Bank 1981) highlighted the problems created by the systematic neglect of agriculture. Lele (1981) focused on the technical problems of reversing Africa's agricultural decline. Eicher and Baker (1982) described the gaps in basic and applied research on agriculture in Africa. Eicher (1982) examined the basis of Africa's food problem and food insecurity. More recently, Binswanger and his collaborators (Binswanger and Deininger 1997; Binswanger and Townsend 1999) have reviewed the problems created when African governments use the agricultural marketing system as a fiscal mechanism and fail to develop rural infrastructure. Gabre-Madhin and Johnston (2001) contrasted Africa's experience with that of Asia's where rapid economic growth was preceded and supported by rising agricultural productivity.

For its part, the Kaunda government devoted a considerable effort to diverting attention from its policies of neglect of agriculture and mining and its misuse of national resources. Official explanations for the economy's problems invariably refer to the difficulties created by changes in copper prices and drought-induced reductions in agricultural output.[27] Although the government sought to deflect blame,[28] the recurrence of wide swings in output

---

27. GRZ (2000, par. 3) noted that "...the intensification of civil wars in some neighbouring countries and the financial crisis in East Asia have largely contributed to the decline in Zambia's export receipts observed over the period 1997–99."

28. The study *Restructuring in the Midst of Crisis* (GRZ 1984) was the first attempt by the government to deal with the country's problems in a comprehensive way. That study, too, regularly refers to the problems created by external events. Only limited attention is given to the problems created by government interference and State-induced inefficiency.

and income in both agriculture and mining has never been a secret. The over-riding policy issue has always been how to manage the swings in ways that would enable the economy to continue growing. Until around 1970, that was done through the pursuit of conservative fiscal and monetary policies, maintaining a realistic exchange rate, and keeping public sector activity consistent with the economy's resource base. The reforms introduced at Mulungushi Rock in 1968 ended that by setting Zambia on a course of public sector expansion that undermined economic growth and development, and from which the economy has yet to recover.

Furthermore, the government made a fundamental policy mistake in the mid-1970s when it did not act swiftly to deal with the consequences of the collapse in mining revenue.[29] That policy mistake has been compounded ever since, due to the unwillingness of successive governments (UNIP and MMD) to make the fundamental macroeconomic changes needed to repair the damage.[30]

3. MMD Policies on Agriculture and Mining

As already noted, all official documents dealing with growth and development in Zambia stress the importance of agriculture and mining.[31] The most significant reform-oriented document produced by the Kaunda government, "Restructuring in the Midst of Crisis," stated:

Agriculture is the priority area in the restructuring effort. It has enormous potential (. . .); it is the one sector that can provide employment for large numbers of people in the short run and can absorb the large population increase of the next twenty years; it is the sub-sector with the greatest capacity for expansion; it uses little foreign exchange; and it is not capital intensive.

The report continued: "(A) turn around in agriculture is a precondition for economic recovery and restructuring in Zambia."[32]

With respect to mining, the report noted:

---

29. For those who might see the above as writing history in reverse, I urge a review the 1977 World Bank *Country Economic Memorandum* (World Bank 1977). At that time, both the World Bank and the IMF were proposing bold measures to deal with Zambia's macroeconomic imbalances. Their advice was ignored.

30. The same mistakes have been repeated. The government's manipulation of the exchange rate throughout 2001 in the guise of "restoring confidence" is one of many examples.

31. That pattern continues (*cf.* Fox and Greenburg 2001, pars.309, 311).

32. GRZ 1984, p.4, pars. 1.19 and 1.20.

For any long-term growth strategy to succeed the mining industry, which is the major provider of foreign exchange, must play a[n] important role. This means that the mining industry, which is facing many technical and financial difficulties, should be restored to previous levels of efficiency to make it once again profitable and competitive in world markets.[33]

These blunt, forthright statements leave no doubt that UNIP officials fully understood where the economy's problems lay and what was required.

Several years later, with both sectors in far worse condition, the MMD *Manifesto* stated:

The MMD is committed to expanding agricultural production and ensuring food is available to all.

It also noted that:

While fully realising that the transition from the present highly distorted situation to a free market will require time and skilled management, the MMD government will liberalise agricultural marketing and processing to put market forces to work.[34]

Similar sentiments can be found in the 1996 *Manifesto*:

The MMD government has set clear policy objectives and strategies to make agriculture the cornerstone of the Zambian economy.[35]

This statement is followed by details for improving food security, sustaining the resource base, using agriculture as a means of generating income and employment, and having the sector contribute to industrial development and improving the balance of payments.

The government would achieve these goals by continuing ". . .with the policy of liberalizing agriculture by enhancing the role of the private sector through a managed transition assisted with adequate transitional arrangements."[36] Since "managed transition" and "adequate" were not defined, the government's intentions were ambiguous. One interpretation is that the government was being careful, given the outcome of its first term during which agricultural output and incomes had fallen. An alternative explanation is that the government was seeking a way to reverse its commitment to liberaliza-

---

33. GRZ 1984, p.4, par.1.18.
34. *Manifesto* 1991, p.5.
35. *Manifesto* 1996, p.7.
36. *ibid.*

tion. The discussion below shows that the government did not "manage" the transition well. Its interference in agricultural marketing was counterproductive. The ban on maize exports and wheat flour imports and the perennial disruption to fertilizer marketing through government imports are obvious examples.[37]

Referring to the mining sector, the 1991 *Manifesto* noted:

> As with other state-owned enterprises, ZCCM's monumental empire shall be reviewed and reorganised.[38]

The 1996 *Manifesto* repeated this commitment, adding that ZCCM will be reorganized and privatized "in line with the overall programme of parastatals."[39]

Neither of these statements was a ringing endorsement of the type of fundamental restructuring required in the mining sector. Nonetheless, the *Manifesto* also included a specific commitment to create an "enabling environment" for the private sector. As Chapter 3 notes, the MMD campaigned on the platform that the "government has no business in business." Its statements, therefore, were fully consistent with the goals of encouraging private sector development supported by "limited government" and motivated by ". . .a renewed spirit of hard work, entrepreneurship, public commitment, honesty, integrity, and public accountability."[40]

Some allowance can be made for exaggeration. Yet, explicit commitments were made in the New Economic Recovery Program (reviewed earlier in Chapter 3). In an excellent assessment of the problems, the NERP stated:

> Agricultural development in the past has been inhibited by excessive government intervention in pricing and marketing, especially with respect to maize. Price controls and subsidies on maize and fertiliser, the system of uniform national pricing, and the cooperatives' monopoly in maize marketing have operated as disincentives to efficient production and optimal land utilisation, while encouraging consumption, stimulating smuggling, and nurturing a bloated and inefficient structure of agricultural cooperatives.

---

37. The Ministry of Agriculture, Food and Fisheries produced a series of policy papers (e.g. MAFF 1995, 1996) reviewing the overall situation in maize marketing. These had optimistic titles such as "The transition programme 1995/96" and "From transition to consolidation. . .1993–1996." As noted in the text, the transition has been shaky and there has been little consolidation.

38. *Manifesto* 1991, p.6.

39. *Manifesto* 1996, p.8.

40. Statements supporting all these points can be found in the MMD *Manifesto* 1991, 1996, pp. 2–4. The quote is taken from the *Manifesto* 1991, p.2.

The Government intends to promote efficient production, ensure food security, and augment exports. Major steps have been taken recently toward elimination of subsidies and liberalisation of pricing policies.[41]

With respect to mining, the NERP noted:

Notwithstanding the Government's efforts to diversify the country's economic base, the copper industry will remain the mainstay of the Zambian economy in the medium term as a major source of foreign exchange and employment. In the past the sector's performance was overshadowed by inefficiencies and high production costs making the copper company (ZCCM) increasingly uncompetitive in world markets. . . . The new Government has put in place policies that will enable the company to operate profitably. . . ZCCM will be restructured and non-mining activities will be divested. Expenditures that are not essential to maintain mining production will be eliminated. Mobilisation of both local and foreign financial resources will enhance the company's creditworthiness. In the light of this programme, it is vital that the expenditure reduction measures be complemented by private investment in ZCCM's undeveloped copper resources. . . .[This will] require considerable foreign investment. ZCCM is currently preparing a long-term strategy for its operations covering divestiture, joint ventures and privatization.[42]

Again these statements leave no doubt that senior government officials (this time from the MMD) fully appreciated the need for fundamental reform in agriculture and mining. The needed reforms did not occur for several reasons.

It was common during the time of President Kaunda and UNIP to attribute poor economic performance to external events. Regularly used explanations were drought and late delivery of inputs in the case of agriculture and declining world prices or transport difficulties in the case of mining. Recognizing that such excuses lacked credibility, the MMD government took a different tack. It emphasized the importance of reform and its determination to vigorously implement the necessary policies. But, as this study has continued to emphasize, the rhetoric was not matched by the actions needed to sustain reform.

In the case of agriculture, the first five years of MMD's tenure coincided with four below average seasons, including the horrendous drought of 1991/92. Only one season (1993/94) was above average. To some degree, therefore, the benefits of improved agricultural marketing and distribution

---

41. GRZ 1992, 1992, pars.59 and 60, p.18
42. *ibid.* par.63, p.19

were offset by bad weather.[43] With respect to maize marketing, however, the government was reluctant to fully withdraw so that the private sector (the majority of whom are farmers) could take advantage of market opportunities. This issue is explored further below.

With respect to mining, there has never been convincing evidence that the MMD government as a whole from President Chiluba down believed that selling the mines was the appropriate strategy. The 1991 *Manifesto* did not refer to privatizing the mines. The 1996 *Manifesto* refers to their sale once and then only indirectly. However, the statement in the NERP (quoted above) was explicit. As subsequent government actions confirmed, the views were largely window-dressing designed to placate the donor community. By the time the mines became too costly to keep, outside circumstances had taken over. The world copper price collapsed in the wake of the Asian financial crisis. With the withdrawal of the Kafue Consortium's offer in 1998, only one buyer, Anglo American, was left. It took almost two years to complete the deal. In the meantime, ZCCM's losses continued unabated, dragging the rest of the economy down.

4. PROBLEMS AND PROSPECTS OF AGRICULTURE

Many factors have undermined agricultural production in Zambia. Most farming remained in private hands although, as a means of promoting food security, the Kaunda government established a number of large state-owned farms. These were inefficient and costly enterprises that added little to total output. Commercial farms produced the bulk of marketed output. Yet, because the majority of these farms was owned by whites (even though many were third generation Zambians), the postindependence government had little interest in policies that would benefit them. Many politicians, including President Kaunda, found it more convenient to press the populist view that commercial farmers should be taxed.

Until the agricultural reforms of June 1989 and September 1990, the government maintained price controls on many commodities, a large number of them derived from agriculture. The system of pan-territorial and pan-seasonal pricing for maize and fertilizer imposed high costs on the budget. It discouraged private storage, promoted smuggling, and resulted in the inefficient use of transport. The system also generated high rates of wastage. On average,

---

43. Benson and Clay (1998) examined the broader impacts of drought in sub-Saharan Africa. Zambia provided its own review of the effects of the 1992 drought (GRZ 1992).

5 to 10 percent of the marketed crop was lost annually.[44] The agricultural payments and commodity delivery systems were abused, creating further losses. Following the drought of 1979, the flows of food aid and fertilizer regularly disrupted local markets, adding to the inefficiency and waste. Taken together these factors undercut agriculture as a dynamic source of output and employment growth. Food production per capita fell, food insecurity intensified, and rural poverty worsened. The description of Zambia as a country with "hungry people on fertile land" was apt.[45]

The UNIP government selectively eased several controls during the 1980s. Beginning in 1981, agricultural exporters were allowed to keep a larger share of additional foreign exchange they earned (in "retention" accounts). In 1989, as part UNIP's New Economic Recovery Program, the government lifted price controls on almost all agricultural products. Controls were maintained on maize and fertilizer.

Following the 1991 elections, the main change in agriculture policy was the liberalization of the price of maize. This action was motivated by budget concerns and not the need to promote agriculture, or reduce rural poverty.[46]

Consistent with the trend started by UNIP, the MMD government indicated that it would be less intrusive. In the months immediately after the 1991 elections, the government quickly removed subsidies on maize meal and fertilizer. Those subsidies had been budget-busters for almost a decade and a half. In 1991 alone they were K10.6 billion against a budgeted amount of K5.7 billion.[47] At the time it removed the subsidies, the government indicated that it would soon remove all remaining restrictions on agricultural marketing and distribution. The large food aid flows to deal with the 1992 drought complicated the implementation of this policy. Nonetheless, to underscore its commitment to market liberalization, the government appointed a task force to review how maize marketing might be reformed and what transition measures were needed to achieve a fully liberalized system.

Despite the government's stated commitment to reform, senior policy

---

44. Losses were higher in bumper years. Sano (1988) reported that approximately 5–10 percent of the "marketable maize" is lost annually through poor marketing and storage. A MAFF report in 1996 put food losses in Zambia at 200,000 tons per annum out of a total of 1,800,000 tons available (MAFF 1996). This is significantly above 10 percent.

45. Harvard Business School 9–797–023 "Zambia's Agricultural Sector Investment Program" January 14, 1997, p.5.

46. The minister of finance's statement to the National Assembly justifying the elimination of the maize subsidy was cast entirely in terms of reducing pressure on the budget. Any advantage for agricultural production was ignored.

47. Statement by Minister Kasonde to the National Assembly (GRZ 1991). *The Economist* October 5, 1991, p.58 reported that the maize subsidy was costing the government approximately half a million dollars per day.

makers underestimated the vigor with which special interests within the Ministry of Finance and the Ministry of Agriculture, Food and Fisheries (MAFF) would resist the removal of controls on agriculture. There are several examples. The timing of the announcement of the ban on maize exports (June 1995) disrupted private sector efforts to import food. The Food Reserve Agency (FRA) has been selectively allowed into areas (e.g., the importation of jute bags) that have no relation to its primary mission. And, though the promise was made every year, the government did not cease importing fertilizer.

The gap between promises and performance convinced many private operators that the government was not serious about allowing agricultural markets to allocate resources or discover prices in an unfettered way. Hesitant to be blind-sided by the government reneging on its commitment to withdraw from maize and fertilizer marketing, private traders offered a limited response to market liberalization, which was seen by many officials as "inadequate."[48] This was precisely the outcome desired by those in government who sought to justify continued state involvement in agricultural marketing. Having created the conditions that deterred private sector involvement, these officials began to argue that it was essential for government to remain involved in maize and fertilizer marketing. For fertilizer, the outcome has been that, despite the government's commitment not to intervene, there have been official imports every year since the 1991 elections.[49]

This pattern of intervention by government has been a feature of agriculture for the last four decades. Both UNIP and MMD governments made a number of efforts to change. All of these, however, have been halting and generally inadequate. Lacking in Zambia has been any broad-based strategy that links agricultural development to food security and economic growth. Action in the sector, by the government and the donors, has been ad hoc. In the remainder of this section, we illustrate this point using examples related to maize marketing, market liberalization, the promotion of sector-wide investment, food aid, and agricultural credit. These examples point to a persis-

---

48. The Harvard Business School case study on ASIP referred to above noted:
The government admitted that in some cases a private monopoly had replaced the state monopoly, with no better prices or service to farmers. Overall, private sector response to the state's retreat from crop buying had been neither as rapid nor as effective as anticipated. (HBS 1997, p.9).

49. Fertilizer imports generated the opportunity for selected officials in the MoF and MAFF to benefit directly from kickbacks. The deal was typically done in South Africa using short-term credit guaranteed by the government. Once the product arrived, some of it was diverted as well. Since the rents were concentrated, they could be easily controlled and divided among those involved.

tent pattern of government intervention in agriculture that, so far, has undermined rather than promoted development.

The Maize Marketing Study: As part of its commitment to liberalize maize marketing, the government assembled a small team of experts headed by Mr. N.P. Mag'ande, then managing director of the Zambia National Commercial Bank (ZANACO). As a former permanent secretary of the Ministry of Agriculture, Mr. Mag'ande was eminently qualified to lead such a team. The terms of reference for the study were to consider how the government could withdraw from maize marketing without undermining food security and without adversely affecting farmers in marginal areas.

The team reviewed Zambia's earlier experience with maize marketing. Since much of the history prior to the September 1990 reforms was well known, the task force focused on the implications of government withdrawal from marketing. Issues considered were the ability of farmers to increase production, the willingness of farmers to store their crops, the availability of transport for moving the crop, the potential response of traders and millers to wider seasonal and geographical fluctuations in prices, the liquidity required to support different marketing scenarios, and strategies for ensuring food security.

The team examined a large amount of evidence, including the experience of countries such as Nigeria that had abruptly liberalized their agricultural marketing systems. The report concluded that both farmers and private traders would respond in ways that avoided major disruptions in the production and supply of maize; that both consumers and producers would adapt to price fluctuations by substitution in production and consumption and the strategic use of storage; and that the financial system could provide the necessary finance on a rolling basis to purchase and evacuate the crop. The report strongly advocated that in order to generate the confidence for the private sector to become permanently engaged in maize marketing, the government needed to fully withdraw from maize and fertilizer marketing. It recommended that food and fertilizer obtained from aid agencies be sold through public tender. The team members, however, recognized that the government had a legitimate role in promoting food security. The report recommended that an independent food reserve agency be established to ensure that a revolving stock of maize be held for food security purposes. This agency would operate on a modest scale through established grain markets. So as not to disrupt local markets, it operations would be announced in advance.

The report was submitted to the ministers of finance and agriculture in October 1993. The team was thanked for its efforts and the report was shelved. Notwithstanding its stated commitment to reform, the government was not ready to place its trust in the private sector to handle the staple crop.

Market Liberalization: The UNIP government had already made some progress in liberalizing agricultural marketing.[50] The MMD government, through the NERP, announced it was committed to continuing that process. As noted earlier, full liberalization was strongly resisted. The government has always found some pretext to continue to intervene. The limited private sector response has been the most common reason. For example, the *PFP* 1994–96 (par.11) stated:

> Government has been unable to attract the private sector into maize marketing as planned. Markets have been completely liberalised (including the removal of export restrictions) but the Government was not able to disengage from maize marketing to the extent envisaged. Private sector activity in maize marketing had to be supplemented by the provision of K20 billion. This amount permitted the purchase—at market prices—of some 3 million bags of maize. The rise in real interest rates, the fall in the regional price of maize, and confusion over the "floor price", deterred private sector participation. The restrictions imposed by the cash Budget prevented Government from supplying additional funds. The purchase and delivery of the crop was completed by issuing promissory notes to farmers. These notes will mature in 1994.

The *PFP* continued (par. 13):

> The disruptions to maize marketing in 1993 have been noted. The combination of an appreciating kwacha, high real interest rates, and uncertainty over official policy should not occur again. Over the programme period, Government expects to fully withdraw from all aspects of maize marketing that can be handled on a commercial basis.

That did not happen. The government established a food reserve and passed legislation for the formation of the Food Reserve Agency (FRA). The agency was expected to operate through market mechanisms to absorb or release food in times of surplus or shortage. It was not long, however, before its goals were perverted. In the process, the FRA has become yet another disruptive force in agricultural marketing.[51]

---

50. Under UNIP, all agricultural prices except maize and fertilizer had been decontrolled in June 1989. Maize and fertilizer marketing were opened up to the private sector in September 1990 (*Zambia: Policy Framework Paper, 1991–1993*, World Bank Sec M91–151, February 7, 1991, pp.5–6, 24–25).

51. *The Post* newspaper in January 2000 published a list of the main defaulters to the FRA. The list included many prominent politicians and MMD supporters.

The problem was that the government's actions undermined market liberalization. From September 1990, the private sector in Zambia has been assured that maize and fertilizer marketing and distribution were activities they could freely enter. Since then, however, the government has always found some reason to re-intervene. In this respect, the MMD government has behaved as its predecessor in generating and maintaining confusion in the agricultural sector.[52] There seem to be two reasons for this behavior. At one level, the government's actions reflect a profound distrust of the private sector's ability to respond in economically sensible ways. At another level, a selected group of government officials have shown that they can still extract large rents by intervening in fertilizer and maize markets.

The government's behavior has been abetted by the actions of donor agencies. Several donors, among them the European Union, the World Food Program of the FAO, Japanese and Danes, have continued providing food and fertilizer as commodity aid. These donors have conditions that, in principle, limit the disruption to markets created by their aid. The agencies, however, cannot (and do not) effectively enforce the conditions. Moreover, since the amounts of these commodities are not known well in advance, private sector marketing agents run the risk (as happened a number of times during the 1990s) of importing commodities only to see their margins undercut by commodity aid.

Both UNIP and MMD fell short of their commitments to liberalize agricultural marketing. UNIP started the process in June 1989. The MMD government under President Chiluba did not complete the task. The effects of the delay are evident in the continued depressed state of Zambian agriculture.

Agriculture Sector Investment Program (ASIP): In principle, ASIP was due to commence in 1994. The intention was to coordinate all donor efforts in agriculture so as to ". . .improve the efficiency of lending for investment and economic growth."[53] ASIP had a number of important features:[54]

- It included all of Zambia's agricultural activities;
- The program was prepared by a Zambian task force;
- It was to be implemented by the MAFF without separate project implementation units;

---

52. Kydd (1986) described in detail how the UNIP government created havoc with the bumper crop of 1985. Approximately 20 percent of that crop was wasted/lost. To make up the short-fall, Zambia had to import 70 thousand tons of maize from Zimbabwe and Malawi.

53. HBS 1997, p.12.

54. The details of ASIP are given in World Bank (1995) and Harvard Business School (1997, pp.12–15).

- It was seen as an integral part of the public sector reforms based on decentralizing control and encouraging beneficiary participation;
- It minimized the use of long-term expatriate technical assistants;
- It was designed to be flexible through a series of annual reviews and adjustments;
- To the extent possible, donor procedures for gaining access to and reporting on the use of their support would be standardized.

In 1991, there were approximately 180 separate donor projects in agriculture. The government had little input into, knowledge about, or control over what was being done. Under ASIP, all of these initiatives would be assembled under a single umbrella project with the objective of directing government and donor resources so as to boost agriculture in ways that alleviated poverty, improved food security, and stimulated rapid economic growth. None of these goals has been, or is being, achieved. Consequently, ASIP has been widely seen as a failure. Indeed, the 1998 budget speech referred to the need to "revitalize ASIP."[55] The 1999 and 2000 budget speeches contained similar language. Ironically, while government officials were stating that ASIP was not working, the World Bank made a special effort to praise the success of ASIP for its role in helping officials "listen to farmers."[56]

The basic problem with ASIP, as with the other sector investment programs (SIPs), is that the administrative requirements are well beyond the relevant capacities available to Zambia. According to the World Bank, a "genuine SIP":

- Is sector-wide in scope;
- Is based on a clear sector strategy;
- Is led by local stakeholders;
- Involves the participation of all main donors;
- Establishes common implementation arrangements;
- Uses local capacity rather than technical assistance.

Observers familiar with the history of development initiatives in Zambian agriculture would recognize that these conditions are impractical. For exam-

---

55. *Budget Speech* 1998, presented to Parliament January 29, 1998

56. World Bank *Findings* 1998, no.105. Curiously, the HIPC "decision point" document conveys the impression that the ASIP is being implemented as planned. It noted: "An Agricultural Sector Investment Program (ASIP) was launched in 1995 with the aim of providing infrastructure to support sustainable, small-scale farming...." The report continued: "...it will now be important to build on these initiatives by preparing and implementing an integrated rural development strategy" (IMF/IDA 2000, par. 25, p.12). With ASIP regularly referred to by government ministers as needing reform, it is not clear what there will be for the integrated rural

ple, a sector-wide project invariably overlaps with other sectors. Should agricultural projects promote improved nutrition or should that be left to health programs? Are feeder roads, which are essential for crop evacuation and food security, the responsibility of the Ministry of Agriculture or the Ministry of Works and Communication? A sector-wide project requires that account be taken of spillovers across sectors. Doing that, however, adds to the administrative burden.

How was the leadership of ASIP to be determined? Who were the stakeholders? All farmers or only those designated by the senior government officials, or the farmers union?

There is no doubt that Zambia would benefit from a clear sector strategy in agriculture. At the official opening of Parliament on the November 29, 1991, newly elected President Chiluba announced:

> . . .the main thrust of [agricultural] expansion will take place in the small scale farming community. . .[57]

He added that the government had every intention of supporting farmers. To do that the government and associate agencies should ". . .get out of their way." This was a bold statement that gave all observers hope that, at last, agriculture would get the priority it deserved. Unfortunately, what President Chiluba told Parliament differs from the MMD *Manifesto* and that, in turn, differs from the commitments in the NERP. The government did not have a clear strategy for the sector. Adopting ASIP did not provide one either.

Donor participation encounters similar problems. The World Bank has been "leading" ASIP although most bilateral donors interested in promoting agriculture do not agree with the bank's approach to conditionality, staffing, procurement, and program supervision. Yet, even if the donor coordination issues could be overcome, the approach adopted by the World Bank still grossly overtaxes Zambia's administrative and technical capacities.

Common implementation procedures can be readily agreed for new activities. But, are new activities meant to adopt the procedures of those that are ongoing, or vice-versa? In principle, local capacity should be used rather than technical assistance. In practice, the marginal net returns generated by well-placed expatriate technical assistants can often be orders of magnitude greater than for locals.

Even if these issues were resolved, a deeper problem remained. If the local

development program to build upon. It should be recalled that Zambia has a long history of previous attempts to promote integrated rural development with their "rural growth poles" and "rural growth areas." These did not succeed.

57. Geisler, 1992, pp.138–139.

capacity is already available to organize donor programs and achieve broad-based growth in agriculture, why has Zambian agriculture not grown? Why hasn't the sector shown dynamism independently of the multitude of donor actions to "stimulate" growth? More important, if the local capacity were available to develop agriculture, why wasn't it fully engaged in that task without the need for ASIP? The answer, of course, is that Zambia has not had (and does not have) the required capacity. Moreover, as personnel losses accelerate due to the spread of HIV/AIDS, Zambia cannot generate that capacity.

For all of these reasons, ASIP was preprogrammed to fail. Its implementation delays and lack of results should have been no surprise.

Food Aid: Within months of taking office, the MMD government was confronted with the effects of the worst drought in Zambia and Southern Africa in more than half a century. With no food reserves, a harvest of approximately 43 percent of the average output of the previous decade (see Table 10–1, Column 8), and no foreign exchange reserves to purchase food imports, Zambia was in dire straits.

Recognizing that it needed to move quickly to prevent a humanitarian disaster, the government approached the donor community. Over the next twelve months several donors provided a total of approximately 900 thousand metric tons of food. This was significantly more than was needed to compensate for the harvest shortfall. Though the harvest improved the following year, it was still below average.

In mid-1995, it became apparent that the food supply would be limited due to the failure of the 1994–95 harvest. The government summoned the donor community to the Mulungushi Conference Centre on August 31, 1995 to plead for special assistance. The minister of finance chaired the proceedings. He noted that the string of bad years had had a highly negative effect on the progress of the government's efforts to promote economic recovery. The droughts had reduced the contribution of the agricultural sector to income and employment, aggravated the food security situation, and required Zambia to divert scarce foreign exchange to cover food imports. He also stated that the repeated failure of the harvests had undermined the effects of the government's efforts to reform agricultural policies.

The minister pointed out that although the government had been conservative when it framed the 1995 budget and balance of payments projections, the harvest had been much worse than expected. These pressures were coming at a time when the economy was being disrupted by problems in the banking sector (principally the collapse of Meridien BIAO bank) and the loss of export revenue due to declining copper prices and copper output.

The minister urged the donors to support the government's request to import 380,000 metric tons of maize. The cost was estimated to be $100 million, of which $75 million would be incurred in 1995 and $25 million in 1996. The minister suggested that balance of payments commitments already in the pipeline could be reprogrammed for the task.

As a result of this appeal the donor community agreed to reallocate some balance of payments support as well as provide additional food aid. Events revealed, however, that the food shortfall had been overestimated and Zambia "got by" with less aid than the amounts originally requested.

Zambia's problem has been that it has received large amounts of food aid on a regular basis since the harvests failed in 1979. In principle, food aid should be irregular and short-term and not a long-term addition to the local food supply. With food aid virtually guaranteed on a permanent basis neither UNIP nor MMD governments have been under pressure to revitalize local food production. Thus, even with large flows of food aid, Zambia's food security situation has deteriorated. Under present arrangements, there is no obvious end to Zambia's "need" for further assistance.

In Chapter 14, we discuss the key dimensions of an "aid exit" strategy for Zambia. An area that requires immediate government attention would be the formulation and implementation of a "food aid exit" strategy. For such a strategy to succeed, agricultural output would have to expand on a sustained basis.

Agricultural Credit: There are no examples of viable government-sponsored credit programs in agriculture since independence.[58] At the macro level, agricultural credit provided through official programs has been a source of waste and inefficiency. Moreover, based on the increase in rural

---

58. Our treatment here is brief. A detailed account of the intricacies of agricultural credit in Zambia would require a separate study. Most of the problems in this area have resulted from government interference and corruption. For instance, Symon's (1996) report on Lima Bank's losses, negative net worth, poor loan recovery, fraud, and politically inspired debt write-offs reveals agricultural credit in Zambia to be both ineffective and scandal-ridden. This is only one of many reports dating from the early 1970s (when credit morality first collapsed) that stress the need for less government interference in agricultural credit. Both UNIP and MMD governments promised reform. Every attempt has failed. Government-sponsored credit schemes remain grant-making programs with the prospect of repayment so low that none of the schemes could ever be viable. The *PFP* 1994–96 offered hope that the government would adopt a pragmatic approach to credit. It noted:

In 1994 and beyond, the private sector will assume a greater role in the supply of agricultural credit. Where Government funding is considered necessary, it will be conditioned on improved financial management of the lending institutions, including higher rates of repayment.

poverty in Zambia over the last two decades, they have exacerbated inequality. The waste has shown up in the repeated recapitalization and concessional support provided to the various agencies—Lima Bank, the Development Bank of Zambia, the Zambia Cooperative Federation, NAMBoard—that have been responsible for providing credit to farmers in cash and commodities.[59] These agencies have all been administered and operated according to the idea that credit is not a resource that has to be accounted for properly, allocated efficiently, and fully recovered when payment is due.

For these reasons, "credit" programs have been misnamed. The government and its various agencies have used agricultural credit as a guise for grant making. For most of the last three decades, every publicly sponsored "credit" operation in Zambia has faced the certain prospect that a large part of the resources involved would be wasted. What has not been known, however, was who would benefit from that waste—farmers who did not repay, officials who did not record repayments and pocketed the proceeds, or officials who appropriated for their own use the commodities being provided on credit. The "rents" created by this waste and inefficiency have generated strong official support for continuing the programs. That can only happen if the donor community, or GRZ, will periodically recapitalize these "credit" agencies. So far, this has been relatively easy. As one donor loses interest in supporting these programs others become engaged.[60]

An example, typical of the operation of credit programs in Zambia, was the Agricultural Credit Management Programme.[61] A report in 1996 noted:

> Following the near bankruptcy of the major agricultural lending institutions, the Government initiated a pilot Agricultural Credit Management Programme (ACMP) in November 1994. The general objective of the ACMP is to develop

---

This statement left the way open for further government interference, for example, as part of ASIP. Given the history of waste associated with such efforts, social welfare in Zambia would improve if the government abandoned any attempt to "push" credit.

59. In his speech at the official opening of Parliament in January 2000, President Chiluba announced that the government would recapitalize the Development Bank of Zambia (DBZ). The cost was to be $10 million. The president gave no indication of the changes that would be made to ensure that *this time* the $10 million would not be wasted. In 1986, the World Bank also provided $10 million to recapitalize DBZ. It noted that the portfolio had been deteriorating since 1983 due to "...continued deterioration of DBZ's arrears situation" (World Bank Report no. 6310-ZA, 1986, p.ii). Subsequent reports on Lima Bank (Symon 1996), and the Agricultural Credit Management Program (MAFF 1996) show that the basic problems of arrears, fraud, and low credit recovery were never effectively addressed.

60. DBZ, for example, has received extensive support from the World Bank and the Norwegian government.

61. MAFF 1996.

the administration of self-sustaining agricultural credit, at the grass-roots level, through private firms. . ..

The ACMP started as a supply-led initiative to deliver fertilizer and seed to small-scale farmers. However, in the second year of operation, farmers were required to make an obligatory 10 percent down payment (equity contribution to the loan) and to buy seed before drawing on the fertilizer loan.

Although the objectives of the scheme were clear, it was not effectively implemented. The program review identified problems of high administrative costs, low credit recovery, and corruption.[62] With recovery rates of under 4 percent, the program was failing in its first year.

The outcome is that agricultural credit has been grossly misused in Zambia. Its principal function has been to redistribute wealth rather than expand agricultural output. Much of the redistribution has occurred at higher levels in the income chain. There is little evidence from village level studies that rural areas as a whole have benefited. For example, there have been no major improvements in the income or wealth or nutritional status of female-headed households in areas where credit agencies have been active.[63]

Access to Land:[64]   The Land Titles Conversion Act of 1975 eliminated freehold tenure. The legislation also stated that land did not have value. Access to land was granted by the state. This provided ample scope for arbitrariness, lack of transparency, and patronage. While title to land could not be sold, the use of land was regularly exchanged or sold through the transfer of instruments granting power of attorney to the purchaser. During the 1980s, the government placed further restrictions on land-holding, making it "virtually impossible for foreigners" to gain access to land.[65]

This unsatisfactory situation created numerous difficulties for the government in its attempt to encourage the expansion of private sector activity. The MMD government recognized this. The NERP stated:

It is essential that more land become available for development. To this end, the Government will ensure that the current leasehold system continues. However, in order to maximize security of tenure, the Government will ensure that subject to conditions and covenants of the lease being complied with by the lessee, the lease shall be deemed to have been extended for a further 99 years period

---

62. MAFF 1996, pp.17–18.

63. Jha and Hojjati 1993; Goldschmidt 1993; Mwenda 1993; Kumar 1994; Hazell and Hojjati 1997.

64. *Policy Framework Paper 1994–1996*, pars.15–18.

65. In 1985, the Land Act was amended, among other things, reducing leasehold tenure for non-Zambians to a maximum of five years (Kydd 1988).

(sic!) upon the expiry of the initial 99 year lease period. The Ministry of Lands will also accelerate the land survey programme in order to reduce the backlog in the issuance of title deeds and will overhaul the land titling system to speed the access to land by new investors.[66]

The government also made a commitment to amend the Land Act. Specifically, it resolved:

> . . .to remove the notion that land has no value; facilitate the sub-division of land; facilitate real estate trading and related transactions; reduce the land and property transfer tax; and take action to provide for the subdivision and sale of state farms.[67]

The 1994 budget speech (pars. 83 to 85) outlined the problems with Zambia's land-holding system:

> A major impediment to new investment is the current legal status of land. At present, the law does not permit freehold tenure. Unimproved land is seen as having no value and is, therefore, of little use as collateral.

The speech had proposals for dealing with these issues. Changes would be made in land ownership, transfer, and registration procedures. A major problem was to rationalize spontaneous settlement or 'squatter' rights. The speech continued (par. 85):

> The Government also intends to introduce legislation to abolish the distinction between Land Reserves and Trust Land on the one hand, and State land on the other; to recognise customary tenure; and to establish a Land Development Fund.

These were bold initiatives. They proved far more difficult to implement than the government anticipated. A major stumbling block was the distinction between Trust and State land. Abolishing the former undermined the existing rural power structure. After considerable debate and some delay, the government amended the Land Act. The outcome remains unsatisfactory. Gaining access to titles over rural land for those bold enough to try remains difficult. There are large backlogs in surveying and titling. Indeed, a prominent goal for the period 2000 to 2002 outlined in the interim poverty reduction and growth strategy that the government presented to the donors in July 2000 was to "develop efficient markets for land under leasehold." This would

---

66. GRZ 1992, par.55, p.17.
67. *PFP* 1994–96, par.16.

be achieved through improvements in the Ministry of Lands' system for managing leasehold applications, and completing plot surveys for ten urban areas by the end of 2000. The land market would be improved by "implement[ing] more effective sanctions for ownership of unutilised land."[68] Since sanctions and incomplete surveys do not foster efficient markets, the government's land policies require further work.

Export Agriculture:[69]   An important and highly encouraging change during the 1990s has been the growth of nontraditional exports. Many of these activities are agriculture-based. There were several reasons for the expansion. First, the progressive removal of exchange controls and impediments to trade led to an acceleration of a trend that had begun with the UNIP-sponsored agricultural liberalization in 1989. Second, some large producers gained access to specialty floriculture and horticulture markets in the U.K. and Europe. Third, transport costs fell as the price of fuel declined and the freight capacity of the major airlines increased. And fourth, most of the growers had learned to insulate their activities from inconsistent domestic policies by dollarizing and making their own arrangements offshore for their input supplies and spare parts.

The expansion of nontraditional exports provided an additional source of foreign exchange for Zambia. Given the general decline in earnings from mining, this was welcome. The expansion of export agriculture has contributed directly to several goals of the economic recovery program. It has increased trade, raised income and employment, provided access to new technology, fostered new managerial skills, boosted productivity, and accelerated the development of agriculture itself.

An encouraging change has been the increase in tobacco production. Based on the scope and scale of the tobacco industries in Malawi and Zimbabwe referred to earlier, the potential for further expansion of tobacco production in Zambia is large. The recent disruptions to tobacco and maize production in Zimbabwe due to the takeover by squatters of commercial farms may provide Zambia with an opportunity to expand output.[70] Whether Zam-

---

68. *Interim Poverty Reduction Strategy Paper*, Lusaka, July 7, 2000, "Zambia Structural Policy Matrix 2000–2002."

69. Some material is taken from a speech McPherson wrote for the Hon. K. Shengamo, M.P., deputy minister of finance delivered to the export growers of Zambia on the occasion of "Export Grower's Day," March 22, 1996.

70. A potential negative factor is that the collapse of the Zimbabwe tobacco crop could undercut Zambian sales. With smaller production in Zimbabwe, world tobacco buyers have less incentive to travel to Southern Africa.

bian producers respond depends on how they perceive the government's long-term approach to macroeconomic management.

One export that Zambia has not promoted, however, is livestock. Major opportunities have been (and are being) lost in this area. The Asian market has undergone a long period of expansion in demand for livestock products that has bypassed Africa. The main beneficiaries have been producers in Argentina, America, and Australia.[71] Those countries are already rich (especially the last two) and have alternative export markets. Asia lacks the comparative advantage in livestock products of Zambia (and its neighbors in Southern Africa). One possible factor constraining livestock exports from Africa is disease. That problem is not insurmountable since many of the livestock diseases endemic to Africa are also present in Asia. What has been lacking so far are entrepreneurs with the vision to make Zambia (and the rest of Southern Africa) a major meat producing area for the Asian market. If exploited, the growth linkages to the rest of agriculture, particularly the linkages to grain producers, would boost to the whole sector.[72]

Zambia's potential for expanding export agriculture is virtually unlimited. The country's share in world markets in all products is negligible. The enterprises engaged in floriculture and horticulture have already shown that agricultural exports can be highly lucrative. Zambia's coffee producers have an international reputation for excellence and its honey producers have found outlets in specialty markets. Neither geography nor distance has been a constraint.[73] International competitiveness has been gained by producing high quality products.

Overview: Government interference in agriculture, combined with its ambivalence about reducing that interference, has seriously distorted incentives for both producers and consumers. By taxing farmers to lower the costs of staple food for urban dwellers and by diverting resources from rural development, successive governments have exacerbated rural poverty. The outcome has been a sustained, broad-based waste of national resources. That waste and inefficiency is deeply embedded in the agricultural system affecting the allocation of land, the distribution and use of credit, the incentive to move into new markets (e.g., in livestock), the organization of donor assistance, and product marketing.

---

71. Shagam 1997; Greene and Southard 1998; Crook, Hsu, and Lopez 1999; Ehui *et al.* 2000.

72. Thinking strategically, one could imagine Zambia as a major grain and store livestock producer with areas more favorably placed (the highlands of Zimbabwe or parts of South Africa close to the coast) as fattening and slaughtering areas for the Asian market.

73. Sachs and Warner 1995; Bloom and Sachs 1998.

The economy cannot grow and develop unless agriculture helps lead the way. No other sector has the potential to create employment, reach the majority of Zambia's poor in such a direct way, or provide Zambia with the prospect of achieving regional development. Furthermore, the development of agriculture is the only activity that, under present and foreseeable conditions, has unlimited potential for Zambia. The potential for expanding output with known technology is enormous. One example will illustrate. In a normal year, the average yield of maize in Zambia is around 12 percent of the average maize yield across the entire corn belt of the United States.

The challenge for the future is to induce the government to begin accepting that local farmers, agricultural agents, agroprocessors, rural transport providers, importers, and exporters, without official intervention, can organize effectively agricultural marketing and distribution. Government intervention to this point has undermined agricultural development and exacerbated rural poverty. There are few prospects that continued intervention offers a way forward. The record clearly shows that it is time the government "got out of the way."

5. Problems and Prospects of the Mining Sector

Despite the urgent need to rehabilitate the mining sector, the MMD government did not treat the privatization of ZCCM as a priority. In view of ZCCM's technical inefficiency and its deteriorating financial situation, privatization was the only option that would allow the mining sector to regain its former dynamism. There was no other practical way to obtain the finance, technical skills, and managerial expertise that could revitalize the sector. This was clearly understood. The problem was that senior officials, including the president, were reluctant to give up state control of the mines.

One fact few Zambians seemed willing to confront was that ZCCM had been poorly managed from the time it was nationalized. The mismanagement had been evident at a number of levels. ZCCM's executives proved incapable of building upon or even sustaining the operations of what were at one time, highly profitable, world-class copper companies. Zambia's politicians proved incapable of providing the economic setting within which ZCCM's contribution to national development would be maximized. Finally, neither presidents Kaunda nor Chiluba were prepared to face the fact that continued government interference in the operations of the mines would ultimately bankrupt ZCCM.

There were numerous indicators of poor management—low (and often negative) profits, rising costs, over-staffing, lax inventory control, an absence of strategic planning, and minimal efforts to prove and develop new ore bodies. These problems were evident at the beginning of the 1980s and, despite a variety of emergency programs to correct them, were not addressed. "Management" at ZCCM consisted of a series of short-term expedients designed to allow the company to "muddle through" rather than prosper. Corporate policy was largely directed to ensuring that ZCCM remained under government control.

The only tactic the government could use to sustain this situation was delay. That took a variety of forms. Ministers who advocated rapid reform of the mines were removed. The *Keinbaum Report* (KR) on privatizing the mines was shelved. The Zambia Privatisation Agency was explicitly excluded from participating in activities related to the potential sale of ZCCM. Nikko Securities was contracted to raise finance for ZCCM to proceed with the Konkola Deep Mining Project (KDMP). Though this effort failed—a foregone conclusion from the start—the ploy successfully delayed action on reforming ZCCM for a further eighteen months. The Anglo-American Corporation was rejected as a suitable candidate to purchase ZCCM even though it supported the government's position that ZCCM should be sold as a single unit.[74]

The Interim Short Term Program (ISTP) designed to prevent further decline in ZCCM was never fully implemented. The copper contingency mechanism was scuttled. Devised by the International Monetary Fund, this scheme set aside funds to support ZCCM's operations when world prices fell. The report of the World Bank team of experts on the state of the mining sector in late 1994 was received with skepticism by the government.[75] When the government finally decided to sell the mines, it appointed the disgraced former chief executive of ZCCM as its principal negotiator. This appointment, more than any other government action, advertised to the world at large that the government was not interested in proceeding rapidly or transparently.[76]

---

74. Holmes 1995.

75. The World Bank assembled, on an emergency basis, a team of twelve mining specialists to review the state of the mines at the end of 1994. Their report was never released but their conclusions became known. One was that if the government did not act immediately to revive the mines, they would be scrap value only. This, in fact, proved to be the case.

76. A subtheme in all of the government's efforts to sell ZCCM has been the potential *private* fortunes that could be made by insiders. Many Zambians readily recall the fortunes made by well-connected individuals when the government bought the mines in 1970 (a deal that was completed over the period September to December 1969). The difficulty facing insiders this time around, however, has been that ZCCM is a wasted asset. With copper prices low and ZCCM in desperate financial shape, potential buyers have had no reason to offer "side payments." The only fortunes to be made have been in stripping ZCCM's assets and skimming proceeds off the top (as in the cobalt deal that became public in early 2001).

Finally, the bid of the Kafue Consortium for the largest part of ZCCM (Nkana and Nchanga) was rejected ostensibly because it was too low. At the time, ZCCM was losing on the order of $15–20 million per month. Holding out for a higher price demonstrated that the government was not concerned about maximizing the net returns from selling ZCCM.[77]

These delaying tactics worked so effectively that by the time ZCCM was sold its net worth was so diminished that the final sale price represented a token payment. In the face of government indecision and delay, Zambia's so-called "crown jewels" were ultimately worth little more than cut glass.[78]

The agreement to sell ZCCM to Anglo-American (originally due to take effect at end December 1999 but held up for "technical reasons" until March 2000) reflected the government's acceptance of the inevitable. ZCCM's asset base had collapsed. Billions of dollars that the government could not provide were required to rehabilitate the mines and cover the debts incurred as ZCCM slid into bankruptcy.

It is beyond the scope of this section to highlight all of the factors that contributed to ZCCM's demise. The process was drawn out and multifaceted. In effect, ZCCM died from a thousand cuts—excessive taxation, incompetent management, political interference, and a progressive decapitalization.

Taxing ZCCM: Over the years, ZCCM was subject to a variety of direct and indirect taxes. IMF staff calculations as part of the copper contingency mechanism give broad estimates of the amounts involved. The mechanism was designed to set aside reserves for ZCCM in periods when copper prices were high (with the resources held in Treasury Bills) for use when copper prices fell. ZCCM's management treated the arrangement as a major imposition. It was, however, a useful way for the government to sterilize "excess" liquidity without subjecting ZCCM to additional taxes.

To determine how much should be set aside under this mechanism, the government and the IMF needed a detailed breakdown of ZCCM's costs. The calculations provide two types of information. The first was the amount of explicit taxes paid by ZCCM. The second was the cost to ZCCM of the dual exchange rate policy (an implicit tax). Calculations for 1992 show that out of total income of K182.1 billion (equivalent to $1071.4 million), import duty and income tax amounted to K18.1 billion (equivalent to $129.6 million).[79]

---

77. These reports proved to be accurate. Based on ZCCM's published accounts the loss over the four-year period 1993–94 to 1997–98 was $606.3 million (IMF Statistical Appendix 1999, Table 15).

78. Some members of the local press recognized that the delay in selling ZCCM was "squandering state resources" (Holmes 1999, pp.12–15).

79. S. Brown "ZCCM – Operating Costs and Financial Condition 1992-Q1 1993" IMF, Lusaka draft, 12 February, 1993.

These taxes raised ZCCM's costs in 1992 to $1.19 per pound, significantly above the combined returns from copper and cobalt ($1.04 per pound). If ZCCM had been able to convert its foreign exchange earnings at the prevailing retention rate (instead of the official rate) its costs would have been 14 cents a pound lower. That is, ZCCM in 1992 was subject to taxes in the form of import duties and income tax of 7.9 cents per pound and in the form of a differential exchange rate of 14 cents per pound. These taxes were being levied on an enterprise that was fundamentally unprofitable, heavily indebted, and so strapped for cash that its expenditure on wages and transport were displacing its expenditure on maintenance and capital expansion.

One might argue that the taxes would not have been a burden on the company if ZCCM had raised its overall productivity. Indeed, the explicit and implicit taxes were draining the company of resources that, if effectively used, might have raised its efficiency.

Keinbaum Report:[80]   While there have been a series of missteps and mistakes along the way in dealing with ZCCM, perhaps the biggest government blunder was the rejection of the KR. This report, completed in 1993, was designed to provide the government with options for privatizing the mines. It included a detailed study of the state of the mines, the alternatives available, and a strategy to dispose of the mines. The report's basic conclusion was that the mines should be "unbundled" and sold as quickly as possible. Since that conclusion was unacceptable to the government, the report was suppressed. Its message, however, was not completely lost, as copies of the report circulated within the government and the donor community.

The essence of the report was to outline and analyze specific privatization options for ZCCM and to highlight some of the work remaining if ZCCM were to be unbundled in ways that served the interests of *all* Zambians. The report focused on maximizing the economic benefits for Zambia from the mining sector. Those benefits were considerable. There was no doubt among the consultants that, with appropriate management, the mines could be turned around in a relatively short period and made profitable on a sustained basis. They stated (KR,p.16):

> The basic premise which underlies the work carried out is that a full revitalization of the Zambian copper mining industry is possible and necessary in order to maximize the long-term economic benefits to the country. Zambia has an immense wealth in her existing and potential mineral inventory.[81]

---

80. Keinbaum and Associates 1993.

81. This was a refreshing perspective after years of World Bank and other views that Zambia's mines were a "wasting resource." Throughout the 1980s World Bank officials had come to believe that Zambia's copper mining potential was in terminal decline. For example, a

The report listed the basic problems with ZCCM. Despite its rich reserves, ZCCM had become a high cost producer.[82] Many of its mines were unprofitable at 90 cents per pound and thus were not viable over the longer term without major improvements. ZCCM's problems had nothing to do with the quality of the ore, its location, or other technical factors. The company was inefficiently run and poorly managed. One illustration of poor management was that there had been no substantive technological advance within ZCCM since the mines were nationalized (KR, p.38). ZCCM was known throughout the industry for its rich deposits. Yet, when compared with other major copper producers, ZCCM had devoted no resources to exploration (KR, p. 67). Consequently, much of the ore upon which the future of Zambia's mining industry rested had yet to be discovered and proven (KR, pp. 29 to 39).

The report noted several potential constraints to privatization. There was a complex tangle of legal agreements. For instance, Anglo-American's 27.31 percent share gave it preemptive rights over any potential sale (KR,p. 42). Many of the ZCCM's debts had convenants restricting the break-up and sale of the company (KR, p. 53).

A more immediate problem was that ZCCM's liquidity crisis restricted its operations (KR, pp.54–58). The consultants noted that the company's viability would be seriously undermined if production levels could not be kept around 400,000 metric tons a year. The scope of the management problems were evident in the data on production costs (KR, pp.70–71). Those costs had risen sharply during the late 1980s and early 1990s for nontechnical reasons (primarily corruption).

World Bank report in 1981 noted "The longer-run prognosis for copper and allied mining activities in Zambia over the next 20 years is declining output and increasing costs of production" (World Bank Report 3007-ZA, 1981, par.42, p.20). The government's 1983 presentation to the Paris Club wrote of the limited life of the mines. Kydd (1986, p.238) echoed this sentiment when he referred to Zambia's final inheritance from the mines. The World Bank Country Economic Memorandum in the mid-1980s discussed how to streamline the mining industry (World Bank 1986, pp.38–41). The memorandum noted: "Zambia's economically recoverable copper reserves are sufficient to maintain current production levels only until approximately the end of the present century" (*ibid.*, p.38). It was widely believed that Zambia needed to begin getting used to (and make the most of) a terminally declining sector (*cf.PFP* 1991–1993, 1991). To its credit the KR dispelled any notion that Zambia's ore bodies were running out. The main problem was that ZCCM had done little exploration or development since the early 1970s. Once Zambia began opening up exploration to outsiders in the 1990s, significant new reserves have been located and proven. The main impediment to profitable mining activity has been (and remains) inappropriate government policy.

82. After surveying market conditions the consultants concluded that a long-term price of 90 cents a pound was to be expected in world markets. At the time of its analysis, most mines and ZCCM as whole, had costs above this figure.

Chapter 3 of the KR examined options for privatizing ZCCM—issuing new shares, selling existing shares, selling the government shares, and selling the company in several "packages." The consultants concluded that because of the need for additional capital to revitalize the mining sector, ZCCM should be sold in packages. One option was to split the company along the lines of the former RCCM (Roan Consolidated Copper Mines) and NCCM (Nchanga Consolidated Copper Mines). Another was to break the company into six parts consisting of Konkola including Konkola Deep Division, Mufulira Division, Chambishi Division (including Chambishi SE), Nkana Division plus Nchanga Division (without Chambishi and with Chibuluma), Luanshya Division (with Baluba, NCR, PMP), and a ZCCM Holding Company. The last-mentioned would consist of the central administration, power division, and other assorted units. It would take over all of ZCCM's liabilities and be the employer of last resort while retrenchment packages were worked out for redundant workers. The consultants suggested that after dealing with ZCCM's liabilities, the holding company be closed.

To compare the likely effects of unbundling the company, the consultants provided three scenarios (KR, pp.159–161). The first was based on the continuation of average production levels and average costs of the five years 1988 to 1992. The second involved privatization with no substantial increase in investment, but major improvements in management. The third gave an estimate of maximum sustainable production. With a world price of US $1 per pound, the consultants concluded that "the potential to increase annual cash operating surpluses may be from less than US$100 million per year to over US$400 million per year. . . ." The implication was that a fully revitalized copper industry could sustain an annual production of 513,000 metric tons of finiahsed copper not including Konkola Deep or Chambishi divisions.

The basic conclusion was that ZCCM could be transformed into a small number of profitable and dynamic companies *if only the appropriate decisions were taken*. The consultants doubted that would occur and their skepticism was subsequently borne out. Most of the actions identified in the KR have been taken in the breach and only after immense damage to the mining sector and the economy.

ZCCM's Management: Stumbling blocks to the attempt to restructure and revive ZCCM were the attitudes and actions of its managers. There was no incentive for the management to cooperate with any exercise that involved the sale of ZCCM. Until the early part of 1994, the management had support from ZIMCO, whose board members and chairman were equally disinterested in selling ZCCM. The dissolution of ZIMCO formally removed this source of resistance.[83]

ZCCM's management was asked in mid-1994 to prepare a memorandum stating its view on privatization. The report entitled "Management's View" (hereafter MV) was completed in September 1994. It was defensive, lacking in vision, and scattered with irrelevant technical digressions. It was a weak apology for the status quo. Its most important failing was that it ignored the fundamental issue of whether Zambia as a nation would be better off with the mines under private management. Seen as an example of the best that ZCCM's management could offer, it was an eloquent case for privatizing the mines as rapidly as possible.

The MV's main weaknesses were that it failed to deal with vital questions related to the capacity of ZCCM to recover financially and of the existing management to oversee that recovery. Questions not discussed included:

- The company's overstaffing and falling labor productivity;
- ZCCM's performance relative to the projections of its ISTP;[84]
- Whether ZCCM had the technical and managerial competence to develop Konkola Deep;[85]
- Why ZCCM had such large arrears when world prices for copper and cobalt were high and, according to management, unit operating costs were falling;
- Why, in the light of these higher prices and falling costs, ZCCM had to borrow an additional $40 million from abroad;
- How the (roughly) $2 billion in additional capital (estimated in the KR) would be raised to maintain production over the medium term;
- What plans ZCCM had to increase exploration and development to boost the company's proven reserves and output over the longer term; and
- ZCCM's management's plans for modernizing the company's mining technology and exploration techniques, and upgrading its managerial capacity.

Perhaps the most important omission from the MV was its failure to recognize the adverse macroeconomic impact of ZCCM's continued inefficiency.[86] This contrasted with the KR's emphasis on efficiency and its conclu-

---

83. President Chiluba was Chairman of ZIMCO. If he had supported the sale of ZCCM, there would have been no resistance from ZIMCO.

84. Just prior to the report being sent to the government, the *Times of Zambia* had carried a statement by ZCCM noting that copper output in 1994 would be well below the 420,000 metric tons projected in the ISTP. In fact, 1994 production was 353,000 metric tons (IMF Statistical Appendix 1999, Table 5). This was a blow to Zambia as world prices had recently increased.

85. The MV recognized that ZCCM could not finance the project.

86. In the year preceding the preparation of the MV, ZCCM had lost approximately $129 million (financial year to March 1994). This amount was almost equivalent to the financing gap identified by the government at the CG Meeting for Zambia in Paris in December 1994.

sion that ZCCM should be unbundled. An important conclusion of the KR, rejected in the MV, was the value of having several mining companies operating in Zambia. The advantages of this arrangement were rising employment, increasing demand for local services and locally manufactured products, the expansion and rehabilitation of infrastructure, new approaches to labor relations, improvements in mine management, the spread of an efficiency-oriented work ethic, and the introduction of new mining technology.

These points were missed in the MV, largely because ZCCM's managers were so intent on defending the status quo. By doing this, they were effectively advocating that Zambia's mining sector remain locked into 1970's technology, 1960's union rules, a Second Republic work ethic, and outmoded and deficient management methods.

The MV rejected the idea of unbundling largely because the separate companies would have to work out what were described as "complex intersdependencies." It was argued that this would reduce efficiency (MV, p.26). The KR had examined this issue and concluded otherwise. Unbundling ZCCM, according to the KR, would produce gains in employment, income, investment, tax revenue, exports, and overall welfare. This was an easy argument to defend since the counterfactual was ZCCM's own history.[87] As a single unit, the company was collapsing undercutting its benefits. Indeed, the period from the latter part of 1993 and first half of 1994 was an immediate example. When ZCCM could not pay its suppliers and meet its tax obligations, the whole economy contracted.

A curious aspect of the MV was its numerous references to CODELCO, the state-owned copper company in Chile. ZCCM's managers evidently felt comfortable comparing their company and CODELCO. Their comparisons, however, were convenient. Many telling dimensions were ignored. For example, ZCCM's costs in 1993–94 were 97.5 cents per pound. CODELCO's were 64.5 cents per pound, and even these were 10 cents per pound *higher* than private copper producers in Chile. CODELCO employed 21,500 workers to produce 1.1 million metric tons of copper. ZCCM had 52,500 workers producing around 350,000 metric tons. While ZCCM had effectively spent nothing on exploration for the decade prior to 1993, CODELCO had been spending close to $20 million per year on that activity.[88] In reality, ZCCM

---

87. It is not clear why ZCCM's managers addressed the issue of "unbundling." The KR had made a solid case that, in the national interest, unbundling the company would increase its value. By arguing to keep the company as a single unit ZCCM's managers were effectively arguing that maximizing national wealth was not a crucial consideration. They also ignored the fact that, if ZCCM were sold as a single unit, its purchaser could increase the value of the company by unbundling it.

88. KR, pp.67–68.

compared unfavorably with CODELCO. ZCCM was grossly inefficient, both economically and technically. CODELCO was neither of these.

As a final point, the MV made a special effort to argue that ZCCM's management had not been responsible for overburdening ZCCM with debt, making the company a high-cost producer, or causing the decline in copper production. According to the MV, the blame rested with the government for using ZCCM as a cash cow, raising mining taxes to levels that discouraged investment, and maintaining a foreign exchange regime that heavily taxed ZCCM's operations. These points are all valid, yet the management cannot deflect blame so easily. No one forced ZCCM's management to buy the Challenger aircraft rather than spend money on research, exploration, and mine development. No one forced ZCCM's management to continually raise wages to levels that could not be justified by ZCCM's productivity or profitability.[89] Finally, no one forced the management to keep such a bloated headquarters staff, to travel abroad so frequently, to grant themselves such lavish perks, or to keep such a large number of redundant workers on the payroll. One would expect ZCCM's managers to defend themselves by pointing out that some of these actions were in response to political pressure. That argument would have been an admission that they were not qualified to manage Zambia's largest (and, once, most profitable) company.

Raising Finance for Konkola Deep Mining Project (KDMP):   One strategy used by ZCCM's management to deflect pressure for privatization was to argue that it could raise the finance needed to develop Konkola Deep. ZCCM proceeded with plans to raise $600 million.[90] The rationale was that, with KDMP starting production, the company would be worth significantly more to a potential private buyer. This claim was not substantiated. At best, the argument was weak; at worst, it would be an exceedingly costly mistake. There was a high probability that any investment by ZCCM in KDMP would subtract value. It would leave ZCCM deeper in debt. More important, it was doubtful that ZCCM's managers would make the choices that potential private buyers would find efficient and cost-effective.

---

89. The ISTP adopted what it termed were radical cost-cutting measures in November 1993. These produced savings of 4 cents per pound. Those savings (and more) were completely wiped out by the 25 percent wage increase granted by ZCCM to its workers in the early part of 1994.

90. ZCCM's managers (MV, p.15) argued that ZCCM had a gearing (debt to equity ratio) that was consistent with world standards for copper companies and thus was in a position to increase its borrowing. World standards were not an appropriate metric for ZCCM. Its output was declining and it had been borrowing simply to maintain production. In effect, its gearing was too high. Potential creditors knew this. It is one reason why ZCCM could not raise the resources to fund KDMP.

Other points were overlooked. It was being proposed that ZCCM should borrow an additional $600 million on commercial terms at a time when its principal owner, the GRZ, had debts of $7 billion (more than twice GDP). These debts were not being serviced. Indeed, the government was actively petitioning the international community to write-off or write-down this debt.[91]

The effort to finance KDMP ended for two reasons. First, Nikko Securities (ZCCM's agent) was unable to raise the finance so that ZCCM could "go it alone." Second, the government began discussions with Anglo-American Corporation to find a solution for moving ahead.[92] Anglo-American indicated that it was interested in developing Konkola Deep if ZCCM were not involved.

The Rothschild Report (RR): The inability of the ZCCM's management to revive the company's fortunes through measures incorporated in the ISTP, and the unwillingness of international lenders to provide the resources to develop Konkola Deep left ZCCM in a precarious position. The government's rejection of the KR increasingly came to be seen, both locally and abroad, as the blunder that it was. The World Bank mining mission in late 1994 had recommended immediate action to improve ZCCM's operations. Several donors, most prominently the British, had urged Zambia to cut its losses by disposing of the mines. An increasing number of donors made their aid conditional on "prompt" action to achieve this objective. Thus, Zambia's leaders were under intense pressure to act. In response, they advertised for experts to report on ZCCM's present financial state and options for privatizing the mines. In late September 1995, Rothschild & Son, a merchant bank, was contracted by the government to "prepare a privatization plan for ZCCM." The consultants delivered the draft report labeled "strictly private and confidential" in April 1996. Copies of the report were soon circulating in Zambia.

In substance, the RR was the KR three years later. The report made the same points about ZCCM's situation.[93] It was a high cost producer—by that time, one of the world's highest. It was heavily in debt and generally cut off from in-

---

91. The author sat through many meetings in which ZCCM outlined its plans for financing KDMP. The discussion had a surreal quality. No one sought to place the $600 million that ZCCM was attempting to borrow in context. At the same time, the government was in the process of having approximately $3.5 billion in arrears written off and written down through the Paris Club and refinanced under an IMF ESAF. It was also in the process of soliciting a grant from donors to organize a debt buy-back of $650 million in commercial debt that could not be serviced. Recognizing Zambia's inability to service debt, many of the major donors had converted all of Zambia's outstanding loans to grants. Germany alone, for example, had written off $650 million. (Chapter 9 covers these details.)

92. The specific points are in the Rothschild Report (1996, Ch.7).

93. RR 1996, pp. 5–11.

ternational finance. Output of both copper and cobalt were falling. As shown above, it had been heavily taxed. Its labor productivity was exceedingly low relative to other large copper companies. And its near-term prospects were poor.

The RR provided a detailed review of the key issues facing ZCCM. Some of these included legal questions related to its break-up and sale, reassignment of its debt, the immediate problems of cutting operating costs, reducing the work force, engaging potential international investors, and dealing with noncore assets.

The consultants reported that no potential buyer was interested in ZCCM as a whole and no potential investor would provide large amounts of cash up-front. There were too many redundant assets and, given the government's start-stop approach to economic reform, taking such a high profile in Zambia was politically risky. Many potential investors were concerned about ZCCM's chronic overmanning and the likely costs of bringing the mines into conformity with international environmental standards. The consultants recommended that ZCCM be unbundled. One scenario was to split the company into five parts with four devoted to mining and the fifth to power distribution.[94]

The completion of the RR and ZCCM's deteriorating financial position forced the government's hand. At a cabinet meeting in late May 1996, the report was accepted. The government agreed that ZCCM would be unbundled and sold. A press release from the minister of finance stated:[95]

Cabinet has accepted the recommendations of the Rothschild's Report on the Privatisation of ZCCM. The Report that has been accepted recommends a two stage privatisation:
- In stage I, substantial majority interests in all of ZCCM's assets would be offered in a number of separate packages to mining companies and other trade investors, with the intention of leaving ZCCM as the owner of minority interests in operating companies controlled and managed by the incoming investors;
- In stage II, the Government will dispose of all, or a substantial part of its shareholding in ZCCM with these shares being offered for sale to the Zambian public as well as financial institutions in Zambia and overseas.

The press release noted that Stage I would be completed in the second half of 1997 and Stage II "in the first half of 1998."

---

94. RR 1996, p.xvi and Chs 13, 14.
95. Press Release *Privatisation of Zambia Consolidated Copper Mines Ltd.(ZCCM)* by R.D.S. Penza MP, minister of finance May 28,1996.

Selling ZCCM: The cabinet decision, though belated, proved to be the easy part. Stage I began and several asset bundles were sold, though less transparently than outside observers had been led to believe by the government. Major interest began to settle on a group, the Kafue Consortium consisting of Avmin Ltd, Commonwealth Development Corporation, Noranda Mining and Exploration Inc., and Phelps Dodge Mining Company.[96] The consortium, launched on February 14, 1997, submitted a bid on February 28, 1997 for Nchanga and Nkana divisions, the Chambishi cobalt plant, and the Chingola refractory ore piles. After much discussion and many false starts, negotiations collapsed in mid-1998.[97] With ZCCM in dire financial condition, having lost K468.1 billion (roughly $294.7 million) in 1997–98 and facing larger losses in 1998–99, the government turned to Anglo-American. That deal was completed in March 2000.

Overview: The failure of the MMD government to quickly resolve the problems of ZCCM profoundly damaged the Zambian economy.[98] Government dithering lowered Zambia's real income, raised the national debt, and prevented the economy from beginning to return to a sustainable growth path. There were many pressures not to reform the mining sector. ZIMCO and ZCCM's managers objected. Key members of Zambia's leadership, including the president, objected. None of this was from lack of advice. Many sensible suggestions were overruled or ignored. The only mining specialist in the government, Dr. Mathias Mpande, deputy minister for mines and minerals, was fired for advocating that the KR be adopted and the mines be unbundled and sold. The RR added little of substance to what was already in the KR. Its contents completely vindicated Dr. Mpande. That, however, was too late to save Zambia from incurring costs of billions of dollars in the form of additional debt, lost output, deflected investment, and foreign aid withheld by the donors.

It is unclear how long it will take to repair the economic damage created by ZCCM's demise. Much will depend on the steps taken by government to cre-

---

96. *The Kafue Consortium* Graphicor 13835, Hortors Print, 1997.

97. Writing just before the deal fell through, *The Economist* (May 9, 1998, p.50) pointed out that the Kafue Consortium had offered $130 million in cash, $75 million in debt assumption, and a commitment to invest $500 million in rehabilitation and expansion. The deal with Anglo American was significantly less generous.

98. Van der Heijden (2000) argued that the failure of the government to dispose of ZCCM in a timely manner was its principal weakness. I take a broader view. The delay in selling ZCCM caused serious economic damage but as the main text and other chapters in this volume show, there were other problems. For instance, the government's continued interference in agriculture undermined welfare and intensified poverty independently of ZCCM's demise.

ate and sustain a setting that stimulates the necessary investment. The manipulation of the exchange rate in the opening months of 2001 was not constructive. Such distortions have to be avoided, though Zambia's historical record is not promising on this score.

6. Concluding Comments

The preceding analysis makes two points. First, agriculture and mining have been performing significantly below their potential in Zambia. Second, any program for future growth and development will hinge on the government's success in creating the conditions needed to revive both sectors. Little can be done about long-term poverty and unemployment without the revitalization of agriculture. And little of consequence can emerge from efforts to stimulate investment, raise incomes, generate wealth, and provide the government with a growing (direct and indirect) source of revenue unless the mining sector regains its former dynamism. Zambia is unlikely to ever become a world-scale copper producer with output approaching one million tons per year (the goal of the Second National Development Plan, 1972–1976). However, it could be a significant producer once more. It has some of the richest copper deposits in the world. The technology for efficiently extracting and processing the ore is available. What has not existed so far has been a policy setting that encourages local and foreign investors to take the risks needed to rehabilitate the sector and expand its capacity. The changes currently underway represent a start in this direction. The "enabling environment" that the MMD undertook to create in its 1991 *Manifesto* has yet to materialize.

A similar conclusion applies to agriculture. Food security remains tenuous as farmers face government-induced market uncertainties. Zambians have had the worst of both worlds. On the one hand, the government does not have the resources to finance the investment and subsidies required to make a state-directed agricultural sector viable. On the other hand, the government does not have enough faith that private operators will respond appropriately if it stops interfering in agricultural markets. To date, the government's interference has not guaranteed food security or raised farmer's incomes. It has, however, deterred producers from taking the decisions required to revitalize the sector.

Will these circumstances change? The mining sector is now in private hands and production costs have declined sharply. New investment is needed to expand the capacity of the mines. With unprecedented levels of poverty and chronic hunger throughout the rural areas, agriculture needs a new direction.

Many of Zambia's present problems in mining and agriculture were avoidable. The basic program for reforming both sectors was set out in the government's 1984 study "Restructuring in the Midst of Crisis." Neither UNIP nor MMD would implement the needed reforms. If agriculture and mining, and ultimately the whole economy, are to prosper, that has to change.

11

A Small Econometric Model of the Zambian Economy

MALCOLM F. MCPHERSON AND TZVETANA S. RAKOVSKI

1. Introduction

This chapter presents a small econometric model of the Zambian economy and discusses its implications. Our objectives are to illustrate empirically some of the main economic trends in Zambia over the last three decades, to draw attention to the connections among key macroeconomic variables, and to provide a basis for making projections about future directions of the economy. The exercise is part of our broader attempt to identify the policies needed to move the Zambian economy towards a path of rapid, sustained growth and development.[1]

We have arranged the chapter as follows. Section 2 gives a brief overview of the Zambian economy from a modeling perspective. Section 3 introduces the model, explains its structure, and reviews the results. Section 4 provides the projection results and discusses possible extensions to the model. Section 5 has concluding comments. There are five appendices. Appendix A has graphs of key macroeconomic series over the period 1967 to 1997. Appendix B defines the variables used in the model and lists the data sources. Appendix C has a brief overview of macroeconomic policy models. Appendix D suggests how the econometric model can be linked to a financial programming framework. Finally, Appendix E uses the basic model to examine aspects of the impact of HIV/AIDS on economic growth.

---

1. This chapter first appeared as an HIID *Development Discussion Paper* no. 672, January 1999. Initial research on this topic was conducted under the "Restarting and Sustaining Growth and Development in Africa" component of the Equity and Growth through Economic Research (EAGER/Public Strategies for Growth with Equity) project supported by USAID.

2. HISTORICAL BACKGROUND

There is now a rich literature on the Zambian economy.[2] Until the mid-1970s, contributions focused on the factors responsible for Zambia's economic progress and the challenges faced by the government as it sought to foster economic development by extending its intervention in the economy. From the mid-1970s onwards, the emphasis shifted to the policies and actions needed to arrest and reverse Zambia's economic decline. From the mid-1980s, most discussions have stressed how Zambia's policies would have to change for the economy to revive.

The broad economic trends in Zambia over the last three decades can be measured in a variety of ways. It is convenient to use the databases of the World Bank, International Monetary Fund (IMF), and the United Nations Development Programme (UNDP). These data are readily available and provide a rich and reliable source of historical and current information.[3] Although some biases and errors are inevitable,[4] the underlying trends have been fully consistent with the economy's actual performance.

The data show that Zambia has become highly indebted, undergone rapid inflation, experienced a profound reduction in copper production, had wide fluctuations in agricultural output with an overall decline in per capita food production, and recorded no substantial increase in formal sector employment for more than two decades. What the data do not reveal is the broad-based shift of economic activity into informal activities as individuals and businesses sought to protect themselves from the costs and distortions associated with pervasive state intervention. The data also do not reveal the

---

2. Some of the scholarly work includes Baldwin (1965), ILO (1969), de Gaay Fortman (1969), Faber and Potter (1971), Bostock and Elliott (1972), Martin (1972), Harvey (1972), Bates (1974), Seidman (1974), Sklar (1975), Markakis and Curry (1976), Dodge (1977), McPherson (1980), Kayizzi-Mugerwa (1988), SIDA (1989), Gulhati (1989), Seshamani (1990), Mwanakatwe (1990), Bates and Collier (1993), McPherson (1995). There are also several comprehensive World Bank studies (World Bank 1977, 1981, 1993, 1995) and some noteworthy Government of Zambia reports (GRZ 1984, 1989, 1992).

3. The key sources are the *International Financial Statistics (IMF)*, *World Development Indicators*, the *Human Development Indicators* and *African Development Indicators (World Bank)*. All of these are available on CD-ROM and most can be retrieved from the internet.

4. An obvious bias shows up in the growth rate of real GDP. As an economy regresses, the rate of collapse tends to be over-stated as activities shift into informal or "unrecorded" activities. The basic reason is that asset-holders and entrepreneurs take steps to insulate their activities and assets from disruption and uncertainty. During periods of recovery, the expansion of real GDP tends to be over-stated as increasing amounts of informal sector activity begin to be recorded.

resources transferred abroad through capital flight[5] or the investment (both local and foreign) foregone because of counterproductive government policies.

In Appendix A, we provide graphs of the major macroeconomic variables in Zambia over the period 1970 to 1998. Figure 11–1 shows the path of the real GDP per capita. There has been no sustained increase in per capita real income since the early 1970s. With population growth of around 3 percent per annum, real per capita income has declined by more than 50 percent over the last twenty-five years. Figure 11–2 plots the annual rate of inflation. Inflation accelerated sharply around 1988. This coincided with the introduction of the government's own program "growth from own resources."[6] The rate of inflation rose because Zambia had too few of its "own resources" relative to the government's expenditure plans. Figure 11–3 shows that as the rate of inflation increased the nominal value of the Kwacha depreciated markedly. By contrast, since 1988, the real exchange rate, shown in Figure 11–4, has tended to appreciate. That is, the rate of depreciation of the nominal exchange rate, though large, has been less than the rate of domestic inflation. With an appreciating real exchange rate, Zambia's ability to compete abroad has suffered.[7] The appreciation of the real exchange rate also explains why Zambia has continued to run large balance of payments deficits. The basic implication, however, is that the Zambian economy has still not adjusted to the sharp decline in *national* productivity as the copper sector become progressively more inef-

---

5. As noted in Chapter 2, the amounts of resources transferred abroad from Zambia have been large—on the order of $12 to 15 billion over the period from the mid-1970s to the early 1990s.

6. Kayizzi-Mugerwa 1990.

7. Some commentators point to the rapid growth of non-traditional exports (NTE) over the last several years to suggest that the real exchange rate has not been over-valued. In relative terms, these activities have been exceedingly successful. In assessing this performance, however, three points should be noted. First, given the small size of NTE's before the government began to liberalize the trade and exchange rate system, there has been a period of "catch-up" growth. Second, many of the NTE's are produced in "enclaves" in Zambia, which have only limited contact with the local economy. And third, most exporters in the sector operate in dollars (or some foreign exchange equivalent) as a means of insulating themselves from local disruptions. None of these points detract from the performance of the NTEs whose dollar value increased by 162 percent between 1990 and 1997 (IMF May, 1999, Table 21). During that period they were the most dynamic aspect of the whole economy. Yet, since 1997, NTE's have generally declined, by 2.5 percent in 1998 (*ibid.*) and by 8 percent in 1999 *Budget Speech* 2000, par. 45). While policy makers in Zambia such as the minister of finance have attributed the decline to external effects such as disruptions in Asia (*ibid.*), the persistent overvaluation of the real exchange rate beginning in 1996:II (IMF May 1999, Table 26) was a factor.

ficient from the mid-1970s onwards.[8] Nevertheless, the economy has continued to adjust (not in the way preferred by the government or donors)
through the continued collapse in real income.[9]

Figures 11–5 and 11–6, respectively, show the annual changes (in real
terms) in mining and agricultural production. These series have fluctuated
widely. When measured in per capita terms, both copper production and agricultural output have fallen steeply.

Figure 11–7 traces foreign aid flows over time. The increase during the
1990s reflects the surge in aid that accompanied the return of multi-party democracy. The blip in 1995 was the result of the completion of the IMF's
RAP.[10] This program gave Zambia access to IMF funding through an ESAF
that refinanced Zambia's arrears to the Fund.[11] It is illuminating to juxtapose
the rise in foreign aid since the mid-1970s against Zambia's growth performance (Figure 11–1). When Zambia was an international creditor, it grew
relatively rapidly. As an aid recipient, Zambia has regressed.[12]

Figure 11–8 plots the annual changes in broad money. Many of Zambia's
economic troubles (rapid inflation, a depreciating exchange rate, declining

---

8. Trends in the inflation-adjusted price of copper show that the real export price of copper
fell sharply during the 1970s and has never fully recovered. The reasons have been discussed in
Chapters 2 and 10.

9. Some form of adjustment always occurs. For developed countries that maintain overvalued real exchange rates for extended periods such as the United Kingdom (from the end of
WWII to 1970), and many European Union countries (before the introduction of the *euro*) the
adjustment comes though a low growth rate. For developing countries, such as Zambia which
have resisted reform, the effects of chronically overvalued exchange rates show up in an absolute decline in income.

10. The three-year ESAF expired in December 1998 without Zambia having successfully
completed one of several formal performance reviews. Undaunted by that experience, the IMF
re-introduced a second ESAF in March 1999 (IMF March 1999). That, too, collapsed within
months (see Chapter 15).

11. As noted in Chapter 2, Zambia's economic difficulties led to the accumulation of large
external arrears. By the early 1990s, its arrears to the IMF exceeded $1.2 billion. Since the IMF
does not reschedule its debts, a mechanism was created to allow the *de facto* rescheduling
through a complicated and drawn-out refinancing. Under the RAP, Zambia could earn the
"right" to repay its arrears using concessionary finance from the IMF under an ESAF arrangement. As described in Chapter 3, after a number of delays, Zambia completed the RAP in December 1995. At that point its arrears were transformed into a concessional credit.

12. An earlier contribution by HIID's team in Zambia (Fernholz *et al.* 1996) argued that the
degree to which Zambia depends on foreign aid had serious adverse effects on the quality of
economic management. (This point is also made in Chapter 14.) For its part, the government
has also recognized that aid created some serious problems (MMD *Manifesto '96*, page 7).
This, however, had no substantive effect on government behavior. The budgets of 1998, 1999,
and 2000 were consistent only if more than 35 percent of the expenditures included in them
were financed by the donor community (see Chapter 3).

real income, excessive debt, and macroeconomic instability) can be traced to movements in this series. The growth of broad money is directly linked to changes in reserve money which is a key policy variable. The government's lack of control over reserve money has created major economic damage.[13]

Figure 11–9 highlights the principal "cause" of the rapid growth of reserve money, namely budget deficits. Since 1975, these deficits have been large. In some years (1975, 1986 and 1991) the deficit exceeded 20 percent of GDP. Persistent deficits of this magnitude have only one source, irresponsible macroeconomic management.

Figure 11–10 shows the increase in Zambia's external debt. Support from the international community of almost $6 billion between 1992 and 1998 made little impression on the debt stock. The problem has been that Zambia continues to run a large balance of payments current account deficit.[14] While this deficit persists, Zambia's debt problem cannot be resolved even if its debts are written off, written down, or forgiven. Certainly any debt relief that Zambia may gain under HIPC (the Highly Indebted Poor Country initiative) will be quickly dissipated if the country's balance of payments deficit continues.[15]

The last two figures (11–11 and 11–12) are, respectively, the world copper and maize prices. Both are in nominal terms. Adjusting them for inflation would show that both series have declined. These trends are indicative of broader movements in other resource prices. Due to technical innovation and shifting patterns of demand and supply, the upward trend in the real price of all commodities evident in the 1970s has been reversed. Zambia has directly lost real income through the decline in copper prices. The severity of this particular "shock" has been substantially modified by changes in other prices.[16]

Taken together, these data summarize Zambia's major macroeconomic problems: stagnating real per capita income, large budget deficits, rapid monetary growth, chronic balance of payments deficits, declining per capita

---

13. The monetary mismanagement in Zambia has been common to other countries. Writing in 1919, Keynes noted:

There is no subtler, no surer means of overturning the existing basis of Society than to debauch the currency. The process engages all the hidden forces of economic law on the side of destruction. . . (Keynes 1963 p. 78.)

14. In technical terms, Zambia continues to "absorb" more real resources than it generates.

15. That appears to be the case. The HIPC 'decision point' document (IMF/IDA 2000, Table 8) shows that the balance of payments current account deficit for 1998 to 2000 averaged 15.7 percent of GDP. For 2001 and 2002, this deficit is expected to average 13 percent of GDP.

16. Even with the surge in oil prices in 1999 and 2000, they remain well below the real levels of 1979 at the peak of the oil crisis. The real costs of computers, communication technology, and international transport (to name some obvious cases) have fallen dramatically as well.

real output in mining and agriculture, high rates of inflation, and an appreciating real exchange rate. None of the major trends has been favorable. As the data show, when improvements have occurred they have been sporadic and, thus far, not sustained. Even the positive effects of the decline in the budget deficit over the last several years have been offset by the negative effects of large balance of payments deficits, sharply increased external debt due to ZCCM's losses, and the liquidity crunch created by ZCCM's arrears.[17] Similarly, while inflation has fallen from the three-digit rates of the early 1990s, it has still been well above comparable world inflation rates.[18]

The main policy question facing Zambia is what measures need to be taken to deal with these constraints so as to enable the economy to move forward. The results of the econometric model reported below provide us with a better appreciation of the inter-connections within the economy. From this we can highlight some of the potential changes that would help promote and sustain growth and development.

3. THE MODEL

Why a Model?

Economic modeling is a rich field of study. Many models of the Zambian economy have now been constructed. One of the first was the "modified input-output" framework formulated by Dudley Seers to complement the work of the UN/ECA/FAO mission to Zambia in 1964. A number of scholars have taken advantage of the excellent set of input-output tables produced in Zambia from 1969 onwards. One noteworthy effort was Charles Blitzer's dynamic simulation model, a precursor to computable general equilibrium (CGE) models.[19] A group sponsored by the European Union has worked for several years to construct a CGE model for Zambia.[20] Other efforts have involved simulation techniques and input-output analysis.[21] Finally, as longer

---

17. The *National Mirror* of June 21–27, 1998 had a front page headline "ZCCM bleeding Zambia" which stated that ZCCM's losses were in the order of K2 billion per day (more than $1 million at the prevailing exchange rate). This datum was consistent with an article in the *Economist* (May 1998) on Zambia's economic troubles. Those losses subsequently intensified. These are discussed in Chapter 10.

18. *World Economic Outlook* October 1998: Table 8, p. 182. These data show that Africa's inflation has been high by world standards. With inflation in the industrial countries below 3 percent per annum since 1994, continued high rates of inflation in Africa erode its international competitiveness.

19. The model is included in volume 4 of World Bank (1977).

20. The group was organized by Christopher Adam of Oxford University.

21. Kayizzi-Muzerwa 1988; Mwanawina 1995.

time series have been assembled, models have sought to combine econometric estimation with input-output techniques.[22]

With so many models available, there is no need to build a model of the Zambia economy from "scratch." Indeed, the model discussed below has been adapted from a well-known equation system.[23] Though small and simple, this model is tractable and relevant. One of its advantages, discussed below, is that it can be directly linked to the standard financial programming framework used by the IMF.

But, why bother with an econometric model? Aren't the main linkages in the Zambian economy obvious? Aren't the principal problems with the economy clear? And, hasn't the performance of the last two decades been so uncharacteristic of Zambia's potential that a formal model could not possibly yield meaningful projections? These questions can be answered in several ways.

Much can be learned about an economy without a formal model. Yet, intuition and casual inspection of time series do not reveal either the strength or direction of the various inter-connections. Statistical estimation of the key macroeconomic relations adds another dimension to the analysis. Formal statistical analysis is the only way to determine the partial correlation, lead-lag relationships, causality, simultaneity, and any feedback that may exist among a number of variables. There are so many inter-connections associated with the behavior of individuals and firms that a formal model is required if only to retain consistency and coherence in the analysis. This behavior reflects the fact that:

- Consumers and producers always face varying opportunities for substitution (both directly and indirectly) among products, factors and services;
- There are transaction costs and market "frictions" (such as agency and menu costs), which consumers and producers encounter as they exercise their market and portfolio choices;
- Competitive pressures differ across sectors and markets;
- Asymmetries exist in the access to information by consumers and producers and their ability to interpret this information;
- The impact of government interventions vary across different groups;

---

22. An example is given in McPherson (1980). That study highlighted the links between employment and growth using a 30-sector input-output decomposition analysis and a seven sector econometric model. It used the World Bank's BSIMULO-X program to derive projections. An interesting footnote is that this model, which covered the period up until 1979, projected major declines during the 1980s in output and employment in the base run scenario of "no policy change." As it turned out, Zambia made few significant adjustments to its economic policies for more than a decade. This led to sharp declines in output and employment, just as the model predicted.

23. Porter and Ranney 1982; Chand 1989; Khan and Knight 1991.

- Consumers and producers have different attitudes to risk;
- The potential rewards of market search differ across consumer and producer groups; and
- The relative attractiveness of international transactions (including capital flight) varies over time.

Other considerations are relevant as well. All economic systems experience positive and negative shocks that reverberate at different rates across sectors and among individuals and firms. Public goods influence the ability of different groups to engage in welfare-enhancing and productive activities. Wide differences exist in the efficiency, prudence and effectiveness with which governments manage the economy. Finally, all economies have links of differing intensity and direction to the world economy. These links, in turn, have their own sets of "knock-on" and "spillover" effects within the domestic economy.[24]

While many of these theoretical points highlight the potential value of using a model, the main practical consideration is whether the estimated model can provide any results relevant to policy. There are two issues. First, in a developing country such as Zambia, which has undergone severe economic disruption, a model may be ill-conditioned. Small changes in specification or lag structure might lead to large changes in the size and direction of key parameters.[25] This outcome can be interpreted in two ways. One is that the model itself is not properly specified. The other is that the ill-conditioned model and its erratic behavior is a valid representation of the unstable nature of the economy. As the data in Appendix A show, most of the major aggregates have fluctuated widely over the last three decades. A major reason has been the lack of consistency and coherence in economic policy and management.[26] An ill-conditioned model may be reflecting this behavior. Properly interpreted, it points to the need for policy reforms that would remove imbalances and return the economy to a stable, sustainable, growth trajectory.

---

24. Many of these spillovers and knock-on effects are the result of growing interdependence and connections created by the globalization of financial, product, factor, and asset markets. The dynamics of many of these linkages have yet to be fully explored (Sachs 1998, Rodrik 1998, Obstfeld 1998.)

25. In technical terms, the system's likelihood function is 'flat.'

26. The lack of consistency and policy reversals in Zambia have been widely documented. A sample of the literature includes: Dresang 1975; Tordoff 1977; ILO 1977; Baylies 1980; McPherson 1980; Mwaipaya 1980; Szeftel 1982; World Bank 1984a, 1986a, 1991a, 1992; Zuckerman 1986; Wulf 1989; Harber 1989; Callaghy 1990; Fardi 1991; Kelley 1991; Economist 1991; West 1992; Bates and Collier 1992; Price Waterhouse 1996; Kasanga 1996, and Hill and McPherson 1998. The last mentioned paper forms the basis for Chapter 15.

Second, in Zambia (as in many other developing countries), prices, exchange rates and interest rates were controlled for much of the period being examined (1967 to 1998). These controls imposed rigidities on the economy that have tended to produce some theoretically unexpected associations. These considerations do not invalidate the use of a simultaneous equations model like the one in this chapter. Such a model is a useful way of capturing (and attempting to measure) the consequences of the controls via their "spillover" effects on the variables that have not been controlled. This is also one way of tracing the (often perverse) trends in the government budget deficit, the balance of payments deficit, the growth of money supply, flows of foreign assistance, changes in imports, and the increase in external debt. Due to the effects of controls, some of the important relationships run contrary to theory. While this can be disturbing, such results cannot be rejected out of hand.[27] They reflect the outcome of all the interactions within the specified system.

Specification of the Model

In constructing the model, we treat Zambia as a small, open developing country, which is exposed to world market fluctuations. The estimated model consists of seven behavioral equations and three accounting identities. Though its structure is simple, the model captures some of the key features of the Zambian economy. In specifying the equations, we have combined theory and institutional considerations.[29] The final version of each equation reported here was obtained after some experimentation with different variables and lag structures. Those not statistically significant were dropped.

Based on the definitions in Appendix B, the model has the following equations.[28]

1. Inflation

$$\Delta p_t = f_1 [\Delta yr_t, \Delta m_t, \Delta e_t, \Delta p_t^f, \Delta p_{t-1}]$$

2. Real Income

$$\Delta yr_t = f_2 [\Delta er_t, \Delta p_t, \Delta min_t, \Delta agr_t, \Delta aid_t]$$

---

27. McPherson and Zinnes (1992) show that economic regression, though the result of inconsistent policies, is a highly systematic process.

28. As noted in Appendix B, lower-case letters denote the logarithm of the upper-case variables.

29. Sources include: McPherson 1980; IMF 1981; Porter and Ranney 1982; SIDA 1989; Chand 1989; Goodhart 1989; Khan and Knight 1991; Rajcoomar *et al.* 1996.

3. Exchange Rate

$$\Delta e_t = f_3 [\Delta m_{t-1}, \Delta p_{t-1}, \Delta i_t, \Delta aid_t]$$

4. Government Revenue

$$t_t = f_4 [y_t, min_t, im_t, aid_t, p_t^{copper}]$$

5. Imports

$$im_t = f_5 [y_t, e_t, aid_{t-1}, im_{t-1}]$$

6. Agricultural Production

$$\Delta agr_t = f_6 [\Delta yr_t, \Delta er_{t-1}, \Delta p_{t-1}^{maize}, rain_t]$$

7. Mining Production

$$\Delta min_t = f_7 [\Delta yr_t, \Delta er_{t-1}, \Delta im_t, \Delta p_{t-1}^{copper}]$$

8. Money Supply

$$\Delta M_t^S = \Delta DC_t + \Delta NFA_t$$

9. Balance of Payments

$$\Delta NFA_t = EX_t - IM_t + CAP_t + AID_t$$

10. Domestic Credit

$$\Delta DC_t = G_t - T_t + \Delta CP_t$$

Inflation: The inflation equation relates the rate of change in the domestic price level to the increase in money supply, the growth of real GDP, the change in the nominal exchange rate, the change in foreign prices, and the lagged inflation rate. These variables are consistent with the standard approach to the demand for money. (The inflation equation is an inverted money demand equation.) The addition of foreign prices, approximated by U.S. consumer prices, and the exchange rate help measure the influence of external events on domestic prices.

Real Income: The growth of real income depends on changes in the real exchange rate and inflation, the growth of output in mining and agriculture, and the change in foreign aid. The equation is a composite of theory and structural variables. In theory, the growth of real income should be related to the growth of factors of production (labor and capital) and variables that capture changes in factor productivity (technology, information, and organization). Some theories also link income growth and the growth of the real money supply. We tried this particular relationship without success. Movements in the exchange rate reflect Zambia's comparative advantage and, indirectly, overall productivity. Finally, the inclusion of foreign aid is an attempt to measure the degree to which aid might compensate for the decline in real income or, by supplementing investment, boost economic growth.

Exchange Rate: The nominal exchange rate equation includes the changes in the money supply, a measure of expected inflation, the change in domestic interest rates, and foreign aid. Apart from foreign aid, which tends to appreciate the exchange rate,[30] the other variables are consistent with standard treatments of exchange rate determination derived from purchasing power parity, interest rate parity, and the monetary theory of the balance of payments. The income variable proved to be statistically insignificant and was excluded from the final version of the equation. The correct term for interest rates should be some measure of the difference between domestic and foreign interest rates. The former were so large and movements so sharp, that they dominated the relation. The intention, however, is to capture the portfolio effects of varying incentives to hold local assets.

Government Revenue: Government revenue is related to the main elements of the tax base—aggregate income, mining production, and imports. Copper prices are included to measure the changes in the value of the export tax base. Aid flows are included for two reasons. Aid adds to total expenditure thereby contributing indirectly to revenue. Aid also tends to change (mainly reduce) the incentive for the government to raise resources domestically.[31]

Imports: Imports are related to income, the exchange rate, lagged aid flows, and lagged imports. Income is a measure of real demand, exchange

---

30. Nyoni (1998) tested the impact of foreign aid in Tanzania on the real exchange rate. Over the period he considered (1970–93) there was a weak positive relation between aid flows and real exchange rate, implying that foreign aid helped to depreciate the exchange rate. The results in Zambia's case differ from these.

31. This may be one reason why foreign aid could be associated with a depreciating exchange rate. By paying fewer taxes, private individuals have higher consumption expenditure. The spillover to imports (and the balance of payments) depreciates the exchange rate.

rates measure the relative costs of tradable goods and services, and the aid variable captures the extent to which foreign assistance raises imports by easing the foreign exchange constraint. (In preliminary runs, we included exports to measure the same effect but their impact was statistically insignificant.) The inclusion of lagged imports is an attempt to measure the delays due to Zambia's distance from major trading centers.[32]

Agriculture: The growth in agricultural output is related to the growth of total income, the change in the real exchange rate, the change in the foreign price of maize, and a variable accounting for rainfall. Aid flows were initially included because of the long history of foreign support to Zambian agriculture. They were statistically insignificant.

Mining Production: The growth of mining output depends upon the growth of aggregate real income, the real exchange rate, imports, and changes in copper prices. The real income variable is meant to capture the linkages of mining to the rest of the economy. The real exchange rate reflects the movements in productivity in Zambia relative to the rest of the world. Imports are included to capture the dependence of mining on key imports, such as machinery, equipment, fuel, and spare parts. The copper price is intended to measure shifts in the relative profitability of mining.

The Identities: The identities impose limits and consistency on key variables and provide closure to the model. The change in money supply is the sum of the change in the net foreign assets and change in net domestic credit. The balance of payments (reflected in the change in net foreign assets of the banking system) is the sum of the trade balance and capital flows including foreign aid. Domestic credit consists of its public and private components. The former captures the effects on the banking system of financing of the budget.

Issues Related to Model Estimation

Statistical methods for estimating simultaneous equations systems capture the mutual dependence among the variables in the model.[33] For the Zambia model, we used Three Stages Least Squares (3SLS). This is a full information

---

32. Students of Zambia's economic history fully appreciated the role of distance in Zambia's development (Robinson 1932; UN/ECA/FAO 1964; Baldwin 1966; Bostock and Harvey 1972). More recently, Sachs and others have argued that Africa's geographical isolation is a barrier to growth (Sachs 1996; Sachs and Warner 1997; Bloom and Sachs 1998). Curiously, when Zambia had prudent macroeconomic policies, isolation did not prevent the economy from growing rapidly.

33. Greene (1993, Ch.16) has a useful treatment of the basic theory.

technique. It uses all the information in the variables including their linkages across equations.

Simultaneous equation methods have several well-known limitations. The classification of variables as exogenous (explained "outside" the model) and endogenous (explained within the model) is subjective. The identifying restrictions (variables excluded from some equations so that parameters might be estimated uniquely) may lead to economically relevant variables being dropped from some equations. The system parameters are assumed to be independent of changes that would make them subject to the Lucas critique.[34] Finally, tractability requires that the system be relatively simple. Otherwise, it takes on the features of a "black box."

The Estimation Results

The 3SLS estimates of the parameters of the model follow. Single and double asterixes denote statistical significance at 0.05 and 0.01.

Dependent Variable: Inflation Rate

Variable	Coefficient	Std. Error	t-Statistics
Constant	-0.05	0.09	-0.63
Δyr_t	0.65	0.73	0.89
Δm_t	0.44	0.19	2.26*
Δe_t	0.27	0.09	3.20**
Δp_t^f	0.61	1.07	0.57
Δp_{t-1}	0.40	0.14	2.80*

Dependent Variable: Real Income Growth

Variable	Coefficient	Std. Error	t-Statistics
Constant	0.02	0.01	3.03**
Δer_t	-0.02	0.02	-0.95
Δp_t	-0.01	0.02	-0.49
Δmin_t	0.18	0.07	2.52*
Δagr_t	0.18	0.05	3.96**
Δaid_t	-0.02	0.01	-1.34

Dependent Variable: Change in Exchange Rate

Variable	Coefficient	Std. Error	t-Statistics
Constant	-0.01	0.11	-0.08
Δm_{t-1}	0.51	0.50	1.01
Δp_{t-1}	0.24	0.38	0.61
Δi_t	0.56	0.19	2.92**
Δaid_t	0.14	0.15	0.89

---

34. Appendix C has more detail on the Lucas Critique and the context in which it applies.

Dependent Variable: Government Revenue

Variable	Coefficient	Std. Error	t-Statistics
Constant	−5.12	2.33	−2.20*
y_t	0.38	0.16	2.45*
im_t	0.60	0.17	3.64**
aid_t	−0.09	0.04	−2.27*
min_t	0.53	0.47	1.13
p_t^{copper}	0.28	0.13	2.09*

Dependent Variable: Imports

Variable	Coefficient	Std. Error	t-Statistics
Constant	−1.92	0.94	−2.03
y_t	0.38	0.16	2.32*
e_t	0.23	0.09	2.59*
aid_{t-1}	0.03	0.04	0.70
im_{t-1}	0.38	0.11	3.34**

Dependent Variable: Growth in Agricultural Production

Variable	Coefficient	Std. Error	t-Statistics
Constant	−0.02	0.04	−0.41
Δyr_t	1.84	0.58	3.16**
Δer_{t-1}	−0.02	0.08	−0.21
Δp_{t-1}^{maize}	−0.003	0.11	−0.03
$rain_t$	−0.003	0.01	−0.50

Dependent Variable: Growth in Mining Production

Variable	Coefficient	Std. Error	t-Statistics
Constant	−0.02	0.02	−1.13
Δyr_t	1.04	0.42	2.46*
Δer_{t-1}	0.06	0.06	1.11
Δim_t	−0.03	0.05	−0.55
Δp_{t-1}^{copper}	−0.02	0.07	−0.27

Inflation is significantly related to the change in broad money and the nominal exchange rate, and to lagged inflation (a proxy for inflationary expectations). It is weakly related to real income but with the incorrect sign. Foreign inflation, approximated by the changes in the U.S. CPI, has not had a direct significant effect on Zambian inflation. That is, inflation has not been "imported."

The growth of real income is highly dependent on changes in agricultural output and mining production. Income growth is negatively and modestly related to changes in aid flows. Given that Zambia has received around 20 percent of GDP in foreign assistance for the last two and a half decades, the *a priori* expectation is that this relationship would be positive and highly significant. The opposite result supports growing evidence that aid to Zambia has been ineffectual, if not counterproductive. This finding is becoming increasingly common with respect to other developing countries as well.[35]

The lack of any significant statistical relationship between real income growth and the change in the real exchange rate is contrary to expectations. Real exchange rate depreciation is supposed to promote growth, yet in all specifications of this equation that we tested, the sign and the significance of the real exchange rate did not change. There are two explanations. First, the effect of the real exchange rate on growth is typically indirect. By raising the price of tradables relative to non-tradables (i.e., depreciating the real exchange rate) Zambia's policy makers would be creating the conditions that lead to the more efficient allocation of all of the nation's resources. This would then stimulate growth.[36] Second, it is likely that over the period examined the direct relationship between the real exchange rate and income growth was overwhelmed by other factors. Exchange controls were progressively tightened. The ensuing distortions led to currency substitution, capital flight, and a flourishing parallel market for foreign exchange. A further distorting factor was the massive flow of external funds in the form of loans and foreign aid. This resource flow supported activity independently of exchange rate movements.

In the exchange rate equation, the change in the money supply (with one lag) has the expected positive sign though the coefficient is not statistically significant. Neither the lagged nor the contemporaneous value of the change in domestic prices has a statistically significant impact on the nominal ex-

---

35. Berg 1996; Brautigam 1996; HIID 1997; Johnson 1997; World Bank 1998; Alesina and Weder 1999. In a more recent analysis, McPherson and Rakovski (2000) developed a multi-equation model that, among other things, linked foreign aid to income growth via an investment equation. Applying the model to 33 African countries over the period 1970 to 1998, they find that the relations between aid and investment and investment and growth are statistically significant and positive. When aid is directly related to income growth in a single equation, the relationship is statistically insignificant. (This is the same result obtained by Burnside and Dollar (2000).) The links between aid, investment, and growth are included in the model in Appendix E.

36. McPherson and Rakovski (1999) use a simultaneous model applied to panel data for 15 African countries over the period 1970 to 1998 to test the mutual interdependence between trade and growth. Unlike the standard single equation (reduced form) approaches, they find that that growth is a positive and highly significant determinant of trade. Trade, measured as imports plus exports to GDP, is a highly significant determinant of the exchange rate. In turn, the real exchange rate is a highly significant determinant of the growth of real income. The model was re-estimated with data for 33 African countries confirming the earlier results (McPherson and Rakovski 2000a).

change rate. Aid flows are weakly related to the movements in the exchange rate. The positive sign is consistent with the fact that, for economies as distorted and unbalanced as Zambia, aid tends to rise in periods of balance of payments difficulties. A common condition for receiving aid is realignment of the exchange rate. Interest rate movements have a positive and significant effect on the exchange rate. (This result was present in all specifications of the exchange rate equation that we tested.) This finding is also contrary to expectations. Rising interest rates should lead to an appreciation of the exchange rate.[37] The observed relationship, however, could have reflected the fact that rising interest rates reduced the rate of depreciation of the kwacha.

Government revenue is significantly related to income, imports and the copper price. These are all elements of the tax base. The estimated coefficient on foreign aid is negative and significant. This result supports the hypothesis that the availability of foreign assistance diminishes the pressure on the government to raise revenue. As such, it points to a negative effect of foreign assistance, namely, that it undercuts the idea of 'self-help.'[38]

Imports are positively related to nominal income and the exchange rate. The latter result is contrary to theoretical predictions. The implication is that depreciation of the exchange rate leads to an increase in imports. A possible explanation is that the economic disruption over the last two decades has led to significant import compression. Devaluation of the exchange rate is then the counterpart of an increase in foreign assistance designed to ease that compression. The direct effect of aid on imports, however, is positive but not statistically significant.

The results of the equations for the change in agricultural and mining production are noteworthy for their general lack of association with other key variables. They both show a strong connection to the growth of real income. The effect of the change in the real exchange rate in both equations is insignificant. We also tested the direct link between agricultural and mining production, and the world market price (with one lag) of maize and copper, respectively. The estimated coefficients of the two price variables are not statistically significant. The rainfall variable (defined as the absolute deviation from the

37. As illustrated during the financial turmoil in Asia in 1997 and 1998, rising interest rates do not necessarily prevent the exchange rate from depreciating. Moreover, as the authorities in Sweden discovered in 1992 when they pushed overnight interest rates to levels above 500 percent before devaluing the kronor, raising the interest rate can be a sign of panic. This makes devaluation inevitable.

38. Once a common principle of foreign assistance (Kennedy in Gardner 1963; Bell 1966; Orme 1995), the general idea is that countries do not receive support for particular activities until and unless they are prepared to co-finance them. The major donors have not emphasized 'self-help' in Africa for decades.

mean rainfall over the sample period) has the correct negative sign. The coefficient is not statistically significant.

4. PROJECTION RESULTS AND POSSIBLE EXTENSIONS OF THE MODEL

Projections

Using the estimated system of equations above, we calculate the projected values of the endogenous variables for 1998 and 1999. These projections are intended to provide some general guidance about the coherence of the model and its structural parameters. The model, however, will not support long-term projections. The structure of the economy has been changing as the economy goes through periods of reform and policy reversals.[39] For the model to remain relevant for projection purposes, it needs to be regularly re-specified and re-estimated.

We have calculated the projections by presetting future values for the exogenous variables. These are based on the estimates for 1998 and the assumptions used in the 1998 Budget Speech for 1999. The specific values are given in Appendix B.

The forecasts for 1998 and 1999 of the inflation rate, real income growth, agricultural and mining output, the change in exchange rate and the levels of government revenue and imports follow. (The exchange rate is K/$, government revenue and imports in K billions; the remaining data are measured as percent per annum.)

Year	Inflation	Real Income	Import Growth	Exchange Rate
1998	32.9	1.2	57.2	3158.2
1999	38.7	1.4	62.2	4877.5

Year	Agricultural Growth	Mining Growth	Government Revenue
1998	−1.9	−0.3	1408.4
1999	−1.6	1.0	1856.1

The projected values for the inflation rate and real GDP growth are close to the estimated outcome for 1998 (29.3 percent and −2.0 percent respectively). The model underestimates the decline in agricultural production (in real

---

39. More recent evidence provided by McPherson, Hoover, and Snodgrass (2000) and sketched out in Appendix E shows that the structure of the economy has been changing as the HIV/AIDS epidemic has intensified.

terms): an estimated -1.9 percent versus an actual decline of 6.1 percent; and the decline in mining production: projected -1.6% versus the actual of -11.0 percent. A partial explanation for the discrepancy for the mining sector is that the sharp fall in production was due mainly to the uncertainty surrounding the future of ZCCM and the institutional impediments to its privatization that were not reflected in the model. The implication is that ZCCM's large losses and the withdrawal of investment due to the low state of confidence will continue to affect adversely the Zambian economy during 1999 and for some time to come.

The nominal exchange rate is predicted to increase by more than 57 percent in 1998 (amounting to a real devaluation of 27 percent) and the kwacha price of the US dollar will approach 3,200. These numbers are consistent with recent government estimates. The projections for imports and government revenue are also consistent with the preliminary numbers for 1998.

None of the projections is especially optimistic. They show that the economy will continue to decline. This outcome, however, is fully consistent with government's overall ambivalence towards economic reform and its general unwillingness to take the steps needed to return the economy to a sustainable growth path.

Possible Extensions of the Model

The model could be extended in a number of ways. The existing system of equations could be specified in a greater detail so as to provide additional policy relevant projections. To help with context, Appendix C has a brief note on policy modeling.

In specifying the model, we have glossed over issues related to productivity improvements, which provide the basis for long-term increases in real per capita income. This would require some attention to production relations across sectors and trends in unit labor costs. The exchange rate equation could be improved (or made more relevant) by adding the foreign exchange premium, especially for the 1980s. More detail in the government revenue equation would allow policy makers to focus on specific components of the tax base.

Adding endogenous variables would expand the equation system and enhance its explanatory power. Obvious examples are equations for investment, labor demand, specific prices (e.g. for food and fuel), output of sectors such as manufacturing, the demand for financial assets, interest rates, and non-traditional exports. Such an expansion would require additional data. It would also make the model more complex to estimate and interpret.

A third modification would be to connect the econometric model with the financial programming analysis undertaken as part of IMF/World Bank efforts in support of structural adjustment. Appendix D discusses the links from the model to financial programming. The model has several evident links. Some of the key elements of the financial programming exercise, such as inflation, real output, and the exchange rate, are endogenous to the model. Short-term projections of these variables using the model provide a consistent framework for the financial programming exercise.

Finally, the model could be adopted to analyze other relevant policy issues. Appendix E, for example, examines the link between economic growth and HIV/AIDS in Zambia.

5. Concluding Comments

This chapter specifies and estimates a tractable, policy-relevant model of the Zambian economy. The value of such a model for policy makers and their advisors is that it provides a framework for systematically examining the principal economic relationships in the economy, their direction, and statistical significance.

The full-information estimation technique (3SLS) offers a simple, though robust, means of deriving the parameter estimates. Although some results are counterintuitive—the outcome of government controls and distortions created by large aid flows—there are few surprises. For most of the period examined, 1967 to 1998, the real side of the economy performed poorly. Output declined and the economy lacked dynamism. On the monetary side, asset-holders have been responding in a predictable way to the extraordinary expansion of domestic credit to finance the large, persistent, budget deficits. By substituting away from local financial assets, these asset-holders have added to the inflationary pressure.

The results have several implications for policy. Zambia has little chance of returning to a path of rapid, sustained growth and development without fundamental changes that eliminate the budget deficit and sharply depreciate the real exchange rate. A major effort is required to enhance productivity.[40] Some

---

40. Zambia has two attractive options. The first is to revive the copper mines, improve efficiency, and bring their output to levels approaching those achieved in the early 1970s. Recent changes in mining technology and innovations in metal processing allow that to be done. Missing so far in Zambia has been the capital and the honest, skilled managers needed to exploit this opportunity. The second is to take advantage of the livestock/grain connection that linkages to the Asian meat market would provide. Rising productivity in maize and other coarse grain production would benefit local consumers and provide producers with the oppor-

recent changes may be moving the economy in that direction. The overall moderation of monetary growth has been encouraging. Inflation, though higher than most international standards, has been relatively stable.

There is, however, a pressing need for marked improvements in growth in agriculture and mining. As suggested in chapter fourteen, the government should also consider measures that would develop an "aid exit" strategy for Zambia. Such a medium term initiative would focus attention on the appropriate changes needed to generate more investment from local resources.

At present, none of these changes is occurring at the rate required to make a fundamental difference to Zambia's prospects for rapid growth and development. The challenge for policy makers is to make the necessary changes and sustain them.

---

tunity to "finish" livestock for the export market. Missing so far has been the incentives that would raise coarse grain production. Also missing has been the initiative, supported by the necessary investment, to increase the production of the types of beef suited to world markets. With increasing pressure on land and rising income in Asia (despite the recent economic turbulence) there are sound prospects for increasing long-term demand for meat and grain. The challenge for Zambian producers is to determine how (not whether) to become involved.

APPENDIX A: BASIC ECONOMIC DATA

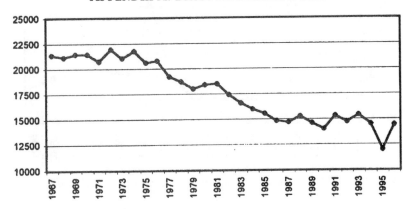

Figure 11-1.   Real GDP per capita (in Kwacha, 1990 prices)

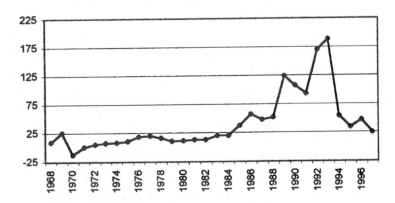

Figure 11-2.   Inflation Rate (percentage change in CPI)

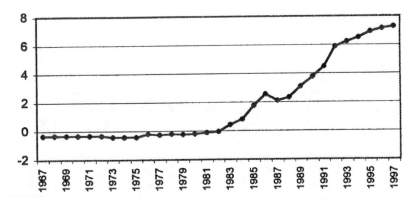

Figure 11-3.   Exchange Rate (in logarithms) Kwacha per US Dollar

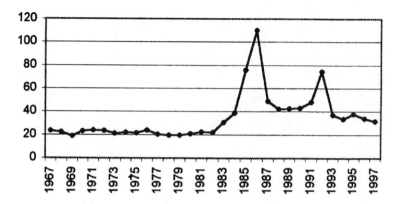

Figure 11-4.   Real Exchange Rate (in logarithms) Kwacha per US Dollar

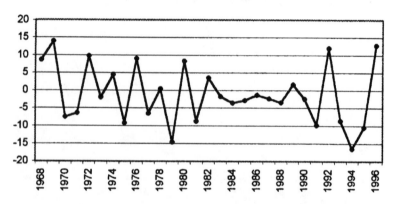

Figure 11-5.   Mining Production Index (1990 = 100) percentage change

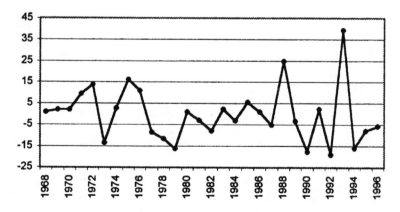

Figure 11-6.   Agriculture Production Index (1990 = 100) percentage change

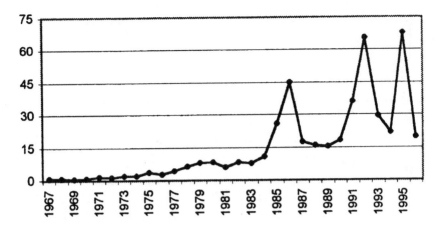

Figure 11-7.   Foreign Aid (percentage of GDP)

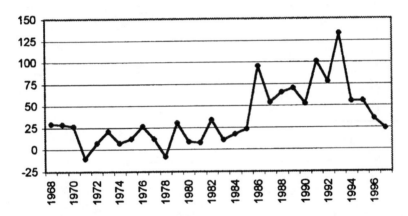

Figure 11-8.   Broad Money (percentage change)

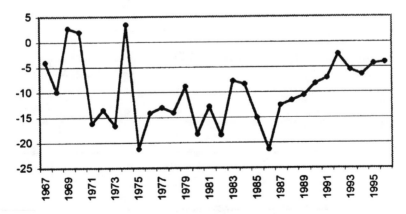

Figure 11-9.   Budget Deficit (percentage of GDP) including Grants

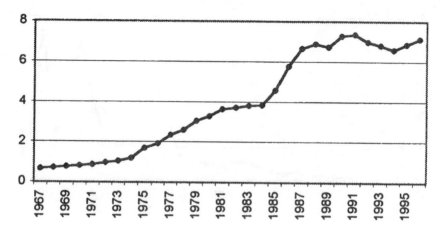

Figure 11-10. External Debt, total (billions of USD)

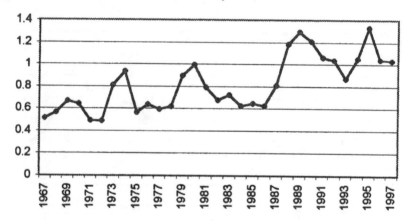

Figure 11-11.   Copper Prices (UD Dollars per pound)

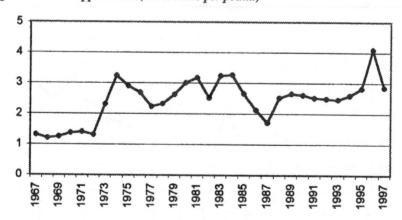

Figure 11-12.   Maize Prices (US Dollar per bushel)

Appendix B: Definitions of Variables and Sources of Data

Δp_t	rate of inflation (based on the CPI, 1990=100)
Δp_t	proxy for the expected inflation rate at time t
Δp_t^f	proxy for foreign rate of inflation (based on the U.S. CPI, 1990=100)
Δy_t	growth rate of nominal GDP
Δyr_t	growth rate of real GDP (1990 prices)
Δagr_t	change in agricultural production index (1990=100)
Δmin_t	change in mining production index (1990=100)
Δi_t	change in domestic nominal interest rate (treasury bill rate, percent per annum)
Δe_t	change in nominal exchange rate (in units of domestic currency per U.S. dollar)
Δer_t	change in real exchange rate (nominal exchange rate adjusted for domestic and foreign prices)
Δm_t	change in nominal stock of money (money plus quasi-money)
P_t^{copper}	world market price of copper (U.K., London, U.S. dollars per pound)
P_t^{maize}	world market price of maize (U.S., Chicago, U.S dollars per bushel)
IM_t	imports of goods and non-factor services (in billions of kwacha)
EX_t	exports of goods and non-factor services (in billions of kwacha)
G_t	government expenditure (in billions of kwacha)
T_t	government revenue (in billions of kwacha)
AID_t	foreign aid flows (in billions of U.S. dollars)
NFA_t	net foreign assets (in billions of kwacha)
DC_t	domestic credit (in billions of kwacha)
CP_t	claims of the banking system on the domestic private sector (in billions of kwacha)
CAP_t	(net) capital flows (in billions of U.S. dollars)
$DEBT_t$	external debt (in billions of U.S. dollars)
$RAIN_t$	weather variable, defined as the absolute deviation from the mean rainfall in inches over 1967–97 at the Momba and Green's farms, Choma, Southern Province.

Note: Lower-case letter denotes the logarithm of the upper-case variable.
Sources:
1) International Financial Statistics, Yearbook 1998; December 1998, IMF.
2) Zambia—Selected Issues and Statistical Appendix, IMF Staff Country Report, November 1997, IMF.
3) World Development Indicators, 1998, World Bank.
4) Macroeconomic Indicators, Ministry of Finance and Economic Development, Zambia, various issues.

Assumptions for the Projections

Growth of nominal money of 30 percent per annum;

Growth of credit to the private sector of 30 percent per annum;

Decrease in the value of exports of 29 percent;

Change in government expenditure of 4 percent;

Increase in nominal interest rate of 15 percent;

Foreign inflation of 2.5 percent;

Decrease in world market copper prices of 41 percent;

Decrease in world market maize prices of 10 percent;

Decrease in foreign aid by 5 percent.

As a proxy for the value of the rainfall variable we use its value from the previous period.

APPENDIX C: POLICY MODELS

Policy models are specified in ways that highlight the linkages between "policy instruments" and "targets." The former are variables over which the authorities (the government or central bank) have some control in the short to medium term. Examples are tax rates, the nominal discount rate on government bonds, the nominal growth of reserve money, and the level of public expenditure on capital projects.

Policy targets are the specific economic variables that the authorities wish to influence. They may include the rate of growth of real income per capita, the rate of inflation, the accumulation of foreign reserves, or the trend path of the exchange rate. The choice of targets and instruments depends on the government's approach to economic development. Governments that see their role as "taking the lead" in promoting development will tend to fix variables they believe are crucial in anticipation that the economy will adjust in ways that justify their original policy actions. By contrast, governments that view their role as creating a setting in which private enterprise can flourish will avoid specific controls. They will seek to influence economic outcomes by indirect means such as the expansion of infrastructure and the enhancement of market incentives.

The general "policy" problem is to determine the changes in the instruments which, given the overall structure of the economy as reflected in the economic model, will have the desired effect on the targets.[41] For example, a

---

41. Following Tinbergen and Theil who developed the theory, there was widespread interest in "optimal" economic policy. The idea was that policy makers should attempt to specify,

central bank wishing to maintain a stable nominal exchange rate has two options. The first is to fix the official exchange rate within a specific "band" and then supply whatever foreign exchange is demanded. The second is to allow the exchange rate to be market-determined but to change interest rates, the growth of reserve money, and the trend path of foreign exchange reserves in ways that counteract any sharp movements of the exchange rate away from its desired level. In both cases, the central bank's "success" in targeting the exchange rate will depend on its influence over other relevant variables and how the remainder of the economy responds to that influence.

Thus, the basic "policy modeling" problem is relatively straightforward. An economic model is specified, the "targets" are designated, and the "instruments" are chosen. The model is estimated and then solved to determine the range over which the instruments have to be manipulated to achieve the desired changes in the targets.

Despite its apparent simplicity, some important formal requirements constrain how a model can be specified and used. One requirement is "consistency". There has to be at least one instrument for each target. A second requirement is "efficiency" in the choice of instruments.[42] The idea is to relate instruments as directly as possible to the targets. For example, an efficient way of dealing with a balance of payments problem is to change the exchange rate. A less efficient way is to impose wage controls in the hope that the reduction in income will curtail the demand for imports adequately to ease the pressure on the balance of payments.

Two other constraints should be noted. The first is "Goodhart's Law" which asserts that variables used as instruments progressively lose their relevance.[43] This occurs because of changes in behavior by those most directly affected by movements in the policy instrument. Monetary policy provides an example. According to monetarist doctrine, a stable relation exists between the growth of money supply and the growth of nominal income. The implication is that by controlling the supply of money, central banks could control the growth of nominal income thereby stabilizing the economy. Based on this doctrine, many central banks began setting specific money

---

in measurable ways, the major objectives of policy. Instruments would then be chosen so as to produce the optimal change in the targets according to policy makers' preferences. Emphasis on this approach has diminished for two reasons. It has been difficult to find suitable measures of preferences that are consistent with aggregation conditions required by Arrow's "possibility theorem." And, in view of the "Lucas critique", the notion of "optimality" does not hold over time. Policy directions cannot be optimally determined in advance. They are time-dependent.

42. This is also called the "assignment" problem.

43. Goodhart 1989, p.100

growth targets. Over time, financial innovation made it more difficult to define a relevant money supply variable that the central bank could control. Measures of velocity (the ratio of income to money) became increasingly unstable, leading central banks to abandon money supply as an instrument.

The second constraint is the "Lucas critique."[44] Economic policy, by its nature, seeks to change economic relationships (e.g., induce individuals and firms to produce more, save more, invest more, consume less, and so on). Thus, if a policy is successful, it systematically modifies the structure of the economy. Since policy models are derived largely from historical data, they do not reflect these changes. In principle, there is no formal way around this problem.[45]

In practice, Goodhart's Law and the Lucas critique do not negate modeling exercises. Variables do not immediately lose their relevance once they are used as instruments and economic structures do not change so dramatically that the effects of policy on them become unpredictable. A practical response to these constraints is for analysts to view their economic models as iterative, path-dependent structures that require regular revision and re-calibration.

A final point is that because an economy is a dynamic interdependent system, the decision *not* to change a particular policy has important economic repercussions. By doing nothing, policy makers implicitly expect the dynamic interactions within the economy to continue producing acceptable policy outcomes. Under the particular circumstances, doing nothing may be the appropriate policy choice. But, in making this choice policy makers should consider three questions. What impact will the choice to do nothing have on public confidence in the economy? Will this decision keep open existing options for the future (or even expand them)? Does the choice to do nothing impose avoidable adjustment costs that are not offset by compensating benefits elsewhere in the economy? (These same questions apply if the policy choice produces some tangible change in the various policy instruments.)

APPENDIX D: LINKS TO FINANCIAL PROGRAMMING[46]

The financial programming framework begins with a projection of nominal GDP. A value of velocity (i.e., the ratio of income to money supply) is de-

---

44. Lucas 1976

45. It has been suggested that economists should specify "policy-invariant" models. This may be possible in developed countries where structural relationships are exceedingly deep and evolve slowly. It is irrelevant to developing countries where the principal object of economic reform and structural adjustment is to fundamentally change the economic structure.

46. See IMF 1981; Chand 1989; Rajcoomar *et al.* 1996.

rived usually from recent experience. Together, the GDP projection and the velocity datum provide an estimate of the growth in the money supply over the program period. Based on the components of the balance of payments—exports, imports, debt service payments, and aid flows—an estimate is obtained for the change in the net foreign assets of the banking system. When combined with the change in the money supply, this estimate allows the change in net domestic credit to be derived. The change in net domestic credit is then divided into its public and private sector components. Since a major objective of structural adjustment is to "make more room for the private sector" the IMF typically allows a generous increase in net credit to the private sector in its programs. The residual provides an upper bound on the potential increase in net credit to the government.

Using data from the projected government revenues and expenditures and the anticipated flows of foreign resources (grants and loans), a preliminary estimate of the budget deficit that has to be funded locally is derived. Expected amounts of non-bank financing (repayment) are subtracted from (added to) this estimate. The result is the projected change in the net credit to government from the banking system. If the estimate is below the upper bound of this variable derived earlier, no further adjustment to the budget is required. If not, additional ways of raising revenue and cutting expenditure have to be found for the financial program to be consistent.

The main advantage of this approach is that it is systematic and consistent. All of the accounts have to add up. It is also a relatively simple way of compressing many complex interactions into a tractable framework that fits on a spreadsheet.

The disadvantage, due to the Lucas critique, is that the estimates only hold over the very short term. Countries in the process of economic reform have policies explicitly designed to transform the structure of the economy. Because financial markets adjust rapidly, the relationships between the variables in the financial program can change significantly. Another disadvantage is that the financial program has no behavioral relations. The velocity variable is assumed. The real growth rate of income and the rate of inflation, which together yield the projection of nominal GDP, are both assumed. The projected movements of the exchange rate are usually derived by assuming that purchasing power parity (PPP) holds. An important objective of structural adjustment is to achieve a sustained depreciation of the real exchange rate. But, by assuming that PPP holds, the financial program understates the desired rate of exchange rate depreciation.

A further problem is that there is no feedback from the controls on monetary variables to domestic interest rates. The financial program makes no allowance for the spillover effects of aid flows. When these are a large component of resource flows, they can significantly alter incentives to reform. In particular, they can induce 'games' by governments and donors to keep the aid flowing. Finally, large aids flows prevent the real exchange rate from depreciating to the degree needed to restore a nation's international competitiveness.

APPENDIX E: LIFE EXPECTANCY, INVESTMENT, AND INCOME GROWTH

This appendix reports the results we obtained by adapting the econometric model presented in the text to derive estimates of the impact of HIV/AIDS on economic growth. The re-specified model has equations for income growth, the growth of investment, the exchange rate, and inflation. We have also added the growth of investment to better model some of the 'endogenous' determinants of income growth.[47] Variables included in the model to incorporate the effects of HIV/AIDS are life expectancy at birth, the age dependency ratio, and the growth rate of the labor force. Both theory and experience have shown that there is a strong positive link between increasing life expectancy and economic growth.[48]

Over the last decade, there has been a strong negative association emerging between the rapid spread of the HIV/AIDS epidemic and falling life expectancy. In Zambia's case, a factor that potentially confounds this relationship has been the continued decline in real per capita income and overall economic welfare. Zambia was experiencing a significant increase in infant mortality even before the rapid spread of HIV/AIDS.

Notwithstanding this qualification, our model helps unravel some important macroeconomic relationships, particularly those that involve the links between economic growth and changes in key social indexes, such as life expectancy at birth and the dependency ratio. At a minimum, the empirical relationships we derive indicate possible directions for further research.

Data: The main data source is the same as in the text, namely the World Bank Africa 2000 CD-ROM database covering the period from 1967 to 1998. Taking first differences and lags into account, the number of observations is 30. There are three new variables, life expectancy at birth, the dependency ratio, and the growth of the labor force. Life expectancy is measured as the average number of years that a person is expected to live given prevailing age-spe-

---

47. An obvious gap in the model included in the text, following the specification of Khan and Knight (1991) upon which the model was based, is that it does not include investment. Endogenous growth theorists (Romer 1994, Grossman and Helpman 1994) emphasize the spillover effects of investment. We added this element to the specification when we re-estimated the model to include the effects of HIV/AIDS.

48. *World Development Report* 1993, Ch. 1.; Gillis *et al.* 1996, Ch.11

cific rates of mortality. The dependency ratio is defined as the number of dependents divided by the working-age population. Because data points do not exist for both series for every year, the missing observations have been derived through interpolation.

Real income and investment are measured in constant kwacha. The exchange rate is kwacha per US dollar. That is, an increase in the exchange rate represents a devaluation of the kwacha. In a slight modification of the main model, domestic inflation is measured by the change in the consumer price index using a base of 1995. The index of foreign inflation is the change in US producer price index (PPI), also with a base of 1995. The real exchange rate is calculated as the nominal exchange rate multiplied by the ratio of the US PPI to the Zambian CPI. Foreign aid is taken as the U.S. dollar amounts reported as Official Development Assistance (ODA).

The Model: The structure of each equation in the model follows.

The equation for the growth in real income reflects the conventional determinants of long run economic expansion on the right hand side—capital accumulation and the growth of labor force. As a proxy for capital accumulation, we have used the growth of real investment. The coefficients on investment and the labor force are expected to be positive. The change in life expectancy enters this equation as a measure of human capital and as a reflection of the impact of HIV/AIDS. Its coefficient should be positive as well.

We include foreign aid in the growth equation as a means of allowing for Zambia's high degree of aid dependence. If aid has been used productively, the estimated coefficient will be positive. We have also added the real exchange rate to this equation. Though the real exchange rate is not considered a direct determinant of real income growth, a large and growing literature justifies its inclusion.[49] A systematic change in the real exchange rate (the price of tradables to non-tradables) is a key indicator of *effective* economic reform. There is now considerable research on why African countries have been marginalized in world trade and exchange. Recent studies have been showing that the major reason is that they are not growing.[50] The research further shows that the lack of growth is associated with major distortions in their key relative prices, of which the real exchange rate is the most important. The coefficient on the real exchange rate is expected to be positive.

The investment equation includes the growth of real income, the growth of the labor force, the change in foreign aid, the dependency ratio, and the change in the real exchange rate. Increases in real income and the labor force should increase the rate of investment. The labor force has two separate ef-

---

49. Gillis *et al.* 1996: Chapter 20; Ghura and Hadjimichael 1996; Calamitsis, Basu and Ghura 1999; McPherson and Rakovski 2000

50. Rodrik 1998; McPherson and Rakovski 1999, 2000a

fects on investment. First, an increase in the labor force raises the output of investment goods. Second, as the labor force expands, producers need to increase investment so as to maintain the amount of capital per worker.

The coefficient on foreign aid is expected to be positive. In principle, a large part of foreign assistance is designed to expand productive capacity. Indeed, one objective of the emphasis given by the World Bank in its 1994 *World Development Report* was to stress the importance for economic growth of improvements in infrastructure. Yet, even in the absence of higher expenditure on infrastructure, foreign aid may increase the supply of investible funds by freeing up government resources that would be spent on other activities.

The specification of the nominal exchange rate equation is straightforward. It incorporates the idea of purchasing power parity and features domestic and foreign inflation as regressors. Real income growth has been added to capture feedback effects within the system of equations.

The inflation equation is derived from the demand for money. The growth of real income, interpreted as a measure of real supply, should be negatively related to inflation. Rapid changes in the nominal money supply raise prices. Hence, the coefficient on the money variable in the inflation equation should be positive. The exchange rate links the inflation equation to the rest of the system. The inclusion of lagged inflation measures the degree to which consumers and producers adjust to changing prices over time.

The Results: As in the main text, we derived the estimated coefficients using three-stage least squares (3SLS). This generalized instrumental variable technique provides consistent estimates in the presence of lagged dependent variables, endogenous regressors and error terms that depart from white noise. The results are in the following table. The first column is the growth equation, the second the investment equation, and so on.

In the growth equation, the investment variable has the correct sign but is not significant at the standard levels. The coefficients on the growth of the labor force (−.39) and the change in the real exchange rate (−.009) are negative. Neither is statistically significant. Life expectancy has the expected positive effect on income growth.[51] The change in foreign aid has a highly statistically significant negative effect on income growth. In this respect, the present sub-model, by including investment, casts further light on the aid/growth relationship in Zambia. The basic conclusion, argued in more detail in chapter fourteen, is that the aggregate effect of foreign aid in Zambia has been counterproductive.

Income growth has a strong first order autoregressive effect. This is statistical confirmation of Zambia's lack of growth over the last three decades: the

---

51. Missing from our analysis is any test for reverse causality. It would require an equation for life expectancy.

Economic Growth and HIV/AIDS: 3SLS Estimation Results

Variables		dlny	dlnINV	dlnE	ddnP
				Equation	
dlny	Real income growth	—	−0.884 (−1.09)	−0.746 (−0.55)	1.375 (2.16)*
dlnINV	Real investment growth	0.023 (1.20)	—	—	—
dlnL	Labor force growth	−0.393 (−1.06)	5.126 (2.11)*	—	—
dLIFEX	Change in life expectancy	0.673 (2.22)*	—	—	—
DepRatio	Dependency ratio	—	−1.159 (−2.90)**	—	—
dlnE	Change in exchange rate	—	—	—	0.256 (1.66)
dlne	Change in real exchange rate	−0.009 (−0.33)	−0.401 (−2.20)*	—	—
dlnM	Growth of money	—	—	—	0.418 (2.10)*
dlnP	Inflation rate (domestic)	—	—	0.769 (2.71)**	—
dlnPf	Inflation rate (foreign)	—	—	−2.328 (−2.09)*	—
dlnAid	Change in foreign aid	−0.026 (−3.01)*	−0.003 (−0.04)	—	—
$dlny_{t-1}$	Lag of real income growth	0.461 (8.32)**	—	—	—
$dlnE_{t-1}$	Lag of change in ex. rate	—	—	−0.170 (−0.87)	—
$dlnINV_{t-1}$	Lag of real investment growth	—	0.443 (6.77)**	—	—
$dlnP_{t-1}$	Lag of (domestic) inflation	—	—	—	0.434 (3.68)**
Constant		0.029 (2.66)**	1.034 (2.53)*	0.191 (1.88)	−0.033 (−0.96)
N	Number of observations	30	30	30	30
"R-sq."		0.79	0.53	0.55	0.83

Note: t-statistics are given in parentheses * coefficient is statistically significant at 0.05; ** at 0.01

present change in income departs little from past changes. The outcome also extends results obtained by Sachs and Warner in their effort to explain "sources of slow growth in Africa". One of the sources of slow growth, which their single equation growth approach ignored, has been slow growth itself. Lacking dynamism, neither locals nor foreigners have been prepared to invest. Indeed, through capital flight they disinvested. Our results reconfirm a standard result (missed in conventional growth regressions) that the lack of growth is self-reinforcing.

The estimated coefficients on the labor force and dependency ratio in the investment equation have the correct signs (positive and negative respectively). Both are statistically significant at 5 percent. A surprising result is that foreign aid and real income growth do not appear to have a significant effect on the growth of investment. The change in the exchange rate has a negative coefficient that is statistically significant. This outcome clearly reflects a jumble of effects—the increased costs of imported capital as the exchange rate depreciates, the inducement to increase economic activity as price distortions are removed, and the fact that foreign aid which raises investment has allowed the real exchange rate to remain overvalued. The lag of the change in investment is positive and statistically significant. The implication is that both producers and consumers have been responding to investment incentives in a structured and adaptive way.

In the exchange rate equation, the coefficients of domestic and foreign inflation have the correct signs and are statistically significant. But they are statistically different from the theoretically prescribed values of 1 and −1, respectively. The differences reflect to the degree to which the exchange rate deviates from the path prescribed by PPP. The negative and insignificant impact of real income growth does not accord with our expectations.

In the inflation equation, the growth of real income behaves in the opposite direction. It has a positive and significant coefficient that proved to be robust to a variety of model specifications. One explanation is that the Zambian economy has major distortions and imbalances that compromise what otherwise should be equilibrium relationship. The policy implication is that the distortions and imbalances should be removed. This would restore the correct negative relationship between inflation and real supply. The growth of the money supply has the positive effect posited by theory. As expected, exchange rate depreciation increases inflation. The coefficient is significant at 10 percent. Based on the lagged inflation term, the rate of adjustment (on an annual basis) to changing prices has been sluggish.

For comparison, we present the results below from a single equation estimation (OLS estimation with robust standard errors) of the growth equation of the system.

OLS Estimation of the Growth Equation

Variable		Coefficient
dlnINV	Real investment growth	0.038 (2.51)*
dlnL	Labor force growth	−0.604 (−1.37)
dLIFEX	Change in life expectancy	0.678 (2.52)*
dlne	Change in real exchange rate	−0.022 (−1.83)
dlnAid	Change in foreign aid	−0.027 (−4.19)*
$dlnyr_{t-1}$	Lag of real income growth	0.456 (9.87)**
Constant		0.035 (2.62)*
N	Number of observations	30
R-sq.		0.81
RMSE		0.02
F		33.71

Notes: t-statistics are given in parentheses

In this relationship, the increase in investment has the expected positive coefficient and is statistically significant. As in the larger system, the change in the real exchange rate has a negative effect on growth. Here, however, it is statistically significant. The other estimates are similar to those obtained from the system of equations.

It is worth noting that in both sets of results, the estimated coefficient on the change in life expectancy at birth is almost identical. This outcome shows that whether or not systemic effects are taken into account, the responsiveness of economic growth to the change in life expectancy is robust. At 0.68, economic growth is sensitive to changes in life expectancy. A one percent reduction in average life expectancy (half a year on average when life expectancy is 50 years) reduces the average growth rate by .68 percent. This is a significant source of income loss. Since HIV/AIDS has been a major factor responsible for the sharp reduction in life expectancy at birth over the last decade and a half,[52] the loss of income growth has been seriously undermining Zambia's prospects for economic recovery.

Concluding Comments: The above results are highly suggestive. The sharp decline in life expectancy during the latter part of the 1990s in Zambia directly reduced the rate of growth. The change in the dependency ratio also produced a significant reduction in the growth rate of investment. These results do not definitively show that HIV/AIDS has reduced the rate of growth. Yet, to the extent that declining life expectancy at birth and a higher dependency ratio reflect the loss of human capital and reduce the capacity of the population to save and invest, the model provides evidence that HIV/AIDS has been undercutting economic growth in Zambia. Since the model is nonlinear (based on growth rates) there is a high likelihood that HIV/AIDS will continue undercutting growth at an increasing rate for the foreseeable future. The policy challenge is daunting. Zambia faces the prospect of attempting to expand its productive capacity as the resources (human, physical, and financial) necessary for that task are being reduced at an increasing rate.

---

52. In Zambia, life expectancy at birth peaked at 51.2 years in 1982. It declined to 49.6 years in 1987. By 1992, it had fallen to 48.4 years. By 1998, it was 43 years.

12

Capacity Building in the Ministry of Finance, Zambia

DEBORAH A. HOOVER AND MALCOLM F. MCPHERSON

1. Introduction[1]

Capacity building was a central component of the Macroeconomic Technical Assistance Project (METAP) in Zambia. The scope of work stated that the project team would carry out the following:

> . . .assist the Government of Zambia to implement the New Economic Recovery Programme; and to enhance the capacity of the staff of the Ministry of Finance to formulate and implement the economic policies to stabilize the economy and lay the foundations for sustainable growth.

Although the term "capacity building" was not specifically defined, its dimensions were clear from the activities required of the project advisors and the requests for support from senior ministry officials. Capacity building was to include policy formulation, training, and institution building. The only details that needed to be determined were the scope and timing of those activities.

This chapter highlights the reasons for the special focus on capacity building in Zambia, the need for such a program within the Ministry of Finance, and the approach adopted under METAP (and later the Computerization and Modernization of Tax Administration Project—CMTAP). We also discuss the problems encountered and the results achieved. We conclude with

---

1. An earlier version of this chapter appears as HIID *Development Discussion Papers* no.704, June 1999.

an assessment of the success of the capacity building effort and the prospects that it will be sustained over the longer term.

2. BACKGROUND

Capacity Building in Perspective

Interest in the importance of capacity building for developing countries was given a major boost following the publication of the World Bank's 1989 study *Sub-Saharan Africa, From Crisis to Sustainable Growth*.[2] This was a timely contribution that required development specialists to re-focus their attention more systematically on activities related to capacity creation or capacity enhancement, some of which dated from the 1950s. The subsequent re-examination of the topic has led to a more structured approach to capacity building, its main elements, and the processes by which it is achieved.

Some of the earliest references to what is now called capacity building appear in the studies of manpower planning and educational development.[3] Governments and donor agencies applied programming and planning techniques to determine the skills needed to foster economic growth and development. Since skilled manpower was seen as a major constraint to growth, attention was directed to using the existing supply of skilled personnel more effectively and filling the manpower gaps through additional training or technical assistance.[4] Zambia adopted such an approach in its *First National Development Plan* in 1966.[5]

Some development agencies responded to the shortage of skills by helping establish "centers of excellence."[6] An early initiative was The Rockefeller

---

2. World Bank 1989.

3. Harbison 1962; Parnes 1962; Harbison and Myers 1965; Maddison 1965; Robinson 1967; UNESCO 1968; Meier 1970:Part V.D; Shaath 1975. King (1991) traces many of these developments from the May 1961 conference on education in Africa sponsored by UNESCO. Arndt (1987) has additional references.

4. It is still seen as a constraint (Richards and Amjad 1994). As noted below, the loss of personnel from HIV/AIDS has tightened the skill constraint.

5. GRZ 1966, pp. 73–78.

6. The idea of "centers of excellence" was ridiculed in V.S. Naipaul's book *A Bend in the River* (1979) which has a thinly disguised description of the Kumuzu Academy in Malawi. Established by President Hastings Banda, the academy was designed to train Malawi's future leaders. Banda, widely seen as eccentric, insisted that the academy achieve and maintain what many saw were outdated and inappropriate standards for an African country. Since education standards have fallen so broadly across Africa (thereby contributing to the continent's marginalization) it remains debatable whether centers of excellence in Africa have been such an outlandish idea. A regular debate in rich countries, for example, is how to promote excellence in education." In-

Foundation's University Development Program. Undertaken in several African countries, the idea was to create a core group of skilled personnel with the capacities needed to foster development.[7] It was succeeded by a more general effort popularly known as "education for development."[8] This approach was widely copied.[9] It drew upon a burgeoning literature that emphasized the role of "human capital" in economic development[10] and the crucial nature of institution building for societies that were in the process of development.[11]

All of these ideas were widely field-tested by agricultural specialists located in the centers that ultimately combined to form the Consultative Group for International Agricultural Research (CGIAR). These centers were responsible for helping to stimulate the development of national agricultural research systems capable of adapting to local conditions the results of the basic research undertaken at the international centers. While reaffirming the importance of institution building, the process also drew attention to the need for special efforts to enhance managerial capacity.[12]

The overall success of these endeavors became apparent as the gloomy predictions of famine and disruption, prominent in the late 1960s,[13] gave way to the progress being made through the spread of the "green revolution." Even with the success of approaches that combined institutional development, skill

---

deed, in the U.S., this topic continues to be widely discussed. A special symposium was sponsored on the issue by the Federal Reserve Bank of New York (FRBNY 1998).

7. The Rockefeller Foundation 1981. This model has proven to be highly resilient. In April 2000, the Rockefeller Foundation combined with Carnegie Corporation, the Ford Foundation, and the MacArthur Foundation to create the "Partnership to Strengthen African Universities." This is a $100 million, five-year effort. Information may be found on www.rockfound.org and www.carnegie.org. Given the need, one must wish these philanthropies well. A curious omission from this program is how universities are to be strengthened without expressly dealing with the problem of HIV/AIDS.

8. Mosher (1965, p. 124) noted:
By "education for development" we mean education that is appropriate for a society that wants to develop. It is education that is selective in its choice of materials for bringing each new generation up to date with respect to the past and is equally selective in the new knowledge, abilities and skills that it tries to help each person acquire.

9. Simmons (1979) reviewed the experience with education for development programs and concluded they had not effectively reached the deprived segments of the population. Education in his words was still a "sieve" (that excluded many underprivileged) rather than an "equalizer" (of opportunities).

10. Harry Johnson (1964) described economic development as a "generalized process of capital accumulation" in which capital was broadly defined to include human and physical capital and institutions. His description drew upon key results in capital theory and the work of Schultz, Becker and others on human capital (Schultz 1959, 1962, 1963; Becker 1964).

11. Blackmore 1965; Hunter 1967, Ch.IV.

12. Moris 1977; Cohen and McPherson 1983.

13. Paddock and Paddock 1967; Ehrlich 1970; Dumont and Rosier 1969.

enhancement through agricultural extension, and special attention to management issues, their potential impact was often undermined by inappropriate economic policies. To remedy this, attention shifted to the task of improving the capacity of policymakers to understand both the technical and economic impacts of their actions (and often lack of action).

Developed countries typically deal with such issues at schools of public administration and business. In developing countries, these matters were largely neglected.[14] The World Food Conference in Rome in 1975 was a wake-up call. A central issue emerging from that conference was how to induce policy makers to create a setting that would support rapid increases in food production. Efforts began to stimulate capacity in the area of policy analysis and policy implementation.[15] Several related aspects of capacity were also identified and emphasized.[16]

The 1989 World Bank study referred to above had been the fourth that the bank produced on Sub-Saharan Africa within a decade.[17] Earlier analyses had highlighted many difficulties in Africa. This was the first time the bank had singled out weak capacity as one of the most pressing problems. The report raised specific questions about the ability of African officials to handle their jobs, and the capacity of key organizations to fulfill their assigned (or adopted) tasks.[18] As a means of creating an institutional structure for improving capacity throughout Africa, the bank promoted the "Africa Capacity Building Initiative" (ACBI).[19] A fund of $100 million was assembled and, in 1991, the African Capacity Building Foundation (ACBF) was created.[20]

---

14. One of the reasons why Harvard University started the Edward S. Mason Program at the Kennedy School of Government in 1969 was in response to the need for more detailed training in economic analysis and public administration (Mason 1986).

15. One outcome was the formation of the International Food Policy Research Institute in Washington, D.C.

16. Mann and McPherson 1981; Honadle 1981; Huddleston and Mann 1986; Grindle, Mann, and Shipton 1989; Loubser 1993; Cohen 1995. Scholars emphasize different aspects of capacity depending on the problem at hand. For example, Mann and McPherson highlighted four dimensions: technical, administrative, strategic, and communications. Their goal was to develop a framework to help policy makers improve food and agricultural policies. Grindle and Hilderbrand (1995, p. 445) defined "capacity" as ". . .the ability to perform appropriate tasks effectively, efficiently and sustainably." They were seeking to understand how state capacity could be improved. The World Bank (1996:5) noted: "Capacity is the combination of human resources and institutions that permits countries to achieve their development goals." This is consistent with the more general approaches taken recently (cf. Loubser 1993). Cohen (1995) provided a detailed review of the operational definitions of capacity.

17. World Bank 1981, 1984, 1986.

18. World Bank 1989, pp. 54–59.

19. World Bank 1991.

20. The initial phase was a four-year pilot project. The objective was to promote and finance indigenous capacity building efforts in policy analysis and development management

Although the World Bank initiative raised the profile of capacity building in Africa, most of the bilateral agencies (USAID, ODA/DFID, SIDA, NORAD, GTZ/KfW, the French CFD, among others) had been generously funding similar activities for years. Moreover, most African governments had readily acknowledged their capacity constraints. Indeed, a frequent criticism by African leaders of the colonial legacy was that it had left their countries with few adequately trained personnel. Most African governments had responded by consistently devoting a large share of their budgets to education and training. After much progress in the years following independence, the momentum had been lost. Economic decline reduced the resources spent on training. Public sector organizations were not making the changes needed to overcome their own structural and staffing weaknesses.[21] The development agenda kept shifting in ways that left existing personnel overstretched and ill-prepared.[22] The overextension of public sectors across Africa undermined efficiency.[23] Mismanagement and corruption added to the difficulties.[24] Finally, many policies were changed but few were sustained, often because of capacity constraints.[25]

Resolving these problems requires, among other things, a sharp reduction in the range of public sector activities as well as increased accountability. These, in turn, require additional capacity including better leadership.[26] A vicious cycle typically emerges in which the conditions needed to improve capacity cannot be met because of weak capacity.

A common method of breaking this cycle in Africa has been to use external

---

throughout SSA, and to strengthen networks of trained professionals, providing an institutional base for them, and encouraging the use of their services by the public and private sectors.

21. This is consistent with Hirschmann's findings in *Exit, Voice and Loyalty,* (1970). He showed that bureaucracies are slow in responding constructively to changes that are potentially harmful to the organization as a whole.

22. For instance, the donor-driven push to promote rural development in the 1970s required a whole new cadre of skilled personnel. The current emphasis on sector investment programs and comprehensive development frameworks is having the same effect.

23. In his study of Uganda, Crawford Young (1971, p. 142) asked "What boundaries upon policy choice are placed upon the policy makers by the limitations in system capability?" By largely ignoring this problem, policy makers across Africa virtually guaranteed that their public sectors would remain inefficient.

24. Young (1982) noted ". . .competency of the state is fundamental to all developmental designs" (p. 320). He added a "highly incompetent state sets all development in jeopardy" (p. 321). In relation to corruption, he argued that: "Neither a market economy nor a socialist economy can function when fettered with a demoralized, corruption-ridden state" (p. 321). The problems of corruption show few signs of diminishing (IRIS 1996).

25. Collier and Gunning 1999.

26. Gray and McPherson 1999.

technical assistance (TA). Many countries have relied heavily on such assistance. A number of development specialists have criticized TA because of its cost, cultural insensitivity, and the limited sustainability of its effects.[27] Yet, few mainstream development economists had questioned its contribution to economic development.[28] Edward Jaycox, then Vice President of the World Bank for Africa, changed that. He argued that external TA to Africa was ineffective, expensive and destructive.[29] In his words:

> After 30 years of technical assistance, and so much money spent, Africa's weak institutions, lack of expertise, and current need for more—rather than less—assistance tell us we [external development agencies] have failed badly in our efforts.

Jaycox argued that donor reliance on foreign experts had been at the expense of qualified African consultants and researchers, and that this had undercut efforts to develop local capacity.

At one level, Jaycox was right. *All* foreign assistance distorts the local economy in some way. TA provides skills that enable particular tasks to be undertaken that local personnel and organizations cannot do. But, it also promotes activities local personnel and organizations would not do. That said, Jaycox's blanket condemnation of TA was unfortunate.[30] The point would have been more effective and accurate if he had argued that some TA to Africa had been counterproductive. For balance, he should also have mentioned that in many cases the problems attributed to TA were generated elsewhere. Donors frequently impose conflicting conditions that result in different groups of technical assistants working at cross-purposes.[31] Many African governments do

---

27. Bauer 1971; Muscat 1986; Jolly 1989. Some of these concerns were reflected in a set of principles designed to make technical assistance more effective (DAC 1991). Gray (1997) has additional suggestions.

28. While there had been some studies critical of technical assistance (e.g., Berg 1993), mainstream views were that TA has been generally successful, even if its effects were harder to measure than, for example, construction projects (Cassen *et al.* 1994, World Bank 1998). Lancaster (1999, Ch. 3) was less convinced. She classified TA as among the least effective of all forms of foreign aid. Chapter 13 examines this issue further.

29. Jaycox 1993.

30. The late Michael Roemer of HIID wrote to Jaycox in August 1993 challenging his views about the effects of TA. A copy of the correspondence is available from the authors. Gray and Hoover (1995) vigorously critique the Jaycox view.

31. Work undertaken in Zambia at the Ministries of Finance and Commerce, Trade and Industry provides an example. Technical assistants at the finance ministry were requested to help revive the economy by promoting liberalization and removing distortions. Technical assistants at the Ministry of Commerce were requested to help Zambia "promote industry." The team at commerce concluded that Zambia needed to protect its industry. This was contrary to liberalization efforts being pursued at finance.

not provide the support needed to make the most effective use of TA. And, all too often, African governments have reversed useful policy reforms irrespective of the analysis undertaken or support being provided by technical assistants.

Nonetheless, the use of TA across Africa has not declined substantially even as organizations such as the ACBF have expanded their programs. Most African countries have found they require additional support to formulate and implement their reform programs. Following war and civil disruption, countries request TA to help them rebuild. Some governments have found that they require assistance to deal with particular areas of reform where crucial systems have broken down (or have proven to be inadequate). Training local staff for these tasks frequently requires resident advisors.

Based on past experience, this situation will continue as many of the tasks needed to promote and sustain reform change over time. For example, the 1997 *World Development Report* on the role of the State[32] raised numerous questions about what governments are meant to do. One of these things, according to the 1998 *WDR Knowledge for Development,* is to help foster the appropriate setting for the creation and dissemination of knowledge. If valid, it has major implications for the *additional* capacities required by African countries. Most of them already require extraordinary efforts to overcome their existing marginalization within the global economy.[33] Many of these challenges cannot be met with local capacity, especially now that losses due to the spread of HIV/AIDS has been reducing existing capacity and undermining the operations of key organizations. In countries such as Botswana and Zambia such losses have reached crisis proportions.

Capacity Building in Zambia

The need for capacity building in Zambia has a long history. Zambia gained independence with barely more than 100 African Zambians having university degrees. Despite the shortage of skills, there was a pressing need to "Zambianize" the upper levels of the work force.[34] Racial discrimination during the colonial period, sustained by an "industrial colour-bar," had prevented African workers from being promoted to high level positions.[35] Even though it was costly, rapid promotion of African workers had become politically essential.[36] Many young and inexperienced personnel were promoted.

---

32. World Bank 1997.
33. Collier 1994; Rodrik 1997; Yeats *et al.* 1997.
34. This was an explicit goal of the First National Development Plan (GRZ 1966).
35. Burawoy 1972.
36. McPherson 1980, Ch. 2.

This created serious management and supervision problems.[37] The state take-overs (initiated with the 1968 Mulungushi Rock speech[38]) simply accentuated those problems.

The principal constraint on capacity in the early years after independence was the tertiary education system. More personnel were required to staff the expanding public sector than the system could produce. That pressure eased after the mid-1970s as the economy began to decline. From that point, the principal constraint was the quality of graduates, not the quantity.

Yet, even in the areas where there has been an adequate supply of well-trained personnel, the emerging pattern of autocratic and arbitrary rule by the party and its government created perverse incentives. The public sector had increasing difficulty retaining skilled personnel. Many highly quali-fied Zambians (doctors, pilots, teachers, accountants, and agronomists) emi-grated.[39] Further complications arose from the increased disorganization and mismanagement within the public sector. Many skilled personnel who re-mained in the public service were used ineffectively.[40]

Over the period 1977 to 1991, in response to the worsening economic situ-ation, the government implemented a total of seven donor-supported struc-tural adjustment programs. Each, in turn, was abandoned. The government even gave up on its own adjustment program, "growth from own resources," that it had launched in 1988.[41]

These developments have led many observers to emphasize the political difficulties of adjustment in Zambia.[42] Difficulties also arose because existing staff could not (and would not) deal with key technical problems.[43] Examples

---

37. "Turner Report" ILO 1969; Jolly 1971.

38. The April 1968 speech, delivered at Mulungushi Rock, was entitled "Zambia: Toward Complete Independence" (de Gaay Fortman 1979).

39. This has been a general problem across Africa, especially for those trained at the univer-sity level (Saint 1992:Ch. IV).

40. Saasa *et al.* 1996. This, too, has been a general problem across Africa. Cohen (1993) and Cohen and Wheeler (1997) examined the issue in Kenya and suggest remedies. Many of these were implemented under METAP.

41. Kayizza-Mugerwa 1990.

42. Callaghy 1990; West 1992; Bates and Collier 1992. One of the many problems created by politicians was that they would not heed sound advice, local or foreign. The two-volume study *Adjustment in the Midst of Crisis* (GRZ 1984), produced largely by government officials, was an excellent and accurate assessment of what was required to reform Zambia. The program was only partially implemented and then dropped.

43. Personal communication with Dr. Kjell Nystrom, Embassy of Sweden, Lusaka, August 1990. Dr. Nystrom indicated that the genesis of METAP was a complaint by President Kaunda to a group of diplomats that he could not get the type of economic advice he needed to help re-form the economy. The assessment was supported in the report by Saasa *et al.* (1996) on capac-ity building. It noted (p. 3):

include debt management, tax reform, financial reform, exchange rate management, and budget reform.

The deterioration of the education system was a direct consequence of economic decline.[44] During the 1980s, expenditure by the government on education as a proportion of GDP was among the lowest in the world.[45] Of the limited amounts available, most was spent on administration and support services. Minimal amounts were devoted to teaching programs, the library, textbooks, and postgraduate studies.[46] Few graduates could meet acceptable international standards.[47] As a result, none of the universities in Zambia or private consulting firms had the capacity or incentive to undertake the kinds of basic and applied research required to move Zambia forward.[48]

The problems in education have been compounded by the deterioration of the health system and growing losses of personnel and productive work time due to HIV/AIDS. Rates of HIV/AIDS infection in Zambia are among the highest in the world.[49] The highest risk group is the young, urban, and educated. Studies by the Ministry of Health note that among the age group 15 to 49 years the death rate is expected to be 70,000 by the year 2000, rising to 120,000 per annum by the year 2005.[50]

HIV/AIDS has had further negative effects on capacity building in Zambia. Government operations, formal training programs, and counterpart training have been regularly interrupted by absenteeism. Many competent teachers and trainers have died. Productivity, already low from disorganization and

---

One of the principal causes of Zambia's social and economic malaise is the absence of national capacity to meaningfully conceptualize; analyze; plan; implement; monitor; and evaluate development. This shortcoming is revealed principally by the government and civil society's severe institutional and human resource limitations in designing policies and strategies that are aimed at realizing the country's developmental aspirations.

44. Kelly 1991, Chs 5, 10; Mathieu 1996.

45. Saasa *et al.* 1996, p. 54.

46. Kelly 1991, p. 182, 185–6, 190. In a cross-country analysis, the World Bank (1995) noted that retention of staff at the university level had been especially difficult in Zambia.

47. World Bank 1986b; Kelly 1991:177–8, 190; Saasa *et al.* 1996:56–7.

48. An example is the study of capacity in Zambia (Saasa *et al.* 1996, esp. Ch. 3). The essence of this report is that Zambians, though lacking the capacity to promote policy reform, understand their capacity constraints and would deal with their problems effectively if only the donor community would provide the necessary resources. Pages 104 to 109 of the report indicate how the donors should allow Zambians to take the lead in formulating their adjustment and capacity building programs. This is followed by an eight-point program which, if implemented, could not be carried out by Zambians. What the study shows is that Zambian scholars remain highly ambivalent about foreign aid. They want control of aid, but do not want it to end. The issue of aid dependency in Zambia is considered further in Chapter 13.

49. GRZ 1997, p. 14. An updated version of this study GRZ (1999) shows that the situation has worsened.

50. GRZ 1997, p. 26

lack of resources, has been reduced further.[51] The motivation to be trained has changed as well.

Overview

Historical experience with capacity building provides a number of lessons. First, there are no easy solutions to the problems of creating capacity on a sustainable basis.[52] Second, capacity building efforts are enhanced if the approaches adopted are flexible and responsive.[53] Third, economic reform imposes special demands on capacity. Successful reform changes the structure of the economy. Some changes can be anticipated; some cannot. A flexible approach to capacity building helps the public sector adapt effectively.

Capacity building has to be seen as a long-term endeavor. The skills needed to promote and sustain economic development only emerge with hard pounding over many years. This requirement, however, is typically stymied by the short-term nature of donor funding for capacity building efforts. To take account of this constraint, most technical advisors stress the *process* of capacity building, especially the importance of activities that strengthen organizations.[54] That was the approach taken under METAP and CMTAP.

3. Capacity Within the Ministry of Finance

The Request for Support

Following the collapse of the government's own structural adjustment initiative in 1988, Zambia's leaders reapproached the donor community. Facing pressure to reform the economy and lacking adequate local capacity, the minister of finance, Gibson Chigaga, requested several donors in 1989 to finance expatriate advisors. The government's proposal identified the need for five resident advisors who would provide technical assistance, policy advice, and on-the-job training. The request also included funding for local and overseas training. The minister specifically identified tax reform, budget reform, debt management, and aid coordination as priorities. He was particularly anxious to have a small advisory team assist the government with the

---

51. *ibid.*, p. 40 At Chilanga Cement, the hours lost due to sickness and funerals increased more than three times over the two-year period from 1992–93 and 1994–95.
52. Gray and Hoover 1995; Grindle and Hilderbrand 1995; Cohen and Wheeler 1997.
53. Gray 1997.
54. Gray and Hoover 1995.

formulation and management of an IMF/World Bank structural adjustment program.[55]

The request by the government can be interpreted in a number of ways. First, it was a genuine plea for help in areas in which Zambia's policies were deficient. Second, it was yet more window dressing by Zambia's leaders intent on rationalizing years of inaction. IMF and World Bank staff and a host of local and external consultants supported by bilateral agencies had made extensive analyses of Zambia's circumstances. What needed to be done was no secret.[56] The key problem was getting it done. The government had repeatedly failed in this, and there was a high probability it would continue to do so. Third, the request was an admission that many of the detailed technical tasks needed to reform the economy could not be accomplished with local staff. And fourth, it provided Zambia with an opportunity to begin rebuilding credibility within the international community. The government had external arrears exceeding US $3 billion. These could not be rationalized without international support.

The donor response to the minister's request was positive but cautious. Donors recognized that the government needed access to credible, timely economic advice. They were also concerned whether the government would effectively use such a team were it provided. After some discussion, the identification of an advisory team was made a condition for the release of a large World Bank credit. Therefore, it was with some urgency that Minister Chigaga wrote in early 1990 to several institutions, including the Harvard Institute for International Development (HIID), requesting expressions of interest in fielding such a team.

HIID staff visited Lusaka in August 1990 to discuss the project with government and donor officials. Their assessment confirmed the need for the support being requested.[57] The initial budget for the technical services and training listed in the terms of reference exceeded the amount earmarked by the donors. Anticipating that additional funds could be found later, the do-

---

55. Information obtained at a meeting with Minister Gibson Chigaga by Malcolm McPherson and Donald Snodgrass of HIID during the Bank/Fund meetings in Washington D.C., September 1990.

56. One author (McPherson) had contributed to a four-volume World Bank study of the Zambian economy in 1977 (World Bank 1977). This study and others (McPherson 1980) highlighted the economy's problems. The government raised many of the same points in its own reports "Restructuring in the Midst of Crisis" and the "New Economic Recovery Program" (GRZ 1984; 1989).

57. There was an important difference. The original TOR called for a trade policy advisor. After discussions with ministry and central bank officials, it was clear that the project should include a macroeconomic data specialist. Most of the key data were months out of date and a special effort was needed in this area.

nors and government agreed to reduce the training program. The government's most immediate problem was *not* access to training funds. Its most pressing need was for technical assistance in formulating and implementing macroeconomic policy.

HIID staff were familiar with what was involved, having undertaken a number of similar projects in other developing countries.[58] Both the original team leader and his successor had extensive overseas experience in policy advisory work and capacity building.[59] Supported by HIID's training office in Cambridge and bolstered by the institute's ongoing experience and research in capacity building, the Harvard team was considered an ideal fit by donors and government officials alike. But, having the team in place only partially addressed the ministry's capacity problems. The effective use of technical assistance required changes in organization and motivation. Those proved to be the greatest challenge.

The Context Within the Ministry

Capacity building is difficult at the best of times. Numerous capacities have to be enhanced simultaneously in circumstances where few staff can be released from their day-to-day activities. The pressure was compounded by the expectation (especially among the donor community) that the Ministry of Finance would take the lead in promoting economic reform. In order for reform to succeed, its staff had to formulate and implement programs such as the liberalization of markets, the lifting of exchange controls, the removal of export and import licenses, and so on. For many years, these actions were contrary to the official party line.

The Ministry of Finance was not well suited to the task of engineering such an about face. Throughout Zambia's post-independence history, finance was never seen or treated as a "strong" ministry. Its minister was a second-tier cabinet officer who ranked below the vice president, the minister of external affairs, the Minister of Defense, and the minister for home affairs. The minister's position had been further weakened during the Second Republic (1972 to 1991) when the party apparatus transcended that of the government.

Thus, the minister of finance had a weak institutional base from which to spearhead the type of reforms needed to revive the economy. The difficulties within the ministry were compounded by the limited technical capacity of its staff. None of its regular staff had been trained beyond the master's degree

---

58. Mason 1986, Chs. 1, 2.
59. McPherson and Radelet 1995.

level. Moreover, much of that training had taken place in Eastern European countries at a time when economic liberalization was not a priority. Moreover, the ministry was disorganized. Two examples make the point. Public debt management was the responsibility of the national debt office in the loans division of the ministry, the national debt office at the Bank of Zambia, and the accounting departments of the various state-owned enterprises that had borrowed abroad. Military debt was a state secret. Thus, there was no way of gaining a comprehensive picture of Zambia's overall indebtedness. A further problem was the institutional split between the current and the capital budget. The latter was the responsibility of the National Commission for Development Planning (NCDP) over which the minister of finance nominally presided. (*De facto*, the NCDP was directed from the president's office.) Responsibility for the current budget rested with the Ministry of Finance. Due in part to the split authority, Zambia had an acute recurrent cost problem that had been untended for years.[60] Evidence of its severity was the advanced state of degradation of Zambia's infrastructure and overall inefficiency of government operations.[61]

A further problem was the lack of incentives for key ministry officials to support economic reform. That problem was not unique to Zambia. It has been common to all economies in transition that rely on the existing bureaucracy to initiate and implement fundamental reforms. Years of economic collapse and start-stop reform make government officials extremely cautious. To minimize the "bureaucratic risks" they faced, many officials had adopted "coping" strategies. They would accommodate whatever policy direction the leadership favored. Few would support initiatives that threatened their positions. Accordingly, officials were reluctant to promote reforms that at the first sign of difficulty were likely to be abandoned. Since Zambia's leaders had a long record of flip-flopping on reform, most officials had become adept at avoiding (or deflecting) actions that might directly associate them with economic reform (and, thus, almost certain failure). Finally, having already experienced years of economic decline, most officials were hesitant to support yet another adjustment program that might make their circumstances worse.

---

60. Gray and Martens 1983; Heller and Aghevli 1985; Peterson 1996.

61. The World Bank Country Economic Memorandum (World Bank 1981, p.13) noted an adverse trend in the ratio of RDCs to wages. The public expenditure review (World Bank 1992, p.iii) noted that the increase in RDC's had seriously lagged the increase in wages over the whole period 1976 to 1991. Later in the report (*ibid.* p.xi, par.44) there is special mention of the difficulties created by the recurrent cost problem.

4. PROJECT DESIGN

It is widely believed in developing countries that TA ". . . is supply-driven and not a response to local demands" and "reflect[s] donor objectives."[62] This was not the case with METAP. During their visit to Lusaka in August 1990, HIID staff asked the Deputy Secretary to the Cabinet why the government was requesting TA. His response was "we do not know where we are."[63] Minister Chigaga, and later Minister Kasonde were aware of the critical need for support to improve capacity within the ministry. They both gave the effort their full support.[64] Indeed, Minister Kasonde was instrumental in pushing for additional assistance to enhance tax administration. This led to the Computerization and Modernization of Tax Administration Project (CMTAP) which focused exclusively on capacity building.

The METAP scope of work interpreted capacity in broad terms. It was understood to involve the technical skills to undertake formal analyses, and the administrative and management skills needed to help the ministry function more effectively and efficiently. Strategic capacity, i.e., the skills needed by senior policy makers to place the key economic and institutional problems in a broader perspective, was not emphasized. This is the most difficult aspect of capacity building to handle. As time was to show, it was a critical gap in the capacity of Zambia's senior policy makers.

According to their terms of reference, each advisor was required to:

- Provide advice in areas of their specialty to policy makers;
- Prepare policy papers for consideration by government officials;
- Train Zambian staff counterparts on the job;
- Develop training programs for Zambian staff;
- Formulate proposals for institutional strengthening; and
- Help strengthen policy formulation and implementation.

Flexibility and responsiveness were incorporated in the structure of METAP in several ways. The goals for each advisor were broad. This provided some discretion regarding the balance between advising and training. Further flexibility was achieved through the use of short-term consultants, local and expatriate. They provided advice on issues such as tax reform, financial supervision, privatization, monetary policy, and exchange rate management.

---

62. Saasa *et al.* 1996, p. 66.

63. Interview with Dr. Jacob Mwanza by Donald Snodgrass and Malcolm McPherson, Lusaka, August 1990.

64. Mr. Chigaga died in March 1991 just as METAP was getting underway.

Typically, the consultants worked directly with several Zambian counterparts. They also assisted with in-country workshops or special task forces in their area of expertise.[65]

Flexibility allows any project to better meet the needs and opportunities of changing social, political, and economic conditions. Its importance for METAP emerged soon after the project commenced when, with losses due to HIV/AIDS mounting, it became necessary to reorient the capacity building program. Priority shifted from long-term overseas training for selected candidates to support for custom-designed short-term courses within Zambia. This change was made after discussions with senior ministry officials. Sending the few officials within the ministry who had bachelor-level qualifications for longer-term training would have seriously handicapped the ministry at the very time these officials were needed to help promote reform.

Other factors were important as well. Given the differences between public and private sector wages, most newly trained personnel would quickly transfer to the private sector.[66] In addition, the expected losses of trained staff due to HIV/AIDS made the cost of long-term training prohibitive. A two-year master's program abroad in the mid-1990s cost close to $120,000.[67] Since METAP had a limited training budget there was a trade-off between sending a few candidates abroad and devoting the resources to broad-based local training efforts. Expected attrition would be high in either case. Spreading training across larger numbers would be a cost effective way of having a more immediate impact on the ministry's operations. METAP continued to support some training abroad but the bulk of the effort and funds shifted to local, short-term courses.

In making this shift, METAP staff sought to emphasize training at all levels within the ministry. Capacity building programs often focus on those most visible—senior members of organizations. They are seen as the staff who can make an immediate difference. This approach ignored the substantial efficiency gains that accrue when better-trained junior staff members support the activities of those in senior positions. Over the years, the ministry had

---

65. This was evident in the assistance provided to the commissioner of taxes and the permanent secretary by Glenn Jenkins, Frank Flatters, and Jim Owens in the background work on the value-added tax and the Zambia Revenue Authority. Richard Goldman organized and presented a shortened version of HIID's macroeconomic management workshop. Graham Glenday worked extensively with the commissioner of customs and his staff to help reform the sales tax system. There were many similar examples.

66. The donors would have liked to impose some bonding arrangements. These have not worked in Zambia.

67. Gray (1997, p. 419) has additional estimates of overseas training costs.

paid little attention to the training of registry clerks, secretaries, entry level accountants, and auditors. In order to raise the efficiency of the ministry as a whole, these groups needed attention. METAP did that.

As part of the reorientation of the capacity building effort it was also decided to give trainees an incentive to concentrate on their training programs, and later, their job performance. Trainees were offered opportunities for further study if they demonstrated high levels of achievement in their courses and if they were applying their learning to their jobs. This approach had the added advantage of engaging supervisors and trainers in regular evaluation of worker performance.

To help reorient the capacity building program, METAP engaged a part-time training coordinator (one of the authors of this chapter). Her primary responsibility was to manage the project's training component. In the original project design, the METAP team leader was to have performed this task in cooperation with the HIID training office in Cambridge. The organizational and management tasks soon multiplied, and it became clear that a local training coordinator was needed. Local specialists handled the course development and provided the training. The training coordinator met regularly with ministry officials, resident advisors, and representatives from local training institutions and other donor-funded training programs. She helped determine training needs, develop programs, explore the potential of local training institutions, target opportunities as they arose, coordinate plans with the ministry's human resource development committee (HRDC), maintain regular communication with the permanent secretary, and arrange for appropriate evaluation of all training programs.

5. PROJECT IMPLEMENTATION

Capacity building in Zambia took place at both the institutional and individual levels. Through regular consultations, the permanent secretary remained engaged in reviewing and approving all capacity building activities. Revisions were made to the program in response to outside reviews, changes in local conditions, and unanticipated opportunities.

Capacity Building: Institutions

METAP staff helped with several institutional changes in the Ministry of Finance. Examples include the reorganization of the ministry, participation in numerous task forces, and the formation and functioning of the debt and data monitoring committees.

Perhaps the most profound long-term change that occurred with the assistance of METAP staff was the reintegration of the national commission for development planning (NCDP) and the Ministry of Finance. This change brought all budget and financial operations under a director of budget (with the rank of permanent secretary).[68] Following the election of the MMD government,[69] the new minister of finance, Mr. Kasonde, requested the METAP team leader to study and report on how the ministry might be reorganized to improve its operations. A draft plan was submitted in April 1992 and modified after discussions with the minister and senior government officials. No action was taken pending the outcome of the broader public sector reform program (PSRP) that began in November 1993. When the ministry was eventually reorganized, the blueprint used was the plan prepared by the METAP team leader. This reorganization was completed in October 1996. The NCDP was folded back into the ministry and the new organization was named the Ministry of Finance and Economic Development (MOFED).[70]

While this process was underway METAP staff helped with many short-term changes in the ministry's operations. Several of these changes were achieved through task forces. The most successful was the tax policy task force (TPTF), the activities of which are described in chapters four and five. Over a period of four years, it helped engineer what has been the most fundamental reform of Zambia's tax structure ever undertaken.[71]

METAP advisors had a vital role in helping to organize the task forces, determine the agendas, provide the technical support, and (where necessary) instruct the members on the key issues involved. Other task forces to which

---

68. A report by staff of the Ministry of Finance (GRZ 1999) describes the structure of the ministry.

69. Discussions about the need for civil service reform were not new. The study *Adjustment in the Midst of Crisis* (GRZ 1984) noted the need for such reform. So did the *MMD Manifesto* (MMD 1991). What was new was action on the issue.

70. With the reorganization, the main challenge has been to raise the efficiency of the ministry and improve morale.

71. The achievements of the task force were not diminished even though successive ministers undercut the reforms through the granting of exemptions. Chapter 5 noted that the 1995 reform of the indirect tax system was undermined in months when the minister approved more than 100 Statutory Instruments granting special exemptions. In 1996, the IMF added a condition to its program requiring that these exemptions be discontinued. The change of ministers in 1998 led to the granting of many more exemptions. The IMF again objected. The 1999 budget speech noted that there were 900 such exemptions extant. The minister of finance announced that they would be examined systematically to determine how the K50 billion in revenue these exemptions cost each year could be reduced. More recently, the HIPC "decision point" document (IMF/IDA 2000, p.7) noted that ". . .the government has reported that it has abstained from granting new tax reductions, exemptions, rebates, or any other preferential tax treatment to any individual or commercial entity since June this year.. . ."

METAP staff contributed were the maize marketing task force (described in Chapter 10), the data monitoring task force (described in Chapter 6), and the debt management task force and the external resource mobilization task force (covered in Chapter 9). The initial work of these task forces was so successful that some became standing committees. For example, the work of the data monitoring task force was eventually brought under the data monitoring committee (DMC). Staffed by officials from both the MoF and BoZ, this committee was charged with overseeing the financial aspects of the World Bank/IMF program and from January 1993, implementing the cash budget.

The support by METAP for local training had a major effect on the capacity of selected local institutions. It enabled them to design and run a number of new courses and raised the quality of existing courses. An example is the assistance provided by METAP to the Zambia Institute for Chartered Accountancy Studies (ZICAS). Support from METAP, and other donors, strengthened the staff and curriculum of ZICAS. The result was that after a detailed review ZICAS became the first organization outside of the United Kingdom to be certified for the full range of accountancy courses under the auspices of the Association of Chartered Certified Accountants (ACCA).

METAP also provided institutional support in the form of policy papers and policy briefs. Many were produced on a wide variety of topics throughout the project. One set of papers written in the latter part of 1991 was especially useful to policy makers. Following the death of Minister Chigaga, the METAP team members were sidelined within the ministry. The new minister, Rabson Chongo, wanted no contact with the advisors. Moreover, with the Kaunda regime unraveling as the October elections approached, there was little the advisors could say about economic management that was of interest to the government.

The permanent secretary, however, took a longer-term view. He asked the METAP advisors to prepare a set of papers on key issues that could be used by the incoming government. When MMD won the election and Mr. Kasonde was appointed minister, he sought technical advice on Zambia's economic problems. The papers prepared by the METAP advisors proved to be extremely helpful and perfectly timed.

Other organizational and institutional changes were achieved through computerization. The Computerization and Modernization of Tax Administration Project (CMTAP) was designed to enhance the operations of the revenue departments through improved tax administration and computerization. The project commenced in September 1992. Its work was deflected when the government decided to create the Zambia Revenue Authority. Once the Authority began operations in April 1994, the intention was to fully integrate CMTAP into ZRA's operations. That integration did not occur because

ZRA staff began developing separate plans for administrative reform and computerization. In March 1995, the senior management of ZRA abruptly ceased all cooperation with CMTAP.[72] At the time many programs, including a computerized VAT system, were being written under CMTAP and large numbers of staff were being trained.

With two years remaining on the CMTAP contract, an alternative was needed. After a hiatus of three months, the minister of finance and the METAP team leader agreed that CMTAP should be moved from the ZRA to the Ministry of Finance. Once that shift was made, CMTAP staff began networking the whole ministry, upgrading its data monitoring and revenue collection systems, preparing manuals and training procedures (including network maintenance), and training specialists so that the system could be regularly maintained and upgraded once the project ended. These activities helped raise the efficiency of the whole ministry.

It is ironic that when the management of the ZRA changed in early 1997, cooperation between CMTAP and ZRA was restored. Many of the applications (customs control, import reporting, the computerized direct tax system, and the bonded warehouse system) that had been completed while CMTAP was part of ZRA were revived and implemented.[73]

Capacity Building: Individuals

The initial METAP budget was designed so that four staff members of the MoF could attend master's level courses abroad each year in public administration, finance, fiscal policy, or macroeconomic policy. Additional funding was available for short-term nondegree training abroad (4–12 weeks) and for short-term workshops, seminars, and short courses in Zambia. On-the-job training was expected although no special funding was provided. Most training under CMTAP was to be on the job and through selected local and regional workshops.

The decision to move towards more localized training (noted earlier) freed up METAP's resources. In particular, it provided the finance for training many ministry officials, who had been regularly passed over. One such group

---

72. It would take a separate essay to recount the events. None of them reflected well on the senior officials involved. A degree of normality was restored when minister of finance Penza was fired, his hand picked chairman of the Zambia Revenue Board was replaced, and a new commissioner general of the ZRA appointed. This provided Zambia with an opportunity to return to the task of achieving some of the national (as distinct from personal) goals for which the move to a revenue authority was designed.

73. All of these applications could have been used by the ZRA. Its managers showed no interest. Each application made tax fraud easier to track and control.

was registry clerks who numbered around sixty. Their role was vital for the movement and tracking of files and messages within the ministry. The ministry's manual filing system had been carried over from colonial times, and procedures were not well understood. Many of the staff in the registry saw their job as a "dead end." METAP engaged a local training organization to work with senior members of the registry to design and organize a course. Its staff then taught the two-week course to four groups of fifteen officials each.

This approach had several advantages. First, it brought together staff in a setting that allowed them to learn methods and procedures relevant to their area of specialization. Second, it gave the staff the opportunity to discuss problems in the operation and organization of the registry with their teachers and co-workers. And third, it provided senior staff with suggestions on what could be done to improve the registry's operations.

The decision to customize and localize training markedly improved the capacity of many ministry officials. A number of trainers were engaged as consultants well before training began. They were requested to design programs that focused on the issues and problems faced by the prospective trainees, and to incorporate task-specific materials and procedures. For training programs located in or near Lusaka, the trainees' supervisors were frequently invited to attend wrap-up sessions where the potential for building on the training experience was discussed. For example, the accountant general frequently attended the final session of the three-week course in management and audit techniques for mid-level auditors conducted by ZICAS. In their course evaluations, participants noted that these exchanges were the first opportunity they had had for dialogue with their supervisors. Upon completion of the training, local consultants interviewed trainees and their supervisors to evaluate the effectiveness of the training and recommend changes.

Special efforts were made to raise the standards of training provided under METAP. For instance, in designing short-term in-country courses for mid-career officers, METAP replicated the program and standards of similar programs offered overseas. An example was a two-week workshop at Siavonga (Lake Kariba) on investment appraisal and risk analysis for the public sector. The 25 participants were drawn from thirteen line ministries. The trainers included three professionals who taught a similar workshop at Harvard University's John F. Kennedy School of Government. The course material had been adapted to fit Zambia's circumstances. The main operational difference was that the trainers had been brought to the trainees, rather than vice versa.

A further example of a customized, short-term, in-country course was a conference on mining sector tax reforms that the Ministry of Finance jointly organized with the Ministry of Mines and Minerals. Thirty-four senior staff from the two ministries, the private sector, and mining company representatives met to debate and recommend legislation related to mining sector tax reforms for the 1994 budget. To assist with the conference and help finalize the recommendations and draft legislation, METAP hired a short-term consultant who was an expert in mining legislation.[74]

Whenever possible, training funds were directed towards targets of opportunity and requests from groups of individuals. For example, at the request of the budget office, METAP organized two three-day workshops on planning and budget reforms, modeled after a similar workshop funded by the World Bank.[75] The sessions were attended by permanent secretaries, controlling officers, and budget office staff. One objective of this support was to begin to have senior policy makers think more broadly about the economy-wide impact of the budget. This was one of the few opportunities the project had to enhance strategic capacity.

Both METAP and CMTAP made a special effort to identify and train women. This proved to be easier than expected. Many qualified and competent women applied for, or were identified for training, and were accepted. In CMTAP, most of the local counterpart staff were women. The project provided them all with advanced training in computer programming and network management.

Occasional in-house lecture courses were devoted to the immediate needs of ministry staff. Practical examples were drawn from the operations of the ministry using contemporary data. This made the training directly relevant to the ministry's work and helped engage lower level staff in discussions of Zambia's most pressing macroeconomic problems.

Capacity building under CMTAP focused on the training of trainers. All three of the resident advisors were engaged almost exclusively in training activities and systems development. Over the course of the project, CMTAP recruited and trained twelve computer programmers and network support officers. This training took the form of frequent, short-term sessions at the Ministry of Finance by the advisors and by consultants from computer firms in South Africa. It was supplemented by occasional short courses at computer

---

74. Making the best use of his time in Zambia, the specialist gave two guest lectures at the Faculty of Law, University of Zambia.

75. There were many other initiatives. For instance, a weekend conference on information technology and tax compliance at Harvard University provided the opportunity for the Zambia commissioner of taxes to be briefed on the latest international practices in tax administration and enforcement. Short workshops were organized in Lusaka on forward budgeting, loan reconciliation, World Bank debt reporting, debt buy-backs, privatization, and Paris Club rescheduling agreements. The main attendees were officials from the Ministry of Finance, the NCDP, and Bank of Zambia.

training centers in Harare and Johannesburg. These same staff members, in turn, trained ministry staff. For example, one of the network support officers trained over seventy-five managers, secretaries, and officers of the ministry in networking, electronic mail, and file-sharing during an eight-month period in 1996–97. Another helped train forty-three economists and analysts from three different ministries in import database analysis. Others were responsible for installing the local area network, debugging and upgrading the systems, and trouble-shooting.

The project also took advantage of numerous local and regional training opportunities. An example was a study tour of the revenue authorities in Uganda and Kenya. Organized by one of the CMTAP advisors for two of the chief revenue analysts, the tour concluded by making constructive revisions to the Zambia Revenue Authority Act. Four members of the tax policy task force visited South Africa to study reforms in customs and excise, value added tax, company tax, and personal income tax. Their final report contained recommendations to the ministry on tax reform that were considered in framing the 1993 Budget.

To enhance sustainability of the training, CMTAP staff compiled a wide range of written manuals and systems specifications. CMTAP advisors and staff members produced a total of fifteen user-friendly system specification manuals on such topics as VAT, customs refunds, company registration, and the ministry's local area network. The advisors also prepared four procedural manuals, including a maintenance guide for the Zambia import monitoring system (ZIMS) and audit guidelines for tax inspectors. After leading a series of three-day workshops at the BoZ for data operators from the preshipment inspection company, one of the CMTAP advisors produced a training kit on how to access the import trade database.

Capacity Building: Counterparts

The original terms of reference stated that each advisor would have a designated local counterpart. The government's idea was that each counterpart would quickly learn the advisor's skills. That did not occur. Three of the five officials initially identified by the ministry as counterparts were also among the few eligible candidates for graduate training abroad. They left for training shortly after the METAP advisors arrived. The remaining two took jobs elsewhere in the public sector. In practice, all METAP advisors worked with many counterparts. This reflected the impracticality of having each advisor work with just one counterpart given the broad range of tasks in which the advisors were engaged.

The literature on technical cooperation has numerous discussions of the expert-counterpart model. The approach adapted by METAP is reflected in the following:[76]

> . . .the intention [of resident advisors] is not to supplant the planning, management and accountability functions of local institutional management; rather the intention is to provide a continuing and independent source of guidance. . ..

Given the imbalance in technical skills between the advisory team and ministry staff, maintaining the distinction between supplanting and guiding was especially important in METAP. The team had four Ph.D. economists. The ministry had none.[77] Team members walked a fine line between too much "fire-fighting" in line-ministry work and providing training to local analysts who might formulate and implement better policies in the future.

The advisor/counterpart relationship remained a lively topic.[78] The METAP advisors worked within a setting where the counterparts varied according to the issues being analyzed. This approach provided extensive on-the-job training and encouraged broad-ranging cooperation among lower level officials in the ministry and other economic agencies. Though this approach had not been foreseen at the start of the project, it ultimately made the most sense. Each advisor was required to work on a range of issues—budgeting, exchange rate management, debt, financial supervision, tax reform, and many more—that no ministry economist alone had the necessary skills to cover.

Capacity Building: Constraints

METAP and CMTAP were designed to deal with some of the ministry's main capacity constraints. But, the effort itself was also subject to constraints. These included the slow pace of civil service reform, the failure of senior ministry officials to rebuild morale within the ministry, policy reversals by the government, and the increased attrition of staff due to illness and death.

The slow pace of civil service reform was a drag on the capacity of the government as a whole. Launched with expressions of determination and pur-

---

76. Saldanha 1993, pp. 149–150.

77. Until early 1995, the ministry had a Zambian advisor who was a Ph.D. economist. The donor community paid his salary at levels well above local rates.

78. It has been an uneasy relationship as well. This is evident in the World Bank study on capacity building (Saasa *et al.*1996) and the manner in which the type of advisory support provided by the HIID team was allowed to wither away as advisors left for other assignments. A visit to Zambia by McPherson in January 2000, long after this essay was originally written, confirmed that the Ministry of Finance was in poor shape in terms of both technical capacity and training.

pose by President Chiluba in November 1993, the public sector reform program (PSRP) remains incomplete. The government found that the political implications of laying off as much as 50 percent of the civil service were far too daunting. Although the implications were understood when the PSRP commenced, the government was unwilling to act decisively. Cost was also an issue. Under Zambian law, civil servants can only be laid off after a large lump-sum payment.[79] Inaction allowed these costs to mount. The government did not take advantage of high rates of attrition. Policy reversals added to the potential cost. Under pressure from the donor community, the civil service fell from around 140,000 in 1992 to 124,000 in early 1997. During a hiatus in the IMF program in early 1997, the government added 17,000 staff to its payroll. The potential cost also increased because the government was unable to hold civil service salaries at levels the budget could sustain. Finally, because the government would not bring the economic reform program back on track in 1996 and 1997, donor support for retrenchment was withheld. This proved to be a major problem in 1998 as well when more than 10 percent of the government budget was programmed to come from donors specifically to pay for staff lay-offs. Throughout this period, the civil service has remained grossly overstaffed, inefficient and—relative to the private sector— underpaid. The government's delays have done nothing to resolve these issues. Moreover, the budget speech in 2000 indicated that future efforts by the government in this area will move away from the task of cutting the civil service.[80]

Similar problems were evident in the Ministry of Finance. The officials responsible for personnel management were in the human resources development office (HRDO). Both METAP and CMTAP staff worked closely with HRDO staff to enhance capacity. The delays and back-pedaling by the government were reflected at his level. For example, it took almost three years for the HRDO to prepare a preliminary staff capacity database for the ministry. Job descriptions did not exist for many positions. Introductory training pro-

---

79. The average cost has been estimated as the equivalent of ten year's salary, of which two-thirds can be taken up-front in cash.

80. Precisely what was intended was not made explicit (cf. budget speech 2000, par. 75). The speech noted:

From a political perspective, the programme must be seen, not as a numbers game, or an aimless surgical exercise, but as a comprehensive exercise aimed at addressing the expectations of our people from the public service.

What this could possibly mean, after seven years of high profile efforts to reform the civil service, was unclear. The shift of emphasis away from retrenchment, however, was a major formal reversal of the government's earlier commitment to create a "leaner, more effective" civil service. The 2000 budget speech did nothing to advance that objective.

grams for new staff, which were the responsibility of the HRDO, had been discontinued. Staff members were not regularly reviewed. Promotions were based primarily on seniority rather than merit. Political interference in personnel matters was common. Many administrative procedures had been allowed to lapse.[81] This was evident in the operation of the human resources development committee. Scheduled monthly meetings were poorly attended and frequently canceled. The chair (a deputy permanent secretary) rarely attended. Meeting agendas were not circulated in advance.

Within that committee, the shift in emphasis by METAP to in-country, on-the-job training was controversial. A major problem was that per diems and allowances for local training were much lower than for training abroad. The incentives were clear. Training was not widely seen as an opportunity to learn or advance within the ministry. Rather, it was generally seen as a means of gaining access to higher take-home pay through per diems. The number of applicants reflected this as well. Competition for training abroad was keen while relatively few staff applied for similar training offered locally.

The skewed incentives within the ministry affected the capacity building program in other ways. The three-year training programs prepared by HRDO staff were the wish lists of department heads. No budgets were attached and staff members were not ranked according to priority or merit. Similarly, HRDO staff allocated government funds for officials to attend management development programs in Swaziland (Trans-Africa Management Institute), where allowances would be paid, but cut the funds for in-house introductory training programs for new employees. In order to improve the skills of his staff, the auditor general requested METAP to contract with ZICAS to provide three-week training sessions in auditing techniques for entry-level internal auditors. The program covered basic auditing, planning, financial control, and an introduction to ministry procedures. At one time, these courses were routinely provided at the ministry.

Lest it appear that we overstress an isolated case, the actions of the HRDO were symptomatic of the distorted incentives and low morale throughout the ministry. The problem started at the top. As noted earlier, the minister of finance was not a senior cabinet position. Minister Chigaga had made a modest attempt to boost the effectiveness of the ministry. His successor Minister Chongo supported the party line and did not use the ministry to promote reform. MMD's first minister of finance, Emmanuel

---

81. In an interview in the local press in early 1996, the secretary to the cabinet (the formal head of the civil service) noted that there were more than 40,000 disciplinary actions pending. In effect, the system of discipline had broken down in the civil service.

Kasonde, was a mover and shaker who was not afraid to raise the profile of the ministry. For a period, his successor, Ronald Penza, did the same. While the reform program was working from mid-1993 to the early part of 1995, Penza provided the ministry with direction and purpose. His influence waned after mid-1995 as government attention shifted from economic reform to manipulating the Constitution so that former President Kaunda could not stand in the 1996 elections. With the elections over, it was expected that the government would turn once more to economic reform. That did not happen.[82] After two years of drift, Penza was replaced by Edith Nawakwi.[83] Her stewardship proved ineffectual and she was replaced by the former minister of health, Katele Kalumba.

Perhaps the most serious constraint on capacity building has been the policy reversals by government. These undercut large amounts of high quality technical work, diverting the attention of key ministry officials from the task of sustaining reform to attempts to contain the damage created by not reforming. Many key reforms were working well in 1993 and 1994 and the economy was responding positively. Policy reversals in mid-1995 pushed the economy into decline. Ministry officials who had earlier supported economic reform began to distance themselves. A pattern of accommodation (and coping), so common during the Second Republic, reemerged.

A further blow was the rate of staff attrition due to HIV/AIDS and other maladies. Their effects had not been anticipated when METAP and CMTAP were formulated. These losses exacerbated the other problems faced by the ministry. For example, the METAP debt advisor noted in 1995 that over the previous four years, seven personnel in the loans division of the Ministry of Finance had died of AIDS or its complications. All of them had been trained locally or abroad with support from METAP and other donors. As part of the training effort under METAP, the training coordinator began working with a gifted local trainer to develop, present, and evaluate a course for the registry staff of the ministry. Before all the staff members were trained, the trainer himself died. Many similar examples exist. The impact has been a dramatic

---

82. A group from the private sector with support from the Embassy of Sweden were to conduct a business forum in November 1998. Not wishing to be upstaged, President Chiluba announced that the government would consult with the private sector at the same time. The event was so evidently orchestrated that nothing substantive emerged. The government claimed success, nonetheless, declaring that it was willing to listen to suggestions and that, having listened, its economic policies were on track. The business forum was called off, and the opportunity for a constructive debate about the economy's performance was lost.

83. Out of office, former Minister Penza became a vocal critic of the government's unwillingness to reform. At the time of his murder in November 1998, he was actively campaigning for the presidency.

loss of trained staff and educated professionals. In the process, a large part of the ministry's institutional memory has been lost.

6. PROJECT ACHIEVEMENTS AND RECOMMENDATIONS

Over the short-term, capacity building under METAP and CMTAP was a success. More than 2000 people were trained, senior ministry officials were exposed to new ideas, and key aspects of economic policy were analyzed in systematic and enlightened ways. The Ministry of Finance was reorganized and restructured, and its operations modernized. Policy issues that for years had been avoided were vigorously debated.

Yet, when judged in terms of sustained impact, both projects probably failed. When the government's commitment to policy reform waned, METAP advisors were sidelined. As their assignments ended, they were not replaced. Senior policy makers ceased being receptive to the advisor's arguments on the need to sustain the economic reforms.[84] It is scant consolation that others inside and outside the government were also unsuccessful in having senior government officials respond constructively.

This was an adverse turn of events. None of the HIID staff who responded to Minister Chigaga's letter in February 1990 expected the GRZ, yet again, to abandon reform. The experience showed that multiparty democracy had done nothing substantive to change the quality of Zambia's leadership. It also reconfirmed evidence from other countries that the provision of TA and training is largely futile when the national leaders do not sustain their commitment to reform.[85] Such a conclusion reflects adversely on the prospective value of TA and future efforts to build capacity in Zambia. What evidence do technical assistants have that any progress they might make in capacity building will be sustained? Why should the donor community support TA for capacity building if the government will not take the necessary measures to enhance the outcomes?

Measured relative to their scopes of work, METAP and CMTAP staff exceeded by large margins all of the specific capacity building goals established at the start of the project. This is evident in the number of trainees, the variety

---

84. Since this was part of their terms of reference, the advisors continued to make the case for economic reform.

85. The same lesson is reported in World Bank (1998). Their cross-country analysis, based largely on the results in Burnside and Dollar (1997), shows that aid is not effective when governments are indifferent to reform. Though not disputing the conclusion, McPherson (2000) shows that the empirical approach Burnside and Dollar use to derive their results is seriously flawed.

of training offered, and the quality achieved. By the time METAP and CMTAP ended in 1998, ten individuals had been trained in one- or two-year master's programs overseas, ninety-one had attended short-term courses or workshops abroad, and more than two thousand had participated in workshops and seminars offered within Zambia. The breakdown is:

Summary of METAP and CMTAP Training 1991–1998

Degree courses	Trainees	10
	Years	12
Short-term courses abroad	Trainees	46
(4–12 weeks)	Weeks	251
Workshops/seminars	Trainees	1,983
(in-country)	Weeks	242
Workshops/seminars	Trainees	45
(abroad)	Sessions	19
Lectures presented	Participants	490
	Sessions	32

While these statistics say little about the "lift" the training gave to the officials, that so many participated over such a long period highlights the popularity and value of the training provided. Not included in these data is the impact of on-the-job training. That was a continuous effort throughout the terms of both projects.

The experience offers a number of lessons:

1. The activities of METAP and CMTAP demonstrated that a systematic approach to policy formulation and implementation, supported by detailed capacity building efforts, can promote economic recovery. For example, a cash budget will work if it is tried. Inflation can be reduced dramatically if the government brings the budget deficit under control. Financial reform can improve the allocation of resources. An unfettered foreign exchange market will help stabilize the exchange rate. Removing import and export controls will stimulate investment and raise incomes and employment. External and internal debts can be restructured in ways that improve investor confidence. Computerization and administrative reform will raise operational efficiency.

2. METAP staff demonstrated the value of a data monitoring committee with responsibility for bringing the key data up to date and keeping them that way. The lesson for policy makers is that economic policy in any meaningful sense is not possible if major problems cannot be anticipated and the outcomes of policy changes cannot be monitored.[86]

86. The relevance of this point has been recently reemphasized because the MOFED has allowed its debt data base to unravel.

3. METAP advisors helped Zambian officials start the process of reducing inefficiency in government by devising a range of constructive policy changes and staff reorganizations. They also helped restructure the Ministry of Finance and rationalize its operations.

4. The local and wide area computer networking developed and installed with the help of METAP and CMTAP staff demonstrated the value of improved information flows and closer working relations among key ministry staff. The skills of all ministry personnel were better utilized as the gaps in information were removed.

5. The projects showed that locally run short-term training programs could address pressing capacity constraints. The short-term custom-designed courses were especially relevant. They were participatory. They responded to recognized problems within the ministry. They were sensitive to the training needs of staff under conditions where HIV/AIDS prevalence is high. The courses were easy to organize especially when they were run through a local training institute. The programs were far more cost-effective than the provision of short- or long-term training abroad. Their evident drawback is that they did not provide trainees with in-depth technical training.

6. There was no evident trade-off between policy advising and capacity building. Under METAP emphasis on both changed over time. The project's flexibility proved useful because the donors and the government had different perceptions of how the project staff should divide their time.[87]

7. The prospect for trainees to gain access to further training based on their performance in existing programs proved to be a major incentive for ministry officials, particularly those at the lower levels. Such training reinforced the need for post-training evaluation and feedback from supervisors.

8. The outcomes in METAP and CMTAP emphasize the complementary nature of capacity building and institutional reform. Each will reinforce the other. In Zambia's case, the government's unwillingness to vigorously promote civil service reform undermined the potential of the capacity building effort.[88]

---

87. This became clear during the midterm review of Phase I of METAP. The donors told the reviewers that they did not want the advisors doing any "fire-fighting" for the government. Government officials, however, stated that they would use the advisors as they saw fit to help advance the economic reform program.

88. In its submission to the Consultative Group in July 2000, the government presented the outline for a thirteen-year capacity building effort to be called the "public sector capacity building project" (PSCAP) (GRZ 2000, par.97). With the "appropriate donor support" it would complete the civil service restructuring, reform the pay scale, introduce more effective management into the civil service, improve accountability and transparency, improve the skills of public servants, improve budgetary resource flow, and improve the government's capacity to carry out the legislative agenda. These are all laudable objectives. They were, nonetheless, many of the same goals of the original public sector reform program launched in November

9. Both projects demonstrated that one way to enhance capacity is for the government to simplify its agenda. This frees up resources (human and financial) to address the most pressing problems of economic reform. When the government is overstretched it cannot create capacity or promote economic reform on a sustained basis.

10. The experience identified the serious gaps that exist in the way governments respond to the problems created by HIV/AIDS. Those gaps, in turn, highlight the general lack of guidance that has been provided by specialists in education, management, organization, social psychology, and other disciplines on how to deal effectively and humanely with personnel who cannot quit working but whose life-spans are being prematurely truncated. METAP and CMTAP responded in a practical way to these matters by adapting the type of training provided. Broader research on these questions would be fruitful.[89]

7. Concluding Observations

Capacity building will remain a pressing need in Zambia. METAP and CMTAP staff made a major effort to enhance the capacity of the MoF to formulate and implement policies designed to sustain growth and development. Project staff also helped reorganize the ministry in ways that would improve its efficiency and effectiveness.

The outcome of METAP and CMTAP reconfirm several well-known lessons. First, capacity building is a process that requires major efforts to sustain. Second, creating capacity is not the same as motivating staff to perform at their peak efficiency. The latter requires a setting that welcomes dialogue, fosters cooperation, and rewards initiative. Third, the effectiveness of capacity building is enhanced when it is supplemented by institutional reform.

In the three years following the 1991 elections, senior policy makers in Zambia welcomed openness, the forthright exchange of views, and the joint search for solutions to the country's economic problems. That setting stimulated many important changes in policy and programs. As a consequence, Zambia's economic performance improved. From early 1995, the pace and direction of reform changed. Policy dialogue and openness gave way to belligerence and secrecy. Instead of cooperating to resolve Zambia's problems, the government and the donor community became confrontational. Capac-

---

1993 that were not vigorously pursued or diligently implemented. Since the government had already shown that it could not implement such a program, the unanswered question is what is being done differently to ensure that the new effort would be implemented?

89. These points are made in Hoover and McPherson (2000).

ity building activities continued under METAP and CMTAP but the results were compromised. Although ministry officials were better prepared to produce the data and analysis required to support policy reform, senior policy makers became progressively less willing to take note of the outcomes.

Both METAP and CMTAP succeeded in reaching their capacity building goals. Yet, in terms of providing Zambia with a solid foundation for moving to a more dynamic and prosperous future, METAP and CMTAP fared no better than the majority of TA projects in Zambia. Unfortunately, all such efforts will fall short of their potential so long as Zambia's leaders remain unwilling to sustain economic reform.

For capacity building to influence economic reform in an enduring way, three matters require further attention. The decline in the quality of education in Zambia needs to be reversed. The loss of skilled personnel and disruption of work due to HIV/AIDS has to be offset by adjustments elsewhere in the system. And, a setting that fosters openness and debate on economic and social policy has to be created. Zambia's dilemma is that all three issues are inter-linked and all three require improvements in capacity. Raising the quality of education requires dedicated scholars and administrators who will set and maintain standards of excellence. Dealing with the consequences of HIV/AIDS requires action by Zambia's leaders to adapt institutions and procedures to deal humanely with the problem while ensuring that productivity does not decline. An important change in this regard would be to reorient education and training, modify management practices, and refocus organizational objectives to accommodate the priorities of the growing number of workers who recognize that their productive life spans have shortened dramatically.

13

Macroeconomic Management and Governance in Zambia

CATHARINE B. HILL AND MALCOLM F. MCPHERSON

1. INTRODUCTION

Beginning in the late 1980s, the donor community increasingly emphasized issues of governance.[1] At first, considerable effort was devoted to defining the notion since the literal meaning of governance, namely, "the act, manner, power, or function of government" (with "government" defined as "the exercise of authority over an organization, institution, state, district") did not adequately cover what was intended.[2] Subsequent usage has made the

---

1. World Bank (1989, pp. 60–61) There are, of course, earlier references to the idea. To illustrate, governance (political and administrative) was listed by Gebrejziabher (1975, p. 3) as one of 10 "crucial functional components" of "integrated rural development." Governance was defined to include:

> ... providing for law and order, security against natural and human disaster (famine, war), policy formulation, resource allocation, revenue collection and redistribution to other components for services and supplies. Equity, equality, freedom, and participation are important features here.

This description is close to the more recent use of the term. It was only in the early 1990s that development specialists made governance a central development theme.

2. *Webster's New World Dictionary* (1964, pp. 627). Govern was defined as "...the exercise of authority in controlling the actions of the members of a body politic and directing the affairs of state, and generally connotes as its purpose the maintenance of public order and the promotion of the common welfare." An early definition of governance used by the World Bank was "the exercise of political power to manage a nation's affairs" (World Bank 1989, p. 60). A decade later, Kaufmann, Kraay, and Zoido-Lobatón (1999, p. 1), all World Bank employees, stated:

> We define governance broadly as the traditions and institutions by which authority in a country is exercised. This includes (1) the process by which governments are selected, monitored and replaced, (2) the capacity of the government to effectively formulate and

term so elastic that Humpty Dumpty would have been proud.[3] It is now common to assert that "good governance" reflects a commitment to transparent administration, accountability, respect for human rights, the refusal to tolerate corruption, sensitivity to gender and environmental issues, and adherence to democratic principles.[4]

There is, however, a more narrow interpretation that can be derived from the literal meaning of "government" and "administration."[5] We take this approach here. Our intention is to stress the point that prudent, responsible, economic management is a crucial dimension of good governance. For Zambia, this is an entirely appropriate exercise. During the election campaign in 1991, the MMD Party pledged that it would govern more openly, more transparently, and more responsibly than had been the case under President Kaunda and UNIP.[6] Those pledges were repeated before the 1996 elections.[7] The record now provides ample evidence to assess this pledge. The value of such an assessment is that it provides a basis for suggesting changes in both governance and macroeconomic management to help move the economy forward.

This chapter is organized as follows. Section 2 sets the context by identifying macroeconomic issues that directly relate to governance. Section 3 examines each of the issues in more detail. Section 4 provides suggestions for improving governance so as to enhance macroeconomic management. Section 5 has concluding comments.

---

implement sound policies, and (3) the respect of citizens and the state for the institutions that govern economic and social interactions among them.

3. "Through the Looking Glass" *The Complete Works of Lewis Carroll* New York: Vintage Books (Introduction by Alexander Woollcott), p. 214.

4. Obasanjo 1987; World Bank 1989; Landell-Mills and Serageldin 1991; World Bank 1989; Hyden and Bratton 1992; Brautigam 1996; Goldsmith 1998; Mkapa 1999; Kaufmann 1999. The Global Coalition for Africa, meeting at Maastricht on November 27–28, 1995, noted that:

Good governance. . .is. . .widely recognised as *the* basic reform underpinning all others. It places emphasis on greater accountability, transparency of decision making, popular participation in public affairs, and conflict prevention.

5. *Webster's New World Dictionary* (1964, p. 19) defines administration as "the management of governmental or institutional affairs."

6. The MMD *Manifesto* (1991, p. 2) stated:

MMD is . . .convinced that a vastly better Zambia can be rebuilt by a renewed spirit of hard work, entrepreneurship, public commitment, honesty, integrity and public accountability.

A campaign poster included in the *Manifesto* noted:

"President Chiluba will answer. . .for all his actions to you! The hour has come for a new President who makes himself answerable, for all his actions, to the people. A man who will also hold himself responsible for the actions of his ministers."

7. MMD *Manifesto* 1996, Section 6.

2. Governance and Macroeconomic Management: The Context

Taken separately, macroeconomic management and governance have been widely studied. The connection between the two has received much less attention, especially in Zambia. We begin by making two distinctions: the *role* of government, and the *performance* of government.

The Role of Government

The proper role of government in any economy cannot be fully settled. Over time, local and foreign circumstances alter; the capabilities and competence of government officials vary; and public perceptions of equity, fairness, and national welfare change. Moreover, the willingness of a particular society to tolerate the costs of public sector activities changes over time as well. These considerations modify the types of activities and policies that a government can, and should, pursue. This can be illustrated by considering one of the conventional justifications for government intervention, namely market failures. These failures stem from the existence of public goods, externalities, increasing returns to scale, and missing markets. It used to be common among social scientists (with economists in the forefront) to argue that one of the government's basic responsibilities was to deal with these failures. The attractiveness of that prescription has diminished markedly in the face of high (and often) rising costs of bureaucratic (or government) failures.[8] Moreover, even in the absence of large-scale inefficiency, it is now widely expected that governments should disengage from commercial activities. The implication is that contemporary analyses of the role of government tend to focus on the relative benefits and costs of changing the existing pattern of government involvement.[9]

The history of disruption and decline in Africa over the last three decades, largely because governments became seriously overextended, has biased the present trend in favor of public sector disengagement.[10] A prominent argument is that governments should confine their efforts to creating an "enabling environment" for the expansion of nongovernment activity. Although this principle has broad acceptance, its implementation has been subject to different interpretations. The extent and pace of disengagement are never

---

8. Wolf 1979, 1988; Burgess and Stern 1993, pp. 764–765.

9. A useful overview is World Development Report "The State in a Changing World" (World Bank 1997).

10. Easterly and Levine 1995, Sachs and Warner 1997; Fischer, Hernández-Catá, and Khan 1998; Calimitsis, Basu, and Ghura 1999; and World Bank 2000.

clearly specified. In some areas, such as health, education, and national food security, a strong case can be made for public sector reengagement, especially to improve the quality of public services.[11] Moreover, recent discussions of governance have emphasized the importance of government reengagement to foster and support civil society in ways that strengthen democracy, accountability, and transparency.[12]

Experience across countries points to government roles that are consistent with accepted standards of good governance. Two common principles are that governments should:

- Disengage from activities that can be more efficiently undertaken by the private sector;
- Pursue activities for which the risk-adjusted net social benefits are positive.

Government bureaucrats, especially in Africa, have demonstrated their lack of commercial skills in many unfortunate ways.[13] Social waste is already high in most poor countries due to excessive official travel, extravagant representation abroad, the under-funding of operations and maintenance, and the accelerated rates of deterioration of public sector capital.[14] That waste has

---

11. Ravallion 1997.

12. Brautigam 1996. The basic argument is derived from an appeal to the theory of public choice and the collective action problem. This idea has been widely stressed in texts on public finance and taxation (Buchanan and Flowers 1975, Chs. 1–6; Mueller 1976; Musgrave and Musgrave 1984; Stiglitz 1988, Ch.1; Ahmad and Stern 1989). The idea has been revived in a variety of contexts. In the wake of the Asian financial crisis, commentators have focused on the public good aspect of financial stabilization (Mussa *et al.* 1999). Transnational problems, such as the prevention of the spread of vector-borne diseases, regional infrastructure development, debt relief, and—more recently—international action to deal with HIV/AIDS are being seen in these terms (Kaul, Grunberg, and Stern 1999). Finally, the recent shift of the IMF from ESAF arrangements to poverty reduction and growth facilities (PRGF) now requires all developing countries that want such support to broadly and collectively consult civil society during the formulation of these programs (IMF March 1999; IDS 2000).

13. World Bank 1995. The performance of Zambia's parastatal sector suffered for years from the inexperience and incompetence of the well-connected bureaucrats who proved to be exceedingly poor managers. As recently as 1992, ZIMCO, the Zambia Industrial and Mining Corporation, was listed among the Fortune 500 enterprises in the world (*Fortune* July 26, 1993, pp. 204, 220). This was largely on the strength of ZCCM's copper and cobalt production. A ZIMCO draft report on the profit and loss of parastatals at December 31, 1993, showed that 43 of its companies (out of 90) had suffered losses in the previous year. The combined loss was K43.3 billion (equivalent to $9.5 million). The largest was ZCCM's loss of K29.2 billion ($6.4 million). ZCCM had been expected to make a profit in 1993 of K131.4 billion ($288 million). These losses were part of pattern that resulted from mismanagement, corruption, and an adverse macroeconomic setting.

14. For obvious reasons, African leaders disagree. In a public address at Harvard University in September 1999, the President of Tanzania stated that all of the aid his country received was

been compounded when governments have bureaucrats managing (often mismanaging) publicly owned commercial assets.

Weighing the benefits and costs of particular activities is fundamental to effective management. Indeed, a standard criterion of public choice is that the prospective (risk-adjusted) benefits of any activity should outweigh the opportunity cost of the resources involved. Public actions derived from this criterion are crucial to the idea of transparency which, as noted earlier, is a central tenet of good governance.

A specific example of the need to carefully assess benefits and costs arises in the case of subsidies. These can be justified if the advantages provided to the group being subsidized add to national welfare. It is relatively straightforward for governments to justify expenditures on drought relief and infrastructure development in isolated regions. Significant numbers of the population would suffer relative to the rest of the population if special actions of this nature were not taken. What is not justified, though it is widespread, is the capture by special interests of public support that gives them a private advantage. Obvious examples in Zambia have been the support provided for the education abroad of children (and relatives) of diplomats, the continued overstaffing of the civil service, and the special advantages conferred on importers through the issuance of Statutory Instruments (SIs) by successive ministers of finance.[15] Few of these subsidies make a positive contribution to national welfare and very few (perhaps none) would be sustained if evaluated on a pure benefit/cost basis.

We recognize that, in practice, it is politically impossible to remove all explicit and implicit subsidies.[16] Nonetheless, as a means of improving gover-

---

being efficiently and effectively used (Mkapa 1999, pp. 11–14). Both locals and foreigners have different perceptions. Information gathered by Transparency International ranks Tanzania as one of the most corrupt countries in Africa, barely above Nigeria (*African Competitiveness Report*, Schwab *et al.* 2000, pp. 214–219).

15. The discussion in Chapter 4 indicated that the selective issue of these instruments by the minister of finance undermined the 1995 customs reform. The practice was abused so grossly that in 1998 one of the IMF's performance benchmarks was that no more exemptions were to be issued by government and as many as possible were to be rescinded. This benchmark was repeated in 2000 (IMF/IDA 2000, par.10, p. 7).

16. The practical difficulty is that regulations often serve a number of functions. For example, the licensing of doctors provides quality control and some ethical oversight but it also generates rents for those in the profession and entry barriers for those seeking to join. Many private sector activities receive some form of implicit protection in this way. It is relatively easy for the IMF (and other donors) to require the government to remove the explicit protection being provided through SIs. It is much more difficult to deal with implicit protection. Common examples include inside tracks on government contracts and special deals (borrowing, lending, purchases) with state-owned enterprises. The government subsidizes public companies by allowing them to keep taxes they collect and not making them pay fees they owe.

nance, subsidies that have no redeeming social value should be removed. Common examples include supporting national airlines that run at a loss, continuing submarket interest rates, and maintaining persistently overvalued official exchange rates designed to artificially raise urban real incomes.

The Performance of Government

Perceptions of the role of government directly influence judgments about its performance. Due largely to the regular, major shifts in the development agendas pursued by the large donor agencies, these judgments are never straightforward.[17] The recent focus on governance is an example. When viewed in isolation, many items that have been added to the development agenda over recent decades can be justified in terms of their potential contribution to social welfare. Problems arise, however, because the cumulative effects of these changes are often adverse. Such additions have cluttered the development agenda in ways that deflect governments from the basic tasks of generating and sustaining rapid growth and development. Most African governments, and especially the government of Zambia, overreached their administrative and financial capacities many years ago. Improved performance requires a drastic simplification and scaling back of public sector activities.

A useful starting point for judging whether a government's macroeconomic performance is meeting acceptable standards of governance can be derived by applying the principles of prudent fiscal and monetary management. Acting in accordance with these principles, governments would finance themselves in noninflationary ways. They would allocate public expenditure to activities with the highest prospective social returns, maintain sovereign debt at levels that can be serviced on a sustainable basis, use public assets to foster public welfare rather than serve narrow sectional interests, enforce tax laws without fear or favor so that *all* groups in society share the costs of public administration, and actively avoid overdependence on foreign assistance. Appropriately implemented, all of these measures would be undertaken pro-actively.

---

17. The World Bank has had a major role in shifting the development agenda. Its annual *World Development Report* serves a number of purposes. It is a detailed review of a particular topic. It highlights the progress being made and the challenges remaining. It serves a third, perhaps unintended purpose, namely of redirecting the development debate. The latter would matter little if African governments had the capacity to effectively evaluate the proposed changes and reject those that are irrelevant. They do not. As a result, the donor community adds new initiatives to an already overloaded agenda. The outcome is that much of what is attempted by most African governments has been preprogrammed to fail. This point is explored further in Chapter 15.

These criteria help us understand some of the important links between macroeconomic management and governance. For discussion purposes, we have grouped them under the following headings:

- macroeconomic stability;
- efficient allocation of government expenditure;
- the responsible accumulation of public debt;
- a high degree of tax compliance;
- a commitment to public welfare;
- avoidance of aid dependence; and
- proactive public policy.

3. CRITERIA FOR SOUND MACROECONOMIC MANAGEMENT

One of the basic requirements for sustained growth and development is macroeconomic balance. Balance in this regard is defined in terms of the relationship between:

- government revenue and expenditure;
- savings and investment;
- imports and exports; and
- debt and productive capacity.

Imbalances or gaps in any of these relationships create "spillovers" or "knock-on" effects. The spillovers can be positive or negative. For example, when recurrent revenue exceeds recurrent expenditure, the government is saving. That saving helps finance the government's capital expenditure. This eases pressure on domestic capital markets and reduces the stock of government debt. Government saving also reduces the rate of monetary expansion. This moderates the growth of nominal income, thereby reducing the demand for imports and freeing a larger share of domestic production for export. These changes improve the balance of trade, raise the level of foreign reserves, and help stabilize the exchange rate.

A major problem in Zambia has been that most of the spillovers have been in the opposite direction with government dissaving raising the rate of monetary growth and the growth of nominal income. Higher income growth (especially in the context of a manipulated, or sluggishly adjusting exchange rate) widens the gap between imports and exports, leading to a loss of foreign reserves, and a build-up of external debt.

The main challenge for macroeconomic managers is to restore balance among these variables in ways that minimize the transition costs. Some costs are inevitable—lost output, higher unemployment, reduced asset values, and shifts in the distribution of income. These costs arise because removing macroeconomic imbalances requires fundamental restructuring of key economic relationships. Many of these costs have been well documented. Indeed, much emphasis has been given in the development literature to the *costs of adjustment*. By contrast, far less attention has been paid to the costs of *not* adjusting. The principal cost to African countries of not adjusting has been economic decline. This has been reflected in what is widely seen as the marginalization of the continent in world trade and exchange.[18]

Zambia is a classic study of a country that has borne a huge cost for failing to adjust. From the time its major macroeconomic imbalances emerged in 1974/75, the Zambian authorities have been urged to adjust. They have resisted. Moreover, that resistance has continued in ways that caused most of the macroeconomic reforms undertaken to be forced upon the authorities, or they have been taken in the breach long after major economic damage has occurred. This has produced general economic regression that has sharply reduced real per capita incomes and sapped the economy's dynamism.

One way of helping countries break out of the cycle of limited and often grudging adjustment is to begin emphasizing the principles of prudent macroeconomic management as a critical dimension of good governance. The following subsections provide examples from Zambia to illustrate the point.

Macroeconomic Stability

One of the most robust econometric results from recent cross-country research has been the destabilizing and growth-inhibiting effects of persistent budget deficits.[19] No developed or developing country has sustained high rates of economic growth and development by running persistently large budget deficits. Indeed, over the last two decades, the majority of OECD countries have implemented broad-based structural adjustment programs designed to reduce their deficits and revive their prospects for sustained growth. In the United States, for example, successive presidents and the Congress spent much of the last decade and a half trying to eliminate the federal deficit. In the European Union, the Maastricht criteria voluntarily bind member governments to keep their budget deficits below a specific, but low, upper limit. Countries hoping to accede to the European Union have to demonstrate their capacity for similar fiscal prudence.[20]

---

18. Collier 1994; World Bank 1995; Yeats *et al.* 1997; Rodrik 1998.
19. Ghura and Grennes 1993; Schmidt-Hebbel 1996; Ghura and Hadjimichael 1996; Calimitsis, Basu and Ghura 1999.
20. Corden 1994, Ch. 9.

There is an obvious lesson here. No developed country has been able to promote sustained economic growth through deficit financing, notwithstanding their deep financial systems, access to international financial markets, effective tax departments, and robust institutions. With few of these institutional advantages, the constraint is even more binding on poor countries. Indeed, history has shown that poor countries cannot grow while they continue to run budget deficits.

Zambia's experience underscores this point. The prospects for sustained economic growth in Zambia disappeared once the Kaunda regime began to rely on deficit financing. From 1970 until 1991, the average budget deficit in Zambia exceeded 12 percent of GDP. The range covers a small surplus of 3.2 percent of GDP in 1974[21] to a deficit of 21.4 percent of GDP in 1986. Such extreme fiscal indulgence generated inflation over that period of around 22,000 percent, the depreciation of the kwacha to almost one thousandth of its 1970 value, and raised the level of foreign debt to US $7.1 billion despite massive foreign assistance (of around US $5.6 billion). The outcome was a decline of per capita real income of 34 percent.

There was some narrowing of the fiscal deficit during the 1990s. Between 1992 and 1998, the budget deficit averaged 5.5 percent of GDP.[22] And with the liberalization of the local financial markets, there has been some attempt to finance the deficit in a noninflationary way. But, even with these improvements, the government has continued to run deficits. This has maintained pressure on prices, interest rates, and the exchange rate. From January 1993 to July 1995, the government and the central bank allowed those pressures to be reflected through commodity prices, the interest rate on treasury bills, and the foreign exchange rate. From mid-1995 onwards, these markets began to be manipulated. The pass-through of changes in the exchange rate to fuel prices was delayed, subsidized credit was provided for commodity imports (such as newsprint and fertilizer), and the Central Statistics Office (CSO) came under pressure from the Ministry of Finance to publish more "acceptable" inflation estimates. The interest rate on treasury bills has been "talked down" through central bank pressure on commercial banks.[23] Finally, the exchange rate was "stabilized" by requiring ZCCM to sell its foreign exchange at

---

21. Except for 1970, 1974 was the only year within the 1970 to 1991 period that Zambia recorded a surplus. (The period can be extended to 2001, implying that Zambia has had an unbroken string of budget deficits since 1974.)

22. Data in IMF/IDA (2000, Table 5) show that the deficit widened in 1999 and 2000.

23. Data in the *Macroeconomic Indicators* (September 1999, Table 2.6) allow this to be checked. Starting at the end of the first quarter of 1997 nominal interest rates began falling. They continued to fall until the second quarter of 1998. By this time, real interest rates were significantly below comparable world levels.

an appreciated rate and, more often than was prudent, the BoZ used its reserves to prevent the exchange rate from depreciating.[24]

These manipulations were made in place of cutting government expenditure and improving tax compliance. The outcome has been chronic inflation (as asset-holders shifted out of kwacha-denominated assets), an inappropriately appreciated real exchange rate, rising levels of foreign debt (largely to cover the foreign borrowing and operating losses incurred by ZCCM), and higher levels of domestic borrowing. But more important, the de facto reintroduction of exchange and interest rate controls seriously eroded confidence in the government's capacity and willingness to manage the economy in an open, transparent way.

Efficient Allocation of Government Expenditure

A common feature of all high-level decision making is the acceptance that political factors invariably require the waste of some national resources. The pork barrel is a well-known expression in the United States that evokes images of politically inspired waste and inefficiency. In advanced democracies, however, the general public expects that the ratio of "pork" to socially productive expenditure will be small. An important feature of these countries is the existence of a wide range of independent agencies whose principal function is to ensure that the use of public funds is monitored in ways that hold their politicians and bureaucrats accountable.[25] Of course, in all advanced democracies, the ultimate protection is voter reaction. Should they choose, the voters can turn irresponsible politicians out of office.

Developing countries have few effective oversight agencies and their fledgling democracies have a limited record of political competition and successful

---

24. There are several indicators of the actions taken by the BoZ to hold the exchange rate. The most obvious has been the depletion of the country's foreign exchange reserves. In this respect, it should be recalled that a principal objective of the ESAF arrangement adopted in December 1995 was to increase foreign exchange reserves. The goal was to have a buffer of reserves, a minimum of three months' import coverage, so that Zambia could withstand external shocks and repay the IMF when the ESAF debt fell due in 2001. Other indicators include the pressure on ZCCM to sell its foreign exchange at a predetermined exchange rate. These manipulations led to the reemergence of a parallel foreign exchange market in early 1998, and the accumulation of a pipeline of funds awaiting the allocation of foreign exchange. In March 1999, the BoZ sold a significant portion of the foreign exchange it had just received from the World Bank to sharply appreciate the exchange rate. And in February 2001, the BoZ, reimposed exchange controls despite denying it had done so. Information on the latter point can be seen on www.boz.zm.

25. In the United States, for example, there are the General Accounting Office, the Congressional Budget Office, various inspectors general for each major department, and a host of bipartisan oversight committees in the Congress.

government transitions. In turn, most governments have a deeply ingrained antipathy to close scrutiny of their operations. The result is that large amounts of socially unproductive expenditures—representation abroad, military outlays, and salary increases unrelated to productivity gains—receive priority in the budget.

This is not a new problem. Efficiency and effectiveness in government expenditure have been stressed for as long as public budgeting has been a coherent field of study. The problem in Africa has been widely studied as well. For example, in the late 1970s a multicountry research effort was launched in West Africa to determine the causes and consequences of the recurrent cost problem.[26] The World Bank has made a major effort to achieve some consistency in public budgeting throughout Africa. It has done this by strengthening national planning organizations. When enthusiasm for planning waned, the Bank's attention shifted to more comprehensive public expenditure reviews (PERs). These reviews stress the need for efficiency, effectiveness, and equity in public sector decision-making. They also give details on how each country could improve its operations in ways that are consistent with these criteria.[27] Finally, the Bank has also provided large amounts of technical assistance and training to improve budgeting.

With the appropriate commitment, this effort could have transformed most government budgets in Africa. Results have been disappointing. A common response by governments has been that the recommended changes are politically too difficult to implement. In reality, few governments perceive major political advantages from adopting measures that improve the allocation of government expenditure. Their assessment (reflected in the lack of budget reform) is that it would be too costly to disrupt established patterns of patronage and support.[28] Direct evidence for this point is the general unwillingness of Africa's leaders to scale back their own benefits. An obvious example is the frequency and lavishness of official travel.[29]

A widespread feature of government expenditure across Africa is the high cost of the civil service. Most countries have now stated officially that their civil services are over-staffed, inefficient, and too costly. As in Zambia during the 1970s and 1980s, wage costs in many developing countries often absorb

---

26. Heller 1974; 1979; McPherson 1979; Gray and Martens 1982.

27. World Bank Report No. 11420-ZA, 1992, par. 1.2.

28. Brautigam 1997; Killick and White 1999.

29. In early 1997, President Chiluba made a fact-finding trip to Asia. His entourage exceeded 60 officials. Robert Chambers (1983, pp. 10–12) derided rural development tourism that occurs when foreign experts briefly visit well-chosen sites in developing countries. A similar phenomenon is widespread among senior officials from developing countries who regularly make "fact-finding" trips abroad.

close to 10 percent of GDP.[30] Yet, effective reform of most civil services has
been exceedingly slow and, in many countries, nonexistent. In some countries, like Côte d'Ivoire, basic reforms were implemented then reversed. The
difficulties typically start at the top. State Houses and Prime Minister's offices
are overstaffed and there are far too many ministers and deputy (or vice)
ministers. This type of political influence peddling reflects the need for weak
leaders (of which Africa has had far too many)[31] to bring everyone "inside the
tent" by creating "jobs for the boys."[32] It has nothing to do with effective government. The rhetoric on public sector reform, now well-worn across Africa,
is that the process will create a leaner, more efficient government. Two dozen
or more (27 in Zambia's case) cabinet ministers is the antithesis of that idea.

Civil service overstaffing is a holdover from the days of controls and government-directed development. Political leaders have been hesitant to reduce
the number of civil servants vigorously for fear of antagonizing the very people they need to carry out their policies. A further complication is that Africa's civil services have often been a refuge for unproductive but well-connected workers.

No one doubts the difficulties involved in reforming civil services, especially the parts of them that have become dysfunctional.[33] But, unless constructive measures are taken to reduce the costs and improve the efficiency of
the civil service, resources cannot be freed up, efficiency will not improve,
and economic growth will not revive.[34]

Zambia's experience illustrates these points. The allocation of government expenditure has been widely analyzed in several PERs, studies by numerous consultants, and the annual *Economic Report*. All of these highlight
trends in expenditure and revenue, and recommend changes in policies that
would improve the overall budget. The discussion in Chapters 4 and 5 illus-

30. Heller and Tait 1983; Robinson 1990; Nunberg 1994; Goldsmith 1999.

31. Gray and McPherson 1999.

32. The practice is common. Upon taking office in 1999, President Obasanjo of Nigeria appointed 47 ministers (Africa News Online, Panafrican News Agency, June 30, 1999).

33. In Zambia, the late Ronald Penza was the minister for commerce, trade and industry
before he became minister of finance in April 1993. While at commerce, Mr. Penza was widely
praised for having reorganized and streamlined the ministry. Yet, when he moved to finance,
Penza showed no such interest in reorganizing the ministry. Indeed, during his tenure, the
minister created an informal network of officials and associates that enabled him to work
around those in established positions.

34. Our colleague, Arthur Goldsmith, has examined whether African bureaucracies are
overgrown (Goldsmith 1999). He finds that relative to their GDP and their total labor forces
the bureaucarcies in most countries in sub-Sarahan Africa are not unduly large. His study,
however, examined the relative size of bureaucracies only. He did not analyze the efficiency of
the bureaucracy and whether or not its activities add or subtract value.

trates that all of this effort has had little positive effect on government budget behavior.

Although the government may have done little with the PER findings, the World Bank has used them to set benchmarks for social sector expenditures. Were the government fully committed to such action, such conditions would have been unnecessary. These sectors, particularly health and education, were emphasized in the 1991 and 1996 versions of the MMD *Manifesto*.[35] The World Bank conditions appear to have made a significant difference in the area of education. For example, the shares of the budget spent on education in 1990, 1997, and 1998 were 9.3, 15.8, and 14.4 percent respectively. For health, the corresponding shares were 10.3, 11.1, and 10.8 percent, respectively. The apparent success of the government in raising (or maintaining) these expenditure shares needs to be set against the overall decline in real expenditures on these activities due to the continued contraction of real economic activity.

A further problem has been that, even when the government agrees to change its budget behavior, the changes are rarely sustained. The experience with the Medium Term Financial Framework (MTFF) is illustrative. Adopted as part of 1996 budget, the MTFF was designed to help different ministries and departments improve the efficiency and effectiveness of their operations. It was also meant to limit government expenditure in areas such as administration so that resources could be shifted to economic and social sectors. Having failed to work as expected in 1996 and 1997, the MTFF was dropped from the 1998 budget and replaced by a three-year medium term economic adjustment program. This latter approach has also been dropped. The recent emphasis has shifted to procedures that support the development and implementation of the World Bank's comprehensive development framework and the IMF's poverty reduction and growth strategy.[36]

The outcome is that the government has not had an approach to budgeting

---

35. MMD *Manifesto* 1991, pp. 8–9; 1996, pp. 13–14, and Section 5

36. The most recent incarnation of the approach is called the "medium-term expenditure framework" (MTEF). It was explained (IMF/IDA 2000, par. 18, p. 10):

As the current medium-term financial framework (MTFF) developed by the Ministry of Finance does not have political approval and is independent from the budget cycle and process, it has not been effective in achieving meaningful prioritization either within sectors or across them. The problems with the MTFF are rooted in the fact that its sector expenditure limits are set by the Ministry of Finance and Economic Development without any commitment from the cabinet or parliament.

This is history written in reverse. Both the IMF and World Bank supported the MTFF before it was developed in 1996 and adopted in 1997. As explained in Chapter 4, the MTFF was formulated as part of the budget exercise. The first of its three years *was* the budget. Furthermore, the MTFF *was* approved by cabinet, and it *was* presented to parliament for consider-

that provides coherence, consistency, and accountability. Lacking such an approach, the budget continues to be a major source of macroeconomic instability, an outcome that is inconsistent with accepted principles of good governance.

Sustainable Levels of Public Debt

A major budgeting problem in African countries has been the general unwillingness of governments to act as though real resources are limited. Expenditure plans typically require far more resources than are available. The resulting deficit raises the level of public debt. One problem is that debt dynamics tend to be ignored in official policy statements. Most budgeting exercises concentrate on flows of current revenue and expenditure. Few of them are derived from the government's consolidated income and wealth accounts.

In principle, however, all budgeting exercises should begin from the resource and debt side of the accounts so that the maximum level of expenditure that can be supported with existing revenue and net borrowing can be determined. A prudent debt strategy would ensure that net additions to the debt stock would not impede the government's ability to raise resources in the present or future.[37]

A basic problem African governments encounter when they allow their debt to rise to insupportable levels is that it triggers events that undermine national wealth and income. Borrowing *does* supplement the flow of national income if the resulting investments earn positive net returns. Frequently, however, the return on borrowed funds has been zero or negative.[38] Governments have often used borrowed resources inefficiently, particularly when attempting to sustain consumption. As debt has risen, a growing share of public resources has been devoted to debt service. This has reduced the resources available for productive investment, thereby lowering the growth of national income.

Governance issues arise at a number of levels. Fiscally responsible governments do not incur deficits that push a country beyond its capacity to service debt on a sustainable basis. Economic shocks might require temporary in-

---

ation. What went wrong? Rather than induce the government to create the conditions that would enable the MTFF to provide a consistent framework for expenditure and revenue analysis, the IMF and World Bank have shifted their focus to an MTEF.

37. This reflects an important principle of prudent management noted below, namely, the need to avoid actions that unnecessarily reduce the decision-makers' options.

38. Collier and Gunning (1999a) reversed their earlier position (Collier and Gunning 1999). They note that the low return on investment has been a source of slow growth in Africa.

creases in debt. Nonetheless, responsible governments make the necessary adjustments so as to ensure that their debt servicing capacity remains unimpaired. Furthermore, responsible leaders do not assume that, because debt is repayable over time (often well beyond their time in office), that repayment is someone else's problem. Under colonial accounting systems, governments used to establish "sinking funds" so that debt repayment remained a charge against the current budget.[39] That practice was dropped by postcolonial governments as their budgets came under pressure and additional ways were needed to gain access to current resources.

Zambia has an unfortunate debt history. Due to the unwillingness of the government to adjust the economy in the wake of the economic shocks of the mid-1970's, the country's external debt rose rapidly. As already noted, debt difficulties quickly emerged with large external arrears evident as early as 1975. Much has been written about the circumstances associated with the rise in debt—falling copper production, fluctuating copper prices, and drought-induced crop failures.[40] As noted in Chapter 14, little has been written (or said) about why international agencies, primarily the IMF and the World Bank, continued to provide additional resources even though the government demonstrated from its first consultative group meeting in 1978 that it would not (or could not) sustain policy reform.[41] In fact, continued support by the donor community allowed Zambia to become completely unbankable and remain that way. Zambia may have become a "ward of the international community" to use Krugman's evocative phrase, but it was fully aided and abetted in this by an indulgent donor community.[42]

Despite massive debt forgiveness and debt restructuring, the period of democratic rule has seen only modest improvement in Zambia's overall debt situation. In 1991, Zambia had a debt stock in excess of $7 billion, of which approximately $3 billion was in arrears. Following the normalization of Zambia's relations with the major donors, there has been a large amount of debt relief, outright forgiveness, a commercial debt buy-back, and $1.2 billion in refinancing from the IMF. (The details are given in Chapter 9.) By the end of 1995, Zambia's debt stock had fallen to around $6.2 billion, the arrears had been paid off, the debt profile had lengthened, and the annual debt service payments had fallen sharply. Beginning in 1996, many of these achievements

---

39. Deane 1953; Overseas Audit Unit 1955, pp. 31–32.

40. GRZ 1984, 1989.

41. An unpublished memorandum by Ben King (1977) examined how the IMF and World Bank regularly overestimated the degree to which the GoZ would honor its commitments to reform and the extent to which copper prices would rise and remain high. Similar comments appear in King (1991).

42. Krugman 1989, p. 184.

were reversed. The most important problem was that the government did not keep its program with the IMF on track. It was compounded by the withdrawal of donor support when the government would not meet acceptable standards of governance, and ZCCM's losses that were estimated to have been around $15–20 million per month.[43]

Although there was evident backsliding on policy reform, senior Zambian authorities continued to look to external scapegoats and solutions. The 1998 budget speech, for example, was highly critical of the donor community for withholding aid because of issues related to governance. Nonetheless, that speech also noted that the availability of the donor-funded Highly Indebted Poor Country (HIPC) initiative was a major opportunity for Zambia to overcome its debt problems. Later, the minister of finance in his 2000 budget speech used more measured language to urge Zambians to strive to create the conditions that would give the country access to debt relief under HIPC.

While many important policy changes had been made with some early success in reducing Zambia's external debt, the government did not sustain the effort. The policy reforms needed to keep Zambia on track so that it would be eligible for HIPC were not taken.[44] The failure to move decisively to sell ZCCM led to a sharp increase in both domestic and external debt.[45]

As a final point, it should be noted that none of Zambia's key policy-mak-

---

43. *The Economist* May 9, 1998, p. 50. Over the five-year period, 1993–94 to 1997–98, ZCCM suffered a loss in all years except 1994/95 when its profit was equivalent to $52 million. The combined loss in the other four years was equivalent to $684 million (IMF, Statistical Appendix, May 1999, Table 15. Exchange rates using in the conversion to dollars were taken from the *Macroeconomic Indicators,* January 2000, Table 1.3).

44. This was illustrated when one of the authors, McPherson, who was principal investigator for a USAID-funded research project, Equity and Growth through Economic Research (EAGER), attempted to interest then minister of finance Penza and secretary of the treasury Mweene in studying the types of measures needed to ensure the economy could meet the HIPC conditions. The proposal, presented to both Penza and Mweene in March 1997, was for the EAGER project to finance a group of Zambian researchers to examine whether the policies then being implemented by the GRZ would provide Zambia with the best chance of meeting the HIPC conditions by the anticipated accession date (December 1998). The exercise was intended to use local research to guide the government on the appropriateness of its policies or the modifications needed to ensure the HIPC conditions would be met. Believing their current policies to be appropriate, neither the minister nor the secretary would approve the study. In the event, Zambia's policies were inadequate and Zambia's accession to HIPC was delayed.

45. As the IMF/IDA (2000, par. 5, p. 6) noted:

In recent years, the fiscal burden of the ZCCM was particularly high, costing about 6 percent of GDP during 1999, and the government had to assume ZCCM's debt obligations, equivalent to about 19 percent of GDP.

The 2000 budget contained a payment of K423 billion (roughly 4 percent of GDP and equivalent to US $158.5 million). These funds were to clear some of ZCCM's domestic arrears (*Budget Speech* 2000, par. 91).

ers act as though they foresee an end to balance of payments deficits. This was evident in both the 1999 and 2000 budget speeches. What is being missed, however, is that unless the deficits are eliminated there is no end to Zambia's debt problems irrespective of the relief that is provided under HIPC, or any other debt reduction initiative. Any government committed to good governance would recognize this point and give highest priority to the elimination of its budget and the balance of payments deficits.

Concern for Public Welfare

Political scientists have many models to explain why collective decisions often undermine national growth and development—interest group dynamics, social pathologies borne of noncooperation, ethnic fractionalization, dysfunctional organizations, and the like.[46] Emphasis has centered on the conflicting pressures which confront policy makers from their constituents, their party and parliamentary colleagues, business associates and business leaders, and church groups, among others. Rationalizing these competing interests in ways that provide a coherent approach to public policy *and* satisfy the policy-makers' personal goals involves many compromises.

Policy-making rarely provides options that are win-win. A crucial dimension of the "art" of effective policy-making is choosing the measures that balance the interests of the winners and losers in ways that allow the public policy agenda to move forward.[47] Under these circumstances the main challenge for policy makers is overcoming the resistance of those who perceive they are harmed by such policies.

The general move towards the restoration of democratic rule throughout Africa (despite setbacks in Niger, The Gambia, and Sierra Leone) has highlighted the need for a broader consensus on the issue of the public good. After many years of repression and arbitrary personal rule,[48] many countries now have democratically elected governments. Since a large number of the new democrats are, in fact, old autocrats (Daniel arap Moi in Kenya for example), constructive changes in economic policy have been slow to emerge.[49] Public discourse rings with the rhetoric of reform. In practice, however, influence peddling is pervasive and narrow special interests (often the newly installed democrats) hold sway.[50]

---

46. Nelson *et al.* 1989; Ayittey 1992, 1998; Bates and Krueger 1993; Kets de Vries 1997; Grindle 1999; Brautigam 2000.
47. Vickers 1983; Dixit 1997.
48. Sandbrook 1987, 1989; Ayittey 1992.
49. Gray and McPherson 2000.
50. Harsch 1993; Ayittey 1998.

These pressures are as strong in Zambia as elsewhere. The consequences have been just as dramatic. Political reform has not been translated into economic reform in ways that generate higher rates of growth and development. Since the MMD government took over in late 1991, living standards and real per capita income in Zambia have continued to erode.[51] The decline in real per capita income over the period 1992 to 2000 has been around 13 percent.[52]

This change is not consistent with good governance. Public welfare will always be undermined by external shocks, droughts and floods, and sheer bad luck stemming from wars or transport disruptions in neighboring countries. Governments, however, can avoid the welfare losses associated with inappropriate policy choices. In Zambia's case, government action has created high rates of inflation, increased the national debt to unsustainable levels, and diminished food security. All three have undermined public welfare; all of them were avoidable.

As noted in Chapters 3 and 4, the exceptionally high inflation in 1991 and 1992, prompted the GoZ to introduce a cash budget in 1993 as a means of bringing down inflation.[53] The effects of the cash budget were dramatic. Inflation fell from an annual rate of 188 percent in 1993 to 54 percent in 1994. But, for reasons highlighted in Chapter 3, beginning in early 1995, the government progressively abandoned the cash budget. This occurred in several ways. Arrears were allowed to accumulate. Bridging finance, in both kwacha and foreign exchange, was provided by the BoZ to the government but was not repaid. Treasury Bills were issued directly to banks and merchants as a means of avoiding expenditure restrictions. And, the "cash budget" principle of blocking expenditure when resources were not available was allowed to

---

51. There are many ways of measuring Zambia's declining standards of living. The WDI (1998, Table 1.3) reported that over the period 1980–96 the distribution corrected decline in per capita consumption was 2.1 percent per annum. The WDI (2000, Table 1.2) shows that the annual decline was 2 percent over the period 1980 to 1998. The *African Development Indicators* (2001, Table 1.1) shows that from 1988 to 1999, real per capita GNP declined by 2.4 percent per annum. The decline in real incomes commenced roughly a decade before. In its presentation to the Consultative Group for Zambia in July 2000, the GRZ offered a long-term vision for dealing with poverty. The document stated (GRZ 2000, p. 1):

The need for a vision has been necessitated by the increasing number of people living in absolute poverty, the generally very low quality of life being experienced by the majority of people of Zambia as a result of the continuing decline in the performance of the economy and the need to guide the development process.

52. This has been derived in two ways—in kwacha from the *Macroeconomic Indicators* and in dollars from the *African Development Indicators* (2001, Tables 1.2 and 2.1). The former yields a decline of real per capita income between 1992 and 2000 of 12.3 percent. The latter yields a decline of 13.2 percent.

53. Bolnick 1997; Adams and Bevan 2000; McPherson 2000. The cash budget is discussed in Chapter 4.

lapse. The progressive abandonment of the strictures imposed by the cash budget showed up as a higher rate of inflation. It was 34 percent in 1995 and 46 percent in 1996. And, while inflation in 1997 was officially reported to be 25 percent, few experts believe that datum reflected reality.[54] Moreover, the exchange rate was manipulated to slow down its rate of depreciation. Thus, the government has failed to sustain measures needed to reduce inflation. It has become commonplace for the budget speech to announce the government's intention to reduce inflation to a low double-digit number and later in the year revise the target upwards. This, for example, was the case in 2000. In January, the minister of finance announced that the target for year-end inflation was 14 percent.[55] By mid-2000 when the government reported to the meeting of the Consultative Group for Zambia in Lusaka, the annual inflation target for 2000 had been revised to 22.3 percent.[56] This was not a one-off slip. In 1999, target inflation was 14 percent. The actual was 20.6 percent.

From a macroeconomic perspective, it is useful to highlight the source of this inflation. None of it has been "imported." Inflation rates in the rest of the world (specifically Zambia's major trading partners) were between 1.4 and 2.4 percent per annum in 1999 and 2000.[57] All of Zambia's inflation over recent years has been domestically generated, the result primarily of the government's inability to eliminate deficit financing and the monetary growth it generates. To illustrate, broad money growth rates in Zambia for 1996, 1997, 1998, and 1999 were 32.1, 21.4, 15.9, and 37.1 percent, respectively. In practice, the government's commitment to reduce inflation has been hollow. This raises questions about the government's commitment to raising welfare. If, indeed, inflation has been the "cruelest tax on the poor" (as President Chiluba asserted) why has the effort to reduce inflation not been sustained?

As discussed in Chapter 9, even with large amounts of rescheduling, refinancing, and outright debt forgiveness, Zambia's external debt was higher at the end of 1998 than at the end of 1991. The main reason has been ZCCM's losses. Major efforts have been made to eliminate Zambia's arrears and restructure its debt (by lengthening the repayment profile and reducing the

---

54. There is every reason to believe that inflation was significantly higher. The GDP deflator increased by 26.5 percent and the import price deflator rose by 11.6 percent (*Macroeoconomic Indicators* September 1999). Since the CPI, the GDP deflator and import prices are interrelated and the share of imports in total supply was .24, the CPI must have increased by at least 31 percent.

55. *Budget Speech* 2000, par. 53.

56. GRZ 2000a, p. 10.

57. *Agricultural Outlook* November, 2000, Table 3, p.28 (published by Economic Research Service of the United States Department of Agriculture). Inflation in the developed countries in 1999 was 1.4 percent and in Asia 2.4 percent.

cost of funds), but the country has continued to accumulate debt through its inability to reduce the balance of payments deficit. The demise of ZCCM led to a steady decline of copper production (from around 427,000 metric tons in 1990 to 280,000 metric tons in 1999).[58] As described in Chapter 6, this situation was aggravated by policies that progressively overvalued the real exchange rate as the decade wore on. The main point is that, from a macroeconomic perspective, Zambia cannot move beyond its insupportable levels of debt while it continues a running balance of payments on itscurrent account that over the period 1992 to 1999 amounted to US $4.21 billion (approximately $526 million per year).[59]

Declining food security has been a long-standing problem in Zambia that first emerged when the drought of 1979–80 cut maize production by 36 percent from a year earlier.[60] Maize production remained low through most of the 1980s with recovery to former peak levels in 1988 and 1989. The drought of 1991–92, however, reduced production to 483 thousand metric tons, a level not seen since 1968 when Zambia's population was 51 percent lower. Massive external support of close to a million metric tons of food averted disaster. Yet, Zambia's food situation has remained precarious. After recovering in 1993 to 109 (1989–91=100), the index of food production per capita in Zambia declined to 82 in 1997 and 77 in 1998. The improved harvest in 1999 raised the index to 83, far too little to reverse the long-term declining trend in food production per capita that began in the late 1970s.[61]

Drought has been a major explanation of the year-to-year fluctuations in food production, but it does not explain the downward trend. Zambia is a country with abundant labor and land, and a large agricultural base. The principal explanation of the country's inability to improve food security over time has been the government's policy choices. These choices generally undermined agricultural incentives during the 1990s. In principle, the government has been committed to a liberal, market-driven agricultural policy. Yet, it has persistently intervened in maize and fertilizer marketing. It has also failed to act, as it promised, to rationalize the use of land so as to encourage

---

58. To allow for annual output fluctuations, a better indication of the downward trend is given by moving averages. Average copper production over the period 1989 to 1991 was 418,000 mts. For the period 1997 to 1999, the average was 302,000 mts. The decline over the decade was 28 percent.

59. *Macroeconomic Indicators* June 1997, April 2000, Table 3.5 It was reported in IMF/IDA (2000, Table 8) that the balance of payments current account deficits for 2000, 2001, and 2002 were projected to be 13.5, 13.1, and 12.4 percent of GDP respectively.

60. Derived from data in Chapter 9. Maize production in 1979 was 1,456 thousand metric tons. In 1980, it was 937 thousand metric tons, a decline of 36 percent.

61. *African Development Indicators* 2001, Table 8.5.

broader investment in agriculture. Finally, through its manipulation of the exchange rate the government has continued to undermine incentives that would lead to the rapid sustained expansion of export agriculture.

High Degree of Tax Compliance

A high degree of tax compliance is an essential dimension of a well-governed society. Responsible governments ensure that they mobilize resources adequate to cover projected expenditures in a noninflationary way. An important means of providing those resources on a sustained basis is to enact *and* administer legislation that ensures a high degree of tax compliance.[62] This topic has received too little attention in the governance literature.[63] For countries like Zambia that depend heavily on donor assistance to close the financing gaps in their budgets, improved tax compliance should be one of their highest priorities. Foreign taxpayers should not be expected to continue supporting governments that do not require their citizens to fully share the burden of raising public revenue. It has been too convenient for African leaders to treat the decline in resource transfers from the rich to the poor countries as niggardliness on the part of the rich countries.[64]

African leaders dedicated to improved governance would ensure that the maximum effort had been made to fairly and effectively raise revenue and economize on expenditures *before* turning to the international community for support.[65] The pattern has been largely the reverse. African governments have found that tapping external sources of finance has been much easier than mobilizing resources locally.

Improving tax compliance has several tangible benefits for an economy. First, ensuring that taxes are paid as required by the law puts to rest one of the principal criticisms by the international community of so-called "soft" or dysfunctional states.[66] Second, better tax compliance improves efficiency throughout the economy. A given amount of revenue can be raised with fewer distortions in economic behavior. Third, a high degree of tax compliance improves equity. Those who are required to contribute to the costs of operating the government do so.

---

62. Experience from The Gambia (McPherson and Radelet 1995) and Magadgascar (Andrianamana 1999; Gray *et al.* 2000) shows that improving tax compliance can have an important impact on macroeconomic management. The problem has been sustaining these initiatives.

63. Glenday (1997) provides evidence from Kenya.

64. Mkapa 1999.

65. This was the principle of self-help stated by President Kennedy in 1963. (References are given in Chapter 14.)

66. Lancaster 1999, Ch. 3.

Until the early 1980s, Zambia was a high tax effort country that had an international reputation for minimal tax fraud.[67] During the 1980s, its tax effort declined sharply. The profitability of ZCCM, a traditional source of revenue, fell due to cuts in investment, overstaffing, an overvalued real exchange rate, and falling standards of management and accountability throughout the company. Furthermore, the rate of economic growth fell as government interference and controls became more pervasive. Finally, the government's overall unwillingness to sustain economic reform undermined business confidence, leading to capital flight and a sharp reduction in productive investment. (These points were covered in Chapters 3 and 6.)

The need to reform the tax system had been recognized for a number of years. Even before the return of democratic rule, the UNIP government had taken steps to overhaul the tax system. The intention was to modernize tax legislation and restructure tax administration. The MMD government built upon this effort. As discussed in Chapter 5, a number of task forces devised several sets of tax reforms. These were implemented in the budget speeches from 1992 to 1995.

By 1995, the government had fundamentally overhauled Zambia's tax system. Laws had been changed. Tax loopholes had been closed. Tax rates were lowered. The tax base had been broadened. Penalties for evasion were increased. In an effort to professionalize tax administration, the government established the Zambia Revenue Authority (ZRA), providing it with significantly more resources so as to enhance tax collection. A major effort was underway to computerize the tax system. But, largely due to high-level influence peddling, the results achieved were well below their potential. Despite what appeared to be some initial improvement when the VAT was introduced, real tax revenue did not increase significantly.[68] It was noted in Chapter 5 that the change in senior management of the ZRA in early 1997 produced some improvement in tax administration. That, however, has been unable to overcome the revenue losses resulting from the general decline in national income. The ZRA has been attempting to maintain real revenues against a background of falling income.

Governance issues have featured prominently in the performance of the ZRA. There was significant pressure to restructure the tax system, but much less to sustain the outcome. To illustrate, much of the effort to broaden the tax base had been undermined by tax exemptions.[69] Furthermore, the admin-

---

67. The 1981 World Bank country economic memorandum noted that "...tax collection is good and tax evasion infrequent" (World Bank 1981, p. 13).

68. Kasanga 1996.

69. The minister of finance has broad powers under the tax code to provide exemptions. These are granted through Statutory Instruments (SIs) published in the *Gazette*. In principle,

istration of the ZRA quickly degenerated under the weight of an intrusive governing board, incompetent expatriate administrators, political interference, and corruption.[70]

While it is easy to point to the deficiencies in tax administration, it should be noted that improving tax compliance in Zambia would have been difficult under the best of circumstances. Years of lax enforcement and economic disruption had convinced most Zambians that cheating on their taxes was an appropriate response to the instability created by the government. Through capital flight and currency substitution many businesses and individuals had shifted their transactions offshore and/or into foreign exchange. These would have been hard to trace even if the capacity of the tax authorities had not declined. Under one-party rule, the revenue departments had been politicized. That did not change under the MMD. The weak position of the Ministry of Finance within the government hierarchy (discussed in Chapter 3) was a further drawback.

Avoidance of Aid Dependence

There are now literally hundreds of studies highlighting both the positive and negative aspects of foreign assistance. (Chapter 14 reviews some of this literature.) Many of the issues associated with aid—the addition to national resources, fungibility, distorted incentives, artificial appreciation of the real exchange rate, the resentment by aid recipients, and moral hazard—were recognized during the implementation of the Marshall Plan.[71] Subsequent discussions have highlighted the complex interplay of motivations and expectations associated with aid. The intersecting interests cover a broad spectrum— politics, economics, diplomacy, international security, and humanitarian concerns. For many commentators, especially senior staff of major aid agencies, foreign assistance is seen as part of the solution to pressing problems of development.[72] As Chapter 14 makes clear, there have always been critics who

publication provides a high degree of transparency, since the information about who is being granted specific tax breaks is part of the public record. In practice, the publication of these tax breaks has made no difference because of the difficulties involved for concerned parties to reverse them.

70. Little has been written on this topic, yet anecdotes abound. For example, in 1995 a cabinet minister with close connections to the business community informed the permanent secretary of finance that the going rate for moving a container through customs at Chirundu (the main border crossing in Zambia) was K1.2 million (around $1,500 at the time). This amount was divided K800,000 for customs officials and K400,000 for the staff of the PSI company.

71. Ohlin 1961; Orme 1995.

72. The speech by the president of the World Bank, James Wolfehnson to the bank/fund meetings in Hong Kong in 1997 was entitled "The Challenge of Inclusion." It addressed the is-

argue that aid is part of the problem. More recently there has been a growing recognition that the pathologies generated by aid dependence need to be addressed directly.[73]

Discussions about ending aid dependence in Africa have an element of blaming the victim. Aid has been provided to African countries for many reasons, most of which had little to do with sustained economic growth and development. They include East-West competition, preventing the weight of external debt from further depressing local economic activity, expanding the influence of multilateral aid agencies, fostering program ownership, maintaining financial stability, promoting the donors' commercial interests, and preventing humanitarian disasters. The outcome has been net transfers to Africa so large and for such extended periods that they have dominated the development agenda. Even without the various "games" which emerge between donors and aid recipients, transfers of such magnitudes distort incentives and maintain the chronic over-valuation of most African currencies.

At some point those who are involved in a dependent relationship need to recognize and deal with the counterproductive dynamics that emerge. What we have been advocating, and discuss in detail in Chapter 14, is that African governments and aid agencies need to acknowledge the adverse effects of their mutual dependence and take steps to overcome them.

Zambia and its many donors have not yet reached that stage. This point was evident in the 1998 budget speech and again in the 1999 and 2000 budget speeches. The 1998 speech (reviewed in Chapter 15) has several statements praising the donors for their support and damning them for their interference. This ambivalence has been a common feature of Zambia's relationship with donors.[74] In many respects, Zambia's situation is a case study of how foreign aid has accentuated economic regression. Because of Zambia's capacity to borrow in the 1970s, it was too easy to finance the imbalances in the economy rather than adjust. As commercial credits became more difficult to obtain towards the end of the 1970s, the IMF and the World Bank provided large amounts of additional resources on the pretext that Zambia was (or would be) taking the measures needed to restructure its

---

sue of how the aid community can fully include those whom fifty years of development support had by-passed. Regarding debt relief, CID (1999) proposed that the poorest countries should have their debt written off and aid increased so that they can develop. Several other efforts are underway. One of these is to induce donors in rich countries (governments, foundations) to provide around $10 billion per year for a global health fund to deal with communicable diseases, especially tuberculosis and HIV/AIDS.

73. Fernholz *et al.* (1996) made this point in a special report on Zambia produced for the Embassy of Sweden. Berg (1996) and HIID (1997) argued that the problem was more general in Africa and needed to be directly addressed by both aid donors and aid recipients alike.

74. Saasa and Carlsson (1996) call the aid relationship in Zambia a "conflict scenario."

economy. The aid continued to flow throughout the 1980s. In the process, Zambia implemented and abandoned numerous structural adjustment programs. By the time the IMF and World Bank decided to get tough on the Kaunda regime, Zambia was deeply in arrears to both organizations. At this point, the problem for the IMF and World Bank was how to extricate themselves in ways that would allow them to recover their loans. The collapse of the UNIP government provided such an opportunity. Zambia's RAP with the IMF was revived and large amounts of aid flowed from both multilateral and bilateral sources.

Progress was made in the first three years of the MMD government in reforming the economy and setting the stage for the transition to higher rates of growth. As already noted, that effort began to unravel in early 1995. It continued to unravel in large part due to the ambivalent response by the donors to the government's nonperformance. Donors withdrew balance of payments support as a sign of their displeasure. Yet, they continued (and in some cases expanded) project support. This reaction simply reconfirmed what Zambia's leaders have known for years. Nonperformance has few (if any) sustained consequences.

Proactive Policy Response

Another dimension of macroeconomic management consistent with good governance is the creation of conditions that enable governments to be proactive in their approach to policy. Such conditions have not been common across Africa. The result is that, too often, African governments have been caught short on key policy issues. Economic management often becomes a continual struggle to catch up with events. A major reason is that governments have adopted agendas that are well beyond their financial and administrative capacities. Underlying this overexpansion has been the failure to adopt a strategic approach to policy formation or economic management. The result has been a lack of coherence in policy characterized by indecision, reversals, and inconsistencies. To paraphrase Lindholm, there is much muddling without any effective "muddling through."[75]

Yet, even if government agendas in Africa were not overextended, their staffs frequently lack the data that allow them to get ahead of the circumstances that directly influence their activities. A further problem that deters African governments from being proactive is the degree to which they depend on foreign aid. As noted earlier, overdependence on foreign aid has un-

---

75. Lindholm (1959) challenged the idea that decision making is a coherent, consistent process based on optimizing behavior. He argued that, due to the constraints under which decision-makers operate, the best they can do is "muddle through."

dermined the ability of African governments to set their own priorities and pursue them consistently. Policies they adopt are largely the result of the pressures that arise in the capitals of their international overseers and bene-factors.

Taking a pro-active stance to policy formation would require a fundamen-tal shift in behavior at the senior-most levels of government. There would need to be a structured program to improve the database, tighten fiscal and monetary policies, and improve the government's capacity to respond to un-expected changes in the macro economy. Experience shows that the place to start is the data. Without adequate, timely data, economic policy cannot be pro-active. At best, the government can react to events as they unfold and then only with a long lag. Typically, a special effort is required to bring up-to-date the data essential for monitoring the economy and to ensure that they remain that way. One approach, which has been effective in several countries, is to establish a joint ministry of finance/central bank data moni-toring committee. This committee is assigned responsibility for monitoring the key macroeconomic data at intervals frequent enough to provide senior policy makers with the information needed to anticipate short-term macro-economic developments.

A second requirement is for the government to review and drastically sim-plify its policy agenda. Priority should be given only to the most urgent and readily achievable policy goals. Many changes are desirable and will eventu-ally have to be made, but a key aspect of a strategic approach to policy reform is to focus on the crucial changes and ensure they are implemented. Most Af-rican governments have been hung up on civil service reform with much of the effort devoted to this task wasted. For their part, civil servants have dem-onstrated that they have no capacity to reform themselves.[76] And, due to im-plied or explicit guarantees of lifetime employment, the costs of redundancy packages are often prohibitive.[77] Guided by the need to simplify their agen-das, governments committed to civil service reform would shut down mar-ginal ministries, lower the age of mandatory retirement to 50 (with special re-tainer provisions for exceptional retirees), and allow attrition to reduce the need for forced retirement. This approach would reform the system by allow-ing the more rapid promotion of younger, better-educated employees.

By simplifying its agenda, the government will be improving its capacity to respond to changes in the macro economy. Two dimensions of this task need emphasis. First, at each decision point, the government should focus on the

---

76. Munene (2000) has a perceptive analysis of the problem in Uganda.

77. In 1995, estimates provided by the Cabinet Office in Zambia showed that the cost of re-trenching an established civil servant exceeded US $50,000. This prohibitive (and highly ineq-uitable) cost has impeded civil service reform.

"next best steps" required to achieve rapid growth and development. Second, the decisions taken should not unnecessarily foreclose future options.

Determining the "next best steps" is the essence of adaptive decision-making. It requires a pragmatic assessment of the basic economic and social objectives that should be pursued, an understanding of the economy's main constraints, and knowledge of the options available for meeting the country's objectives within the context of those constraints. One of these constraints is globalization, an issue with which few African governments have come to grips. This is evident in the common approach to budgeting. The typical approach, as illustrated by the way Zambia's budgets were framed during the 1990s, is to begin from domestic expenditure requirements and match these against projected domestic revenues. The inevitable "resource gap" is then filled by an exercise which consists of cobbling together a range of multilateral and bilateral support from Zambia's development partners.

This approach is repeated so often across Africa that it *is* the institutionalized form of budgeting. From a policy perspective it is fundamentally wrong. The *domestic* budget exercise should begin with the constraints imposed by *external* resources. If adopted, such an approach would have the beneficial effect of focusing African governments on the policies needed to ensure that external resources supplement rather than supplant local efforts. Ironically, this was a commitment made by the MMD government immediately it assumed office.[78] So far, that commitment has not been kept.

An important principle in deciding on the "next best steps" is to avoid making policy choices that foreclose potentially useful options. Political pressures frequently lead decision-makers to favor government involvement rather than the creation of incentives that would expand the private sector. Having made that choice, however, governments often discover that further intervention is required because of a lack of private sector response. The fault, however, lies not with the private sector especially when governments provide mixed signals. By remaining involved, the government directly (and often strategically) discourages the private sector.[79]

Zambia provides an interesting set of contrasts in these areas. Beginning in September 1992 the government made a concerted effort to bring the key

---

78. At the donor/creditor meeting in Paris on December 11, 1991, the government submission (GRZ 1991a, p.1) stated:

...your financial assistance, so generously provided in the past, must in future supplement our own savings and efforts, and *not* replace them. (emphasis in original).

79. Zambian government participation in the importation of fertilizer has been driven by these considerations. Government officials have regularly created circumstances such that their intervention allows lucrative public sector contracts (for the officials involved) to be negotiated to the detriment of private sector expansion in fertilizer marketing.

macroeconomic data up-to-date. The initial effort was based on the input of an *ad hoc* committee formed by BoZ and MoF staff. With the decision to implement the cash budget in 1993, the minister of finance formally appointed a Data Monitoring Committee (DMC). Its members were instructed to devote whatever effort was needed to bring all of the relevant monetary, fiscal, debt, and trade data up-to-date and keep them that way. Initially, the committee met on a daily basis. Having got on top of the numbers, it met three times a week. The result has been that the Zambian authorities (principally the governor and the minister of finance) have been fully briefed on the performance of the economy since early 1993.

They have also been adequately warned of potential stresses and difficulties. Whatever macroeconomic missteps since then have not been due to the lack of information. They have resulted primarily from the failure of senior policy-makers to act appropriately and in time. As noted in Chapter 14, a particular instance was in December 1995 when the government failed to meet six of the ten performance criteria agreed with the IMF under the ESAF arrangement. Senior policy-makers were warned well in advance that several benchmarks were in jeopardy. No corrective action was taken. In early January 1996, senior policy-makers were informed that the benchmarks, in fact, had been breached. When this situation was confirmed, they were advised to respond preemptively and forcefully and bring the program back on track. The policy-makers (led by the minister of finance) preferred to do otherwise. This set in motion many of the subsequent difficulties that Zambia has had with the international community. Another example has been the unwillingness of the government, despite its commitments, to fully liberalize agricultural marketing and distribution. Selected senior government officials found the temptation to reintervene too strong, and too lucrative (see Chapter 10).

Overview

The main point has been repeated a number of times. Prudent macroeconomic management is a crucial dimension of good governance. Furthermore, good governance is reflected in the types of macroeconomic choices that governments make. In addition to eliminating deficit financing, the government of Zambia would significantly enhance both macroeconomic management and governance by sharply cutting its policy agenda.

4. Achieving Good Governance

Having identified some of the key areas where the links between good governance and macroeconomic management have broken down, what remedial actions might be possible? Political scientists regularly point to the rise of a well-informed middle class as the principal means by which the power of the rulers and ruling class is curbed. This is not a short-term option in countries such as Zambia, or in other parts of Africa where political reforms have been relatively recent and have yet to take hold. The economic retrogression of the past two and a half decades has undermined middle-income groups, diminished their standards of education, and pushed a greater proportion of the population into a "coping" mode.[80]

With the start-stop attempts at economic reform exacerbating the decline in average real per capita incomes in Zambia, there is little prospect that a vibrant middle class will emerge to begin pressing for economic reform. Much of the pressure for reform in Zambia will come from external sources. One source will be other countries in Southern Africa.[81] Another will be the international community. Yet, with the donors and Zambia so heavily mutually dependent, the continued need for the donors to dispense aid compromises their ability to pressure the GRZ to reform. Donor sanctions, at best, will remain relatively ineffective.

There are other mechanisms that might ensure continued progress in the areas of governance. One is international publicity. Zambia's leaders have been highly sensitive to adverse publicity in Africa and further afield. Being accused on the front pages of *The Times, Le Monde, or The New York Times* of human rights violations or antidemocratic behavior seriously damaged the Chiluba government's international image. Those accusations increased following the October 1997 attempted *coup.* They undercut President Chiluba's efforts to portray his regime as one that is law-abiding, committed to democracy and human rights.[82] Few people, including international observers, have missed the irony that Chiluba campaigned against the excesses of the Kaunda regime only to adopt many of the same practices himself.

A second mechanism, which so far has not been used effectively, is to stop

---

80. Moser (1996) provides examples.

81. In 1996, a group of Southern Africa leaders headed by Nelson Mandela, president of South Africa, expressed its profound concern at the way Chiluba and the MMD were manipulating the Constitution. This intervention proved fruitless. Nonetheless, it signaled that countries in the region were becoming less tolerant of gross abuses of the principles of good governance.

82. The BBC (Monday February 19, 2001) had a headline "Zambia coup plotters were tortured." A report by an independent commission concluded that the 79 coup suspects had been tortured and that 21 police officers should be retired in the national interest. The government rejected the report. Such headlines have not been isolated. The *International Herald Tribune* in early August 1996 reported "Zambia's Success Story Turning Sour." It noted:

...once hailed as a model of transition [Zambia's government] stands accused by its international supporters of backpedaling on democracy and tolerating the kind of repression it once condemned.

the flow of foreign aid. To date, the major donor groups have expressed their displeasure with the government's performance by suspending balance of payments support. No major cuts in project aid or technical assistance has yet occurred. Thus the Chiluba government has *not* been put under the same pressure as Kaunda and UNIP.

There are two implications. First, aid donors have separated the behavior of President Chiluba and the MMD government from the perceived needs of the Zambian people for whom the aid is intended. Second, even though governance issues have been a problem, the situation has not deteriorated as dramatically as it had under President Kaunda. More important, unless elections are suspended or the Constitution manipulated,[83] there is a clear limit to the time that the Zambian people and the international community have to tolerate the excesses and deficiencies of the Chiluba administration. For this reason, continued foreign assistance to Zambia could be viewed as a "holding operation" until the government changes its policies, or a new government is elected.

A third mechanism is for the local business community to lobby the government to change. So far, there has been minimal pressure from this quarter. Above all else, members of Zambia's business community are survivors. Experience has repeatedly demonstrated that if they are to survive in Zambia's business climate, their enterprise and entrepreneurial capacity have to be confined to the opportunities sanctioned by government officials or those that emerge from direct links they can create with the outside world. To defend their interests, Zambian businessmen and women have typically avoided activities that put them in direct competition with the quasicommercial activities of the government, politicians, and well-connected civil servants. The example of fertilizer imports has already been given. There are numerous others: gemstone production and sales, cellular telephone communication, the local production of batteries, petroleum imports, textile production, and flour imports.

A fourth mechanism is improved macroeconomic management itself. The most important effect of this change will be to enhance competition. This would reverse a major shift that occurred in the years immediately after independence. Under the influence of State-directed development, none of the key entities in the country—businesses, skilled labor, farmers, public sector employees—was required to compete.[84] This sapped the economy's dyna-

83. For much of 2001, President Chiluba encouraged his supporters to change the Constitution so that he could run for a third term. The effort met stiff resistance in Zambia and ultimately failed.

84. The *coup de grace* was the creation of the Second Republic that made political competition with UNIP and, by extension, with President Kaunda himself illegal.

mism. The economic reform in Zambia from 1989 onwards (tentative and partial though it has been) has progressively broadened the scope of competition. Some liberalization, such as the removal of exchange controls, was belated recognition that the official controls had failed. Other changes such as the reduction in tariffs have been part of a structured program to lower the general degree of protection in the economy. In this respect, the genie is out of the bottle. Zambia has to learn to compete or the economy will continue to sink.

A fifth way of promoting "better" governance is through the conditions attached to the IMF and World Bank programs. To date, these conditions have proven to be blunt instruments. Moreover, largely due to the breadth of the agenda being pursued by both agencies (the Bank more so than the Fund) the conditions have been largely ineffectual in redirecting economic policy. The basic problem with the IMF conditions is that the sloppy implementation of the RAP convinced senior Zambian policy makers that all performance criteria were fungible. Under the RAP, the incentives to complete the program were reversed. The IMF needed a successful outcome to the RAP so that Zambia's arrears to the Fund could be cleared (see Chapter 14). When Zambia moved from the RAP to an ESAF, its senior officials expected the same degree of indulgence from the IMF. That was not possible. World Bank conditions have been equally ineffectual. The World Bank has imposed such a large number of conditions that its only option for performance evaluation has been a scorecard approach. Under these circumstances, meeting conditions is a game in which the Zambian authorities have to create the impression that most conditions are being met. Because the World Bank has relented on Zambia's noncompliance with many conditions and modified others so often, its programs have lacked discipline and structure. Furthermore, Zambia's leaders understand as well as anyone that World Bank officers have to "move the money." To break this cycle, a major effort is needed to reestablish the direction and coherence of Fund and Bank support. This will require, among other things, a drastic reduction in the number of conditions (especially from the Bank), a narrowing of their scope, and more rigid enforcement.

A final mechanism for improving governance is that members of civil society continue their campaign of exposing inefficiency and waste in government. While the government may not respond directly or immediately, the process of having groups prepared to speak out and challenge the government strengthens the "voice" option in society.[85] Democracy and good governance can only improve if they are practiced. That requires participation

---

85. Hirschman (1970).

rather than resignation. It is time-consuming and it requires effort, and often courage. Former United States Senator Barry Goldwater once noted "extremism in the defense of liberty is no crime." Accordingly, Zambians have no option other than to jealously guard their liberty. The best way of doing that is to continually hold the government accountable. This is something the MMD government should have expected. Moreover, given its promises about good governance before the 1991 and 1996 elections it is something the MMD should have welcomed.

5. CONCLUDING COMMENTS

In this chapter, we have argued that there is a direct link between macroeconomic management and good governance. Governments committed to principles of good governance seek non-inflationary ways to finance their operations. They also ensure that taxes due are collected fairly and in full, that their debt burden remains at sustainable levels, that their dependence on international aid does not become excessive, and that their approach to policy formation and implementation is proactive.

Macroeconomic management in Zambia has many deficiencies in these areas. Senior policy makers have not yet made the fundamental decision to cut public sector spending in ways that are consistent with the longer-term availability of resources. They have also failed to ensure that the resources that are available are used in the socially most productive manner. The outcome has been a persistent waste of public resources. Some important attempts have been made to improve macroeconomic management. The reforms adopted in 1992 are an example.

As the decade progressed, however, there was widespread slippage. Why this occurred is not completely clear. It may be an unavoidable consequence of having such a "new" democracy. It may also have been a consequence of having leaders that had no incentive to continue acting in the national interest. The ineffectiveness of international pressure and competition among Zambia's numerous interest groups were relevant as well.

Whatever the explanations, Zambia's future prospects for growth and development have been diminished by the failure of its leaders to abide by the principles of good governance and effective macroeconomic management. No one disputes the fact that governments can do what they want. The GRZ has certainly determined its own course of action. Its leaders have been ready to demonstrate that they would not be pushed around by the IMF, or by the other donors. Unfortunately, none of the actions they took to register their independence broadened the scope for rapid growth and development. Indeed, the government's actions foreclosed many useful options. Zambia's external debt has increased, the civil service has remained inefficient and (in parts) dysfunctional, ZCCM was not privatized in a way that maximized the benefits to the economy, and donor support that might have been constructively used was delayed or withdrawn. In the process, the government undermined the international good will that had been cultivated during the transition from the Second to the Third Republic.

The outcome, thus far, has been disappointing. It is a decade since democracy was restored. Annual copper production has fallen by over 40 percent, Zambia's external debt (after more than $4 billion in debt rescheduling, refinancing, and write-offs) ended the 1990s higher than it was at the start, food security has been more precarious than during the Second Republic, inflation remains high relative to Zambia's trading partners, key areas of the economy are manipulated even as the government asserts they have been liberalized, domestic savings have not increased, and per capita real incomes continue to decline. Corruption and human rights abuses are reported in the international press.[86] None of these developments indicates that the MMD government met its promises to abide by principles of good governance. For sustained growth and development to become a reality in Zambia, this has to change.

---

86. The United States Department of State's report on human rights for 2000 referred to Zambia's poor human rights record. The *African Competitiveness Report* (Schwab *et al.* 2000, Table 1, p. 71) ranked Zambia as among the most corrupt countries in Africa. Reporting on President Chiluba's bid for a third term, *The Economist* (March 17, 2001, p.44) noted:

If [Chiluba] leaves office, he could face some awkward questions. Corruption seems to mar virtually every thing his government does, from piping oil to buying maize to avert famine.

14

Ending Aid Dependence in Zambia

MALCOLM F. MCPHERSON

"Community Based Rehabilitation is the Answer.
Do Not Give Alms to Street Beggars"
(Lusaka Street Sign, 2001)

1. INTRODUCTION

The above quote is prominently displayed on several Lusaka streets. It replaced a sign that read "Do not allow people to become dependant (sic!) on you, Do not give alms to street beggars." Both of these signs were attempts by the government's department of community development to address the worsening poverty situation in Zambia, namely the growing number of people eking out a living on the streets of the major cities. Both messages convey the assertion (and hope) that community development will move street beggars beyond the need for charity. The messages raise an interesting message for the nation as a whole. If community development will move beggars beyond charity, can't the same principles be applied to the nation itself? Could economic development move Zambia beyond its acute dependence on international support?

A basic problem is that adverse expectations generated by the prospect (and fact) of charity have blocked economic development. Just as individuals provide alms when they recognize that there is no community development to keep beggars off the streets, so the donor community provides external aid because it recognizes that Zambia is not developing. The reverse holds as well. Beggars have few incentives to participate in community development activities when they know that charity will be provided. Similarly, economic development becomes less pressing for the nation as a whole when donors continue providing large amounts of aid. In both cases, and at both levels, the expectations are self-fulfilling. Development does not occur.

This chapter argues that for Zambia to grow and develop on a sustained basis it needs to devise and implement an "aid [or alms] exit" strategy. The idea is that the government and the donors would agree on a program whereby aid to Zambia would be systematically reduced over a fixed time period.[1] At the end of that period (perhaps ten, but no more than fifteen years), Zambia would be receiving less than 2 percent of GDP in concessional support.

The rationale for designing such a strategy is that sustained growth and development are impossible while Zambia remains as dependent on foreign resources as it has been since the early 1970s. Evidence is easy to find. First, Zambia has regressed economically during this period despite massive amounts of external assistance. Over the period 1975 to 2001, Zambia received in excess of $16 billion of foreign assistance. This was equivalent to almost 20 percent of GDP.[2] With Zambia having passed the Highly Indebted Poor Country (HIPC) decision point, several more billion dollars will be forthcoming. Second, poverty has increased despite this aid. Third, the aid did not stimulate a major restructuring of the economy. Fourth, without a fundamental change in the relationship between the government and the donor community a large amount of aid to Zambia will continue to be wasted.[3] Fifth, until the GRZ begins taking *its own* steps to replace donor funding with resources that *it* raises (through a combination of improved tax compliance,

---

1. In this essay, foreign aid means ". . .the transfer of concessional resources from one government to another.. . ." (Lancaster 1999, p.1). My focus will be on economic assistance although I recognize that military aid frees up resources as well. Like Lancaster, I also appreciate that "foreign aid . . . is a tool of statecraft." Nonetheless, to keep the discussion manageable, the emphasis will be official development assistance (ODA) as defined by the Development Assistance Committee of the OECD.

2. This datum can be derived from Tables 2.5 and 12.1 of the *African Development Indicators* 2001. Aid flows to Zambia averaged $204 million over the period 1975–1984, $411 million for 1985 to 1989, and $821 for the period 1990 to 1999. The HIPC decision point reached at the end of 2000 (IMF/IDA 2000) will provide $3.8 billion in debt relief. Thus, over the period 1975 to 2000 the aid has been on the order of $16.1 billion. From Table 2.5 of the *ADI* and the HIPC document, the aggregate GDP generated in Zambia over that same period has been around $82.2 billion. That is, aid has been equivalent to 19.6 percent of GDP. This is over two-and-a-half times the average aid flows for countries in SSA (excluding South Africa and Nigeria).

3. This paper does not address the issue of aid from private sources. Relative to official aid flows, private sector support has been small. Moreover, since this aid is provided by and overseen by private individuals and firms it is likely to be effectively used.

expenditure cuts, and actions that encourage financial deepening), sustained growth and development will not be achieved.

After three decades of the misapplication of resources by the government and the donor community in Zambia, there is almost zero prospect that foreign aid can be made "effective" (a term regularly used by the World Bank)[4] while Zambia remains so highly dependent on such large amounts of "easy money." Restructuring the mechanisms by which foreign aid is provided and used in Zambia will require explicit action by the government and the donors to change what the historical record shows has been a counterproductive relationship. That is, for Zambia to grow and develop, foreign aid as we know it has to end.[5]

My argument is not that aid to Zambia should be *eliminated*. As a practical matter, the forces allied against such an outcome, both inside and outside Zambia (and Africa more generally), are too formidable and too well organized for that to happen. Nevertheless, there is a strong case for substantially reducing aid to Zambia so that economic performance can be enhanced. Indeed, the two would be mutually reinforcing. Reduced aid would spur improved economic performance; the latter would make the flow of aid to Zambia (especially in the exaggerated amounts of recent years) unnecessary.

The need for an end to aid dependence in Zambia rests on two premises. First, as foreign assistance to Zambia is currently being administered, most if not all aid agencies (and their NGO satellites) have lost sight of the reasons for providing economic assistance. Second, the Zambian government has been so "hooked" on foreign aid that the pressure to ensure that aid continues flowing has distorted the government's whole approach to economic management.

Section 2 discusses the rationale for aiding Zambia. Section 3 examines the volume of foreign assistance to Zambia and reviews indicators of aid dependence. Section 4 considers what aid was meant to achieve in Zambia. Section 5 outlines a program whereby Zambia can work itself off foreign assistance in ways that will enhance the economy's capacity to grow and develop. Section 6 concludes the chapter by asking whether there is an easier way to foster growth and development than by moving Zambia off foreign aid.

---

4. World Bank 1998. The bank now has an *Annual Review of Development Effectiveness.*

5. This is an intentional allusion to the attempt by the United States to restructure its welfare system (Saving 1997). Dissatisfaction with the U.S. welfare system arises from the perception that both the government and welfare recipients have become dependent upon a system that does not effectively reduce intergenerational poverty problems yet is so entrenched that needed reforms are blocked.

2. The Rationale for Aiding Zambia

To place the issue of foreign aid in context, three points need to be made at the start.

First, there is nothing fundamentally wrong with the principle of foreign assistance. Some countries have benefited extensively from aid flows. The basic problem in Zambia (and other African countries) has been the type of open-ended, game-inducing, growth-dissipating transfers that donors have provided over the last three decades.

Second, foreign aid comes in a variety of forms from cash and commodity grants, to technical assistance and training, soft loans, and long-term credits. Most African countries receive all types of aid. Because of spillover effects the impact of particular aid flows is difficult to measure.[6] Nonetheless, no African country (especially Zambia) can conclusively show that foreign aid has been critical for economic development.[7] In fact, the point is more general. All of the currently industrialized countries (including the newly industrialized "gang of four") progressed without foreign aid of the type and in the amounts, relative to GDP, that most African countries have received since 1960. It is true, however, that the prudent use of *some* foreign aid in *some* countries has played a positive role in stimulating growth and development.[8]

Third, there is nothing new about the argument that aid should be substantially cut, if not ended completely. Critics from both the right and the left have made the point. My focus is not on the quantity of aid; rather, it is on ways to end aid dependence.

There are now literally dozens of studies of foreign aid with more underway. All of these studies reaffirm the general proposition that the provision of foreign assistance has been motivated by the desire to stimulate growth and development. None of the studies starts from the premise that foreign aid is meant to undermine a recipient country's prosperity and dissipate its wealth. Correlation does not imply causation. Yet, the majority of African countries has experienced a decline in their capacity to grow and develop as their reli-

---

6. Goldsmith (1998) tested the effects of foreign assistance on state capacity in sub-Saharan Africa. His results show that aid has helped and it has hindered. There is no evidence, however, that aid has been essential for strengthening any state.

7. This point was made by Bauer (1976, p. 78) when he noted that there is "no axiomatic case for aid." In his view, ". . .if the mainsprings of development are present, material progress will occur even without foreign aid." This point had emerged during a debate on the impact of U.S. aid to countries such as Pakistan, Colombia, and others during the 1960s (Ohlin 1966, pp. 35–36).

8. Both Collier and Gunning (1999, pp.104–5) and Lancaster (1999, Ch.3) note that particular types of foreign assistance have been generally ineffective. More recent evidence (World Bank 2001) confirms this.

ance on foreign aid has increased. Evidence of this connection is especially strong in Zambia.

A further presumption, explicit in the early literature on economic development,[9] is that poor countries should achieve the greatest possible mobilization of local resources so that over time these economies can become absolutely and relatively less reliant upon foreign assistance. That has not happened in Zambia, or more generally across Africa. Under current circumstances, there is little prospect that it can, or will. One reason has been that donor agencies have been locked into open-ended programs of resource transfers that do not support growth and development. Another reason is that most African governments have come to depend too heavily on donor resources to change the present arrangements.

Why should foreign governments and international agencies provide financial and other assistance to African countries including Zambia? The amount of support has been large[10] with the majority of African countries receiving net financial and other support from abroad that, for most of the last two decades, has exceeded 10 percent of their respective GDPs. What have these countries done to warrant such assistance? These questions have short and long answers. The short answer is that due to a combination of bad luck and poor economic management most African countries have exceedingly large external debts. From the early 1980s, these debts could not have been serviced without extraordinary donor support.[11] The problem with providing this support, however, is that it deflected the attention of African governments from the fundamental changes required to get their countries out of debt and off aid.

The long answer has its roots in the basic reasons why countries provide aid intermingled with the political and economic aspects of postcolonial relations across Africa. The literature on official foreign assistance is huge, and we make no attempt to review it. Yet even a brief reading of that literature

---

9. Lewis 1956, p.8; Chenery 1963, pp. 37–39; McKinnon 1964; Meier 1970, pp. 284–291; Selowsky 1991.

10. Based on World Bank data, the flow of *net* ODA to SSA (excluding South Africa and Nigeria) was 3.1 percent of GDP in 1970. It increased to 15.1 percent of GDP in 1994 and has subsequently fallen to around 10 percent of GDP. Over the entire period 1970 to 1997, the average annual flow of net assistance was 7.7 percent of GDP. Source: *World Development Indicators 1999*, CD-ROM. Data from the *African Development Indicators* 2001, Table 12–9 show that net aid flows averaged 6.1, 8.4 and 11.4 percent, respectively, in the periods 1975–84, 1984–89, and 1990–97. In the latter period the net flows were $15.1 billion per year.

11. This is the modern equivalent of the German reparations problem discussed by Keynes (1919). Keynes' point, which remains valid, was that heavy debt payments divert national savings from investment in the export-oriented activities required to generate the balance of payments surpluses needed to service the debt. That is, a heavily indebted country cannot generate the surplus needed to grow rapidly enough to service the debt.

shows that debates on the merits and demerits of foreign assistance cover the whole spectrum of opinion.[12]

Early discussions of official foreign assistance tended to emphasize moral and ethical issues.[13] The notion of supporting, assisting, and having compassion for those who are less fortunate is basic to all major moral philosophies. A prominent view, which still has widespread support, is that rich societies have a moral obligation to help those that are poor.[14]

Yet morality was not the most pressing concern when the United States provided emergency support to Europe and Japan following WWII. This assistance was justified on several grounds—humanitarian concerns, internal security, economic revival, and as a counter force to communism. Moral issues probably strengthened the case, but they were not decisive. Indeed, a number of scholars argued that international relations have little to do with morality; rather they hinge on questions of power, self-interest, and influence.[15]

The positive results of the Marshall Plan in Europe and U.S. support for Japan (1947–1963) demonstrated that assisting allies and former enemies could be prudent and constructive. That the assistance had the added advantage of reviving the economies of Europe and Japan and forestalling the communist threat made foreign aid, for the United States at least, a matter of national interest.[16] Having repaired the wartime damage in Europe and Japan, the attention of the United States turned elsewhere.

---

12. Brief surveys appear in Krueger (1986), Cassen *et al.* (1986, 1994), Chenery (1989), and Lancaster (1999).

13. Ohlin 1966, pp. 22–24; Asher 1970; Opeskin 1996.

14. Ward (1964) argued that overcoming backwardness required broad-based revolutions—social, intellectual, scientific, and medical. A revolution was needed so that these countries might rise above their "inherent conservatism" which led them to ". . . preserve rather than create. . . ." Aid brought "Western ideas" which "stirred up" the desire and pressure to "develop." In her view, there was so much that needed to be done that rich countries had an obligation to help.

15. Mason (1957) identified four reasons for the United States to provide foreign aid: humanitarian, economic, political, and security. There was no compelling reason for the first two. There were enough humanitarian tasks within the United States. No country directly gained by giving away resources. This left political and security concerns as the main rationales for aid.

16. In his message to Congress on the Foreign Aid Bill, President Kennedy stated (March 1961):

. . . widespread poverty and chaos lead to a collapse of existing political and social structures which could inevitably invite the advance of totalitarianism into every weak and unstable area. Thus our own security would be endangered and our prosperity imperiled. A program of assistance to the underdeveloped nations must continue because the nation's interest and the cause of political freedom require it. (John F. Kennedy in Gardner 1962, p. 146.)

There were some important successes. Economic support to Korea and Taiwan, initially for security purposes but later to foster economic growth, began to yield spectacular results in the late 1960s and early 1970s. Some failures were also noteworthy. Western support for Gamal Abdul Nasser in Egypt did not diminish Soviet influence in that country. The Vietnam debacle (before and after U.S. military intervention) showed that foreign aid can undermine economic development. And, the successive support for Ethiopia by the West (for Haile Selassie) and by the Soviet Union (for Haile Meriam Mengistu) demonstrated that aid, irrespective of its ideological basis, does not necessarily promote growth and development. Though other failures occurred, there were enough successes to support the view that foreign assistance was something which the rich countries, especially the United States, should continue providing.

Arguments about ending foreign aid come from both the extreme right and extreme left. Conservatives object to foreign assistance because it strengthens governments at the expense of the private sector. Liberals object to aid because it strengthens elites aligned with governments at the expense of the poor. In the late 1950s, Milton Friedman argued that foreign assistance would be unnecessary if only countries would remove restrictions that undermined growth.[17] Friedman asserted it was dangerous (and contradictory) for the United States to require national plans as a condition for countries to receive aid. This requirement, he believed, used American resources to strengthen authoritarian and interventionist regimes.[18] The Heritage Foundation continues this critique. Its studies have shown that despite aid from the United States for four decades (longer in several cases) a large number of poor countries had failed to grow.[19] Indeed, real per capita incomes in more than a dozen countries, one of which was Zambia, have declined.

From the other side of the political spectrum, Bauer rejected the notion that aid promotes growth and development.[20] Others writers view foreign aid as an instrument of imperialism, as furthering the goals of neocolonial finance capital, perpetuating (the Marxist version of) dependency, and intensifying underdevelopment.[21] These arguments have provoked a range of re-

---

17. Viner 1951, pp. 371–372; Friedman 1958; Krauss 1983.

18. This point was also noted by Nurske (1953, pp.94–95) who argued that there was a major inconsistency between the U.S. support for planning in the use of aid as a means of reconstruction and development, and the fundamental rejection of "planning" within the public sector in the U.S. Inconsistency or not, the Department of State endorsed the use of "plans" as one of its eight principles of support for African countries (USDS 1964).

19. Johnson 1997.

20. Bauer 1976, 1991.

21. According to Frank, Santos, Amin, and others, a dependent economy is one that is trapped within a web of interlocked (and typically exploitative) international relationships. A

sponses. Some observers have called for ending aid altogether. Others have argued that aid should be reformed by removing donor conditions, and empowering those for whom the aid was (or should be) intended.[22]

The mainstream donor community has dismissed these suggestions. Its members argue that for all its shortcomings, aid has worked and continues to be effective. Their argument has two parts. First, many former aid recipients (countries in Western Europe, Japan, Singapore, Korea, and Taiwan) have grown and developed rapidly. Second, since most poor countries are "unbankable," aid has to continue if they are to obtain access to the resources required for them to grow and develop. This mainstream view has recently added two subthemes. One is that since only reforming countries benefit from aid, the international community should focus on this group.[23] The other is that the heavily indebted countries require additional foreign assistance so they can retire their debt and promote growth and development.[24]

Proponents of aid have been able to defend their positions through appeals to the evidence. They openly acknowledge that problems exist with aid. But, they suggest that the effects have been incidental. To date, this tactic has provided a formidable defense of the *status quo*. All empirical results are subject to a wide range of interpretations, and analytical methods and data can always be challenged.[25] Evidence on the effects of aid derived from cross-country regres-

---

standard perception is that these relationships are fostered and sustained by multinational corporations. Dependence of this nature keeps a country systematically underdeveloped. The essence of this view is that the economy's international relations have an adverse asymmetrical impact on its capacity to grow and develop. Further subtlety is added by suggestions that the local elite benefits from the exploitative relationships (Pearce 1989, p. 102; Yasane 1980, Ch.1; Austen 1987, Ch.10).

22. Hayter (1971), Moore Lappé, Collins and Kinley (1981), Hancock (1989), Maren (1997), and Johnson (1997) argue that aid has been administered in ways that reinforce the power of entrenched minorities in poor countries. The implication is that aid does not (and cannot) reach the poor.

23. Devarajan, Dollar, and Holmgren (2001) summarize ten case studies of aid in Africa. They found no general evidence that aid had been essential for growth and development. Aid had played a role in helping countries that had appropriate (i.e., reform-oriented) policies. They conclude that aid should be directed more selectively to reforming countries. They suggest that nonreformers should be supported through TA to help strengthen the organizations needed to promote reform.

24. CID (1999). This study makes the case for additional aid. It fails to address the issue of how countries that are currently ineffectively using aid will be induced to improve their performance.

25. There are many criteria upon which the result can be challenged—the time period chosen, variables included and excluded, the form of the functional relationship, the country coverage, whether a statistical issue (simultaneity, heteroskedasticity, autocorrelation) has been tested for and/or corrected, and the definition of the terms included in the empirical analysis. The list could be extended. A more recent change has been to redefine the concept of aid.

sions has often been inconclusive. Moreover, by switching definitions of aid, for example, from the widely used official development assistance (ODA) to effective development assistance (EDA), analysts generate enough ambiguity to deflect criticism.[26] The issues, however, sharpen up significantly when the focus shifts from cross-country analysis to individual countries. For instance, in the multiequation model of Zambia in Chapter 11, over the period 1970 to 1998, the growth of real income and aid flows were negatively related.

Work sponsored by the World Bank has shown that aid is not effective when economic policies create distortions.[27] According to this research, aid has only been effective when it is supported by the appropriate policies and is directed to growth-enhancing activities. These results, however, have not been used to challenge the efficacy of aid. More important, this research has sidestepped the issue of whether the aid has led to the adoption, or continuation, of inappropriate policies.[28] Largely as a reflection of the forces defending the *status quo*, aid relationships that lead to substandard economic performance have not been faulted. Solutions focus on renewing efforts to make the aid work better[29] and reducing aid flows to countries that are not reforming. Neither of these approaches addresses the fundamental questions of why aid, despite its long history, has not been effective and why countries, despite being provided with large amounts of aid, have not been reforming. Both solutions simply push the problem back one level.

Notwithstanding the mainstream aid community's tactics to deflect criticism, the critics' views merit attention. Foreign aid has been administered in ways that strengthen the public sector, relative to the private sector and foreign aid has strengthened existing power relations to the detriment of the poor. Detailed studies showing that aid has been counterproductive in selected circumstances are also convincing.[30]

---

26. Burnside and Dollar (1997, 2000) shift from official development assistance (ODA) to effective development assistance (EDA) by focusing on the grant component of aid. McPherson (2000) criticizes this approach on two grounds. No members of the aid community (providers or recipients) base their economic behavior on the notion of EDA. At the aggregate level (i.e., the level at which Burnside and Dollar conduct their analysis), the correlation of ODA and EDA is exceedingly high (i.e., above .95) especially in African countries.

27. Isham and Kaufmann 1995.

28. Goldsmith (1998), cited above, examined whether states were weak in Africa because they received aid or the reverse. His results for SSA as a whole were inconclusive. Earlier, Brautigam (1996) had argued that the ineffectiveness of aid could be traced to the lack of state capacity.

29. This is the essence of the message in Kaplan (1967), Krueger (1986), Cassen *et al.* (1986, 1994), Hyden (1993), World Bank (1998), Lancaster (1999), and *The Economist* (June 26, 1999).

30. Morss (1984) described how foreign aid had undermined institutions. This has occurred most frequently when donors have supported the establishment of parallel implemen-

This evidence, however, has done little to dramatically scale back or modify the flow of aid to Africa. Much has been made of the cuts in aid to Africa, but even with them, aid to Africa during the 1990s was higher than in any other decade.[31] Although aid flows are historically high, it is also clear that, apart from any special efforts that may be made to deal with HIV/AIDS, there is no compelling case for expanding aid to Africa, or Zambia. Few African countries, including Zambia, have performed in ways that would allow additional foreign assistance to be used effectively and efficiently. Furthermore, far fewer aid officials are now willing to see Africa's poor economic performance as the result of external developments.[32] In light of Africa's post-colonial history and the mayhem created by the procession of thugs and tyrants who have held power across Africa, scholars (many of them African) have argued that most of Africa's problems have been generated locally.[33]

There have been other changes within the aid community. High level officials in the largest agencies have become more insistent that continued assistance from members of the Development Assistance Committee (DAC) occurs within the context of better economic management, evidence of improved governance, and local efforts to promote growth and development. These sentiments are fully consistent with emerging political realities in the DAC member countries. Voters there broadly support the principle of foreign assistance. But, when the questions shift to specific cases, support erodes. There are few influential lobbies advocating an expansion of foreign support. Indeed, the traditional supporters of foreign assistance have lost ground to groups who argue that foreign assistance is not working.[34]

---

tation agencies because the existing ministries and departments are "dysfunctional" (a term used by Collier and Gunning 1999).

31. Some commentators have been highly critical of these cuts. Yet, perspective is needed. Net ODA to Africa (excluding South Africa and Nigeria) increased from around 3 percent of GDP in 1970 to 14.3 percent of GDP in 1994. It declined to 12.5 percent in 1995, 10 percent in 1996, and 8.6 percent in 1997 (*African Development Indicators* 2001, Table 12.9).

32. There is a major disconnect in the approaches being taken. Western countries are seeking to move on (European Union 1996). With the support of the OAU, African countries have been pushing for reparations (Mazrui 1994).

33. This argument has been made by Africans (Ayittey 1992, 1998; Frimpong-Ansah 1993) and others (*The Economist* May 7, 1994, pp. 19–21, September 7, 1996 "Africa for the Africans"). It is noteworthy that some of Africa's most ardent supporters have changed their minds. For example, Basil Davidson, long an admirer of Africa and of many of its leaders, took an entirely different position in *Black Man's Burden* (Davidson 1991). He argued that most of Africa's problems are internal—corruption, inefficiency, and armed thuggery. One barely needs to be reminded of Robert Mugabe's exploits to realize the distance many African countries have to make up before standards of governance and accountability rise to internationally accepted levels.

34. The statement by Senator Jesse Helms that "aid to Africa is money down a rat-hole" (*The Economist* December 10, 1994, p. 101) was graphic and to the point. No one in the mainstream development community condemned it, nor did they produce data to refute it.

There are several dimensions to the problem. Voters are increasingly aware of the pathologies induced by aid dependence. The financial assistance to Mexico in 1994 and then to countries in Asia have been widely portrayed as "bail-outs." Since voters in rich countries recognize that some of these countries have unsavory and unaccountable leaders, efforts to insulate those leaders from the consequences of their own mismanagement and corruption have been opposed. Furthermore, because many countries in Africa have been subject to disruption, pillage, and carnage at the hands of an equally unsavory group of leaders, these same voters see little point providing additional resources to sustain them.

During 2001, there was a concerted movement underway among Western academics and NGOs to press their governments to support the purchase and distribution of drugs to treat HIV/AIDS. The program started by condemning the pharmaceutical companies for the high costs of these drugs. Under threat of patent-busting production of generics, the companies agreed to reduce the cost of drugs sold in Africa. Attention has since shifted to convincing the U.S. and other governments to underwrite the cost of treatment.[35] Incredibly, little attention has been given to the capacity of African countries to deliver the drugs effectively, fairly, and continuously.[36] Furthermore, from the discussion in Chapter 12, little attention has been given to the broader problems of reviving the societies and economies where the ravages of HIV/AIDS have been most severe.[37] The aid donors may ultimately respond by providing additional resources to deal with HIV/AIDS. If they do, radical changes will be needed in the way aid is distributed by donors and how it is used by African countries.

3. Aiding Zambia

To place in context foreign assistance to Zambia, the country's history since WWII can be broken into two periods. During the first period (1945 to 1973), Zambia received minimal amounts of foreign assistance.[38] The economy grew rapidly with average real per capita income rising by close to 4 percent per annum.[39] Zambia was one of the richest countries in SSA with what most observers saw as vast potential for continued growth and development.

---

35. Attaran and Sachs 2001.

36. Gray and McPherson 2001.

37. McPherson, Hoover and Snodgrass 2000.

38. Throughout the period 1954 to 1963, while Zambia was part of the Central African Federation, funds actually flowed from Northern Rhodesia (Zambia) to the other two members, Nyasaland (Malawi) and Southern Rhodesia (Zimbabwe).

39. McPherson 1980, Ch. 2

Throughout the second period (1974 to the present), Zambia has received large amounts of foreign assistance both in absolute terms and relative to its GDP. This has coincided with a sharp deterioration in economic performance. That performance has shown no sign of sustained improvement. Zambia's regression has been so broad-based that donor agencies have been induced to provide extraordinary amounts of support in an attempt to reverse the trend. The trend has not been reversed and Zambia now ranks among Africa's poorest countries.

The World Bank report *Assessing Aid* emphasized Zambia's decline. That report has estimates showing that if Zambia had used all of its resources efficiently over the last three decades, its per capita income in 1998 would have exceeded $10,000. At that time, Zambia's per capita income was sinking towards $300. While allowance should be made for the World Bank's exaggerated portrayal of Zambia's nonperformance,[40] the general point is beyond dispute: with better policies Zambia's real per capita income would now be significantly higher. Perhaps the most telling indicator is that if, since 1960, Zambia had grown only at the rate of the rest of SSA (which has lagged badly by world standards) average real per capita income in 1997 would have been 78 percent higher than it was.[41]

How did this situation arise? Zambia gained independence in 1964 with abundant foreign exchange reserves, a prosperous, dynamic mining sector, a large tax base, and minimal foreign debt. It was considered to be a middle-income country with the capacity, if necessary, to borrow on commercial terms. At independence, foreign economic aid was not needed, nor was it a major issue.[42] The most pressing problem for Zambia was how to augment its

---

40. Taken literally, the World Bank's estimates imply that Zambia's GDP would now exceed $100 billion. Such a result could not have been achieved even if all of Zambia's investible resources had been placed in the New York stock market where, for the three decades prior to 1998, the Dow Jones Industrial Average has increased at an average annual cumulative rate of roughly 9.1 percent. What the World Bank researchers ignored is that, even though economic policies were poor, there were some factors that affected performance over which Zambia had no control. The Mufulira mine did collapse; copper prices did fall during the energy crisis; the cost of energy did rise; the border at Livingstone was closed; there were civil wars in Mozambique, Zimbabwe, and Angola that spilled over to Zambia ; and there were several bad droughts.

41. Data from *World Development Indicators*. In 1960, real per capita income in Zambia in 1995 prices was $616. For SSA, the corresponding datum was $451. The two income levels were equal (at $612) in 1977. By 1997, Zambia's per capita income was $408 and that of SSA was $528.

42. The World Bank's basic economic review of 1977 contains a detailed analysis of the main economic trends from independence until the mid-1970s (World Bank 1586b-ZA 1977). Additional material can be found in McPherson (1980, Ch. 2).

underdeveloped human capacity.[43] The donor community responded by providing technical assistance and training, primarily in areas related to health, education, and agriculture.

It was only after the mid-1970s that aid flows to Zambia rose dramatically. The aid had three features:

- The amounts were large;
- The government met few of the conditions associated with the assistance;
- Aid flows displaced local efforts to mobilize resources.

Since the data have been reported in Chapters 2, 3, 6, and 11, some brief details will suffice. At the time Zambia gained independence, it was receiving virtually no aid. It had a healthy balance of payments surplus and, as a middle income country, it was required to borrow from the International Bank for Reconstruction and Development (IBRD) and not the International Development Association (IDA). By 1970, net ODA from all sources was only 0.75 percent of GDP, an inconsequential amount. At that time, Zambia had adequate supplies of maize and an expanding crop area that over the next eight years would produce adequate supplies of food.

Aid flows began to increase sharply in 1975 following the dramatic fall in copper prices and the stresses associated with the doubling of petroleum prices. In 1975, net aid was 3.6 percent of GDP. At 5.3 thousand metric tons, food aid was minimal. By 1979, however there had been a dramatic shift. Real income per capita had been falling sharply since 1977 and the harvest was poor. Net aid jumped to 8.3 percent of GDP and food aid was 166.5 thousand metric tons.

Net aid hovered around 8–9 percent of GDP until 1985 at which time it increased to 14.3 percent of GDP. Net aid in 1986 was 27.3 percent of GDP. This coincided with the program of liberalization adopted by the Kaunda government when it began to auction foreign exchange. Zambia also received significantly higher levels of food aid, the result of poor maize harvests, a need to meet the demands of a growing urban population, and the shortage of foreign exchange.

Following the break with the IMF in 1987, aid flows declined. They were equivalent to 12.8 percent of GDP in 1988 and 9.4 percent of GDP in 1989. Rapprochement with the donors led to a rise in assistance in 1990 and 1991. Once multiparty democracy was restored, the flows of external assistance expanded further. For example, over the period 1992 to 1997, net aid averaged 29

---

43. See First National Development Plan (GRZ 1966). Reprinted in Meier (1970, pp. 646–656).

percent of Zambia's GDP. The drought in 1991–92 stimulated a large inflow of food aid. A total of 898 thousand metric tons was provided. This was equivalent to 57 percent of the total output of maize in Zambia in 1991 and 1992.

By any standards of comparison, the aid provided to Zambia has been large. As noted earlier, the total net aid between 1975 and 2001 was approximately $16 billion, just under 20 percent of GDP. What is truly sobering about this total is that the bulk of the assistance was provided from 1985 onwards. Aid flows did not precipitate Zambia's economic crisis although the extravagant flows of assistance undoubtedly have prolonged the country's difficulties by enabling its leaders to postpone adjustment.

The Macroeconomic Effects of Aid: Aid flows became so large in Zambia that they soon dominated the macroeconomic agenda. Coming so quickly after the 1975 "watershed speech" in which President Kaunda had declared Zambia's economic independence, this development was ironic. In per capita terms, aid has represented a major gross addition to the flow of resources. Used efficiently, they could have greatly boosted Zambia's productive capacity. That did not occur. They were primarily used to sustain private and public consumption.[44]

The international community cannot be accused of neglecting Zambia. If anything, the donors, have been extraordinarily indulgent. Zambia was able to cover its resource gaps without major cuts in government consumption or serious pressure to restructure the economy.

Not only were the resources inefficiently used, but there is little evidence that the foreign assistance helped Zambia respond to shocks in a constructive way. Indeed, a general measure of the ineffectiveness of aid to Zambia is that, despite large amounts of food aid since the late 1970s with special emergency shipments in 1992, the nation's food security situation has not improved. Per capita food availability has declined (see Chapter 10).[45]

The Microeconomic Effects of Aid: Official government to government (nonmilitary) aid comes in various forms—programs, projects, commodi-

---

44. White and Estrand 1994, p. 14.

45. This shows up in a number of ways. The growth of productivity of major crops has been exceedingly low. Furthermore, since 1985 the productivity has fallen for all major crops except sunflower and tobacco. Over the 1985–89 period productivity (output per hectare) fell by 6.4 percent per annum in maize. Over the period 1990–99, it declined by 0.1 percent per annum. This is reflected in the per capita food production index in Zambia. Measured on a base of 1989–91 = 100, it was 94 in 1980 and 83 in 1999 (*African Development Indicators* Tables 8.5 and 8.13).

ties, TA, grants for education and travel abroad, debt relief (including debt cancellation), and direct debt service. Furthermore, members of the DAC support the multilateral agencies (World Bank, African Development Bank) that have activities in most of the above areas. Official support is also channeled through third parties such as NGOs. They, in turn, run projects and provide commodity aid and TA.

All of these activities have a microeconomic impact. Wages are paid, fuel and supplies are acquired, drugs are provided, and capital equipment is purchased. Some activities, such as the program against malnutrition (PAM), begun during the 1992 drought to distribute relief, have increasingly drawn on local resources. Other projects such as the health activities in Western Province, funded by the Dutch government, have had to rely almost exclusively on expatriate doctors. It has proven almost impossible to induce local doctors to live in remote areas.

The basic issue at the microeconomic level is that by adding to and/or redirecting the flows of resources within the local economy, foreign aid has modified the incentives to work, produce, save, take risks, and be entrepreneurial and enterprising. A common example, widely cited in the literature has been the impact of food aid on rural incomes. This form of assistance raises the supply of food in the economy. It has two effects. First, it directly affects welfare as individuals facing deprivation gain access to food. The donor-supplied food aid in 1992 prevented starvation in many areas of Zambia. Since the principal objective of such aid is humanitarian, the main issues are whether the aid is distributed equitably and at low (relative) cost. Second, food aid lowers the rewards to local food producers and those whose livelihoods depend on them.

There is now a large literature on the disincentives associated with food aid.[46] The effects are well known and have been widely debated. Not much is done to ameliorate those effects when the country's food security is threatened. The lack of dynamism in agriculture has kept the food supply under threat since the late 1970s.

Donor support in the form of commodity aid, particularly food and fertilizer, had an adverse effect on the profitability and risks of agricultural production in Zambia during the period (1975 to 1992) when prices were fixed pan-seasonally and pan-territorially. Aid flows helped perpetuate that system. The policy was ultimately abandoned, but not because it was exacer-

---

46. Much has been written about the advantages to farmers in the United States and Europe of commodity aid programs in disposing of their "surplus." The flip side of those advantages is the disincentive that such programs have for local production of the commodities and their close substitutes (Schultz 1960; FAO 1961; Johnson 1967, pp. 92–94).

bating rural poverty. It was dropped because of its adverse impact on the budget.[47]

Donor support for credit programs has been almost universally unsuccessful. The main problem is that there were no penalties for those who did not repay. In some respects, this behavior mirrored that of the nation. Since 1975, the GRZ has progressively defaulted on its external debt setting an unfortunate example for all Zambians. Official credit schemes have been largely ineffective (and often counterproductive) wasting large amounts of donor (and some local) resources. Because of bad debts and poor management, the Development Bank of Zambia (DBZ) has had to be recapitalized several times.[48] The cooperative societies have lost billions of kwacha on their credit operations. Some of these losses have been covered by GRZ borrowing from the BoZ. However, most of them have been refinanced by the donors. The rural credit system could not have staggered along for so long without the continued (and largely uncritical) support of the donors.[49] Paradoxically, the outcome has been financial regression rather than financial development.

On the positive side, there is evidence that the support provided through

---

47. In late 1991, Finance minister Emmanuel Kasonde addressed Parliament on the question of removing subsidies on maize, fertilizer and other commodities. He stated:

Mr. Speaker, the programme of reducing subsidies is of great priority because without it, none of our [economic] objectives will be met. Taking no measures at all would raise the subsidy bill to over K20 billion next year. Such a high figure cannot, obviously, be sustained by the budget.. . . As it is our objective to have a balanced budget within two years, the reduction of subsidies will go a long way in achieving this objective.

48. At the state opening of parliament (21 January 2000), President Chiluba announced that the government would spend $10 million to recapitalize DBZ. He did not announce how this initiative, which has been repeated a number of times, would be sustained.

49. A review by the Ministry of Agriculture Food and Fisheries (MAFF) of its agricultural credit management program (ACMP) for the 1994–95 and 1995–96 seasons found widespread abuse. Some of the problems included loan officers cheating farmers, farmers who would not repay the lending agencies, and lending agencies that would not repay the government. This cascading pyramid of uncollected and unpaid credit is a pattern that has been repeated many times. Indeed, the ACMP was established primarily to compensate for the *de facto* bankruptcy of Zambia's traditional agricultural credit agencies CUSA (Credit Union and Savings Association) and Lima Bank. Barely two years old, the ACMP was failing as well. The report noted (MAFF 1996, p.ii):

In the first year of operation, Credit Managers experienced very low rates of loan recovery. This has been attributed to: late delivery of inputs, lack of sound credit policy, political utterances, and drought.. . . The disappointing part is that Credit Managers are also having problems in recovering the 10 percent down payment! Most farmers indicated that they paid back a significant part of the 1994/95 loan. In addition, all farmers indicated that they paid the 10 percent of the loan value before they received inputs. Therefore, Credit Coordinators have deliberately kept the 1994/95 loan recoveries and the 10 percent down payment.

foreign aid for the development and maintenance of infrastructure has been vital to the economy's performance. Donor support to rebuild and repair roads and bridges, and rehabilitate the electricity generation system has directly lowered operating costs throughout the economy. These spillover effects have often been short-lived because the government has failed to provide the recurrent resources needed to maintain the infrastructure once it has been repaired. It has now been common for the donors to rehabilitate capital assets only to see them fall into disrepair through insufficient maintenance.

The Social Effects of Aid: Zambia's economic collapse has been mirrored by an equally profound collapse in most major social indicators. As economic performance in all major areas deteriorated there was a corresponding (though delayed) decline in the key social areas as well.[50] The health system deteriorated and the quality of education declined.[51] The standard of living, especially for middle-income Zambians, sank. Poverty has intensified, particularly in the rural areas.[52] The decline in health standards has been reflected in rising infant mortality. In this respect, Zambia has been one of only a limited number of countries in the world, untouched by civil strife, that experienced increasing infant mortality even before the large-scale effects of HIV/AIDS took hold.[53]

The donors have directed large amounts of assistance to the social sectors, particularly health and education. The aid has been mainly for two purposes. The first has been to prevent further deterioration. The second has been to spread the services more broadly throughout the population. These have been difficult tasks. Population has been growing rapidly in Zambia at rates that until recently were around 3 percent per annum. The rising toll of HIV/AIDS over the last decade has overburdened the health system. The premature death of teachers, doctors, nurses, and healthcare workers has im-

---

50. Data from *African Development Indicators* 2001, Section 13 show that over the period 1984–1997, 86 percent of Zambians were classified as being in poverty (with less that $1 of income per day). Infant mortality increased from 88 per thousand live births in 1982 to 114 per thousand in 1998. Overall literacy was declining and school enrollment was falling, though only marginally (*ibid.* Table 13.13).

51. Achola 1990; Kelley 1991; Saasa 1996. Chapter 12 has additional references.

52. World Bank 1981, 1986, 1993; GRZ/UNICEF 1986, 1995; Iliffe 1987; ILO 1977, 1992

53. *World Development Indicators 1999*, Table 2.17. Life expectancy at birth in Zambia was 51 years in 1980 and 44 years in 1996. Over the period 1970 to 1997, it shows the following profile: 46 (1970), 47 (1972), 49 (1977), 50 (1980), 51 (1982), 50 (1987), 49 (1990), 44 (1996), and 43 (1997), and 43 (1998) (World Bank *WDI* 1999, CD-ROM and *African Development Indicators* 2001, Section 13).

paired the capacities of the health and education systems. The decline of real per capita income has diminished the scope for the expansion of private sector alternatives to public health and education.

Overview: Zambia has been a major recipient of foreign assistance for the last two decades. Many government activities have come to depend on the continuation of that assistance. While aid flows remain so large and their effects so intrusive at both the macro and micro levels, there is little prospect that Zambians can (or will) take the steps needed to grow and develop in a sustained way. An adverse cycle of mutual dependence has emerged. Donor agencies provide services and facilities (and emergency support) because the government is deficient in key areas. Seeing the donors willing to respond to these deficiencies, the government faces little pressure to remedy them. Over the short-term, the situation is convenient for both parties. Over the longer term, it has undercut efforts to move the country forward.

One negative consequence of the volume and scope of donor support has been that the government has become convinced that with donor support, it is making far-reaching, comprehensive, and bold attempts to adjust.[54] Accordingly, it has been easy for the government to attribute setbacks to problems related to donor assistance. Reasons regularly used to explain the government's poor performance include donors' rigid disbursement procedures, the time taken for projects to come on-line, conflicting donor conditions, and shocks to ongoing government activities when support is withheld. Perhaps the most profound effect of donor assistance is that it has allowed attention to be deflected from the government's performance. Extended over the last three decades, donor assistance has institutionalized government under-performance of the tasks for which it alone is responsible.

---

54. For those who believe this overstretches the point, one need only read back-to-back the reports the government prepares each year for the CG to Zambia. The 1995 report (GRZ 1995) stated:

Much has been accomplished in the past four years. The government has implemented far-reaching reforms. Markets were liberalized and price controls abandoned (p.1).

Two years later the 1997 report noted (GRZ 1997):

Upon coming to office in 1991, the MMD government has implemented an ambitious reform programme to achieve macro-economic stability, reduce poverty and put the Zambian economy onto a high and export-led growth path. Much has been accomplished since that time (p.1).

4. Indicators of Aid Dependence

Zambia's Reliance on Aid

There are many statistical measures of aid dependence. In the mid-1990s, the World Bank began reporting "aid dependence" in its *World Development Indicators* as the ratio of gross aid flows to GDP. This, however, is only one of a number of partial measures of what in reality is a highly complex relationship. Other measures include:

- The length of time a country has been receiving aid;
- The size of aid flows relative to resources mobilized for public capital formation;
- The share of locally generated resources used for external debt service;
- The import coverage provided by aid flows;
- The aid flows relative to the budget deficit and the deficit on the current account of the balance of payments;
- The changes in the external debt stock due to the country's own financing efforts;
- The proportion of the health, education, and infrastructure budgets that are aid-financed;
- The expected results of aid and penalties (if any) for underachievement;
- The processes used by government and donor agencies to increase aid flows;
- The existence of a program to systematically reduce aid flows.

Although Zambia has been receiving some form of aid, especially TA, since independence (1964), that support was a minor part of the total resources available to the government until the mid-1970s. Since then, aid has been a major component of resource flows. To illustrate, donor assistance has been around 35 percent of total resources in the 1998, 1999, and 2000 budgets.

From the early 1980s as Zambia's domestic savings rate declined, aid has accounted for a large share of gross domestic capital formation. The same applies to aid in relation to external debt service. Indeed, for most of the last two decades, Zambia has made no net local contribution to external debt service.

Zambia's economic decline has been characterized by the stagnation of exports. As consumption expanded, imports rose rapidly. Export receipts did not increase commensurately and the balance of payments deficit widened. During the initial stages the deficit was financed through external reserves and foreign borrowing. As those options petered out, the growth of imports became more closely related to the availability of aid. Import compression, in turn, constrained the growth of income. The econometric model in Chapter 11 captures some of these dynamics.

Since Zambia has run budget and balance of payments deficits for most of the last three decades, it has been continually adding to its internal and external debt. Moreover, since Zambia has not had the real resources to finance either of these deficits, their persistence has been entirely due to the indulgence of the donor community (and creditors willing to take the chance that donors will pay when the government defaults). In the absence of foreign assistance, both deficits would have been forced to zero. In fact, the constraint would have been tighter. Because of its debt overhang, Zambia would have been forced to provide cash-in-advance financing for its external purchases. Such a situation emerged briefly following Zambia's break with the IMF in 1987.

Based on trends over the last two decades, there has been no fundamental change in Zambia's debt stock due to the government's own efforts. From Chapter 9, all net reductions in external debt have occurred because of donor-sponsored initiatives. Through the Paris Club, some bilateral creditors have forgiven outstanding principal and interest and rescheduled trade credit and government-guaranteed debt. Through the provision of additional resources, the World Bank has refinanced debt owed to the IMF. Several bilateral donors have provided "fifth dimension" support to repay the World Bank. Still others financed the commercial debt buy-back.

Just as in the case of debt, the government's contribution to education and health expenditure has been small. That contribution has primarily covered wages and some RDCs. The shares of health, education, and infrastructure financed by the donor community particularly over the last decade have been high, regularly exceeding 90 percent.[55]

Official statements on the expected results of aid are always positive. ASIP, the Agricultural Sector Investment Program, discussed in Chapter 10 is an example. Several government statements suggest that many of the key aspects of ASIP have failed.[56] None of the parties involved wishes to admit that aid has been ineffective, that the support is being provided simply to ensure Zambia repays the IMF, or that even with an expansion of aid under the present conditions, Zambia is unlikely to grow or develop.[57]

When donors began assisting Zambia on a large scale they, and the government, believed they were responding to a temporary emergency. The collapse in copper prices in 1974–75 was a shock matched only by the copper price collapse during the Great Depression. The problem has been compounded by aid agencies proceeding as though additional support will enable Zambia to

---

55. These data are available in successive editions of the government's *Economic Report*.

56. In one of its *Findings*, the World Bank provided an upbeat assessment of the role of ASIP in promoting dialogue (World Bank 1998a).

57. Internal assessments by the World Bank of its assistance to Zambia suggests that most projects and programs over the last two decades have failed (World Bank 1996).

restore macroecomic balance. This has been, and remains, the premise upon which the IMF has been aiding Zambia almost continuously since 1977. The ESAF arrangements in 1999 (now the Poverty Reduction and Growth Facility) and more recently the HIPC decision point are variations on the same theme.

In principle, the structural support provided by the World Bank and IMF and cofinanced by the other donors, if used appropriately, would ultimately allow Zambia to exit from aid. Structural adjustment by its very nature is meant to provide a foundation for growth and development. That has not happened. The ESAF arrangement introduced in December 1995 collapsed within months. The same occurred with the ESAF program approved in March 1999. As pointed out in Chapters 2 and 3, these failures have been part of a long-established pattern. The donors and the GRZ have been down this well-worn path before.

Yet, when seen from another perspective much of the assistance provided during the 1990s had little to do with creating the foundation from which Zambia could grow and develop. The food aid in 1992 prevented a humanitarian disaster. The Paris Club debt relief and donor-funded commercial debt buy-back were further confirmation that Zambia could not repay its debts. That aid simply rationalized what were, in fact, sunk costs. The same applied to IMF support under the RAP. Zambia was required to meet IMF conditions for an extended period so that it could gain the right for the IMF to move $1.2 billion from its bad debts ledger to its accounts receivables. Zambia still owes the $1.2 billion, an amount that will only be repaid when the donor community provides the necessary finance.

The record suggests that neither donors nor the government expected much to be achieved with foreign aid during the 1990s. These low expectations translated into weak sanctions for Zambia's noncompliance. Literally hundreds of conditions were imposed. Some were acted upon such as the donors' insistence that the president remove cabinet members implicated in drug running and that the government close Zambia Airways. Yet, despite its confrontations with the government, the donor agencies continued (and even expanded) their project support. These actions jumbled the messages. The government response was similarly mixed. It took some conditions seriously. Most of them were ignored in the knowledge that noncompliance carried no significant consequences.

A final indicator of donor dependence is the process whereby aid is provided. For some donors, like the World Bank, the process has been highly institutionalized. The Bank's mandate to promote development has given it a broad agenda. That agenda is regularly updated and extended through the themes of the *World Development Report* (WDR). Over the last decade, Zambia (like other African countries) has seen World Bank concern over health, poverty, environment, infrastructure, workers, knowledge, governance, the role of the State, and globalization wax and wane as these topics have worked their way through the WDR cycle. Other aid agencies have had their own shifting priorities. For the government, the main problem has been matching donor enthusiasm for various activities with the country's capacity to absorb assistance. Some areas, such as infrastructure, have been in such obvious need of reconstruction that the main problem is one of scheduling the work. Other tasks, such as the formulation of environment action plans, have been entirely donor-driven.

In aggregate, these activities have done little to enhance the medium-term prospects for growth and development in Zambia. The GRZ has been too intent on keeping the aid flowing and the donors have been too focused on pushing their specific agendas. There has been no coherent effort to ensure that the overall program comprises a consistent, feasible, and sustainable approach for moving Zambia forward. Perhaps this is the ultimate indicator of Zambia's dependence on aid. Current aid flows cannot be stopped without major economic disruption. And, since no formal plan exists for phasing out or substantively reducing aid flows, stopping them at some future date would be similarly disruptive.

Aid, Games, and Strategic Behavior

There are further difficulties. The above indicators highlight specific dimensions of aid dependence. They do not adequately measure the effects of the games, strategies, and tactics associated with the way that aid is generated, distributed, and used. From this perspective, aid dependence is reflected in the way the main decision-makers behave. A common feature of this behavior is that foreign aid has become the first rather than the last resort. When senior Zambian policy-makers confront a resource deficiency, they do not, as a matter of principle, exhaust every opportunity locally to raise revenue or economize on expenditure *before* turning to the donor community. Similarly, members of the donor community do not typically insist that every effort be made locally to raise resources *before* they provide assistance.[58] Indeed, aid re-

---

58. This comes directly from my experience in numerous African ministries of finance including long-term assignments in The Gambia (1985 to 1989) and Zambia (1992 to 1996). Public evidence of dependence is the endorsement by the OAU of the Lagos Plan of Action (OAU 1980) and the Alternative Structural Adjustment Programme (ECA/OAU 1989). Both of these plans called for major increases in aid to Africa. Neither of them included actions to strengthen efforts to mobilize domestic resources so that aid could be phased out.

lationships have become so highly institutionalized that each donor has strategic objectives and senior policy makers in Zambia are fully aware which donor can be tapped for each type of support.

These games undermine the value of the financial programming exercise that is a routine part of macroeconomic management. The financing gap that emerges from this exercise is meant to reflect the country's best efforts at adjustment. In practice, the government has seen performance criteria established by the IMF as the maximum requirements for adjustment and not as performance targets that should be exceeded. That is, the financial program represents a compromise consisting of the minimum amount of adjustment that IMF managers require to move Zambia's program past their board, the best guess about the amounts of resources being provided by other donors, and the total available funding from the IMF and World Bank.

If additional resources are required to close the gap, the government is expected to take revenue measures and/or the donors are canvassed for extraordinary financing either as additional debt relief or balance of payments support. This is where further gamesmanship is often evident. The IMF staff and its board express their willingness to move forward with a program. The country requires an IMF program to give it access to resources from other donors. The World Bank requires an IMF program so that it, too, can support structural adjustment. The principal game is with the IMF. Side games emerge when the IMF and World Bank begin to disagree on the nature and pace of reforms. On some conditions, the IMF has been at odds with other members of the donor community. For example, to reduce the budget deficit, the IMF has tended to focus on cutting expenditure. These cuts often fall on recurrent expenditure clashing with the requirement by other donors that the GRZ provide local counterpart funds. In practice, these resources are not forthcoming (even if they are budgeted) with donor-funded capital projects regularly underperforming.[59]

Gamesmanship also emerges when the overall program is formulated and a financing gap remains. The gap could be closed if the government would make additional policy changes. That is usually not its intention. With the IMF and World Bank having already indicated their maximum commitment to the program, pressure increases on other donors to provide additional resources or risk seeing the program fail.

This is where the Paris Club and the consultative group (CG) meetings have proven to be so useful for Zambia (and other African countries). Addi-

---

59. This is the essence of the recurrent cost problem which was examined extensively in the Sahelian countries in the late 1970s and early 1980s (McPherson 1979; Gray and Martens 1982; Heller and Aghelvi 1985).

tional finance can usually be obtained by stretching the scope of Paris Club debt relief. (For example, the GRZ did not meet the conditions of the ESAF arrangement at the end of 1995. The government and other donors, however, proceeded as if the Paris Club meeting planned for March 1996, but not held, had in fact granted the expected relief.) CG meetings are largely theater. Such meetings are never convened unless it is known beforehand that they will be "constructive." Having indicated their potential levels of assistance to the World Bank weeks in advance, officials from the aid agencies gather. They listen to the IMF and government present the case for additional assistance. They then indicate that they will help close the financing gap ensuring (as the case requires) that their message conveys their collective approval or disapproval of the government's efforts.

Lost among all this bureaucratic posturing is the basic principle of self-help that, at one time, was central to foreign assistance. This principle, fundamental to the success of Marshall Plan,[60] was seen as being vital to the promotion of growth and development. Its intention was unmistakable. As President Kennedy noted in his 1961 message on foreign aid to the US Congress:

> . . .It is essential that the developing nations set for themselves sensible targets; that these targets be based on balanced programs for their own economic, educational and social growth, programs which use their own resources to the maximum. . . Thus, the first requirement is that each recipient government seriously undertake to the best of its ability on its own those efforts of resource mobilization, self-help and internal reform, including land reform, tax reform and improved education and social justice, which its own development requires and which would increase its capacity to absorb external capital productively. . ..[61]

This principle was instrumental in the phase-out of the United States's economic assistance to Japan and later to South Korea and Taiwan. It was meant to apply to aid programs for African countries as well.[62] The idea was ultimately buried as the aid business expanded and new procedures for dispensing and evaluating aid emerged. Those rules were influenced by several factors. The number of donors increased. The multilateral agencies (particularly the World Bank) began to dominate the aid agenda, especially in Africa. The nonaligned nations called for a new international economic order. Tensions between East and West during the Cold War led to large aid flows unrelated to a country's economic performance. Finally, the criteria for aid dis-

---

60. Orme 1995.
61. John F. Kennedy in (ed.) Gardner 1962, p. 150.
62. USDS 1964.

bursement and its continuation became increasingly fungible. A major casualty of these developments has been the idea of self-help.

As a result, Zambia (like many other African countries) has treated foreign assistance as an entitlement reinforced by the institutionalization of aid through the operations of the multilateral agencies, the Paris Club, and donor consultative groups. In the process, Zambia has become hooked on aid and most donor agencies have been co-opted into providing long-term, open-ended support.[63]

What are the implications for Zambia? Since the mid-1970s, it has received extraordinary amounts of foreign assistance. The economy has regressed rather than progressed. Some might argue the counterfactual that, without aid, the regression would have been more pronounced.[64] History refutes this argument. Before Zambia began receiving large amounts of foreign aid, it grew and developed rapidly.

How might Zambia break out of the cycle of aid dependence?

5. AN AID EXIT STRATEGY FOR ZAMBIA[65]

My argument so far has been that the mutual links between the donor community and GRZ have systematically undermined the prospects for growth and development. What remedies are available?[66] What might foreign aid achieve if this mutual dependence diminishes and the games between both sides are redirected to the achievement of growth and development? What action can the government take to end aid dependence? My suggestion is for the government to formulate and implement an aid exit strategy.

---

63. In proposing "basic concepts and principles" under which U.S. foreign assistance would be "prudently and effectively used", President Kennedy did not envision that countries would become dependent on aid. The eight items he specified were all aimed, directly and indirectly, at "self-sustaining growth." Of the eight, the one that is most relevant to the present argument is: "special attention to those nations most willing and able to mobilize their own resources, make necessary social and economic reforms, engage in long-range planning, and make the other efforts necessary if these are to reach the stage of self-sustaining growth" (John F. Kennedy in (ed.) Gardner 1962, pp. 149–150).

64. For the rest of Africa, the counterfactual is the experience of Botswana and Mauritius. Without agenda-dominating aid flows, these countries have grown and developed while (most) other African countries have stagnated or declined.

65. Should Zambia bother? White and Estrand (1994, p. 106) argued that, even with additional support, conditions will remain difficult in Zambia:

The prospects for growth in Zambia are not promising, despite the very large amounts of aid required. But if the aid were not to be forthcoming then Zambia would plunge further into crisis and living standards continue to fall.

66. *The Economist*, June 26, 1999, "Helping the Third World: How to make aid work."

Formulating An Aid Exit Strategy

The principal requirement for an aid exit strategy is that it has to be desired and designed by Zambians. Donors cannot be part of the fundamental process by which Zambia's leaders decide that the prospects for growth and development can only be enhanced when the society as a whole becomes significantly less reliant on external support.[67] Once Zambia's leaders have taken that decision and have begun to formulate the strategy, external agencies willing to support the effort can be invited to contribute. Specific areas where they can help would be to determine the types of complementary actions, such as debt relief, disaster relief, and foreign investment that will enable Zambia to move beyond the extraordinary levels of aid it has been receiving.

An aid exit strategy will not necessarily end foreign assistance to Zambia. What such a strategy will accomplish is to encourage Zambians to take full responsibility for promoting growth and development. This, in turn, will give impetus to the activities that will end aid dependence.

There are several ways to formulate an aid exit strategy. A group of senior ministers could draw up a set of proposals. The cabinet could then approve the proposals and they would be adopted as part of government policy. Since one of the main problems in Zambia over the last three decades has been that policies once adopted are frequently reversed, this approach is unlikely to work.

Another method would be for the government to appoint a technical working group drawing members from government, business, and civil society. Its members would be given the task of deriving a ten- to fifteen-year program to promote growth and development that achieves a reduction in the flow of foreign assistance from its current levels of 15–20 percent of GDP to 1–2 percent of GDP. From international experience, the latter datum is a normal level for countries that are truly developing. The technical working group would be empowered to elicit the views of local and foreign experts to identify relevant issues. To ensure discipline, the group would be given a specific, short-term, deadline for completing its report.

---

67. Judging from recent submissions by the government, that point is a long way off. The acuteness of the government's dependence upon the donors was underscored by its statement about how the national poverty reduction action plan (NPRAP) would be financed (GRZ 2000, par. 29):

> In all, NPRAP contains 33 sector wide programs whose implementation is planned to be done in three phases [over four years]. US $4.9 billion is required and 43 percent of this amount is reported as having been already committed while the government is projected to provide three percent of the required finances.

The implication is clear. The GRZ will reduce poverty so long as the international community pays almost all the cost.

The task force would need to make realistic assessments of the following:

- The flows of aid from all sources and their contributions to growth and development;
- The capacity of the government, in particular, and public sector, more broadly, to provide the services which are truly of a social nature—basic health, education, law and order, food security, and infrastructure;
- Activities in areas where continued foreign assistance could genuinely and quickly enhance the government's capacity;
- Areas of opportunity within the private sector for the rapid growth of output, exports, and employment and the public sector activities (if any) required to promote these opportunities;
- The main constraints—skills, finance, international competition, managerial limitations, macroeconomic policy—that prevent expansion of the private sector. Attention would focus on constraints associated with government regulations and policies and how the constraints these impose might be removed.

The objective of these assessments is to understand the possibilities for:

- Cutting government expenditure;
- Running a large public sector surplus;
- Stimulating local private sector investment;
- Enhancing production in the key growth sectors, especially agriculture, mining, tourism, and energy;
- Reducing the nation's external and internal debt to genuinely sustainable levels;
- Creating the institutions that ensure the public sector remains restrained so that deficit financing and overreliance on aid financing do not reemerge.

The Donor's Role

The task force's assessment would provide the government with an overview of its own capacities—technical, administrative, and financial—necessary to promote growth and development. What role might the donors have?

It is easy and, as evident in the World Bank study *Assessing Aid* referred to earlier, in vogue to ascribe Zambia's poor record of growth and development to policy failures. This is the counterpart to the regular assertions by President Kaunda and members of his regime that Zambia's economic deficiencies resulted from external factors. Missing from the list is the formal admission by government and aid agency officials that some of Zambia's poor performance can be attributed to foreign assistance. A close reading of the World Bank's study reveals a special effort to avoid the issue of whether aid contributed to poor economic performance.

Given its present heavy reliance on aid and its current debt burden, Zambia cannot immediately or precipitously reduce the aid it receives. An aid exit strategy would not do that. The goal is to focus the attention of public officials, local business leaders, and donor agency staff on the types of changes that have to be made *and sustained* if Zambia is to move beyond debt and aid in a structured way.

During the formulation of the aid exit strategy, members of the donor community would be approached to discuss areas where their contribution is vital. To return to an old, but too frequently ignored theme: the principal role of the donor community should be to *supplement* Zambia's own efforts not supplant them. One area needing detailed attention is debt. Fundamentally, Zambia cannot exit from aid unless it can exit from debt as well. Properly conceived, an aid exit strategy would include a debt exit strategy. A simple and direct approach would be for the government and donor community to agree on complete relief of all debt service on all outstanding external debt prior to an agreed cut-off date. That date would be set so as not to induce a round of borrowing or build-up of arrears. The overall agreement would take effect once the government, as a confidence-building measure, takes irrevocable steps to implement the aid exit strategy. The task force should propose those steps. This action would effectively remove a major part of Zambia's foreign debt. (Whether donors write off the debt, agree to fifth dimension funding if it cannot be written off, or include it under further enhancement of HIPC would be left to them to determine.) In return for this commitment from the donor community, Zambia would agree to refrain from new external borrowing. This would be reinforced in the aid exit strategy by ensuring that the government, and more generally the public sector, runs a large surplus. The reasoning is simple: Zambia can never escape from debt and aid until it stops borrowing.

The donor community would also be asked to continue supporting sector programs for which the government is providing more than 50 percent of the funding. The latter is a crucial condition. An exit from aid is not possible unless the government is willing to adopt a strategy of self-help. A schedule for phasing out donor support can be worked out as the government begins directing its resources away from value-subtracting and nonproductive activities to areas that the task force identifies are vital for sustained growth and development.

During a prearranged transition period (e.g., three years), the donor community should continue its direct support for projects in social sectors and infrastructure. There are many examples and well-established procedures for support to health, education, water and sanitation, infrastructure (roads, bridges, village grain stores), and legal and regulatory reform. The aim would be to continue to strengthen the relevant institutions and directly enhance the welfare of the Zambian population. Whether the donors work through established government arrangements or provide their support directly should not be predetermined. The mode of support for each program should be assessed on its merits based on an explicit set of benefit/cost and efficiency criteria. The requirement is that the donors and the government maintain only those mechanisms of cooperation that are efficient and effective.

Because of the special problems imposed by the loss of technical and administrative capacity due to HIV/AIDS both the task force and the donor community should recognize the need to respond flexibly and pragmatically. For the task force, the loss of skills and technical capacity within the government implies that its agenda should be scaled back even more sharply than otherwise. For its part, the donor community should be prepared to consider providing additional TA to maintain and, if possible, strengthen areas that government officials believe are vital to its scaled-back role.

In devising an aid exit strategy two issues will arise: donor funding for NGOs, and disaster relief. NGOs have become a powerful, persistent lobby for a host of activities, many of which have little to do with growth and development. Since donors cannot be prevented from financing whomever they please, the government should not interfere so long as the NGOs operate according to their respective memoranda of understanding and any Zambian laws that relate to their activities. (For instance, NGOs should not distribute out-of-date medicines if this contravenes Zambian health standards.) But, while the government should not interfere, the donor community should not presume that any support they provide to NGOs is official aid. International charity does not cease because a government has decided to move beyond its dependence on aid. But, aid dependence for the nation as a whole cannot end if the donors cut aid to the government only to redirect the resources through NGOs.

Because Zambia is now, and for the foreseeable future likely to remain, at the edge of its (food and foreign exchange) reserves, disaster relief will be required from time to time. But disaster relief, if appropriately provided, would be irregular, specific, and close-ended. It would cease once the calamity has passed. To ensure transparency, the government should separately account for any disaster relief that it receives. Since disasters of some form always occur, the aid exit strategy should also include a government provision (preferably an amount separately budgeted and set aside each year) for disaster relief. Such action is consistent with the principle of self-help. A disaster may overwhelm the government's capacity to respond, requiring additional international support. However, that support will only be effective if it supplements the government's own contribution.

Finally, the conditions attached to donor support should be explicit, time-bound, easy to monitor, and implemented in ways that do not overtax the government's limited capacity.[68] Moreover, any conditions on donor assistance should be mutually agreed, not imposed. If these criteria are met, then both the government and the donors have an obligation to meet them.

Zambia's Economic Structure After Reducing Its Dependence on Aid

Formulating a strategy to reduce Zambia's dependence on aid is one thing. Having an idea of where the economy can go is another. The goals of any aid exit strategy would be to create an economic system in which the public sector can be sustained by the country's resource base and performs in ways that raise economic output and enhances the welfare of all Zambians.

Based on Zambia's experience of the last thirty years, this will imply a major reduction in the size of government (as measured by revenue and expenditure) and a drastic simplification of its agenda. In particular, the government should focus only on the main factors that promote growth and development. While opinions will differ on the details, the following parameters offer a guide.

At the end of the ten- to fifteen-year period during which aid declines to low, sustainable levels, the macro economy, functions of government, and basic structure of the overall economy would be as follows:

Public Sector

Government revenue	16% of GDP
Government recurrent expenditure	12% of GDP
Government budget surplus (i.e. savings)	4% of GDP
Government capital expenditure	4% of GDP
Public enterprise operations	Fully commercial or fully subsidized through the budget with no government guarantees.

Macroeconomic Indicators

Sustainable growth of GDP	6% per annum
Capital/output ratio	5 (and continuing to fall)[69]
Gross domestic savings	25% of GDP
Gross domestic investment	30% of GDP

---

68. Much ink has been spilled over whether conditions are needed, or are effective, or should even be applied. Helleiner (1986) argued that it was not clear if conditions worked or could be made to work. The ECA/OAU (1989) argued in the Alternative Structural Adjustment Programme for Africa that aid flows to Africa should be increased and conditions removed. This would give African governments more flexibility to reform their economies as they saw fit. Notwithstanding the evidence or the logic, conditions are likely to be integral to any assistance provided to African countries for the foreseeable future.

69. "The Long Term Development Vision for Zambia" presented to the CG meeting in

Resource balance/capital inflow	5% of GDP
Current account deficit on BoP	5% of GDP
o/w foreign aid	2% of GDP
foreign direct investment	3% of GDP
Change in foreign debt	Zero
Change in domestic debt	Zero (except for monetary policy purposes)
Real exchange rate	At a value that sustains the inflow of foreign direct investment and ensures that Zambia's unit labor costs remain low by international standards
Interest rates	Fully market determined but some measure above comparable rates in international financial markets.
Inflation	Equal to, but preferably below, rates of inflation in Zambia's major trading partners.

Structural characteristics

Exports	Mineral products, agriculture products (grain), livestock products, horticulture products, some processed agricultural commodities, tourism, energy (electricity) and some light manufacturing
Growth sectors	Tourism, energy, financial services, mineral products, agriculture, horticulture, and livestock.
Health	Rising life expectancy at birth, improving access to health care, enhanced food security
Education	Increasing school enrollments, rising quality of education, improved literacy among the non-school population
Political	Broad-based participation in a muti-party democratic system.

Merits and Demerits of an Aid Exit Strategy

There are several advantages of formulating and implementing an aid exit strategy. It would represent an explicit attempt by Zambia, as a nation, to move beyond the experience of the last three decades during which massive foreign assistance has been accompanied by a sharp rise in poverty. It would focus attention on the key issues—sustained growth and development—that are essential for Zambia's future as a thriving coherent entity. Finally, it would provide a framework that enables Zambians to take the initiative in promoting sustained economic recovery. At present, the initiative lies with international officials who assemble from time to time in Paris, Brussels, London, and Washington.

Lusaka in July 2000, proposed a scenario in which Zambia's per capita income would reach $1,400 in 2025. This would require a GDP growth rate of 9 percent per annum. Since investment was assumed to be 25 percent of GDP, the implied capital-output ratio was 2.8 percent, lower than in the United States. This was unrealistic. Even the more modest goal of doubling Zambia's income by 2025 with a 25 percent investment rate, implies a capital-output ratio of 4.3. This, too, is ambitious. The level of 5 noted in the text will be a stretch but it represents the level of efficiency required to achieve the desired rate of growth.

There are, however, disadvantages to such a strategy. The first is that with ten formal structural adjustment programs since 1977, all of them abandoned, the government has not demonstrated that it can sustain reform. The government has no credibility in this area. A program to exit from aid is likely to be seen as wishful thinking. Indeed, many of Zambia's partners in development will probably see the government's interest in such a strategy as yet another ploy to divert them from developing their own comprehensive development framework (CDF) or becoming fully engaged in the poverty reduction and growth exercises that are now required for IMF support.[70]

A second disadvantage is that the formulation of an aid exit strategy would be an official acknowledgement of the extreme mutual dependence that has emerged between Zambia's public sector and the donor community. Aid agencies, particularly the World Bank, have been reluctant to admit that their support to Zambia (and Africa more generally) has been counterproductive. As noted earlier, recent research suggests that this might be changing. The question for the World Bank (and others) is how do they make their aid more effective.

A third disadvantage is that for an aid exit strategy to succeed, the government cannot avoid simplifying and sharply cutting its development agenda. In the process, the privileges of many interest groups will have to be curtailed. The priorities now attached to a host of current activities such as an action plan for the environment, SIPs for agriculture, the public sector wage bill, the military, representation abroad, and official foreign travel will have to be re-ordered. Many will have to be slashed. This will require Zambia's leaders, for the first time in almost three decades, to begin acting in ways consistent with the broadest interpretation of the national interest. All of the needed cuts are politically sensitive. Many will be resisted by local interest groups. Fearing that activities they are pushing will be cut, donors may resist as well.

6. Concluding Comments: Is There an Easier Way?

Do the disadvantages of an aid exit strategy so thoroughly outweigh the advantages that such an approach should be dismissed out of hand? Isn't it possible for Zambia's policy-makers to regain the initiative by taking charge of the CDF and PRGS exercises and use these to foster rapid, sustained, growth and development? This is not likely to happen for three reasons.

---

70. Attempts by the World Bank to promote CDF's are the opposite of what we are suggesting. We argue that Zambia has to drastically simplify its agenda. Under a CDF, the agenda remains too ambitious and beyond Zambia's implementation capacity.

First, the CDF is not Zambia's initiative. It has been a World Bank attempt to apply the principles of sector investment programming to the whole economy. Second, Zambia lacks the capacity to organize and implement the elements of the CDF. The program is too detailed. Existing capacity is already inadequate and, due to HIV/AIDS, being eroded. Zambia's past attempts to implement comprehensive approaches to economic and social development have failed. Making them more complicated, as is the case with the CDF and the PRGS, further reduces their chance of success. Third, such an approach does not ensure that the government will undertake the tasks that it can handle while leaving remaining activities to the private sector.

Where does this leave Zambia? How should the government treat foreign assistance? International experience has already confirmed that, if properly administered and effectively used, foreign aid can boost growth and development. How can Zambia and the donors build on this experience? Four ways stand out.

First, Zambia should, as matters of principle and practice, only accept donor support that is specifically designed to accelerate economic growth and development.

Second, the government should formulate and begin implementing without reservation or diversion its own adjustment program. A key feature of that program should be measures that progressively reduce Zambia's use of foreign assistance.

Third, once the government has such a program underway, the donor community should agree to remove (through debt write-offs or a structured program of annual payments) the burden of all past external debts.

Fourth, both the donors and the government should agree to a mutually binding set of conditions for monitoring and judging the performance of the economy. These conditions should relate directly to the goals of rapid growth and development.

Such a program would be a time-bound, structured effort by both the donors and the GRZ to systematically reduce Zambia's reliance on foreign aid. The program would markedly improve the efficiency of foreign assistance. It would shift the aid relationship away from its current status of an entitlement. It would focus attention on breaking the endless cycle of IMF/World Bank supported adjustment programs, debt rescheduling, debt reduction, and extraordinary finance. The first requirement for jump-starting this approach is an honest assessment by the GRZ and its donors of areas where their mutual association has become counterproductive.

Whether the donor community *and* the GRZ are prepared to restructure the present aid relationship remains an open question. Critics of the aid exit strategy outlined above have argued that no one (donors or African officials) has any incentive to change the current arrangements.[71] There is no doubt that without effort by both parties that raises them above their present short-term dependence, any attempt to end aid "as we know it" is doomed. Worse, the continuation of aid under present conditions is likely to further erode Zambia's capacity to deal with its economic problems.

---

71. An anonymous referee made this point when an article setting out the aid exit strategy was reviewed for publication.

15

Sustaining Rapid Growth and Development in Zambia: The Way Forward

CATHARINE B. HILL AND MALCOLM F. MCPHERSON

1. INTRODUCTION

What needs to be done to move the Zambian economy onto a path of high sustained growth and development? We shall attempt to answer this question by drawing on the arguments developed in earlier chapters. Our aim is to suggest ways in which Zambia can move beyond the start-stop adjustments of the past, enabling the economy to begin fulfilling its enormous, and largely untapped, potential.

The least ambiguous message from our research is that for Zambia to achieve sustained growth and development, the government has to promote economic reform consistently and persistently. Anything less will fall short of what is required. Zambia's history of intermittent and partial reform since the mid-1970s has undermined economic growth, dissipated the nation's wealth, and deepened poverty.

The government will need to sharply scale back its development agenda, cease interfering in ways that benefit narrow groups, foster market mechanisms in all areas where it lacks the capacity for socially beneficial intervention, and systematically reduce its dependence on external support. Readers familiar with Zambia's economic history will not miss the irony of Zambia's present circumstances. What needs to be done to revive the economy is the direct opposite of what President Kaunda and his UNIP associates believed would be the foundation of Zambia's future prosperity. The requirements, however, are far more radical than the measures President Chiluba and the MMD government were prepared to implement.

When former President Kaunda began the program of state takeovers in 1968, his goal for Zambia was "economic independence." When President Chiluba and the MMD party were elected, they promised to meet the "challenge of change." With more than three decades of state interference, Zambia has become acutely dependent, both financially and economically. For the foreseeable future, most of the economic policies adopted by the Zambian government will be the result of agreements reached by bureaucrats meeting in Brussels, London, Washington, and Paris. That could be changed. But, it would require an effort that Zambia's leaders have heretofore been unwilling to make. We are encouraged to imagine that at some point in the future, Zambia's development will become Zambia's business.

Section 2 presents an overview of recent economic trends. Economic programs, including the programs developed in 2000 and 2001 are briefly reviewed to help place the overall policy stance in context. Section 3 considers the circumstances under which these programs could be successfully implemented. Section 4 offers our suggestions for moving Zambia forward. Section 5 has concluding comments.

2. The General Pattern of Reform

Zambia has little to show in terms of poverty reduction and improved economic performance since the 1991 elections. President Chiluba's government, however, did make many policy changes that the Kaunda regime would have found totally unacceptable. The Chiluba government did not implement the reforms rapidly enough, nor did it sustain them.

Rationalizing the government's role in the economy has been a critical need. A large number of state-owned enterprises (SOEs) were dismantled or sold. Some remain. That process needs to be completed without further delay. Attempts have been made to improve the efficiency of government administration. These efforts have to be more vigorous if the effectiveness and efficiency of the civil service are to be restored. The government still has too many employees, its budget is too large relative to the country's economic base,[1] and its activities remain far too economically intrusive.

Sustained growth and development in Zambia also will require the revival of mining and agriculture. With an appropriately valued real exchange rate

---

1. The 2000 budget speech stated that it was the government's goal to keep the public sector wage bill below 5 percent of GDP.

and overall macroeconomic stability, both sectors would be highly competitive in international markets. Were these sectors to revive, all activities connected to them would benefit as well.

Action by the government in these areas will have important spillover effects, particularly with respect to governance. Maintaining an appropriately valued real exchange rate will require macroeconomic management that eliminates the budget deficit, reduces inflation to a rate consistent with international norms, and reorganizes the public sector in ways that minimize waste and inefficiency. It will also raise the question of how the government can reduce its overwhelming dependence on foreign aid. That goal would be furthered if, as a means of improving its economic management, the government formulated and began implementing an "aid exit" strategy. An essential aspect of improved economic management will be the elimination of the budget deficit. With Zambia now past the "decision point" for the Highly Indebted Poor Country (HIPC) initiative, the only possible way that debt sustainability can be achieved and maintained is if the budget deficit is eliminated.[2]

Events typically unfold slowly in Zambia. Economic reform has been no exception. Zambia began the 1990s with a new government promising fundamental change. That did not occur. Zambia ended the 1990s with most of its main problems still unresolved. Worse, because of delays and backsliding in key areas, Zambia has been confronting the new decade with its financial and institutional capacities impaired.

During the 1990s, the mining sector was seriously decapitalized, the per capita productive capacity of agriculture fell, and Zambia's total debt stock relative to GDP rose. Furthermore, with the spread of HIV/AIDS, Zambia has lost a large number of the skilled personnel whose talents could have helped stimulate growth and development. Economic and political events during the 1990s seriously undermined the confidence of voters, consumers, and investors. The relief and celebration associated with the change of government in 1991 were genuine but short-lived. Democratically elected officials have proven to be as unwilling as their autocratic predecessors to sustain the reforms needed to revive Zambia's fortunes.

Zambia has now been reforming off and on for most of the last thirty years. As the country moves towards its fourth decade of attempting to rebalance the economy, the pace and content of economic reform remain un-

---

2. Technically, debt sustainability can be achieved if debt grows at a rate below the long-term growth of real income, and exports expand at a rate in excess of the average rate of interest on the debt. Zambia's record with fine tuning of this order is so poor that a more practical guide is to eliminate the deficit.

even. On paper, the MMD government's approach to economic reform during the 1990s was bold, broad-based, comprehensive, and far-reaching. Some important changes occurred but the drift and delay that characterized Zambia's reform efforts during the Second Republic resurfaced in too many areas. The economy did not improve and poverty intensified.[3] The main problem has been that the implementation of several critical initiatives has not been vigorously pursued. For example, the pace and direction of civil service reforms were inadequate. The copper company, ZCCM, incurred major losses and created serious financial stress among its suppliers while the government dithered over the terms and conditions of its sale.

Upon taking office, the MMD government promised to move quickly to revive ZCCM and improve its management. The Keinbaum Report offered a program for selling ZCCM that would have quickly disposed of the company, while yielding some income for Zambia. That course of action was unacceptable to the government. With the help of ZIMCO (of which President Chiluba was chairman), ZCCM's management blocked action to dispose of the company. Conditions deteriorated on two fronts. ZCCM began to suffer large losses, and the donor community began withholding financial support because of the government's inaction. After a further report by Rothchilds, a merchant bank, the government agreed to sell ZCCM. Some parts (Kansanshi and the power division) were disposed of quickly. The sticking point came when the Kafue Consortium offered to buy the core mining assets. Senior members of the government were in no hurry to complete the transaction. They delayed the proceedings by appointing, as principal negotiator, the disgraced former managing director of ZCCM.

Predictably the negotiations collapsed in mid-1998. Notwithstanding some heroic efforts by minister of finance Edith Nawakwi to revive the consortium's interest, its members had experienced enough bad faith on the government's part. The only option, apart from simply shutting the mines, was to invite Anglo American, one of ZCCM's shareholders, as the buyer of last resort. After protracted discussions during which times ZCCM's losses continued to mount, an agreement was reached. The final sale was concluded in March 2000. The story has yet to be written on why the government allowed so much of Zambia's wealth to dissipate by dragging the sale of the mines out

---

3. In 1999, President Chiluba made several references to rising poverty in Zambia. He mentioned it at the state opening of the National Assembly in January and apologized to the Zambian public for the lack of economic progress. Reporting on a State House press conference in December, *The Post* (December 2, 1999) noted that "President Chiluba . . .admitted that Zambians were subjected to acute poverty which had led to their miserable standard of living."

over eight years. It had taken less than six months for the government to purchase the mines in 1970.[4]

The government and the IMF reached agreement on a second ESAF arrangement in March 1999. (Its content is discussed below.) Like the first ESAF introduced in December 1995, this arrangement quickly fell apart. The IMF responded in July 1999 by significantly revising the program's performance criteria. Though no official explanations were provided, ordinary Zambians might wonder how the government and the IMF *for the second time* could agree to conditions that were not going to be met.

Zambia's economic leadership has seen some rapid turnover. Within a period of eighteen months (during 1998 and 1999), two ministers of finance were fired. In addition to his well-known presidential ambitions, Minister Penza was reported to have pushed too hard for the government to sell ZCCM. The accomplishments of his successor, Minister Nawakwi, were undistinguished, with her tenure adding to the general atmosphere of uncertainty and doubt. Minister Nawakwi's successor, Katele Kalumba, was formerly the minister for health. His immediate task was to revitalize a seriously depressed, highly indebted economy that, because of the government's inability to deal with the budget deficit has chronically high inflation.

During the 1990s, losses due to HIV/AIDS have increasingly depleted the government's administrative capacity and reduced its supply of technically competent workers. There is little evidence that the present cycle of debility and death from HIV/AIDS in the broader population will, or can, end soon. Chapter 12 explains that local and foreign specialists in education, management, and administration (and other disciplines) have yet to devise ways for Zambia to compensate for the losses. In the meantime, people with these skills are being lost as well.

The economic damage associated with the delayed sale of the mines and losses due to HIV/AIDS has been compounded by the government's counterproductive approach to macroeconomic management. The most obvious indicator is that Zambia's rate of inflation has been significantly out of line with world inflation.[5] Zambia's inflation is entirely the consequence of domestic policies. Since 1997, the economy has been losing international reserves. That should have produced deflation by reducing the money supply. But, fuelled by large budget deficits, domestic credit has grown rapidly keeping pressure on inflation.

Three high profile murders (former Minister of Finance Ronald Penza, UNIP official Wezi Kaunda, and MMD official Paul Tembo) have added

---

4. Martin 1972, Sklar 1975.
5. *World Economic Outlook*, Statistical Appendix, October 1999, Table 3.

some uncharacteristically vicious elements to Zambian politics and high-level business activities.[6] These events shattered Zambia's once credible reputation as a haven of peace and stability within Southern Africa.

Some changes, however, have had a positive effect. The easing of the Asian financial crisis raised the world prices of copper and cobalt. Real interest rates on Treasury bills became significantly positive during 1999 and 2000 as nominal interest rates rose. The increase in the nominal exchange rate provided welcome, though inadequate, depreciation of the real exchange rate.[7] Progress was made in moving past the HIPC "decision point."

Yet, these changes have been insufficient to reverse the economy's decline. For that to happen, fundamental modifications in government policy are needed. It is still unknown whether the government and its partners in development have the capacity to move beyond their habitual responses for that to happen. The endorsement by the donor community of the government's renewed effort to promote growth and reduce poverty is welcome. Yet, such statements have been made so often in the past that observers may wonder whether *this time* the Zambian authorities will meet their commitments.

3. THE POLICY SETTING

These developments have unfolded within a setting that has been structured, in large part, by the various agreements that the government has concluded with the major international agencies. These agreements start with a review of economic trends. They assess where the economy is headed and the types of policies that the government contemplates taking (or has agreed to take) to achieve its objectives. In the remainder of this section, we shall summarize the policy framework paper (PFP) 1999–2001, the 2000 budget, and the program presented to the donor community at the consultative group (CG) meeting for Zambia held in Lusaka in July 2000.

---

6. Two well-known commercial farmers were murdered as well.

7. A review of the situation in Zambian agriculture noted (Saasa *et al.* 1999, p. 4):
External trade performance in Zambia has been closely linked to the country's exchange rate policies. The experience of the country over the 1980 to 1994 period confirms the strong correlation between export volumes and the real exchange rate, and the government's decision to liberalize the latter is in recognition of this reality. Nontraditional exports increased by close to 80 percent following the introduction of the reforms in 1983. When Zambia abandoned SAP in mid-1987, which resulted in a considerable appreciation of the real exchange rate, export growth in the nontraditional sector reversed so dramatically that by 1990 the export levels were similar to the 1983 ones.

The Policy Framework Paper 1999–2001[8]

The PFP 1999–2001 was the basis for the government's second attempt to implement an enhanced structural adjustment facility (ESAF). Yet, within two months the ESAF arrangement was off track and the government made no serious attempt to rectify the situation. The difficulty was that the assumptions used to derive the program were unrealistic.

The Program: For the period 1999 to 2001, the government had three goals. They were sustaining economic growth of 5 percent per year, reducing inflation to a rate of 4 percent per annum by 2001, and restoring gross official reserves to the equivalent of three months of projected imports by the end of 2001. To achieve these goals there would need to be a rebound in copper production, agricultural output, nontraditional exports (NTEs), and a sharp rise in the investment/GDP ratio financed by higher private domestic saving. The annual growth rates assumed were 10 percent for copper production, 7 to 8 percent for agriculture, and 13 percent for NTEs. The investment rate was expected to rise from 14.5 percent of GDP in 1998 to 20 percent in 2001.

According to the PFP, the fiscal deficit would fall in ways that would ". . .allow Zambia to reduce over the medium term its dependence on external assistance as a source of budget financing."[9] To reduce the fiscal deficit the government would raise the revenue to GDP ratio (by 1.5 percentage points) primarily by "strengthening. . .tax administration." Some of the deficit reduction would also result from restructuring government revenue and expenditure. The program anticipated that wage expenditure and internal debt service would decline as a share of total expenditure. This would free up additional domestic resources for investment. Better controls over the budget were anticipated. The PFP noted: "To improve fiscal performance, the government will give high priority to the strengthening of commitment controls and the elimination of domestic payment arrears." Both revenue and expenditure were expected to increase relative to GDP over the PFP period.[10]

To stimulate growth, action would be taken to make monetary policy more effective. Trade liberalization would be continued, primarily by lowering average tariff duties. With respect to exchange rate management, the PFP noted that the "BoZ intends to continue its policy of refraining from interventions in the exchange market that go against underlying market trends." It added:[11]

---

8. IMF 1999 (March).
9. *Ibid.,* p. 4.
10. *Ibid.,* p. 5.
11. *Ibid.,* p. 6.

The authorities will closely monitor conditions in the exchange market and developments in other major countries in the region, with a view to adapting policies if exchange rate developments jeopardize the inflation objective or the profitability of Zambia's tradable goods sector.

Regarding institutional reform, the government made a number of commitments in the area of privatization and public enterprise reform, public sector management, financial sector reform, and governance. On the first point, several SOEs were to be sold, or preparations were to be accelerated so they might be sold. A 'new' initiative was commercialization of the Tanzania/Zambia (TAZAMA) oil pipeline.[12] A notable addition to the list of enterprises being sold was the Zambia National Commercial Bank (ZANACO).

To improve public sector management, the government reiterated its commitment to further reduce the number of public sector employees. The government also restated its long-standing promise to review the "possibility of altering the computation of pension benefits to retrenched civil servants and the feasibility of sending retrenchees, once identified, on forced leave so that they cannot benefit from future wage increases or changed pay scales. . .."[13] With respect to financial sector reform, the basic issue was to ensure that the BoZ would refrain from financing insolvent financial enterprises.

The government reaffirmed its "high priority to further improving political and economic governance."[14] The PFP pointed out that "the government is preparing a comprehensive governance program for discussion with its external partners."

Sectoral policies dealt with agriculture, mining, tourism, transport, water, and energy. A priority for agriculture was to implement the agricultural sector investment program (ASIP). In mining, the government intended to "formalize" gemstone mining and trading. It would also "improve the efficiency of government services" to the mining sector. In tourism, the government would emphasize infrastructure development. Transport activities will focus on the implementation of ROADSIP, a 10-year donor-funded road rehabilitation and maintenance program. Railways would also receive attention. With respect to water and sanitation, activities would concentrate on expanding access to safe drinking water. Finally, in the energy sector there would be efforts to improve the performance of Zambia Electricity Supply Company (ZESCO) and Zambia National Oil Company (ZNOC). Some of their activities would be commercialized.

Regarding issues related to poverty reduction, human resource develop-

---

12. In 1993, the government promised swift action to rehabilitate and privatize TAZAMA.
13. IMF 1999, p. 7.
14. *Ibid.*, p. 7.

ment, and the environment, the government noted that the incidence of poverty ". . .has declined only marginally in recent years. . .." Poverty would be addressed by devoting "at least 36 percent of domestic expenditure (excluding debt service) to the social sector in 1999–2001" and promoting home ownership through the president's housing initiative (PHI). Explicit attention would be given to health, education, and the environment. On-going programs would be emphasized.

The final section of the PFP dealt with external financing requirements. These covered additional balance of payments support, project assistance, and debt relief from donors that have regularly supported Zambia—the World Bank, the African Development Bank, the European Union, and several bilateral agencies. Based on a debt sustainability analysis, the PFP showed that Zambia's external debt was well beyond the country's current and projected debt servicing capacity. The PFP noted that ". . .Zambia will seek exceptional debt relief. . ." through the HIPC initiative.[15]

An important strength of the PFP was that it highlighted all of the themes essential for generating donor support. That, however, was also a major weakness. Because the government's technical and administrative capacities are limited, the ESAF arrangement could not be implemented. The agreed agenda was so far beyond the government's capacity that the ESAF was, in effect, preprogrammed to fail.

This, however, was only one of several reasons why the ESAF collapsed. First, for the macroeconomic projections to be valid, Zambia had to reduce inflation to levels close to those in the rest of the world, and do it rapidly. Too many attempts had been made in the past to "soft land" the economy. All had failed. Further attempts to reduce inflation gradually would do nothing to raise consumer and investor confidence. The only way that inflation could be reduced quickly was for the government to move the budget sharply into surplus. That was not part of the PFP.

Second, the PFP recirculated too many promises that had *not* been implemented. There was no indication in the PFP why this time, after so many false starts, the government would now meet its commitments. Some of the long-standing promises included reducing the civil service, lowering inflation to single-digit rates, cutting the wage bill, commercializing ZNOC, and meeting the conditions for access to HIPC.[16] Had these actions been taken, they would have greatly benefited the economy. Yet, when the government could

---

15. *Ibid.*, p. 14.

16. To help the government reduce its commitments, a team of officials should review earlier PFP's and similar policy statements (including reports to the CG and Paris Club) and compare promises made with results achieved. That exercise would reveal that most of the commitments in the 1999–2001 PFP were included in earlier programs. Making commitments has never been the government's problem; keeping them has.

not (or would not) implement them, they should have been dropped, or reformulated in ways that would have made their implementation more probable. That, too, was not done.

Third, as the PFP was structured, it took no account of the government's diminished capacity due to debility and death from HIV/AIDS of technical specialists. Much of what was being required of the government, and what it promised, could not be attained because of administrative and technical constraints. In this regard, the PFP was far too ambitious. Zambia's policy makers could have readily noted the experience of fast-growing Asian countries. None of them attempted to do everything (or even many things) at once. They made a few important changes and took steps to ensure that those changes endured. They then moved forward from there.[17]

Fourth, a major deficiency in the PFP was the presumption that both government revenue and expenditure would increase. This represented a fundamental misunderstanding of Zambia's macroeconomic predicament. If the government were fully committed to restarting growth and development, it would have taken steps to *reduce* its revenue and expenditure for the foreseeable future. Revenue needed to decline in order to reduce the real burden of taxation in Zambia. Real per capita incomes have fallen in Zambia since the mid-1970s. The government's attempts to raise the tax ratio have added to the real burden of taxation. To help restore macroeconomic balance, a reduction in tax revenue should have been matched by a corresponding reduction in expenditure. These actions would have raised net after-tax incomes, allowing private expenditure to rise. In view of the government's long record of inefficient use of resources, this reallocation would boost overall efficiency of the economy. With compelling evidence that the government's efforts to promote growth and development have had the opposite effect, the PFP should have anticipated allocating fewer resources to the public sector.[18]

Fifth, as discussed further below, some of the projected growth rates were inconsistent with the economy's more recent performance. Mining output was expected to rise. At the time, it was falling. NTE's were expected to expand rapidly. They, too, were declining. Agricultural output did increase in 1999 as a result of favorable rains. But, based on past performance and the government's policies, there was no justification for expecting agriculture to grow on a sustained basis at 7 to 8 percent per year. Inflation was being pro-

---

17. Perkins 1992, 1994, pp. 655–661.

18. In the PFP, government stated: "(T)he cost effectiveness of the public service has declined significantly over the past ten years" (IMF 1999, p. 6). It continued:

...even the available manpower is not used efficiently because of inappropriate management and organizational structures. Consequently, the public service has become unresponsive to the country's needs.

grammed to fall sharply. Due to continued credit creation to finance the budget deficit that could not happen.

Sixth, the commitments on monetary and exchange rate policies made no sense independent of action to eliminate the budget deficit. With the government committed to building up its external reserves, the foreign exchange rate would have had to depreciate sharply. This would have raised the growth of the money supply. To offset that, the budget would have needed to be in surplus. As already noted, that that was not part of the program.

There were other problems with the PFP. This, however, is not the point. There is a broader issue: the PFP did not represent a feasible program that the government, even if it were operating efficiently or effectively, could have implemented. That would have required a drastic reduction in the scope of the program. None of the parties involved, government or donors, contemplated such a development.

The Consultative Group Submissions, July 2000

The budget speech for 2000, the main points of which were briefly covered in Chapter 3, had attempted to chart a new beginning for Zambia. Yet in order to move the economy to a higher growth path, the government had to repair the financial and economic damage created by the failure of ZCCM to meet its domestic obligations (to the power company, fuel suppliers, and other local merchants). As a start, the government devoted a large portion of the budget to paying down ZCCM's arrears. That action scuttled the 2000 budget as a means of reviving growth or reducing poverty. It also made impractical the government's stated intention of reducing year-end inflation.[19]

The government did not have to wait long for evidence that its budget objectives (4 percent real growth, significantly lower year-end inflation, and rebuilding foreign exchange reserves) could not be achieved. That was already clear in the first quarter as the government turned its attention to an IMF review of the ESAF, by then renamed the poverty reduction and growth facility (PRGF),[20] and a CG meeting that was to be held in Lusaka in July 2000.

Although the government had not met the major performance benchmarks, the IMF review was more positive than officials had anticipated. This outcome was not the result of anything the government had done. Rather, the IMF needed to deal with a "hump" in Zambia's debt payments

---

19. Every budget since MMD took office contains the commitment to reduce year-end inflation. Only one (1993) met that goal.

20. The IMF changed the name of the program without changing its substance. The same conditions apply and, as a means of engaging African countries, the preparation and approval process has been extended.

that, unless addressed through extraordinary measures, would have created serious debt service problems in 2001. The hump in payments was not unexpected. It had been noted specifically by IMF staff in 1995 when they evaluated whether Zambia could fulfill the conditions of the first ESAF. Under the ESAF, the government was to build up foreign exchange reserves adequate to meet the surge in debt payments when the ESAF's grace period ended. The government failed to do this. Rather than have Zambia default, the IMF changed the rules for HIPC eligibility in Zambia's favor.[21]

This special treatment simply reconfirmed, yet again, Zambia's aid dependence.[22] The irony of this situation is worth noting. At the time the ESAF was approved, in 1995, one of its major goals was to rebuild Zambia's foreign exchange reserves in order to provide additional foreign exchange to repay the surge of debt (the hump) when the ESAF grace period expired in 2001. This particular requirement remained unmet because the government always found it more convenient to use the reserves rather than accumulate them. The foreign reserves were used to prevent the kwacha from depreciating, maintain a subsidy (through ZNOC) on petroleum, finance emergency imports of fertilizer on an annual basis, and several other activities that were inconsistent with the reform program. And, by delaying the sale of ZCCM, the government postponed any prospect that economic activity could revive to replenish Zambia's foreign exchange reserves.

The government presented several papers at the July CG meeting. Four of them are of interest—the government's report to the consultative group on the economy's performance, the Interim PRGF (I-PRGF), a statement of the government's long-term vision for Zambia's development, and suggestions on "scaling-up" activities related to HIV/AIDS. We briefly review their main points. This will highlight the government's views on the economy's performance, and the types of short- and long-term measures needed for the economy to make progress. It also provides a useful backdrop for the final section that contains our suggestions on moving the economy forward.

The report on the economy's performance was entitled "2000: CG Report." It begins by announcing that the ESAF agreed to in March 1999 had encountered "difficulties." To compensate for that rocky start, the IMF and government had designed a new program for March 2000 to March 2003. After a brief description of Zambia's achievements in establishing relative macro stability the report reviewed events of 1999. The goals of the PFP were

---

21. IMF 1999; Gondwe 2000.

22. Having approved the PRGF, the IMF was not about to sit by as Zambia's access to HIPC unraveled. With the change in rules Zambia was cleared to pass the decision point for HIPC. (The details can be found in Chapter 9.)

real growth of 4 percent, year-end inflation of 15 percent, an increase in official external reserves to 1.2 months of imports, and an overall budget deficit limited to 1.8 percent of GDP. In fact, growth was 2.4 percent, year-end inflation was 20.6 percent, international reserves were seriously depleted (amounting to less than one weeks' import coverage), and the overall budget deficit (including grants) was 4 percent of GDP.[23] The targets were missed by wide margins. Yet again, the main reason was that the sale of ZCCM had been delayed longer than expected, prompting donors to withhold support. (The PFP noted that of $818 million pledged only half of that had been dispensed.)

As a result of these developments, Zambia's economic situation had deteriorated and poverty was increasing. Government data showed that 73 percent of the population was classified as poor. The balance of payments deficit remained large, at around $500 million, HIV/AIDS prevalence was rising, and external debt ($6.52 billion after Naples terms write-offs) was beyond what the economy could service.

The government stressed its determination to improve the situation and outlined initiatives in education, public welfare (the Public Welfare Assistance Scheme), health, HIV/AIDS, and special measures to strengthen the social-safety net.

To support its efforts in these areas, the government announced its macroeconomic objectives for the period 2000 to 2002. These were real growth of 4 to 7 percent per annum, a phased reduction of inflation to 22.3 percent in 2000, 16.5 percent in 2001, and 11.5 percent in 2002, the rebuilding of international reserves to three months' import coverage by 2002, and the reduction of the budget deficit to 0.2 percent of GDP on a cash basis. All of these were constructive goals. Achieving them would depend on sharp increases in mining, agriculture, nontraditional exports, trade, and manufacturing.[24] It was also assumed that the investment rate would rise from 14.5 percent of GDP (its 1998 value) to 23 percent in 2002.

Noting that the "...ultimate objective of these policies is to reduce the incidence of poverty in Zambia over the medium and long-term" (p.10), the government then outlined its long-term development vision for Zambia. The theme was restoring "... prosperity through the pursuit of excellence with justice." Its principal objective was to double per capita income to $600 by

---

23. The budget deficit on a cash basis in 1999 was 4 percent of GDP. Excluding grants it was 11.9 percent of GDP (IMF/IDA 2000, Table 7).

24. The expected growth rates were: mining 6.5 percent, agriculture 7 percent, nontraditional exports 13 percent, trade 4.5 percent, and manufacturing 5 percent.

2025.[25] That would require a sustained rate of growth of 6 percent per annum.

As in the PFP, the program foresaw that agriculture would grow at 7 percent per annum. This target immediately confirmed that the strategy was infeasible. Such a sustained growth rate in agriculture had no historical precedent. Moreover, it implied that the contribution of agriculture to GDP would rise over time. This inverted pattern of growth has been observed only in countries that are regressing. Since that was not the government's intention, the implications of the various assumptions needed to be recast.[26]

That was not done. Instead the government sought consistency in its objectives by turning to the donor community (par.54):

> Achievement of the above macroeconomic objectives for 2000 and reduction in poverty in particular will partly be dependent on receipt of additional assistance from the cooperating partners.

To ensure that the budget remained on track, the government restated its intention to implement (and enforce) a commitment monitoring system (paragraph 56). It would also base its funding of the budget on the "yellow book" totals. These promises had been made several times before. The key issue, therefore, was not commitment but implementation.

The Interim Poverty Reduction Programme was derived from the government's own Poverty Reduction Strategic Framework that had been intro-

---

25. Three different goals can be found in the documents presented to the CG. One stated that the income level would be raised to $700 by 2025. Another set the target of $1400 by 2025. The third, as noted, indicated $600. This target is more realistic though it will be a stretch unless there are major improvements in efficiency and additional domestic resources are mobilized.

26. The approach to agriculture needs to be completely rethought. The following passage (par. 47) suggests that government officials have learned nothing substantive from the failure of government interference in agriculture over the last three decades:

> In agriculture, new focus is on increasing hectarage planted and yields by small-scale farmers. This will be achieved through providing advisory services to farmers to improve the quality of farming. Farmers will be assisted to increase agricultural production and productivity through adoption of proven technological innovations and provide a strong linkage between farmers and farm support organizations responsible for marketing, credit and farm input supplies. Extension officers will drive this new focus. Farmers will be taught management and marketing skills to operate on a commercial basis and appreciate farming as a business in a market driven environment. In livestock, the focus will be on improved control of animal diseases and for fisheries it will be on facilitation of the production of fingerlings, capacity building and improved enforcement of the regulatory framework to promote sustainable fishing methods.

duced in May 1998. The program aimed to achieve a broad-based reduction in poverty by:

- Encouraging economic growth through agriculture and rural development;
- Providing public physical infrastructure;
- Increasing productivity in urban microenterprises;
- Developing human resources;
- Coordinating, monitoring, and evaluating poverty reduction programs.

To combat poverty, the government would focus on reviving activity in the major sectors. For agriculture, the government would emphasize liberalization and decentralization.[27] In tourism, it would improve infrastructure. Mining would be left to the private sector. In transport, the government would implement ROADSIP. With heavy involvement from the donors in both the organization and financing, ROADSIP was already proceeding as planned. The government noted, however, that in order to preserve the roads once the rehabilitation and reconstruction were over, the rail system needed to be refurbished. The poor state of the railways had been costly to the economy as a whole, by adding to the wear-and-tear on the road system.[28]

The report concluded with three further subsections. These were public sector reform, the introduction of a "good governance" initiative, and the request to the donors for financial support. The government announced that the number of government employees had fallen from 139,000 in April 1997 to 101,000 by April 2000 (par. 95, p.22). Given that civil service reductions had unraveled a number of times during the 1990s, this was progress. It was noted, however, that a donor-supported public sector capacity building project (PSCAP) would be launched. Due to commence in August 2000, this thirteen-year program would complete the restructuring, reform the pay scales, introduce more effective management, foster accountability and transparency, enhance the skills of public servants, facilitate budgetary resource flows, and improve the government's capacity to carry out its legislative agenda.

These intentions are laudable. However, two points were overlooked.

---

27. A useful starting point in stressing sector policies would be an honest assessment of the government's role. With respect to agriculture, the poverty reduction strategy made a poor start. For example, the report noted: "Input supply and crop marketing have been left in private hands, prices are set in free and open markets and restrictions on domestic and international trade have been removed" (par. 63). At best, this is a misrepresentation. Agriculture has performed poorly in Zambia, primarily because the government will not stop interfering.

28. The report noted: "The shift from trains to road traffic is estimated to have cost the Zambian economy US $100–150 million per year in increased road deterioration and fuel costs" (par. 74, p.18).

First, there was no indication how rapidly improvements were meant to occur. If it were spread over thirteen years, this program would do nothing to immediately address the inefficiency of the civil service so that growth could increase. Second, there was no mention of the need to deal with problems of workers with HIV/AIDS (a point covered in Chapter 12).

The "good governance" initiative began on March 31, 2000. It was entitled the National Capacity Building Programme for Good Governance. After a decade of questionable governance involving many disputes with the donor community, the shift in direction raises several questions, especially about the government's motives. The priorities established were:

- constitutionalism and human rights;
- accountability and transparency;
- economic management;
- democracy, decentralization and local government.

Since all of these were promises made by the MMD in its 1991 *Manifesto,* the initiative further underscores Zambia's acute dependence on the donors. Unable to improve governance, despite its extended tenure, the government switched direction with a program intended primarily to co-opt the donor community.

The report concluded with a discussion of financing needs. These were not trivial. The amounts are $766 million in 2000, $906 million in 2001, and $890 million in 2002. It was noted that these amounts would change marginally if Zambia gained access to HIPC in 2001. A concluding paragraph (par. 117) asserted that Zambia could not make the necessary program changes without donor support.

The report on "scaling-up" action on HIV/AIDS followed a format developed by the World Bank. The goal was to engage NGOs and 14 sectoral ministries in the implementation of priority actions (outlined in Section 4 of the report). The three-year program was estimated to cost $56 million and would consist of 42 "catalytic" projects. The activities would involve:

- Preparing a detailed statement of issues;
- Procuring donor support;
- Providing a statement by members of civil society at the CG meeting;
- Coordinating the statement prior to the CG to emphasize issues;
- Fully integrating priorities into poverty reduction work;
- Monitoring public expenditures on HIV/AIDS;
- Including HIV/AIDS as a priority in poverty reduction work;
- Determining performance indicators to incorporate in PRGF and HIPC documents;

- Devoting budgetary savings from HIPC to HIV/AIDS;
- Urgently soliciting bilateral creditors to support the HIV/AIDS response.

There is no doubt that constructive measures are needed to deal with HIV/AIDS. Nonetheless, the issue needs to be kept in context. During MMD's tenure roughly half a million Zambian children had become orphans through AIDS.[29] President Chiluba's commitment to dealing with the issue did not even extend to attending the international conference on HIV/AIDS held in Lusaka in 1999. The above actions represent a wish list that might be undertaken if the donors provide the resources directly or through HIPC. That the proposed effort was beyond any capacity the authorities could marshal was clear from the document. It indicated that the government would need special support for capacity building to monitor and evaluate the impact of the proposed activities. Instead of scaling-up, the government should have been seeking ways to scale back, so that whatever actions were taken responded effectively to the HIV/AIDS situation.

4. The Way Forward

It is probably far too easy to review the promises of the MMD government and criticize its shortcomings. Yet, after a decade in power, the government is well beyond any reasonable learning period. At times, and in some areas, the government made useful progress. At other times, and in particular areas (such as the sale of ZCCM) making progress was not the government's intention. In this regard, the Chiluba government has not operated in the broad public interest even though it was elected on the promise that it would raise the welfare of all Zambians. Holding any government accountable is difficult in a system where one of the objectives is to improve accountability. There is always room for strategic backsliding that can then be blamed on the weak system of accountability.

What the above review and earlier chapters show is that, in all its activities, the government has been severely overstretched administratively, financially, and technically. What has not been fully integrated into any of the programs that the government has devised (either on its own or with the cooperation of the donor community) is that the agenda always has been, and remains, infeasible. Implementation shortfalls and outright failure have been inherent in the reform program. Thus, even if the government had been fully committed to implementing its reforms, it would have failed.

---

29. GRZ 1999, pp. 35, 57.

A key principle in moving the economy forward is that the government has to sharply scale back its agenda. The main task should be to focus only on activities that it can implement effectively. Without this fundamental change, every effort to help Zambia revive growth and development will fail. This is not an issue that can be fudged. Zambia's history, both under UNIP and MMD, demonstrates otherwise.

The implication is that, however well intentioned the annual budgets or how well articulated the various PFPs, PGRFs, and CG documents, the basic problem is agenda overload. Without major cuts, sustained forward movement cannot occur.

The program we propose builds from this point. We see the role of the government as being focused on creating the conditions that will generate and sustain rapid rates of economic growth and development. Good governance includes and requires effective macroeconomic management. All Zambians, except the rich and well-connected, have suffered three decades of economic decline. The cost in diminished welfare and foregone opportunities has been staggering. Reversing this will require major improvements in public administration and economic management.

For the immediate future, steps will be needed to unravel the effects of ZCCM's losses, make headway on civil service reform, improve macroeconomic management, address governance issues, and develop a structured program to reduce Zambia's extreme dependence on foreign aid.

The government was correct when it noted in the 1998 budget speech that ". . . the most powerful mechanism for the reduction of poverty in the long-term is achieving broad-based economic growth."[30] It could have added that rapid growth is the most powerful mechanism for short-term poverty reduction as well. Direct government action to alleviate poverty has had little effect in Zambia. Indeed, the opposite has occurred. The government's numerous attempts to promote growth and development over the decades have failed. Poverty reduction is a critical and worthy goal. The basic issue has always been to determine the most constructive way that the government can contribute to that process. Based on our assessment of the record, the following activities will be needed.

Reviving Mining and Agriculture

With the sale of ZCCM now complete, the pressing concern is to restore the mines to full production in the shortest time possible. When this is accomplished, Zambia will once more benefit from higher rates of income gen-

---

30. Budget speech 1998, par. 83.

eration, employment, and wealth creation. Government revenue would also increase.

With world copper prices well below $1 per pound, recovery in Zambia's mining fortunes will not be dramatic. Yet, major progress is likely now that the mines are being managed by world class mining companies that can afford state-of-the-art technology. These changes will allow the much overdue process of reconstruction and reorganization of the mines to proceed with positive spillover effects for the Copperbelt and all activities connected to mining.

The main challenge for the government (and donors) will be to unravel ZCCM's losses in ways that do not further damage the economy. If handled appropriately by the government most of ZCCM's debts and related losses will be absorbed by the donors. That is already underway now that Zambia has reached the HIPC decision point. Yet, the country as a whole will only benefit if the government continues to improve its macroeconomic management and takes the measures needed to enhance governance.

Although it is difficult to overemphasize the importance of reviving mining activity, it is equally critical that agriculture grows rapidly. As noted in earlier chapters, the government has made numerous efforts to influence agriculture in some form or other over the last four decades. Missing from these efforts, however, have been consistent macroeconomic policies and microeconomic initiatives that encouraged all agricultural producers, both large and small, to act in ways that raised their incomes and wealth. Instead, farmers and livestock herders have responded defensively to official intervention.

The outcomes have been predictable. Producers have shifted their output-mix away from crops and livestock activities that were heavily taxed or controlled. They found ways to avoid repaying their credit advances, and they worked out mechanisms for diverting government-sponsored commodity inputs to higher value uses. They also found ways around government restrictions banning exports, especially of maize.

There are now many suggestions for improving agriculture. Based on Zambia's history, none of these can succeed if the government continues to interfere in agricultural marketing and distribution, and if macroeconomic managers attempt to sustain an overvalued real exchange rate. The inability of the government to implement its flagship initiative, ASIP, since 1995 should add to the official caution. Unfortunately, the government's submission on agriculture to the CG meeting in mid-2000 was chilling. It proposed more, not less, official intervention. The government lacks the capacity to do more than develop rural infrastructure and create the legal and regulatory frameworks to support the full liberalization of all agricultural markets. Even these tasks will be major challenges. Anything else will be counterproductive.[31]

Progress on the Public Sector Reform Program (PSRP)

The main outstanding issues with respect to the PSRP are how large a civil service is needed to administer Zambia effectively, what size wage bill is appropriate, and how can that bill be sustained by the country's economic base? Estimates of the costs involved should include the transition costs, such as those associated with retrenchment, and the additional costs of paying a smaller civil service at higher rates on a sustained basis.

The government's retrenchment packages are well beyond the country's financial capacity. Under existing law, the government has been obliged to offer laid-off civil servants a lump-sum payment equal to two-thirds of their total pension. This can result in immediate payments equal to 3–6 times an employee's annual salary. For senior civil servants, the amount has been roughly $50,000. What has been ignored so far is that the government has a public responsibility to reduce the cost. To date, its attention has been focused on the legal entitlements of retirees. Members of the donor community have stated on numerous occasions that they will help finance retrenchment. Does this represent the most efficient use of donor resources? With poverty so pervasive, it is grossly inequitable to be devoting around 150 times Zambia's average annual income to pay for the removal of one redundant civil servant.

Cheaper ways need to be found. While many have been available, the government has shown little initiative in devising a less costly package. Options include cheaper voluntary packages that circumvent the legal requirements, changing the law to lower the cost, or keeping workers on the payroll but not using them. The overriding issue, however, is not retrenchment but raising the quality of the civil service. A cost-effective way of doing this would be for the government to furlough unproductive workers on full pay, but without access to future wage increases. (That possibility, suggested by one of the authors in 1992, resurfaced in the 1999 PFP.)

One element that needs to be addressed in a systematic way is how to improve the capacity of the civil service in the face of mounting losses due to

---

31. This statement may be seen as extreme. Proponents of intervention will point to the need for extension and credit. The historical record demonstrates that the government has no capacity to support these activities effectively. We would add, however, that the conventional model of agricultural extension is totally inadequate in the face of the HIV/AIDS epidemic. What does the government have to extend to teenage heads of household and grandparents who now comprise the fastest growing groups of producers in rural areas?

HIV/AIDS. We have already discussed (in Chapter 12) the problems of training, managing, and motivating workers under these circumstances. The government informed the CG meeting in July 2000 that, if funding were forthcoming, it would promote a thirteen-year capacity building effort in the civil service. That plan did not take account of the impact of HIV/AIDS.

Improved Macroeconomic Management

The fundamental issues with respect to macroeconomic management are to eliminate the budget deficit and to engineer a large sustained devaluation of the real exchange rate. Zambia's history since 1970 (when large deficits first emerged) has shown that without a responsible approach to government finance (a crucial element of governance), nothing else in the macroeconomic picture can be consistent. Pressure has to be relieved on debt creation at all levels. That is not possible while the government continues running a budget deficit. Furthermore, Zambia cannot regenerate the dynamism in its export and import-competing sectors that it requires to grow rapidly without a significant, sustained realignment of the real exchange rate.[32] Zambia's mines are no longer (as they once were) among the lowest cost sources of copper in the world. Zambian wages are not low relative to average worker productivity. Thus, the only way to reduce unit (labor) costs in a sustained manner is through real exchange rate devaluation.

There are several ways to proceed. Eliminating the budget deficit requires a mechanism such as a cash budget advanced by at least one month. Such a device would ensure that the budget remained in surplus irrespective of expenditure pressures.[33] Sharply devaluing the real exchange rate will require the BoZ to continue manipulating the exchange rate (as it has since mid-1995) but in ways that encourages devaluation rather than resists it. The BoZ could easily do this by aggressively rebuilding its external reserves.

Government actions must contribute to national savings. The "public good" dimensions of economic stability—low inflation, relatively low interest rates, and an appropriately valued exchange rate—deserve the highest pri-

---

32. The model in Chapter 11 provides evidence.

33. The cash budget advanced by one month implies that the government would operate with a full month's revenue as a cushion. For example, expenditure (including commitments) in June would be limited to revenue collected in April. The cash budget that operated in Zambia during 1993 and 1994 operated in a way that kept revenue ahead of expenditure by roughly two weeks. This system broke down, not because it was failing, or could not work. It was inconvenient for senior government officials to restrain expenditure sufficiently to build up and maintain a revenue cushion. The cash budget broke down as the government began funding its operations with monthly advances from the BoZ and having BoZ pay government debt service outside the budget.

ority. On a benefit/cost basis, there is no program of deficit spending that the
government can implement that will generate more social welfare than the
stability that will result from eliminating the deficit.[34]

Bringing the budget under control will require action to clear the government's arrears. Several steps are needed. First, the outstanding stock of arrears has to be verified. [35] Second, future budgets need to make adequate provision to clear the arrears. Third, procedures to avoid new arrears have to be
followed.[36]

A variety of changes would help. Since unexpected and *ad hoc* expenditures always arise, the contingency reserve in the budget has to be adequate to
cover the most urgent of these unexpected items. Expenditure cuts have to be
made. Official travel and representation abroad should be slashed. The strategic underfunding of crucial budget items (such as interest payments and operations and maintenance) is simply window-dressing. The budget process
needs to be realistic, with all items included at their full cost. The retrenchment packages could be reworked or, through the mechanism described earlier, avoided. Tax defaulters should be prosecuted to the full extent of the law.
The 1998 budget speech provided a tax amnesty and referred to the "dire
consequences" for defaulters.[37] That threat has to be given substance, without
fear or favor. The viability of the several sector investment programs (SIPs)
should be reexamined. The problems with ASIP demonstrate that the government lacks the capacity to implement such administratively intensive projects.[38] Instead of learning from the demise of ASIP, the donors and the government have undertaken several other SIPs, in education, health, and
infrastructure (ROADSIP). With the education and health efforts already encountering capacity constraints and ROADSIP dominated by the donors, a
more efficient and effective approach for the government would be to concentrate on improving the quality of primary education and preventive
health care. When Zambia's real income increases, the agenda can be expanded.

---

34. The background to the introduction of the cash budget described in Chapter 3 is relevant to this point.

35. Chapter 4 describes how Zambia "avoided" arrears by sweeping all expenditure overruns into "X-accounts" at the central bank at the end of each year.

36. The 1994 budget sspeech noted that arrears had been a problem in 1993. During 1994,
arrears of K17 billion were paid. In 1995, the government paid arrears of K22 billion; in 1996,
the total was K42 billion. In 1997, K68.9 billion in arrears were cleared even though there was
no provision for them in the budget. Large payments were made to "clear" arrears in both 1998
and 1999. The 2000 budget contained over K400 billion to clear some of ZCCM's arrears. Additional amounts were needed to pay government arrears as well.

37. Budget speech 1998, par. 146.

38. The history of ASIP has been covered in Chapter 10.

Continued Promotion of Exports

Promoting exports does not require explicit action by the government. It does, however, require a conducive economic setting at both the micro and macro levels. The government can contribute to such a setting by taking the measures needed to eliminate the budget deficit, devalue the real exchange rate, and support the agricultural sector through improvements in basic infrastructure. Zambia's exporters are already linked to foreign markets and can gain access to finance if their potential output is competitively priced. Neither of these requires new initiatives by the government. What is required, however, is for the government to take seriously its pledge, first enunciated in the 1991 MMD *Manifesto* of "creating an enabling environment" for private sector activity.

Explicit Attention to Governance

That same *Manifesto* committed the MMD party to transparency, accountability, and honest administration. Whether intended or not, President Chiluba and his team set high standards when they took office in 1991.[39] Indeed, it was these commitments that induced the majority of Zambian voters and key donor agencies to provide their support. The government's record on governance has been spotty at best.

Though much has been said and written about the governance, some important issues remain muddled. An example from the 1999 PFP is the government's statement that it was "...preparing a comprehensive Governance Program for discussion with its external partners."[40] This has the process backwards. Governance does not (or ought not) involve what Zambia's "external partners" urge upon Zambia's leaders. The government may usefully draw on experience elsewhere. At its most fundamental level "political and economic governance" is what Zambians do for themselves. Zambians lose when they do not insist that their leaders behave forthrightly, honestly and humanely, no one else. Moreover, if Zambia's leaders have to look abroad for international endorsement of their behavior, they misunderstand what leadership entails.

Evidently lost is the point that governance rests on the relationship between those who lead and those who follow. If neither group has faith in the other, no amount of documentation prepared for and shared with "external

---

39. Chapter 13 points out that both the 1991 and 1996 MMD *Manifestos* state the need for, and the government's commitment to, good governance.

40. IMF 1999, p. 8.

partners" will create a viable, accountable, government. The principles are clear. They need to be observed.

This takes time and practice. In Zambia's case, time is not on the government's side. Since the restoration of multiparty democracy a decade ago, real per capita income has fallen rather than risen, and poverty has intensified. These circumstances persist because the government has been unwilling to implement and sustain the types of policies that would promote growth and development. In effect, the government has not met the standards of governance that it set itself at the start of its tenure.

It has also been counterproductive for Zambia's leaders to bristle when they are criticized on issues of governance.[41] This reaction garners little sympathy, locally or abroad. Donor agencies have been under pressure to withhold aid from governments that tolerate corruption, lack transparency, demonstrate contempt for the rule of law, engage in antidemocratic behavior, and show indifference to human rights.

The government's challenge is to restore public confidence in its commitment to good governance. Purposeful steps are needed to convince Zambians that the government is fundamentally concerned with their welfare—that the promises in the MMD *Manifestos* were not hollow. One way to start repairing the damage would be to begin implementing the program outlined above—revive the mining sector, raise the efficiency of the civil service, eliminate the budget deficit, depreciate the real exchange rate, and stop interfering in agricultural markets. To succeed, these will all require transparency, honest administration, and accountability.

Reduced Aid Dependence

The government's efforts to improve governance would be enhanced if it reduced its acute overdependence on the donor community. A major benefit of formulating an "aid exit" strategy (described in Chapter 14) is that it would require wide-ranging, positive, changes in government behavior. We do not make such a recommendation gratuitously. We recognize that Zambia is a poor country and under normal circumstances could benefit from international transfers. Yet, since the early 1970s, the processes through which foreign aid has been generated and used have blocked growth and development.[42] Both the government and donor agencies have become enmeshed in

---

41. This is evident in their public statements, for example, those already cited from the 1998 budget speech. Towards the end of his term, President Chiluba intensified his criticism of the donor community (*The Post*, December 2, 1999).

42. Though the World Bank continues to lend heavily to Zambia, its internal assessment of the contribution of Bank support to Zambia have been highly negative (World Bank 1996).

a destructive cycle of adverse expectations. Government officials do not expect Zambia to move beyond aid in the foreseeable future. Donor officials have similar expectations. Consequently, foreign aid has become the financing of first, rather than last, resort. For evidence, one needs look no further than social expenditure. Activities that should be the government's highest priority are often financed by the donor community.[43]

An important aspect of an "aid exit" strategy is a program to achieve an exit from debt.[44] The donors have already made major progress in this area on Zambia's behalf (see Chapter 9). But, to repeat a familiar point, an exit from debt will be impossible if the government continues running a deficit and resists the devaluation of the real exchange rate needed to allow the external accounts to move into balance.

Some scholars have argued that an aid exit strategy is too severe and, for a poor country, unwarranted.[45] In Zambia's case, however, aid has become so counterproductive that a fundamental break with past practices and behavior is required. On this count, it is worth recalling that in 1970 Zambia had minimal foreign assistance, low foreign debt, high rates of saving and investment, a positive resource balance, a budget surplus, low inflation, and a positive rate of per capita income growth. Comparisons with 1980, 1990, and 2000 reveal an entirely different situation. By these dates, real per capita income had fallen, the rates of saving and investment had declined sharply, and foreign debt had risen to levels that could not be serviced. Zambia had ceased relying on its own resources and had become acutely dependent on foreign aid.

An aid exit strategy would also bring some rationality to the policy making process. Over the last two decades, the flows of foreign resources have been so large that policy making in Zambia has been dominated by the need to keep the resources flowing.[46] Foreign aid has exacerbated Zambia's economic

---

43. For evidence, readers need only consult recent *Economic Reports* or *Public Expenditure Reviews* to see that the bulk of the financing (more than 95 percent) for development activities in areas such as education, health, and infrastructure is provided by the donors.

44. We recognize that there are many debt reduction strategies have been proposed. The HIPC initiative has been revised a number of times (details are on the IMF website). Scholars at the Center for International Development at Harvard University have offered suggestions (CID 1999). These and other plans, however, do nothing to ensure that countries will remain out of debt. Moreover, they only deal with debt dependence, not aid dependence. Indeed, the CID proposal requires donors to write off the debt *and* substantially increase the flow of aid to the HIPCs.

45. Our colleague at Harvard, Clive Gray, disagrees with this approach. In McPherson and Gray (2000) he rebutted the idea of an "aid exit" strategy. In his view, if countries fully implemented the IMF/World Bank adjustment program, they would grow and develop and graduate from aid. His views also appear in Chapter 16.

46. The *Times of Zambia* (May 12, 1998) carried a story "Zambia plans Club 'assault.' " It

problems because it has allowed the government (both UNIP and MMD) to finance imbalances rather than adjust. The 1998 budget included external financing equivalent to 35 percent of total expenditure.[47] Subsequent budgets have been similarly dependent upon external financing. The way out of this impasse is for the donors and the government to adopt measures that disentangle their mutual dependence.

In the 1998 budget speech, the minister of finance stated: "... the people of Zambia do not want charity. They want a chance to move ahead."[48] Since this presumably represents the feelings of the government, there should be no resistance to the idea of designing and implementing an aid exit strategy. Zambia would then have the chance to move beyond the aid and aid-induced behavior that, so far, has scuttled all of the country's efforts to grow and develop.

5. CONCLUDING COMMENTS

Zambia has the advantage of abundant natural resources (many of which have not been developed), adequate fertile land, and the basic infrastructure to support modern economic growth. The conventional approach, however, has been to assume that Zambia needs additional resources if it is to grow and develop. History has shown that resources are not the constraint. Over the last three decades, Zambia has had access to large amounts of domestic and external resources. Those resources have not been used efficiently, effectively, or equitably. The outcome has been economic regression not economic growth.

Economic reform in Zambia has now been through several false starts under both the UNIP and MMD governments. Will the recent changes in the mining sector result in brighter prospects for growth? Or, will they be another dead-end? Are there now conditions emerging in Zambia where sustained growth and development, after being on hold for almost three decades, might

---

explained how, at the CG meeting in Paris, the Zambian team would make its case to the donors in order to restore the flow of aid.

47. BS 1998, par. 104. Though his expenditure plans relied heavily on external funding, the minister emphatically denied that Zambia was dependent on foreign aid. In a subtle twist, the minister stated: "Zambia's case is not one of growing dependency on donor support" (budget speech par. 159). Though this might have been true, it was inconsistent with the MMD *Manifesto* in 1996 which stated that Zambia needed to reduce its dependence on foreign assistance so that (among other things) it could control its policies. Since 1996, Zambia's dependence on the donors has not declined. With the HIPC initiative now in place, its dependence has increased.

48. BS 1998, par. 158.

once more materialize? As Zambia's history has shown, the answers will depend on its leaders and, if they respond constructively, on how rapidly business and consumer confidence revives. Zambia continues to have enormous capacity for rapid growth and development. Policies and politics have conspired to undermine that capacity.

Will circumstances be any different now than they were in 1984 when UNIP launched its program for "restructuring in the midst of crisis," or in 1992 when MMD initiated its new economic recovery program (NERP)? We sincerely hope so. Our study has underscored the changes that are needed for recovery and sustained growth.

Whether that happens will depend on the responses of the government and the donor community. Their actions cannot guarantee that Zambia will prosper but their reactions to the emerging opportunities, if inappropriate, will guarantee that Zambia continues to stagnate.

Zambia needs a fresh start. It needs a fundamental break with past government behavior. With the mines now in private hands, the opportunity exists for national income and wealth to increase on a sustained basis. Making the changes we suggest will not be easy. Many groups will find their interests threatened. The government, however, could readily counter that by explicitly focusing on Zambia's largest interest group, namely, the 86 percent of the population (by World Bank estimates) that are poor. None of the poor is helped by high inflation. None of them gains from an overvalued real exchange rate that undercuts economic growth. None of them benefits from government intervention that reduces agricultural income. Finally, none of the poor is helped when the government promises far more than it can deliver.

16

Critical Review: Lessons from Zambia for Sub-Saharan Africa

CLIVE S. GRAY

1. Economic Regression

Catharine Hill and Malcolm McPherson paint a sad picture of economic regression in Zambia. A country that at independence in 1964 ranked third in sub-Saharan Africa (SSA) in per capita GDP, by 2000 was tied with one other country in 26th place, out of 46 SSA countries ranked by the World Bank.[1] And this, despite having at independence an agricultural sector that ensured food self-sufficiency, along with one of the world's most modern copper industries. The latter had just benefited from a period of expansion and technological innovation (a lot of it generated in Zambia) that followed the 1949 devaluation of sterling and increase in demand accompanying the Korean War boom.

The sorriest component of this gloomy picture is the opportunity that was lost after the MMD party succeeded in ousting Kenneth Kaunda and his discredited UNIP administration on a reform platform in 1991. After nationalizing and unifying the copper industry under ZCCM in 1970, UNIP had severely weakened it. Production of around 400,000 tons in 1990–91 was only 55 percent of the 1970 level, and annual outlays on exploration and development, a *sine qua non* to keep any mining industry competitive, had long been close to zero, lower than in any other major producing country.

According to the World Bank's *World Development Report* for 1995, during 1980–93 Zambia's per capita GDP declined at an average annual rate of

---

1. Computed by the writer from 2001 *World Development Indicators* database, World Bank website, 7/16/01.

3.1 percent. UNDP's *Human Development Report* for 1995 puts per capita income at $370 in 1992. Before the 1991 election, most observers believed that Zambia and its copper industry had nowhere to go but up.

Hill and McPherson show us they were wrong. MMD's first eight years in office saw a further 24 percent drop in copper production.[2] A 1993 consultancy report put ZCCM's sale price at around $750 million. When the government finally completed privatization in 2000, the nominal price received for the company covered only a fraction of the debt that it had incurred.

As for per capita income, World Bank data show it declining once more, to $300 in 2000. Hill and McPherson note in their introduction that the U.N.'s Human Development Index (HDI) dropped Zambia from No. 136 in the world in 1992, to No. 153 in 1999.

To be sure, some external factors complicated the MMD regime's life—notably drought, volatility in the real copper price, and disruption in neighboring countries (Zimbabwe, Mozambique, Angola). Nonetheless, Hill and McPherson show conclusively how these problems were exacerbated by the regime's policy choices—a massively overvalued exchange rate, continued interference in agriculture, an over-extended agenda, plus unwillingness to sustain reform.

2. The Political Dimension

The terms of reference of the Harvard advisory project under which Hill and McPherson served and whose work provides most of the material for the book related specifically to economic policy. In the author's view, the book does a superb job of reviewing the factors that caused Zambia's economy to decline under 27 years of UNIP rule; outlining policies that would have reversed that decline under the MMD administration; and proposing a strategy for the immediate future that would restore the economy to a respectable growth rate.

As the authors note, they do not *directly* address political development and related issues.[3] However they conclude their introductory chapter with the observation that Zambia's "growth and development has been blocked by the unwillingness of Zambia's political leaders to assemble a government that would implement and sustain the policies required to realize [the country's] potential."

It may be useful to dwell for a moment on the causes of this "unwilling-

---

2. Chapter 10 *supra*, Table 1 gives output of 376,900 tons in 1991 and 287,100 tons in 1999.
3. Chapter 1, Section 5.

ness." There are two alternative ways of looking at it: either Zambia's political system failed to provide incentives to give the necessary "will" to political leaders who would otherwise have been capable of implementing and sustaining the required policies; or, alternatively, the system replaced Kaunda's circle with a set of individuals motivated from the outset by a desire to use the government machinery to acquire and manipulate personal power and wealth, who would have resisted donor efforts to impose progrowth policies under any circumstances. *And,* continuing the second explanation, the system failed to produce other individuals who could hold those politicians accountable and eventually displace them.

Both explanations must be partially true. Chiluba's first cabinet contained two individuals so notoriously involved in drug running that the donor community issued an extraordinary ultimatum: replace those ministers, or no new aid. The Chiluba administration reluctantly complied, installing one of the two (Vernon Mwaanga) as secretary of the MMD. (He returned to the cabinet during Chiluba's second term.) It is difficult to imagine these individuals implementing and sustaining progrowth policies in their respective agencies under any circumstances. Other individuals whom the donors did not pinpoint have joined in looting the national treasury and/or ZCCM's assets.

Regardless of which explanation holds greater weight, it is clear that Zambia's political system has so far catastrophically failed the nation. It has given the MMD leadership confidence that it could act with impunity to misuse political power against the interests of the macroeconomy and the population at large, and it has failed to provide credible alternative leadership. It has even ushered in assassination as a political *modus operandi*—cf. the activities of the "black maamba" during the 1996 election campaign and the more recent murders of Kenneth Kaunda's son, and of ex-MMD official Paul Tembo.

After five years of misrule, the MMD was returned to power in 1996. It was helped, to be sure, by the constitutional manipulation banning Kenneth Kaunda's candidacy, but reviewing his nearly three decades in power, it is difficult to describe him as a credible alternative leader.

Zambia is not alone in Africa (or indeed in other continents) in this regard. The writer will cite briefly two other African countries, in which he has worked, whose political system has thus far similarly failed them. In Kenya, following 13 years of corrupt misrule by President Daniel arap Moi, aid donors obliged him in 1991 to open up a one-party system to free elections. Initially a largely united opposition was given a strong chance of winning. Within a few months the opposition had fragmented and Moi pulled through with only 36 percent of the national vote. The past records of the three opposition presidential candidates and their leading supporters gave little hope that the election of any of them would have produced a sea change in the direction and quality of the national leadership. In 1997 Moi won again, this time with 43 percent of the vote.

In Madagascar, President Didier Ratsiraka was ousted by popular unrest and went into exile in France in 1991 after 16 years of miring the economy in a pseudo-Marxist trap. His successor, Albert Zafy, was impeached by parliament in 1996 after four years of misrule had left the economy little better off. Ten or so candidates contested a new presidential election in late 1996. Which two candidates received a plurality? None other than Messrs. Ratsiraka and Zafy. Ratsiraka eventually won with 50.6 percent of the runoff vote. Back in power, he was overheard saying that, with the economy on an even keel (4 percent GDP growth), he was going to take care of his children. Shades of Indonesia's Suharto!

Local political scientists with whom the writer has spoken attribute the perseverance of Moi and Ratsiraka to little more than name recognition by the respective electorates. One is thus tempted to say that improved outcomes depend on increasing education levels. However, as a result of fiscal pressure associated with slow or negative growth, most observers (including Hoover and McPherson in Chapter 12 *supra*) report a declining trend in the quality of secondary and higher education in all three countries.

If education levels will not improve in the near future, what alternative solution is there? The writer will define "salvation" as achievement of the goal set by African leaders through the Economic Commission for Africa to halve poverty—the proportion of a country's population with per capita income under some official threshold—by 2015. In his view, given persistent trends, this goal is no more likely to be achieved than was the World Health Organization's objective, set at the Alma Ata conference in 1978, of Health for All by the Year 2000.

Salvation for the three (and most other African) countries is most likely to come, if at all, from the chance appearance of visionary leaders who appeal to, and succeed in attracting a critical mass of support from, both the elite and substantial portions of the electorate. How soon is this likely to happen in Zambia, Kenya, or Madagascar? Sorry, no idea. The writer is acquainted with talented individuals in Kenya and Madagascar (as well as in other African countries) who have the vision and technical skills required to implement and sustain policies that will achieve the 2015 goal. Hill and McPherson know Zambians of whom they would say the same thing. But so far none of these individuals has applied the charisma needed to acquire significant political power.[4]

---

4. This section borrows heavily from the argument of the writer's joint article with McPherson, "The Leadership Factor in African Policy Reform and Growth," *Economic Development and Cultural Change*, vol. 49, July 2001, pp. 707–40.

3. DONOR STRATEGIES

Perhaps the most controversial thesis of the book, and certainly the one that will raise hackles in Washington and London, is the argument that the donors and IMF have aided and abetted the MMD regime in its mismanagement of the economy by failing to enforce aid conditionalities. Instead, they have come through with money to forestall anticipated financial crises notwithstanding the regime's failure to meet previously agreed economic benchmarks.

Chapter 1 cites "IMF indulgence" in the government's failure to implement the 1992–95 Rights Accumulation Program (RAP), thereby undermining subsequent arrangements under the Enhanced Structural Adjustment Facility (ESAF). Chapter 3 accuses the World Bank and other donor officials of being motivated more to meet perceived institutional targets for commitment of aid funds, than to manage the funds as a "carrot," obliging the government to adhere to sound policies.

This writer has not had the opportunity to talk with donor officials specifically about their management of aid to Zambia. But he has had numerous discussions in which donor (and IMF) officials outlined an ultimate objective of helping the government of one or another country avoid a financial crisis that they felt could threaten the regime by provoking popular and/or military unrest. For example, a senior IMF official described to the writer a 1979 discussion with then Sierra Leone President Siaka Stevens in which Stevens said, in effect, "if IMF doesn't accept a budget deficit that covers rehabilitation of our army's barracks, the army is going to overthrow my government."

The IMF's mandate does not explicitly provide for rescuing regimes like Sierra Leone's whose kleptocratic leaders have bankrupted them, but the political forces that ultimately control the Fund are generally averse to military takeovers or, even worse, disintegration of central authority. The Fund and donors kept the Stevens regime and several successors afloat until central authority collapsed and Sierra Leone joined the ranks of failed African states in the late 1990s.

What would have happened had the IMF refused to finance Stevens's 1979 deficit and let the army take over then and there? Would central authority have been preserved longer than actually occurred, and would Sierra Leone be in better shape now? What would have happened in Zambia had the IMF and World Bank adhered to their conditionalities, possibly allowing financial crises that would make those recorded by Hill and McPherson look like Sunday School picnics? Would the Zambian army have taken over, and would it have conducted the country's affairs better than the MMD administration has done?

This writer does not purport to know the answers. However, to be entirely fair to the IMF and World Bank, one should explore this counterfactual, which Hill and McPherson refrain from doing.

4. AID EXIT

The writer has previously debated this issue with McPherson, and neither of us has backed off from opposing positions outlined in a paper written in 2000 under the USAID-funded EAGER Project.[5]

McPherson argues in Chapter 14 that Zambia's government could improve the economy's performance by defining and pursuing targets for ending its current heavy dependence on foreign aid within the medium term.

The simple, let's say for the sake of argument, naive, counterargument is that the World Bank and other donors today have taken over a major part of the role that private investors in 19th and early 20th century Europe, led by Britain, played in supplying capital to the U.S., Canada, Australia and other countries of recent settlement, and thus financing the investment that helped underwrite those nations' development. Today's developing world, so the argument goes, is afflicted by much greater political instability than applied in the previous era, hence most of the required financing for infrastructure will not be provided by bond-buyers in industrial countries.

Accordingly, the argument continues, a low-income country can accelerate its development through additional investment financed by capital borrowed or obtained on grant terms from the World Bank and bilateral donors, which serves to complement the country's domestic saving. The same holds for technical assistance that donors provide to complement the skills of an under-educated labor force.

If this argument holds, it means that a competent Zambian government, led by individuals sharing the Hill-McPherson (and Gray) "vision" of pro-growth policies, could exploit donor aid to accelerate growth. From this viewpoint, the McPherson thesis raises two questions: does continued access to aid (1) make it less likely that such individuals will eventually take political control, and (2) if they do take control, does it make it less likely that they will wish, or be able, to implement pro-growth policies?

McPherson's argument implies a positive answer to both questions. That is, he believes that continued access to aid (1) strengthens the hold on power of elements such as the current MMD administration whose objective is to misuse it for personal advantage rather than to promote economic growth, and (2) is likely to divert or even corrupt the inclinations of pro-growth ele-

---

5. McPherson and Gray 2000.

ments should they succeed in displacing the MMD (and outlasting other competitors for power).

Evidence supplied by Hill-McPherson suggests that the continued inflow of aid notwithstanding, the GoZ's noncompliance with policy condition-alities may have forestalled financial crises greater than the nontrivial ones reported by the authors, which might have shaken the MMD's hold on power. This would support foregoing hypothesis No. 1. On the other hand, the corollary, that stricter enforcement of the conditionalities would have curbed the MMD's economic mismanagement, is not proven. Zambia would not be the first African country in which the leaders simply packed up their accumulated loot (stored conveniently in Swiss bank accounts) and flew the coop when a firm stance by the donor community threatened their hold on power.

In any case this writer would argue that hypothesis No. 1 is essentially ir-relevant, because McPherson is not preaching to the current MMD regime. They are not likely to change their ways in response to the merits of the case for rejecting the aid that enables them to continue looting their country.

The relevant question is therefore whether McPherson's second hypothe-sis is correct: that a continued inflow of substantial aid would undermine pro-growth policies of a "visionary" administration, whose leaders should recognize this and voluntarily renounce the aid (or a large part of it). It is this hypothesis that the present writer regards as uncertain and definitely not proven.

McPherson is right that substantial aid inflow enables a country to support a higher exchange rate (more dollars for, say, 1,000 units of the national cur-rency) and therefore diminishes the incentive for production of exports and import substitutes presented by a lower rate. On the other hand our putative "visionary" leaders could follow a policy of temporarily sterilizing those com-ponents of the aid inflow that did not immediately generate supplemental imports of capital equipment. The impact of the inflow would thus be limited to creating additional infrastructure, thereby reducing production costs and stimulating exports and import substitution.

Turning to the technical assistance component of aid, one implication of McPherson's original (and persuasive) thesis about the growing impact of HIV/AIDS on the capacity of Zambia's public administration (see especially Chapter 12) is that Zambia's growth prospects might be furthered by an in-crease, rather than decrease, in that vehicle of aid. The implication that McPherson himself draws in several chapters, of course, is also correct: that the government must limit its currently unrealistic ambitions regarding tasks entrusted to the public sector.

But some tasks are inherent to any country's public sector: for example, the formulation of macroeconomic policy. One of the capacity building targets of the Harvard project was the creation of an economic policy unit in the finance ministry. After seven years of training and advisory assistance, due to staff attrition and lack of interest on the part of successive senior ministry officials, the unit remained an empty box.

A new "visionary" administration in Zambia would certainly seek support from such a unit. It would be well advised to offer sufficient compensation to attract competent Zambian economists willing to work in the country, but these are few and far between, and demand for them in commerce and other state agencies such as the Bank of Zambia outstrips supply. Hence it is likely that the "visionary" administration would seek renewed help from a foreign team such as the one Hill-McPherson led, whose advice during the MMD era mostly fell on deaf ears.

What is the bottom line? This writer agrees with McPherson that the visionary administration's first priority should be to define and pursue sound economic policies that curb wasteful expenditure and inflation, enhance domestic saving, attract private foreign investment, and provide solid incentives for production of tradables. This will trim and eventually eliminate Zambia's dependence on the kind of emergency balance of payments assistance to which the MMD regime has repeatedly resorted.

But should the government go further and prepare medium-term financial plans that forego all or most capital and technical assistance from multi- and bilateral agencies? In this writer's view such a policy would amount to cutting off one's nose to spite one's face. Given the income gap between poor and rich countries, and the latter's recently heightened fear that persistent poverty creates a breeding ground for terrorism, overseas development assistance will be around for a long time. The challenge to a future "visionary" Zambian administration will be to make constructive use of it, rather than reject it (or waste it as the UNIP and MMD regimes have done).

5. Technical Assistance for Capacity Building

The chapter by Hoover and McPherson on capacity building in the finance ministry details a program that formed a major part of the Harvard projects' terms of reference. Led by the authors themselves, the team put even more effort into this component than was envisaged initially. During 1991–98 METAP and CMTAP organized and financed twelve person-years of overseas degree training and 251 person-weeks of foreign short-term courses, sent forty-five ministry staff to foreign workshops/seminars, and put more than 2,000 staff through local short courses.

The chapter does not offer an estimate of the proportion of the approximately $14 million spent on the two projects that was devoted to capacity building. That is always difficult when a major part of each resident adviser's assignment is training counterparts on the job. Allocating the shares of his/her time devoted to advising and capacity building is a highly subjective exercise.

The task of estimating the economic returns to such investment in human capital is no easier. Subjectively, the chapter gives a discouraging view of the returns. First, there was the normal attrition that occurs when foreign training equips civil servants to earn much higher compensation in foreign agencies or the private sector than the government is willing to pay them. This was compounded by alarming staff losses due to HIV/AIDS (and loss of staff time in activities such as attending funerals and so on).

But the negative element that permeates the whole capacity building scene is the dysfunctional organizational setting of the finance ministry under an MMD leadership that was more interested in personal aggrandizement than in economic reform. This is to blame for the situation described in a footnote in Chapter 12, to the effect that a visit by McPherson two years after the Harvard project ended found the finance ministry "in poor shape in terms of both technical capacity and training."

In the present writer's experience, the majority of ministers and top civil servants in the finance and planning ministries of developing countries are too preoccupied by short-term crises and/or in jockeying for influence at higher levels of government (and sometimes defrauding the government), to pay much attention to capacity building in their agencies. The tenure of ministry management is almost always far shorter than the term required to achieve positive returns from investment in human capital. Virtually all of HIID's resident advisory projects invested significant time and money in training local staff, but only in a few cases did ministry managers make the effort required to recruit and/or retain individuals qualified to perform policy analysis.[6]

Does this mean that the capacity building element in Harvard's Zambia projects was ill fated from the outset and should never have been attempted? The answer to this question is linked to one's estimate of the overall return to the Harvard projects. During the projects' term, 1991–98, Zambia's per capita GDP dropped another 20 percent. Did the activities of the Harvard projects mitigate this decline by adding, say, at least that much to the net present value of Zambia's present and future GDP, adjusted by some shadow price for income distribution?

---

6. See Gray 1997.

The volume makes no claim along those lines, indeed it gives the impression that, most of the time, the MMD regime was so resistant to the team's input that lasting benefits cannot be demonstrated. In 1997–98 the donor consortium funding the projects concluded that, due to this resistance, continued technical assistance of this type would not be cost-effective, and the projects came to an end.

Thus, it could be argued that, with hindsight, the donors would have been best advised not to have responded favorably to finance minister Chigaga's request, initially made in 1989, to fund a team of expatriate advisers. Perhaps they would have been best advised not to spend the money in Zambia at all, but to pick other targets more susceptible to reform, or even return the money to their respective taxpayers.

On the other hand, had the regime not resisted or ignored the team's advice, the projects could easily have generated a strongly positive return, probably even a multiple of their cost. In that event, the bureaucratic environment would most likely also have supported the absorption of trained local staff and motivated a significant proportion of them to apply effectively their training in the finance ministry.

To the extent the projects have any impact over the long term, it will be because the exposure to competent, motivated foreign economists, as well as the formal training the projects generated, has added value to the performance of local staff during their remaining careers. The improved performance may not even take place in the finance ministry—the economic pay-off may come in other government agencies, parastatals, academe, or the private sector.

Any projection of this added value would be subject to so wide a margin of error as to be scarcely worth undertaking. However, it can be said with some confidence that the Harvard team managers acted in Zambia's best interest by putting as much effort into staff development as they did. Moreover, in the absence of Harvard or another agency playing Harvard's role, only a minute fraction of the capacity building that occurred during 1991–98 would have taken place.

6. Conclusion: What Lessons for Other African Countries?

A large number of African countries have followed a path of disjointed structural adjustment analogous to Zambia's, marked by almost as many (or more) steps backward as forward. Earlier we mentioned Kenya and Madagascar. Research coordinated by McPherson and the present writer under the afore-mentioned EAGER project during 1998–2001 included five country studies by local economists on "restarting and sustaining growth and development."[7] The five countries were Ghana, Kenya, Senegal, Tanzania, and Uganda.

All five obtained structural adjustment credits (SACs) from the World Bank and enhanced structural adjustment facilities (ESAFs) from the IMF during the 1980s and 1990s, subject to policy conditionalities many of which were not fulfilled. This led to periodic suspension or cancellation of disbursements and then renegotiation of the aid. All five governments received abundant technical assistance to improve their policy performance, although as far as the writer is aware, none hosted as large an integrated advisory team in its finance ministry as did Zambia during 1991–98.

Each of the structural adjustment programs (SAPs) in question involved as a basic element amending macroeconomic management to (1) reduce budget deficits and inflation, and (2) reorient the economy towards exports and efficient import substitution based on market-clearing exchange rates. In this writer's view, the present volume puts the advice offered by Harvard's Zambia team in the mainstream of structural adjustment strategies propounded for African countries. As already noted, the volume's criticism of the Bretton Woods institutions is based primarily on their failure to enforce policy conditionalities that closely paralleled advice the Harvard team was offering from its internal vantage point.

The strand of analysis and policy advice that strikes this writer as most original concerns the implications, for policy formulation and management, of a high HIV/AIDS infection rate, afflicting disproportionately educated persons and, among them, government officials. Hoover and McPherson point to greatly reduced life expectancy not only for persons diagnosed with the disease, but for many others who don't yet know that they have it, but suspect they may, or assume fatalistically that sooner or later infection will come their way.

This has significant implications for civil service morale, ambition, and ethics, and hence efficiency. How many officials work hard with no expectation of future benefit? Why not grab what one can and get maximum enjoyment out of one's remaining life span? Implications for human resource management include the following:

- A unit staffed with a given number of officials will suffer greater turnover and produce less, hence government must compress the functions it appropriates for itself, e.g. management and supervision of commercial activities through parastatal corporations or economic regulation;

---

7. Two of these are McPherson (2002, 2002a) with others to follow.

- To the extent functions cannot be compressed, redundant staffing is required to maintain the same level of effort and institutional memory;
- Closer supervision is required to forestall misappropriation of public property;
- Maintaining a given level of senior capacity through degree training becomes so expensive that resources must be more heavily concentrated on short-term training;
- After a period in which many writers (and governments) believed African countries had acquired sufficient local talent to dispense with foreign advisers, technical assistance may once more prove to be an agency's only recourse.

Zambia's estimated rate of infection of persons aged 15–49 ties it with two other countries for fifth place in SSA—cf. UNAIDS data as of end-1999:[8]

SSA countries with rate > 13%	Estimated adult infection rate (%)
1. Botswana	35.8
2. Swaziland	25.3
3. Zimbabwe	25.1
4. Lesotho	23.6
5. Namibia (tie)	20.0
6. South Africa (tie)	20.0
7. Zambia (tie)	20.0
8. Kenya	13.9
9. Central African Republic	13.8
10. Mozambique	13.2

No data are available on infection rates among middle- and senior-level government personnel, but a reasonable hypothesis is that they are closely correlated with overall infection rates. Hence the need for other African governments to start orienting their human resource management along similar lines, however uncomfortable the thought.

8. UNAIDS website, report issued June 2000.

17

Postscript: Prospects for Moving Forward?

CATHARINE B. HILL AND MALCOLM F. MCPHERSON

1. Introduction

The essays in this volume have been compiled and edited over several years. Some noteworthy developments within Zambia and the sub-region have occurred since the narrative in the text ended in mid-2000. In this postscript, we provide a brief overview of recent trends and examine whether, and how, they affect our conclusions about what is required to move Zambia forward. Section 2 considers economic developments, Section 3 reviews recent political changes, and Section 4 discusses social issues. Section 5 has a summary and concluding comments.

2. Economic Developments

Perhaps the most significant economic development relates to the mining sector. Once the sale of ZCCM was completed in March 2000, the fortunes of the mining sector improved noticeably. For example, copper production in 2001 was significantly higher (by 15 percent) than in 2000.[1] Unfortunately, world market conditions weakened throughout 2001 and projections showed that the situation would continue. Faced with that prospect, the Anglo American Corporation announced in January 2002 that it was withdrawing from the Konkola Copper Mine (KCM) venture. Thus the incoming government

---

1. *Macroeconomic Indicators* May 2002, Table 6.3, Lusaka, Ministry of Finance and National Planning.

headed by Levy Mwanawasa was faced with the problem of how to sustain Zambia's mining activities without reengaging the government in the sector, or commiting the government to support that may eventually cost hundreds of millions of dollars. The government's obvious preferences are to keep KCM operating and to encourage the development of Konkola Deep Mining Project (KDMP). Still unknown, however, is how low prices will fall and how long world demand for copper and cobalt will remain weak.

The economy has other challenges. The grain harvest has fallen well below expectations because of drought. Due in part to mismanagement of Food Reserve Agency funds and political intervention in grain marketing (described in Chapter 10), food reserves were low before the season started. Widespread deprivation and starvation can only be avoided if the international community provides adequate food aid. Several donors have indicated they will help and have begun to do so.[2] The food shortages demonstrate that no fundamental progress has been made over the last decade to boost food security. As noted in Chapters 3 and 10, a critical food shortage emerged in 1992 just after the MMD government took power. Despite that experience and a number of poor harvests subsequently, the government failed to provide adequate reserves (of food and foreign exchange) so that Zambians could be properly fed.[3] The current situation also confirms that government and donor efforts failed to promote agricultural development through the Agricultural Sector Investment Program (discussed in Chapter 10). Finally, though the dimensions of the effect are not fully understood, the spread of HIV/AIDS has added to food insecurity by undermining the country's rural economy. This matter is discussed further in Section 4 below.

Even with a full decade of debt relief and debt rationalization through buy-backs, fifth dimension support, Paris Club agreements, and related programs, Zambia's total debt is as large in 2002 as it was in 1992. ZCCM's losses were one factor. The basic problem, however, is that Zambia has continued to run large budget deficits in the context of a chronically overvalued exchange

---

2. The situation has not been helped by Zambia's refusal to accept grain that has been produced using advanced biotechnology. President Mwanawasa added to the confusion by referring to these genetically modified foods as "poison." Since Mwanawasa has made numerous trips to the United States (where GM food is ubiquitous) and not been poisoned an unavoidable conclusion is that he and his senior officials are playing politics with drought relief.

3. Those who believe Zambia is acutely aid dependent would argue that the government's experience in 1992 (during which the donors more than adequately made up for the country's food shortfalls) convinced the country's leaders that food security was not a high priority. As current events show, once more the donors will provide emergency assistance to forestall starvation in Zambia.

rate. Balance of payments deficits have remained high.[4] While these deficits persist, the economy will continue to be submerged in debt whether or not the HIPC "completion point" is reached or any other follow-on debt relief is provided.[5]

Inflation is chronically high and, given the current budget stance, cannot decline. The budget brought down in March 2002 programs a deficit of 3 percent of GDP, most of which will be financed by domestic credit creation.[6] Since this has been the pattern since 1974 (the last time the government ran a budget surplus), the year-end inflation target of 13 percent (given in the budget speech)[7] is out of reach. Based on mid-year data, inflation for 2002 will be 20 percent.[8] To achieve the lower inflation target, the government would have to fundamentally change its budget policy. That is unlikely. Additional price pressures will result from the accelerated depreciation of the exchange rate since the start of 2002. From December 2001 to May 2002 the kwacha declined 10.6 percent relative to the US dollar. This shift is long overdue but much more will be needed if the real exchange rate is to fall to a level that helps stimulate exports, raise agricultural output, and boost tourism. Furthermore, any prospect that the government and the donors might have of diversifying the economy (a recently revived development theme) will founder unless there is a sustained devaluation of the real exchange rate.[9]

Some recent economic news provides encouragement. There is renewed, though slow, growth in nontraditional exports, tourist arrivals have increased, and mining firms other than Anglo-American are actively consolidating their positions. Some firms, such as First Quantum Minerals, are expanding and upgrading their capacity. Over the last several years, mineral

---

4. *Macroeconomic Indicators* May 2002, Table 3.5 shows that the balance of payments current account deficit as a percent of GDP over the period 1998 to 2001 inclusive has been 17.7, 15.2, 18.3, and 20.9 respectively.

5. The government's Letter of Development Policy (available on www.imf.org/zambia) of May 2002 indicates that HIPC relief, though generous, will not be adequate to resolve Zambia's debt problems.

6. *Macroeconomic Indicators* May 2002, Table 4.5; 2002 budget speech presented by the minister of finance and national planning The Hon. E.G. Kasonde, M.P., March 1, 2002, par.52.

7. 2002 budget speech, par.55.

8. *Macroeconomic* Indicators May 2002, Table 1.1.

9. This theme is not new. It was central to Zambia's first three national plans, the World Bank's economic memorandum from the mid-1970 (World Bank 1977), and the "Restructuring in the Midst of Crisis" document (GRZ 1984). Yet, before Zambian policy makers re-embrace this goal, they would greatly benefit from some reflection (and analysis) why earlier efforts to diversify did not succeed. Taking time to learn from the past would provide useful lessons on moving the economy forward and ultimately diversifying effectively consistent with the country's comparative advantage and resource endowment (physical and human).

exploration has increased Zambia's reserves by a significant margin. If unit costs can be reduced and kept down, mining activities will continue to support Zambia's growth and development. Keeping costs under control, however, will require that the government resists any temptation to re-engage in mine management.

Regional developments offer hopeful signs for future growth and development as well. Peace in Angola and relative stability in the Democratic Republic of Congo enhance the prospects for achieving greater cooperation in removing trade barriers, expanding markets, and developing infrastructure. The increasing assertiveness of South African enterprises in regional markets holds the promise of gains from closer market integration and economies of scale across the whole subregion. Economic decline in Zimbabwe is an obvious drawback. Yet, the economic framework that has been taking shape under the auspices of the newly formed African Union and through the New Partnership for African Development (NEPAD) provide a means for containing the adverse spillover effects from Zimbabwe, providing an opportunity for the rest of Southern Africa to move forward.[10]

3. Political Developments

Political developments in Zambia from mid-2001 to mid-2002 have been path breaking. They may eventually have profound implications for other African countries. A concerted campaign by opposition parties and civil society derailed President Chiluba's bid for a third term.[11] An overabundance of presidential candidates scuttled any chance for voters to register a clear choice. Ten candidates contested the election demonstrating in practical terms the breadth of the opposition that has emerged over the last decade and how intense political competition has become.

The elections (held in the final days of December 2001) passed without major disturbances or disruption. The winning presidential candidate (Mwanawasa) received only 30 percent of the vote. MMD gained the most seats in the National Assembly but not a majority. Opposition candidates accused the ruling party of fraud. European Union delegates concluded that the elections involved "clear, glaring irregularities"[12]

---

10. de Waal 2002; Hope 2002.

11. Civil servants began a campaign of encouraging those who opposed a third term to honk their car horns at 5 p.m. every day. The political message was unmistakable.

12. A report on CNN, the international news network (January 16, 2002) stated: "Monitors from the EU and the influential Zambian groups the Foundation for Democratic Process (FODEP) and Afronet have said that the elections were marred by irregularities and interference from state security agents."

This was an inauspicious beginning for President Mwanawasa and his administration. Disregarding local and external criticism, Mwanawasa appointed a cabinet and started to govern. Opponents accused the new president of being a stooge for former President Chiluba. That matter was quickly put to rest as the press and Mwanawasa himself made public damaging allegations about activities by Chiluba and his associates. The implications of these matters will take time to unfold. In the interim, President Mwanawasa's actions are setting new standards for openness, accountability, and good governance. The challenge for all Zambians will be to ensure that those standards are maintained.

Zambia's leaders gained few admirers, locally or abroad, by their hasty conclusion that Zimbabwe's elections in March 2002 represented a fair expression of the voters' preferences. Whether this was a reflection of MMDs own questionable election record is not clear,[13] Zambia's endorsement of the vote rigging and violence perpetrated by Robert Mugabe was artless at best. Under Mugabe, the economy of Zimbabwe has collapsed, poverty has increased, food insecurity has intensified, tourism has plummeted, and violence has become a regular means of achieving political and economic goals.

With political influence diffused, the government's policies are likely to be vigorously debated and actively discussed. Democratic processes will be strengthened. Civil society will benefit. Given Zambia's constraints (inflation, debt, deficits, and investor uncertainty about the future of mining), greater political activism may not deliver higher sustained growth, but it will stimulate the debate and deliberation needed to move the country forward.

These developments can only strengthen the country's political institutions, a process that is being boosted by international developments. For instance, the war on terrorism undertaken following the events of September 11, 2001, in the United States has sharply reduced international tolerance for nondemocratic and nonaccountable governance, particularly in small states. Actions by politicians that increase the prospect of instability and thereby provide a setting conducive to terrorism and lawlessness (including gunrunning, drug-running, and money-laundering) may provoke retribution by the international community. The unmistakable message from the major industrial nations, the United Nations Security Council, and related security organizations is that nondemocratic behavior that threatens peace and security is unacceptable.

Other pressures have emerged within Africa. African leaders seeking to end the continent's marginalization in world affairs have become increas-

---

13. Opposition parties petitioned the courts to have the results of the December 2001 elections overturned.

ingly critical of countries that undermine peace and stability. A crucial dimension of NEPAD (mentioned earlier) is a peer review mechanism that increases pressure on African leaders to sanction their counterparts whose behavior breaches accepted norms.[14] Although the details remain to be resolved, the clear intention is for African leaders, under the auspices of the African Union, to ensure that security and stability are achieved and preserved.

Zambia has been leading by example in some of these areas. The new emphasis through NEPAD and the African Union will strengthen political reform, making the prospect of backsliding less likely. This is fortunate because political development and democratization are two areas where Zambia can no longer afford to indulge its long-running pattern of start-stop reform.

4. SOCIAL DEVELOPMENTS

Perhaps the most important social development over the last decade and one that will pre-occupy Zambian policy makers for years to come is the rapid and devastating spread of HIV/AIDS. The HIV prevalence rate for adults in 1990 was around 1 percent. Recent data show that it exceeds 20 percent. Girls aged 15 to 19 years have been especially vulnerable for reasons related to poverty, sexual predation (by older men), and the imbalance of power in their sexual encounters.[15] The spread of HIV/AIDS has affected every aspect of Zambia's political, economic, and social development in complex ways. Many of these are still unfolding and remain to be understood. The most damaging impact by far has been the loss of human capacity, reflected in the loss of personnel and time, and disruptions to organizations and work routines.

The spread of HIV/AIDS has been systematically undermining the growth processes in countries that have been especially hard hit (like Zambia). Evidence (presented in Chapter 11) also indicates that, as the epidemic intensifies, it becomes progressively more difficult for developing countries to create the conditions needed to promote rapid growth and development. One problem, which has already affected Zambia, is that it becomes increasingly difficult to sustain economic reform.[16] HIV/AIDS undermines institutions and

---

14. Information on NEPAD can be found on www.nepad.org.

15. GRZ 1999.

16. As noted in McPherson (2001, 2002), the basic reason can be related to the behavioral changes resulting from the collapse of decision horizons among those who are HIV positive. When HIV prevalence rates are low, such shifts in behavior are inconsequential for the economy as a whole. At prevalence rates of 20 percent or more of the adult population, the behavioral changes have major macroeconomic effects.

compromises organizations. Zambia's difficulties with respect to food security reflect, to a large extent, the problems that arise when rural households are de-capitalized and agricultural production systems are disrupted through the loss of semi-skilled and skilled labor.

The donor community (especially the World Bank) and the government have been committed to scaling up activities designed to deal with the impact of HIV/AIDS. One question that neither the bank nor the government has answered is how the country can scale up its activities when the human capacity required for that task is being undercut by the disease? Based on the discussion in Chapter 12, this question has not been effectively answered because the implications of the loss of human capacity to HIV/AIDS on output and institutions have not been adequately understood. Much more work, by Zambians, is needed so that senior policy makers can effectively address this issue.

The challenge for Zambia (and other countries in Southern Africa) is to respond systematically to the pressures created by the spread of HIV/AIDS. There are (at least) three dimensions. First, means are needed to economize on the use of available human capacity. Work routines need to be reorganized, the development agenda needs to be cut and streamlined, and other productive factors that can substitute for skilled operators need to be found.[17] Second, more effective methods are required to train staff.[18] The idea that education can be a leisurely enterprise stretched over years (e.g., four years to train a nurse) is not tenable. Innovative pedagogical techniques that allow medical orderlies, nurses, teachers, accountants, and other professionals to be trained rapidly need to be developed and adopted. Third, serious attention should be given to the problems resulting from the psychosocial trauma that has accompanied rising debility and death rates. The growing numbers of orphans need to be dealt with constructively and humanely.[19]

An over-riding goal in all these activities should be to make the most effective use possible of all existing skills and talents that the country has available, and improve the productivity of all workers. Means for enhancing productiv-

---

17. Examples include the use of software for undertaking medical tests, calibration equipment to keep motors and machinery operating at peak efficiency, and distance-learning mechanisms to draw on a broader range of information and skill in training professionals.

18. In addition to training, there are issues of managing, motivating, and disciplining the staff.

19. In this respect, it is simply not enough to vote resources to prevent mother-to-child transmission of HIV as Senator Jesse Helms has done (Helms 2002). Being HIV-positive, the mother will eventually die and the HIV-negative child will be orphaned. If Helms were determined to help children (as he professed) he would have included funds for their support once their HIV-positive mothers succumb to AIDS.

ity over time, even in the face of continued losses from HIV/AIDS, are required. For developing countries, these changes are compelling whether or not HIV/AIDS is a problem. When the prevalence of HIV/AIDS is high, such changes become essential.

A further social issue that has dogged Zambia since the late 1970s has been the increase in poverty. World Bank data, reflected in the table "Zambia at a Glance,"[20] show that in 2001, 73 percent of Zambians lived on less than $1 per day in purchasing power parity (PPP) terms.[21] In practice, deepening poverty is reflected in rising infant mortality (even when AIDS losses are taken into account), the widening regional differences of income and opportunity, the general deterioration in education, and decreased food security.

Poverty has intensified in Zambia for several reasons. The most obvious has been the inexorable decline in real per capita income since the mid-1970s due, in large part, to the failure of successive governments to adopt and sustain growth-oriented policies. Poverty has been exacerbated by the declining quality of health and education. This has lowered productivity, diverted savings from productive investments to consumption, and eroded the incentives individuals have for deepening their capacities. The spread of HIV/AIDS has compounded the poverty situation for many families and communities by undercutting the income earning capacity of workers, depleting family savings, and diverting resources that might otherwise have been used for productive investment to consumption expenditures.

5. SUMMARY AND CONCLUSION

There is nothing unfamiliar about the main problems that Zambia's policy makers confront in order to move the economy forward. The budget and balance of payments are in deficit, inflation is high by international standards and not coming down as programmed,[22] foreign debt remains unserviceable,

---

20. Table dated 9/13/01 may be found on www.worldbank.org.

21. The government's own assessment of poverty (*Zambia Poverty Reduction Strategy Paper 2002–2004*, Ministry of Finance and National Planning, Lusaka, May 2002) indicated that in 1998, 72.9 percent of the population was poor with 57.9 percent in "extreme poverty." 83.1 percent of the rural population was poor. The corresponding datum for urban poverty was 56 percent (*ibid.*, p. 23).

22. The official attitude to inflation has been exceedingly casual. To illustrate, the government's *Economic Report* 2001 (Lusaka: Ministry of Finance and National Planning February 2002), discusses inflation (and the exchange rate) in the most cursory terms (*ibid.*, pp. 36–38). Inflation in 2001 was above its year-end target (18.7 percent versus a target of 17.5 percent). Officials saw the performance of the exchange rate as highly positive. (Due to rigging by the BoZ, the exchange rate appreciated 7 percent for the year.) Properly construed, however, both

export growth is sluggish, the demand for imports outstrips the economy's capacity to generate foreign exchange, poverty has been increasing, food insecurity haunts the majority of Zambians, and aid dependence is acute.

The essays in this volume have analyzed the origins of these problems, discussed the attempts that have been made to deal with them, and explored potential remedies. None of the remedies requires rocket science. They do require that Zambian policy makers abandon their long history of start-stop reform and create a stable macroeconomic setting so as to encourage Zambians and foreigners alike to invest in productive activities.

That setting will be characterized by low inflation, rising levels of productivity in the public sector, and a real exchange rate that allows Zambian firms to compete aggressively in world markets. Four elements will be crucial to achieving macro stability. The budget deficit will be eliminated (leaving the budget balanced over the business cycle); the nominal exchange rate will be actively depreciated to ensure that Zambia's unit labor costs are low by international standards; the government will have a development agenda matched to its human, financial, and administrative capacities; and Zambian individuals and firms will find local opportunities and incentives adequate encouragement for keeping their resources "on shore" rather than shifting them abroad.

Again, none of this is rocket science. The problem and the challenge will be to convince the relevant policy makers that Zambia cannot create the conditions for sustained growth and development by actions and policies that generate budget deficits, keep inflation at rates well above world norms, overstretch the capacities of public resources (human and financial), and systematically overvalue the real exchange rate.

As always, Zambians and their leaders face a choice. They can become serious about economic reform and take whatever actions are needed to fundamentally readjust the economy. Or, they can continue their pattern of drift, benefiting from neither growth nor development. The government cannot begin to resolve the country's problems unless it is prepared to address their fundamental causes and sustain relevant solutions. The economy and society as a whole has suffered exceedingly heavy losses. More are in store unless the approach to reform changes. The basic challenge, which has to be met on several fronts, is to create the conditions whereby some of these losses can be counteracted and even offset. Though this will require hard pounding, it could be done. We remain hopeful that it will.

---

the high rate of inflation (relative to world norms) and the adverse movement in the exchange rate (relative to Zambia's capacity to compete in world markets) were disastrous. The official account gave no impression that anything was amiss.

References

Abed, G.T. *et al.* (1993) *Fiscal Reform in Low-Income Countries: Experience under IMF—supported Program.* International Monetary Fund Occasional Paper no. 160.

Ablo, E. and R. Reinikka. (1998). "Do Budgets Really Matter? Evidence from Public Spending on Education and Health in Uganda." World Bank *Policy Research Working Paper,* no. 1926.

Achola, P.P.W. (1990) "Implementing Educational Policies in Zambia." World Bank *Discussion Papers,* no. 90.

Adam, C.S. and D.L. Bevan (1993) "Stabilization and The Risk of Hyperinflation Issues in Zambian Macroeconomic Performance 1992–1993." Draft report for GRZ and European Development Fund, March.

Adam, C.S. and D.L. Bevan (1996) "Aid and the Credit Squeeze in Zambia: Causes and Consequences." Centre for the Study of African Economies, Oxford University, October.

Adam, C.S. and D.L. Bevan (2000) "The Cash-Budget as a Restraint: The Experience of Zambia." Chapter 8 in eds. P. Collier and C. Pattillo *Investment and Risk in Africa* Basingstoke: Macmillan & Co.

Aguirre, C. A., and P. Shome, (1988) "The Mexican Value-Added Tax (VAT): Methodology for Calculating the Base." *National Tax Journal,* vol. 41, no. 4, pp. 543–54.

Ahmad, E. and N. Stern, (1989), "Taxation for Developing Countries," in eds. H.B. Chenery and T.N. Srinivasan *Handbook of Development Economics,* vol. II, Amsterdam: North-Holland.

Alesina, A and D. Weder (1999). "Do Corrupt Governments Receive Less Foreign Aid?" NBER *Working Paper,* no. 7108.

Alm, J., R. Bahl, and M. N. Murray, (1991). "Tax Base Erosion in Developing Countries." *Economic Development and Cultural Change,* vol. 39, no. 4, July, pp. 849–872.

Amin, S. (1974) *Accumulation on a World Scale*. Sussex: Harvester Press.

Amin, S. (1977) *Imperialism and Unequal Development*. Hassocks: Harvester Press.

Anderson, Per-Ake and S. Kayizzi-Mugerwa (1989) "Mineral Dependence, Goal Attainment and Equity: Zambia's Experience with Structural Adjustment in the 1980s." Department of Economics, School of Economics and Legal Science, University of Goteborg, April.

Andrianamanana, P. *et al.* (1998) "Amelioration de la Transparence dans l'Administration Fiscale" EAGER/Public Strategies for Growth with Equity. Final Report, Tsipika Editeur, Anatananarivo, Malagasy Republic, May.

Arndt, H.W. (1987) *Economic Development The History of An Idea*. Chicago: University of Chicago Press.

Aron, J. (1992) "Political Mismanagement of a Mining Parastatal: The Case of Zambia Consolidated Copper Mines Limited." Draft. The World Bank and Center for International Development Research, Duke University.

Aron, J. and I.A. Elbadawi (1992) "Parallel Markets, the Foreign Exchange Auction, and Exchange Rate Unification in Zambia." Policy Research Country Economics Department *Working Paper*, World Bank, Washington D.C., May.

Asher, R.E. (1970) *Development Assistance in the Seventies Alternatives for the United States*. Washington D.C.: The Brookings Institution.

Attaran, A. and J. Sachs (2001) "Defining and Refining international donor support for combating the AIDS pandemic." *Lancet*, no. 357, pp. 57–6.

Auerbach, A.J. and M. Feldstein, (1985) *Handbook of Public Economics*. Amsterdam: Elsevier Science Publishers B.V.

Austen, R.A. (1987) *African Economic History: Internal Development and External Dependency*. Portsmouth: Heinemann.

Auty, R.M. (1993) *Sustaining Development in Mineral Economies The resource curse thesis*. London: Routledge.

Ayittey, G.B.N. (1992) *Africa Betrayed*. New York: St. Martin's Press.

Ayittey, G.B.N. (1998) *Africa in Chaos*. New York: St. Martin's Press.

BIS (1988) "International Convergence of Capital Measurement and Capital Standards." The Basle Committee on Banking Regulations and Supervisory Practices, Basle, July [also in *Analyst* vol. 2, no. 5].

BoZ (various dates), *Main Economic Indicators*. Bank of Zambia, Lusaka.

BoZ (various dates), *Statistics Fortnightly*. Bank of Zambia, Lusaka.

BoZ (1981). *Manual of Exchange Control Regulations to Authorized Dealers*. 3rd Edition. Lusaka: Government Printer.

BoZ (1993) "Liberalization of Exchange Controls." Processed. June.

BoZ (1994). *Financial Statements for 1989 & 1990, Statement of Affairs 1991 & 1992*. Lusaka: Universal Zambia.

BoZ (1995) "Financial Highlights for the Zambian Banking Industry for the Period

Ending 31 December 1994." Financial Analysis and Regulatory Policy Financial Systems Supervision, Bank of Zambia, Lusaka, May.

BoZ (1995) *Bank of Zambia Annual Report 1994*. Lusaka: Interlink Corporate Communications.

BoZ (1996) *Bank of Zambia Annual Report 1995*. Lusaka: Interlink Corporate Communications.

BIS (1999) "A New Capital Adequacy Framework, (E)." Bank for International Settlements: The Basle Committee on Banking Supervision, no. 50.

Baldwin, R.E. (1965) *Economic Growth and Export Growth A Study of Northern Rhodesia 1920–1960*. Berkeley: University of California Press.

Bancroft, J.A. (1961) *Mining in Northern Rhodesia*. Bedford: The British South Africa Company.

Banda, M. *et al.* (1988) *Report on the Proceedings of the Seminar on the Exchange Rate*. Lusaka: Economic Association of Zambia Occasional Paper, no. 1, June.

Barber, W.J. (1961) *The Economy of British Central Africa: A Case Study of Economic Development in a Dualistic Society*. Stanford: Stanford University Press.

Bates, R.H. (1974) "Patterns of Uneven Development: Causes and Consequences in Zambia." University of Denver Monograph Series in World Affairs, vol.11, Monograph no. 3.

Bates, R.H. (1981) *Markets and States in Tropical Africa*. Berkeley: University of California Press.

Bates, R.H. and P. Collier (1992) "The Politics and Economics of Policy Reform in Zambia." Duke University, Papers in International Political Economy, no. 153, January [also published in *Journal of African Economies*, vol. 4, issue 1, 1995, pp. 115–143].

Bauer, P.T. (1971) *Dissent on Development*. Cambridge: Harvard University Press, [revised edition, 1976].

Bauer, P.T. (1991) *Aid, End it or Mend it!* Center for Economic Growth (Reprint Series), San Francisco.

Baylies, C. (1980) "The State and the Growth of Indigenous Capital: Zambia's Economic Reforms and their Aftermath." *Centre for African Studies*, University of Edinburgh.

Beckerman, P. (1997) "Central Bank Decapitalization in Developing Countries." *World Development*, vol. 25, no. 2, pp. 167–178.

Bell, D.E. (1965) "The Quality of Aid." *Foreign Affairs*, vol. 43, pp. 601–607.

Benson, C. and E. Clay (1998) *The Impact of Drought on Sub-Saharan African Economies: A Preliminary Examination*. Washington D.C.: World Bank Technical Paper, no. 401, March.

Berg, E. (1993) *Rethinking Technical Cooperation Reforms for Capacity Building in Africa*. New York: United Nations Development Programme.

Berg, E. (1996) "Dilemmas in Donor Aid Strategies." Paper prepared for Workshop on External Resources for Development, Rotterdam, May 13–14.

Berger, E.L. (1974) *Labour, Race, and Colonial Rule: The Copperbelt from 1924 to Independence.* Oxford: Clarendon Press.

Becker, G.S. (1964) *Human Capital.* Princeton: Princeton University Press

Binswanger, H.P. and K. Dreninger (1997) "Explaining Agricultural and Agrarian Policies in Developing Countries." *Journal of Economic Literature,* vol. 35, no. 4, December, pp. 1958–2005.

Binswanger, H. and R.F. Townsend (2000) "The Growth Performance of Agriculture in Subsaharan Africa." *American Journal of Agricultural Economics,* vol. 82, no. 5, pp. 1075–1086.

Blackmore, J. (1965) "Creating Needed Institutions." Chaper 9 in ed. E.O. Haroldsen *Economic Development of Agriculture The Modernization of Farming.* Ames: Iowa State University Press.

Bloom, D.E. and J.D. Sachs (1998) "Geography, Demography, and Economic Growth in Africa." *Brookings Papers on Economic Activity* no. 2, pp. 207–295.

Bolnick, B.(1991), "Monetary Management in Sub-Saharan Africa: Conditions and Prospects in Malawi." Harvard Institute for International Development, Cambridge, processed.

Bolnick, B. (1995), "Establishing Fiscal Discipline: Implementing the Cash Budget in Zambia." Northeastern University, Boston, processed.

Bolnick, B.R. (1997) "Establishing Fiscal Discipline: The Cash Budget in Zambia." Chapter 11 in ed. M.S. Grindle *Getting Good Government: Capacity Building in the Public Sectors of Developing Countries.* Cambridge: Harvard Studies in International Development distributed by Harvard University Press.

Bostock, M. and C. Harvey eds. (1972) *Economic Independence and Zambian Copper: A Case Study of Foreign Investment.* New York: Praeger Publishers.

Bouton, L., C. Jones, and M. Kiguel (1994) "Macroeconomic Reform and Growth in Africa: Adjustment in Africa Revisited." Policy Research Working Paper no. 1394, World Bank, Washington D.C., December.

Bratton, M. (1992) "Zambia starts over." *Journal of Democracy,* vol. 3, no. 2, pp. 3–69.

Bratton, M. *et al.* (1999) "The Effects of Civic Education on Political Culture: Evidence from Zambia." *World Development,* vol. 27, no. 5, May, pp. 807–824.

Brautigam, D. (1996) "State Capacity and Effective Governance." Ch. 2. in eds. B. Ndulo and N. van der Walle *Agenda for Africa's Economic Renewal* New Brunswick: Transactions Publishers.

Brautigam, D. (1997) "Winners and Losers: The Politics of Participation in Economic Policy Reform." Paper for USAID Seminar on Economic Growth and Democratic Governance, Washington D.C., October 9–10.

Brautigam, D. (1999) "Aid Dependence and Governance." Paper prepared for the Division for International Development Cooperation, Ministry of Foreign Affairs, Sweden.

Brautigam, D. (2000) "Interest Groups, Economic Policy and Growth in Sub-Saharan Africa." Draft for EAGER Project, HIID, March [Chapter 8 in ed. McPherson 2002].

Brown, L.R. and E.C. Wolf (1985) "Reversing Africa's Decline." Washington D.C.: Worldwatch Paper no. 65, June [Also appears as Chapter 10 in *State of the World 1986* New York: Norton].

Brown, L.R. (1978) *The twenty-ninth day: accommodating human needs and numbers to the earth's resources.* New York: W.W. Norton.

Bruno, M. (1988) "Opening Up." Chapter 10 in eds. Dornbusch and Helmers *op. cit.*

Bruno M. *et al.* eds. (1991) *Lessons of Economic Stabilization and Its Aftermath.* Cambridge, MA: The MIT Press.

Bruton, H.J., (1998) "A Reconsideration of Import Substitution." *Journal of Economic Literature,* vol. 36, no. 3, June, pp. 903–936.

Buchanan, J.M. and M.R. Flowers (1975) *The public finances: An introductory textbook 4th ed.* Homewood, Ill: Richard D. Irwin Inc.

Burgess, R. and N. Stern (1993) "Taxation and Development." *Journal of Economic Literature,* vol. 31, no. 2, pp. 762–785.

Burawoy, M. (1972) *The Colour of Class on the Copper Mines.* Lusaka: Institute for African Studies, Zambian Paper no. 7.

Burnstein, M. *et al.* (1997) "TBTF Fixing FDICIA A Plan to Address the Too-Big-To-Fail Problem." Federal Reserve Bank of Minneapolis *The Region.* 1997 Annual Report.

Burnside, C. and D. Dollar (1997) "Aid, Policies, and Growth." World Bank *Working Paper* no. 1777, June, Washington D.C.: World Bank.

Burnside, C. and D. Dollar (2000) "Aid, Policies, and Growth." *American Economic Review,* vol. 90, no. 4, September, pp. 847–868.

Busshau, W.J. (1945) *Report on the Development of Secondary Industries in Northern Rhodesia.* Lusaka: Government Printer.

CID (1999) "Implementing Debt Relief for the HIPCs." Center for International Development, John F. Kennedy School of Government, Harvard University, August.

CSO (1994) *Social Dimensions of Adjustment Priority Survey II 1993 Tabulation Report.* Republic of Zambia: Central Statistical Office, December.

Calamitsis, E., A Basu and D. Ghura. (1999) "Adjustment and Growth in Sub-Saharan Africa." IMF *Working Paper* 99/51 Washington D.C.

Callaghy, T.M. (1990) "Lost Between State and Market: The Politics of Economic Adjustment in Ghana, Zambia, and Nigeria," in ed. J.M. Nelson *The Politics of Economic Adjustment in Developing Nations.* New Jersey: Princeton University Press.

Camdessus, M. (1996) Address to the Board of Governors of the IMF, October 1, Washington, D.C.: International Monetary Fund.

Camdessus, M. (1998) "Africa: A Continent on the Move." Address by the Managing Director of the IMF at the Summit of Heads of State and Government of the OAU, Ouagadougou, June 8.

Cassen, R. *et al.* (1994) *Does Aid Work?* 2nd ed. Oxford: Clarendon Press [First edition 1986].

Chambers, R. (1978) "Project Selection for Poverty-Focused Rural Development: Simple is Optimal." *World Development*, vol. 6, no. 2, pp. 209–219.

Chambers, R. (1983) *Rural Development: putting the last first.* Essex: Longman Scientific & Technical.

Chand, S.K., (1989) "Toward a Growth-Oriented Model of Financial Programming." *World Development*, vol. 17, no. 4, pp. 473–490.

Chenery, H.B. (1963) "The Objectives and Criteria for Foreign Assistance," in (ed.) R.A. Goldwin *Why Foreign Aid? Two Messages by President Kennedy and Essays.* Chicago: Rand McNally & Co.

Chenery, H.B. (1987). "Foreign Aid." in eds. J.Eatwell, M. Milgate, & P. Newman, *The New Palgrave Economic Development.* New York: W.W. Norton, pp. 137–144.

Chenery, H.B. *et al.* (1974) *Redistribution with Growth.* Oxford: Oxford University Press.

Chenery, H.B. and M. Syrquin (1975) *Patterns of Development 1950–1970.* London: Oxford University Press for the World Bank.

Chenery, H.B. and T.N. Srinivasan eds. (1989) *Handbook of Development Economics,* in two vols. New York: Elsevier Science Publishers.

Cho, Yoon Je (1986), "Inefficiencies from Financial Liberalization in the Absence of Well-Functioning Equity Markets." *Journal of Money, Credit and Banking,* vol. 18, no. 2, pp. 191–199.

Chu, K-Y, H. Davoodi, and S. Gupta, (2000), "Income Distribution and Tax and Government Social Spending Policies in Developing Countries." IMF Fiscal Affairs Department, Working Paper WP/00/62, March 1.

Clegg, E. (1960) *Race and Politics.* London: Oxford University Press.

Cobbe, J.H. (1979) *Governments and Mining Companies in Developing Countries.* Boulder: Westview Press.

Coclough, C. (1988) "Zambian Adjustment Strategy – With and Without the IMF." IDS *Bulletin.* vol. 19, no. 1, pp. 51–60.

Cohen, J.M. (1993) "Importance of Public Sector Reform: the Case of Kenya." *The Journal of Modern African Studies,* vol. 31, no. 3, pp. 449–476.

Cohen, J.M. (1995) "Capacity building in the public sector: A focused framework for analysis and action." *International Review of Administrative Sciences,* vol. 61, pp. 407–422.

Cohen, J. and M.F. McPherson M.F. (1983) "Aga Khan Center for Training in Rural Policy and Management." Paper Commissioned for the Aga Khan University Study, Harvard University.

Cohen, J. and J.R. Wheeler (1997) "Building sustainable professional capacity in African public sectors: retention constraints in Kenya." *Public Administration and Development*, vol. 17, pp. 307–324.

Collier, P. (1991) "Africa's External Economic Relations: 1960–90." Chapter 6 in ed. D. Rimmer *Africa 30 Years On*. London: The Royal Africa Society in association with James Currey.

Collier, P. (1994) "The Marginalization of Africa." *International Labour Review*, no. 134, pp. 541–557.

Collier, P., and J.W. Gunning (1999) "Explaining African Economic Performance." *Journal of Economic Literature*, vol. 37, no. 1, March, pp. 64–111.

Collier, P. and J. W. Gunning (1999a) "Why Has Africa Grown Slowly?" *Journal of Economic Perspectives*, vol. 13, no. 3, Summer, pp. 23–40.

Collier, P. and C. Pattillo eds. (2000) *Investment and Risk in Africa*. Basingstoke: Macmillan & Co.

Cooper, R. (1991) *Economic Stabilization in Developing Countries*. San. Francisco: ICS Press.

Corbo, V. and J. de Melo (1985) "Liberalization with Stabilization in the Southern Cone of Latin America." *World Development*, vol. 13, pp. 863–66.

Corden, W.M. (1994) *Economic Policy, Exchange Rates and the International System*. Chicago: The University of Chicago Press.

Cornia, G.A., R. Jolly and F. Stewart eds. (1988) *Adjustment with a Human Face*, in two vols. Oxford: Clarendon Press.

Crook, F.W., H-H. Hsu, and M. Lopez (1999) "The Long-Term Boom in China's Feed Manufacturing Industry." *Agricultural Outlook*, December, pp. 13–16.

Crown Agents (1991) *Zambia Ministry of Finance Report Commissioned from Crown Agents*. Two vols. Crown Agents, Sutton, U.K., March.

DAC (1991) "Principles for New Orientations in Technical Cooperation." Development Assistance Committee, OECD/GD(91)207, Paris.

Daily Mail, The (1998) "ZCCM advised on the way forward." Letter to the Editor, April 23rd.

Daseking, C. and R. Powell, (1999) "From Toronto Terms to the HIPC Initiative – A Brief History of Debt Relief for Low-Income Countries." IMF, Policy Development and Review Department. WP/99/142.

de Gaay Fortman, B. ed. (1969) *After Mulungushi – The Economics of Zambian Humanism*. Nairobi: East African Publishing House.

de Waal, A. (2002) "What's new in the 'New Partnership for Africa's Development'?" *International Affairs*, vol. 78, no. 3, July, pp. 463–475.

Deane, P. (1953) *Colonial Social Accounting*. Cambridge: Cambridge University Press.

Devarajan, S., D. Dollar, and T. Holmgren (2001) *Aid and Reform in Africa: Lessons from Ten Case Studies*. Washington D.C.: The World Bank.

Diaz-Alejandro, C. (1985), "Good-Bye Financial Repression, Hello Financial Crash." *Journal of Development Economics*, vol. 19, pp. 1–24.

Dixit, A.K. (1997) *The Making of Economic Policy A Transaction-Cost Politics Perspective.* Cambridge MA: The MIT Press.

Dodge, D.J. (1977) *Agricultural Policy and Performance in Zambia.* Berkeley: Institute of International Studies, University of California.

Donker, S.M.K. and O.Ohiokpehai (1998) "The Relationship Between Food Security and Good Governance in Africa." [on www.toda.org/conferences/durban].

Dollar, D. (1992) "Outward-oriented Developing Countries Really Do Grow More Rapidly: Evidence from 95 LDC's 1976–1985." *Economic Development and Cultural Change,* vol. 40, no. 3, April, pp. 523–544.

Dornbusch, R. and F.L.C.H. Helmers eds. (1988) *The Open Economy: Tools for Policymakers in Developing Countries.* New York: Oxford University Press for the World Bank.

Dresang, D. (1975) "The Political Economy of Zambia." in ed. D. Dresang *The Political Economy of Africa,* New York: John Wiley and Sons.

Duesenberry and McPherson (1992), "Monetary Management in Sub-Saharan Africa: Key Issues." *Journal of African Finance and Economic Development*, vol. 1, no. 1, Spring, pp. 25–36.

Duesenberry, J.S., A.A. Goldsmith, and M.F. McPherson (1999) "Restarting and Sustaining Growth and Development in Africa." HIID *Development Discussion Papers* no. 680, February.

Dumont, R. (1962) *L'Afrique noire est Mal Partie.* Paris: Editions du Seuil [Reprinted in English as *False Start in Africa* 1967].

Dumont, R. (1966) *Opportunities for Development in African Agriculture.* Rome: United Nations Food and Agricultural Organization.

Dumont, R. and B. Rosier (1969) *The Hungry Future.* New York: Praeger Books.

Dumont, R. and M-F. Mottin (1980) *L'Afrique Etranglée: Zambie, Tanzanie, Senegal, Côte d'Ivoire, Guinee-Bissau, Cap Vert.* Paris: Editions du Seuil.

ECA/OAU (1989) *African Alternative Framework to Structural Adjustment Programmes for Socio-Economic Recovery and Transformation (AAF-SAP).* United Nations Economic Commission for Africa E/ECA/CM.15/6/Rev.3, Addis Ababa.

Easterly, W. (1999) "The Lost Decades: Explaining Developing Countries' Stagnation 1980–1998." World Bank, Washington D.C. Draft, November.

Easterly, W. (2000) "How did Highly Indebted Poor Countries Become Highly Indebted? Reviewing Two Decades of Debt Relief." World Bank, Development Research Group, *Working Paper,* no. 2225, June.

Easterly, W. and K. Schmidt-Hebbel (1993) "Fiscal Deficits and Macroeconomic Performance in Developing Countries." *The World Bank Research Observer,* vol. 8, no. 2, July, pp. 211–237.

Easterly, W. and R. Levine (1995) "Africa's Growth Tragedy A Retrospective, 1960–89." The World Bank Policy Research *Working Paper* no. 1503, August.

Easterly, W. and R. Levine (1998) "Troubles with the Neighbours: Africa's Problem, Africa's Opportunity." *Journal of African Economies*, vol. 7, no. 1, pp. 120–42.

Economist, The (1991) Zambia Country Report, no. 4, 1991, London: The Economist Intelligence Unit.

Economist, The (1994) "Africa: A Flicker of Light." March 5, pp. 23–28.

Economist, The (1994) "Down the rathole." December 10, p. 101.

Economist, The (1994). "Why aid is an empty promise." May 7, pp. 19–22.

Economist, The (1999) "Helping the Third World." June 26, pp. 23–25.

Edwards, S. (1993) "Openness, Trade Liberalization, and Growth in Developing Countries." *Journal of Economic Literature*, vol. 31, September, pp. 1358–1393.

Edwards, S. and S. van Wijnbergen (1989) "Disequilibrium and Structural Adjustment." Ch. 28 in eds. H.B.Chenery and T.N.Srinivasan *Handbook of Development Economics*, vol. 2, New York: Elsevier Science Publishers.

Edwards, M. & D. Hulme. (1996) "Too close for comfort? The impact of official aid on non-governmental organizations." *World Development*, vol. 24, no. 9, pp. 961–974.

Ehrlich, P.R. (1970) *The Population Bomb.* New York: Ballantine Books.

Ehui, S. *et al.* (2000) "China: Will They Buy or Sell?" *Choices*, Third Quarter, pp. 8–12.

Eicher, C.K. (1982) "Facing Up to Africa's Food Crisis" *Foreign Affairs*, vol. 61, no. 1, Fall, pp. 154–174.

Eicher, C.K. (1992) "African Agricultural Development Strategies." Ch. 3 in eds. F. Stewart, S. Lall and S. Wangwe *Alternative Development Strategies in sub-Saharan Africa.* New York: St. Martin's Press.

Eicher, C.K. and D.C. Baker (1992) "Agricultural Development in sub-Saharan Africa: A Critical Survey." in ed. L.R. Martin, *A Survey of Agricultural Economics Literature*, vol. 4. Minneapolis: University of Minnesota Press for the American Agricultural Economics Association.

Elliott, C. ed. (1971) *Constraints on the Economic Development of Zambia.* Nairobi: Oxford University Press.

Essex, M. (1999) "The New AIDS Epidemic." *Harvard Magazine*, September-October, pp. 35–39.

European Union (1996) "Green Paper on Relations between the European Union and the ACP Countries on the Eve of the 21st Century: Challenges and Options for a New Partnership." European Commission Study Group Partnership 2000, Brussels, November 14.

Faber, M. and J. Potter (1971) *Towards Economic Independence.* Cambridge: Cambridge University Press.

Fardi, M.A. (1991) "Zambia: Reform and Reversal." Chapter 16 in eds. V. Thomas et al. *Restructuring Economies in Distress: Policy Reform and the World Bank*, New York: Oxford University Press.

Faria, A. and Z. Yucelik. (1995). "The Interrelationship between Tax Policy and Tax Administration." ed. P. Shome, *Tax Policy Handbook*, Washington D.C.: International Monetary Fund, pp. 267–72.

FRBNY (1998) "Proceedings of a Conference on Excellence in Education." Federal Reserve Bank of New York *Economic Policy Review*, vol. 4, no. 1, March.

Fernholz, F. *et al.* (1996) "Zambia's Economic Prospects over the Period 1997 to 2001." HIID, Macroeconomic Technical Assistance Project, Ministry of France, Lusaka.

Financial Times, The (1997) "Zambia." Financial Times *Survey*, March 4.

Fischer, S. (1997) "Financial System Soundness." *Finance & Development*, March, pp. 14–16.

Fischer, S. (1998) "Reforming World Finance: Lessons from a Crisis." *IMF Survey*, Special Supplement, October.

Fischer, S. (1999) "On the Need for an International Lender of Last Resort." Paper prepared for delivery of the joint luncheon of the American Economic Association and the American Finance Association. New York, January 3.

Fischer, S. (2001) "Exchange Rate Regimes: Is the Bipolar View Correct?" Distinguished lecture on Economics in Government American Economic Association, AEA meeting, New Orleans, January 6.

Fischer, S., E. Hernández-Catá and M.S. Khan. 1998. "Africa: Is This the Turning Point?" International Monetary Fund Paper on Policy Analysis and Assessment, 98/6, May. Washington D.C.

Fortune (1997) "Zambia: A Model for Africa." Special Advertising Section, July 25.

Fox, J.W. and D.E. Greenberg (2001) "How Zambia Can Achieve Export-Led Economic Growth." Draft report to the GRZ supported by USAID, February.

Franck, T.M. (1960) *Race and Nationalism The Struggle for Power in Rhodesia and Nyasaland*. New York: Fordham University Press.

Frankel, S.H. (1938) *Capital Investment in Africa Its Course and Effects*. London: Oxford University Press.

Friedman, M. (1958). "Foreign Economic Aid: Means and Objectives." *Yale Review*, Summer [Reprinted in Ranis *op.cit.*, pp. 24–38].

Friedman, M. (1992) *Monetary Mischief: Episodes in Monetary History*. New York: Harcourt, Brace, Jovanovich.

Frimpong-Ansah, J.H. (1991) *The Vampire State in Africa: The Political Economy of Decline in Ghana*. Trenton: Africa World Press.

Frimpong-Ansah, J.H., S.M. Ravi Kanbur, and P. Svedberg eds. (1991) *Trade and Development in Sub-Saharan Africa*. New York: Manchester University Press.

Fry, J. (1974) *An Analysis of Employment and Income Distribution in Zambia.* Unpublished Ph.D. thesis, Faculty of Social Studies, Oxford University.

Fry, J. and C. Harvey (1974) "Copper in Zambia." Chapter 9 in eds. S.L. Pearson and J.L. Cownie *Commodity Exports and African Economic Development.* Lexington: Heath & Co.

Fry, M. (1988), *Money, Interest and Banking in Economic Development.* Johns Hopkins University Press, Baltimore.

GCA (1996) *African Social and Economic Trends 1995.* Annual Report for the Global Coalition for Africa, Washington D.C.

GRZ (1966) *First National Development Plan 1966–1970.* Lusaka: Office of National Development and Planning, July, pp. 73–8 [Reprinted in G.M. Meier 1970, pp. 646–656].

GRZ (1971) *Second National Development Plan.* Lusaka: Ministry of Development Planning and National Guidance.

GRZ (1984) *Restructuring in the Midst of Crisis,* in two vols. Lusaka: Republic of Zambia for Consultative Group for Zambia, May 22–24.

GRZ (1985) "An Action Programme for Economic Restructuring." Paper presented to the Consultative Group for Zambia, June 4–5.

GRZ (1988) *Annual Report of the Mines Development Department for the Year 1988.* Lusaka: Ministry of Mines.

GRZ (1989) *New Economic Recovery Programme Economic and Financial Policy Framework 1989–1993.* National Commission on Development Planning, Lusaka, August.

GRZ (1990) *Progress Report on the Implementation of Economic Measures.* Consultative Group for Zambia, Paris, April.

GRZ (1990) "Public Investment Programme 1990–1993." Consultative Group for Zambia, Paris, April.

GRZ (1991) "Statement by the Government of Zambia to the Donor/Creditor Community." Paris, December 11, 1991.

GRZ (1991) "Ministerial Statement by Hon. E.G. Kasonde Minister of Finance and National Commission for Development Planning on Maize, Fertilizer and other Related Subsidies." Lusaka, National Assembly, December.

GRZ (1992) *The Social Action Programme 1992–1995 Report to the Consultative Group Meeting.* Paris, Social Action Programme Secretariat, Lusaka, March.

GRZ (1992) "Zambia: Implementation of the Economic Recovery Programme, 1992–1993." Informal Meeting of the Consultative Group for Zambia, Paris, December 11.

GRZ, (1992), *Tax Policy Task Force, Recommendations on Tax Reform for the 1993 Budget.* Ministry of Finance, Lusaka, October 30.

GRZ (1992) *New Economic Recovery Programme Economic and Financial Policy*

Framework 1991–1993. Ministry of Finance and National Commission for Development Planning, Lusaka, April.

GRZ (1992) Speech by President F.T.J. Chiluba on the Occasion of the Meeting with Donors at State House, December 3.

GRZ (1992) "The 1992 Zambian Drought: Impacts, Responses and Costs." Prepared by the Government of Zambia, March.

GRZ (1992) *Zambia Economic Perspectives Building a Firm Base.* Lusaka: Government of Republic of Zambia.

GRZ (1993) *Zambia Implementation of Economic Recovery Programme Efforts and Policies of the Government of Zambia.* Lusaka, November.

GRZ (1994). *Zambia: Consolidating Macro-Economic Stability and Promoting Economic Growth and Social Development, The Challenge of the Next Three Years.* Report presented to the Consultative Group Meeting for Zambia, December 8–9.

GRZ (1995) *Zambia Consolidating Policy Reform for Economic Growth and Poverty Reduction.* Report Presented to the Meeting of the Consultative Group for Zambia, Lusaka December 13–15.

GRZ (1995) *National Strategic Health Plan for 1995–99.* Lusaka: Ministry of Health.

GRZ (1996) *Educating our Future.* Lusaka: Ministry of Education.

GRZ (1996) "Privatisation of Zambia Consolidated Copper Mines Ltd. (ZCCM)." Press Release by Minster of Finance, May 28.

GRZ (1997) "Government and IMF Mission Reach Agreement." Press Release by Minister of Finance and Economic Development, December 17.

GRZ (1997) *Zambia Demographic and Health Survey 1996, Preliminary Report.* Lusaka: Central Statistical Office and Ministry of Health.

GRZ (1997) *Enhanced Structural Adjustment, Economic Growth and Poverty Reduction: Policies of the Government of the Republic of Zambia.* Report Presented to the Consultative Group Meeting for Zambia, Paris, July 9–11.

GRZ (1997) "Zambia – Public Sector Reform and Export Promotion Credit (PSREPC) – Letter of Development Policy." Ministry of Finance and Economic Development, Lusaka, September 30.

GRZ (1998) *Economic Report 1997.* Lusaka, Ministry of Finance and Economic Development, January.

GRZ (1999) "HIV/AIDS in Zambia: Background Projections Impacts Interventions." Ministry of Health, Central Board of Health, Lusaka, September.

GRZ (2000) "Interim Poverty Reduction Strategy Paper." Lusaka: Republic of Zambia, Ministry of Finance and Economic Development, July 7.

GRZ, (2000) "Mobilizing for Sustained Economic Growth and Poverty Reduction: Scaling up the Zambia HIV/AIDS and Orphans and Vulnerable Children Response to Accelerate Poverty Reduction." Paper presented to 12th Consultative Group Meeting for Zambia. Lusaka, July 16–19.

GRZ, (2000) "2000 CG Report." Ministry of Finance and Economic Development, Lusaka, June 30.

GRZ, (2000) "The Long-Term Development Vision for Zambia." Paper presented to the Consultative Group Meeting, Lusaka, July 16–19.

GRZ, *Budget Address.* Ministry of Finance, Lusaka, Government Printer, various years.

GRZ, *Monthly Digest of Statistics.* Lusaka: Central Statistical Office published monthly.

GRZ (various dates), *Macroeconomic Indicators.* Ministry of Finance and Economic Development, Lusaka.

GRZ/UNDP (1995) *Prospects for Sustainable Human Development in Zambia More Choices for Our People.* Lusaka: United Nations Development Programme.

GRZ/UNICEF (1986) *Situation Analysis of Children and Women in Zambia.* GRZ/UNICEF Programming Committee, Lusaka, June.

Gallup, J.L. and J.S. Sachs (1998) "Agricultural Productivity and Geography." Draft. HIID Cambridge MA, January.

Gallup, J.L. and J.D. Sachs with A. Mellinger (1998) "Geography and Economic Development." Paper presented at the Annual Bank Conference on Development Economics, The World Bank, Washington D.C., April.

Gandhi, V.P., E. Sidgwick, and D.A. O'Sullivan, (1990) "Malta: Ideas for Indirect Tax Reform, 1991–1994." IMF Fiscal Affairs Department, Washington D.C.

Gardner, J.W. (1962). *President John F. Kennedy To Turn the Tide.* London: Hamish Hamilton.

Gebrejiabher, B. (1975) *Integrated Development in Rural Ethiopia.* Bloomington Ill: International Development Research Center.

Geisler, G. (1992) "Who is Losing Out? Structural Adjustment, Gender, and the Agricultural Sector in Zambia." *The Journal of Modern African Studies,* vol. 30, no. 1, pp. 113–139.

Gemmell, N., (1996). "Evaluating the Impacts of Human Capital Stocks and Accumulation on Economic Growth: Some New Evidence." *Oxford Bulletin of Economics and Statistics,* vol. 58, pp. 9–28.

Ghura, D. and T.J. Grennes (1993) "The Real Exchange Rate and Macroeconomic Performance in Sub-Saharan Africa." *Journal of Development Economics,* vol. 42, pp. 155–174.

Ghura, D. and M.T. Hadjimichael (1996) "Growth in sub-Saharan Africa" *IMF Staff Papers,* vol. 43, no. 3, September, pp. 605–634.

Gillis, S.M., D.H. Perkins, M. Roemer, and D.R. Snodgrass, (1992) *Economics of Development.* 3rd ed. New York: W.W. Norton and Company.

Glenday, G. (1995) "Capacity Building in the Context of the Kenya Tax Modernization Program." HIID, Cambridge MA, November.

Goldschmidt, J. (1993) "An Analysis of Commercial Farm Debt in Zambia, 1993." Draft report, Lusaka.

Goldsmith, A.A. (1998) "Africa's Overgrown State Reconsidered: Bureaucracy and Economic Growth." *World Politics,* vol. 51, no. 4, July, pp. 520–546.

Goldsmith, A. A. (1999) "Slapping the Grasping Hand: Correlates of Political Corruption in Emerging Markets." *American Journal of Economics and Sociology,* vol. 58.

Goldwin, R.A. (1963) *Why Foreign Aid? Two Messages by President Kennedy and Essays.* Chicago: Rand McNally & Co.

Gondwe, G.E. (2000) "Change in HIPC Rules Will Help Zambia A Letter to the Editor." *Financial Times,* December 8 [http://www.imf.org/external/np/vc/2000/120800.htm].

Good, R.C. (1973) *U.D.I. The International Politics of the Rhodesian Rebellion.* London: Faber & Faber.

Good, K. (1986) "Systemic Agricultural Mismanagement: The 1985 'Bumper' Harvest in Zambia." *The Journal of Modern African Studies,* vol. 24, no. 1, pp. 257–284.

Good, K. (1989) "Debt and the One-Party State in Zambia." *The Journal of Modern African Studies,* vol. 27, no. 2, pp. 297–313.

Goode, R.B. (1959) "Adding to the Stock of Physical and Human Capital." *American Economic Association Proceedings,* vol. 49, no. 2, May.

Goodfriend, M. and J.M.Lacker (1999) "Limited Commitment and Central Bank Lending." Federal Reserve Bank of Richmond *Working Paper* no. 99–2, January.

Goodhart, C.A.E. (1988) *The Evolution of Central Banks.* Cambridge: The MIT Press.

Goodhart, C.A.E. (1989) *Money, Information, and Uncertainty.* 2nd ed. Cambridge: The MIT Press.

Goodman, S. (1971) "The Foreign Exchange Constraint." Chapter 8 in ed. C. Elliott *Constraints on the Economic Development of Zambia.* Nairobi: Oxford University Press.

Gray, C.S. (1997) "Technical Assistance and Capacity Building for Policy Analysis and Implementation." in ed. M.S. Grindle, *op. cit.*

Gray, C. and A. Martens (1983) "The Political Economy of the 'Recurrent Cost Problem' in the West African Sahel." *World Development,* vol. 11, no. 2, pp. 101–117.

Gray, C.S. and D.A. Hoover (1995) "Capacity Improvement in the Ministry of Finance." Chapter 15 in eds. M.F. McPherson and S.C. Radelet, *op. cit.*

Gray, C.S. and J.S. Duesenberry (1996) "Exchange Rate Management in Senegal." Chapter 8 in J.S. Duesenberry *et al. Improving Exchange Rate Management in Sub-Saharan Africa.* Draft monograph HIID, Cambridge.

Gray, C.S. and M.F. McPherson (1999) "The Leadership Factor in African Policy Reform and Growth." HIID *Development Discussion Papers* no. 703, May [Published in *Economic Development and Cultural Change,* vol. 49, no. 4, July 2001, pp. 707–740].

Gray, C.S. *et al.*, (2000) "Enhancing Transparency in Tax Administration in Madagascar and Tanzania: Final Report." Equity and Growth through Economic Research/Public Strategies for Growth with Equity, Harvard University, March.

Gray, C.W. and D. Kaufmann (1998) "Corruption and Development." *Finance & Development*, vol. 35, pp. 7–10.

Gray, R. (1960) *The Two Nations.* London: Oxford University Press.

Greene, J. and L. Southard (1998) "U.S. Red Meat and Poultry Markets in a Global Setting." *Agricultural Outlook*, June-July, pp. 10–12.

Greene, W.H. (1993) *Econometric Analysis.* 2nd ed. Englewood Cliffs: Prentice-Hall.

Grindle, M.S. ed. (1997) *Getting Good Government: Capacity Building in the Public Sectors of Developing Countries.* Cambridge: Harvard Studies in International Development, distributed by Harvard University Press.

Grindle, M.S. (1999) "In Quest of the Political: The Political Economy of Development Policy Making." *CID Working Paper Series* no.17, (Harvard University), June.

Grindle, M., C.K. Mann, and P. Shipton eds. (1989) *Seeking Solutions: Framework and Cases for Small Business Development Programs.* West Hartford: Kumarian Press.

Grindle, M.S. and M.E. Hilderbrand (1995) "Building sustainable capacity in the public sector: what can be done?" *Public Administration and Development*, vol.15, pp. 441–463.

Grossman, G.M. and E. Helpmann (1995) "Technology and Trade." in eds. G.M. Grossman and K. Rogoff *Handbook of International Economics*, vol.III, Amsterdam: North Holland.

Gulhati, R. (1989) "Impasse in Zambia: The Economics and Politics of Reform." World Bank, *EDI Development Policy Case Studies.* Analytical Case Studies, no. 2.

Gupta, S., M. Verhoeven, and E. Tiongson, (1999), "Does Higher Government Spending Buy Better Results in Education and Health Care?" IMF *Working Paper* WP/99/21, February.

HBS (1997) "Zambia's Agricultural Sector Investment Program." Harvard Business School case 9–797–023 revised January, Boston MA.

HIID (1997) "A New Partnership for Growth in Africa." Harvard Institute for International Development, Cambridge, MA, February.

Haggard, S. and R.R. Kaufman eds. (1992) *The Politics of Economic Adjustment.* Princeton: Princeton University Press.

Hall, R. (1965) *Zambia.* London: Pall Mall Press.

Hancock, G. (1989). *Lords of Poverty: the power, prestige and corruption of the international aid business.* New York: The Atlantic Monthly Press.

Hanke, S.H. and K. Schuler (1994) *Currency Boards for Developing Countries.* San Francisco: ICG Press (no. 9 in ICG Sector Studies Series).

Harber, R.P. (1989) "Zambia's Foreign Exchange Auction: A Description and Analysis of its Functioning and Effects, October 1985 – May 1987." In *Economic Policy Reform in Zambia (1982–1987)*, Robert R. Nathan Assocs., Washington D.C., March.

Harbison, F.H. (1962) "Human Resources Development Planning in Modernising Economies." *International Labour Review*, vol. 85, no. 5, May [Reprinted in G.M. Meier 1970, pp. 612–619].

Harbison, F.H. and C.A. Myers (1964) *Education, Manpower and Economic Growth.* New York: McGraw-Hill.

Harsch, E. (1993) "Accumulators and Democrats: Challenging State Corruption in Africa." *Journal of Modern African Studies*, vol. 31, no. 1, pp. 31–48.

Harvey, C. (1972) "Economic Independence." Chapter 1 in eds. M. Bostock and C. Harvey *Economic Independence and Zambian Copper*, New York: Praeger Publishers.

Hayter, T. (1971) *Aid as Imperialism.* New York: Penguin Books.

Hazell, P. (1999) "Agricultural Growth, Poverty Alleviation, and Environmental Sustainability: Having it all." 2020 *Brief* no. 59, IFPRI March.

Hazell, P.B.R. and B. Hojjati (1999) "Farm/Non-Farm Growth Linkages in Zambia." *Journal of African Economies*, vol. 4, no. 3, pp. 406–435.

Heller, W.W. (1954) "Fiscal Policies for Underdeveloped Economies," in ed. H.P. Wald *Conference on Agricultural Taxation and Economic Development.* Cambridge: Harvard Law School [Reprinted in G.M. Meier 1970, pp. 190–194].

Heller, P.S. (1974) "Public Investment in LDC's with Recurrent Cost Constraints." *Quarterly Journal of Economics*, vol. 88, May, pp. 251–277.

Heller, P.S. (1979)."The Underfinancing of Recurrent Development Costs." *Finance & Development.*

Heller, P.S. and Tait, A.A. (1983) "Government Employment and Pay: Some International Comparisons." International Monetary Fund *Occasional Paper* no. 24.

Heller, P.S. and J.E. Aghevli (1985) "The Recurrent Cost Problem: An International Overview," in ed. J. Howell *Recurrent Costs in Agricultural Development.* London: Overseas Development Institute.

Helleiner, G.K., (1982) "Balance of Payments Problems and Macro-economic Policy in Small Economies." Chapter 9 in ed. B.Jalan *Problems and Policies in Small Economies.* New York: St. Martin's.

Hendricks, D. and B. Hirtle (1997) "Bank Capital Requirements for Market Risk: The Internal Models Approach." *Economic Policy Review*, vol. 3, no. 4, December.

Hill, C.B. and A. Pellechio, (1996), "Equivalence of the Production and Consumption Methods of Calculating the Value-Added Tax Base: Application to Zambia." IMF *Working Paper* WP/96/67. Washington, D.C.

Hill, C. B. and M. F. McPherson (1998) "Economic Growth and Development in Zambia: The Way Forward." Paper prepared for Embassy of Sweden, June 1998.

Hirschman, A.O. (1970) *Exit, Voice and Loyalty.* Cambridge: Harvard University Press.

Holmes, J.A. (1995) "The Anglo Group's Views on the Future of ZCCM." Address to ZACCI and Economic Association of Zambia, Pamodzi Hotel, Lusaka, March 15.

Holmes, T. (1999) "Theory and Hypothesis." *Profit*, March, pp. 12–15.

Honadle, B.W. (1981) "A Capacity-Building Framework: A Search for Concept and Purpose." *Public Administration Review*, vol. 41, no. 5, pp. 575–580.

Hoover, D.A. and M.F. McPherson (1999) "Capacity Building in the Ministry of Finance, Zambia." HIID *Development Discussion Papers* no. 704, June.

Hoover, D.A. and M.F. McPherson (2000) "Capacity Building Programs – Facing the Reality of HIV/AIDS." in *HIV/AIDS in the Commonwealth 2000/01*. London: Kensington Publications for the Commonwealth Secretariat, pp. 60–63.

Hope, K.R. Sr. (2002) "From Crisis to Renewal: Towards a Successful Implementation of the New Partnership for Africa's Development." *African Affairs*, no. 101, pp. 387–402.

Hunter, G. (1967) *The Best of Both Worlds?* London: Oxford University Press.

Hyden, G. (1983) *No Shortcuts to Progress: African Development Management in Perspective.* Berkeley: University of California Press.

Hyden, G. and M. Bratton eds. (1992) *Governance and Politics in Africa.* Boulder: Lynne Rienner Publishers.

IDS (2000) "Poverty Reduction Strategies: A Part for the Poor?" *IDS Policy Briefing* Issue no. 13, April, Institute of Development Studies.

IFPRI (1995) *A 2020 Vision for Food, Agriculture, and the Environment The Vision, Challenge and Recommended Action.* Washington, D.C.: International Food Policy Research Institute, October.

ILO (1969) *Report to the Government of Zambia on Incomes, Wages, and Prices in Zambia: Policy and Machinery.* Prepared by H.A. Turner, Geneva: International Labour Organization ["The Turner Report"].

ILO (1977) *Narrowing the Gaps. Planning for Basic Needs and Productive Employment in Zambia.* Addis Ababa: International Labour Office.

ILO (1992) "Employment and Income Generation in Zambia." Draft. International Labour Organisation, Geneva.

IMF (1977) "Zambia: Recent Economic Developments." SM/77/34 Washington D.C.: International Monetary Fund, February.

IMF (1981) *Financial Policy Workshops: The Case of Kenya.* Washington D.C.: The IMF Institute.

IMF (1983) *Interest Rate Policies of Developing Countries.* Occasional Paper no. 22, International Monetary Fund, Washington D.C.

IMF (1993) "Zambia: Staff Report for the 1993 Rights Accumulation Program." EBS/93/48 Washington D.C. International Monetary Fund, March 24.

IMF (1994), *International Financial Statistics Yearbook.* Washington D.C.: International Monetary Fund.

IMF (1995) "Aide-Memoire International Monetary Fund Mission to Zambia March 28 – April 4, 1995." Draft, International Monetary Fund, Lusaka.

IMF (1995) "Zambia – Interim Report on Policy Actions and Economic Developments." EBD/95/122, International Monetary Fund, September 6.

IMF (1995) "Policy Framework Paper 1995–98." Paper prepared by the staffs of the IMF and World Bank, Lusaka, November.

IMF (1997) *Zambia – Midterm Review Under the First Annual Arrangement Under The Enhanced Structural Adjustment Facility.* Report EBS/97/20, International Monetary Fund, Washington D.C., February 12.

IMF (1997a) *Zambia – Staff Report for the 1997 Article IV Consultation.* Report EM/97/226, International Monetary Fund, Washington D.C., August 29.

IMF (1997b) *Zambia – Selected Issues and Statistical Appendix.* Report SM/97/243 International Monetary Fund, Washington D.C., September 24.

IMF (1998) *Evaluation of the Enhanced Structural Adjustment Facility: Report by a Group of Independent Experts.* Washington DC: International Monetary Fund.

IMF (1999) "IMF Approves ESAF Loan for Zambia." Press Release no. 99/10, March 26.

IMF (1999) "Zambia Enhanced Structural Adjustment Facility Policy Framework Paper 1999–2001." International Monetary Fund, Lusaka, March.

IMF (1999) *Zambia: Statistical Appendix.* IMF Staff Country Report, no. 99/43, Washington D.C., May.

IMF (2000) "The IMF's Poverty Reduction and Growth Facility (PRGF)." Washington D.C.: International Monetary Fund, July 31 [available on http://www.imf.org/external then click on prgf].

IMF (2000) "Zambia to Receive $3.8 Billion in Debt Service Relief: The IMF and the World Bank Support Debt Relief for Zambia under the Enhanced HIPC Initiative." Press Release no. 00/67, December 8, on http://www.imf.org/external/np/sec/pr/2000/pr0067.htm

IMF (2001) "IMF Concludes 2001 Article IV Consultation with Zambia." Public Information Notice (PIN) 01/123, International Monetary Fund, Washington D.C.

IMF *International Financial Statistics Yearbook.* Washington D.C.: International Monetary Fund, various years.

IMF/IDA (2000) "ZAMBIA Decision Point Document for the Enhanced Heavily Indebted Poor Countries (HIPC) Initiative." Document prepared by the Staffs of the International Monetary Fund and the International Development Association, Washington, D.C., November 20.

IRIS (1996) *Governance and the Economy in Africa: Tools for Analysis and Reform of Corruption.* College Park: Center for Institutional Reform and the Informal Sector.

Iliffe, J. (1987) *The African Poor: A History.* Cambridge: Cambridge University Press.

Isham, J., D. Kaufmann, and L. Pritchett, (1995). "Government and the Returns on Investment." World Bank Policy Research *Working Paper* no. 1550.

Isham, J. and D. Kaufmann (1995) "The Forgotten Rationale for Policy Reform: The Productivity of Investment Projects." The World Bank *Policy Research Working Paper* no. 1549, November.

Jaycox, E.V.K. (1993) "Capacity Building: The Missing Link in African Development." Address to Conference sponsored by the African American Institute, Reston, Virginia, May 20.

Jha, D. and B. Hojjati (1993) "Fertilizer Use on Smallholder Farms in Eastern Province, Zambia" *IFPRI Abstract.* Research Report no. 94, July.

Johnson, H.G. (1964) "Towards a Generalized Capital Accumulation Approach to Economic Development," in OECD Study Group in the Economics of Education *The Residual Factor and Economic Growth.* Paris: OECD.

Johnson, H.G. (1967) *Economic Policies Toward Less Developed Countries.* Washington D.C.: The Brookings Institution.

Johnson, B.T. (1997) "Economic Freedom, Foreign Aid, and Economic Development." Chapter 2 in eds. K.R. Holmes, B.T. Johnson and M. Kirkpatrick *1997 Index of Economic Freedom.* New York: The Heritage Foundation and Wall Street Journal.

Jolly, R. (1971) "The Skilled Manpower Constraint." Chapter 2 in ed. C. Elliott *op. cit.*

Jolly, R. (1989) "A Future for UN Aid and Technical Assistance?" *Development,* vol. 89, no. 4, pp. 21–26.

Jourdan, P. (1986) "The Mining Industry in Zambia." *Raw Minerals Report,* vol. 4, no. 4, pp. 14–27.

Kaldor, N. (1963) "Taxation for Economic Development." *Journal of Modern African Studies,* vol. 1, no. 1 [Reprinted in G.M. Meier 1970, pp. 194–198].

Kane, E.J. and T. Rice (2000) "Bank Runs and Banking Policies Lessons for African Policymakers." NBER *Working Paper* no. 8003, November.

Kapur, I. *et al,* (1991) *Ghana: Adjustment and Growth, 1983–1991.* Occasional Paper no. 86, International Monetary Fund, Washington D.C.

Kasanga, J.M. (1996) *Study of "Enclave" Approach to Tax & Customs Administration in Zambia.* The World Bank, Lusaka, June.

Kasonde, E. (1994) "Structural Adjustment and Long-Term Development in Sub-Saharan Africa." in eds. L. van Drunen and F. van der Kraaij *Structural Adjustment in Sub-Saharan Africa Research and Policy Issues.* Poverty and Development Analysis and Policy no. 11, The Hague, September.

Kaufmann, D. (1997) "Corruption: the facts." *Foreign Policy*, Summer, pp. 114–131.

Kaufmannn, D., A. Kraay, and P. Zoido-Lobaton (1999) "Governance Matters." World Bank Policy Research *Working Paper* no. 2196, Washington D.C.

Kaul, I., I. Grunberg, and M.A. Stern eds.(1999) *Global Public Goods International Cooperation in the 21st Century*. New York: Oxford University Press for the United Nations Development Programme.

Kaunda, K. (1969) "Zambia Towards Complete Independence." Chapter 3 in ed. B. de Gaay Fortman (1969) *After Mulungushi – The Economics of Zambian Humanism*. Nairobi: East African Publishing House.

Kaunda, K. (1969a) *Report on Second National Convention on Rural Development, Incomes, Wages and Prices*. Kitwe: Republic of Zambia.

Kaunda, K. (1975) *The "Watershed" Speech*. Lusaka, Government of Republic of Zambia, June 30-July 3.

Kayizzi-Mugerwa, S. (1988) *External Shocks and Adjustment in Zambia*. Economic Studies no. 26, Goteborg University.

Kayizzi-Mugerwa, S. (1990) "Growth from Own Resources: Zambia's Fourth National Development Plan in Perspective." *Development Policy Review*, vol. 8, pp. 59–76.

Keinbaum Associates. (1993). *Report on the Strategic Options for the Privatisation of ZCCM*. Lusaka: Kienbaum Associates.

Kelley, M.J. (1991) *Education in a Declining Economy The Case of Zambia 1975–1985*. Economics Development Institute Development Policy Case Series no. 8, The World Bank, Washington D.C.

Kets de Vries, M.R.F. (1997) "The Leadership Mystique," in ed. K. Grint, *Leadership: Classical, Contemporary, and Critical Approaches*. New York: Oxford University Press

Keynes, J.M. (1919) "Inflation" [Reprinted in J.M. Keynes 1963].

Keynes, J.M. (1936) *The General Theory of Interest, Money and Employment*. New York: Harcourt, Brace.

Keynes, J.M. (1963) *Essays in Persuasion*. New York: W.W. Norton & Co.

Khan, M.S. and M.D. Knight (1991) "Stabilization Programs in Developing Countries A Formal Framework," in eds. M.S. Khan, P.J. Montiel, and N.U. Haque *Macroeconomic Models for Adjustment in Developing Countries*. Washington D.C.: International Monetary Fund.

Killick, T. (1987) "Balance of Payments Adjustment and Developing Countries: Some Outstanding Issues." Chapter 4 in ed. M. Posner *Problems of International Money 1972–85*. Washington D.C.: International Monetary Fund.

Killick, T. and H. White (1999) "Poverty in Africa: Why Economic Growth Will Not Be Enough." Talk at ODI, June 9 [on www.oneworld.org/odi/speeches].

Kindleberger, C.P. (1989) *Manias, Panics and Crashes: A History of Financial Crises.* Revised ed. New York: Basic Books.

King, B. (1988) "From Dutch Disease to Dutch Auction." Draft paper. The World Bank, Washington D.C., December.

King, K. (1991) "Education and Training in Africa: The Search to Control the Agenda for their Development," in ed. D. Rimmer *Africa 30 Years On.* The Royal African Society in association with James Currey, London.

Kitchen, R.L. (1986) *Finance for Developing Countries.* Chichester: John Wiley and Sons.

Klitgaard, R E. (1988) *Controlling Corruption.* Berkeley: University of California Press.

Klitgaard, R.E. (1990) *Tropical Gangsters.* New York: Basic Books.

Krauss, M.B. (1983) *Development without Aid.* New York: New Press.

Kreuger, A.O. (1986) "Aid in the Development Process." *World Bank Research Observer,* vol. 1, no. 1, January, pp. 57–78.

Krueger, A.O., (1997), "Trade Policy and Economic Development: How We Learn." *American Economic Review,* vol. 87, no. 1, pp. 1–22.

Krugman, P.R. (1989). "Developing Countries in the World Economy." *Daedalus,* vol. 118, no. 1, pp. 183–203.

Kumar, S.K. (1994) *Adoption of Hybrid Maize in Zambia: Effects on Gender Roles, Food Consumption, and Nutrition.* Research Report no.100, International Food Policy Research Institute, Washington D.C.

Kuznets, S. (1966) *Modern Economic Growth: Rate, Structure and Spread.* New Haven: Yale University Press.

Kydd, J. (1986) "Changes in Zambian Agricultural Policy since 1983: Problems of Liberalisation and Agrarianisation." *Development Policy Review,* vol. 4, pp. 233–259.

Kydd, J. (1988) "Coffee After Copper? Structural Adjustment, Liberalisation, and Agriculture in Zambia" *The Journal of Modern African Studies,* vol. 26, no. 2, pp. 227–251

Lancaster, C. (1999) *Aid to Africa: So Much to Do So Little Done.* Chicago: The University of Chicago Press for The Century Foundation.

Landell-Mills, P. and I. Serageldin (1991) "Governance and the Development Process." *Finance & Development,* September, pp. 14–17.

Lavy, V. (1992) "Alleviating Transitory Food Crises in Sub-Saharan Africa: International Altruism and Trade." *The World Bank Economic Review,* vol. 6, no. 1, January, pp. 125–138.

Legum, C. (1966) *Zambia: Independence and Beyond.* London: Nelson.

Lele, U. (1981) "Rural Africa: Modernization, Equity, and Long-Term Development." *Science,* February 6, pp. 547–553.

Lele, U. (1989) "Sources of Growth in East African Agriculture." *The World Bank Economic Review,* vol. 3, no. 1, January, pp. 119–144.

Lewis, W.A. (1956) *Development Planning The Essentials of Economic Policy.* New York: Harper & Row.

Lewis, J.D. and M.F. McPherson (1994) "Macroeconomic Management: To Finance or Adjust." Chapter 4 in eds. D. Lindauer and M. Roemer *op. cit.*

Lewis, J.D. and M.F. McPherson (1996) "Exchange Rate Management in Zambia." Ch. 7 in J.S. Duesenberry *et al. Improving Exchange Rate Management in Sub-Saharan Africa.* HIID, Cambridge MA.

Lindauer, D.L., and B. Nunberg. (1994). *Rehabilitating Government: Pay and Employment Reform in Africa.* Washington D.C.: World Bank.

Lindauer, D. and M. Roemer eds. (1994) *Asia and Africa Legacies and Opportunities in Develepment.* San Francisco: ICS Press.

Lindblom, C.E. (1959) "The science of muddling through." *Public Administration Review,* vol. 19, no. 2, Spring, pp. 79–88.

Loney, M. (1975) *Rhodesia: White Racism and Imperial Response.* Baltimore: Penguin Books.

Lopez, J. A. (1999) "Using CAMEL Rating to Monitor Bank Conditions." *FRBSF Economic Letter* no. 99–19, June 11.

Loubser, J. (1993) "Capacity Development – A Conceptual Overview." in eds. P. Morgan and V. Carlan *Emerging Issues in Capacity Development Proceedings of a Workshop.* Aga Khan Foundation Canada and CIDA Ottawa, November 22–24.

Lucas, R.E. (1976) "Econometric Policy Evaluation: A Critique," in ed. K.L. Brunner *The Phillips Curve and Labor Markets.* Supplement to the *Journal of Monetary Economics.* pp. 19–46.

MAFF (1995) "A Review of Maize Marketing Liberalization During 1994: The Transition Programme 1995/96." Lusaka: Ministry of Agriculture, Food and Fisheries Food Security Division, March.

MAFF (1996) "Zambia From Transition to Consolidation – A Critical Review of the Liberalization of Maize and Input Markets, 1993–1996." Ministry of Agriculture, Food and Fisheries Marketing Management Assistance Project, June.

MAFF (1996) "Review of the Agricultural Credit Management Programme in Zambia 1994/95–1996/96." Ministry of Agriculture Food and Fisheries Market Liberalization Impact Studies no.16, Lusaka, June.

MMD (1991) *Movement for Multi-Party Democracy Manifesto.* Lusaka MMD Campaign Committee.

MMD (1996) *MMD Manifesto '96* Lusaka: Movement for Multi-Party Democracy Campaign Committee.

MoFED (1999) "Restructuring Report." Lusaka: Ministry of Finance and Economic Development, December.

MacKenzie, G.A. (1991) "Estimating the Base of the Value-Added Tax (VAT) in Developing Countries." *IMF Working Paper* WP/91/21, February.

Mackenzie, G.A., D.W.H. Orsmond, and P.R. Gerson (1997) "The Composition of Fiscal Adjustment and Growth Lessons from Fiscal Reforms in Eight Economies." *Occasional Paper* no. 149, International Monetary Fund, Washington D.C., March.

McKinnon, R.I. (1964) "Foreign Exchange Constraints in Economic Development and Efficient Aid Allocation." *Economic Journal*, vol.74, pp. 388–409 [Reprinted in ed. J. Bhagwati *International Trade*. Baltimore: Penguin Books 1969].

Madavo, C. and J-L. Sarbib (1997) "Africa on the Move: Attracting Private Capital to A Changing Continent." *SAIS Review*, vol. 17, no. 2, Summer-Fall, pp. 111–126.

Maddison, A. (1965) *Foreign Skills and Technical Assistance in Economic Development*. Paris: OECD.

Mann, C.K., and M.F. McPherson, (1981) "Improving Food Policy." *IADS report 1981* International Agricultural Development Service, New York, pp. 27–33.

Mann, C.K. and B. Huddleston eds. (1986) *Food Policy Frameworks for Analysis and Action*. Bloomington: Indiana University Press.

Markakis, J. and R.L. Curry (1976) "The Global Economy's Impact on Recent Budgetary Politics in Zambia." *Journal of African Studies*, pp. 403–427.

Martin, A. (1972) *Minding their Own Business: Zambia's Struggle Against Western Control*. London: Hutchinson.

Mason, E.S. (1957) "United States Interests in Foreign Economic Assistance." in ed. G. Ranis *op. cit.*

Mason, E.S. (1986) *The Harvard Institute for International Development and its Antecedents*. Lanham: HIID and University Press of America.

Mathieu, J.T. (1996) "Reflections on Two African Universities." *Issue A Journal of Opinion* "Issues in African Higher Education," vol. 24, no. 1, pp. 24–28.

Mauro, P. (1997) "Why Worry About Corruption?" International Monetary Fund *Economic Issues* no. 6.

Mazrui, A.A. (1980) *The African Condition: A Political Diagnosis*. Cambridge: Cambridge University Press.

Mazrui, A.A. (1994) "Global Africa: From Abolitionists to Reparationists." *African Studies Review*, vol. 37, no. 3, December, pp. 1–18.

McDonough, W.J. (1997) "The Changing Role of Supervision." Federal Reserve Bank of New York *Annual Report* 1997, pp. 3–13.

McKinnon, R. (1973), *Money, Capital and Economic Development*. Washington D.C.: Brookings Institution.

McKinnon, R. (1991), *The Order of Economic Liberalization*. Baltimore: The Johns Hopkins University Press.

McPherson, M.F. (1979) *An Analysis of the Recurrent Cost Problem in The Gambia*.

HIID, Cambridge, MA (consultant report for USAID Sahel Recurrent Cost Study).

McPherson, M.F. (1980) *A Study of Employment in Zambia.* Unpublished Ph.D. thesis, Harvard University [Widener Library].

McPherson, M.F. (1993) "Potential Sources of Growth in Zambia." Macroeconomic Technical Assistance Project, Ministry of Finance, Lusaka, August.

McPherson, M.F. (1995) "The Sequencing of Economic Reforms: Lessons from Zambia." HIID *Development Discussion Papers* no. 516, November.

McPherson, M.F. (1996). "The State of the Zambian Economy Mid-1996." Draft. HIID, Cambridge MA.

McPherson, M.F. (1999) "Looking for an aid exit strategy." *Profit*, vol. 7, no. 8, February, pp. 7–9.

McPherson, M.F. (1999) "Seignorage in Highly Indebted Developing Countries." HIID *Development Discussion Papers* no. 696, April.

McPherson, M.F. (2000) "Malcolm McPherson on 'The Cash Budget as a Restraint: The Experience of Zambia by Christopher S. Adam and David L. Bevan," in eds. P. Collier and C. Pattillo *Investment and Risk in Africa*. Basingstoke: Macmillan & Co.

McPherson, M.F. (2000) "Aid, Policies, and Growth: A Comment." Belfer Center for Science and International Affairs, John F. Kennedy School of Government, Harvard University, October.

McPherson, M.F. (2001) "The Collapse of the Meridien/BIAO Bank in Zambia." Paper prepared for the Center for International Development Capacity Building for Economic Decision Making project, Ministry of Planning and Finance, Maputo, Mozambique, April.

McPherson, M.F. ed. (2002) *Restarting and Sustaining Growth and Development in Africa.* Bethesda MD: Franklin Printers for USAID.

McPherson, M.F. ed. (2002a) *Promoting and Sustaining Trade and Exchange Rate Reform in Africa.* Bethesda MD: Franklin Printers for USAID.

McPherson, M.F. and C.F. Zinnes (1991) "Economic Retrogression in Sub-Saharan Africa." Paper presented at Northeast Universities Development Conference, October 4–5, Harvard University, Cambridge, Massachusetts.

McPherson, M.F. and C.F. Zinnes (1992) "Economic Retrogression in sub-Saharan Africa." HIID *Development Discussion Papers* no. 423, May.

McPherson, M.F in association with D. Hoover and D. Snodgrass. (2000) "The Impact on Economic Growth in Africa of Rising Costs and Labor Productivity Losses Associated with HIV/AIDS." Paper prepared for the Consulting Assistance for Economic Reform (CAER-II) Project, Kennedy School of Government, Harvard University, August 11.

McPherson, M.F. and T. Rakovski. (1999). "A Small Econometric Model of the Zambian Economy." HIID *Development Discussion Papers* no. 672.

McPherson, M.F. and T. Rakovski (2000) "Trade and Growth in Sub-Saharan Africa: Empirical Evidence." Revision of 1999 draft. HIID, Cambridge.

McPherson, M.F. and T. Rakovski (2001) "Understanding the Growth Process in Sub-Saharan Africa: Some Empirical Estimates," in ed. M.F. McPherson *Restarting and Sustaining Growth and Development in Africa.* Revised draft. EAGER Project, John F. Kennedy School of Government, Harvard University, January.

McPherson, M. and C. S. Gray (2000) "An 'Aid Exit' Strategy for African Countries: A Debate." Chapter 9 in ed. M.F. McPherson *Restarting and Sustaining Growth and Development in Africa.* Draft manuscript, Belfer Center, John F. Kennedy School of Government, Harvard University.

McPherson, M.F. and S.C. Radelet (eds.) (1995) *Economic Recovery in The Gambia:Insights for Adjustment in Sub-Saharan Africa.* Cambridge: Harvard University Press.

Meier, G.M.(1970) *Leading Issues in Economic Development.* 2nd ed. New York: Oxford University Press.

Meier, G.M. (1989) *Leading Issues in Economic Development.* 5th ed. New York: Oxford University Press.

Merle-Davis, J. ed. (1967) *Modern Industry and the African.* 2nd ed. London: Cass & Co.

Mikesell, R.F. (1988) *The Global Copper Industry Problems and Prospects.* London: Croom Helm.

Mills, T.C. and G.E. Wood, (1993). "Does the Exchange Regime Affect the Economy." Federal Reserve Bank of St. Louis *Review*, vol. 75, no. 4, July/August, pp. 3–20.

Mitrany, D. (1951) *Marx against the peasant: a study in social dogmatism.* Chapel Hill: University of North Carolina Press.

Moore Lappe, F., J. Collins, and D. Kinley, (1981). *Aid as Obstacle.* San Francisco: Institute for Food and Development Policy.

Moors, E.R. (1984) "Institutional Destruction Resulting from Donor and Project Proliferation in Sub-Saharan African Countries." *World Development*, vol. 12, no. 4, pp. 465–470.

Moris, J.R. (1977) "The Transferability of Western Management Concepts and Programs: East African Perspective." Chapter 5 in L.D. Stifel *et al. Education and Training for Public Sector Management in Developing Countries.* New York: The Rockefeller Foundation.

Moser, C.O.N. (1996) "How Do the Urban Poor Manage in an Economic Crisis?" *Finance & Development*, vol. 33, no. 4 December, pp. 42–44.

Mosher, A.T. (1965) *Getting Agriculture Moving.* New York: Frederick Praeger for The Agricultural Development Council.

Mueller, D.C. (1979) *Public Choice.* New York: Cambridge University Press.

Munene, J. (2000) "Some of the Cultural Values and Practices that Matter in

Uganda: A Comparative Study of Social Capital in a Modernising University and Traditional Public Service." Paper prepared for the EAGER study "Enhancing and Sustaining Growth in Uganda." Makerere Institute for Social Research, Kampala.

Muscat, R.J. (1986) "Evaluating Technical Cooperation: a Review of the Literature." *Development Policy Review*, vol. 4, pp. 69–89.

Musgrave, R.A. and P.B. Musgrave (1989) *Public Finance in Theory and Practice.* Fifth Edition New York: McGraw-Hill Co.

Mussa, M. *et al.* (1999) "Moderating Fluctuations in Capital Flows to Emerging Market Economies." *Finance & Development,* September, pp. 9–12.

Mwaipaya, P.A. (1980) *The Importance of Quality Leadership in National Development, With Special Reference to Africa.* New York: Vantage Press.

Mwanakatwe, J.M. (1990) "Reflections on Long-term Perspectives for Sub-Saharan Africa with Particular Reference to Zambia." *The Long-Term Perspective Study of Sub-Saharan Africa,* vol. 1, Country Perspectives. The World Bank, Washington D.C.

Mwanawina, I. (1990) *An Input-Output and Econometric Approach to Analysing Structural Change and Growth Strategies in the Zambian Economy.* Dissertation University of Konstanz.

Mwanza, J. (1973) *Modern Sector Employment Growth in East Africa (with Special Emphasis on Zambia).* Unpublished Ph.D. thesis, Cornell University, June.

Mwenda, A. (1993) *Credit Rationing and Investment Behaviour under Market Imperfections Evidence from Commercial Agriculture in Zambia.* Goteborg: University of Goteborg Studies in Economic Development.

Mwenda, A. (1999) "Monetary Policy Effectiveness in Zambia." Chapter 6 in ed. S. Kayizzi-Mugerwa *The African Economy Policy, institutions and the future.* London: Routledge.

Nasution, A., (1983), *Financial Institutions and Policies in Indonesia.* Singapore: Institute of Southeast Asian Studies.

Ndulo, M. (1999) "Transforming Economic and Political Structures for Growth The Zambian Experience." Chapter 13 in ed. S. Kayizzi-Mugerwa *The African Economy Policy, institutions and the future.* London: Routledge.

Ndulu, B. and N. van de Walle (1996) *Agenda for Africa's Economic Renewal.* Washington D.C.: Overseas Development Council.

Nelson, J. ed. (1989) *Fragile Coalitions: The Politics of Economic Adjustment.* New Brunswick, NJ: Transactions Books for the Overseas Development Council.

Nelson, J. ed. (1990) *Economic Crisis and Policy Choice: The Politics of Adjustment in the Third World.* Princeton: Princeton University Press.

Nelson, J. (1993). "The Politics of Economic Transformation: Is Third World Experience Relevant for Eastern Europe?" *World Politics,* vol. 45, pp. 433–463.

Nkrumah,K. (1965) *Neo-Colonialism: The Last Stage of Imperialism.* New York: International Publishers.

Nunberg, B. (1994). "Experience with Civil Service Pay and Employment Reform: An Overview," in eds. D.L. Lindauer and B. Nunberg *Rehabilitating Government: Pay and Employment Reform in Africa.* Washington DC: World Bank.

Nurkse, R. (1970) *Problems of Capital Formation in Underdeveloped Countries and Patterns of Trade and Development.* New York: Oxford University Press [originally published 1953].

Nyang'oro, J.E. (1989) *The State and Capitalist Development in African Declining Political Economies.* New York: Praeger Publishers.

Nyoni, T. S. (1998) "Foreign aid and Economic Performance in Tanzania." *World Development,* vol. 26, no. 7, pp. 1235–1240.

OAU (1979) *What Kind of Africa by the Year 2000?* Proceedings of the Monrovia Symposium, Addis Ababa: Organisation of African Unity.

OAU (1980) *The Lagos Plan of Action for the Implementation of the Monrovia Strategy for the Economic Development of Africa.* Lagos: Organisation of African Unity, April.

ODI (1982) "Africa's Economic Crisis." Overseas Development Institute *Briefing Paper* no. 2, September.

OXFAM (1995) *The Impact of Structural Adjustment on Community Life: Undoing Development.* Boston: Oxfam America.

Obasanjo, O. (1987) *Africa in Perspective: Myths and Realities.* New York: Council on Foreign Relations.

Obstfeld, M. (1998) "The Global Capital Market: Benefactor or Menace?" *The Journal of Economic Perspectives,* vol. 12, no. 4, Fall, pp. 9–30.

O'Faircheallaigh, C. (1984) *Mining and Development Foreign-Financed Mines in Australia, Ireland, Papua New Guinea and Zambia.* New York: St. Martin's Press.

O'Faircheallaigh, C. (1986) "Mineral Taxation, Mineral Revenues and Mine Investment in Zambia, 1964–1983." *American Journal of Economics and Sociology,* vol. 45, no. 1, January, pp. 53–67.

Ohlin G. (1966) "The Evolution of the Aid Doctrine." *Foreign Aid Policies Reconsidered.* Geneva: OECD.

Opeskin, B.R. (1996) "The Moral Foundations of Foreign Aid." *World Development,* vol. 24, no. 1, pp. 21–44.

Orme, J. (1995) "The Original Megapolicy: America's Marshall Plan," in eds. J.D.Montgomery and D.A. Rondinelli *Great Policies: Strategic Innovations in Asia and the Pacific Basin.* Westport: Praeger Publishers.

Osterberg, W.P. (1997) "The Hidden Costs of Mexican Banking Reform." FRB Cleveland, *Economic Commentary,* January 1.

Overseas Audit Unit (1955) *An Outline of Colonial Accounting and Financial Procedure.* London: Knapp, Drewitt and sons, Ltd.

Paddock W. and P. Paddock (1967) *Famine 1975! America's Decision Who will Survive?* Boston: Little, Brown Co.

Parfitt, T.W. and S.P. Riley (1989) *The African Debt Crisis.* New York: Routledge.

Parnes, H.S. (1962) *Forecasting Educational Needs for Economic and Social Development.* Paris: OECD.

Poulson, J.A. (1993), "Some Unresolved Issues in African Financial Reforms," in ed. L. White, *African Finance.* San Francisco: Institute for Contemporary Studies.

Pearce, D.W. (1989) *The MIT Dictionary of Modern Economics.* 3rd Ed. Cambridge: The MIT Press.

Perkins, D.H. (1992) "China's 'Gradual' Approach to Market Reforms." United Nations Conference on Trade and Development *Discussion Papers* no.52, December.

Perkins, D.H. (1994) "There Are At Least Three Models of East Asian Development." *World Development,* vol. 22, no. 4, pp. 655–661.

Peterson, S.B. (1996) "The Recurrent Cost Crisis in Development Bureaucracies." *Policy Studies and Developing Nations,* vol. 3, pp. 175–203.

Pinstrup-Andersen, P. and R. Pandya-Lorch (1995) "Agricultural Growth Is the Key to Poverty Alleviation in Low-Income Developing Countries." 2020 Vision *Brief* no. 15, IFPRI April.

Pletcher, J. (2000) "The Politics of Liberalizing Zambia's Maize Markets." *World Development,* vol. 28, no.1, January, pp. 129–142.

Potter, B.H. and J. Diamond, (1999) "Guidelines for Public Expenditure Management." International Monetary Fund, Washington D.C.

Price Waterhouse (1996) "The 1996 Zambia Budget Highlights." Lusaka: Price Waterhouse, January.

Pritchett, L. and G. Sethi, (1994) "Tariff Rates, Tariff Revenue, and Tariff Reform: Some New Facts." *The World Bank Economic Review,* vol. 8 no. 1, pp. 1–16.

Porter, R.C. and S.I. Ranney (1982) "An Eclectic Model of Recent LDC Macroeconomic Policy Analyses." *World Development,* vol. 10, no. 9, pp. 751–765.

Posner, D.N. (1998) *The Institutional Origins of Ethnic Politics in Zambia.* Ph.D. thesis Department of Political Science, Harvard University, Widener Library.

Post, The (1998) "Economy Records Severe Recession." Issue no. 1114, Monday, November 30.

Premchand, A. (1993) *Public Expenditure Management.* Washington D.C.: International Monetary Fund.

Rajcoomar, S, M. Bell, *et al.* (1996) *Financial Programming and Policy: The Case of Sri Lanka.* Washington, D.C.: The IMF Institute.

Ranis, G. ed. (1964) *The United States and the Developing Economies.* New York: W.W. Norton.

Richards, P. and R. Amjad eds. (1994) *New Approaches to Manpower Planning and Analysis.* Geneva: International Labour Office.

Robinson, E.A.G. (1967) "The Economic Problem" Part 3 in J. Merle Davis *Modern*

Industry and the African. 2nd ed. with an Introduction by R.I. Rotberg. London: Frank Cass and Co. [First edition 1932].

Robinson, R.D. (1967) *High-Level Manpower in Economic Development: The Turkish Case.* Cambridge: Harvard Middle Eastern Monograph Series.

Robinson, D. (1990). *Civil Service Pay in Africa.* Geneva: International Labour Organisation.

Rodrik, D. (1997) "Trade Policy and Economic Performance in Sub-Saharan Africa." Paper prepared for the Swedish Ministry for Foreign Affairs, November.

Rodrik, D. (1998) "Trade Policy and Economic Performance in sub-Saharan Africa." NBER *Working Paper* no. 6562, May.

Rodrik, D. (1998) "Symposium on Globalization in Perspective: An Introduction." *The Journal of Economic Perspectives,* vol. 12, no. 4, Fall, pp. 3–8.

Rockefeller Foundation (1981) *Agricultural Sciences Seminar.* The Rockefeller Foundation Working Papers New York, March.

Romer, P. (1986) "Increasing Returns and Long-Run Growth." *Journal of Political Economy,* vol. 94, pp. 1002–1037.

Rothschild, N.M. & Sons (1996) "Phase I Privatisation Report Prepared for the Government of the Republic of Zambia, Zambia Consolidated Copper Mines." Draft (marked strictly private and confidential), Lusaka, April.

SIDA (1989) *Zambia Exchange Rate Policy.* Koping: Swedish International Development Authority.

Saasa, O.S. (1987) *Evaluation of Zambia's attitudes, policies and procedures concerning technical assistance personnel.* Report prepared for the Embassy of Sweden, Lusaka.

Saasa, O.S. et. al. (1996) *Capacity Building for Economic Development in Zambia: Challenges and Prospects.* The World Bank: Washington D.C., October.

Saasa, O.S., *et al.* (1999) "Comparative Economic Advantage of Alternative Agricultural Production Activities in Zambia." *SD Publication Series.* Office of Sustainable Development, Bureau for Africa, Washington, D.C., Technical Paper no. 104, December.

Sachs, J.D. (1996) "Growth in Africa: It can be done." *The Economist,* June 29, pp. 19–21.

Sachs, J.D. (1998) "International Economics: Unlocking the Mysteries of Globalization." *Foreign Policy* Special Edition on the "Frontiers of Knowledge" no. 110, Spring, pp. 97–11.

Sachs, J.D. and A.M. Warner. (1995), "Natural Resources and Economic Growth." HIID *Development Discussion Papers* no. 517a, Cambridge, MA.

Sachs, J.D. and A.M. Warner (1997) "Sources of Slow Growth in African Economies." *Journal of African Economies,* vol. 6, no. 3, pp. 335–376.

Sahn, David E. (1992). "Public Expenditures in Sub-Saharan Africa During a Period of Economic Reforms." *World Development,* vol. 20, no. 5, pp. 673–93.

Sahn, D.E. ed. (1994) *Adjusting to Policy Failure in African Economies.* Ithaca: Cornell University Press.

Saint, W. (1992) *Universities in Africa Strategies for Stabilization and Revitalization.* The World Bank, Africa Region, Washington D.C.

Saldanha, C.D. (1993) "Capacity Development: Issues, Constraints and Strategies for Donor Agencies." in eds. P. Morgan and V. Carlan *Emerging Issues in Capacity Development.* Aga Khan Foundation Canada and CIDA, Ottowa, November.

Sandbrook, R. (1986) "The State and Economic Stagnation in Tropical Africa." *World Development,* vol. 14, pp. 319–332.

Sandbrook, R. (1987) *The Politics of Africa's Economic Stagnation.* Cambridge: Cambridge University Press.

Sandbrook, R. (1993) *The Politics of Africa's Economic Recovery.* Cambridge: Cambridge University Press.

Sano, H-O (1988) "The IMF and Zambia: The Contradictions of Exchange Rate Auctioning and De-Subsidization of Agriculture." *African Affairs,* October, pp. 563–577.

Saving, J.L. (1997) "An End to Welfare as we Know it?" FRB of Dallas *South-West Economy,* Issue no. 1, January-February, pp. 6–8.

Sayers, R.S. (1957) *Central Banking After Bagehot.* Oxford: Clarendon Press.

Scheuer, D.J. and S.L. Topping (1990) "Report on Government Finance and Money and Banking Statistics Mission to Zambia." Bureau of Statistics, International Monetary Fund, Washington D.C., March.

Schioler, E. (1998) *Good News from Africa: Farmers, Agricultural Research and Food in the Pantry.* Washington D.C.: International Food Policy Research Institute.

Schmidt-Hebbel, K. (1996) "Fiscal Adjustment and Growth: In and Out of Africa." *Journal of African Economies* Supplement to vol. 5, no. 3, part I, pp. 7–59.

Schultz, T.P., (1999) "Health and Schooling Investments in Africa." *Journal of Economic Perspectives,* vol. 13, no. 3, Summer, pp. 67–88.

Schultz, T. P. and A. Tansel. (1997) "Wage and Labor Supply Effects of Illness in Côte d'Ivoire and Ghana: Instrumental Variable Estimates for Days Disabled." *Journal of Development Economics,* vol. 53, no. 3, pp. 251–86.

Schultz, T.W. (1959) "Investment in Man: An Economist's View." *Social Science Review,* June.

Schultz, T.W. (1960) "Value of U.S. Farm Surpluses to Underdeveloped Countries." *Journal of Farm Economics,* vol. 62, December, pp. 1019–1030.

Schultz, T.W. (1962) "Reflections on Investment in Man." *Journal of Political Economy,* Supplement, October.

Schultz, T.W. (1963) *The Economic Value of Education.* New York: Columbia University Press

Schwab, K. *et al.* (2000) *The Africa Competitiveness Report 2000/2001.* New York: Oxford University Press.

Seers, D. (1966) "The Use of a Modified Input-Output System for an Economic Program in Zambia." Chapter 8 in eds. I. Adelman and E. Thorbecke *The Design of Economic Development.* Baltimore: The Johns Hopkins Press

Seidman, A. (1974) "The Distorted Growth of Import-Substitution Industry: The Zambian Case." *The Journal of Modern African Studies,* vol. 12, no. 4, December, pp. 601–631.

Selowsky, M. (1991) "External Financing and Adjustment." *Finance & Development* June, pp. 22–24.

Seshamani, V. (1990) "Towards Structural Transformation with a Human Focus: The Economic Programmes and Policies of Zambia in the 1980s." UNICEF, Innocenti Occasional Papers no. 7, October.

Shaath, N.A. (1975) "African Manpower Needs and the Role of Technical Assistance." in eds. A.H. Rweyemamu and G.Hyden *A Decade of Public Administration in Africa.* Nairobi: Kenya Literature Bureau.

Shafer, D. M. (1990) "Sectors, States, and Social Forces Korea and Zambia Confront Economic Restructuring." *Comparative Politics,* January, pp. 127–150.

Shagam, S. (1997) "World Beef and Cattle Trade: Evolving & Expanding." *Agricultural Outlook.* December, pp. 6–10.

Sharer, R.L., H.R. de Zoysa and C. A. McDonald, (1995), *Uganda: Adjustment with Growth, 1987–94.* Occasional Paper no. 121, International Monetary Fund, Washington D.C.

Shaw, E. (1973), *Financial Deepening in Economic Development.* New York: Oxford University Press.

Sheng, A. (1996) *Bank Restructuring Lessons from the 1980s.* Washington D.C.: The World Bank.

Shome, P. (1999) "Taxation in Latin America: Structural Trends and Impact of Administration." IMF *Working Paper,* WP/99/19, February.

Simmons, J. (1979) "Education for Development, Reconsidered." *World Development,* vol. 7, no.11/12, November/December, pp. 1005–1016.

Simons, K. (1996) "Value at Risk – New Approaches to Risk Management." *New England Economic Review.* Federal Reserve Bank of Boston. September/October.

Sklar, R.L. (1975) *Corporate Power in an African State.* Berkeley: University of California Press.

Smithies, A. (1955). *The Budgetary Process in the United States.* New York: J. Wiley & Sons.

Sparrow, F.T., B.H. Bowen, and Z. Yu (1999) *Modeling Long-Term Expansion Options for the Southern African Power Pool (SAPP).* Purdue University, West Lafayette, Ind.

Squire, L. (1991) "Introduction: Poverty and Adjustment in the 1980s." *The World Bank Economic Review*, vol. 5, no. 2, May, pp. 177–186.

Stella, P. (1997) "Do Central Banks Need Capital?" *IMF Working Paper* WP/97/83, July.

Stevens, E. (2000) "Evolution in Banking Supervision." Federal Reserve Bank of Cleveland *Economic Commentary*, March 1.

Stiglitz, J.E. and A. Weiss (1981), "Credit Rationing in Markets with Imperfect Information." *American Economic Review*, vol. 71, no. 3, pp. 394–410.

Stiglitz, J.E. (1988) *Economics of the Public Sector*. 2nd ed. New York: W.W. Norton & Co.

Stiglitz, J.E. (1993) *Economics*. New York: W.W. Norton & Co.

Stiglitz, J.E. (1993), "The Role of the State in Financial Markets." *Proceedings of the World Bank Annual Conference on Development Economics 1993*. World Bank, pp. 19–62.

Stiglitz, J. (1998) "Concrete Targets for Developing Countries." Op-ed article in *The Herald Tribune*, April 16.

Stiglitz, J.E. and L. Squire. (1998). "International Development: Is it Possible?" *Foreign Policy* Special Edition "Frontiers of Knowledge," no. 110, Spring, pp. 138–151.

Svedberg, P. (1991) "The Export Performance of Sub-Saharan Africa." *Economic Development and Cultural Change*, vol. 39, pp. 549–564.

Symon, W. (1995) *Lima Bank Limited A Report on Certain Aspects of Privatization*. Lusaka, draft report.

Syrquin, M. and H.B. Chenery (1989) "Patterns of Development: 1950–1983." *World Bank Discussion Papers* no. 41, The World Bank.

Szeftel, M. (1982) "Political Graft and the Spoils System in Zambia – The State as a Resource in Itself." *Review of African Political Economy*, no. 24.

Tanzi, V. and H. Davoodi (1998) "Roads to Nowhere: How Corruption in Public Investment Hurts Growth." International Monetary Fund, *Economic Issues* no. 12.

Taylor, L. (1996) "Sustainable Development: An Introduction." *World Development*, vol. 24, no. 2, pp. 215–225.

Thirsk, W., ed. (1997) *Tax Reform in Developing Countries*. Washington, D.C.: World Bank.

Thomas, T. (1996) "Africa for the Africans A Survey of Sub-Saharan Africa." *The Economist*, September 7.

Tordoff, W. (1977) "The Politics of Disengagement." *African Affairs*, vol. 76, no. 203, January, pp. 60–69.

Tordoff, W. (1984) *Government and Politics in Africa*. Bloomington: Indiana University Press.

Tseng, W. and R. Corker (1991), *Financial Liberalization, Money Demand, and Mone-*

tary Policy in Asian Countries. Occasional Paper no. 84, International Monetary Fund, Washington D.C.

UNAIDS (2000) *AIDS Epidemic Update.* UNAIDS Joint United Nations Programme on HIV/AIDS, Geneva: UNAIDS/WHO, December.

UN/ECA/FAO (1964) *Economic Survey Mission on the Economic Development of Zambia.* Ndola: Falcon Press [The "Seers Mission" report].

UNESCO (1968) *Manpower Aspects of Educational Planning.* Paris: United Nations Education and Scientific and Cultural Organisation.

USDA (1990) *World Agriculture Trends and Indicators 1970–1989.* Washington D.C.: US Department of Agriculture, Economic Research Service Statistical Bulletin no. 815, September.

USDS (1964). "U.S. Economic Aid to Africa 1950–64." *Africa Report,* December.

United Nations (1986) *Report on the Preparatory Committee of the Whole for the Special Session of the General Assembly on the Critical Economic Situation in Africa.* United Nations 13th Special Session Supplement No. 1 (A/S-13/4) June.

van der Heijden, H. (1997) "The Flow of Aid Resources to Zambia 1992–1996 Greater Dependency or More Self-Reliance?" Draft. Ministry of Finance and Economic Development, Lusaka.

van der Heijden, H. (2000) *Zambia's Economic Reform Program.* Draft manuscript, Lusaka.

van de Walle, N. (1996) "The Politics of Aid Effectiveness." Ch. 13 in ed. S. Ellis *Africa Now: People, Policies, and Institutions.* London: Heinemann.

Vickers, Sir Geoffrey (1983) *The Art of Judgement: A Study of Policy Making.* London: Chapman and Hall.

Villanueva, D. and A. Mirakhor (1991), "Strategies for Financial Reforms." *IMF Staff Papers,* vol. 37, no. 3, pp. 509–536.

Viner, J. (1951) *International Economics.* Glencoe, Ill.: The Free Press.

von Braun, J. T. Teklu, and P. Webb (1998) *Famine in Africa: Causes, Responses, and Prevention.* Baltimore: The Johns Hopkins University Press for IFPRI.

WINROCK (1993) *Agricultural Transformation in Africa.* (ed. D. Seckler), Arlington, VA: Winrock International Institute for Agricultural Development.

Ward, B. (1962) *The rich nations and the poor nations.* New York: W.W. Norton.

Washington Post, The (1998) "Cash, Pork and Politics," in National Weekly Edition, April 13, pp. 6–12.

Welch, J.H. and D. McLeod, (1993). "The Costs and Benefits of Fixed Dollar Exchange Rates in Latin America." Federal Reserve Bank of Dallas. *Economic Review.* First Quarter, pp. 31–44.

West, T. (1992) "The Politics of the Implementation of Structural Adjustment in Zambia 1985–1987." Chapter 8 in *The Politics of Economic Reform in Sub-Saharan Africa* (Final Report). Center for Strategic and International Studies, Washington D.C.

White, H. and T. Edstrand (1994) "The Macroeconomic Impact of Aid in Zambia." SASDA (Secretariat for Analysis of Swedish Development Assistance) Working Paper no. 19, August.

Widner, J. A. (1996) "The Courts as Restraints." Paper prepared for Conference on Risk and Restraint: Reducing the Perceived Risks of African Investment. HIID, September 5.

Williamson, O.E. (1996) *The Mechanisms of Governance.* New York Oxford University Press.

Williamson, J. (2000) "Designing a Middle Way Between Fixed and Flexible Exchange Rates." Paper presented to conference on Monetary and Exchange Rate Policies: Options for Egypt." Egyptian Centre for Economic Studies, Cairo, November 19–20.

Wolf, C.R.Jr. (1979) "A Theory of Nonmarket Failure." *Journal of Law and Economics,* vol. 22, no. 1, April, pp. 107–139.

Wolf, C.R.Jr. (1988) *Markets or Governments Choosing between Imperfect Alternatives.* Cambridge: The MIT Press.

Wolfensohn, J.D. (1997) "The Challenge of Inclusion." Address to the Board of Governors, The World Bank Group, Hong Kong, September 23.

Wolfensohn J.D. (1998) "The Other Crisis." Address to the Board of Governors, Washington D.C., October 6.

World Bank (1977) *Zambia: A Basic Economic Report.* Four vols. 1586b-ZA Washington D.C.: East Africa Regional Office, October.

World Bank (1981) "Zambia Country Economic Memorandum." Report No. 3007-ZA, Eastern Africa Programs, World Bank Washington D.C., February 27.

World Bank (1981a) *Accelerating Development in Sub-Saharan Africa: An Agenda for ACTION.* Washington D.C.: The World Bank.

World Bank (1984) *Towards Sustained Development in Sub-Saharan Africa.* Washington D.C.: The World Bank.

World Bank (1984) "Zambia Industrial Policy and Performance." Report No. 4436-ZA Industrial Strategy and Policy Division, World Bank, Washington D.C., April.

World Bank (1986) *Zambia: Wage Policy and the Structure of Wages and Employment.* Report no. 5727-ZA, The World Bank, Washington D.C., May.

World Bank (1986) *Financing Adjustment with Growth in Sub-Saharan Africa,1986–90.* Washington D.C.: The World Bank.

World Bank (1986) *Zambia: Specialized Training Study.* Report No.6071-ZA, Education and Manpower Development Division, Eastern and Southern Africa Regional Office, Washington D.C.: The World Bank.

World Bank (1986) *Report to the Consultative Group for Zambia on the Public Expenditure Reform.* The World Bank Eastern and Southern Africa Regional Office report ZAM 86–7, Washington D.C., December.

World Bank (1986) *Staff Appraisal Report Zambia Third Development Bank of Zam-*

bia Project. World Bank, Industrial and Development Finance Division Eastern and Southern Africa Region, September.

World Bank (1986) *Zambia Country Economic Memorandum Economic Reforms and Development Prospects.* World Bank, Country Programs Department I, Eastern and Southern Africa Region, report no. 6355-ZA, November.

World Bank (1986). "Zambia: Wage Policy and the Structure of Wages and Employment." No. 5727-ZA, The World Bank, Washington D.C., May 7.

World Bank (1988) *Report on Adjustment Lending.* Country Economics Department, World Bank, Washington D.C., August.

World Bank (1989) *Zambia: Policy Framework Paper 1989–93.* Report Sec M89–1115 prepared by the staffs of the World Bank and IMF, Washington D.C., August.

World Bank (1989) *Sub-Saharan Africa From Crisis to Sustainable Growth A Long Term Perspective Study.* Washington D.C.: The World Bank.

World Bank (1990) *The Long Term Perspective Study of sub-Saharan Africa.* Four vols. Washington D.C.: The World Bank.

World Bank (1991) *The African Capacity Building Initiative.* Washington D.C.: The World Bank.

World Bank (1991) *Republic of Zambia: Public Sector Management Review.* Report no. 9827-ZA Africa Region, World Bank, Washington D.C., October 31.

World Bank (1991) "Draft Report on The Commercial Banking System in Zambia." Industry and Energy Division, Southern Africa Department, The World Bank, November 11.

World Bank (1992) *Republic of Zambia Public Expenditure Review.* Report no.11420-ZA, Africa Region, World Bank, Washington D.C., December 1.

World Bank (1992) *Agriculture Sector Strategy: Issues and Options.* Draft. Washington D.C., January 20.

World Bank (1993) *The East Asian Miracle Economic Growth and Public Policy.* A World Bank Policy Research Report, Washington D.C.: The World Bank.

World Bank (1993) *Zambia: Prospects for Sustainable and Equitable Growth.* Report No. 11570-ZA Country Operations Division, Southern Africa Department, Washington D.C., August.

World Bank (1994) *Zambia Poverty Assessment.* Two vols. Report No. 12985-ZA Human Resources Division, Africa Regional Office, Washington D.C., November 10.

World Bank, (1994) *Adjustment in Africa: Reforms, Results and the Road Ahead.* New York: Oxford University Press.

World Bank (1995) *Labor and the Growth Crisis in sub-Saharan Africa.* Regional Perspectives on World Development Report 1995 Washington D.C.: The World Bank.

World Bank (1995) *Bureaucrats in Business: The Economics and Politics of Govern-*

ment Ownership. A World Bank Policy Research Report New York: Oxford University Press.

World Bank (1995) *Reducing Poverty in Zambia: Getting from Ideas to Action.* Washington D.C.: The World Bank.

World Bank (1995) "Retaining Teaching Capacity in African Universities: Problems and Prospects." *Findings,* Africa Region, no. 39, May.

World Bank (1995) "Consultative Group for Zambia Paris 8–9 December, 1994, Chairperson's Report of the Proceedings." The World Bank, Paris, CG 95–9, February.

World Bank (1996) *Zambia Country Assistance Review.* World Bank Operations Evaluation Department, Washington D.C., March 4.

World Bank (1996) "Zambia: Country Assistance Review Summary." World Bank OED report no. 15675, June.

World Bank (1996) "Partnership for Capacity Building in Africa" Office of the Vice President, Africa Region, The World Bank, January 31.

World Bank (1996) "Privatization in Africa: The Zambia Experience." *Findings,* Africa Region no. 72.

World Bank (1997) *African Development Indicators.* Washington, DC: The World Bank.

World Bank (1997) *World Development Report 1997 "The State in a Changing World"* Washington D.C.: Oxford University Press for The World Bank.

World Bank (1998) "Listening to farmers: Participatory assessment of policy reform in Zambia's agriculture sector." *Findings* no.105, February.

World Bank (1998) *World Development Indicators.* Washington DC: The World Bank.

World Bank (1998) *Assessing Aid What Works, What Doesn't, and Why?* Washington D.C.: The World Bank.

World Bank (2000) *Can Africa Claim the 21st Century?* Washington D.C.: The World Bank.

World Bank/UNDP (1989) *Africa's Adjustment and Growth in the 1980's.* Washington D.C.: The World Bank and UNDP.

Wulf, J. (1989) "Floating Exchange Rates in Developing Countries: The Case of Zambia." *The Journal of Modern African Studies,* vol. 27, no. 3, pp. 503–579.

Yansane, A.Y. ed. (1980) *Decolonization and Dependency Problems of Development of African Societies.* Westport: Greenwood Press.

Yeats, A. J. *et al.* (1996) "What Caused sub-Saharan Africa's Marginalization in World Trade?" *Finance & Development,* December, pp. 38–41.

Yeats, A. *et al.* (1997) *Did Domestic Policies Marginalize Africa in World Trade* Washington D.C.: World Bank Directions in Development Series.

Young, M.C. (1971) "Agricultural Policy in Uganda: Capability and Choice" Chapter 7 in ed. M.F. Lofchie *The State of the Nations Constraints on Development in Independent Africa.* Berkeley: University of California Press.

Young, M. C. (1982) *Ideology and Development in Africa.* New Haven: Yale University Press.

Zuckerman, E. (1986) "A Study in Red: Zambia succumbs to its debts." *Harper's Magazine.*